The Northern Frontiers of Roman Britain

For Brian Dobson

The Northern Frontiers of Roman Britain

David J. Breeze

BOOK CLUB ASSOCIATES LONDON

First published 1982

This edition published 1982
by Book Club Associates
By arrangement with
B.T. Batsford Ltd, London

Printed in Great Britain

Contents

Plates

Maps and Diagrams

Acknowledgments

The author and publisher wish to thank the following for permission to reproduce the photographs and plans appearing in this book: *Scottish Development Department Ancient Monuments Branch*, plates 1, 9, 10, 18, 19, figure 25; *Royal Commission on the Ancient and Historical Monuments of Scotland*, plate 4; *Cambridge University Committee for Aerial Photography*, plates 2, 3, 5, 6, 12; *Newcastle Museum of Antiquities*, plates, 7, 11; *National Museum of Antiquities of Scotland*, plates 13–17; *Mr Peter Connolly*, plate 8; *Society for the Promotion of Roman Studies*, figure 5; *Mr C.M. Daniels*, figures 17, 36, 37.

The jacket illustration, of a watch-tower on the Gask Ridge, has been kindly prepared by Mike Moore.

A Note on Terminology

Modern political divisions complicate life for the ancient historian. The Romans knew no such place as Scotland. They called the whole island *Britannia*, and the only distinction within that was the geographical territory of the British tribes. However, Tacitus, writing of the campaigns of his father-in-law Agricola in the first century, spoke of *Caledonia*. Unfortunately it is not clear whether this refers merely to the tribes inhabiting the Highlands, or to all the tribes north of the Forth-Clyde isthmus. For that reason, and because its usage by the Romans will have changed over the years, this term is eschewed. That part of Britain north of the Tyne-Solway isthmus is referred to throughout this book as north Britain. Areas within that area are related to modern geographical names or to ancient tribes.

The Romans called the people living beyond the empire, barbarians, a term they had inherited from the Greeks, to whom they had once been barbarians. The term is frequently used below in relation to the northern tribes: it does not imply any slur upon their state of civilisation, but merely emphasises that they were not Roman.

Preface

Hadrian's Wall holds a perennial fascination, as the visitor numbers to such important sites as Housesteads and the considerable success of Chesterholm-Vindolanda demonstrate. However, Hadrian's Wall is only one of several Roman frontiers in Britain, which survive to greater or lesser extent. In Scotland the Antonine Wall, though much less well preserved, has been well known for centuries, while recent research has cast light upon Agricola's lost frontier on the Forth-Clyde isthmus and its apparent successor in Perthshire. All these frontiers are the subject of this book, leaving aside only the Saxon Shore along the south and east coast of England, which has recently been discussed in detail in two monographs.

These Roman frontiers did not stand in isolation. They were built in reaction to something – or rather someone: the native peoples of north Britain. The northern tribes – the Caledonians and their successors the Picts – therefore form as much a part of this book as the Roman frontiers and the soldiers who manned them. It is unfortunate that we know so little about the enemies of Rome, largely because no written record of theirs has survived, and much of what we do know emanates from Roman sources, hardly an unbiased point of view. However, archaeology can go some way towards redressing the balance.

It is important also to place the British frontiers within the overall setting provided by the Roman empire. Hence this book commences with a look at the rise of Rome and a discussion of the conquest of Britain. An examination of the northern tribes in Britain at the time of the Romans forms the body of the next chapter. The northern frontiers are then discussed in chronological order: Agricola on the Forth-Clyde isthmus, the 'Gask frontier', Hadrian's Wall and the Antonine Wall. The next chapter deals with the history of the northern frontier following the abandonment of the Antonine Wall, while a final chapter draws together the various themes of the book. At all stages an attempt has been made to interweave the Roman and native material to create a meaningful story, reflecting not only the building, occupation and abandonment of the frontiers, but their development and their impact upon the native peoples living in their vicinity and the barbarian tribes to the north.

No book is the product of one man. One person may write it, but he has previously assimilated facts and beliefs brought to his attention by others, some of which are bound to be incorporated, consciously or subconsciously, into the book. I am pleased to acknowledge one major and formative influence on this book: the teachings of the Department of Archaeology in the University of Durham. In particular I owe a considerable debt to Eric Birley, John Mann and Brian Dobson who first encouraged and nurtured my interest in Roman Britain and in Roman military studies, the last not least serving as my research supervisor through five years and two theses. I would also like to acknowledge my debt to other members of the 'Corbridge School': John Gillam, Charles Daniels, George Jobey, Valerie Maxfield and the late Jock Tait. While none would agree with all the views expressed in this book, and some would regard many as downright heretical, these scholars have nevertheless wittingly or unwittingly helped to create and mould those views. Finally I must thank the adult students who have attended my courses, and especially those on the Hadrian's Wall course run jointly with Brian Dobson and Valerie Maxfield, for asking difficult questions, offering solutions to difficult problems and generally forcing me to think again (and again) about different aspects of the frontier.

This book has been read in draft by Brian Dobson, Iain MacIvor and Anna and Graham Ritchie. To them I offer my grateful thanks for all their suggestions and comments aimed at improving the text. I would also like to thank John Barber, Gordon Barclay and Ian Hodgson for discussing various problems with me, Tom Borthwick for preparing figs 1, 2, 7, 11, 12, 21, 28, 35 and 39, Mike Moore for executing the reconstruction drawings (figs 9, 14–16, 18, 22 and 24), Charles Daniels for generously making the drawings of Housesteads and Wallsend available in advance of publication, W.S. Hanson for similarly allowing me to use the plan of Croy Hill, and all who so kindly provided photographs. Thanks are also due to Graham Webster and Peter Kemmis Betty for inviting me to write this book. Finally, my best thanks must go to my wife who has had to live with Hadrian's Wall and the Antonine Wall for far too long.

Edinburgh
March 1981

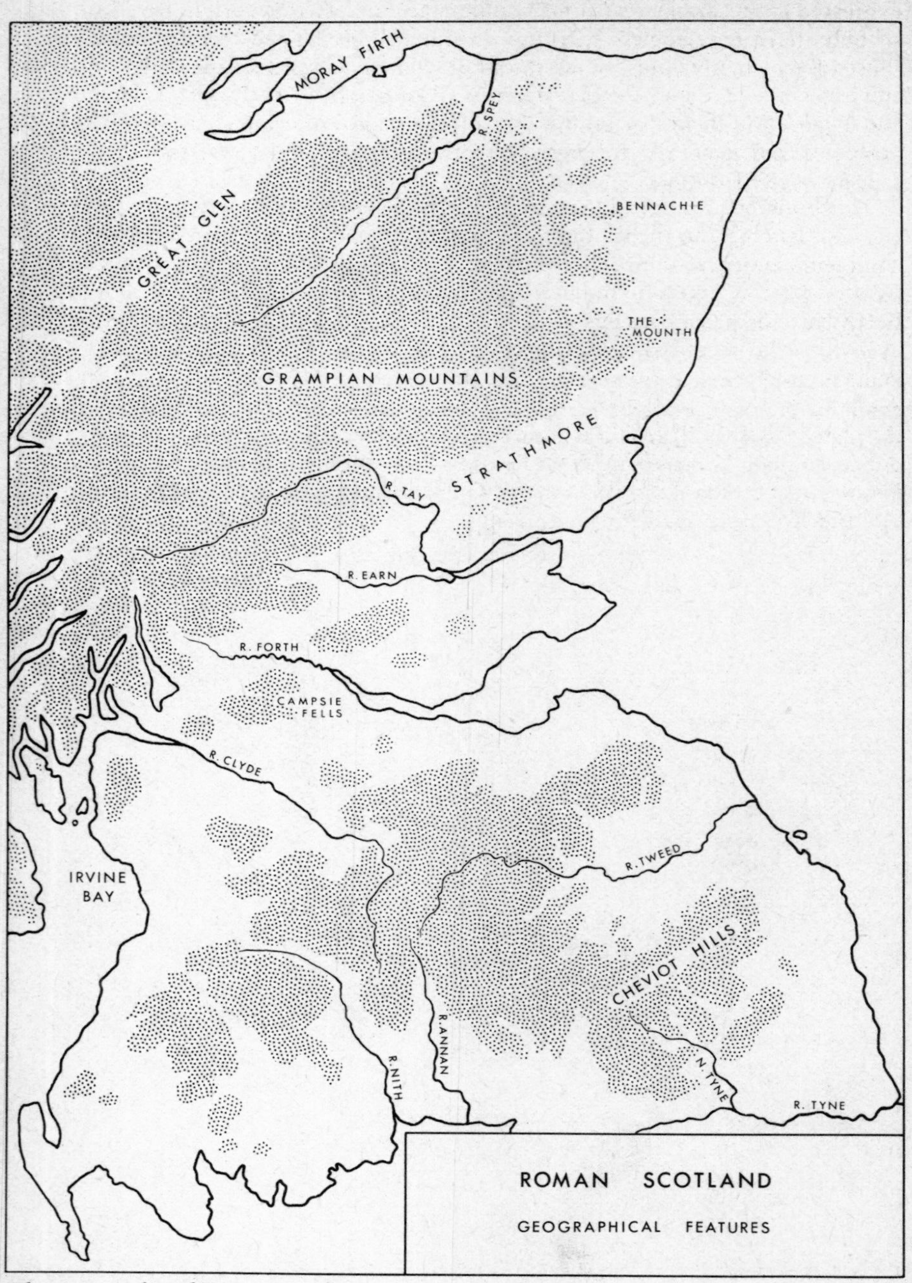

The Geography of Roman Scotland

I

Romans

The arrival of Roman armies in north Britain in the 80s AD coincided with the establishment of the first frontiers in the Roman empire. Before that time the empire, of course, had boundaries but not frontiers in the sense of patrolled and defended lines of control or, as they were to become in the second century AD, barriers. The construction of these frontiers reflected a changing attitude on the part of the Romans to the extension of their empire. The possibility that their empire might not continue to expand indefinitely was first recognised, paradoxically, in the testament of the greatest expansionist of them all, Augustus. The construction of the lines of control in the 80s was the second step, and the hardening of these into linear barriers a third. But throughout these years, and beyond, the empire was still expanding, though not in the grand way of previous centuries. Claudius, Nero, Vespasian, Titus, Domitian, Trajan, Antoninus Pius, Marcus Aurelius, Septimius Severus all expanded, or attempted to expand, the Roman empire, and it was the advent of the civil wars in the mid-third century and the swing in the balance of power against the Romans that led at first to a halt to this expansion and then a gradual, and long drawn out, contraction; long drawn out, for the Roman empire did not end until the fall of Constantinople in 1453. Within this time scale the frontiers of the Roman empire such as Hadrian's Wall and the Antonine Wall had a very short life. Further, while ostensibly reflecting the might of Rome, viewed against the background of the twenty-two centuries from the traditional foundation of Rome to the fall of Constantinople in 1453, they may be regarded as expressions of failure.

The expansion of Rome

Patrolled lines of control along a frontier had no place in the early history of Rome. The city's first concerns were to rid herself of the oppression of her foreign masters, and then to defend herself against her neighbours. Through successive struggles with the peoples of Italy Rome gradually came to control the whole of the peninsula: by the end of the third century BC all Italy lay within her grasp. What drove Rome on was fear of her enemies, fear of being conquered and subdued by them. During the course of these struggles Rome perfected a military machine, a vehicle which eventually was to bring her to the control of the whole Mediterranean basin. This vehicle was the legion. Copied from the Greek phalanx this body of 4,000–5,000 men was rendered more flexible by its organisation into three lines, each advancing through gaps in the line ahead to present fresh troops to the enemy. The Romans were also prepared to learn from other peoples: the Greeks might provide one example but weapons and armour were also adopted from the Gauls. The legion was primarily an infantry unit; the cavalry element in the army was provided by Rome's allies.

The legion was fully incorporated into the Roman state. It was formed from the citizens of Rome and the farmers of its territory; its commanders were drawn from the ruling oligarchy of Rome. However, these men were not a separate military caste: when not fighting they were civil magistrates and administrators. Thus military affairs permeated the whole Roman state, and was not a distinct and separate element in society.

Her skill in warfare and administration, the loyalty and resilience of her people, were to stand Rome in good stead in her fiercest fight, that against the Carthaginians. Over half of the sixty years 264–204 BC were spent fighting this people. Again the war grew out of fear, fear that the only other major power in the western Mediterranean would come to subjugate Rome unless prevented by forceful action on the part of Rome herself. However, in this war Rome moved first and carried out a pre-emptive strike by crossing the Straits of Messina into Sicily to occupy the city of Messina which she believed was about to be occupied by the Carthaginians. Menacing activities by her enemies were to be used again and again as an excuse for war by Rome even against the weakest foe: she always liked a *casus belli*, even if this was a patent fabrication. The first Punic war ended with the victory of Rome and the acquisition of its first overseas territory, Sicily – which was quickly followed by Sardinia and Corsica. The victorious conclusion of the second Punic war saw the absorption of the Carthaginian territories in Spain into the Roman orbit.

So far as possible the new provinces were left to govern and administer themselves, and this was to be a continuing feature of Roman provincial administration. The new territories were already divided among city states and Rome perpetuated this organisation, later creating new cities where necessary. To govern each province a magistrate was sent out from Rome. His duties included administering the law, raising taxes and keeping the peace. In carrying out such functions he would have assistance, from, for example, a financial secretary (also sent out from Rome annually), and from the army. However, unless these provinces were troubled by bandits, as in Sardinia, or an external enemy as in Spain, army units were not usually permanently stationed in them: there was no need to control the local cities by a military presence, for they could be controlled by the mere existence of the army. A serious revolt within a few years of the establishment of a new province was a regular accompaniment of the expansion of the empire, but thereafter for the most part the provincials settled down peaceably under their new masters (though internal disturbances and insurrections broke out occasionally in both the Republic and the Empire).

The second Punic war by chance also brought Rome an interest in the eastern Mediterranean. Macedonia had declared war on Rome after Hannibal's victory at Cannae and thus drew on herself the wrath of Rome after her success over the Carthaginians. Thus was Rome drawn into the maelstrom of eastern politics. At first she seemed to be content merely to hold the ring, but this changed in the middle of the second century BC when, losing patience, she destroyed Carthage, incorporated Africa and Macedonia into her empire and then proceeded to expand further in the eastern Mediterranean by the simple expedient of inheriting kingdoms from childless monarchs. Eighty years after the destruction of Carthage practically all the Mediterranean basin was in Roman hands – Egypt was the only major exception – and Rome was turning her attention to its hinterland.

This era of expansion brought new tensions to Rome. Now a permanent field army was required. The conscription of men from Rome and Italy on an annual basis and for a limited number of years was no longer tolerable or efficient. The old ways, the old Roman army, ended for ever when in 107 BC Marius enrolled volunteers for the war in north Africa. A new problem was created in turn, for these soldiers owed their allegiance not to the Roman state but to their commanders. Further, the state was finding it increasingly difficult to control overweening and unscrupulous nobles. These strains tore the republic apart and resulted in the creation of the principate under Augustus' guidance. Through these years, however, the empire continued to expand. The best known war of conquest was conducted by Julius Caesar in Gaul – best known because he left his own record of his exploits. The Gallic War reveals clearly the Roman military machine, Roman strategy and tactics and Roman diplomacy at work.

The conquest of Gaul was unprovoked. The Romans, of course, had their excuse for intervention – the migration of the Helvetii, then the presence of Germans in Gaul (who had incidentally, as Caesar records, been invited there by one of the Gaulish tribes), and finally the reaction of the Gaulish tribes to the Roman intervention. But the main purpose of Caesar's war was to enable him to keep an army in the field, and as a result increase his power (he gained important prestige through his triumphs) and obtain booty for his army. When Gaul seemed to have been subdued, Caesar turned his attention to Britain and led two expeditions there. He also reconnoitred across the Rhine. In both cases he had excuses for intervention and might well have gone on to further conquests but for insurrections in Gaul and then a changed political situation in Rome which led to his interests being directed elsewhere. When he actually became master of Rome, Caesar significantly did not return to Britain but turned his attention towards Parthia.

The fighting in Gaul was carried out by legions supported by troops raised from the less civilised parts of the empire or from the Gallic allies. The number of legions steadily increased from four to 11, new ones being raised from Italy when required. Support – or auxiliary – troops included Cretan archers, slingers from the Balearic islands, light armed infantry from Numidia in north Africa, Gaul and, in later years, Germany. An important element in the army was the Gallic cavalry, in total something over 4,000 men, raised from friendly or allied tribes, even during the rebellion of Vercingetorix from German allies. This force was of great value in reconnoitering and raiding, as well as supporting the legions in battle. The cavalry occasionally fought engagements by themselves, and in a set-piece battle served an important function in following up the victory won by the legions: Caesar lamented that the lack of cavalry in Britain in 55 BC prevented him from achieving his usual success.

Caesar was a civil magistrate as well as a military commander during his governorship of Cisalpine Gaul (actually north Italy), Transalpine Gaul (southern France: modern Provence) and Illyricum (the west coast of Yugoslavia). Each winter he returned to his provinces to supervise their administration and dispense justice. In the spring he gathered his army together and set out on campaign. The fighting and diplomacy during these campaigns was carried out at Caesar's behest: he never appears to have consulted the Senate in Rome on any matter, though he sent regular dispatches and justified his actions retrospectively. Some of the Gallic tribes were allied to Rome and Caesar was quick to exploit the jealousies and differences between the tribes and indeed within each tribe. He controlled all the tribes, both friendly and hostile, by taking hostages from among their chief men and by the presence of his army and himself – or by the threat of his presence (though this did not always prevent revolts from breaking out). Caesar does not mention the construction of a single permanent fort in Gaul during the eight years of campaigning there and none of this date have been found by modern archaeologists working in France. At the end of each season the army returned to winter quarters. At first all the legions were placed together close to the existing province, but later they were split into separate groups, though never less than a legion in size, and quartered in the territory of newly conquered tribes. During the summer the army lived off the land as much as was possible and then laid in supplies for the winter months. The winter quarters, temporary timber huts, were protected from attack by a rampart and ditch and such camps were also constructed on campaign.

The situation in Gaul in the years following Caesar's conquest is far from clear. When the position becomes clearer, early in Augustus' reign, the army units are found on the Rhine: it seems probable that legions were first stationed there permanently between 16 and 13 BC. Here the units were poised for intervention either in Gaul, where insurrections might break out – as in 12 BC, or in Germany, which was to be the scene of the next step forward.

The bringing of new order to the empire by Augustus resulted in new order on the frontiers. As soon as Augustus had achieved an internal settlement, with the establishment of the principate in 27 BC, he turned his attention to the problems of the frontiers. It is possible that Augustus' activities, which at first sight appear to have no thread or purpose, in fact were carefully considered and executed according to a coherent plan.

In the years 27–13 BC Augustus concentrated on trying to impose lasting settlements on all the frontiers of the empire except the northern. He reorganised the remaining African kingdoms by annexing Numidia and moving its king, Juba, to Mauretania. Shortly afterwards, in 25–24 BC, he sent an expedition into Arabia, during which Aden was sacked, and probed up the Nile: it was clear that nothing was to be feared from these quarters. Internal dissensions in Parthia led to success on the eastern frontier merely by threatening invasion: sabre rattling by Tiberius on the frontier in 20 BC led to the return of all Roman prisoners and captured standards in a truly cheap victory. At the same time Augustus ratified Antony's reorganisation of the local client kingdoms. Meanwhile in western Europe Augustus completed the conquest of Spain, which had been dragging on for nearly two centuries, subdued the Alpine tribes, organised the affairs of Gaul (which seem to have been left untended since Caesar lost interest) and achieved some sort of diplomatic settlement with Britain. During these years minor campaigns were fought elsewhere, in Illyricum, Pannonia and Moesia, along the Danube and in Asia Minor. The assimilation of the tribes up to the Danube was achieved by 15 BC, though, as often happened, serious revolts broke out some years later. Most of this military and diplomatic activity was carried out by Augustus himself, by Tiberius and Drusus his stepsons, or by Agrippa, his closest friend and later his son-in-law.

The successful settlements on all the frontiers except the north left Augustus free in 13 BC to consider the conquest of Germany. It has been argued that Augustus saw the conquest of Germany as imperative for the security of the empire. Whether Augustus would have stopped on the Elbe, which was seemingly the initial objective, is uncertain. The Romans at this time thought the world was limited in extent and Augustus could well have considered that the subjugation of Germany was merely the first step towards the control of all the world beyond the Danube. Augustus had many excuses for invading Germany, for since Caesar's time there had been several forays into Gaul by the Germans.

Starting in 12 BC Drusus conducted four campaigns into Germany as far as the

Elbe. After his death in 9 BC Tiberius and L. Domitius Ahenobarbus took over, the latter even crossing the Elbe. At the same time the North Sea coast was explored as far north as the northern tip of Jutland. Periodic revolts by the tribes living in the provinces immediately south of the Danube accompanied the campaigns of these years. In AD 6, while Tiberius was attacking the Marcomanni, who had given no offence to Rome save by maintaining a well equipped and trained standing army, a most serious revolt broke out in Pannonia and Illyricum which led to the abandonment of the campaign and the start of fierce fighting in the Danube provinces. No sooner was this revolt put down than P. Quintilius Varus was defeated in Germany: his army of three legions and an unknown number of auxiliaries were massacred in the Teutoburg Forest. Augustus was now an old man in his seventies. He lacked the resilience of earlier years and these two events – the Illyricum revolt and the loss of the legions in Germany – resulted in a loss of faith, retrenchment and the famous advice to his successor not to extend the empire any further (advice which he had signally failed to follow himself).

The Varan disaster of AD 9 has clouded the Augustan achievements in Germany up to that date. It is clear, however, that Roman strategy and tactics in conquering and organising a new province were no different now from what they had been forty years before under Caesar. Following the *casus belli*, taken up in 12 BC, Rome had first conquered the German tribes and then set about reducing the land between the Rhine and the Elbe to the status of a province. During the course of these operations reconnaisance expeditions crossed the Elbe just as Caesar had crossed the Rhine and the English Channel, and treaties were concluded with the tribes beyond the river. An altar and cult of Augustus was established at Cologne on the Rhine to be the focus for provincial unity and loyalty, in emulation of an earlier establishment at Lugudunum for the Gallic tribes. Later another altar to Augustus was erected on the Elbe. Cities and markets sprang up, Germans joined the Roman army and the country appeared to be largely pacified. However, even now, in AD 9, there were few forts in Germany. Timber forts constructed along the Lippe, the main route into Germany, were possibly not occupied all year. Other forts in the new province are mentioned by Roman writers, but these have not been located and it is probable that they were only occupied during the summer, for still the main body of the army retired each winter into Roman territory, as Caesar had done while conquering Gaul. By AD 9 the pacification of Germany was so far advanced that taxation and Roman law were being imposed on the new provincials. Whether this action, Varus' temperament or simply German restlessness led to the subsequent – successful – revolt is difficult to determine. Certainly the situation in Germany followed that in other provinces: initial Roman success, revolt(s), eventual Roman victory, often after bitter and protracted fighting. The important difference now was that Augustus was too old to recover from the blow and preferred to retreat, abandon the forts across the Rhine, and re-establish that river as the empire's frontier.

The methods used to defend that frontier, and others, were simple and straightforward. The five or six legions on the Rhine were placed so that they could intervene in either Gaul or Germany. The forces were concentrated in large army groups. Only four military bases dating to the years before 12 BC have been found on the Rhine, though others may have existed. These bases were all, with possibly one exception, apparently capable of holding two legions, though they may not all have been occupied at the same time. They were usually placed beside access routes into Germany. The auxiliary units were stationed at, or close to, the legionary bases, though a few guarded important points such as river crossings. Such dispositions continued, with the modification of an extra base at Cologne on the Rhine and forts along the Lippe and possible elsewhere in Germany, until the Varan disaster. It was only after AD 9, or possibly AD 16, when Germanicus was recalled, that new forts were established on the Rhine, in positions indicating that they were more concerned with defence than offence.

This situation was reflected elsewhere in the empire. In the east, for example, the army units were not spread out along the frontier, but placed astride the great trade routes, which of course also served as invasion routes, so that they could not only control the local population within the empire but also move out against the adjacent kingdoms. The main base on the eastern frontier lay at Antioch where three or four legions were stationed at the western end of the caravan route into Parthia.

The second method of defence was by means of client kingdoms, a device long used in the eastern Roman world. Much of the eastern Mediterranean was controlled through client kingdoms, Rome often preferring to establish a new king when one died without an obvious heir rather than to incorporate the kingdom into the empire. The client kings were responsible for maintaining law and order within their own territory and for defending their states from external agression: in many ways they were useful buffer states for Rome. At Rome's behest they would have to provide troops for Rome's armies, but they were not allowed their own foreign policy and if they demonstrated too much independence they were simply replaced. In this way Rome controlled great areas with the minimum of trouble and cost. Augustus' own statement of his achievements, the *Res Gestae*, makes it clear that Rome regarded the client states as subject to her and therefore part of the empire.

Rome's defence was thus her latent power, supported by the visible expression of the force behind that power, her armies. Client kings could be kept under control by the threat of Roman intervention: diplomacy – and the payment of subsidies – to such kings and to peoples beyond the empire, was cheaper than military intervention. Order was maintained within the empire, and the frontiers defended by troops placed at strategic points, usually close to but not actually on, the frontiers of the empire. Army groups stationed at such points were also in a position to move forward to conquer new lands as and when necessary: there was no point in stringing the army units out along the frontier simply because there was no permanent frontier, there was only the boundary of this year, or this decade, and before long the unconquered Roman army would move forward again and incorporate new tribes and cities within the empire. And indeed this happened regularly up until AD 9. The Varan disaster brought about a pause in Rome's expansion, a pause which was to last throughout the remaining years of Augustus' principate and, with the exception of Germanicus' abortive and costly campaigns in Germany, throughout the twenty-three years of Tiberius (14–37), and, in spite of the preparatory moves and gestures of Gaius (37–41), was not to end until AD 43 when Claudius (41–54) began the conquest of Britain.

The thirty years between the Varan disaster and the invasion of Britain saw a number of changes in the Roman army, changes partly resulting from the inertia of those years. The army was gradually settling down to a life on the frontier and adapting itself to that life. By AD 43 no soldier in the army, apart from a few long serving centurions, would have known the days of expansion and exploration under Augustus: those days were now over a generation ago. The army of Claudius, although in theory similar to that of his great-uncle, was subtly modifying itself to suit its new role. This process can first be seen in Germany.

In the years following the recall of Germanicus in AD 16, the virtual end of Roman pretensions in Germany (at least for two generations), there was a move away from the garrisoning of two legions together in the same base. In the army of lower Germany the two-legion base at Cologne was abandoned, the garrison being provided with separate fortresses elsewhere, though two legions remained at Vetera. In the army of Upper Germany two legions remained at Mainz, but the other two legions were split between separate fortresses. Now also there was a move to fill, at least in part, the gaps between the legionary fortresses along the Rhine by auxiliary forts, linked by a road along the river and connected in certain areas by fortlets. This was accentuated in Upper Germany after the withdrawal of the legion at Strasbourg for service in Britain in 43. This move was compensated for by the establishment of auxiliary forts spread over a wider area, but still not abandoning the principle of military strong-points for a linear arrangement. In Raetia (modern Bavaria), further to the south-east, under Claudius there was, however, a move towards the establishment of a linear defensive system along the Danube. Here, for the first time, the south bank of the Danube was defended by the construction of a series of forts – ten have so far been assigned to these years – and this probably reflects the abandonment of Roman designs on the tribes beyond the river.

The conquest of Britain

The change in military thinking can perhaps best be seen in Britain for here the system of defence and control started *de nouveau* in 43 and is not obscured by earlier dispositions. The real reason for the invasion of Britain in 43 is probably given by the Roman writer Suetonius: Claudius required a triumph. Claudius had come to the throne in 41 after the murder of his nephew Gaius (better known by his nickname Caligula), in not too auspicious circumstances. There was a rebellion a few months later, quickly put down, but Claudius, who had no military experience, and indeed had had to wait until the age of 47 before being made consul, required military prestige – so necessary for an emperor – to strengthen his position. He chose Britain, long considered a legitimate Roman sphere of interest, presumably considered not too difficult a task, and for which he had a pretext – the expulsion of a king, Berikos (almost certainly Verica of the Atrebates), by his brother. Further Claudius could be seen to be emulating the actions of his ancestor, the great Julius Caesar, while the conquest of land considered by the Romans to be at the end of the world would bring its own mystique.

The invasion force consisted of four legions, *II Augusta*, *IX Hispana*, *XIV* and *XX*, with probably an equivalent number of auxiliary soldiers. The main opponent was the kingdom ruled by Caratacus and Togodumnus, sons of King Cunobelin, who had died about three years before. Their realm embraced the tribes of the Catuvellauni and Trinovantes in central southern England and Essex. The Roman army dealt with the opposition expeditiously, though not without some hard fighting, and in one skirmish Togodumnus was killed. Claudius himself arrived for the final blow against Colchester, capital of the kingdom. The vanquished sued for peace, Caratacus fled westwards, and other tribes submitted. Claudius in Britain was hailed as Imperator, the senate voted him the title of Britannicus, and awarded him a triumph. Claudius had indeed won his military prestige and was not challenged by rebellion during the remaining eleven years of his reign, though he did use other means to strengthen his position, such as his marriage to Agrippina.

Following the return of Claudius to Rome Aulus Plautius, the governor of Britain, was left to conquer 'the rest', a meaningless phrase which is incapable of interpretation: it could imply the completion of the conquest of those parts of the island designated by Claudius as the province, or the rest of the island, excluding the client kingdoms, which it was felt in time would be incorporated within the empire. Plautius' army quickly overran the south and midlands of England. Little is known of these operations. Vespasian, later to become emperor, was legate of II Augusta at this time and fought thirty engagements and captured more than twenty *oppida* (probably mainly forts rather than towns) in southern England, including the Isle of Wight. Otherwise the strength of the opposition to the Roman armies is not known: the hints in the relevant Roman literature suggest that opposition was not great – Vespasian's achievements were recorded only because he later became emperor.

Although little evidence survives concerning Roman campaigning methods in Britain during the early years of the conquest a clear picture of campaigning in Britain does emerge when the various comments in the books of Tacitus (in particular his biography of his father-in-law the Flavian governor, Gnaeus Julius Agricola) are gathered together. The pattern that emerges when these various statements, often made almost as throw-away lines, are combined to form a continuous narrative, is little different from that provided by Caesar's *Gallic War*.

At the beginning of the campaigning season the governor concentrated his army and marched out to try to locate the enemy, a task in which he was not always successful. Intelligence was gathered from a variety of sources, including merchants, and this information included details of the tribes to be attacked, their political organisation, their strongholds, the lie of the land and landing places and harbours where appropriate. Where an excuse for attack was needed a pretext was manufactured. In 43 there was a fugitive British prince in Rome and while Agricola was considering the possibility of invading Ireland he had an Irish prince to hand. His excuse for attacking the Caledonians a year later was that he had heard of threatening movements made by the tribe. It was only after the Roman invasion that the northern tribes 'without provocation' – a statement very reminiscent of that concerning a similar incident in the Gallic war – attacked a Roman fort.

Much time on campaign was clearly spent fighting the terrain and weather rather than the enemy. Each night the army defended itself from attack by the construction of temporary camps, a device shown to be of special value in Agricola's sixth season when, after he had divided his army into three divisions (a move approved by modern military tacticians), one division was attacked. It might take several seasons to defeat the enemy, but Roman generals were used to such problems and more than one governor of Britain had experience of mountain warfare in more difficult parts of the empire.

At the end of each campaigning season the army retired into winter quarters, which, until the enemy was subdued, always lay within the province. It was only after the defeat of the enemy that forts were built in his territory; until then it was controlled by the army's presence, or threat of its presence, and by the taking of hostages as recorded in the second season and after Mons Graupius. After its defeat the enemy, or rather the new provincials, would be disarmed. Finally, it may be noted that campaigning was only the summer's activity. In the winter the governor, as had Caesar, turned to the problems of administration and justice in the more settled parts of the province.

The main distinction to be drawn between Tacitus' account of campaigning and Caesar's, lies in the nature of the winter quarters. Caesar, each winter, divided his army into groups never less than one legion strong, and generally two or three legions in strength. These were placed either in friendly territory or in the area of newly conquered tribes in order to intimidate and control them. The position in Britain is not clear during the very early years after the invasion but when a pattern does emerge it is not of such concentrations. On the contrary, the units are now spread between a large number of forts, echoing the pattern apparently developing at the same time in Germany. In part this reflects the increasing importance of the auxiliary regiments, which for the first time in the Flavian period (69–96) formed a battle-line without help from the legions.

The arrangements made by the first governor of Britain, Aulus Plautius, for the organisation of this province are fairly clear. Certain tribes – the Catuvellauni, Trinovantes, Coritani, Dobunni, Durotriges and Dumnonii – were formed into the province. Each tribe was organised into the north-west European equivalent of the city state prevalent in the Mediterranean basin, the tribe being translated into a *civitas*. The *civitas* consisted of the territory of the tribe, possibly modified from pre-conquest days, with the chief urban centre of the tribe forming the city of the *civitas*. Much controversy surrounds the question of the strict definition of the *civitas* and it is not possible to be sure whether the Romans saw the organisation as essentially a city with a surrounding territory, on which lay lesser settlements, or as a tribe with a town chosen to be its administrative and religious focus: so far as one can tell the former is more likely to be nearer reality. These *civitates* would take some time to create and it is possible that in the early years, while the local aristocracy was being introduced to Roman ways, each was governed by a prefect sent out by Rome. When this period was over the *civitates* would be left to govern themselves within the administrative, legal and financial framework provided by the governor and procurator of the province.

After the conquest not all tribes were incorporated into the province. Some were made, by treaty, into client kingdoms. These were the Iceni in East Anglia, the Atrebates in Wessex, and the Brigantes in northern England. These client states extended the area under Roman influence to the later provincial boundary, though with the notable exception of Wales. They were a device frequently used by Rome when incorporating new territory into the empire, partly, no doubt, in order to relieve pressure on the army in those early days. Certainly Rome would have regarded them essentially as parts of the empire and felt free to intervene in their affairs at will – as she was later to demonstrate in her dealings with the Iceni in 47 when the governor sent troops to disarm the tribe and with the Brigantes on a number of occasions. These tribes were, however, for the most part left to run their own affairs, and, so far as can be seen, left ungarrisoned by Roman troops. As the client kings died, the treaties between them and Rome lapsed and were either renegotiated with their successors (though there is no evidence for this) or their kingdoms were incorporated into the province. Thus on the death of Prasutagus of the Iceni in 60, apparently with no male heir, his kingdom was taken into the province; this led, as was so often the case when client kingdoms were absorbed by Rome, to a bloody revolt. Ten years later the expulsion of Queen Cartimandua from her Brigantian kingdom resulted in the incorporation of that client state into the province. The kingdom of Cogidubnus of the Atrebates was also presumably absorbed into the province on his death and was divided into possibly as many as three *civitates*.

The tribes who submitted to Rome and were formed into the province had to be controlled and defended from attack. Little is known of the disposition of the auxiliary units in these early years, so it is not possible to determine whether or not they were grouped round the legionary fortresses in the concentration of forces still found at this time on the continent. The placing of the legions is rather more certain. One was established at Colchester, the former capital of the kingdom of the Catuvellauni and Trinovantes, and now to become the capital of the new province. A second legion was placed in the south-west, a third in the northern part of the province, the east midlands, while the fourth presumably lay somewhere in between in the west midlands. It is possible that in some areas legionary detachments were garrisoned away from the main legionary fortresses, though this would be unexpected in view of the situation still pertaining elsewhere in the empire. The discovery of a fort at Verulamium, the main town of the new *civitas* of the Catuvellauni, suggests that military units, presumably auxiliary units, may have been stationed at all the new tribal centres in the early years after the conquest.

The army must soon have started the construction of roads to link the new forts. One of these roads, the Fosse Way, ran from Exeter to Lincoln. This has been described as the first frontier in Britain, but in reality it is merely a road connecting the forts situated in a broad zone along the western and northern boundaries of the province and no more. The boundary of the province at this time would presumably have been the western and northern boundaries of the tribes which submitted to Rome. There would have been no point in defending such a boundary; rather the troops would be placed in the most convenient geographical positions in order to intercept any attacks on the province. Furthermore, there is no need to envisage these forts as being occupied throughout the year. In the summer, as the contemporary accounts of activity in Britain make clear, the army would be out on campaign. The strategy behind the disposition of the military forces was not to change throughout the many fluctuations in success. The main factors governing the position of forts were that they should be so placed that the army could control the local population and defend it from attack, units in the 'front line' being supported by others placed on the roads leading into the interior of the province.

Military affairs in Britain did not proceed smoothly. After the initial flurry, culminating in suitable prestige for Claudius, his interest seems to have flagged and for the remaining twelve years of his reign the only recorded recurrence of his interest was when Caratacus was captured and paraded through Rome. Britain also appears to have been left in a backwater during the early years of Nero's reign (54–68). When, in 57, he took up the reins of government himself he at first seems to have considered abandoning the province – no doubt after securing a suitable settlement in Rome's favour. In the end he decided to retain control and press forward the conquest of the island, commencing with the Welsh tribes. This advance lost some impetus when Nero's new governor, Quintus Veranius, died after only a year in office, and then ground to a halt in 60 when the Iceni revolted during their absorption into the province following the death of Prasutagus. Britain again reverted to being a backwater through the remaining years of his reign and during the succeeding civil war; this was reflected in the withdrawal of *legio XIV* from Britain in 66. The accession of Vespasian (69–79) brought to the throne a soldier who had previously served in Britain. He replaced the withdrawn legion and initiated an advance in the island which culminated in the defeat, fourteen years later, of the final major enemy in Britain, the Caledonians.

The erratic way in which events proceeded in Britain was due almost entirely to the interest and involvement of the emperor. When he was actively concerned to deal effectively with frontier problems, they were dealt with expeditiously; at other times they were left as a running sore. Under the Flavians, Vespasian and his two sons (69–96), no other events intervened for thirteen or fourteen years to slow up or stop the forward progress of Roman arms in Britain. During this time the size of the province was almost doubled.

In Britain the major task facing Vespasian was the recovery of Roman influence in Brigantia after the expulsion of Queen Cartimandua by her consort Venutius during the Roman civil war. The kingdom was invaded by the new governor Petillius Cerealis, Venutius and the opponents of Rome were defeated, and the construction of forts commenced. The next governor, Julius Frontinus, plucked out the thorn which had long been in the side of the Roman forces in the west of Britain by conquering and garrisoning the Welsh tribes. The activities of both generals could be seen, in some ways, as the completion of unfinished business. It was not until the next governorship, that of Julius Agricola, that the Roman army pushed forward into new lands.

It is under the Flavian governors that the pattern of the military occupation of Britain first becomes clear. The legions were widely spaced as before, though all were moved at this time. Under Petillius Cerealis *IX Hispana* was moved from Lincoln to York and under Julius Frontinus *II Augusta* was established at Caerleon in South Wales and *II Adiutrix* transferred to a new base at Chester. *XX Valeria Victrix* appears to have remained at Wroxeter for some time, but took *II Adiutrix*'s place at Chester when that legion was sent to the continent probably in 86. These legions were carefully placed for effective action. *II Augusta* could oversee the Silures in south Wales, with *XX Valeria Victrix* poised to provide support, and to keep watch on the Ordovices in north Wales. *II Adiutrix* was positioned so that it could intervene either against the Ordovices or the Brigantes where it would be able to support *IX Hispana*, whose sphere of activity would include defence of the northern frontier.

While the legions were concerned with larger strategy the local situation was covered by the auxiliary units based on a network of forts connected by roads. So little is known about the internal layout of these forts, or their garrisons, that it is not possible to determine if normally one unit was assigned to each fort, or if units were divided between a number of forts, or combined in other instances. An added complication is that units may not have become fully standardised in size and internal organisation. In the only widely investigated fort of this period, Pen Llystyn, there were twelve barrack-blocks suggesting either the brigading together of two small cohorts, or the existence of a large unit of double size not attested anywhere else. There are peculiarities too in the barrack-blocks within the Scottish 'type-site', Fendoch, which may imply that the fort was not built, as is generally assumed, for a thousand strong infantry unit. What is clear, however, is that the forts are not specially grouped round the legions in preparation for offensive protection or advance, but are spread across the country, concerned rather with the strategy of control: there was of course in Wales no enemy beyond the province poised to attack.

The Roman army in Britain

The nature and size of the force charged with keeping peace in the province and protecting it from attack also becomes clearer in the Flavian period. The four legions each contained something over 5,000 infantrymen with a small detachment of 120 cavalrymen, Roman citizens all. Each infantryman wore articulated plate armour, known as the *lorica segmentata*, an iron or bronze helmet and carried sword, dagger, two throwing spears, or *pila*, and a large shield; the cavalryman probably wore mail, but otherwise was similarly armed. Well armed, the legionaries were also highly trained and disciplined. They were used to fighting the set-piece battle but also carrying out major building programmes: each legion contained its own engineering corps, building and maintenance staff, medical service and artillery corps. The legion was divided into ten cohorts, subdivided in turn into six 80-strong centuries, with the exception of the first cohort, which in some, possibly most, legions was composed of five double-sized centuries. The century was commanded by a centurion, usually a soldier who had risen from the ranks: these professional officers formed the core of the army. The cohort had no administrative organisation, though it had an important tactical role in battle, and sometimes served as a conveniently sized detachment for duties away from base. The senior officers of the legion were drawn from the aristocracy of the empire, the legate and the senior tribune, his second-in-command, from the senatorial families and the prefect of the camp and the junior tribunes from the equestrian nobility.

The other main branch of the provincial army was the *auxilia*. This was originally formed from the friends and allies of Rome to give support to the legions, but now auxiliary units were raised from the frontier tribes of the empire and thereafter locally recruited. The term *auxilia* covered a variety of units of different sizes and organisation. There were three basic types of unit: the infantry cohort of six centuries, the cavalry *ala* of 16 troops and the mixed cohort of six centuries and four troops. In the Flavian period a double-sized unit of each type was introduced. Although the units were in theory double in size – milliary as opposed to quingenary – in fact they were not quite so large, the infantry cohort containing ten centuries, the *ala* 24 troops and the mixed cohort ten centuries and eight troops. Epigraphic evidence allows the strength of this branch of the British army to be closely defined in the early second century. During the reigns of Trajan and Hadrian (98–138) the minimum number of auxiliary units in Britain seems to have been as follows:

The '*Auxilia*' in Britain during the reigns of Trajan and Hadrian (98–138)

	number	**total strength**
ala milliaria	1	800
ala quingenaria	14+1?	7,000+500?
cohors milliaria equitata	4	4000
cohors milliaria peditata	1+1?	800+800?
cohors quingenaria equitata	23+1?	13,800+600?
cohors quingenaria peditata	14	6,720
	57+3?	33,120+1,900?

It seems unlikely that the strength of the *auxilia* in Britain in the Flavian period was less than the above total of between 33,000 and 35,000 men. There were losses from the British army between the retirement of Agricola and the second century, for

Tacitus records the presence of four Batavian cohorts at Mons Graupius while only one is later attested in Britain. There were certainly a number of occasions when troops could have been withdrawn from Britain, but none when new units are likely to have been sent to the province, in the late first century or early second. Furthermore, a number of units are attested in Britain, but not in the Trajanic-Hadrianic period so the above total is most probably on the conservative side.

The table clearly demonstrates that the most common unit in the British army was the *cohors quingenaria equitata*, the smaller mixed unit, about 600 men strong. The *ala quingenaria*, 500 men strong, and the similarly sized cohort, the *cohors quingenaria peditata*, were present in approximately equal sizes. The milliary, thousand strong units, of all types were rare now as always: there was only one *ala milliaria* in this, or any other, province. The auxiliary century seems to have contained the same number of men as the legionary century – 80, while the cavalry troop was 32 men strong. The infantry centurion and the cavalry decurion were soldiers risen from the ranks, and the commanding officers, prefects and tribunes, were members of the equestrian nobility. The auxiliaries were armed in a similar manner to the legionaries, though they wore mail rather than plate armour. Auxiliaries were not Roman citizens, but awarded that honour on retirement.

The Roman army was, in the main, a volunteer army, though conscription was on occasion employed. A tolerably good level of regular pay was a powerful inducement to recruiting. Legionaries and auxiliaries both served for twenty five years, though centurions and decurions had no set length of service. The senior officers served for much shorter periods, generally about three years and had much less military experience than the men they commanded. Provincial governors such as Agricola had only acquired about six years service before commanding an army of about 50,000 men. It is indeed remarkable that with commanders of such limited military experience the Roman army did not lose more battles!

2

Barbarians

This book is concerned with the frontiers which Rome built in Britain along its northern boundary – or perhaps boundaries would be more accurate as the line fluctuated – over a period of sixty years from the end of the first century to the middle of the second. The enemy which these successive frontiers faced was primarily the Caledonii and their successors the Picts who lived north of the Forth. There is no evidence that the tribes of the Scottish Lowlands ever gave the Roman army any serious cause for concern, yet as these people were those more immediately close to the longest-surviving Roman frontier in north Britain – Hadrian's Wall – it is essential to consider their archaeology and history, as well as the Caledonians', and also their relationship to Rome.

The tribes of north Britain

The earliest surviving description of the tribes of Scotland is by the Alexandrian geographer Claudius Ptolemaeus writing in the mid-second century AD. He wrote two books, the *Almagest* and the *Geography*. It is the latter which contains the references to Britain and it is simply a list of geographical features, tribes and places with their latitudes and longitudes. As such the *Geography* is an incomparable source, but it suffers from three defects so far as Scotland is concerned. Firstly, Ptolemy made a basic error in his measurements in relation to north Britain and as a result Scotland north of the Forth is twisted round at 90°. Secondly, it is possible that Ptolemy had no astronomical data from the British Isles, locations being determined by measurements from Marseilles. Finally, Ptolemy probably simply read names off a map, placing in his list under the tribal heading those place names which appeared on the map in the general area of the tribe. This map has not survived but it was probably also used to provide the basic information in the later document known as the *Ravenna Cosmography*. As a result of these defects many places mentioned by Ptolemy cannot now be identified, and even when a name appears under the heading of a tribe the possibility that it has been wrongly attributed by Ptolemy cannot altogether be dismissed. One final general point should be mentioned: it is not clear whether the place names listed by Ptolemy in northern Britain are native sites or Roman forts or even camps. (The places listed in Ireland clearly cannot be Roman forts, so there is equally no need for all the places in Scotland to be Roman sites.)

South of the Forth Ptolemy lists four tribes: the Votadini of eastern Scotland, the Selgovae in the centre, the Novantae in Dumfries and Galloway, and the Damnonii or Dumnonii who occupy the Clyde basin and spread northwards through Strathearn into south Strathmore (fig. 1). The location of the Votadini and the Novantae is not in doubt, but there are problems concerning the territory of the Selgovae and the Damnonii. Four places, probably all Roman forts, are placed within the territory of the former. Only one of these places can be identified,

Trimontium, Newstead in the middle Tweed basin. However, the co-ordinates of the other three places suggest that they are further west and one ought to lie at the mouth of the Nith, where there is a fort known, Ward Law. It seems improbable, though not impossible, on geographical grounds that the same tribe should occupy the middle and upper Tweed valley and also Annandale and Nithsdale. Further, if *Trimontium* were a Selgovian seat this would be a salient pushed into Votadinian territory which included not only the coastal plain from the Tyne to the Forth but also some of the valleys in the hinterland of that plain including Redesdale. *Trimontium* is placed at the end of the list of Selgovian places and it seems possible that Ptolemy has simply got his tribal attribution wrong and the fort really lay in Votadinian territory.

The second point of doubt concerns the territory of the Damnonii. This stretched from Irvine Bay in Ayrshire across the Clyde, through Menteith and the upper Forth valley into Strathmore. Again this might seem improbable on geographical grounds, reinforced in this case by the political history of the area for Strathmore later undoubtedly fell within the southern division of the Picts. Ptolemy clearly made a mistake with one of his northern tribes, the Vacomagi, as he assigned them places in Angus and the Mearns and in Banff and Moray. In fact it seems more probable that this tribe should be placed in the more northerly position on the south shore of the Moray Firth. It is possible that Ptolemy also made a mistake with the Damnonii and assigned them the territory and places of two tribes, one, presumably the Damnonii, occupying the Clyde basin, and the other, whose name is now unknown, lying north of the Clyde in Strathmore: equally possibly a tribal name has slipped out of Ptolemy's list in later copying.

North of the Forth there are similar problems concerning tribal areas: one has already been noted. The general outlines are clear, however. The Caledonii occupied the Great Glen and the central Highlands, the Vacomagi probably the Moray plain, the Taezali the modern Grampian Region, and the Venicones Fife. The populous area of Strathmore was, according to Ptolemy, assigned to the Damnonii. Along the western and northern littoral of Scotland there were a further eight tribes, their names only appearing in Ptolemy and none of the later sources, unless some are the garbled names in the Ravenna Cosmography.

Some of the place names listed by Ptolemy can be assigned to known Roman forts. The best example is *Trimontium*, the modern Newstead, beside the three Eildon Hills. Others include *Uxellum*, also assigned to the Selgovae and which ought to be Ward Law at the mouth of the Nith, and *Bremenium*, High Rochester on Dere Street, in Votadinian territory. But considerable doubt surrounds the identification of the remaining 19 'places'. In certain cases, even when the approximate location of the 'place' can be determined, there is no known Roman fort in the area to qualify for the name: thus *Vindogara* must lie in the vicinity of Irvine though no Roman fort has been recognised there. One final interesting point remains concerning these place-names. Ptolemy includes within the territory of the Votadini *Curia*, in the land of the Selgovae *Coria*, and amongst the Damnonii *Corda*. These all appear to derive from the same Celtic word, *curia*, meaning hosting, and by extension hosting-place or meeting place, and may refer to the capitals of those three tribes. It is unfortunate that the location of none of these places can be determined, though the Selgovian *Corda* would appear to lie in Upper Annandale, or less likely Upper Nithsdale, while the Votadinian *Curia* seems to be on the southern shore of the Firth of Forth and may lie at or towards Traprain Law.

It is probable that Ptolemy and his sources, one of whom was Marinus of Tyre,

1 The tribes of north Britain in the first century (after Ptolemy)

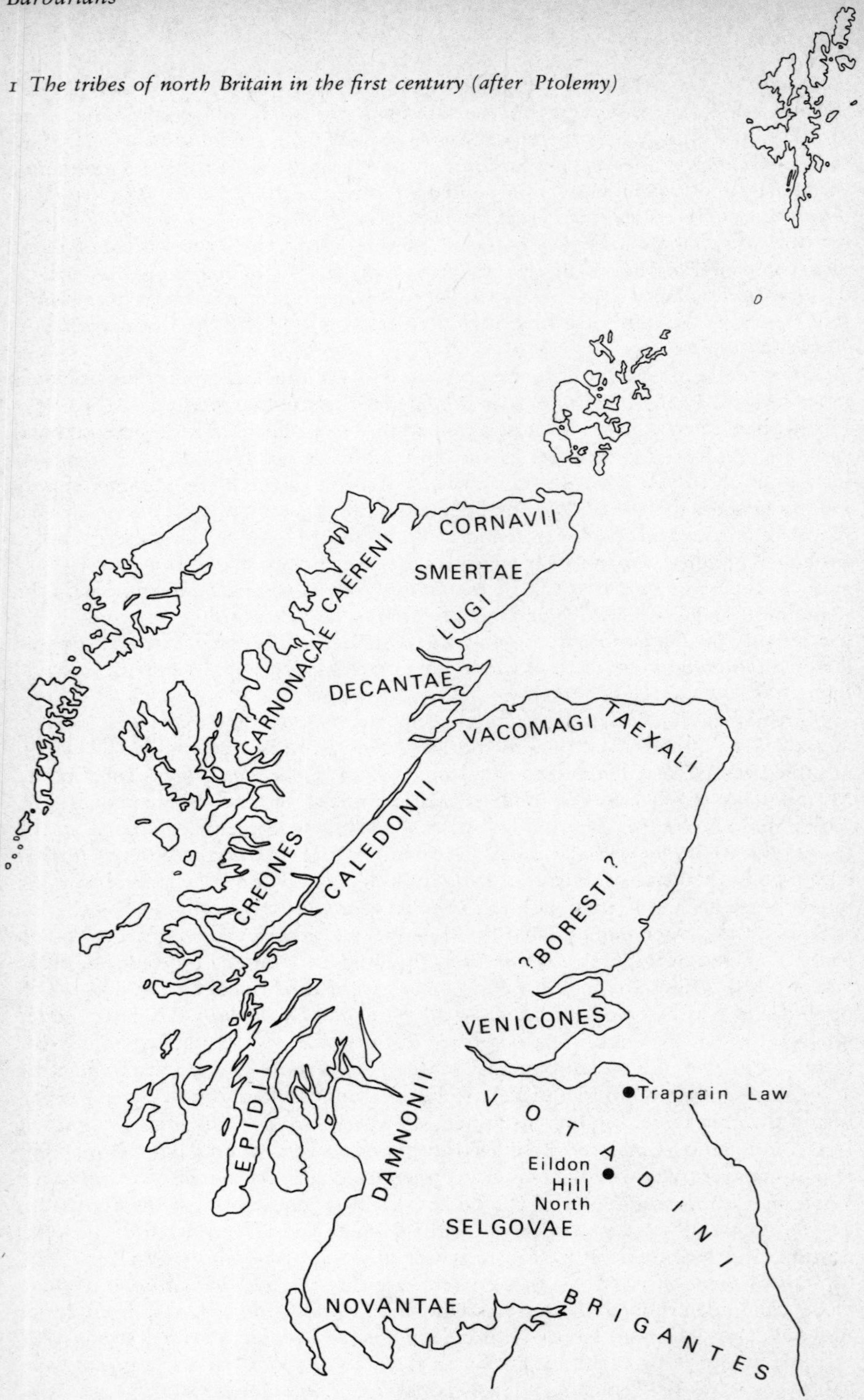

2 The distribution of Iron Age monuments in north Britain (after Childe and Gillam)

acquired most of their information from the records of Agricola's campaigns and voyages in Scotland in the 80s. Tacitus, in his accounts of Britain, mentions very few place-names, and several of these, such as Mons Graupius and Portus Trucculensis, cannot now be identified. He records an otherwise unattested tribe, the Boresti. We are not informed where these people live, but Agricola marched into their territory after Mons Graupius and returned thence to his winter quarters: it seems to be not impossible that the Boresti were the lost tribe of Ptolemy and were located in Strathmore, though it is also possible that they should be placed in the Moray plain.

The names of two northern tribes in Ptolemy's list, the Damnonii of the Clyde valley and the Cornavii of Caithness, are also found in England. The former inhabit the south-west peninsula, where they are termed the Dumnonii, while the latter, here the Cornovii, occupy the west Midlands. It has been suggested that the occurence of the same tribal name in southern Britain and in Scotland points to a northward movement of people, presumably on a fairly substantial scale for the tribal name to be maintained, possibly as a result of the Roman invasion. Support for this hypothesis has been sought in the discovery of artefacts imported from the south.

This folk movement, or at least contact, has also been extended to Ireland, for three tribal names appear here as well as in western England. The Brigantes are found in south-east Ireland as well as northern England; the Gangani, recorded in the *promontorium Ganganorum* of Caernarfonshire, are also found in Galway; while the Lagin appear to have given their name to Leinster and Lleyn. The recurrence of so many tribal names may point to the existence of a cultural province round the Irish Sea, as has been recognised at other times, or at least regular contact.

There is, however, more than one interpretation of both forms of evidence, documentary and archaeological. Tribal names do recur among the northern and western fringes of the empire. The name Brigantes, beside appearing in north England and Ireland, occurs as Brigantii in Raetia, while the Parisi are found in east Yorkshire and – as the Parisii – in the Seine valley in Gaul. There is no known connection between the Brigantes of the British Isles and the Brigantii of the upper Danube, but the occurrence of similar burial rites in the territories of the Parisi and Parisii has been taken to imply a close connection between these two tribes, possibly even a common origin. This suggestion is, however, incapable of proof. A further difficulty lies in the nature of the documents used by Ptolemy in compiling his Geography. His source material depended essentially upon the interpretation of a Roman scribe writing down the names of unfamiliar tribes. It seems not impossible that when hearing a name which sounded familiar the scribe, perhaps unconsciously, wrote down that known name, or one similar to it. This itself may be significant, but without supporting evidence, which may be difficult to identify, the connections drawn out of the identification of tribal names should be treated with caution.

A small number of imports were certainly entering Scotland throughout the Iron Age. Some seem to have been transported up the west coast, and include finger rings, glass beads, dice, querns and crucibles. Elsewhere imports were generally high-status goods. They include the Torrs pony cap and horns, probably manufactured in central England in the second century BC, a gold torc terminal with East Anglian parallels, and horse-trappings from East Anglia: other objects have been considered to have connections with Ireland. In no case is the way by which the object found its way north definitely known. Some may have come as a result of trade or plunder, others with craftsmen or refugees. The Middlebie hoard in Dumfriesshire includes objects almost certainly imported from East Anglia and others made locally either by or for the owner of the imports. There is no documentary evidence for refugees, though elsewhere it is known that some fled before the Roman advance. In each case, however, the refugee was a king or noble: Commius fleeing from Caesar and Caratacus from Claudius, for example. This may reflect the inadequacy of our sources, or may correctly demonstrate that it was only the aristocracy who had the wish, freedom and means to escape: refugee craftsmen were probably unusual.

A further complicating factor is that so many of the late Iron Age objects have demonstrable Roman connections. This may take the form of the inclusion of Roman objects in hoards of native Iron Age material, such as the Carlingwark Loch hoard from Kirkcudbrightshire or the Blackburn Mill hoard in Berwickshire which contained a second century Roman *patera*: both hoards were almost certainly votive deposits in a pool or loch. Other Iron Age hoards or collections containing imports have been found near to Roman forts, such as the Middlebie hoard, which was buried less than a kilometre from the first century fort at Birrens. It is difficult to determine the part the Roman army, rather than native refugees, craftsmen or traders, played in the distribution of this material.

North-east Scotland saw a flowering in metalwork in the late first century and extending into the third century. This was clearly the result of closer contact between this area and the south but with no known predecessors in the area it would be difficult perhaps to postulate that the massive terrets, armlets and snake bracelets now manufactured were made by local craftsmen influenced by external styles rather than that incoming smiths introduced new items or adapted local styles. In fact the range in size and variation in quality of both types of armlets have led to the suggestion that the objects were first made by incoming smiths and were then copied by local craftsmen. However, the place of origin of the incoming smiths is a matter of debate, both northern England and Ireland having been suggested. It seems further possible that insufficient allowance had been made for the innovatory skill of the local Caledonian craftsman.

In summary, there is no definite proof of northward folk movement in the immediate pre-Roman Iron Age which would account for south British tribal names reappearing in the north, and little for individual refugees fleeing before the Roman advance. Certain artefacts, however, point to direct contact with schools of metalwork elsewhere and it seems possible that this contact was through refugee craftsmen and nobles, though the number of refugees seems to have been small. The Roman army also played a considerable part in introducing material from the southern part of the island to the northern tribes. Indeed when all the hoards with possible Roman connections are removed from the distribution maps remarkably few collections remain, suggesting less contact between northern and southern natives than often assumed.

There was in north Britain a distinctive division between the tribes north and south of the Forth. This great estuary was to become the southern boundary of the Picts, as is clearly demonstrated by the distribution of 'pit' place names and Pictish symbol stones as well as historical documentation (fig. 39 and pl. 18–19). Yet earlier the Forth also appears to have been a boundary, for in Neolithic times the distribution pattern of carved stone balls is very similar to that of Pictish symbol stones. In the Iron Age the distributions of brochs, duns and timber-laced forts all emphasise the position of the Forth as a cultural division. Further, the Forth also appears to have been a linguistic divison for the tribes of Lowland Scotland spoke a P-Celtic language while those to the north spoke a different, or rather two different languages. Here, it has been suggested, the mass of people spoke a pre-Celtic, non-Indo-European language, while later arrivals, settling mainly along the coast between the Forth and south-east Sutherland, spoke a Gallo-Britonnic language similar to, but not the same as, the P-Celtic spoken further south. This division was to be reflected in the Roman frontier organisation.

One later source, the Anglo-Saxon historian Bede, mentions a distinctive feature concerning the Picts. He stated that 'whenever doubt arises they choose a king from the female royal lineage rather than from the male: which custom, as is well known, has been observed among the Picts to this day'. The lists of Pictish kings demonstrate that, apart from two possible cases towards the end of the Pictish kingdom, no son succeeded his father, though brothers followed one another; this appears to support Bede's statement. This form of succession is not known in Celtic nations and it is possible therefore that Bede is describing a pre-Celtic practice surviving here, uniquely, in Britain.

Roman accounts of the barbarians

The Celts had long been known to the Romans and many accounts of them appeared in Roman literature, though few have survived. The differences between the various tribes were distinguished by some writers – by Caesar, for example (not that the people of the three areas of Gaul that he conquered differed from one another in language, law and customs). Roman descriptions of Celtic practices in continental Europe can therefore only be transferred to Britain with extreme caution, not least because the Celtic settlement of the island is primarily a matter of deduction based on archaeological and philological evidence: the only historical reference to the migration of Celtic peoples to Britain is Caesar's description of the emigration of Belgic tribes from Gaul. Nevertheless it is worth considering Roman comments on Celtic society for they help paint a general picture, in broad outlines relevant to Britain.

In Gaul, Caesar noted, each tribe was divided among rival factions, each headed by a member of the warrior aristocracy. These men, called knights by Caesar, formed one of the two leading classes of society, the other being the priests. Below these were the common people. These had no say in the governing of the tribe but, oppressed by debts or taxation, were bound to the service of the knights: Caesar comments that they were treated little better than slaves. The craftsmen were highly regarded and seem to have fallen between the aristocracy and the free peasants in the social hierarchy. Slaves may have existed but there is no clear evidence for them.

Inter-tribal fighting was a regular pursuit. Wars took place in Gaul nearly every year, with the knights taking the field at the head of their retainers: the size of his following was the main indication of a knight's status. Later Irish literary sources support the accounts of classical writers. According to these medieval traditions cattle raiding and feuding were important aspects of Celtic life, being followed by the warrior aristocracy as a way of life.

The priestly class also possessed considerable power. Not only did they officiate in religious affairs, but they also acted as judges and were the main repositories of tribal knowledge and traditions. Eloquence was highly valued in the Celtic world and in an heroic society the bards served an important role in lauding the achievements of the warriors. Britain was said to be the main centre of Druidic learning, but there is no evidence either now or later for Druids in Scotland. One gruesome practice linked warriors and priests: head-hunting. Enemies' heads were collected as trophies and suspended over house entrances. This also had a religious significance for the human head was believed to contain powers of good which would ward off evil. Heads fashioned out of stone are another manifestation of this cult. It may be noted that head-hunting was not restricted to the Celts, for it was also practiced by the soldiers of the Roman army, as is amply demonstrated by Trajan's Column.

Women do not appear to have had an equal place with men in Celtic society, at least according to Caesar. In Britain wives were shared between groups of ten or twelve men, especially between brothers and between fathers and sons, but the offspring of such unions were counted as the children of the man with whom a particular woman first cohabited. In Gaul husbands had powers of life and death over their wives and children. Against this may be set the existence of two British queens, Boudica of the Iceni and Cartimandua of the Brigantes.

Caesar's description of the Britons is clearly only relevant to the southern part of the island, and cannot be extended to the northern tribes. He stated that the Britons dyed their bodies with woad, which had a blue colour, giving them a more terrifying appearance in battle, but this cannot be connected with the possibility that the name *Picti* derives from the fact that the northern tribes tattooed their bodies – though it may hint that the warriors fought naked or semi-naked, as did a famous group of Gaulish mercenaries in the second century BC.

Tacitus in the *Agricola* furnishes the first account of the peoples of north Britain. He provides the only description of the physique and complexion of the Caledonian: he had large limbs and red hair, in contrast to the Silurian of south Wales who had a swarthy complexion. Tacitus' account of the nature of British society is strongly reminiscent of Caesar's earlier description. The main strength of the British tribes lay in their infantry. Some tribes also fought from chariots, a practice long abandoned on the continent, and the account of Mons Graupius reveals that the Caledonians fought in this way. The chariot was driven by a nobleman who was supported by his dependants on foot. The warrior aristocrats drove up and down between the rival armies, challenging their enemies to fight, but after these individual contests, when the serious fighting began, the charioteers retired from the field to return and fight on foot.

Obedience to kings, states Tacitus, had given way to rivalry between tribal factions headed by chieftains. This rivalry extended to the tribes themselves, as in Gaul in Caesar's time, and Tacitus wryly notes that it was unusual for two or three states to unite to repel a common danger, and in this way they were easily overcome by the Roman armies. The affinity of institutions between the tribes of southern England and Gaul was noted, but this does not necessarily imply that those of the more northerly tribes were much different.

Tacitus also discussed the climate of Britain: it was objectionable with frequent rains and mists, but there was no extreme cold. The shortness of the night in the north was noted, no doubt during the voyage round Britain at the close of Agricola's seventh season. The soil is fertile and can bear all produce, except the olive, vine and other species native to warmer climes. Crops are slow to ripen, but quick to grow, both facts due to the extreme moistness of the climate.

The most detailed account of the northern tribes is by Dio in the preface to his discussion of the Severan campaigns in the early third century and it seems probable that the position described at this time was very similar to that pertaining 120 years before. The passage is worth quoting *in extenso*.

> There are two principal nations of the Britons, the Caledonians and the Maeatae, and the names of the others have been merged in these. The Maeatae live by the wall which divides the island in half and the Caledonians beyond them. Both inhabit wild and waterless mountains and desolate and swampy plains, and possess neither walls, cities nor cultivated land, but live on their flocks, wild game and certain fruits, for although the stocks of fish are limitless and immense they leave them untouched. They live in tents, unclothed and unshod, possess their women in common and bring up their children together. Their government is for the most part democratic and because they are very fond of plundering they choose the bravest men to be their rulers. They fight both in chariots with small swift horses, and on foot, when they run very fast and also stand their

> ground with great determination. For arms they have a shield and a short spear with a bronze apple on the end of the shaft which they can shake and clash to terrify the enemy; and they also have daggers. They can endure hunger and cold and any form of hardship; for they plunge into the swamps and exist there for many days with only their heads above water, and in the forest they live off bark and roots; and for all emergencies they prepare a certain kind of food and when they have eaten a portion of this the size of a bean they do not become hungry or thirsty.

Dio also mentions a conversation between the wife of a Caledonian Argentocoxus, possibly a hostage, and the Empress Julia Domna, consort of Septimius Severus, in about 210. In reply to a comment by the Empress on the freedom of Roman women to have intercourse with whom they pleased, the Caledonian replied that, while Roman women allowed themselves to be seduced in secret by the worst of men, the Caledonian women had intercourse openly with the best men. This could be connected with the matrilinear succession recorded by Bede: in a society with free sexual practices, succession through the female line will have been an advantage.

Herodian's account of the northern barbarians includes many items already recorded by Dio, but also some new comments:

> . . . most of Britain is marshland because it is flooded by the ocean tides. The barbarians usually swim in these swamps or run along in them submerged to the waist: they are practically naked and do not mind the mud. They are unfamiliar with the use of clothing but decorate their waists and necks with iron, valuing this metal as an ornament and as a symbol of wealth in the way that other barbarians value gold. They tattoo their bodies with various patterns and pictures of all sorts of animals. Hence the reason why they do not wear clothes, so as not to cover the pictures on their bodies. They are very fierce and dangerous fighters, protected only by a narrow shield and a spear, with a sword slung from their naked bodies. They are unaccustomed to breastplates and helmets, considering them to be a hindrance as they cross the marshes. A thick mist rises from the marshes, so that the atmosphere in the country is always gloomy.

Archaeology and the northern tribes

Many items in the above accounts are clearly myths or travellers' tales. Archaeology has amplified and amended the picture of the northern tribes as painted by the Roman writers. In spite of the tribal and linguistic differences dividing the peoples of the Scottish mainland on the eve of the Roman invasion their life styles were not materially different.

The ubiquitous form of dwelling in southern and eastern Scotland was the round timber house. The houses varied in diameter from about 6 to 15m though the average size was about 9m across. They were built in a variety of styles. Generally, however, the houses seem to have had low walls of wattle and daub or logs and high conical roofs of thatch or skins. The main weight of the structure rested on a circle of principal uprights but in some instances these were supplemented by central posts. Some houses were divided internally into rooms. Cooking was normally carried out on open fires placed more-or-less centrally. Sometimes houses were placed on natural or artificial islands or platforms in a lake or river. This form of settlement, the crannog, was popular in certain parts of Scotland until the medieval period.

A single family might occupy one or two houses, thus forming a farmstead: analysis of the population of similar modern houses in Africa and elsewhere suggests that on average between five and nine people might occupy a house about

10m in diameter. Sometimes several families grouped themselves together in a village or homestead, containing perhaps up to twenty houses, often defended by ramparts and ditches. The slight nature of such defences emphasises that many must have been simply to keep out wild animals – wolves and bears roamed Scotland at this time – but some were clearly built against warring neighbours and can be fairly termed forts. Such forts might have two, three or even four rows of ramparts and ditches. In certain cases the defences were strengthened by extra outworks or other measures at the entrances. One particular form of extra defence was the *chevaux de frise*, a series of small projecting pointed stones or stakes set in the ground and intended to break an infantry or cavalry charge.

Forts, often placed on top of hills, abound in the Borders. Most are less than half a hectare in area but the size of some – about 8 hectares and above – is such that they have been suggested as the strongholds of tribal chiefs or chieftains. It is not possible to relate these major forts closely to the known tribes or to use them to suggest divisions within the tribes. However, Traprain Law in East Lothian is generally recognised as one of the chief seats of the Votadini if not their capital: it is the only known hill fort in southern Scotland to have continued in occupation through the Roman period and furthermore it survived, seemingly, with its defences intact. Another major hill forts in the Borders was that on Eildon Hill North, by Newstead (Pl. 1). Nearly 300 hut platforms are still visible within the 10 hectares enclosed by the defences and it has been calculated that the population of the 'town' might have been between 2,000 and 3,000 people. Nevertheless it is possible that such hill forts were not occupied all year round. Some may have been refuges or strongholds to which the local population, possibly with their herds, could retire when attacked. They may also have been the 'castles' of the aristocracy. In view of the account of the Celtic way of life with endemic warfare, raiding and feuding, this may not be too fanciful a picture. The warrior aristocrat in his fort may have controlled an area, the people of that area paying taxes to him, helping in the construction of his 'castle' and forming his following in battle.

Hill forts are not only found in the Lowlands, but also north of the Forth in eastern and north-eastern Scotland, though in smaller numbers. Many of these were built in a distinctive manner, with timber-laced ramparts. This form of construction is found mainly in the area between the Forth and Moray Firths and along the west coast from Galloway to Cape Wrath, but there are outliers elsewhere. These distinctive ramparts owe nothing to the Romans, or even the Gauls, for some were built as early as the seventh century BC.

In the far north and west of Scotland different forms of settlement are found (figs. 32–33). Here stone was more plentiful, or perhaps simply more easily won, and as a result many settlements were constructed of this material. Stone houses were built as early as the fourth millennium BC in northern Scotland but in, or shortly before, the second century BC a new form of dwelling appeared in north Scotland, the broch. Brochs are dry-stone built towers, with small, low entrances, and no other openings on their external elevations. The highest surviving broch is on an island in the Shetlands and is 13m high. Brochs were clearly used as dwellings, but they are so small that animals could not be brought in as well with any degree of comfort. They are also clearly defensive, but who was the enemy? It used to be considered that they may have been built against Roman slave raiders, but as they have now been shown to originate well before the arrival of the Romans that theory is no longer tenable.

There are very few brochs in Argyll on the west coast of Scotland, but here as elsewhere in the western islands are found many small stone-walled forts or duns.

Duns vary in shape and in internal area, though most are up to 375 square metres in floor area, and have lower walls than brochs; many indeed were probably little more than stoutly defended houses. The majority of duns have been found on the west coast but there are also groups in the central valley of Scotland and in the far south-west. The large forts found in south and east Scotland generally do not appear in north and west Scotland and while this undoubtedly to some extent results from variations in topography it may also suggest a rather different social organisation.

The people of the Scottish tribes carried out a mixed farming economy. They reared cattle and sheep, hunted wild animals, especially deer, fished, collected wild berries, shellfish and fruit and also grew cereals. Barley has been found in archaeological contexts dating to the fourth millennium BC, and wheat (emmer) has also been found in prehistoric settlements in Scotland. Farming implements survive from at least the second millenium BC, and marks made by the plough or ard have been recognised in archaeological contexts. The deterioration in the climate of the British Isles some centuries before the beginning of the Christian era may have made cultivation of cereals in Scotland more difficult. During the first half of the first millenium BC rainfall increased and the temperature fell, though it was still probably a degree or two higher than the average temperature today. In the later Iron Age in many parts of Scotland the temperature may have been insufficient during the summer months to ripen the grain, and this may have led to the abandonment of existing fields, which in some areas became overgrown by peat. Other fields no doubt reverted to pasture for herds and flocks. Nevertheless some fields associated with settlements of this period may have been used for cultivation while there is evidence for ploughing in the Iron Age. Plough marks have been found below several sites on Hadrian's Wall, though in no case is the ploughing dated. It seems improbable that all date to the years immediately before the construction of the Wall in the 120s, and perhaps unlikely that all are Bronze Age in date: some or all could date to the Iron Age. One site in particular must have been inhospitable then as it is now, for the ploughing at Carrawburgh is on an exposed hillside with a clay subsoil. If such land could be cultivated then it seems likely that agriculture at this time was more widespread than usually considered. Indeed evidence for ploughing in the Iron Age has recently been discovered on Arran. Parts of two ploughs have also been found in Lowland Scotland. Near Lochmaben in Annandale was found in 1870 a wooden beam from an ard, now dated by radio carbon analysis to the second or first century BC. Excavations at Milton Loch Crannog in Kirkcudbrightshire have revealed an ard head and stilt, possibly a votive deposit, again dated by radio carbon analysis, but in this instance to the fifth century BC. Part of a rotary quern was also found at Milton Loch, and quern stones and barley grains have been discovered in Iron Age contexts elsewhere. Grain could have been traded like any other commodity but it seems probable at this time that cereals continued to be grown in certain favoured situations.

The previous clearances of forest in the Neolithic and Bronze Ages had been to some extent temporary for as the land became exhausted through cultivation the farmers moved on and the woodland was allowed to recolonise. The major and more or less permanent deforestation appears to have started in the late pre-Roman Iron Age in the north and have continued through the Roman period. It was probably mainly in order to provide more pasturage for animals, though other factors in certain areas will have played a part: the construction of stockades and also timber-laced forts will have required considerable quantities of timber. On the eve of the Roman advance into Scotland then the landscape would still have been well forested with clearings, most containing pasturage for cattle and sheep, but some with fields for cereals such as wheat and barley. The animals would have provided a wide variety of raw materials in addition to food. These included wool, skins and leather for clothing, leather for containers of all kinds, fastenings and bindings, hair for ropes, fat for food, cooking, lamps and soap (used by the Celts in Gaul according to Roman writers), horn and hoof for glue, artefacts and possibly medicine. Some animals, cattle especially, may have been used to measure the wealth and status of their owners, though no Roman writer mentions this.

The domesticated animals were not of course the modern improved breeds. Generally they were smaller than modern specimens. Cattle were of the Celtic shorthorn variety, the closest modern representative today being the Kerry breed and the Welsh Black. Sheep were slender legged animals similar to Soay and Shetland sheep, with less meat and wool than modern improved breeds, though an improved breed was probably introduced to Britain either before or during the Roman period. The pig was a more agile type than modern specimens, being left free to forage in scrubland rather than kept in farmyards or the in-fields. Horses too were small by modern standards; the animals that pulled the war chariots were little bigger than today's ponies. At the Roman fort at Newstead the bones of two types of ponies were recovered during the excavations early in this century: the unimproved native British breed similar to the modern Shetland pony and the small slender limbed pony such as the Exmoor or the 'Celtic' pony of Iceland. Both types were under 12 hands high. Also found were the bones of larger ponies between 12 and 13 hands high and the bones of horses from just under 14 to nearly 15 hands.

Cattle bones are usually more numerous than the bones of sheep, pig or wild animals on late Iron Age sites in north England, so it seems probable that beef formed the major part of the meat diet here and presumably further north. In northern England it was possible to keep animals over the winter, demonstrating that there was no problem of winter fodder. The majority of cattle and sheep at one settlement were slaughtered between 12 and 30 months of age, when a moderate weight would have been achieved.

Archaeology too has clothed the barbarian warrior described by Tacitus, Dio and Herodian. The sword of the barbarian generally appears to have been rather longer than the auxiliary cavalryman's *spatha*, as Tacitus implies. It was of iron with a distinctively Celtic tang and its scabbard was usually of wood or leather, sometimes decorated with bronze fittings. Spears were often of ash with leaf-shaped iron tips. The rectangular shield depicted on the second century AD Bridgeness distance slab and other Roman and Pictish sculpture probably represented the shield carried by the Caledonian and his allies (pls. 17 and 19). It was probably constructed of wood and leather with a central boss, usually of iron.

Chariot burials dating to the Iron Age have been found in East Yorkshire and although cemeteries similar to those in East Yorkshire have been discovered in Scotland no chariot burials have yet come to light. However, examples of horse equipment do survive. Terret rings and snaffle-bits were both probably used on chariot horses rather than cavalry mounts. Terrets were mounted in pairs on the yoke to guide the reins: sets of five indicate a double harness. Such items of horse equipment were sometimes highly ornamented with enamel.

The warrior himself will also have worn elaborate ornaments. Armlets and torcs, in one case of gold and imported probably from eastern England, are known and a single example survives of an elaborate collar of bronze, though this probably belongs to a period contemporary with the Roman occupation of Scotland. Herodian states that the Caledonians fought naked and this is not impossible as Polybius records that Gaulish mercenaries fought naked at the battle of Telamon in 225 BC. Roman writers testify to the noise created by the Celtic army preparing for battle. The whoops of the charioteers joined with the yells of the infantryman to form a deafening cacophany. Human voices were supplemented by the war trumpets. Part of one such trumpet, the Deskford Carnyx, from Banff, survives. It was in the form of a boar's head with, originally, a moveable wooden tongue and eyes. No doubt each army would have possessed several trumpeters leading each warrior's retinue.

Little is known about the clothing worn by the Caledonian. Wool, leather and skins were available and presumably used: Caesar specifically mentions skins, while Dio describes Boudica as wearing a thick plaid over a voluminous patterned cloak. A type of check woollen cloth was popular in the Roman period in north Britain and may have been worn earlier. The woollen cloak with a hood, the *cucullus*, known on sculpture, and the longer, heavier cape, the *byrrus Britannicus*, recorded in Diocletian's edict on prices, may have had a respectable, but unknown history in northern Britain. Certainly spindle whorls from prehistoric contexts attest the spinning of wool before the arrival of the Romans, while even woollen textiles have occasionally been found. Pins and brooches, usually of bronze, for fastening clothing are known. Bone pins survive, and also bone combs. One final decorative item may be mentioned, the finger ring.

It is too easy to depict the Caledonian as a wild and savage barbarian, devoid of political organisation and prey to internecine strife. There are, fortunately, reminders that this is a false picture. The splendid tomb of Maeshowe, constructed over 2,500 years before the Roman conquest, bears witness to the architectural skill and achievement of the northern peoples. The broch tower of Mousa, which has weathered 2,000 years of storms and a Norse siege, is testimony not only to the barbarian's prowess in design and building technique but also to the existence of itinerant architect-engineers, the economy to support such craftsmen, and the social organisation to order the construction of these dwellings.

The Caledonian peoples and their allies must have enjoyed a profit-making agricultural economy for many generations. Agricultural surplus would have had to have been produced to support not only the architect-engineers, but miners, smiths and presumably the aristocracy. Little is known of religion in Scotland at this time, though what there is demonstrates affinity with practices in the mainstream of the Celtic world. Several ritual deposits in pools emphasise the veneration of springs and rivers, while the cult of the human head – which in Celtic eyes was symbolic of divinity – also seems to have been current. It is not impossible therefore that a priesthood, which we have already met in the Druids in Gaul and southern Britain, existed in Caledonian society and if so would have required to be supported by the community at large.

The political sophistication of the tribes is a more difficult area to probe. There is no reason to believe that the northern tribes were not ruled by kings who manifestly existed in southern Britain. Certainly, too, in the face of the common Roman enemy, the barbarian tribes were capable of sinking their differences and combining their forces against that enemy. Tacitus records that in preparation for meeting the Roman army at Mons Graupius the northern tribes negotiated treaties with each other in order to field as large a force as possible, and, it would appear, chose one of the many tribal leaders to be their general. The accounts of the

Agricolan and Severan campaigns abound with references to the barbarians' strategic skill and their military intelligence. For example, they knew which division was the weakest in Agricola's sixth campaign when the army was divided into three columns, while their tactics in the face of Severus' overwhelming numerical superiority were clearly carefully thought out and executed, even though not successful. In such a fight the odds were heavily stacked against the more wayward Celts.

Even the recording of their customs, as we have seen, was in the hands of their enemies and the final indignity is undoubtedly their anonymity. The best known Caledonian, Calgacus, leader of the northern tribes in their fight against Agricola, was possibly named by the Romans, leaving only Argentocoxus, whose wife met the Empress Julia Domna about 210, and Lossio Veda, grandson or nephew of Vepogenus, a Caledonian, who dedicated a votive plaque at Colchester in the reign of Severus Alexander (222–35).

3
Agricola and the first frontier in Britain

Agricola

The career of Gnaeus Julius Agricola, governor of Britain for almost six and a half years, is better known than that of any of his colleagues. This is simply because he had the good fortune to have the historian Cornelius Tacitus as his son-in-law. Tacitus wrote a biography of his father-in-law, which is one of the few such works to survive from Roman times. The biography naturally extolled the virtues of its hero and can hardly be considered an unbiased account of the events of these years. Nevertheless in spite of this, and in spite of the paucity of geographical names in the *Agricola*, the work provides an invaluable account of events in Britain for forty years from the conquest to the recall of Agricola.

There is one outstanding problem concerning the governorship of Agricola. Tacitus does not give the dates of his term of office and they have therefore to be calculated from other evidence. The governorship began in either 77 or 78: both dates have their followers and it is not possible on present evidence to be sure which is correct. For the sake of convenience therefore the events of Agricola's governorship will be related to the year of his governorship and not absolute dates.

Agricola was an unusual governor of Britain in that he had previously served twice within the province: it was not unusual for a man to have two of his three or four military postings in the same province, but Agricola is unique in having all three of his in the one province. The reason for this is probably connected with the general political situation in the empire. In 68 and 69 there was a bitter struggle for the throne following an abortive coup, a rebellion which nevertheless caused Nero to commit suicide. Agricola espoused the cause of the eventual victor, Vespasian, even before he had been proclaimed emperor. This action was to bring him suitable rewards, including an accelerated career and, four or five years later, elevation to patrician rank. As a loyal supporter of the Flavian dynasty Agricola was a safe man to put in charge of one of the three largest provincial armies, even though he might have acquired many contacts there as a result of his previous service in the island. It was also equally safe to leave him there for an unusually long term of office. The dislike – even fear – of Agricola by Vespasian's son Domitian, recorded in the *Agricola*, may well be overplayed by Tacitus as Domitian did award Agricola triumphal ornaments, the most prestigious battle honours, on the completion of his governorship of Britain, which he himself allowed to extend to six years, while it was Agricola who excused himself from the governorship of Asia, not Domitian who refused it him. Tacitus may be purposefully distancing Agricola from the tyrant Domitian who after his death had his memory damned. In the days of Trajan's reign, when the *Agricola* was written, it would have been embarrassing to have been too closely associated with Domitian and that emperor's natural act of regularly enquiring after Agricola, an old family friend, during his last illness, as Tacitus faithfully records, may have been wilfully re-interpreted in a more sinister light in the changed political situation.

Agricola's close relationship with the Flavian dynasty was to colour – and cloud – his whole career. It is impossible to say how successful he might have been if Nero had lived, but it seems unlikely that he would have enjoyed the governorship of Britain for six years nor have acquired the reputation of being a great general. As it is, through his unusually long governorship, defeat of the major Scottish tribe, and posterity's blind belief in the words of his son-in-law, Agricola has acquired a reputation which he may not have altogether deserved.

Agricola's career, up to his governorship of Britain, was normal. He served in Britain as a military tribune on the staff of the governor Suetonius Paulinus at the time of the Boudican rebellion. His next position was as quaestor (financial secretary) of Asia and two appointments in Rome followed. Vespasian sent him back to Britain at the beginning of his reign as legate of *legio XX Valeria Victrix*. The governorship of Aquitania followed, then the consulship in 77, at the age of 37, well below the official minimum of 42. In 77 or 78 Agricola returned to Britain for the third time, as governor.

Agricola arrived in Britain late in the year and spent the latter part of the summer quashing a revolt of the Ordovices in north Wales. Tacitus does not name the area where Agricola campaigned in his second season but it is usually considered to be northern England – the territory of the Brigantes. Petillius Cerealis, governor in the early 70s, had conquered this tribe, but may not have had time to consolidate his victory by the construction of a full network of forts. It is clear that Agricola fought no battles in this season but was concerned to mop up local resistence and complete the fort-building programme started by Cerealis. As Tacitus records that several tribes submitted to Agricola, it is possible that his activities extended beyond the Tyne-Solway isthmus, beyond Brigantian territory. As it is only in the next season that he ventured into the territory of new tribes, it is possible that Cerealis had already made contact with the tribes who were incorporated into the province in Agricola's second season.

In his third season, his second full season, for the first time Agricola passed beyond the limits of earlier campaigning. Moving through the territory of new nations he reconnoitred as far as the river Tay. His route is not known but he must have moved either up the east coast, probably following the line of the present A68, or up Annandale and down Clydesdale – the route of the present A74 – or both. He passed through the territory of several tribes, but Tacitus states that the enemy did not attack the Roman army and devotes some space to discussing the appalling weather of that summer. He goes on to remark that there was even time to construct forts that year: clearly the Lowland tribes gave Agricola little trouble.

In 79 the Emperor Titus was acclaimed *imperator* for the fifteenth time as a result of the achievements of Agricola in Britain. It is not possible to be certain whether the occasion for the acclamation was the results of the second or third season of campaigning: an equally good case can be made out for both years. The move north was also commemorated in another way for a Caledonian bear appeared at the opening of the Colosseum in Rome in June 80.

Tacitus opens the discussion of the following season, Agricola's fourth, with a remarkable phrase: if the valour of the army and the glory of Rome had allowed it, a halting place would have been found within the island. He then goes on to state that the neck of land between the Forth and Clyde estuaries was secured by a line of garrisons. This is the first known suggestion in the history of the province of Britain that a frontier might be established within the island: in other words this is the first known explicit rejection of the idea of total conquest of the island. Previously, expansion of the province had moved forward erratically, but there had been no hint that any of the halting points had been intended to be permanent. It seems probable that the line of forts established now was intended to be the permanent boundary of the province, and the peculiar phraseology of Tacitus may merely reflect (as he knew with hindsight) that the boundary was not in fact permanent as the army moved on two years later. However, there is another consideration. Roman governors generally served for three years at a time, and this was Agricola's fourth campaigning season in the province – towards the end of the year he would have passed the third anniversary of his arrival in Britain. Roman emperors carefully controlled the activities of their governors and no doubt Agricola had been sent to the province with specific instructions. Usually, it would appear, in these years emperors provided their governors with tasks which might be expected to last three years. Thus Petillius Cerealis, the first Flavian governor of Britain, was charged with subduing the Brigantes, while Julius Frontinus, his successor, completed the conquest of Wales. Agricola's task would seem to have been to complete Cerealis' work in north England and then move on to take another convenient grouping of tribes into the province. He had successfully completed this by the end of his third season and in that year and the following he moved on to the second stage of the operation, namely the control and protection of the newly conquered tribes by the construction of forts. He then, it may be presumed, had completed the task he was sent out to do. The construction of forts across the Forth-Clyde isthmus may or may not have been part of his original instruction: almost certainly they were not.

Tacitus' mention of a halting place on the Forth-Clyde isthmus emphasises that this line of forts was unusual. During the course of his third season Agricola had reached the Tay and from there he will have seen the Highlands barring his passage to the north. Word of the country ahead must have been brought to him by the scouts habitually employed by the army and no doubt more information was obtained from the local tribesmen and captives. Agricola may have realised the difficulties of operating in that mountainous terrain and advised the emperor, Titus, of this. In that case Titus, acting on the intelligence received from Agricola, may have decided to halt the expansion in Britain on a convenient line. It seems unlikely that Agricola wished to advance further north but was held back by Titus and Tacitus gives no hint that his hero's ambitions were thwarted at this time only to triumph two years later. Agricola had not only completed the tasks allotted to him by the Emperor Vespasian but gone as far in Britain as the Romans now intended to go.

Little is known of Agricola's frontier on the Forth-Clyde isthmus, but before examining the surviving remains it would be better to consider the overall pattern of the occupation of northern England and southern Scotland at this time. This pattern was largely dictated by the geography of the area. On either side of the Pennines a road led north, connecting the forts along the route, and where appropriate these major lines of communication were linked by roads across the hills. At this time two new legionary fortresses were constructed. In the east *legio IX Hispana* was moved up from Lincoln to York, while in the west Wroxeter was abandoned and *legio XX Valeria Victrix* established at Chester, where it was strategically placed for intervention in either Wales or north England. On either side of the Pennines the auxiliary units were placed in forts about 20–30 kilometres apart, approximately a day's march. These forts generally appear to have varied in size from 1.5 to 2.5 hectares: the forts on the roads across the hills were usually smaller at about 1.2 hectares. Little is known of the garrisons of these forts. Each of the smaller stations was presumably garrisoned by the smallest auxiliary unit of the Roman army, the 480 strong infantry unit, the *cohors quingenaria peditata*. No doubt many of the other forts were garrisoned by its sister unit, the *cohors quingenaria equitata*, which contained a cavalry complement of 120 men in addition to the 480 infantry.

Forts were established at other points beside these, at Brough-on-Humber, for example, in the territory of the Parisi, and at Malton, north-east of York. One area does not appear to have had troops placed within it at this time, the present-day Lake District. No forts seem to have been established here until the early second century.

In southern Scotland too geography dictated routes and many troop dispositions. The eastern and western roads continued north. The eastern road, Dere Street, stayed close to the line taken by the modern A68 while the western road followed the line of the modern A74 up Annandale and down into Clydesdale. Again these two main roads were linked by cross routes, one running westwards from Newstead towards Irvine Bay, and the other south-westwards from Newstead into Annandale and Nithsdale.

In each of the major river valleys there was placed a large fort, usually about 3 hectares in size and containing a composite garrison (fig. 4). In the Tyne valley lay a large fort, about 10 hectares in extent. This was found on trial examination to contain some store-houses and it may be that this was a base or depot rather than a fort proper. Further north lay Newstead in the Tweed valley, Camelon on the Forth, Milton in Annandale, Dalswinton in Nithsdale, while in Clydesdale was constructed Castledykes. Elsewhere there were smaller stations: forts capable of holding a single auxiliary unit such as Oakwood or Easter Happrew, small forts such as Crawford acting as the bases for units which had men posted elsewhere, and fortlets like Birrens or Gatehouse of Fleet containing a detachment of 80 men or thereabouts. These forts and fortlets were also generally about 20–30km apart, though the distances varied considerably depending upon the topography.

The forts and fortlets and the road connecting them formed the sort of network which might be expected in any territory recently conquered by Rome, the idiosyncracies dependent on the topography. The only unusual feature was the line of forts built across the Forth-Clyde isthmus. Although Tacitus records the construction of these stations few have been recognised archaeologically. The major fort at Camelon in the Forth valley is strategically not one of these stations. On the other side of the isthmus the fort at Barochan, rediscovered in 1972, lies on the low hills overlooking the Clyde and may or may not be one of the forts specifically built to guard this neck of land. In between in 1977 a new small fort was located at Mollins about 4km south of the Antonine Wall. Excavation in 1978 confirmed a late first century date for this 0.4 hectare fort and it seems most likely therefore that it was one of the stations built under Agricola.

Two other fortlets on the line of the later Antonine Wall have been assigned to Agricola: the enclosures under the forts at Croy Hill and Bar Hill. Excavations in 1975 at the former site demonstrated conclusively that this structure dated not to the governorship of Agricola, but to the reoccupation of Scotland in the 140s. Examination of part of the enclosure under Bar Hill fort failed to produce any first century artefacts while the filling of the ditch would argue for an early Antonine rather than an Agricolan date.

No other structure on the Forth-Clyde isthmus can be assigned to the governorship of Agricola, but it seems not improbable that more may yet come to light through the medium of aerial photography. Artefactual evidence, however, may play a part in determining the position of Agricola's forts. Glass and samian pottery dating to the first century has been found at Castlecary and Cadder, two forts on the Antonine Wall (fig. 21). First-century bronze coins have come to light at Mumrills, Castlecary, Balmuildy and Kirkintilloch, all on the line of the Antonine Wall: first-century bronze coins had a short life so it is possible that these sites were occupied in the Flavian period. Finally, pre-Hadrianic, and possibly Agricolan, coarse pottery has been recorded at Mumrills, Castlecary, Balmuildy and Old Kilpatrick. These artefacts may suggest that all or some of the forts of Mumrills, Castlecary, Kirkintilloch, Cadder, Balmuildy and Old Kilpatrick were the sites of Agricola's stations being garrisoned by Roman forces, large or small, but to date no structural evidence has come to light to support these chance finds, and the possibility that many of the finds were brought by the later Antonine builders should not be ignored.

Agricola would normally have expected his governorship to end after three years and, as discussed above, it seems probable that his term of office was planned with that in mind. However, he was to continue as governor for a further three years, thus achieving an unprecedented – for Britain at least – governorship of over six years. The two final seasons of Agricola's governorship were spent campaigning and fighting north of the Forth, but the year before, Agricola's fifth season, was spent elsewhere. The operations began with a sea voyage, clearly in the west of Britain for Agricola drew up his troops facing Ireland, and involved the subduing of tribes hitherto unknown. It has been suggested that Agricola moved down into Ayrshire and Galloway to conquer the Novantae who, because of their isolation, had been by-passed on the march north, or sailed across the Clyde to campaign in Argyllshire, or perhaps carried out both operations during that season. A further possibility, proposed by Mr W.S. Hanson, is that the reference to the sea voyage may imply that Agricola sailed, from his winter quarters, perhaps at Chester, to Scotland at the opening of the campaigning season.

It seems a reasonable assumption that the main campaign of this season was into south-west Scotland: this is the most appropriate part of north Britain to be described as facing Ireland. Further, it is quite possible that this area had been ignored in the move north through the Scottish Lowlands in the same way as earlier Agricola had by-passed the Lake District. The route taken by the army is not known, but if it moved directly from its winter quarters it may have passed along the north shore of the Solway, the route at present taken by the A75. The only physical indication of its presence may be a marching camp at Girvan in south Ayrshire.

Tacitus records that Agricola considered the possibility of conquering Ireland. He had a fugitive Irish prince with him, who would provide a pretext for intervention, and strategic reasons – or excuses – in that, as Ireland was considered to lie between Britain and Spain, it would provide better communications between those two parts of the empire and also extinguish the torch of liberty beyond the frontier. There is a further possibility, not recorded by Tacitus. Agricola had been ordered to stay in Britain but may not have been given any specific task. He may have been collecting information on Ireland in order to offer it as a possible area of expansion, possibly for his successor rather than himself, now that the intention of conquering northern Scotland had been abandoned. It may be that Agricola went so far as to prepare a report for the emperor; certainly he gathered intelligence on harbours and landing places, the climate and the tribes, and calculated how large a force would be required for the subjugation of the island – a legion and a few auxiliaries. This estimate is generally considered to be too low, but it may not have been too far wrong for in 1315–16 Edward Bruce conquered Ireland with a similar sized army.

However, Ireland was not to be brought within the Roman empire. In the following year Agricola turned north, crossed the Forth and began an operation which ended with Roman victory at Mons Graupius a year later. Tacitus records the pretext: the enemy gave provocation. The relevant passage in the *Agricola* deserves close examination for it records that Agricola 'feared a rising of the northern tribes' and so moved across the Forth; only then did the enemy retaliate and 'without provocation' attack a Roman fort. The *Agricola* is unmistakable: the first move was by the Romans, who moved to prevent a real or imagined threat (though it is hard to see how the Caledonians could seriously have threatened Rome). This was the sixth year of Agricola's governorship and whichever dating system is adopted was certainly within the reign of the Emperor Domitian (81–96). It is noteworthy that this emperor commenced his reign with warfare on another frontier, for in Germany he fought a war with the Chatti. This probably commenced in the spring of 83, at first under the direction of Domitian himself. The Roman sources do not state the reason for the war and it is possible that the emperor wished to demonstrate his military prowess, having lived for so long in the shadow of his elder brother Titus. The advance in Britain may have been for the same reason; it was certainly not in response to unprovoked aggression by the northern tribes.

Agricola spent two seasons campaigning north of the Forth (fig. 3). He advanced by land and by sea, using the fleet to supplement his army weakened by withdrawals for service elsewhere, but also to reconnoitre the harbours. In the first season he failed to bring the Caledonians to battle but was attacked himself, nearly losing a third of his army, including *legio IX*, in a night assault on their temporary camp. He also had to suffer a mutiny by a regiment recently raised in Germany and still undergoing basic training in Britain. In the next season he was more successful. He brought the Caledonians to bay at Mons Graupius and soundly defeated them. This is the only battle between the Romans and the Caledonians (or the Picts) described in ancient literature and it is therefore worth examining in some detail.

In this season Agricola sent his fleet ahead to plunder and spread consternation among the enemy while the army marched light. Agricola and his army met the Caledonians at Mons Graupius (the Graupian Mountain) where the barbarians were drawn up on ground of their own choosing. The northern tribes had made careful preparations for the battle. They had put aside their differences and entered into treaty relationship with each other so as to be able to assemble the full force of all the tribes – an action worthy of special note in view of the statement by Tacitus that seldom did the British tribes combine together to fight the Romans. The barbarians mustered, according to Tacitus, more than 30,000 men and these were arranged on the hillside, with the van on the level ground at the bottom and the rest riding up the gentle slopes behind.

The Roman army was drawn up in front of their camp. In the van lay the auxiliary infantry, and on the flanks the cavalry, while the legions were kept in reserve. Tacitus does not give a total for all the Roman forces present, but he does state that there were 8,000 auxiliary infantry and 3,000 cavalry in the battle line, while an additional 2,000 cavalry were kept in reserve. Included within the infantry

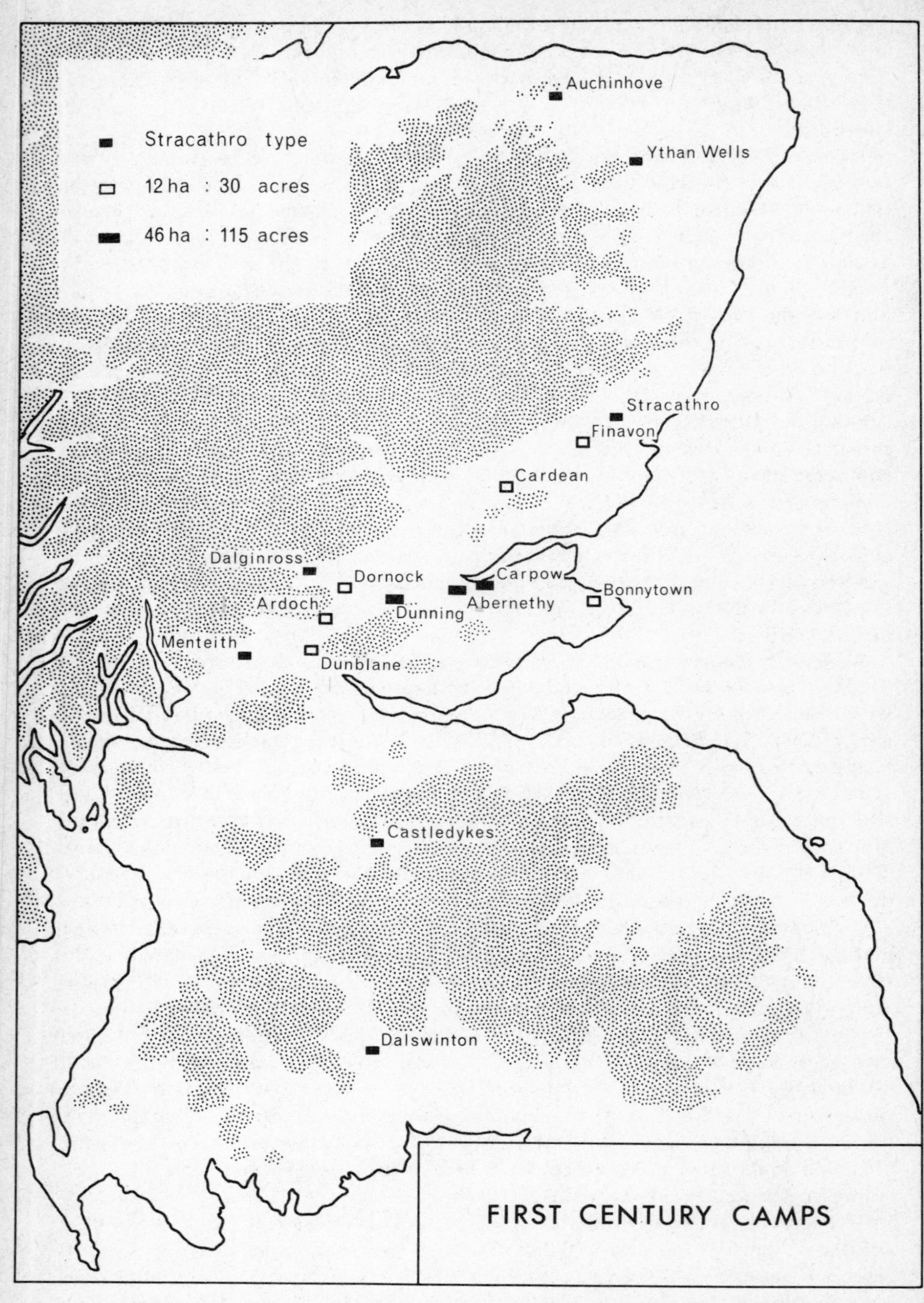

3 *Marching camps in Scotland considered to date to the Agricolan campaigns*

were four cohorts of Batavians and two of Tungrians, though it is not known whether these were 500 or 1,000 strong. The army also contained soldiers recruited in Britain and it seems probable that these were serving in the auxiliary units. Presumably all four British legions were present at Mons Graupius, but none were at full strength. While nominally 5,200 strong, headquarters staff, recruits and training officers would no doubt have remained at base. In addition, however, detachments from all the legions were at this time serving elsewhere. A single detachment, probably 500 or 1000 strong, from each legion had been sent to the Rhine for service in the Chattan war, while an extra detachment from *IX Hispana* was also operating in the same area. The legionary strength, in theory something over 20,000, may therefore have been reduced to 15,000 or even less. Agricola's army is unlikely to have numbered more than 28,000 men, and may have been considerably smaller.

Tacitus' description of the battle includes preliminary set-piece speeches by the two commanding officers. It is not known whether speeches were actually made, though it seems probable that Agricola did address his men in the usual Roman manner, but the speech of Calgacus, the Caledonian leader, as relayed by Tacitus is clearly merely Roman rhetoric put into the mouth of Rome's enemy. Calgacus made a classic anti-imperialist speech, dwelling on the freedom of the Caledonians and the success, albeit limited, of other opponents of Rome, and included the famous phrase that the Romans created a desert and called it peace. Agricola referred to the bravery of the Roman army and the cowardice of the enemy, emphasising that this was the final victory they required to complete the conquest of the island.

Before the battle commenced the Caledonian charioteers rampaged up and down between the two armies. In the face of such a substantial force Agricola spread his battleline dangerously thin, but this was to prevent being out-flanked. The battle itself began with an exchange of missiles. Then Agricola ordered the Batavian and Tungrian cohorts to advance. Now the Caledonians were at a disadvantage. The Romans were armed with short stabbing swords and protected, in addition to their normal armour, by large shields. The Caledonians, on the other hand had smaller shields and long slashing swords unsuitable in close encounters. The Roman auxiliaries, stabbing with their swords and pushing with the bosses of their shields, routed the enemy on the plain and pushed on up the hill, quickly overcoming the men on the lower slopes. They were now joined by the cavalry who had been seeing off the chariots. The very speed of the initial Roman advance, however, nearly proved to be their undoing, for now, faced by the main body of the Caledonian force and the rough hill-slope, their advance ground to a halt, while the presence of cavalry amongst the Roman infantry led to disarray in the ranks. The Caledonians on the higher ground began to advance and threatened to envelop the rear of the Roman army, so Agricola set this cavalry reserve of four regiments against them and broke their attack. The Caledonians were now faced by the Romans on both sides and broke rank, being driven back to some woods. Here they rallied, but the Roman infantry and the dismounted cavalry ringed the wood and drove forward, pushing back the Caledonians. Seeing no chance of victory the barbarians turned and fled, pursued by the Romans. Night brought an end to the fighting and when the Romans counted the dead they found, according to Tacitus, that only 360 Romans had fallen as opposed to 10,000 Caledonians.

According to the account of Tacitus there was only one point when the battle seriously turned against the Romans, and then the situation was saved by the timely action of Agricola in throwing in the cavalry reserve. The legions, also kept in reserve, were not required, the whole brunt of the fighting falling on the auxiliaries; as a result not a drop of 'Roman', that is legionary, blood was shed. In only using his auxiliaries Agricola was not innovatory. Exactly the same tactic had been used by Petillius Cerealis fifteen years before during the Batavian revolt. This action was part of the increasingly important role played by the auxiliary units in different aspects of military affairs. It is clear, however, that Agricola kept a close control over the movement of the battle and, of course, was successful in achieving victory. The Caledonians fell before the superior weapons, armour, discipline and tactics of the Romans.

The day following the battle Agricola sent scouts to search for the enemy. However, finding that they had all fled, he made no attempt to pursue them further but made preparations for returning south. He led his army into the territory of the Boresti, an otherwise unknown tribe, and there collected hostages. He ordered his fleet to sail round Britain (during the voyage they discovered the Orkney Islands and sighted Thule), while he marched south with his army.

One major problem concerning the battle of Mons Graupius is that its location is not known. Tacitus makes no attempt to locate the site: it would appear to lie beside the Boresti, but, as this tribe is otherwise unknown, this piece of information is of little value. The battle clearly lay north of the Forth and the line of first-century marching camps appears to stretch as far as Auchinhove in Banffshire. It seems possible therefore that Mons Graupius lay beyond the Mounth, the point where the Highlands nearly reach the sea at Stonehaven. Various locations have been suggested for the battle. One argument would place it near the later battle of Culloden, for here the Caledonians would have been compelled to fight for the same reasons as the Jacobites: if they had retreated further the army would have split into different sections as the tribes fell back on their homelands, north, south and west of Inverness. More recently the hill of Bennachie, 32 kilometres north-west of Aberdeen, has been proposed as the site of the battle. While many of the topographical features support this allegation there are still some discrepancies. In fact it is most unlikely that we will ever know the exact site of the battle and the most that can be said is that it probably lies north of the Mounth.

Agricola's achievements were welcomed in Rome and he was awarded the ornaments of a triumph, the highest honour a general could receive as the triumph itself was reserved for members of the imperial family, and the erection of a statue. Agricola, having served over six years as governor of Britain, soon after Mons Graupius, it would appear, retired, handing over his province to his successor. Thereafter he was to hold no public office, declining even the offer of the prestigious proconsulship of Asia.

Agricola's governorship is the longest known in Romano-British history. However, it seems unlikely that this was due to any special military merit on his part. Agricola's loyalty to the dynasty rendered him a safe candidate for the governorship of a major military province like Britain, and even an extended governorship, though this was probably the result of the 'accident' of the death of the Emperor Titus. The duration of the governorship was the equivalent of two more normal-length governorships and this may not have been coincidental. Such long terms of office were rare at this time though the Emperor Tiberius fifty years before had kept some governors in post for as long as 10 and 25 years, while Didius Gallus had been governor of Britain for five or six years in the 50s and Trebellius Maximus for six years in the 60s. Two emperors died during the course of

Agricola's governorship: Vespasian in the middle of either the first or second full year and Titus at the end of either the third or fourth. Of these two deaths the more important was that of Titus, for it fell about the time when Agricola might normally expect his governorship to end: it may have been easier for Domitian to leave Agricola in Britain than immediately find a replacement. Whichever date is prefered for the commencement of the governorship it will still have been Titus who ordered the halt on the Forth and Domitian the advance two years later. Agricola's task was to implement the policies initiated by his emperor, though he could of course recommend a course of action himself, as he may have been preparing to do in his fifth season when he drew up his troops facing Ireland. Agricola was duly rewarded for faithfully and successfully obeying his orders.

The award of the ornaments of a triumph to Agricola suggests that the conquest of Britain was now considered to be completed – the great triumphal monument at Richborough was probably erected at this time and points to the same conclusion. The position of the most northerly marching camps attributable to the campaigns of Agricola on the south shore of the Moray Firth would allow it to be said that Agricola had reached practically the end of the island and he had certainly defeated his major foe. There is no hint in the *Agricola* that during these last two campaigning seasons Agricola built any fort north of the Forth. The most northerly forts recorded in the biography are those on the Forth-Clyde isthmus, unless the fort attacked in the sixth season lay in Strathmore or Strathearn. It would not be unusual for the mopping-up operation following a battle such as Mons Graupius to be left to his successor. It seems probable therefore that all, or at least most of, the forts now built north of the Forth were the work of Agricola's successor. It is possible that the position of some had already been determined by Agricola himself, but that is speculation; there is no need to consider that Agricola viewed himself indispensable in the matter of British affairs: such decisions could be left to his successor.

The aftermath of Mons Graupius

There are two main groups or lines of forts north of the Forth (fig. 4). The outer line hugs the edge of the Highlands, the forts usually being placed within the very mouths of the glens. Seven forts are known in the line, eight if Barochan on the Clyde is included. The forts stretch north-east from Drumquassle at the south-east corner of Loch Lomond through Malling at Menteith, Bochastle at Callander, Dalginross at Comrie and Fendoch at the mouth of the Sma' Glen to the legionary fortress at Inchtuthil. The inner line lies in the centre of the valleys Strathearn and Strathmore, following the line taken by the Roman road leading north from Camelon. The first fort in the series may be presumed to have lain at or near Stirling guarding the crossing of the Forth: it is as yet undiscovered. Beyond there were forts at Ardoch (pl. 4), Strageath, Bertha, Cargill, Cardean and Stracathro: the extra-long gap between the last two sites suggests that another fort remains to be discovered.

The forts on both the inner and the outer line follow an interesting pattern of alternating small and large enclosures. The smaller forts vary from about 1.5 to 1.8 hectares in size while the larger ones cover about 3 hectares. Most of the smaller forts will have held only one auxiliary unit, though it seems that Strageath may have been garrisoned by a force in excess of a single regiment. The larger forts will no doubt usually have contained more than one unit: Ardoch may have been

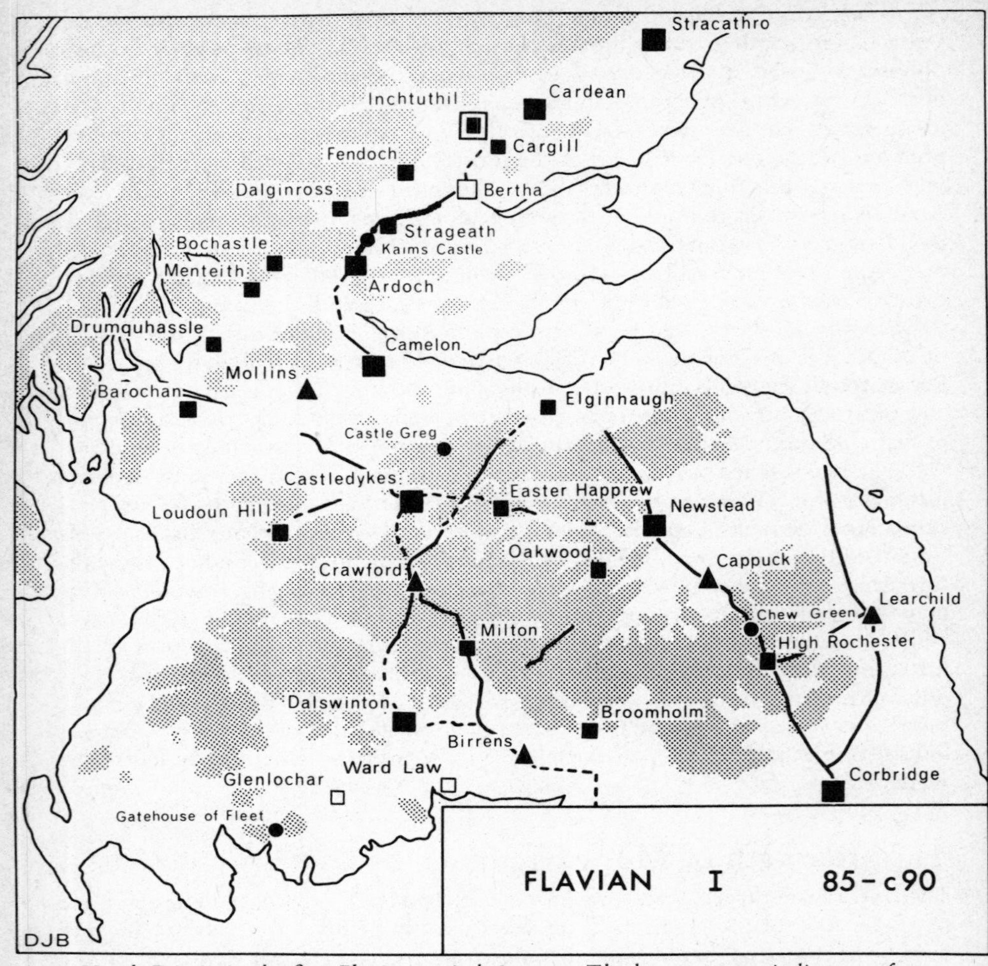

4 *North Britain in the first Flavian period, 85–c.90. The larger square indicates a fort 2.8 hectares (7 acres) or excess in area, the smaller square a fort of 1.4–2.4 hectares (3.5–6.5 acres), the triangle a small fort of about 0.4 hectares (1 acre), the larger circle a fortlet, while the Gaśk towers are marked as small circles. Inchtuthil is denoted by a double square. An open square indicates occupation uncertain*

garrisoned by an auxiliary unit and a legionary detachment. This arrangement obviously reflects a carefully planned use of manpower and resources: as the same arrangement was adopted for both lines it may suggest that the outer line had no special significance.

It appears that none of the forts north of the Forth were occupied for long. None could have been constructed before Agricola's third season, 79 or 80, when he first reached the Tay, while pottery evidence points to the abandonment of all forts north of the Forth-Clyde isthmus by about 90. Further, the legionary base at Inchtuthil was abandoned before it was completed while excavation at two of the auxiliary forts, Fendoch and Cardean, has demonstrated that they were given up after brief occupations. Thus the construction, occupation and abandonment of at least 12 forts, two with two phases of occupation, have to be squeezed into a period of no more than ten years, and possibly less. No literary sources survive for this period and epigraphic and numismatic evidence is slight: purely archaeological dating methods cannot be refined so closely as to distinguish between the occupation of forts within five or even ten years. In the light of these difficulties the history of the area north of the Forth in these years has to be determined by reference to 'historical' and 'logical' arguments rather than literary documentation and concrete fact.

It is not possible to determine the exact sequence of events; all that can be done is to suggest the probable pattern, or patterns, in the knowledge that the truth will never be known. More than one explanation, on present evidence, is possible and, where appropriate, will be discussed. One final problem remains to be mentioned. It seems possible that the Roman network of forts north of the Forth was never completed. Thus we are trying to link together not just the pieces of a partially surviving jigsaw, many fragments having been lost through the passage of nearly 2000 years, but the pieces of a jigsaw which was never complete.

Agricola first reached the Tay in his third season, 79 or 80. However, the frontier line established in the following season lay on the Forth-Clyde isthmus. It is possible therefore that he built no forts north of the isthmus. On the other hand in the discussion of his sixth campaign, the first against the Caledonians, it is recorded by Tacitus that a Roman fort was attacked, and it is usually presumed that this lay north of the Forth. There is no warrant for this assumption, for the Caledonians clearly had the mobility to attack a fort on, or even south of, the Forth-Clyde isthmus. Nevertheless, for what it is worth, this passage may imply that one or more forts had been built during or before the sixth season north of the Forth. The obvious candidates are those on the road to the Tay. At two of these forts, Ardoch and Strageath, two phases of occupation in the first century have been discovered. The first may date to Agricola's third season, though equally possibly both phases may fall within the years following Agricola's retirement.

In fact it is probable that no forts were constructed by Agricola north of the Forth. No fort building is mentioned in the *Agricola* during the last three seasons when Agricola drew up his troops facing Ireland and campaigned against the Caledonians. The last fort building recorded in that book was in the governor's fourth season when he consolidated his hold on the Lowland tribes and placed a chain of garrisons across the Forth-Clyde isthmus (though perhaps too much reliance should not be placed on the essentially negative evidence of Tacitus). During his last two seasons Agricola was concerned with the conquest of the Caledonians and it was only after that tribe and their allies had been defeated that attention would have turned to the construction of forts in their territory. As Agricola did not have time to do this – he seems to have left Britain immediately after Mons Graupius – the work was left to his successor.

The construction of forts north of the Forth by Agricola's unknown successor ties in well with other evidence from Inchtuthil. The legionary fortress at Inchtuthil was still being built when it was abandoned (fig. 5). The reason for this change in plan must have resulted from the withdrawal of *legio II Adiutrix* from Britain. The exact date of this is not known but evidence from the continent points to the winter of 85/86 or 86 as being the most likely time. Inchtuthil, in common with a number of other Scottish forts, Camelon, Strageath, Stracathro, Crawford, Newstead and possibly Cramond, Castledykes and Barochan, has produced a number of *asses*, coins, of 86 in unworn condition, demonstrating that it – and the other forts – was

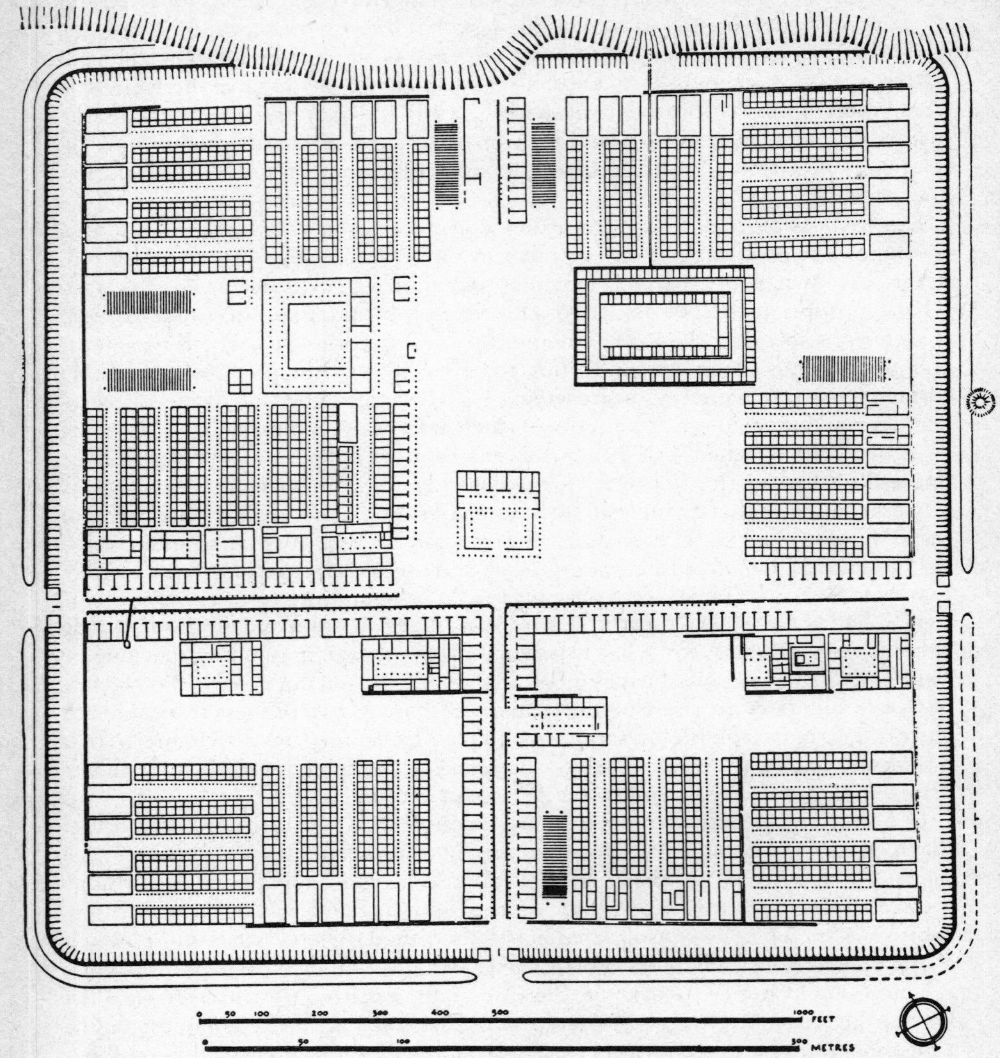

5 The legionary fortress at Inchtuthil. The fortress contains sufficient barrack-blocks for the 10 cohorts, but granaries for only 6, a small headquarters building in the centre, hospital and workshop behind. No house for the legate had been built and only 4 of the 7 senior officers' houses. (Drawn by I.A. Richmond)

garrisoned in that year, or shortly after. It seems probable that these coins were specially imported into Britain to allow the army to implement the soldier's pay raise which occurred sometime in the reign of the Emperor Domitian. Inchtuthil was modified, even before it was completed, by the addition of a stone face to the turf rampart. Outside the fortress lie labour camps used by the troops engaged in the building operations and these exhibit two phases of use. It is possible therefore that if Inchtuthil was, on the coin evidence, being built in 86 (or after) work had not started before 85, the year following the retirement of Agricola. All three lines of argument, although unsatisfactory or uncertain in themselves, point to the same conclusion: building operations commenced at Inchtuthil no earlier than 85 and were abandoned in 86, or shortly afterwards, when *legio II Adiutrix* was withdrawn for service on the continent.

It seems perfectly possible that a legionary fortress, or rather most of it, could be constructed in two years. It is clear from Caesar and Josephus, for example, that complex siege works could be constructed with speed in a matter of a few weeks and modern experiments in fort building support the testimony of ancient authorities. Presumably the legion which was to occupy the fortress was mainly engaged on its construction while gangs from other legions were occupied building the auxiliary forts.

The fact that the network of forts north of the Forth was probably not completed renders the definition of the role of some of the forts difficult. This is an acute problem in relation to the glen forts. They have usually been interpreted as 'glen-blocking forts', guarding the mouths of the glens and preventing access to the province by the Caledonians to the north and west. This is possible and was certainly a device used on other frontiers of the empire, in particular in north Africa, though in later years. This argument presumes that the Romans considered that the occupation of the Highlands of Scotland was beyond their capabilities. To assume this is to ignore the more hostile terrain – and tribes – overcome in other parts of the empire such as Asia Minor, north-west Spain and the Alps. It is in fact possible that the construction of the glen forts formed the first step towards the occupation of the Highlands: they were the springboard for an advance up the glens, an advance which never materialised because the plan was abandoned uncompleted.

There is one other important piece of evidence: the position of the legionary fortress at Inchtuthil. Two factors generally influenced the position of legionary fortresses: they could either be springboards for an advance or supports for the frontier system, though at times and in certain places the two are difficult to distinguish. The early fortresses in the Empire seem to fall into the former category and as the province was being extended in Britain at this time it might be expected that Inchtuthil would also. This assumption might be considered to be supported by the position of the fortress, which lies on the very edge of the province in front of a river. The tactical position of the fortress suggests that defence was not a prime consideration, otherwise its relationship to the river would presumably have been reversed; while its isolation suggests that strategically it was to be the base for a major extension of the province north and westwards.

It seems best therefore to regard the glen forts as the springboards for advances up the glens: indeed forts may have been built up some of the glens and still await discovery. The glens would have been convenient lines of advance for an army intending to penetrate the Highland massif: in the not dissimilar mountainous terrain of Wales the valleys had been used in such a manner by the Roman army. No evidence survives relating to the use of the glens by the Caledonians. Montrose in the seventeenth century frequently moved along the glens but on occasions he led his army over the mountain ridges and there is no reason to believe that the Caledonians could not have done likewise and that the Romans would have found this unexpected. In such circumstances the Roman army may have found the position of the glen forts cramped their movements. This would, however, be of no account if the forts were part of an offensive forward movement up the glens. Certainly the glen forts, including Inchtuthil, do not form a defensible frontier and it is noteworthy that in the second century when outpost forts north of the Antonine Wall were occupied no forts were placed at the mouths of the glens.

Agricola clearly felt that having defeated the Caledonians he had completed the conquest of the island, and this view was shared by Domitian for he was duly rewarded. It would have been natural for this victory to have been followed by the establishment of a network of roads and forts in the area of the conquered tribes, the Highlands. The forts along the edge of the Highlands, in the mouths of the glens, would thus be best seen as the basis for advances up those glens in order to establish a pattern no doubt similar to that created by the Hanoverians 1700 years later. As it happened, Roman defeats on the Rhine and Danube led to the withdrawal of troops from Britain and the abandonment of Roman plans for the occupation of the Highlands of Scotland.

Roman and Native

While the province lay at its furthest extent we shall pause to consider the effect of the Roman advance upon the natives. Twelve hill forts in Scotland, in the Borders and in north-east Scotland, are known to have been abandoned uncompleted and it has been suggested that this was connected with the Roman advance. Some forts were abandoned in early stages of construction while others were abandoned as their original defences were being extended or improved. This work, it has been proposed, was being carried out as the Roman army advanced north, the Scottish tribes belatedly realising the danger that they were in. However, none of the unfinished hill forts are dated. Some, possibly many, could date to several years, even centuries, before the Roman advance and a variety of reasons could account for their unfinished state. Tribal or factional warfare could have ended work, financial or other difficulties on the part of the builder could have led his workforce to disperse. However, it is not impossible that some were constructed in the face of the Roman advance. Even if this was the case none of these forts, nor any others, was strong enough to force the Roman army to pause and construct the siege works in which they excelled.

The Roman advance through the territories of the Lowland tribes was swift and apparently uneventful: Tacitus remarks that the Roman army was not attacked. It is even possible that the Lowland tribes submitted voluntarily to Rome. Trajan's Column vividly portrays their fate if they had resisted the Roman advance. Scenes on the Column show the burning of enemy villages, the flight of their inhabitants, fighting between Roman and barbarian, the defeat and death of the barbarians or their imprisonment in stockades, and on surrender the separation of husbands from their families; on defeat the Dacian king, Decabalus, committed suicide. Following their defeat, or peaceful submission, the tribes would be incorporated into the province. No doubt Agricola commenced this operation in his third and fourth seasons when he paused on the Forth-Clyde isthmus. Those who had opposed the Roman advance will have become *dediticii*, conquered peoples without rights. Some may have been sold into slavery, others drafted into the army, though this, if it took place at all, was probably limited in scale. All the new provincials will have been subject to the census, so that their liability for taxation could be assessed, to the requisition of supplies such as corn and hides, though at set prices, and to forced labour on the roads. All will have fallen under military jurisdiction and there is no evidence either now or later that the Roman administration attempted to organise the northern tribes into *civitates*, self-governing tribal units.

Local law was probably allowed to operate as before, so long as it was not in direct contravention of Roman law. One difference is that the new provincials would now have the dubious advantage of appeal from their tribal court to the governor: in practice no doubt usually the local army commander. The army would, when necessary, have kept the peace as there was no separate police force in the Roman world. Many surviving documents from Egypt bear witness to the extra-military duties of soldiers. They were asked to investigate many crimes: theft, assault, arson, malicious damage, trespass, and even the settlement of disputes over wills and the search for missing persons.

It is difficult to determine the attitude of the Lowland tribes to the Roman advance. It is frequently stated that the Selgovae, Damnonii and Novantae opposed the Roman army, but not the Votadini. Suppositions concerning the attitude of the Votadini to Rome and their subsequent history depend mainly upon the history of Traprain Law. This hill fort had a long life from the Bronze Age into at least the fifth century AD. Unlike any other known hill fort within the province it continued in occupation through the Roman period. Indeed it reached its greatest extent at this time, the defences being extended in the late first or early second century so that the area within them grew from 12 to 16 hectares. The size of the fort, its continuing occupation and the range of important finds from the site combine to suggest that this was the capital of the Votadini. It seems possible therefore that this tribe voluntarily submitted to Rome, possibly even before the army entered her territory, and as a result a treaty was negotiated between the two. It is even possible, as Traprain Law continued in occupation, that the tribe became a client state and that the status continued through several generations. Such a position would not be unusual on Roman frontiers.

It is interesting to compare the situation at Traprain Law with that at Eildon Hill North, by Newstead, for a timber signal-station or watch-tower was planted in the centre of this hill fort. The exact date of the construction of the tower is not known: it could have been erected in either the first or second centuries. It might be expected that the construction of a Roman watch-tower would have led to the abandonment of the hill fort, and this might indeed have been the case, but the presence of second century coins and pottery of the second, third and fourth centuries points to renewed, if not continuing, native occupation.

The abandonment of many other native forts can be demonstrated for in the second century open settlements sprang up often spreading over the ramparts of former forts (fig. 32): it seems probable that such sites were abandoned as a result of the Agricolan rather than the Antonine advance. At Camelon, a defended homestead, and possibly other houses, was abandoned either now or in the mid-second century when the army constructed a large fort a few metres away. However, the site appears to have been re-occupied when the army withdrew.

The distribution of Roman forts may also hint at the attitude of the tribes to their conquerer. Forts were planted in the territory of the Selgovae and the Damnonii, but they are rarer in the area attributed to the Votadini and Novantae (fig. 4). However, the situation is not straightforward. Firstly, it is probable that the known distribution of Roman forts is incomplete. Few military sites have been discovered in Galloway, the land of the Novantae. This may be not so much because there were no forts, but as a result of the underlying geology which renders parts of this corner of Scotland unresponsive to aerial photography. In the east only one fort has been located east of Dere Street – at Low Learchild – but again more may have existed. Another factor is that Roman forts were situated with strategic as well as tactical considerations in mind. Thus forts would be placed on Dere Street in order to provide support for troops on the frontier as well as with the intention of controlling the local population: there was no need to establish garrisons throughout the territory of a tribe which had submitted, it could be controlled by units beyond its boundaries. A further difficulty lies in the fact that the boundaries of the tribes are not known. Finally, Rome's attitude to the tribes, friendly or otherwise, must be considered. Rome regarded even client states as part of the empire even though technically they were independent. In Britain this is demonstrated by the disarming of the Iceni in 47 by the governor Ostorius Scapula in spite of their client status. If the Votadini had been a client state, or at least been philo-Roman, it is possible that garrisons were still planted in their territory, for their protection if not to control them. If the army had wished to place a watch-tower or signal-station within the hill fort of a friendly tribe there is no doubt that it would have gone ahead and constructed the observation post: the appearance of such a watch-tower on the summit of Eildon Hill North is therefore not a secure indication of the status of the occupants of the site. The distribution of forts is accordingly of little help in determining the attitude of the tribes to their new lords.

With the move across the Forth-Clyde isthmus in Agricola's sixth year of office the Roman army met a new enemy. It is clear from the account of Tacitus that the Caledonians and the other northern tribes attempted to sink their differences in the face of the common threat. Treaties were negotiated between the various tribes in order to solve areas of disagreement and field as large an army as possible. From the available tribal leaders one was chosen to be the leader of the army, Calgacus. This was the first step in a process of amalgamation of tribes beyond the empire forced on them by the presence of Rome. In the event, the joint action of the northern tribes was to no avail for they were defeated at Mons Graupius. The process of assimilation of these tribes into the province would be repeated, though again nothing is known of this.

The sudden arrival of a monetary economy and of well-paid Roman soldiers requiring food, clothing, leather and other goods, might have been expected to bring about changes in the northern economy and society. Farmers no doubt turned to producing agricultural commodities for the army rather than for their old masters while traders and merchants would have been attracted north to sell goods and services to the troops. However, neither changes in the agricultural landscape in Scotland nor civil settlements outside forts have been certainly recognised at this time.

If such changes are difficult to recognise archaeologically it is certain that artefacts – brooches, glass vessels, pottery as well as coins – found their way into the hands of the new provincials, though these objects cannot speak of the method of their transmission – trade, stealing, plunder? Few objects have been found beyond the province (fig. 6). No more than 10 coins, brooches, or sherds of pottery, of first-century date, have come to light in the highlands and islands of Scotland; and some of these of course could have been lost several years after they were manufactured. This would seem to imply that there was little contact, certainly little friendly contact, as indeed might be expected, between Roman and barbarian: the contact between those who had fled before the Roman advance and the tribesmen to the north has already been discussed.

The Roman army imposed peace. And with peace came other 'benefits': taxation, slavery, forced labour, and so on. If hill forts were abandoned no new settlements of this period have yet been identified. Nor can any other results of the imposition of Roman rule on the north British tribes be identified archaeologically, though the flowering of metalwork among the tribes beyond the province in the late first century and beyond almost certainly arose from the presence of Rome.

6 The distribution of Roman finds on non-military sites in Scotland in the first century (after Robertson)

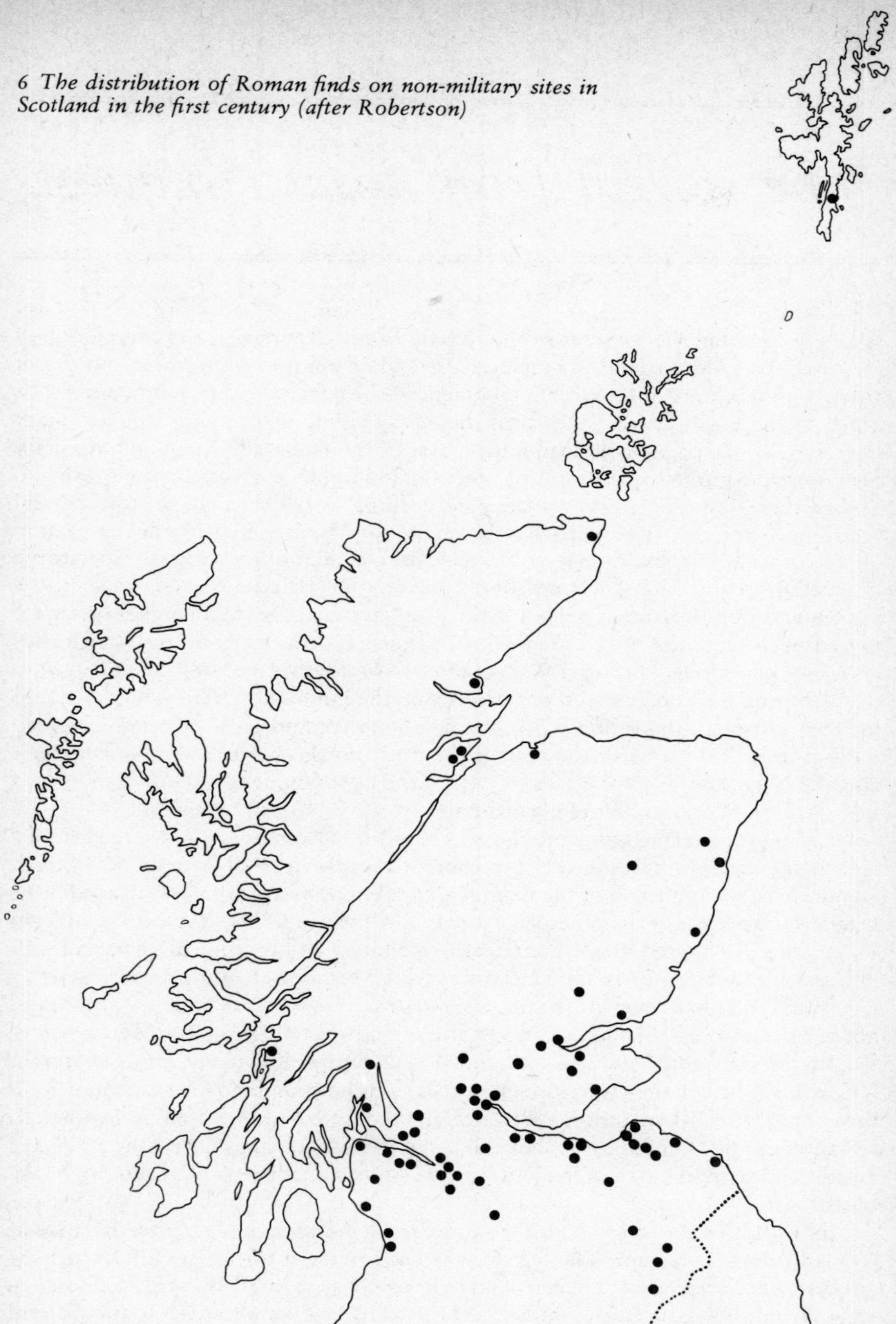

4

The retreat from total conquest

We have seen that the Romans probably saw Mons Graupius as the completion of the conquest of the island. Thereafter Agricola's unknown successor, no doubt acting on the orders of Domitian, commenced the construction of forts and roads north of the Forth-Clyde isthmus in the newly conquered territory. A legionary fortress was placed at Inchtuthil a little east of the Dunkeld Gorge and auxiliary forts were positioned at the mouths of the main Highland glens. To the south and east of these lay more forts on the road leading north through Strathearn and Strathmore as far as Stracathro, north-west of the Montrose Basin: the occupation of at least some of these forts seems to have been contemporary with the glen forts. It seems probable that the forts built at this time reflect the first stage in the implementation of Roman plans for the occupation of the Highlands. Forts were placed in the mouths of the glens, not to block Caledonian raiding, which they could not have done, but to act as springboards for the advance of Roman forces up the glens and the construction of forts within the Highlands. This would account for the position of the legion so far north: when the plans were fully implemented the legion would be far to the rear of the most northerly forts. A major disaster elsewhere within the empire was to lead to the abandonment of Domitian's plans for northern Scotland before even the first stage was fully completed.

In 85 an army of Dacians, from the area of modern Romania, crossed the Danube and in the ensuing fighting the governor of the province of Moesia was killed. Domitian took command of the Roman defence, but in a retaliatory attack on the Dacians the prefect of the praetorian guard, Cornelius Fuscus, was killed and *legio V Alaudae* annihilated. the Roman forces withdrew and regrouped and as a result of a second invasion in 89 the Dacians accepted terms, becoming a client state of Rome and in return receiving a subsidy and other assistance. Peace was, however, not permanently established for in 92 tribes living west of Dacia, the Marcomanni, Quadi, Jazyges and Sarmatians, invaded the empire destroying another legion, *XXI Rapax*, before they were driven out. To aid the Danubian armies troops were brought in from other frontiers: Britain supplied *legio II Adiutrix*. This legion was certainly on the Danube by 93, but other slight evidence suggests that it may have been withdrawn as early as the winter of 85/86 or 86, at the very beginning of the crisis.

The withdrawal of *legio II Adiutrix* marked a decisive change in the balance of Roman forces in Britain. The legion was not to return to the province, nor was another sent to replace it. The garrison of Britain was permanently reduced to three legions and this reduced the capacity of the army to take offensive action beyond the frontier: the withdrawal of the legion was thus an important factor in determining that the rest of the island would never be conquered by Rome.

As a result of the movement of *II Adiutrix* to the continent the legionary fortress at Inchtuthil was abandoned even before it was completed. All the barracks had been constructed, most of the granaries, several of the officers' houses and the principal buildings, with the exception of the commanding officer's palace. So far as is known the auxiliary forts, where building had commenced, had been completed, but it is possible that other forts in this line along the edge of the Highlands were planned but had not been started. The legion destined for Inchtuthil, probably *XX Valeria Victrix*, was instead moved to Chester to take the place of *II Adiutrix*. The abandonment of Inchtuthil was almost certainly accompanied by the withdrawal of the garrisons from the glen forts. It is not known where the units in these forts moved to but it is possible that they, or others, accompanied *II Adiutrix* to the continent. The abandonment of Inchtuthil, and the glen forts, must also have led to the relinquishing of whatever plans Rome had for the occupation of the Highlands.

The Gask frontier

Although the abandonment of Inchtuthil presumably carried with it the withdrawal of garrisons from the glen forts to the south-west, it is possible that no other forts were abandoned at this time. Several of the forts on the road north from the Forth had a more complicated history than the glen forts. Two first-century forts have been recognised at Ardoch while excavation has revealed two phases in at least part of the fort at Strageath. Nothing is known of the next fort to the north, Bertha at the crossing of the Tay, but the situation at Cargill, at the crossing of the Isla, is now complex. The fort, first century in date, lies only 3 kilometres south-east of the legionary fortress at Inchtuthil. Furthermore, an undated fortlet lies beside the fort. It is not possible to do more than speculate about the sequence of events. The fort may have been occupied at the same time as the fortress for the two served different functions, yet on the other hand their proximity may argue that they were not contemporary, one, presumably the fort, succeeding the other: the fortlet is an altogether unknown quantity. The continuing occupation of these 'road' forts after the abandonment of Inchtuthil may carry with it the two forts to the north, Cardean and Stracathro. The rebuilding of the more southerly forts in this line was probably occasioned by the abandonment of Inchtuthil: these forts were presumably initially built either at the same time as the glen forts, or perhaps in Agricola's third season, possibly, in view of the closeness of the two lines, being abandoned briefly when the glen forts were occupied.

Along the road north are a number of timber watch-towers and these are probably best dated to this time (figs 4 and 7, pl. 3). Each consisted of a timber tower, 3–4m square, based on four main timber posts, and surrounded by an earthen bank and one or two ditches. The towers fall into two sectors. From Ardoch northwards along the road to Strageath four have been found. The distance between Ardoch and the first tower, between each of the three towers and between the third tower and the fortlet at Kaims Castle, is in each case just under 1,000m. The fourth tower at present stands by itself, some distance to the north of Kaims Castle, and presumably more remain to be discovered in this stretch.

The distances between the eleven towers known along the Gask Ridge running eastwards from Strageath vary considerably from 760m to 1520m, though it is possible that some long gaps were broken by as yet undiscovered towers. The only indentifiable difference in planning between the regularly spaced towers from Ardoch to Kaims Castle and those on the Gask Ridge is that the former are surrounded by two ditches and the latter by only one.

The watch-towers are too close together to have been signal-stations: many

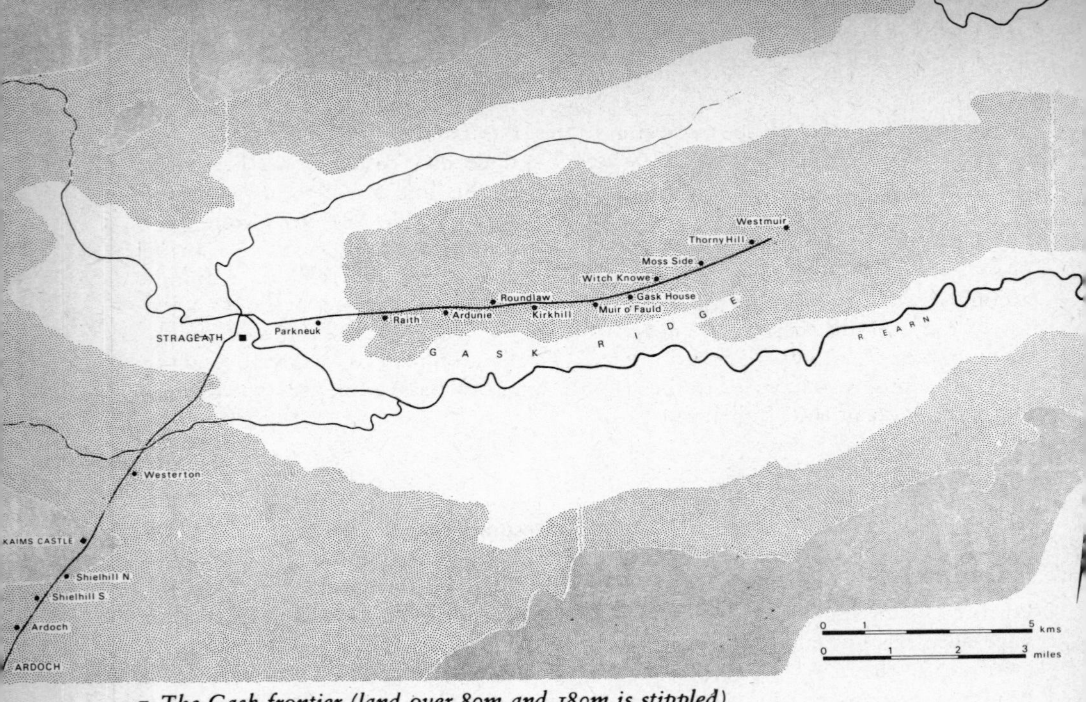

7 The Gask frontier (land over 80m and 180m is stippled)

would have been superfluous as they could have been by-passed by fire or smoke signals (pl. 8 for towers and bonfires along the Danube). The purpose of the posts was presumably to keep watch on the cleared strip of ground on either side of the road beside which they lay (fig. 9). The watch-towers, and the forts along the same line, therefore formed a frontier, or at least a line of control, a device to help the army monitor the movement of people into and out of the province. The garrison of the towers by itself was insufficient to prevent infiltration by the barbarians and bandits outside the province, but the system would enable the army to see what was happening and take appropriate retaliatory measures.

Regulations governed the movement of people into and out of the empire. No such regulations survive for Britain, but almost contemporary incidents concerning frontier regulations are recorded by classical writers. In 70 the Tencteri, a tribe living on the east bank of the Rhine, complained that they could only have access to the *Colonia Agrippina* – Cologne – unarmed and practically naked, under guard and after paying a fee. At the end of the first century Tacitus recorded how the Hermanduri from across the Danube had the privilege, unique among the Germans, of trading not just on the bank of the river but deep inside a Roman colony and could enter and leave without guards. These accounts, from two separate areas of the empire, would suggest that similar regulations were in operation on the northern frontier in Britain. The watch-towers can accordingly be seen as an attempt to operate such regulations, to ensure that tribesmen from beyond the province entered the province unarmed, were escorted to agreed markets, and charged a fee for the privilege.

This frontier system – the 'Gask frontier' (see note at end of this chapter) – is not closely dated. It is not mentioned in the documentary sources for Roman Britain and there are only two surviving sherds of pottery from the eight watch-towers investigated to date: both date to the late first century. By itself this is little evidence to date a whole frontier complex, but there are two other considerations: firstly the

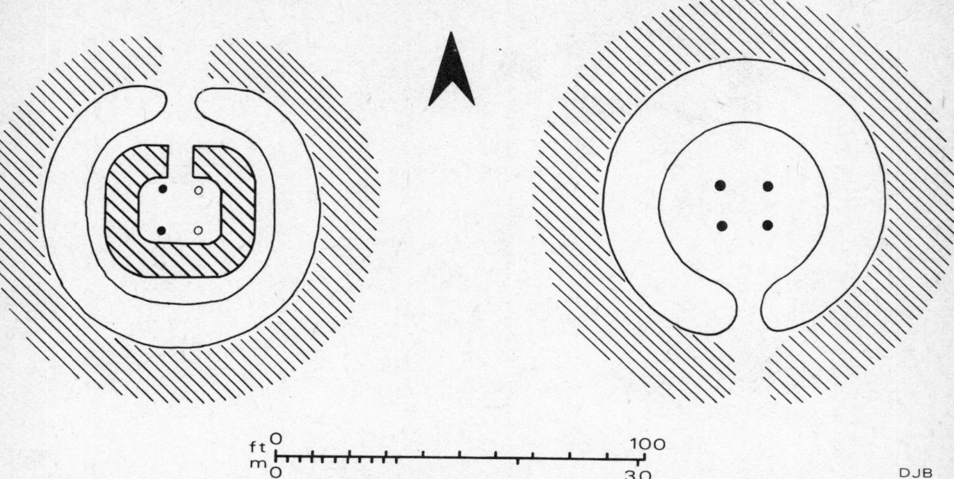

8 Plans of towers on the Gask Ridge: Parkneuk (after Robertson) and Witch Knowe (after Christieson)

relationship of the watch-towers to the history of the northern frontier and secondly the relationship of the British watch-towers to those in Germany.

There are a number of occasions when the watch-towers could have been constructed: during Agricola's move north in his third season, during the campaigns north of the Forth in his sixth and seventh seasons, as support for the glen forts, or during the years following the abandonment of those forts.

A frontier such as that under consideration is not compatible with the fluid military situation that existed during the years of Agricola's governorship. We have already seen that the first mention of a possible frontier in Britain was in Agricola's fourth campaigning season. It seems unlikely that a frontier would have been constructed 30 kilometres to the north in the preceding year. In the sixth and seventh seasons, on the other hand, Agricola was fighting the Caledonians and concerned neither to build forts nor frontiers. In the following years when Inchtuthil and the glen forts were being constructed it seems unlikely that a second line of defence should have been built to their rear, leaving, in particular, the legion beyond the line of watch-towers. The best time for the construction of the watch-towers therefore would seem to be in the years following the abandonment of Inchtuthil and the glen forts. As such they would represent the line to which the army fell back on the abandonment of the more northerly and westerly forts. Finally, it may be considered that the watch-towers served as extra protection in front of the Antonine Wall in the mid-second century, but this would seem to be out of character with the frontiers of the period and unparalleled on any other of the empire's frontiers at that time.

If the Gask watch-towers have been correctly dated they were exactly contemporary with similar structures in Germany. In the 80s the Emperor Domitian waged war against the Chatti east of the Rhine. The war probably started in the spring of 83 and at first the Roman army achieved victories: Domitian celebrated his triumph in the summer of 83. However, the war dragged on for at least another year and when it ended, probably as a result of the outbreak of more

9 The Gask Ridge, view from the west. Reconstruction showing two of the fortified towers. (Drawn by M. Moore)

serious trouble on the Danube, it led to the acquisition of very little territory by Rome. Nevertheless two most important events followed. The first was the creation of two new provinces, Upper Germany and Lower Germany. Hitherto there had been two army groups based on the Rhine, ostensibly waiting for orders to move forward and conquer the rest of Germany. On the completion of this operation the army groups would become the garrison of the new provinces. Now it was tacitly recognised that this move forward was unlikely to materialise. Secondly, a new frontier was laid out encompassing those areas brought into the empire as a result of the Chattan war. New forts were established through the Wetterau and Taunus from the junction of the Rhine and the Mosel to the Neckar. Still within the period of the Chattan war, it appears that these forts were supplemented by the construction of timber watch-towers, which were placed beside the path linking the forts. These towers were normally 500–600m apart, though under certain circumstances – on level ground and given good visibility – the distance might be as much as 1,000m. It seems probable that this new frontier should be associated with a statement by Julius Frontinus, a former governor of Britain and a member of Domitian's staff during the Chattan war, in his book, *Stratagems*. Here he states (1,3,10) that following raiding by the Germans Domitian advanced the frontier of the empire along a stretch of 120 miles (200km): the total north-south length of the new frontier is 120 miles. The construction of this type of frontier, for the first time anywhere in the empire, together with the establishment of the two new provinces marks a fundamental change in Roman attitudes towards frontiers, though of course this was not recognised at that time: a few years later Tacitus remarked in the *Germania* that the conquest of Germany was taking a long time, not apparently realising that Roman pretentions in Free Germany had been abandoned, at least temporarily, and the fact recognised by the establishment of the provinces and the frontier.

The creation of a similar frontier in Britain came a few years after that in Germany. Essentially the two were the same. Forts and towers connected by a road marked the frontier which was probably defined by a cleared strip of ground. This would allow for the observation of people coming into and out of the province, though of course it would not prevent it: the addition of the towers was merely to allow the Roman army better powers of observation and control.

The watch-towers in Scotland are at present known only for a distance of about 18km through Strathearn, along the line of the road leading north into Strathmore. It is possible that if they are part of a frontier system, as argued above, they started further south, possibly at Camelon, and continued further north. They presumably continued – that is if the construction of the frontier was ever completed – at least as far as Bertha on the Tay. No watch-towers have been recognised beyond the Tay, but it is possible that some had been built there, or had intended to be built, but were not constructed owing to abandonment of the project.

The Gask frontier would appear to have had a short life. It cannot have been constructed until after 86, if the preceding arguments are accepted, yet pottery evidence suggests that all sites north of the Forth Clyde isthmus were abandoned by about 90. At this time the forts and watch-towers were dismantled and burnt. The Gask frontier therefore, occupied for perhaps no more than three years, marks a brief pause before another major withdrawal south. Rome presumably considered that if intentions to occupy the Highlands were abandoned she could still maintain control over the peoples south of the Highland Line. But that was not to be. Whether the abandonment of all pretensions north of the Forth was the result of more troop withdrawals from Britain or simply a more realistic reappraisal of resources is not known.

The abandonment of Scotland

The forts abandoned at this time included all those north of the Forth and several to the south. The most northerly line of forts now lay on or, just to the north of, the Cheviots. They included Newstead, probably Oakwood, Milton, Dalswinton and Glenlochar (fig. 10). The evidence for the continuing occupation of these forts is ceramic and structural. At Newstead, Oakwood and Glenlochar two structural phases have been recorded in excavations, at Milton two or possibly three first-century phases are known, while Dalswinton had as many as four. In addition Newstead and Dalswinton have produced late first-century samian pottery. Two other sites must be mentioned: Castlecary on the Forth-Clyde isthmus has produced late first-century samian ware though the first-century site here has not been discovered, while as many as four first-century phases have been recorded at the small fort at Loudoun Hill in Ayrshire.

Four of the forts in the Scottish Lowlands at this time, Newstead, Milton, Dalswinton and Glenlochar, all on the same axis, were larger than usual. Newstead was rebuilt, probably at this time, and was both larger and more massively defended than its predecessor. It is possible that these large forts were the bases of garrisons charged with long-range patrolling and the maintenance of surveillance over those lands recently abandoned. Such an explanation might account for the occupation of stations further to the north and west: Castlecary and Loudoun Hill. Forts to the rear, on the roads north in the east and at Broomholm in the west, also continued in occupation.

These forts were not to be occupied for long before there was yet another

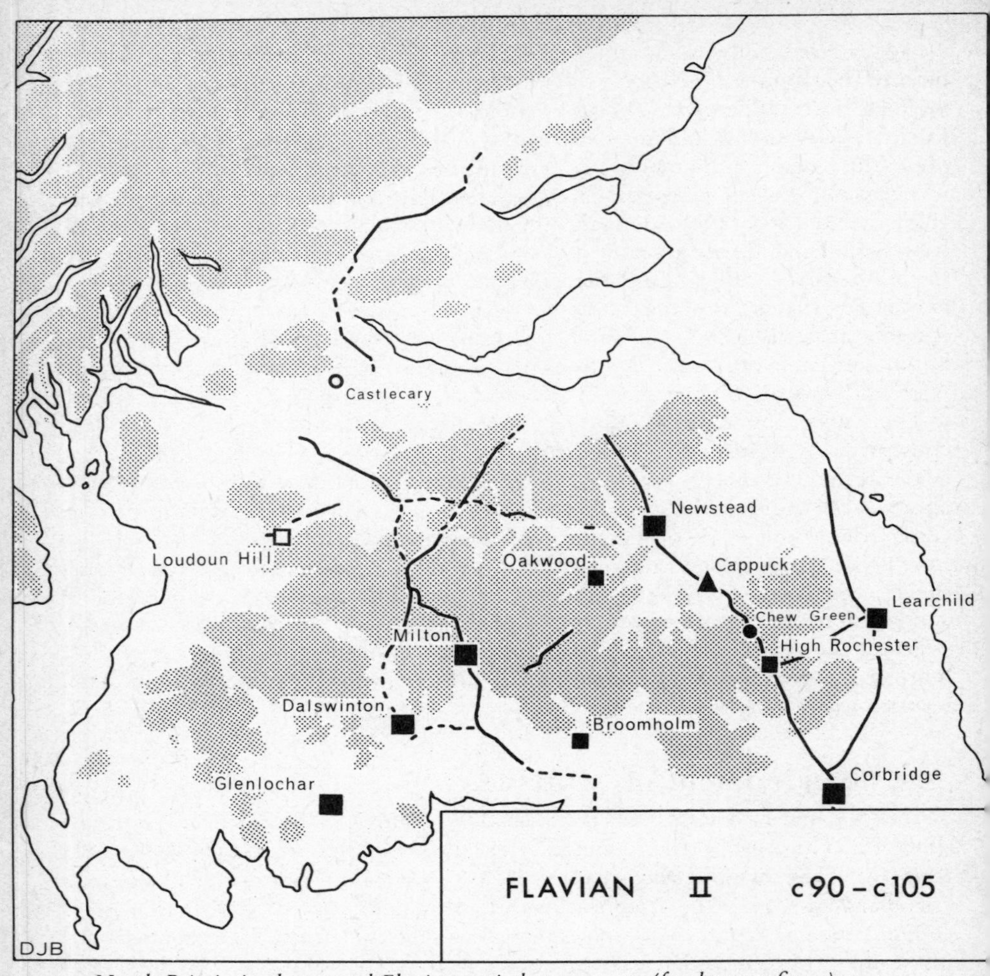

10 North Britain in the second Flavian period, c.90–c.105 (for key see fig. 4)

withdrawal, this time south to the Tyne-Solway isthmus. There are two pieces of evidence which combine to suggest a date in the first decade of the second century for this withdrawal. Firstly, the samian pottery from the sites north of the isthmus carry their occupation down to the last years of the first century or the first years of the second. Secondly, in 1973 a coin of 103 was found in a construction trench of the Trajanic fort at Corbridge on the Tyne. This must date the building of this fort to 103 or later. Again the abandonment of forts in southern Scotland and Northumberland may have been because troops were withdrawn from Britain for in 105 Trajan commenced his second war against the Dacians and this may have led to empire wide troop movement, though we can point to no positive evidence for this in relation to Britain.

There is a further possible occasion for the withdrawal of army units from southern Scotland. *Legio IX Hispana* was still at York in 107/8 when it was recorded on a building inscription but it had almost certainly left by 122 when *legio*

VI Victrix was sent to Britain from Lower Germany, presumably to replace it and provide more men to help in the construction of Hadrian's Wall. Its departure may have been sooner rather than later after 108. Archaeological evidence from York suggests that there was a reduction in the density of occupation of the legionary fortress from *c.*110–*c.*125/30. It seems likely that the legion was not at York during these years, and of course *VI Victrix* when it arrived went straight off to build Hadrian's Wall which accounts for the continuing lack of pottery on the site.

There were two significant events in Trajan's reign (98–117) which might have led to major troop movements in the empire: the Dacian wars of 101–106 and the invasion of Parthia 114–117. The earlier was before the building work by *legio IX Hispana* at York – unless the consequence of the incorporation of Dacia into the empire continued to be felt in the form of troop movements for some time after 106 – but the latter may be relevant. A tile stamp and a *mortarium* stamp found at the legionary fortress at Nijmegen on the Lower Rhine would fit this date and allow *IX Hispana* to be transferred to the continent as part of widespread troop movements connected with the Parthian war and thence east to be destroyed either in the Jewish revolt of Hadrian's reign or in the Parthian invasion of 161. The legion was certainly not destroyed before the end of the 120s, as the careers of certain officers of the legion demonstrate. If *IX Hispana* was withdrawn from Britain about 114 it might have been accompanied by auxiliary units and even if this was not the case the departure might have been the occasion for a rearrangement of the frontier garrisons in order to compensate for the loss of this force.

A date of about 114 for this reorganisation would be rather later than the pottery and structural evidence suggests for the establishment of the Tyne-Solway isthmus as a frontier. There is also, as is often the case, a complication. Tiles of *legio IX* have been found at Scalesceugh, about 4.5km south-east of Carlisle. These may date to the late first or early second century, though this is far from certain. It has been suggested that at this time *legio IX* was engaged in the construction of a new legionary fortress in the neighbourhood of Carlisle preparatory to evacuating York. Building work would take some time and presumably require the presence of a large part of the legion. This might account for the lack of pottery at York in these years, while the continuing, though small, army presence might explain why the fortress was not given over to civilian use, which would surely have happened if it had been abandoned completely. But this is speculation. The reason for the presence of tiles of *IX Hispana* at Scalesceugh is not known. The legion has left no record in Britain after 108 and it does not appear on the many building stones from Hadrian's Wall. All, perhaps, that can be said is that the movements of *legio IX Hispana* in these years are unclear and as a result none of the above possibilities can be ignored.

Many of the forts abandoned in the early second century were burnt and it is not impossible that this was the result of hostile action. Destruction material from the burning of timber buildings has been found to cover the whole area of the fort at Corbridge, but the most evocative evidence is from Newstead on the Tweed. Here, in pits, have been discovered burnt wattle and daub from timber buildings, damaged military equipment and human skulls. It has been argued that this all results from the destruction of the fort by the northern tribes, buried by the Romans after they had retrieved the situation. Yet a peaceful scenario is equally possible. The burnt wattle and daub could have resulted from the destruction of the buildings by the Roman army itself on abandonment of the site: this was the usual procedure. The buildings were demolished, usually it would appear in a methodical way, and the wattle and daub panels and the main timbers burnt. Sometimes the main timbers were not removed but were burnt *in situ*. Sometimes the fort's rampart was slighted, at other times not. The damaged equipment at Newstead could have been that in the workshops awaiting repair when word came that the fort was to be evacuated, and abandoned as surplus to requirements, or to transport capabilities. The skulls appear alone, without associated long bones. Human heads are shown on the almost contemporary Trajan's Column as trophies held by Roman soldiers. Heads, presumably Dacians', appear on poles placed in front of a Roman fort, while in another scene Roman soldiers themselves carry heads as they fight, held by the hair from their teeth. The skulls at Newstead therefore could be the remains of such heads buried when the fort was abandoned. The evidence for the cause of the evacuation of these forts north of the Tyne-Solway isthmus in the early second century is not clear, nor is the date certain. However, the action is definite enough and it led to the construction of a new frontier across this southern isthmus. This frontier, often called the Stanegate frontier, is as yet imperfectly understood. It will probably always be imperfectly understood because it was in part an addition to an existing screen of forts, while it was, it would appear, modified during its lifetime. Further, by its very nature, composed as it was of a number of disparate and separate elements, it is more difficult to understand and appreciate its growth and function.

The Stanegate 'frontier'

When the forts north of the Tyne-Solway isthmus were abandoned in the early years of the second century the handful of forts across the isthmus became the most northerly line of military stations in Britain (fig. 11). Occupation at three forts at this time has been proved by archaeology and it is possible on other grounds that a further one or two forts should be added to this group. In the east lay Corbridge, strategically placed beside the lowest crossing of the Tyne, just below the confluence of the North and South Tynes and where Dere Street passed northwards into *barbaricum*. A road, the Stanegate, crossed the isthmus from here to Carlisle where the western route north bridged the Eden. In between lay a fort at Chesterholm, 22km west of Corbridge, which was occupied at this time, and a second at Nether Denton, 18km from Chesterholm and 22km from Carlisle. This fort has not been excavated but is generally considered to date to this time. These forts, at a day's march apart, were probably all on sites chosen twenty years before even though they might have been rebuilt and moved slightly in the meantime. Their spacing is normal. Almost exactly halfway between Chesterholm and Nether Denton, however, lies another fort at Carvoran. Again the date of this fort is not known, but aerial reconnaissance here, as at Nether Denton, has revealed a large, 3.2 hectare, military enclosure below the known fort, which may be an Agricolan foundation at the north end of the Maiden Way. This road branches off the Stainmore road at Kirby Thore to pass northwards through Whitley Castle and connect with the Stanegate. Certainly there would appear to have been first century occupation here for the site had produced the famous Carvoran *modius* which dates to the reign of Domitian.

These five forts therefore would appear to have been the late first-century bases across the isthmus. They did not form a frontier at that time but lay within the province and their spacing and strength was no different from those of sites on, for example, the Stainmore road leading across the Pennines from Catterick to

Brougham. Now, the gradual withdrawal stopped and this line was strengthened, in time by the construction of Hadrian's Wall. The existence of the Tyne-Solway isthmus no doubt led to the halt here, but it may not be entirely coincidental that this marked the northern boundary of the Brigantes, a tribe undoubtedly regarded as part of the empire since it had accepted client status fifty years before.

The reign of Trajan saw major modifications to the line of forts across the isthmus, and this work may have continued into the early days of Hadrian's reign. Firstly, some of the existing forts may have been rebuilt. The fort at Corbridge was burnt down and reconstructed after, probably shortly after, 103, and indeed this work is one of the main pointers to the date of the withdrawal from the more northerly forts and the strengthening of the installations on the isthmus. At Chesterholm too one of the three pre-Hadrianic rebuildings may date to this time. Aerial photographs reveal that the fort at Nether Denton was remodelled at least once during its life and this may date to these years. At Carlisle the position is not known. Secondly, new forts were built across the isthmus. In the east, beyond Corbridge, a fort, apparently of two periods, has been discovered from the air at Washing Well, Whickham. The site is not excavated, but ought to be earlier than Hadrian's Wall, and therefore may well fit into Trajan's reign. In the west, beyond Carlisle, two forts are now known, at Burgh-by-Sands, a little south of the Hadrianic fort, and at Kirkbride, south of Bowness at the end of the Wall. The spacing is interesting, and indicative of what is to come, 8km and 9.5km. On the Stanegate a new fort was built at Old Church Brampton, between Carlisle and Nether Denton to break the gap of 22km, but no fort can positively be identified between Corbridge and Chesterholm, though fourth-century Newbrough, roughly halfway between, may have had a second-century predecessor. The spacing between most of the forts had now been reduced from about 22km to 9–11km, though the east, where the Tyne formed a clear line of demarcation, may have been more sparsely covered. Moreover the line was now extended both east of Corbridge and west of Carlisle.

To these forts a new element was added, the small fort. Only two such sites have been securely identified, Haltwhistle Burn between Chesterholm and Carvoran and Throp between Carvoran and Nether Denton, and only at the former site are the internal buildings known. It is clear from these buildings that Haltwhistle Burn is not a fortlet, but a small fort, a generic term indicating that the station was the base for the parent body of a military unit most, or many, of whose men were outposted elsewhere. Haltwhistle Burn contained a small building in the centre, possibly serving the purpose of a headquarters, a granary and a barrack-block, leaving space for several small buildings, but not another barrack-block: the plan is reminiscent of a *numerus* fort in Germany. The fort seems to have had a life of some years and pottery suggests occupation in the early years of the second century. It seems possible that the fort was constructed on, or shortly after, the move south to form part of a new system of frontier control.

The men from this, and other small forts, might have been sent to man the watch-towers which were erected in the years preceding the construction of Hadrian's Wall. Two of these towers lay on the high ground to the north of the Stanegate, as if providing extra eyes for the garrisons of the forts. That at Walltown, later to be incorporated into the Wall as turret 45a, produced, on excavation, no pottery earlier than the opening years of Hadrian's reign. At Pike Hill and Mains Rigg no pottery at all was found. It is possible, therefore, on the basis of the findings at Walltown, that these towers did not form part of the basic Trajanic plan, but were later additions to it.

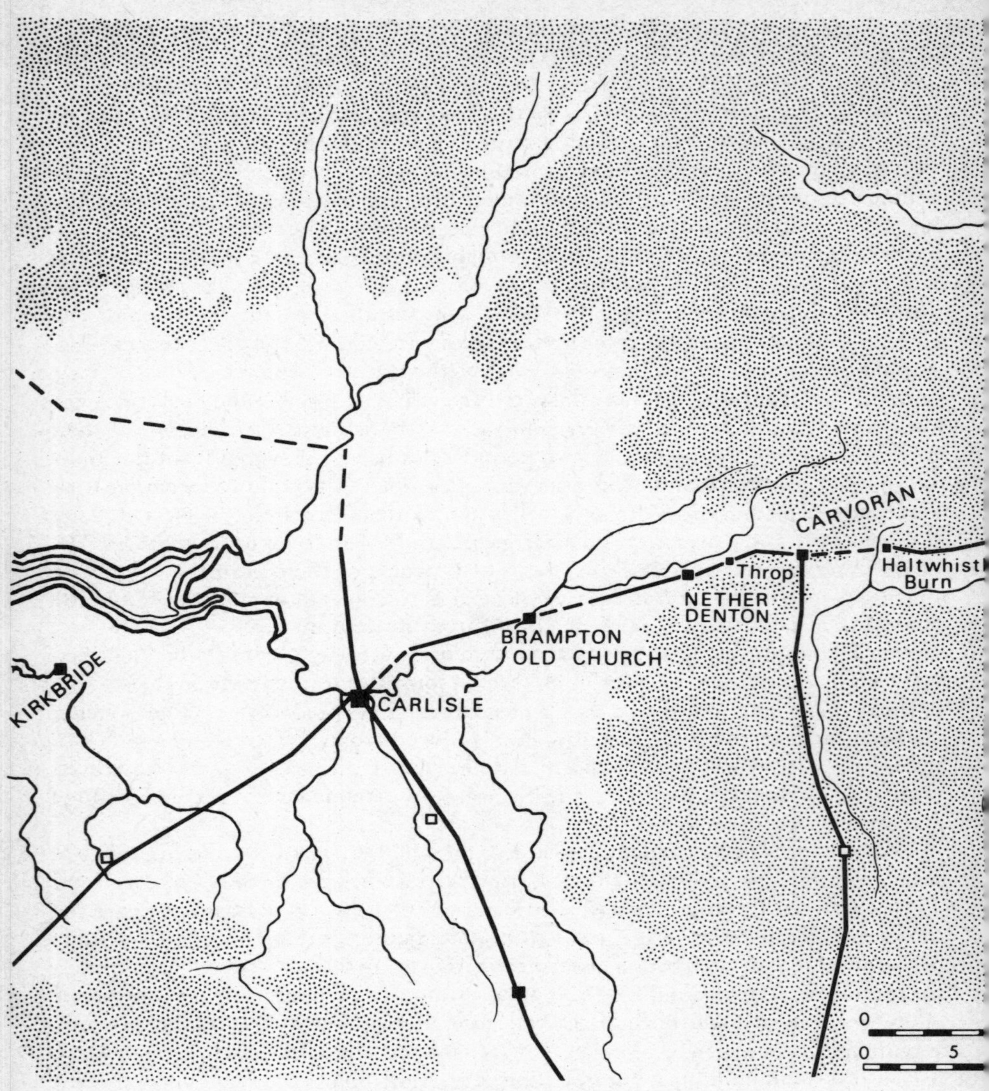

11 The Stanegate 'frontier' (land over 180m is stippled)

In spite of the uncertainties the main outlines of the new system of frontier control are now clear. Existing forts were renewed, probably with garrison changes, new forts built on the lower Tyne, west of Carlisle, and between certain of the existing forts. The main purpose of this greater troop concentration would be in order to help defend the province from attack. The close spacing of certain forts, however, and the addition of small forts, draws attention to the new concern with frontier control. Some soldiers were clearly as much involved with frontier police duties as with general defence. Finally, perhaps some years after the first moves to strengthen the Stanegate forts, watch-towers were built on the north rim of Tynedale. There appears, however, to have been no attempt to recreate the line of

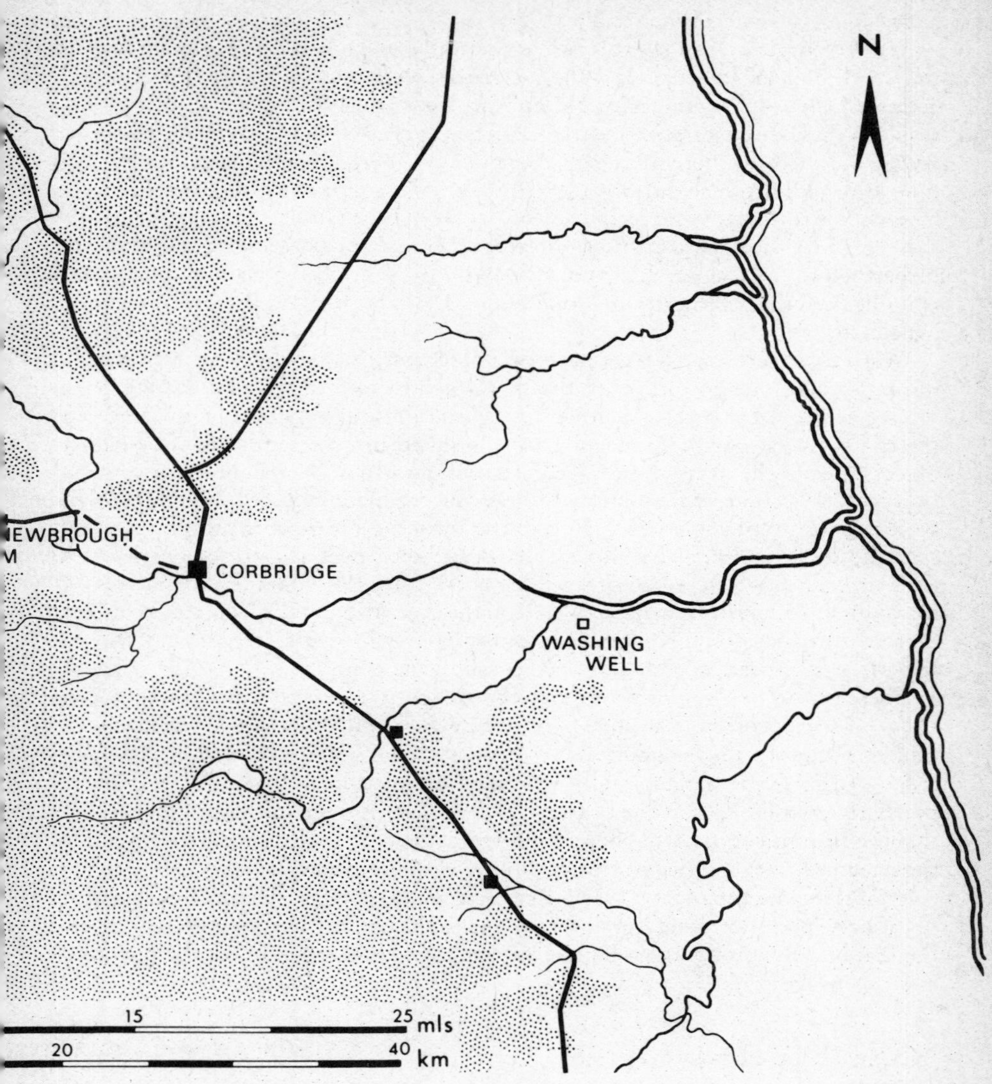

timber watch-towers such as had previously existed along the road from Ardoch to Bertha.

One recently discovered feature which has been connected with the Stanegate remains to be noted. Beneath the 'Stanegate' fort at Burgh-by-Sands Professor Barri Jones has located from the air and subsequently examined through excavation a circular ditch and rampart containing a four post watch-tower or gate-tower. Pottery from one of the post-holes included black-burnished ware, which only entered this area about 120. The timber tower was succeeded after a short interval by the fort, again associated with early second-century pottery. It would appear that modifications were being made to the frontier arrangements in this sector in the very early years of Hadrian's reign.

Also at Burgh-by-Sands Professor Jones found a ditch and palisade underlying the north gate of the fort, and these features were later recognised at Fingland 4.5km to the west, again, it would appear, associated with a watch-tower. As a result of these discoveries Professor Jones has suggested that between Carlisle and the sea at Kirkbride there was a palisade and ditch, perhaps not continuous but only filling the gaps between the mosses, with a patrolling garrison housed in the watch-towers. It is too early to be certain of the nature of the military works in this area or their history, not least because Professor Jones' work remains unpublished. Nevertheless it is clear that the military works in this area are much more complicated than hitherto realised and no doubt further discoveries can be expected.

No forts are known to have been occupied north of the Tyne-Solway isthmus during Trajan's reign following the withdrawal south in the first decade of the second century. Little too is known of the relationship between the province and the tribes to the north. Traprain Law continued in occupation but few Roman objects specifically of this time have been found north of the isthmus. It is possible, however, that some of the objects of first-century manufacture found in Scotland were not lost until some years later, in the second century. It is certainly unlikely that the Roman army abandoned all surveillance over the tribes north of the province. Through the reign of Trajan – and Hadrian – Roman army patrols will no doubt have continued to keep watch on the areas beyond the frontiers in order to try to ensure that nothing happened against Roman interests. In pursuit of this end they do not appear to have been altogether successful.

There is only one hint at warfare on the northern frontier during Trajan's reign. *Cohors I Cugernorum*, stationed in Britain, was awarded the title *Ulpia Traiana* in return for meritorious conduct sometime between 103 and 122. The occasion and scene of this event remains unknown, but the most likely place for it is on the northern frontier. Also at the beginning of Hadrian's reign his biographer records that the Britons could hardly be kept under control. Again the most likely place for the event which gave rise to this comment is the northern frontier. However, in spite of these disturbances it was possible, it would appear, to reduce the garrison of the province by moving *legio IX Hispana* to the continent. As so often is the case the main evidence of contact between Roman and native lies in the realms of war and not peace.

Note: The Gask frontier

The frontier formed by the line of watch-towers through Strathearn has no formally recognised name. Most of the known sites lie on the Gask Ridge, but Gask Ridge Frontier would be an inadequate title. Similarly Strathearn Frontier might be rendered too restricted by further discoveries. A title based on the date of the frontier is clumsy and again might be affected by later discoveries. A name based on the geographical location seems most appropriate and as the watch-towers were first noted on the Gask Ridge the Gask frontier is here suggested as the best description of the line.

5

Hadrian's Wall

It seems likely that the additions and modifications to the military establishment on the Tyne-Solway isthmus during the reign of Trajan, and possibly the early years of his successor, were in order to try to control more effectively movement into and out of the province. However, the construction of Hadrian's Wall in the 120s would appear to suggest that these measures did not meet with complete success. Hadrian's Wall provided the only effective method of frontier control by the provision of a new element, the linear barrier. As first planned Hadrian's Wall was intended to be a fairly simple and straightforward modification to the existing chain of forts. The barrier was to consist of a curtain of stone or turf to run across the isthmus from a new bridge to be constructed on the Tyne at Newcastle to Bowness on the Solway, with provision for military and civilian passage through this barrier in the form of gateways defended by small fortlets or milecastles and with observation towers placed at one third of a mile intervals (fig. 13). Nothing is known of the garrison of the milecastles or the turrets, but as it is clear that the pre-existing forts behind the Wall were to continue in existence it may be presumed that the units stationed there would provide the troops for the new establishments. The Wall was placed in the most sensible geographical position. In the east it ran along the north rim of Tynedale, linking up in the centre with the Whin Sill (pl. 5). In the west it came off the Whin Sill onto the escarpment above the River Irthing, following the north side of that river's valley until reaching the Solway Estuary. From Carlisle, where the Wall crossed the Eden, the Wall lay on the southern shore of the estuary until a convenient point was found to stop at Bowness.

The purpose of Hadrian's Wall was given by Hadrian's biographer who stated that the Wall was constructed for 80 miles (120km) from sea to sea to divide the barbarians from the Romans. This is manifestly correct for the barbarians beyond the province were separated from the empire by the most obvious and clear method: a wall.

Movement was provided for and allowed, but it was to be controlled. The addition of a curtain wall, a linear barrier, to the earlier forms of control – forts, small forts and watch-towers – was Hadrian's contribution to the development of Roman frontiers, and it is therefore appropriate that Hadrian's Wall is the best preserved and best known of all Roman frontier defences.

It may be considered that there was a special reason for the construction of a Wall in Britain at this time. When Hadrian succeeded his great-uncle Trajan in 117 his biographer remarks that Britain could hardly be kept under control. It is not known whether this refers to an internal revolt or a disturbance on the northern frontier, though the latter seems to be the most probable. There may also have been trouble in Britain during Trajan's reign as discussed above. Yet at the same time it seems that the garrison of the province was reduced by the transfer of *legio IX Hispana* from Britain to the continent during the years between 108, when it is last attested at York, and probably 122 when *legio VI Victrix* arrived. It seems that this

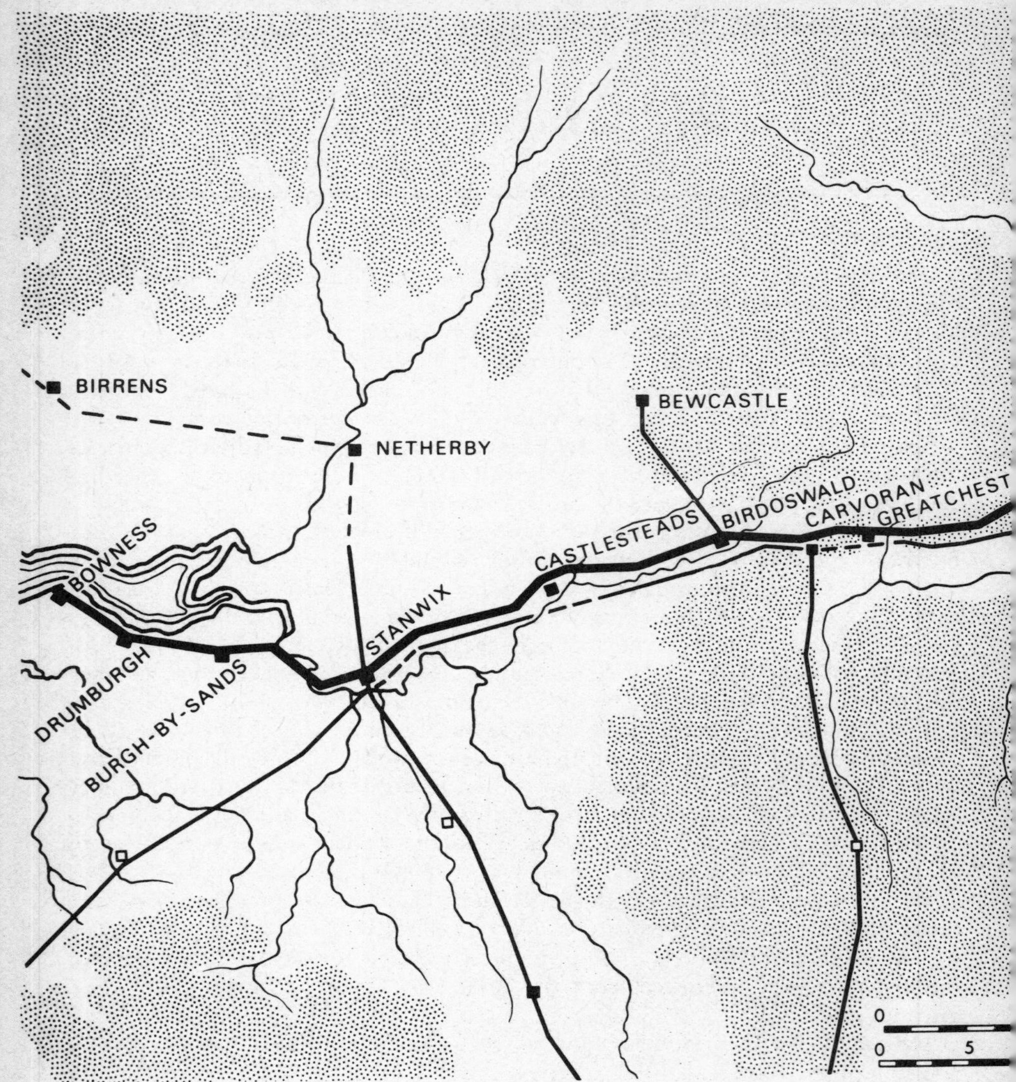

12 *Hadrian's Wall under Hadrian (land over 180m is stippled)*

move occurred between earlier warfare in Trajan's reign and the disturbance at the end of it, unless the warfare arose out of the reduction of the provincial garrison.

The disturbance in Britain at the beginning of Hadrian's reign appears to have been serious. Forty years later Cornelius Fronto wrote to the Emperor Marcus Aurelius (161–80), his former pupil, to console the emperor for the heavy losses of his army in the Parthian war, by recalling the serious losses incurred by Hadrian in Judaea in the mid 130s and in Britain. There is no reason to doubt that the losses occured in Britain during the disturbance recorded by Hadrian's biographer: there is certainly no knowledge of a later war in Britain in this reign.

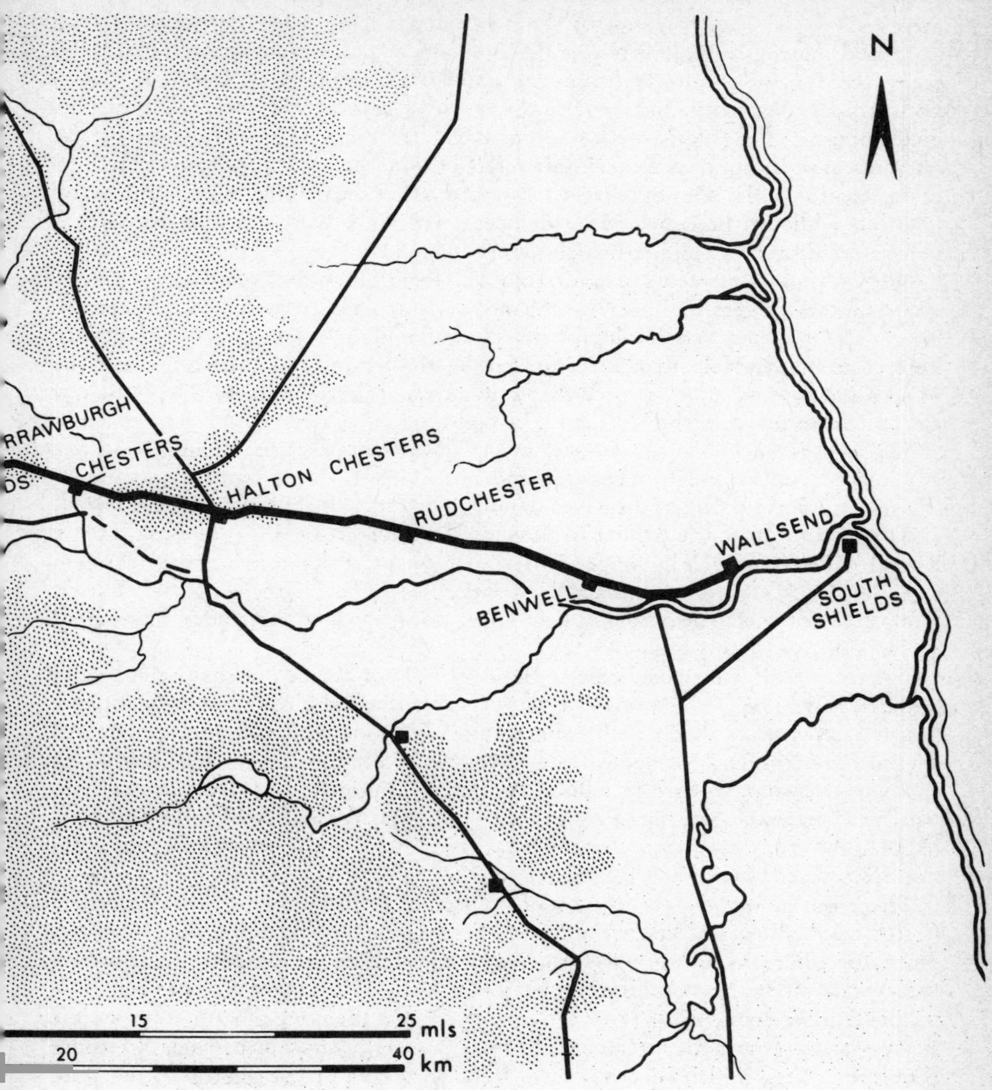

However, such warfare almost certainly had little to do with the construction of Hadrian's Wall, for two reasons. Firstly, Hadrian's Wall was concerned, not with the major attacks on the province, the only ones which might earn a unit military honours, and achieve mention in imperial records, but with the more small-scale, day-to-day problems of frontier control. If there had been a serious threat to the province at this time it would have been dealt with by the army units based in northern England, including those on the Tyne-Solway isthmus, and possibly with help from the legions, but the construction of a Wall would not have helped to deter or prevent such attacks. The defeat – and prevention – of such attacks could only be achieved by the strengthening of the army units in the area. Secondly, almost certainly Hadrian's Wall was not the first artificial frontier of this type to be constructed in the empire. Hadrian came to Britain in 122 from Germany and in both Upper Germany and in Britain he was responsible, according to his biographer, for the construction of artificial frontiers. The discussion of the frontiers in the biography is so closely related to the account of the visits as to lead to the natural, and no doubt correct, assumption that the frontiers were initiated by Hadrian while in the respective provinces. Hadrian's Wall was therefore not a unique solution to a unique British problem.

Nor were all the elements in Hadrian's Wall new. Thirty-five years before closely spaced watch-towers had been established on the Gask frontier in Strathearn in order to keep observation along the line of control. Fortlets, in use in Britain since the conquest, provided linear ancestors for the smaller milecastles. In both cases the towers and fortlets supplemented the main garrisons based in forts. The only new element introduced in the 120s was the continuous barrier.

The most remarkable fact about Hadrian's Wall is its very size. The curtain was planned, it would appear, in two sectors. The first was to run from Newcastle on the Tyne to the crossing of the River Irthing, a distance of 45 Roman miles (73km), and the second from the Irthing to Bowness on the Solway, a shorter length of 31 Roman miles (50km). The longer part was to be constructed in stone, 10 Roman feet (3m) thick and up to perhaps 15 Roman feet (4.5m) high, while the shorter, western sector was to be of turf 20 Roman feet (6m) thick at base and perhaps up to 14 Roman feet (4.3m) high.

The stone wall was placed on a shallow foundation formed of rough flags set in puddled clay. The facing stones were of roughly dressed blocks of sandstone, the finished appearance of the wall being defined in modern terminology as coursed rubble. The core was formed of rough stones usually bonded by mortar, though clay was occasionally used as a bonding material. In most areas the facing stones were of manageable size measuring about 15cm high by 22cm long, tailing back up to 40cm into the core, but in certain areas large blocks up to 40cm long and 30cm high were used.

There was an offset on both sides of the wall after either the first or the third or fourth course. It is not known how the top was finished off. On other frontiers, especially where the barrier was formed by a fence, there was patently no provision for a patrol along the top of the barrier. The width of Hadrian's Wall has led to the unsubstantiated conclusion that there was a sentry walk along the top. It is possible that provision was made for such a walkway, but this cannot be proved. No stones have been found which shed any clear light on the nature of the top of the wall, though two unusual L-shaped stones found at Cawfields may derive from the upper part of the wall. Most reconstructions complete the wall top as crenellated, on the model of the later city walls of Rome and the provinces: in view of the lack of contemporary parallels such reconstructions can only be accepted with reservation. However, the near contemporary Rudge Cup (pl. 7) and Amiens Skillet do suggest that the wall top was crenellated.

Earth Wall should be a better description than Turf Wall for the western sector of Hadrian's Wall for turf was not the only material used. In some places beaten clay was the material of construction, and in one area 'clods' dug out of a marsh or pond were used. Such differences probably reflect changes in the local vegetation cover, which in turn was largely dependent upon the underlying geology. Roman military manuals laid down the regulation size for turves: 18 by 12 by 6 inches, but actual Roman turves revealed by excavation can rarely be shown to approach that size. The wall was placed on a bed of coursed turf, three or four layers thick. Above this both faces rose steeply. The highest archaeological section dug through the wall revealed that the front was at first near vertical, while the back rose at an angle of 1 in 4. The top is as much a mystery as that of the stone wall. If there was a sentry walk there must have been wooden duck-boarding along the top, such as appears on Trajan's Column. There may also have been a breastwork, perhaps of brushwood rather than split logs.

The reason for the different use of materials in the construction of Hadrian's Wall is not known. It has been suggested that good building stone is lacking in Cumberland, or that a scarcity of limestone in this area led to construction in turf, but as the Turf Wall was later rebuilt in stone neither explanation seems to contain the whole truth. A further element has therefore been added and that is that external considerations required the speedy construction of the Wall in the west. Such considerations can only have included a threat to the Roman forces or the province by dissident tribesmen to the north and this in turn has been linked with the placing of three forts beyond the Wall at Bewcastle, Netherby and Birrens. However, there seems to be no special military reason for outpost forts here: advance patrolling and scouting would have no doubt been carried out to the north of the Wall as a matter of course all along its length by the troops in the forts behind the Wall, while in event of a major attack these army units would advance beyond the Wall and combine to protect the province: in some ways with the Wall in existence isolated outpost forts may have been more of a liability than an asset, though this may not have been understood at the time. The discovery of an inscription to Brigantia at Birrens may provide the answer for the outpost forts, for this may suggest that part of this tribe extended beyond the Wall into modern Dumfriesshire and that therefore the outpost forts were constructed to protect these people, still part of the province, but left beyond the military boundary by the erection of the Wall. It might be expected that the Wall was built on the most convenient geographical line and that this did not coincide with the political boundary of the province, or for that matter the most convenient line for military forces operating in order to defend the province from attack. Finally, it may be remarked that if there was a threat to the security of this area during building operations it would have been dealt with by the army independently of building work: it is a totally false picture to imagine Hadrian's Wall being constructed by troops on the defensive and possibly even fighting off attacks while building. Such trouble as there may have been, and the evidence for this is uncertain, would have been seen to by the army before building work was allowed to commence.

The reason for the building of part of the Wall in turf is therefore unknown. It may be that with all the other building operations on the Wall proceeding the army may have decided that it was wiser to build part of the Wall in turf initially and then rebuild it as and when necessary in stone at leisure rather than allow carting and supply difficulties to drag the building works out even longer. The existence of outpost forts to the north may have been felt to affect in some way the requirements of the Wall to the rear. It must, however, be noted that when compared to other frontiers it is not the turf sector of the Wall that is unusual, but the stone.

Hadrian's stone wall is indeed unusual. The contemporary frontier in Germany was merely a timber fence, while the linear barrier in north Africa, the *Fossatum Africae*, parts of which could be contemporary with Hadrian's Wall, was of dry stone walling or earth. Other, later, frontiers were also of timber, earth or turf, with the single exception of the frontier in Raetia (modern Bavaria) which consisted of a stone wall, though only 1.3m wide. The narrowness of this wall, removed in time and space from Hadrian's Wall, emphasises the unique nature of the English frontier. It has been suggested that the massive nature of Hadrian's Wall could be a compensation for the abandonment of territorial pretensions to the north, an alternative memorial to Hadrian, as indeed it is. Further, Hadrian was a great builder – the Pantheon, his villa at Tivoli, cities and another frontier were all his inspiration – and the wall which still bears his name may be a further reflection of this facet of his character: great builders seldom seem to require justification for their actions! It may be that the stone wall was built so massively because the Roman engineers were not sure that a narrower wall could stand without buttresses – this was, after all, the first such linear barrier – and decided that it was as easy to construct a broad wall as a narrower wall with buttresses. This would allow for the later narrowing of the curtain when it was discovered that a narrower wall would stand without support, and the even narrower wall in Raetia. The Romans were used to constructing large buildings and understood stresses and such problems, but this was the first such engineering project they had tackled and they might well have leant on the side of caution. In truth, however, the reason for the scale of the stone wall is not known and almost certainly never can be: further all suggestions fail satisfactorily to explain the use of turf in one sector rather than stone throughout.

In front of the wall, and separated from it by an open space or berm, lay a wide and deep ditch. This varied considerably in size, from 8 to 12m wide and from 3 to 4m deep, though the smaller figures seem to have been the more normal. Its profile appears to have been the normal V-shape. The material from the ditch was spread out on the north side to form a broad mound or glacis. The berm too varied in width. On the stone wall it was usually 20 Roman feet (6m) wide and on the turf wall 6 Roman feet (1.8m), but a width of 40 feet (12m) has been recorded at one place on the turf wall and here and elsewhere it appears that the berm was widened to take account of unstable geological conditions. A number of places are known where the ditch was not completed, nor the glacis smoothed off. Along the front of the crags, purposely, no ditch at all was dug, while in certain areas along the Solway shore no ditch was dug for the sea was considered sufficient barrier.

At several places the Wall crossed a stream or river. Streams would no doubt have been channelled through the wall, a straightforward operation on the stone wall, but more difficult in the turf sector, while the rivers were bridged. The two main river crossings were at Chesters where the North Tyne afforded a formidable obstacle, and at Willowford where the Irthing lay at the foot of a steep bank, Harrow's Scar. There was to be no attempt to carry the wall itself over the rivers, merely a walkway. At Chesters, where more is known of the earlier, and presumably Hadrianic, bridge, at least four piers, with cutwaters up and down stream, made provision for a walkway 3m wide. The ditch may have simply run out at the rivers, but at Willowford the end of the berm was protected by part of the abutment of the bridge.

The wall, of either turf or stone, and the ditch formed the linear barrier. The two main types of structures placed on this barrier were the milecastles and turrets. The milecastle, the linear descendant of the earlier fortlet, was attached to the rear of the wall (fig. 13). On the stone wall it generally measured about 60 by 50 Roman feet (18 by 15m) internally, being constructed of stone, while the turf and timber milecastle on the turf wall appears to have been usually about 10 feet (3m) larger in

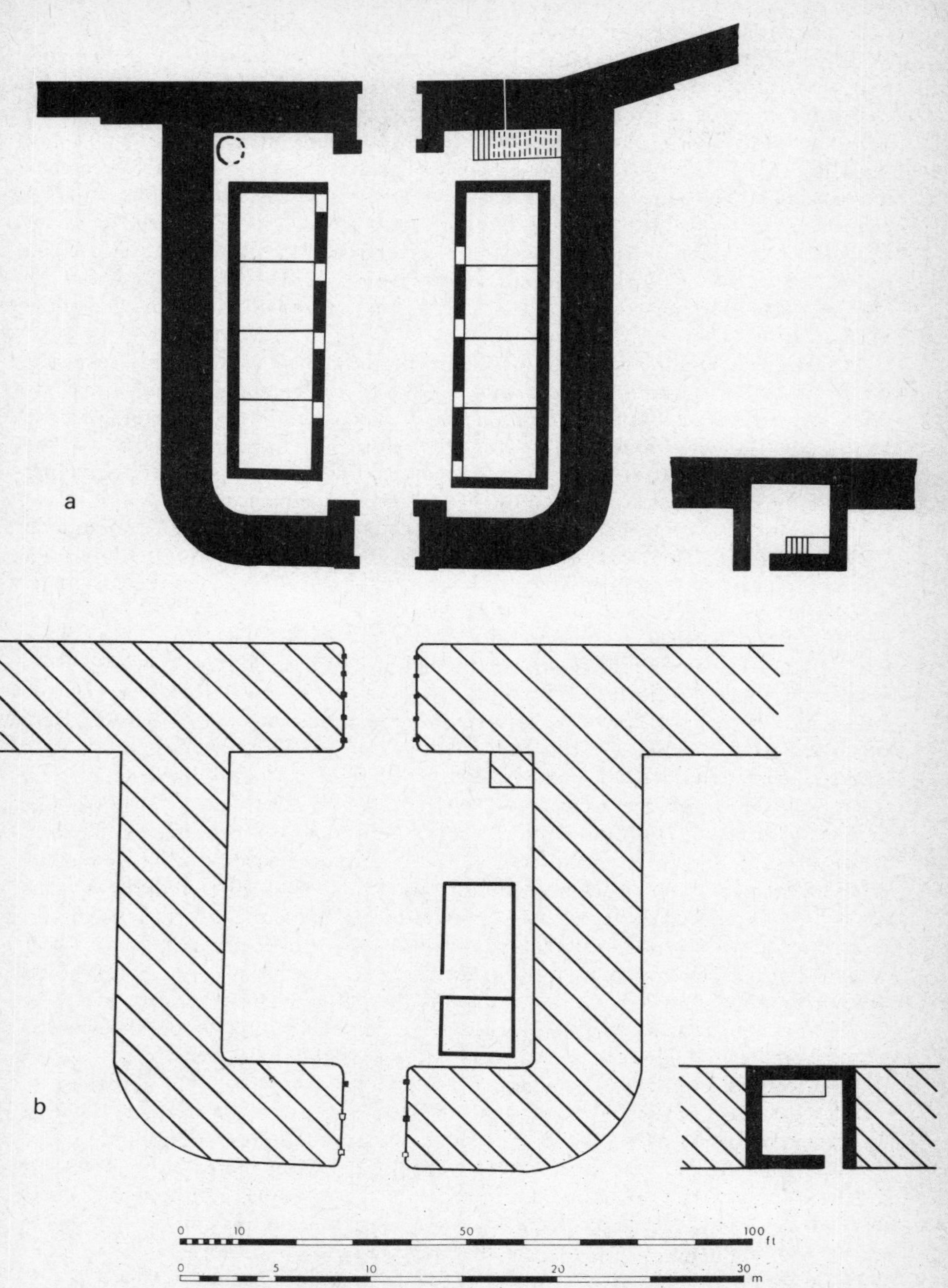

13 Milecastles and turrets on Hadrian's Wall: (a) MC 48 (Poltross Burn) and T 18a (Wallhouses East); (b) MC 50 TW (High House) and T 52a (Banks East)

both directions. In the north wall of the milecastle a gate led through Hadrian's Wall, while a second entrance led into the milecastle from the south. It is probable that both gates were surmounted by towers, the northern one forming part of the chain of towers or turrets along the Wall. Inside each milecastle there generally appears to have been a small barrack-block, sometimes an extra storehouse, an oven and also a flight of steps. These steps will probably have led to the tower, they may also have led to the wall top. They survive best at MC 48 Poltross Burn and by calculation it is possible to suggest that the wall top was 3.7m high at the rear and, because of the slope of the ground, 4.3m at the front. At MC 37 Housesteads so much survives of the north gate that it is possible to calculate that the height of the arch was 3.6m, the voussoirs adding another 60cm to give a minimum height for the wall of nearly 4.3m.

Milecastles were not generally protected by ditches, though in four cases the provision of a single ditch has been noted (MCs 23, 25, 29 and 51). In one case the ditch was unfinished, but it is difficult to argue that an original proposal to provide all milecastles with ditches was dropped before full implementation, for the milecastles with ditches were constructed at different times in the building programme. Finally, it is remarkable that there is evidence for a causeway across the Wall ditch in front of the north gate of only two milecastles (MCs 50 and 54, both on the turf sector). It is not known how the Wall ditch was crossed at the other milecastles: it is conceivable that a bridge was used, but if that was the case, why were these two milecastles treated differently?

Two towers or turrets lay between each milecastle (fig. 13). These were constructed of stone on both the stone and turf walls. On the former they were built with wing walls in order to aid bonding, while on the turf wall they were built as free-standing towers. The turrets were about 4.3m square internally and were recessed into the thickness of the Wall. The doorway was placed in the south wall. Turrets often contained a hearth and a stone platform, which in most stone wall turrets appears to have been the base for a stair or ladder to an upper floor. The height of the turret is unknown, but a minimum height of 7 to 9m for the roof, which presumably served as an elevated observation platform might be expected (cf. pl. 8 for towers on the Danube bank). The Rudge Cup (pl. 7) and the Amiens Skillet, which appear to have been souvenirs of the Wall, suggest that the towers had a flat top with crenellations and stood about twice the height of the wall. There was probably an intermediate floor at the same level as the wall top. This would allow continuous passage along a wall walk, if such movement was required; the building-up of the recesses when turrets were demolished may suggest that such access was desired, though it is also possible that this work was to protect an otherwise weak point in the curtain.

Little is known of the garrisons of the milecastles and turrets. Artefacts found at the sites have been used to argue that the troops were similar in status and type to those in the adjacent forts, and that they were not. Certainly there is no evidence for a separate force on the Wall and it is probably best to assume that the soldiers who manned the milecastles and turrets were sent out from the forts on the Stanegate, and possibly further south, in the manner attested on many Roman military documents. It is not known how long these soldiers might be expected to serve on the Wall, but documentary evidence from another unit based on the Eastern frontier demonstrates that 100 years later soldiers could be away from their base on detached duty for periods of three years and more, while contemporary documents furnish ample evidence for the practice of troops serving away from the colours.

Above: *The hill fort on Eildon Hill North. The ramparts of the fort are visible, while within the hut* *cles show up as* 'pock marks'

Below: *Burnswark Hill looking north. The ramparts of the hill fort are clearly visible. To the near side* *the south camp with the Antonine fortlet in the north-east corner*

3 Above: *The Gask Ridge looking west. The circular earthworks of the watch-tower at Gask House lies few metres to the south of the road*
4 Below: *The fort at Ardoch looking south-east. The complicated ditch system to the east and north of the fort represents several periods of occupation*

Above: *Hadrian's Wall at Cawfields looking east. MC42, Cawfields, lies in the foreground, while the ll snakes along the crags and the Vallum crosses the lower ground to the right*

Below: *The fort at Housesteads on Hadrian's Wall looking west. The headquarters building, nmanding officer's house, granaries and, in the right foreground, fourth-century barracks, are all visible*

7 Above: *The Rudge Cup, probably made in the mid-second century, appears to be representation of the Wall with turrets. Presumably one of a pair, this contains the names of the seven western forts on the Wall:* A MAIS ABALLAVA UXELLODUM CAMBOGLANS BANNA

8 Below: *Two towers and two bonfires on Trajan's Column. There is a balcony at first-floor level on each tower, while a torch projects from a window. The towers seem to be of stone, the balcony and palisade of wood*

9 Right: *The Antonine Wall on Croy Hill look east. In the foreground the rampart lies on the of the crags and the ditch at the bottom. Furth east an area of 'dead' ground lies in front of th Wall*

10 Below right: *The fort at Rough Castle on t Antonine Wall looking north. The Antonine W crosses diagonally and to the south two ditche defining the fort are visible. The annexe, with south ditch and three east ditches, lies to the e*

11 Above: *A model of the Romano-British native farmstead at Riding Wood in Northumberland*

12 Below: *The fort at Chesterholm looking sou with the civil settlement to the west: the militar bathhouse lies in the right foreground*

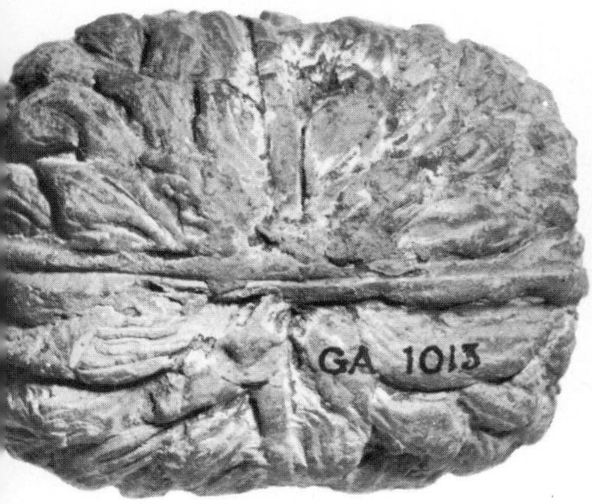

.bove: *A terra cotta model of a bail of hides or es found at Dun Fiadhairt, Skye. It is probably tive offering made by a merchant from the an empire*

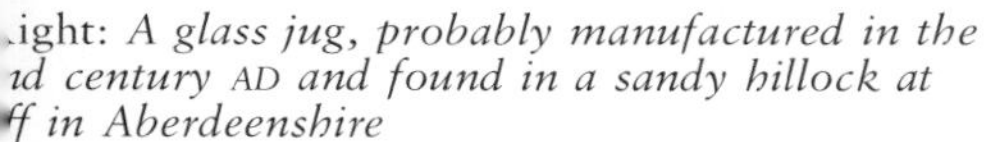

.ight: *A glass jug, probably manufactured in the d century* AD *and found in a sandy hillock at ff in Aberdeenshire*

ight above: *This stone, found at Traprain Law, nscribed on it the letters, A, B, C and part of is possible that when complete the stone ined the whole alphabet*

elow: *Five objects from the late fourth–early century Traprain Treasure. The treasure was ably either booty, almost certainly from the nent, or part of a subsidy paid by Rome to Votadini*

17 Above: *The Bridgeness Distance Slab recording the construction of about* $4\frac{2}{3}$ *miles of the Antonine* *by soldiers of legion* II Augusta. *To the left a Roman soldier rides down a group of four barbarians, u* *to the right a sacrifice is celebrated*

18 Above: *The Glamis Pictish symbol stone, dating to the seventh century. Inscribed on the stone are a serpent, fish and mirror, all common symbols: there is possibly a second fish at the top*

19 Right: *The Aberlemno churchyard cross, dating to the eighth century. The rear face has a Z-rod and disc at the top, while below is a scene including both cavalry and infantry, armed with spears and protected by helmets and round shields. There appear to be two groups of warriors, those on the right turning to flee: a dead warrior lies in the right-hand lower corner*

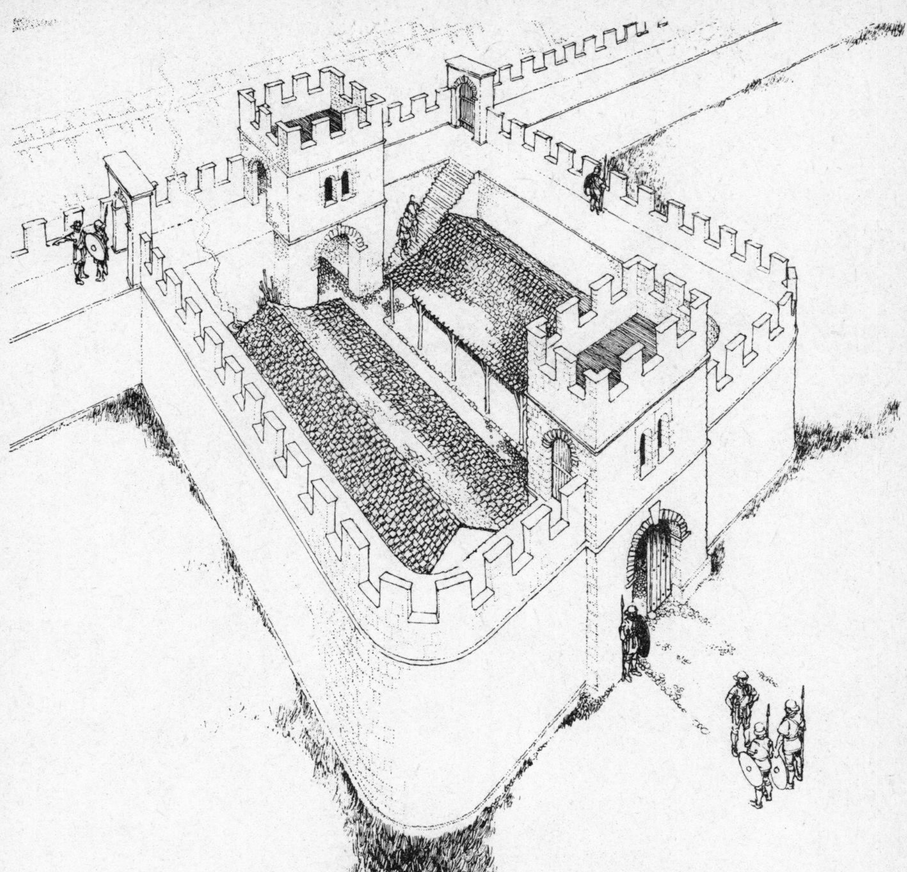

14 A stone milecastle on Hadrian's Wall, view from the south east. Reconstruction showing a barrack-block, storehouse, oven and steps. (Drawn by M. Moore)

The size of the garrison of the milecastles and turrets is another problem. The full complement of barrack-blocks is only known for six milecastles. In four cases the barrack was a small two-roomed block, while in the other two examples two blocks provided approximately four times as much accommodation. The smaller two-roomed unit was roughly equal in size to a double room in the barrack-block of a normal fort and may therefore have contained the same number of men, eight. The two larger milecastles may accordingly have provided accommodation for four times that number, 32 men.

There is no evidence to determine whether the soldiers on duty at the turrets normally lived there, or went out each day from the milecastles. The hearths within turrets, and the quantities of pottery found at all, point to the preparation of food, but not necessarily sleeping. The space available in a turret was not inconsiderable. The lower floor was little smaller in area than a small barrack-room and there was presumably an upper floor available in addition. If soldiers went out to the turrets from the milecastle each day, then the total garrison for the Wall line might have been about 650 men. If, as perhaps seems more likely, some soldiers lived at the

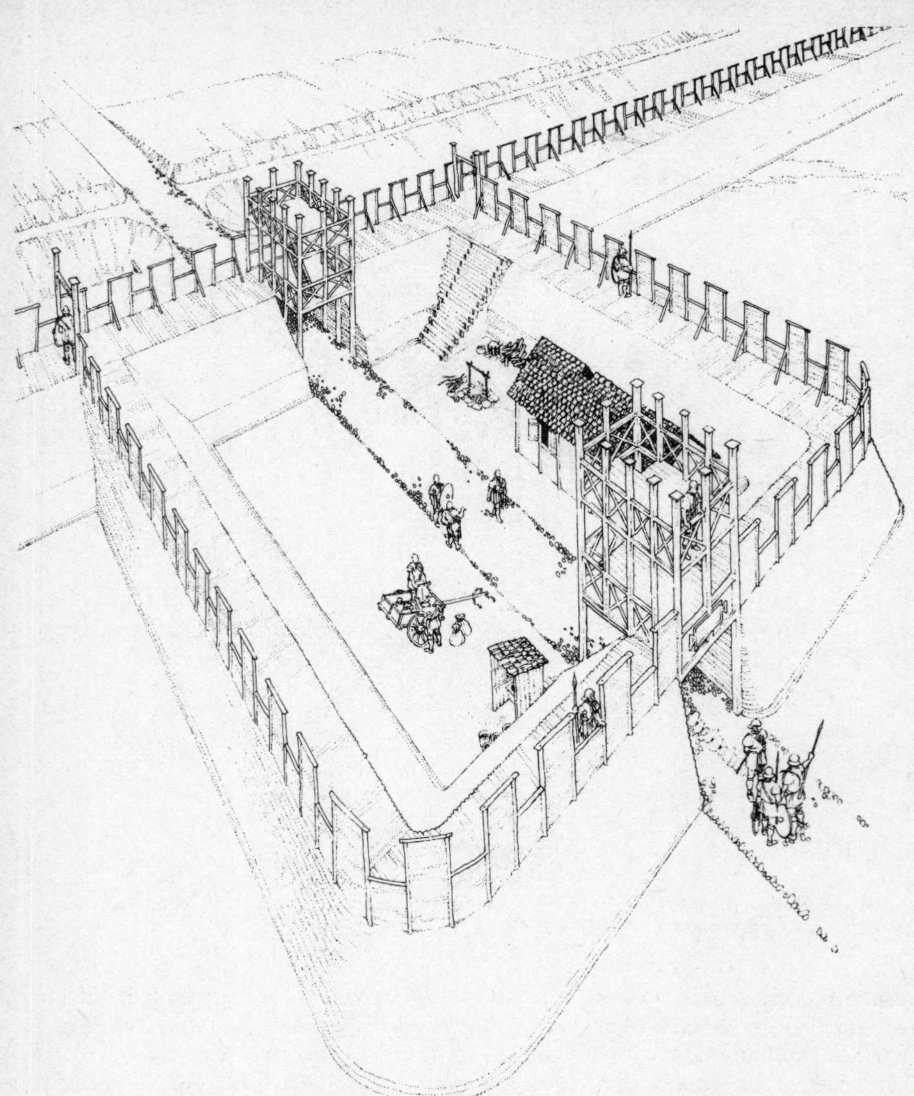

15 A turf and timber milecastle on Hadrian's Wall, view from the south-east. Reconstruction of MC 50 TW. (Drawn by M. Moore)

turrets then the strength of milecastle and turret garrisons combined might have been between 1700 and 1900.

It is possible to suggest the size of the garrison of the milecastles and turrets in a different way. It seems probable that each turret and each milecastle north tower will have required two soldiers on duty at any one time. The milecastle gates might be expected to have had an additional guard of two men. If the soldiers worked in eight-hour shifts then 24 men will have been required to man a milecastle and the turrets on either side, a total of nearly 2,000 men for the whole Wall line, which is close to the putative combined garrison of the milecastles and turrets based on the available accommodation. This figure seems more likely to be close to the correct total, for quartering both milecastle and turret guards at the milecastles each night might be thought to place intolerable burdens on the accommodation available there.

The planning – and construction – of the Wall, with its attendant milecastles and turrets, seems to have been accompanied by activity in the forts on the Stanegate. The fort at Corbridge was probably rebuilt at this time and its garrison changed, while one of the several pre-Wall phases at Chesterholm may be contemporary. To the east one of the two phases recognised on the aerial photographs of the unexcavated fort at Washing Well may date to these years. Beyond Carlisle both the newly discovered forts at Burgh-by-Sands and Fingland may be contemporary with this initial scheme for the Wall. It thus appears that work on the construction of the linear barrier was accompanied by the reorganisation of the army units immediately behind the Wall, presumably in order to allow these units to relate better to the changed frontier conditions.

The Cumbrian coast

Although the Wall stopped at Bowness the system of milecastles and turrets continued down the Cumbrian coast, though there they are termed milefortlets and towers. The spacing was the same, and also the materials of construction: stone for the towers, turf and timber for the milefortlets. It has been considered that milefortlets were only provided with one entrance, placed either front or rear, but recent work suggests that there may usually have been two. The system of milefortlets and towers has been traced for nearly 40km down the Cumbrian Coast to just beyond Maryport, by modern Workington. It is possible that it continued for a further 22km to St Bee's Head, which was a convenient stopping point, though no structures have been noted in this area. A further 32km on at Ravenglass a fortlet, of the same size as the milefortlets to the north, has been found under the later fort, and there is the possibility that another may lie 1.5km (a mile) to the south. This may suggest that the system, or at least part of it, continued for nearly 100km beyond the end of the Wall at Bowness, though at present the regular series of milefortlets and towers can only be traced as far south as Tower 26b.

The provision of the cordon so far along the coast may reflect concern at a threat from beyond the Solway. Certainly the Galloway coast looms very close, even at Maryport, 37km beyond Bowness, but there is no evidence that the tribes of this region were ever troublesome to Rome. It may well be that the Cumbrian Coast chain was simply a product of the rigid mind so clearly at work elsewhere on the Wall. The spacing of milecastles, and milefortlets, turrets and towers, with scant regard for topography, points to the planning of the frontier far away from the area through which it was built: the Cumbrian Coast may be no more than a reflection of this.

A word must be said about the latest discoveries on the more northerly sector of the Cumbrian Coast. Professor Barri Jones has located from the air parallel ditches in various places between Bowness and Silloth. The milefortlets and towers lie between the ditches, and although no obvious breaks for access can be seen on the aerial photograph, excavation has revealed that one milefortlet had both front and rear entrances thus allowing movement across the ditches. Ditch is the most obvious term to describe these features but in fact they are little more than trenches. Generally they are no more than 40cm wide and deep, and some appear to have held a thorn hedge. In some areas the trenches were recut, elsewhere the double line of trenches was replaced by a single palisade. This palisade consisted of twin stakes set about 40cm apart, presumably supporting a wattle fence. It has also been suggested that in an early phase in the sequence there may have been timber towers on the Cumbrian Coast, but the evidence for this consists of one platform of clay on the site of the later Tower 4b. The major difficulties in interpreting these recent discoveries lie in their incompleteness and in the fact that they have not yet been definitively published. It is to be hoped that Professor Jones' camera and pen will help to remedy both deficiencies.

The function of Hadrian's Wall

How was Hadrian's Wall to operate? The barrier certainly separated the barbarians from the Romans, in the phrase of Hadrian's biographer. The wall would hold up both small-scale raiding and major attacks, but would not prevent either: this could only be done by the army. Certainly raiding parties would now find it most difficult to operate with a barrier blocking their access to the peaceful, undefended settlements of the province, and, more importantly, hindering their swift return north. It may have been possible to enter the province quietly, but much more difficult to escape laden with booty, especially as that booty would have probably included flocks and herds.Thus the Wall will have aided the peaceful economic exploitation of the province to the south, protecting the inhabitants of the province, and their goods, from the tribes to the north who presumably still continued with their ancient and traditional warlike activities.

These activities occasionally erupted in full-scale warfare. The late second and the late fourth centuries were particularly disturbed times in the north when the tribes beyond the province gave the Roman army serious cause for concern. At such times the Wall would be – and was – largely irrelevant to both sides. It would be a hindrance to movement, but that was all. The tribal army would be a sizeable force no doubt able to overpower the smaller garrison present at whichever point on the Wall it chose to cross. The Roman army would be concerned to seek a successful conclusion to the invasion in the field, where the Romans knew they were predominant. To the Romans the Wall merely got in the way. Scouts would have maintained surveillance over the territory north of the Wall and, in the original plan, would have communicated with the units behind the Wall on the Stanegate. If warning of an attack was received the army units strung out in forts along the Stanegate and further south would assemble to attempt to intercept the enemy, reports presumably being sent back to York to inform the legionary commander of the local situation. The Wall would not aid such an army and it is instructive to note that no provision was made for the establishment of units on the Wall line at this time.

The very massiveness of Hadrian's Wall invites comparison with a medieval castle or town wall, but in reality the comparison is false. Medieval battles were generally between two forces roughly equally armed and from similar political and social backgrounds. The armies were capable of fighting set-piece battles and undertaking or sustaining sieges. The battles of Roman Britain, on the other hand, were not fought between equally armed or equally disciplined forces. Furthermore, one army was paid to fight while the other fought to defend its territory. In this unequal struggle might was on the side of the Romans. Indeed they had become so used to success that their army was not armed with defensive weapons such as

16 Hadrian's Wall, view from the east. Reconstruction showing a turret and, in the distance, a milecastle. (Drawn by M. Moore)

would be required during a siege. The Roman army was an offensive army, and would seek to decide the issue in the field and this was so much part of the military traditions and practice that it found itself at a disadvantage when besieged in its own camps or forts. In one famous siege the Roman soldiers were reduced to throwing turves at their attackers because they had not appropriate weapons to fight with. Although, according to the second-century writer Arrian and the fourth-century commentator Vegetius, Roman soldiers should be trained in the use of the bow there is no evidence that this was treated as a serious form of defence, while documentary and archaeological sources both imply that soldiers were not normally supplied with this weapon: generally bows and arrows were restricted to the specialist units of archers, such as the Hamians stationed at Carvoran in the second century nor was this deficiency rectified by the provision of alternative weapons such as spears. The normal issue for each soldier was two javelins and, so far as can be determined, no extra quantities were kept in case of siege.

The Wall itself was also a serious obstacle to its use as a fighting platform. The top must have been fairly narrow, perhaps 2–2.5m wide on the broad wall, but as little as 1.3m wide on the later narrow wall and about 1.3–1.6m wide on the turf wall. Access too was restricted, there being steps up to the Wall top only at milecastles and turrets one-third of a Roman mile apart. There was no provision for enfilading fire on the Wall, and none for artillery, which in any case was not usually available to auxiliary troops at this time.

All arguments combine to reinforce the conclusion that the Wall was not a fighting platform, merely a barrier to free movement, a means by which the army could control the movement of people across the frontier and channel it through certain guarded points.

The Wall, although probably not the actual boundary of the province for all or even part of its length, may well have become the customs boundary: it was after all the most convenient place for the examination of merchants and the exaction of tolls. Foreign trade, at least across the Eastern frontier, was charged a duty of 12½ percent, which was relatively high in relation to the tolls of 2–2½ percent levied on internal trade and collected at internal boundaries or towns. It was also strictly controlled, at least in the later Roman empire. In the east foreign trade was only allowed at a few licensed places. The export of certain articles, such as iron, bronze, arms and armour, was banned, no doubt for security reasons and customs officials were posted at these trading posts to control the trade and tax both incoming and outgoing goods. The taxing of imports and exports demonstrates that this was not a protective tariff, merely a means of raising revenue. The customs officers at the time of Hadrian were private individuals to whom the imperial government farmed the collection of taxes and over whom they maintained a close scrutiny. From the later second century, however, these *conductores* were replaced by a system of direct collection under imperial procurators.

Surviving documents demonstrate that customs officers had the right of search, and undeclared goods were forfeit. However, if they chose to search and found nothing the customs collector had to reimburse the merchant for the expense of unloading and provide written confirmation that all goods had been declared. Some tax officers exceeded their authority and an edict issued in the late second century ordered such unscrupulous officers to desist from demanding extra charges and from blackmailing merchants into paying for quicker treatment.

It may be presumed that the movement of people across Hadrian's Wall would be governed by regulations such as have been discussed in relationship to the Gask frontier. Access was only allowed at certain points, meeting places were stipulated, traders had to be unarmed but were nevertheless guarded, and finally these relations were taxed. It is possible that members of any client state which might have existed to the north might have had the regulations relaxed for them, as they were relaxed for the Hermanduri. Finally, it may be noted that there may have been two types of officials involved, the tax collectors and the army – though this is not certain, for soldiers in some parts of the empire acted as customs officers, collecting tolls on the frontier. Later, in the late second and third centuries, special army officers, *beneficiarii consularis* appear in the north of England. Elsewhere in the empire these were appointed to special frontier stations where they served as customs officials, frontier guards, intelligence agents and police officials. These soldiers are attested at Housesteads, Chesterholm and Risingham and in the hinterland at Lanchester, Binchester, Greta Bridge, Catterick and Lancaster. Although none are attested as early as Hadrian's reign, it is possible that their predecessors had some responsibility for customs and frontier control on the Wall.

It is not clear how and where the frontier regulations were enforced. There were two types of gates through the Wall, the regularly spaced milecastle gateways and those at roads. Only two of the latter may be presumed. Nothing is known of the gate by Stanwix where the road led north to Netherby, Birrens and beyond, but on Dere Street a special gate has been found on the top of Stagshaw Bank at the Portgate, though only its mere existence has been attested by archaeology: other special gates may have existed. It seems probable that these gates may have been customs stations where taxes were levied on goods in transit and *bona fide* travellers allowed into the province. Whether soldiers then escorted such travellers to villages, such as those which sprang up outside forts, or at Corbridge or Carlisle, is a matter for speculation.

The milecastle gateway can be seen in another light. While each milecastle on the Wall was provided with a gate through the barrier the provision of milefortlets down the Cumbrian Coast demonstrates that the guarding of such gates was only part of their function. Milecastles were probably more important as bases for the surveillance garrison of the Wall, with the gate provided almost as a matter of chance. In view of the regulations operating on other frontiers it seems probable that if travellers did try to cross the Wall at a milecastle they would be escorted to a customs post. The major restriction on the use of the milecastle gateways would appear to be the lack of a causeway across the ditch in front of the gate. While this might have been of little consequence for civilian traffic, it would have been a serious matter for the army for whose use, it might otherwise have been argued, the gates were provided. Clearly much has yet to be learnt about the function of the milecastles.

The building of the Wall

Inscriptions demonstrate that the Wall was constructed by soldiers from the three legions of Britain: *II Augusta* from Caerleon in South Wales, *XX Valeria Victrix* from Chester and *VI Victrix*, newly arrived in Britain from Lower Germany and the new occupant of the legionary fortress at York. There is no evidence that native levies played any part in the building operations, though it is possible that they helped with the fetching and carrying.

Constructional differences in the milecastles, turrets and curtain wall suggest that three different groups took part in the building operations and inscriptions confirm that these groups can be identified with the legions: differences have been noted between the milefortlets and the towers on the Cumbrian Coast but it is not possible to relate these to legions.

On both the stone and turf walls there are areas where only one particular type of milecastle, turret and wall base is found, with no other type intervening. In these sectors it is reasonable to assume that one legion was responsible for the discrete block of work which contains only these types. It appears that inscriptions, recording the name of the emperor, legionary builder and occasionally governor, were erected over both the north and south gates of the milecastles. Only one inscription survives from the turf wall for these were of timber, but four inscriptions from three milecastles on the stone wall firmly establish the type of milecastle built by *legio II Augusta*, and by extension its type of turret and curtain wall. There is still an element of doubt concerning the attribution of the other milecastle, turret and curtain types to the other two legions. The recent discovery of an inscription at T 33b Coesike suggests that the traditional allocation of milecastle, turret and curtain types to legions *VI* and *XX* should be reversed. Be that as it may, the evidence accumulated to date allows a picture to be built up of the order and progress of work on the Wall.

It is clear that building on the stone wall started at the east: there is no evidence for the turf wall. On both stone and turf sectors the constructional work was divided into lengths of 5–6 Roman miles (8–9.6km), each the responsibility of a single legion. Within that block the milecastles and turrets were generally constructed first, with work probably proceeding on the foundations of the wall at the same time. One legion at least also commenced the construction of the curtain wall before it had completed all the milecastles and turrets in its sector. Where bridges fell within a block of work priority appears to have been allotted to these as well as to the milecastles and turrets. The relationship of the excavation of the ditch to these operations is not known: apart from where solid rock approached close to the surface this was a straightforward operation and presumably could be completed quicker than the building work. The speed of work on the stone and turf walls and the attendant structures would have varied considerably in relation to the proximity of supplies of turf, stone, limestone for mortar, timber and water as well as the nature of the terrain. The discovery of military building inscriptions – centurial stones – on the stone curtain implies that an attempt was made to supervise the work and ensure that standards were kept broadly similar. Each legion marked the end of its length of wall with an inscription, and within that each cohort marked both ends of its allocation and finally each century similarly denoted its workload. In some areas these centurial stones have been found in sufficient number to suggest that the length of the stretch allotted to each century was about 40m. The stones were generally placed on the south side of the wall, but some have been found on the north face.

The figures of 5–6 Roman miles for the length of a legionary block can be recognised on both the turf and stone walls. The turf wall divides neatly into six such lengths, presumably representing two three-legion blocks, though only one such legionary block can be identified as a result of excavation. On the stone wall, about which much more is known, the situation is more complicated. There is a short length of 3 Roman miles (5km) at the east end which does not appear to fit into any pattern, then follows a 15-mile (24km) sector divided into three legionary lengths. Thereafter, however, the legions seem to have been split, one legion continuing working westwards towards the North Tyne, while the other two moved further west and commenced building in the 20km running eastwards from the Irthing leaving a 14km gap to be completed later. These sectors, and probably some of the previous allocation, were not completed to the original specifications for before the work was finished the wall was reduced in thickness from its original 10 Roman feet (3m) to either 8 or 6 Roman feet (2.35 and 1.80m). This decision appears to have followed another, the transfer of many troops from constructing the wall to building new forts. It was presumably in order to speed the work of the remaining gangs that the wall was narrowed. When this order was given all the milecastles between the North Tyne and the Irthing had been erected, at least so far as can be determined, and most of the turrets, but work on the curtain was not so well advanced: in fact on the crags the foundation of the wall was not laid in many areas, partly owing to the difficulties of transporting water, stone and mortar in this hill country, partly because it was not everywhere necessary as the bedrock was so close to the surface.

In the meantime most of the soldiers hitherto working on the wall had started to implement a major policy change which had far-reaching consequences. Previously there had been no forts on the Wall itself, but it was now decided to abandon those behind the Wall on the Stanegate and construct new forts on the line of the Wall itself. This decision was not undertaken lightly, for it involved the abandonment of at least eight forts, the demolition of several turrets, one milecastle and several yards of curtain, the infilling of lengths of the Wall ditch, and the construction of 12 new forts (pl. 6). The decision to move the forts up onto the Wall, presumably grew out of the realisation that once the Wall was constructed it would create a barrier to the free movement of the army. In order to get to grips with an enemy north of the Wall the army would have had to move up from their forts on the Stanegate and pass through small milecastle gateways. A desire to deal with this problem would appear to have lain behind the construction of the new forts astride the Wall, wherever the terrain allowed, even though in some instances this resulted in the demolition of more curtain and the infilling of more ditch than would otherwise have been necessary. The forts were constructed with a third of their area and three of their four gates north of the Wall (fig. 18). Communication with the province to the south was improved by the unique addition of two side gates, at either end of the *via quintana*. The result of this unparalleled arrangement was that the equivalent of six single-portal milecastle gateways now lay in the northern part of the fort, north of the Wall, while four portals opened to the south. Thus movement was considerably facilitated.

The position of the forts astride the Wall emphasises the nature of the problem that the army authorities were trying to combat. There were three possible positions for forts in relation to the linear barrier: behind, in front or on the Wall line. Patently the position of forts behind the Wall was unsatisfactory. Presumably forts in front of the Wall would have suffered in a similar way, for the Wall would again have got in the way of the free movement of the army; while in the event of a serious attack the divorce of an army unit from colleagues to the south by the Wall itself might have been embarrassing. As a result the solution adopted was to place the forts astride the barrier, thus enabling troops stationed in each enclosure the freest possible movement both north and south. There is no reason to assume that this major change was brought about as a result of native opposition to the construction of the Wall. It would have been obvious to the Roman commanders that the River Tyne and the Irthing Gorge, lying between the forts and the new Wall, would have been a serious hindrance to communication: it may be no coincidence that the earliest forts to be built on the Wall were apparently Benwell and Halton Chesters in the east, precisely those whose predecessors would have experienced the most difficulty of communication with the Wall. Without a Wall the Stanegate was a sensible enough line for the frontier troops, but as soon as the Wall was built it became a nonsense to leave the troops there.

The new forts, with one probable exception, were each designed for a single auxiliary unit (fig. 17). In view of the rigidity of planning displayed on Hadrian's Wall, this is not surprising, but it was a relatively new concept at the time. Up to the end of the first century many forts were built either for detachments or for composite garrisons. The forts on Hadrian's Wall may have been the first group of forts to be built for one single, complete auxiliary unit. They were also perhaps the last for most of the forts on the Antonine Wall were designed for detachments not whole units. The average distance between each of the new forts was about 11.5km, that is about half a normal day's march. The distances varied a little for account was taken of the major rivers on the Wall line when positioning the forts. Chesters, for example, was moved a little to the east so that it lay beside the North Tyne, while Stanwix was moved about 1.5km to the west so that it could lie beside

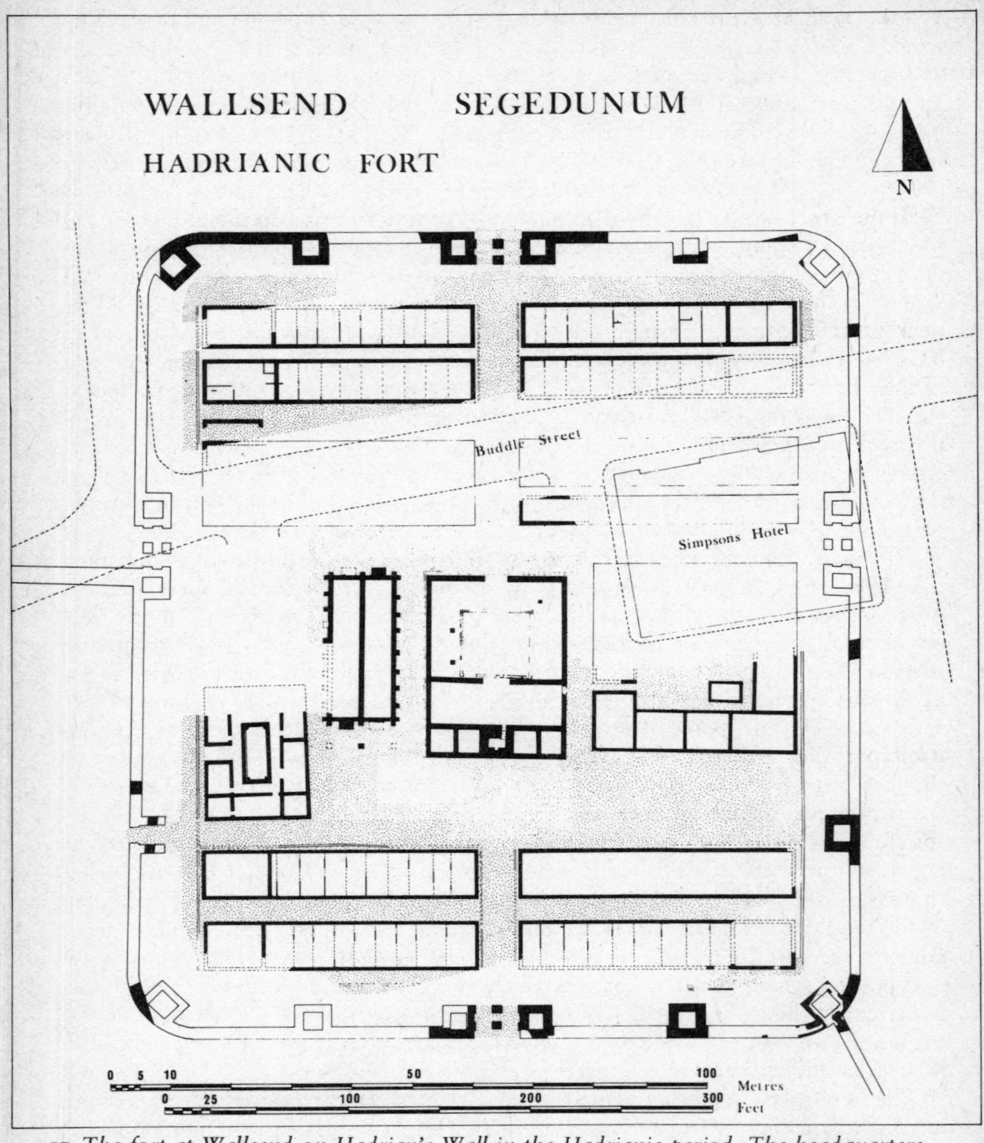

17 The fort at Wallsend on Hadrian's Wall in the Hadrianic period. The headquarters in the centre is flanked, left by a granary and hospital, right by the commanding officer's house. To the north and south lie barrack-blocks and ?stables. (Drawn by C.M. Daniels)

Carlisle and the main road north. It was also decided at this time to extend the Wall 4 Roman miles down the Tyne to Wallsend where the most easterly fort on the Wall was now built.

The new forts, in their materials of construction, closely followed the Wall. On the stone wall the fort walls and apparently all the principal building were of stone.

The barrack-blocks, stables and storehouses, however, appear in most cases to have been completely of timber or at least timber on stone sill walls. On the turf wall all the forts seem to have been constructed with turf ramparts and timber buildings, with the exception of Birdoswald, at the eastern end of the turf wall, which was constructed of stone.

The forts on the Wall were strengthened by the addition of new forts on the flanks, built, or at least planned, now. In the east lay South Shields at the mouth of the Tyne, but on the southern side of the estuary. In the west two forts appear to have been added to the Cumbrian Coast at Beckfoot and at Moresby, while further south Ravenglass was built later in Hadrian's reign and may have been planned at this time; the fort at Maryport appears to have been built at an earlier date, though still within Hadrian's reign.

Inscriptions demonstrate that both legions *VI* and *XX* took part, no doubt over several years, in the construction of these forts, while the similarity between the masonry in the *legio II* milecastle gateways and certain fort gateways suggests that this legion was also involved in this task. As in the milecastles and turrets there was a certain amount of standardisation in fort planning. Four forts, for example, were 177m long or wide, Benwell, Chesters, Birdoswald and Stanwix, while the opposing measurement at Stanwix, 213m, is close to the length of Bowness on Solway, 216m. It is interesting to note, too that the only five Hadrianic bath-houses known on the frontier – Benwell, Chesters, Carrawburgh, Netherby and Bewcastle – were clearly all built to the same blue-print even though the forts to which they were attached fall into three different groups: Benwell and Chesters were primary forts, Carrawburgh secondary, while the other two were outpost forts.

The new forts on the Wall, and possibly also on the Cumbrian Coast, took the place of existing forts to the rear yet the units in the Stanegate forts were not apparently moved up into the nearest fort on the Wall. Certainly the *cohors milliaria equitata* which abandoned Corbridge did not move to Halton Chesters 5km up Dere Street. It seems probable that the disposition of forces on the Wall line was carefully planned. The senior officer on the Wall was stationed at Stanwix for here was placed the senior auxiliary unit in the provincial army, the *ala milliaria*. There were only 10–11 of these units in the empire and never more than one in each province. The commanding officer was in the final stage of his career in the auxilia and would expect to pass on to other commands, notably procuratorships, including the governorship of minor provinces. But his rank did not accord him any special position, any authority over his colleagues commanding other units on the Wall: the nearest officer with authority over the auxiliary commanding officers was the legionary legate at York. The *ala milliaria* was presumably placed at Stanwix because of the central position of this fort and because it lay beside one of the two major roads north: there is no need to assume that there was a special threat to the province from the west which led to the placing of the unit here.

Only one other cavalry unit is definitely known to have been stationed on the Wall, the *ala Augusta ob virtutem appellata*, the unit named *Augusta* for valour, at Chesters by the North Tyne, though the plan of the fort at Benwell suggests that a cavalry unit may also have been stationed there. Most of the units on the Wall seem to have been either infantry or the mixed infantry and cavalry type. It may not be coincidental that the infantry units all appear to have been placed in the centre of the Wall in the forts furthest from the roads north and facing inhospitable country.

The additional units required to garrison the extra four forts on the isthmus, and also the three outpost forts, appear to have been drawn from the Pennines and Wales where archaeological evidence suggests that a number of sites were abandoned at this time.

The construction of the forts did not proceed without change. Although most of the forts were constructed astride the wall, some were not. These include Greatchesters, among the last of the forts to be constructed, and Carrawburgh, an addition to the Wall. It seems that, once the forts were on the Wall line, it was realised that it was not necessary for them to project to the north. Thus in addition to this modification the gates at some forts seem to have early fallen into disuse, as if there was overprovision of entrances. Finally, it may be noted that none of the forts on the Antonine Wall were built astride the rampart.

One fort, it should be noted, does not fall into the neat categories discussed above. Asymmetrically between Burgh-by-Sands and Bowness-on-Solway a small fort was placed on a convenient knoll at Drumburgh. The original fort was of turf and timber and was incapable of holding a complete unit. The relationship of the fort to the turf wall is not known, though they are probably broadly contemporary, and both were replaced in stone later. It seems probable that the difficult terrain of the Solway estuary had here compelled a different arrangement of the forts.

The placing of the forts on the Wall itself confused and muddled two distinct functions – that of the control of movement across the frontier and the protection of the province from attack. That distinction had been clear in the earlier plan for the Wall, but it was now no longer so obvious.

One further addition to the Wall remains to be considered, the Vallum. This earthwork extends along the whole length of the Wall from Bowness to Newcastle, with the exception of the short extension to Wallsend (pl. 5). It consists of a ditch with a mound set back on either side. The Vallum is essentially incorrectly titled for the main feature is the ditch, the *fossa*, not the mounds, the *valla*, but it was so named by the Venerable Bede over a 1,000 years ago and the name has been retained, hallowed by tradition. The Vallum, 120 Roman feet (35m) across, offered no advantage to either side, but it served to mark the rear of the military zone which was now clearly defined by the ditch to the north and the Vallum to the south: it was the Roman equivalent of barbed wire. The importance of the Vallum is emphasised by the care taken to ensure that its ditch was completed, unlike the Wall ditch. Thus at Limestone Corner the Vallum ditch was dug through solid rock and finished while the gangs digging the Wall ditch failed in their appointed task.

Passage through the Vallum was only possible at a fort or presumably where one of the two main roads to the north crossed the Wall. The Vallum often diverged from its straight line to avoid a fort, and here gaps were left through the mounds and a causeway provided over the ditch. The causeway was protected by a gate, closed from the north. Civil settlement in the area between the Vallum and the Wall was forbidden and when civilians came to build their houses outside forts these had to be constructed south of the Vallum. At Housesteads, where there is the only known Hadrianic civil settlement on the Wall, the buildings were erected well beyond the Vallum on a low hill some 200m south of the fort. The effect of the Vallum was to reduce the ease with which the Wall could be crossed. Hitherto it had been necessary to walk no more than half a Roman mile in order to cross the Wall, but it was now necessary to walk up to 4 miles (7km) in order to gain passage through the Wall.

It seems probable that the construction of the Vallum was designed to increase Roman control over the movement of people across the frontier. The regulations

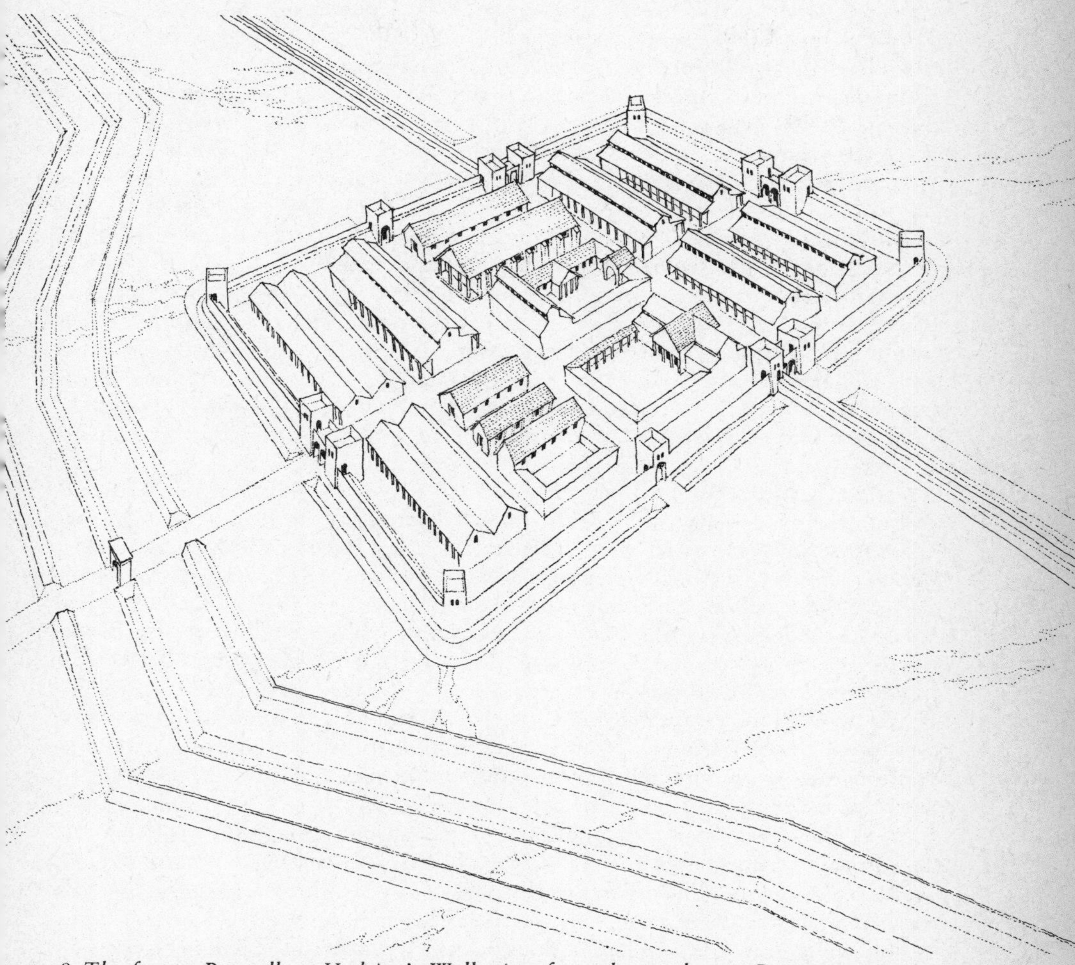

18 The fort at Benwell on Hadrian's Wall, view from the south-east. Reconstruction showing the fort, stone wall, ditch and glacis, Vallum and the crossing south of the fort. (Drawn by M. Moore)

had, up until now, presumably been enforced by the soldiers in the milecastles, but now they were to be enforced by the officers at the forts: possibly it was felt that the soldiers had been – or were likely to be – too slack in carrying out their duties. It has been suggested that the Vallum demonstrated that the local inhabitants of the area had showed their opposition to the construction of the Wall, possibly because it cut across their traditional pasturage routes. The construction of the Wall will obviously have affected the free movement of people, possibly affected their farming practices, but there is only one instance where the Wall appears to have had a visual impact on the local inhabitants of the Wall. Between the Wall and the

Vallum at Milking Gap, 3.5km west of Housesteads, a farm or settlement of five huts appears to have been swept away by the army because it lay within the military zone. But there is no evidence that there was any military opposition to the construction of the Wall or any attacks on the army during building operations. It seems possible that the Vallum was merely an attempt to increase the bureaucratic control of the army over the passage of civilians across the frontier.

One feature not constructed on Hadrian's Wall was a road to link the forts. Hitherto the Stanegate had formed the line of communication between the forts across the isthmus from Corbridge to Carlisle, where the two main roads led north. After the forts moved up onto the Wall the disadvantage of not having a road along the Wall line may not have become immediately obvious. Light road-metalling has been discovered on the south berm of the Vallum at three places and in one place on the north berm. Thus it seems possible that the Vallum was used as a line of communication. But there were hindrances to this. The only gaps in the south mound of the Vallum and causeways across the ditch, with the exception of one certain and a second possible example, were at forts. There were, on the other hand, apparently original gaps in the north mound of the Vallum. Thus the way would be open for traffic to cross the Vallum ditch at a fort and proceed along the north berm to a milecastle where access was possible through a gap in the north mound.

Hadrian's Wall took many years to build. It seems probable that it started during or soon after Hadrian's visit to Britain in 122. In that year, in July, a new governor Aulus Platorius Nepos, arrived in the island. He came from Lower Germany, and it seems probable that he accompanied the emperor, who also came to Britain from there. A third arrival from that province was *legio VI Victrix*. The date of the arrival of the legion is not known, but it certainly had arrived before the close of Nepos' governorship and it is tempting to assume that it came with the governor – and the emperor. If that was the case it is possible that Hadrian had already decided to build a Wall in Britain before he arrived, presumably in the wake of a similar decision in Upper Germany. However, it is equally possible that he only took the decision after seeing for himself the position of the northern frontier in Britain and then sent for the legion, and perhaps also the governor.

Aulus Platorius Nepos was an old friend of Hadrian, though they were later to fall out, and it seems probable that he was specially chosen by the emperor to carry out this undertaking. Since military glory was not possible under Hadrian, Nepos was being allowed the nearest equivalent: only his name appears on building stones in addition to Hadrian's. Before building work commenced the line to be taken by the Wall would have to be surveyed, troops informed and marshalled and a start made collecting materials. New bridges were required, across the Tyne at Newcastle, where the bridge was named Pons Aelius in honour of the emperor, across the North Tyne at Chesters, and over the Irthing at Birdoswald. It would be logical to commence the construction of these first, in order to aid communication, and there is some evidence to suggest that the bridge at Newcastle came early in the building sequence.

It is not known how long it was expected the Wall would take to construct. The division of work into legionary blocks might suggest that each block was planned to take a year to complete. In this case the original estimate was three years. However, the addition of the forts, and to a lesser extent the Vallum, will have lengthened the programme considerably.

It seems probable that originally the legions were divided into gangs working simultaneously on the stone and turf walls and possibly also on the Cumbrian Coast. Once soldiers were taken off the construction of the Wall itself in order to build forts, work must have proceeded in an apparently haphazard fashion to anyone trying to follow the proceedings. The construction of the Wall in the crags sector had already been held up by the difficulties of the terrain. Now there were many milecastles and turrets unconnected by the curtain wall, short lengths of curtain completed, possibly to full height, longer lengths of foundation, all being linked together slowly by one legion, while other soldiers built forts and yet more dug the Vallum. Work on the Vallum in some areas proceeded quicker than the erection of the Wall and it seems that in the area of Carrawburgh the Vallum was dug before the Wall, planned years earlier, was built.

Other changes took place during the building operations. Greatchesters was built wholly behind the Wall, unlike most other forts, but it is possible that when this decision was taken work had already commenced on the site for the fort sits uncomfortably within its ditches. Further, when the curtain was constructed in that area the new builders ignored the foundation which had already been laid and placed their wall in front of the overgrown remains. Twenty-three kilometres to the east a new fort was added at Carrawburgh, which necessitated the obliteration of the Vallum dug shortly before. Modifications continued to be made to the Wall throughout Hadrian's reign. The fort at Carvoran had been specifically excluded from the Wall zone by the construction of the Vallum which diverged to the north to avoid the fort, which was therefore presumably abandoned, or at least intended to be abandoned. In 136 or 137 work was proceeding on the building or rebuilding of Carvoran in stone. It is not clear whether the intention was to rebuild the whole of the turf wall, but by the time Hadrian died only the eastern 8 km had been replaced.

Hadrian's Wall must have caused its designers some headaches. The rigidity in the spacing of milecastles and turrets in the original scheme suggests that the Wall was not planned by someone locally. It suggests a designer working at some distance from the north of England, possibly the governor in London, perhaps even the emperor. The forts showed more concern for the terrain and topography, but even they were regularly spaced. Nevertheless many aspects of Hadrian's Wall reveal flexibility in the minds of the planners and builders. In the first place the Wall was unique. Not only had no such frontier ever been built before in the Roman empire, but its only predecessor, the Upper German frontier, was itself almost certainly still being built when Hadrian's Wall was being planned. Furthermore Hadrian's Wall bore little resemblance to the German frontier. That barrier was of timber, not stone or even turf and did not have the same provision of fortlets, or, it would appear, the same rigidity of planning. Once building was well advanced two other unique elements were introduced, the position of the forts astride the Wall, and the Vallum. And then, when it was discovered that it was not necessary to place the forts astride the Wall once they were on the frontier itself, the positions of the later forts were modified and they were built attached to the rear of the barrier. All these changes, several of them unique experiments in an attempt to deal with a unique situation, more than many others during the long life of the empire, demonstrate in a tangible form the flexibility of the Romans, the flexibility even of the military mind. It is unfortunate that more is not known of the response of the locals to the construction of this monumental frontier.

The construction of Hadrian's Wall appears to cut off contact between provincial and barbarian, but that was not necessarily the case. The purpose of the

Wall was to regulate such contact, not prevent it. Few artefacts of the first forty years of the second century have been found north of the Wall, and what finds there have been could equally well have been lost in the middle rather than the early years of the century. That, however, is not to say that there was no contact either between civilian or between soldier and civilian. The construction of the Wall would not automatically have resulted in the loss of interest by the army in the events to the north. Army units would no doubt continue to patrol the lands to the north. It is possible that relations with the tribes of the Scottish Lowlands were governed by treaty, as was the case on other frontiers. Certainly it is to be expected that the Votadini would have been party to a treaty with Rome: there is no definable break in the flow of Roman goods to their capital on Traprain Law in these years. However, as always the activities and attitudes of the barbarians remain obscure.

6

The Antonine Wall

The move north

The Emperor Hadrian died on 10 July 138. By the following year Britain had a new governor, Quintus Lollius Urbicus, and the building projects initiated by this governor in that year demonstrate unequivocally that a new policy for the northern British frontier had been promulgated. An inscription from Corbridge recording the construction of a granary in 139 is the first indication of this new policy, which is recorded in the *Life of Antoninus Pius*, Hadrian's successor: 'for he conquered the Britons through the governor Lollius Urbicus and after driving back the barbarians built a new wall of turf'. The activity of Urbicus is recorded not just at Corbridge, but at High Rochester in Northumberland and at Balmuildy on the Antonine Wall. There is no doubt what was initiated at this time, but the reasons are another matter.

There are two schools of thought on the reason for the abandonment of Hadrian's Wall and the construction of a new Wall, the Antonine Wall: they might be termed the insular and the empire solutions. The first emphasises that trouble on the northern frontier led to a reappraisal of the Roman position, while the second suggests that the advance in Britain was merely a political move, a foreign adventure, by an emperor who needed to strengthen his position in Rome.

The phrase 'drive back the barbarians' in the passage in the biography of Antoninus Pius certainly seems to imply that forcible action was necessary on the part of Lollius Urbicus and this receives some support from an enigmatic aside by Pausanias in his *Description of Greece:* 'Antoninus deprived the Brigantes in Britain of most of their territory because they too had taken up arms and invaded the Genunian district, the people of which are subject to Rome'. This passage as it stands makes little sense. The Brigantes were already within the province and could therefore hardly be deprived of their lands, while the Genunian district is not known. Various interpretations of the passage have been offered: 'Brigantes' simply means Britons rather in the same way that English is used as a synonym for British; the Brigantes were those members of the tribe in modern Dumfriesshire left outside the province by the construction of the Wall; Genunia is a corruption of Novantae, the tribe of Dumfries and Galloway; Pausanias, perhaps relying on memory, transferred to Britain events which really happened in Raetia (modern Bavaria) where a tribe of similar name, Brigantii, and the Genauni, are attested. In view of the uncertainty surrounding this passage it is hardly possible to use it to support the theory that warfare on the northern frontier caused Antoninus Pius to move the frontier forward 160km: the trouble, if it had existed, could have been dealt with more straightforwardly by military intervention.

It has also been suggested that although Hadrian's Wall was a tactical success it was a strategic failure because it was built in the wrong position: on the Tyne-Solway isthmus it was out of contact with the main centres of opposition to Rome, the tribes of the Highlands of Scotland. It is certainly true that there is no evidence that the Lowland tribes ever gave the Romans any serious cause for concern. Opposition to Rome, in the first century, the late second and early third centuries and in the fourth century, always came from the Highland tribes. But there is no evidence that these tribes were creating a disturbance on the northern frontier in the early years of the Emperor Antoninus Pius, or the last years of the reign of his predecessor. If they had, it might be expected that such warfare would be mentioned in the biography of Antoninus Pius, in the spirit of the justification of military action prevalent at the time. As it is, Pius' biographer contents himself with a colourless reference to driving back the barbarians, which may be no more than a literary allusion to Tacitus' comment in the *Agricola* that after the construction of a chain of garrisons across the Forth-Clyde isthmus the enemy had been pushed, as it were, into another island. The passage may have been intended to mean simply that: the construction of the new Wall had pushed back the boundaries of barbary. Unlike the references in the *Lives* of Hadrian and Marcus Aurelius to serious disturbances in Britain at the beginning of their reigns, the biographer of Antoninus Pius is curiously reticent about the events, real or otherwise, in the late 130s. It may be fair to conclude that there was no warfare on the north British frontier at this time that required military intervention by Rome and the construction of a new frontier.

The alternative explanation for the advance into Scotland in the early 140s rests on an appreciation of power politics in Rome. Antoninus Pius was not Hadrian's first choice as successor. The old emperor had no children but both his sister and his sister-in-law had descendants. However, while seriously ill in 136 Hadrian had become suspicious of his sister's husband, the 90-year-old L. Julius Servianus, and his grandson, Cnaeus Pedanius Fuscus Salinator, and, although he had already hinted that Servianus might succeed him, on his recovery he forced both to commit suicide. Hadrian now chose as his successor L. Ceionius Commodus, who took the names L. Aelius Caesar. The reason for the choice is unclear, but it is possible that Commodus was chosen as a placeholder until his real successor Marcus Aurelius, then only 15, was old enough to reign: Marcus was the grandson of Hadrian's wife's half-sister, Rupilia Faustina. However, Hadrian's careful plans were upset by the death of Commodus on 1 January 138. Two months later Hadrian named his new successor, T. Aurelius Antoninus, the maternal uncle of Marcus Aurelius. Less than five months later Hadrian was dead and Antoninus succeeded him without opposition.

The new emperor had played a small part in public service, sufficient only to fulfil his honourable obligations to the state, but he had never served in the army and had only held one appointment outside Italy, the proconsulship of Asia, probably in 134–35. This was the only time he had ventured out of Italy. His qualifications for office seem to have been that he was an honourable man, without ambition, and a close relative of Marcus. However, Marcus had other relatives, in particular L. Catilius Severus his step-grandfather and prefect of Rome in 138 until removed from office by Hadrian, apparently when he allowed his ambition to show. Severus had been one of Trajan's marshals, indeed the only governor of the short-lived province of Armenia abandoned by Hadrian in 117. He had considerable experience of civilian and military affairs and was also, having held the consulship twice, senior in status to Antoninus.

Although Antoninus' succession was peaceful there were therefore tensions beneath the surface. The new emperor had been designated Caesar less than five months before, apparently mainly because of his relationship to the young Marcus

Aurelius, while another relative of this young man had revealed his ambition for the purple. The adoption of Antoninus in February 138 had caused ill-feeling, according to contemporary sources, and no doubt many in the leading circles of government felt they had an equal claim to be emperor. Finally, Antoninus was the nominee of a man cordially disliked by the senatorial aristocracy. In those early months he may well have cast round for a means of strengthening his position. The most straightforward way to gain popularity, and the support of the army, was through a successful military venture. Tacitus remarks how important military prestige was to an emperor and it worth noting that from Augustus to Septimius Severus no emperor, apart from during the civil wars of 68/9 and 193, was removed by the army. Britain may well have seemed a good place to gain military prestige, as Claudius had realised almost 100 years before. Any military expedition there could be limited by geography, and also no doubt presented as a reclamation of former provincial territory. At the same time it was so far away that the successful general would not be in a position to get too ambitious himself.

There are two aspects of the war which lend support to this interpretation. Firstly, this was the only war for which Antoninus Pius accepted the imperial acclamation. During his reign there was a serious revolt in Mauretania in the 140s, while at the beginning of the reign a disturbance in Dacia led to the appointment of a special commanding officer. Later the frontier in Upper Germany and Raetia was advanced a short distance. Yet Pius accepted no salutation for the successful conclusion of these wars, most notably for the advance in Germany. This would suggest that the British war held a particular significance in his eyes. The second point concerns Fronto again. The orator wrote that 'although the emperor committed the conduct of the operations to others while remaining in the Palace at Rome, yet like the helmsman at the tiller of a warship, the glory of the whole navigation and voyage belongs to him'. While this passage is no doubt largely flattery it again appears to emphasise the close relationship between the emperor and the British war.

While the reason for the advance north in Britain is uncertain we do not move onto much firmer ground in discussing the events themselves. Building work commenced at Corbridge in 139, so it would appear that Antoninus decided on his new policy within months of his accession. Pius accepted his imperial salutation in 142 and in that year or early in the following a new coin issue commemorated the victory. Building work in Scotland commenced under Lollius Urbicus, but as his name does not appear on most of the building inscriptions from the Antonine Wall it seems probable that the bulk of the construction work was carried out under his successor.

Nothing is known of the fighting itself, but it is unlikely that the tribes which had given Agricola no trouble sixty years before, and which had presumably been under surveillance since then, would provide serious cause for concern to the Roman army at this time. In fact it seems possible that the Roman 'invasion' was little more than a formality. Preparations will have taken some time. They included the rebuilding of the fort at Corbridge which was required now that Dere Street would be utilised as one of the two main routes into Scotland. In addition to the reconstruction of this and other forts supplies would need to be gathered. This activity, if carried out thoroughly might take at least a season to complete: certainly building was going on at Corbridge in 139 and 140. In that case the army may not have moved until 141 to complete the re-occupation of the land up to the Tay in a single season, prior to Antoninus' acceptance of the title of Imperator in 142.

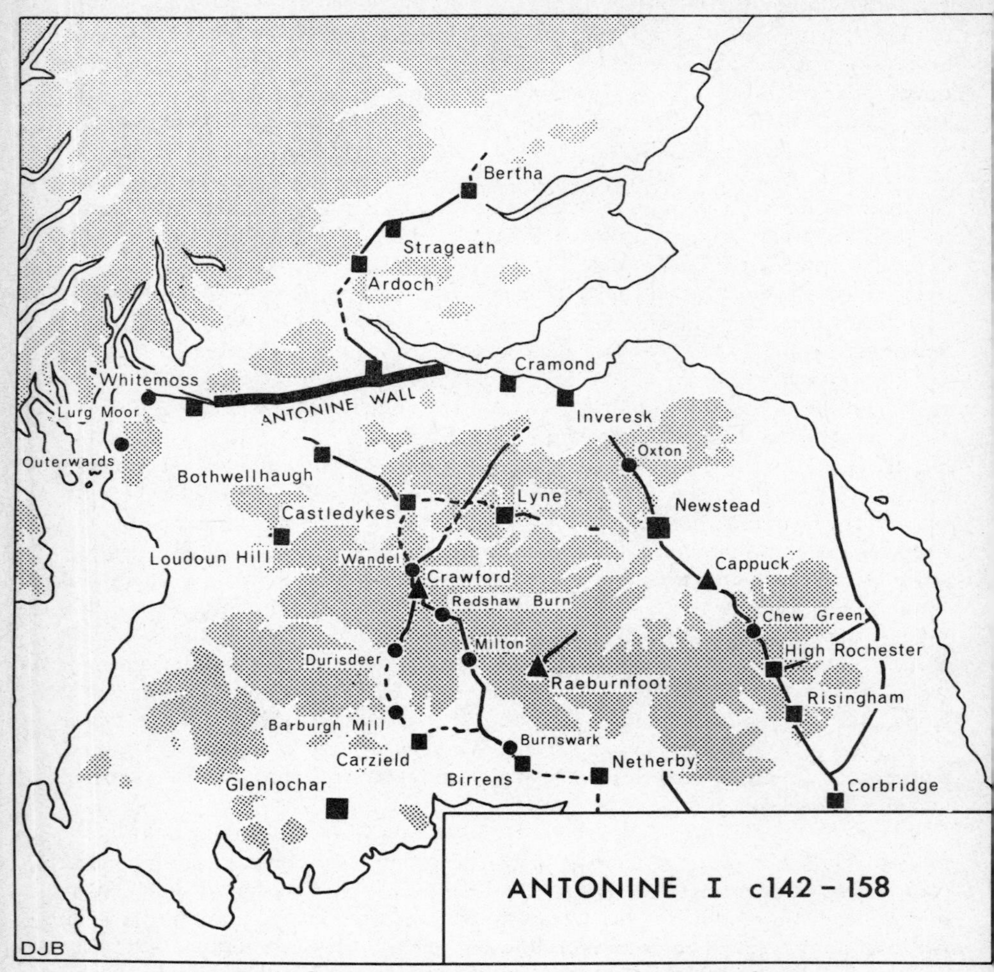

19 North Britain in the first Antonine period, c.142–58 (for key see fig. 4)

Once the tribes had been formally incorporated into the empire the army turned to the task of controlling and protecting them (fig. 19). The Lowlands of Scotland were covered by a network of forts and fortlets connected by roads: a milestone from Ingliston near Cramond, dated to between 139 and 144, was presumably erected when the road thereabouts was repaired. Many of the forts were placed on or near their Agricolan predecessors. The pattern of forts was in fact very similar to that of sixty years before, though generally the garrisons were rather smaller. There was, however, one distinctive difference. Much greater use was made in the second century of the fortlet. Such sites cluster especially thickly in the valleys of south-west Scotland, Annandale, Nithsdale and Clydesdale. Eight or nine of these fortlets are known, each capable of holding a garrison of between 40 and 80 men. The most

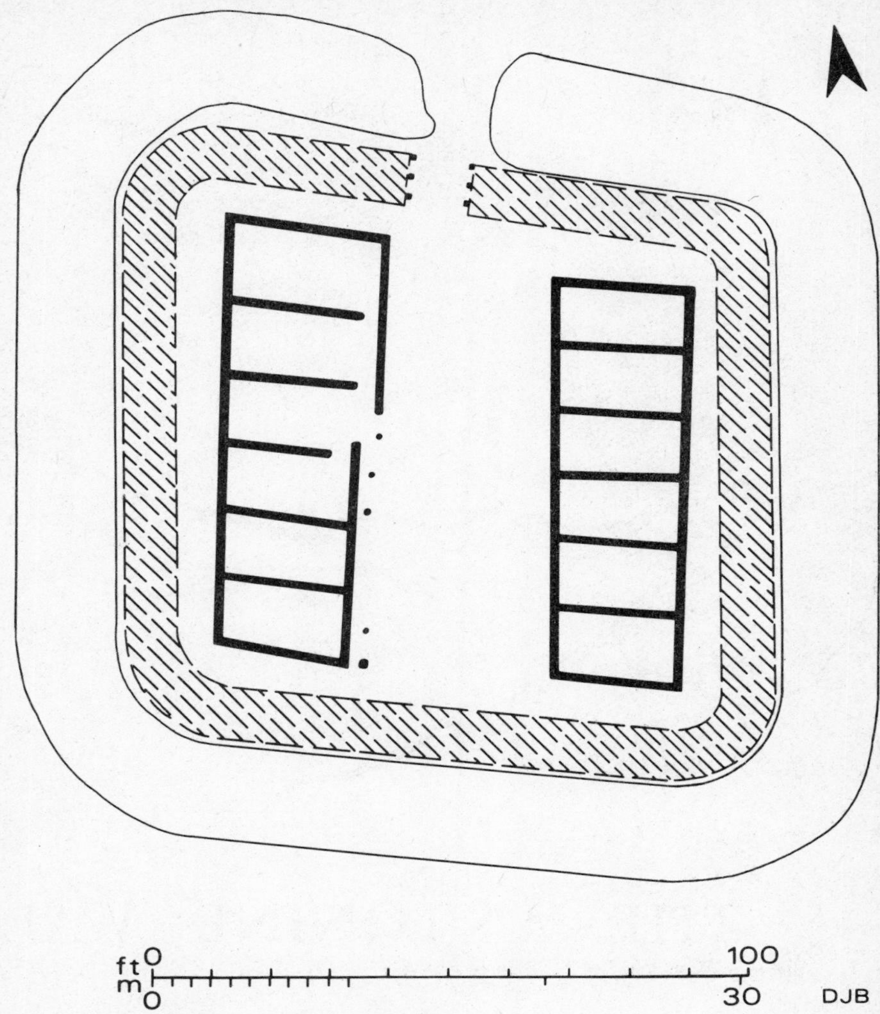

20 *The fortlet at Barburgh Mill in Dumfriesshire*

extensively excavated site at Barburgh Mill in the Nith valley contained two timber barrack-blocks suitable for an infantry century 80 strong (fig. 20). In between certain of these fortlets have been found timber watch-towers or signal-stations presumably forming links in the communications between forts and fortlets.

The organisation of the Scottish Lowlands was carefully planned. The garrisons of the fortlets were outposted from certain forts where no provision was made for their accommodation. It would thus appear that these detachments were expected to remain permanently outposted, though the individual soldiers might interchange. Elsewhere complete units might be kept together. Carzield in the lower Nith valley, for example, appears to have been garrisoned by an *ala* which had no men outstationed.

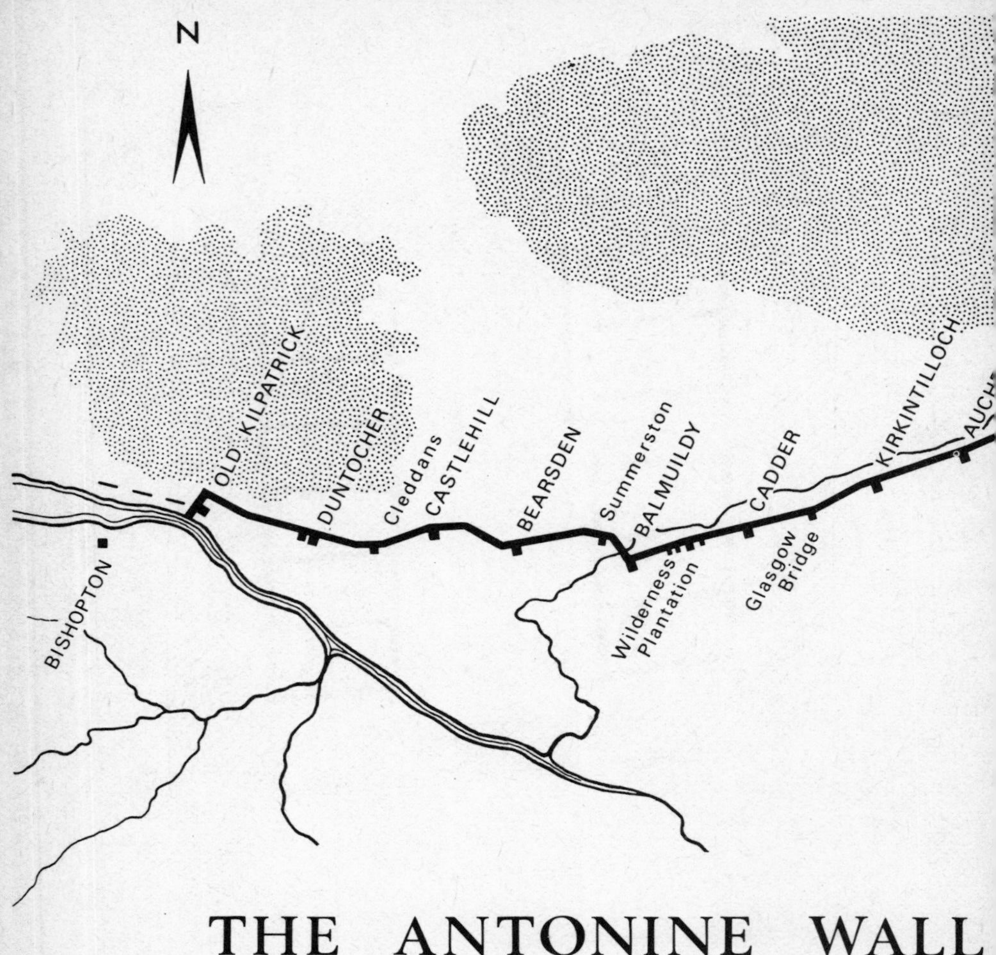

21 The Antonine Wall (land over 180m is stippled)

The Antonine Wall

To the north of these forts lay the Antonine Wall. This new Wall was exactly half the length of its predecessor, 40 Roman miles. It ran from modern Bo'ness on the Forth to Old Kilpatrick on the Clyde, ending beside the Erskine Bridge. For the first 6–8km from the east the Wall ran along the raised beach overlooking the Carse of the Forth. Thereafter until 11km short of the western termination the Wall utilised the Central Valley of Scotland, the valley formed by the River Carron in the east and the River Kelvin in the west. The Wall lay on the southern slopes of this valley overlooking the Campsie Fells to the north and the flat, marshy ground between (pl. 9). For the western 11km, however, where there was no such convenient geographical feature to follow the Wall jumped from high point to high point before reaching the Clyde low enough downstream to guard most of the fording points. Although the tactical position of the Antonine Wall was often stronger than

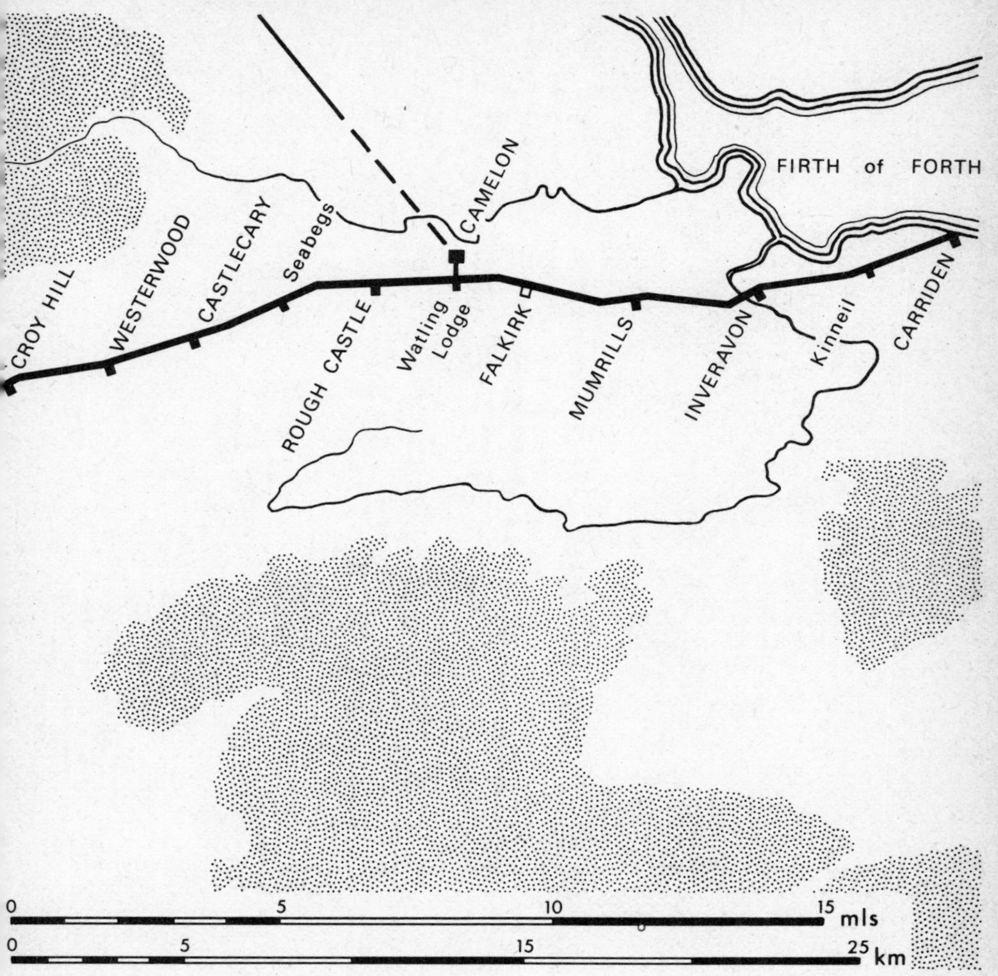

that of Hadrian's Wall it did not slavishly follow the best ground. Thus on Croy Hill there was a wide area of 'dead' ground in front of the Wall while for the most western 3km the lie of the land lay against the Romans.

The new wall, as Pius' biographer recorded, was of turf. Excavation has confirmed this, but also demonstrated that where good turf was not available blocks of clay were used. The turves – or clay blocks – were placed on a base of stone. Formed of rough boulders, bordered by dressed kerbs, this base was generally about 15 Roman feet (4.35m) wide. The height of the rampart is not known. In the 1890s experiments with the turf lying round a section through the rampart demonstrated that it could be restored to a height of nearly 3m. This is, of course, a minimum figure for the rampart. On its solid base it is possible that it rose as high as the turf sector of Hadrian's Wall. The excavators of the 1890s pointed

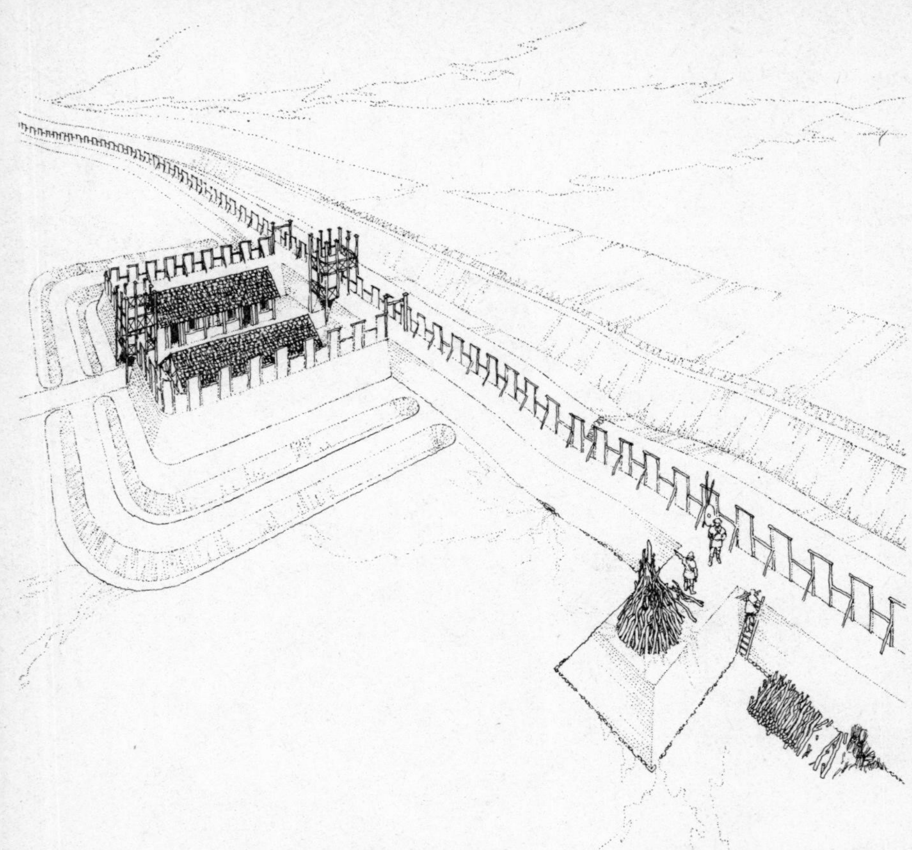

22 *The Antonine Wall, view from the east. Reconstruction showing the turf rampart, ditch and glacis, milefortlet in the background and beacon-platform (expansion) in the foreground. (Drawn by M. Moore)*

out that if a batter of 1 in 3 was allowed on both sides of the rampart, and a walk 2m wide on the top, then the wall may have been as high as 3.6m; if the width of the wall top walk was reduced then the rampart could have been built higher. There is even less evidence from the Antonine Wall to suggest how the wall top was completed, for no Rudge Cup or Amiens Skillet survives from the Scottish Wall. However, if it is assumed that provision was made for passage along the wall top then some protection would have had to be provided. This probably took the form of a wattle breastwork rather than, say, a fence of split logs: analysis of burnt debris found in front of the east rampart of the fort at Bearsden, debris probably deriving from a timber breastwork, included branches of willow and ash three to five years old and some 1–1.5cm in diameter, entirely appropriate for such a fence.

In front of the rampart, and separated from it by a berm, lay a ditch. This varied in width from nearly 6m to 12m and in depth from 2m to 4m. The larger measurements only pertain in the central sector of the Wall from Falkirk to Bar Hill; both east and west of these points the ditch usually conformed to the narrower figures. The width of the berm generally varied in relation to the width of the ditch. Where this was 12m wide, then the berm was 6m in width, but when the ditch narrowed then the berm widened to about 9m. It would thus appear that the main marking out lines were the front of the rampart and the centre of the ditch, the intention being to keep the two lines the same distance apart even though the ditch might narrow. In some areas this was not possible. Croy Hill provided the most difficult terrain for the army to cross, yet even here where crags rendered it superfluous the ditch was always dug, except for two points where the hardness of the bedrock defeated the Roman navvies. In order to provide a ditch the berm had to be allowed to widen, and in some places it not only achieved widths of up to 30m, but it also lay 14m and more below the level of the rampart on the top of the crags.

As on Hadrian's Wall the earth excavated from the ditch was not required for the construction of the wall and it was therefore tipped out onto the north side to form a wide, low outer mound or glacis. Where the rampart has long since been destroyed this upcast mound often survives. Strangely the turf from below this mound does not appear to have been stripped for use in the rampart before being buried. In some areas at least the northern edge of the upcast mound was marked by a low bank before dumping commenced.

At regular intervals along the Wall forts were constructed. Some forts were planned or built before the rampart, others added later. Recent work has suggested that these belong to two quite separate schemes: like Hadrian's Wall the Antonine Wall was subjected to changes in plan during its construction. The first plan appears to have been for six forts on the Wall, about 13km apart, and each capable of holding a single auxiliary unit. Between each fort, at approximately one Roman mile intervals, were to be fortlets, similar in size, and no doubt function, to those on Hadrian's Wall. At present only nine such fortlets are known, out of a possible original total of 29, or thereabouts, but in each instance the fortlet was contemporary with the rampart, or even preceded it, demonstrating that they were part of the original plan. The Antonine Wall in fact was planned to be similar to its predecessor as completed: forts at half a day's march apart with fortlets in between. The only element lacking was the turret. No turrets or towers have been found on the Antonine Wall, but if they were of timber and placed within the thickness of the rampart they would be difficult to find. A slightly different structure has, however, been discovered. Aerial photographs have revealed the existence of small enclosures attached to the rear of the rampart. Three such enclosures are known in the Wilderness Plantation-Balmuildy sector. They measure about 12m within a single ditch and, together with the fortlet at Wilderness Plantation, they form a sequence of four sites at roughly regular intervals of 250m: one-sixth of a Roman mile. This spacing, half the distance between turrets on Hadrian's Wall, may not be coincidental. Excavation of one enclosure in 1980, however, failed to reveal any structure in the interior so in the meantime their precise function must remain uncertain. It is not even definite that they formed part of the original plan for the Antonine Wall, nor that they continued along the whole length of the barrier.

One totally new element was added to the Antonine Wall: a road. With the Stanegate in existence behind much of Hadrian's Wall the need for a road on the Wall line itself may not have been strongly felt. But on the Antonine Wall there was no pre-existing road and the need will have been obvious from the first: there is some evidence to suggest that the road, the Military Way, was part of the original plan for the Wall. This road presumably ran along the whole length of the Wall, though it has not been found east of Watling Lodge, and it continued beyond the west end of the Wall, perhaps heading for a Roman harbour in the vicinity of modern Dumbuck or Dumbarton.

This plan for the Antonine Wall was modified, probably before it was completed. The modification took the form of the addition of a further 10 or 11 forts, possibly even 13, to the Wall. Excavation has revealed that several of these forts were simply attached to the rear of the existing rampart, and presumably all followed a similar pattern. The new forts were all smaller than the primary forts and many were incapable of holding even the smallest auxiliary unit in the Roman army. Some forts replaced earlier fortlets. At Duntocher the fortlet was incorporated within the new enclosure, but at Croy considerations of topography led to the construction of the fort some 50m to the east of the fortlet (fig. 25). Elsewhere it seems probable that some forts were placed in entirely new positions, for different reasons governed the siting of fortlets and forts. Thus at Bearsden, in spite of extensive investigations, no fortlet has been discovered in the immediate vicinity of the fort, which is presumed to be secondary.

The forts, both primary and secondary, were similar in materials of construction to those on Hadrian's Wall. The ramparts were of turf, sometimes on a stone base, with the exception of two of the primary forts, Balmuildy and Castlecary, which had stone walls. The reason for this is quite uncertain. Balmuildy in fact was provided with stone wing walls as if the builders were expecting to bond in with a stone wall rather than a turf rampart. The fort was one of the earliest to be built on the Wall, perhaps the earliest, for it is the only site which has produced an inscription of Lollius Urbicus, and the provision of the stone wing walls may hint that at one time the Roman commanders were considering building the Antonine Wall in stone.

Within the fort ramparts lay both stone and timber buildings. Stone was generally used for the principal buildings such as the headquarters, commanding officer's house and granaries, while the barrack-blocks, storehouses, stables and workshops were of timber (fig. 23 and pl. 10). Most of the forts were provided with an annexe, an enclosure commonly found attached to forts in Britain, though not on the continent. Annexes are not found on Hadrian's Wall, presumably because they were not necessary: the Vallum formed a sort of elongated annexe along the whole length of the Wall. As there was no Vallum on the Antonine Wall recourse was had to the annexe. This enclosure was provided in order to protect the military buildings which could not be accommodated within the fort. Thus the bath-house often lay within the annexe, though sometimes it was built within the fort and in at least one instance in neither: at Camelon the annexe contained furnaces and smithing hearths. The annexe was not for the use of civilians: the exclusion of civilians from the space between the Vallum and the wall on Hadrian's Wall emphasises this. No protection was provided for civilians by the army.

In one important particular the forts on the Antonine Wall differed from those on Hadrian's Wall and that is in the direction of their main axis. On Hadrian's Wall the forts were separate entities, clearly on the Wall line for convenience only. The headquarters building faced along the long axis even though this might result in the fort facing east rather than north. On the Antonine Wall, however, with the single exception of Cadder all the forts faced north even though this might result in the headquarters building facing along the short axis. The impression is therefore given of forts more closely tied to the frontier line than before.

The forts varied considerably in size from Duntocher, less than 0.2 hectares in internal area, to Mumrills containing 2.6 hectares and holding the only cavalry unit attested on the Wall. Most other forts were garrisoned by auxiliary units or detachments of such units, but in some cases it appears that legionaries were used to

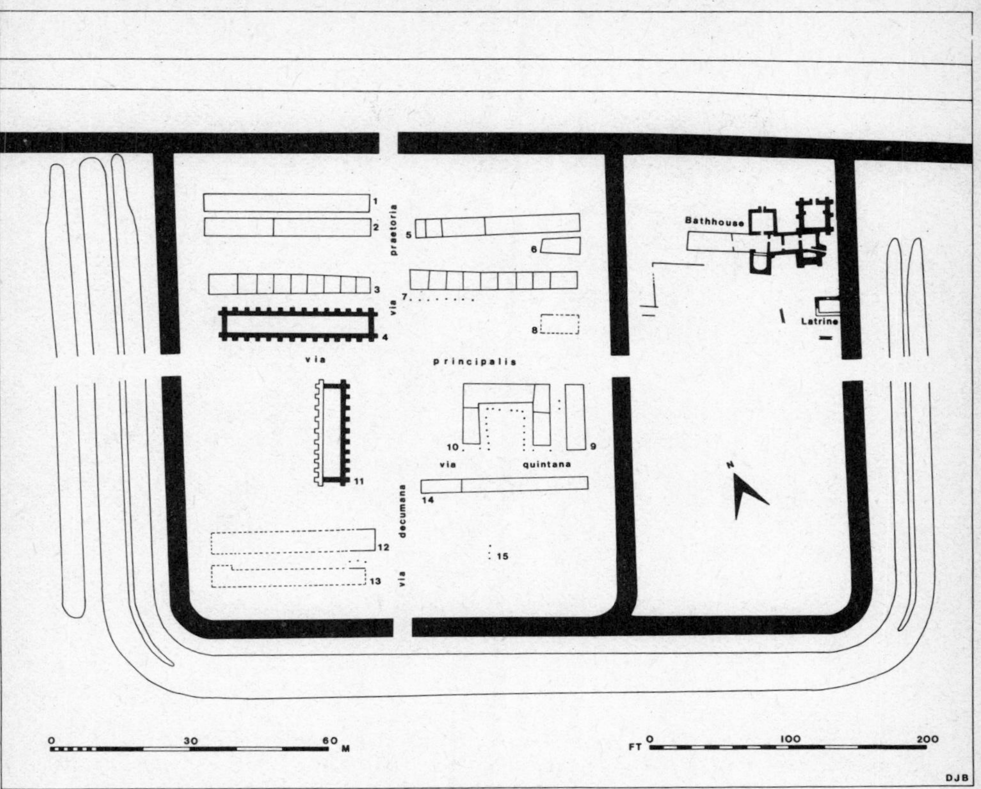

23 The fort at Bearsden. 3, 7 and ? 13 barrack blocks; 1, 2, 5, 6 and ? 12 stables; 4 and 11 granaries; 9 storehouse; 10 workshop; 15 works area ?; 8 and 14 unknown

supplement the Wall garrison. The weight of this garrison lay towards the western end of the Wall. Here the Campsie Fells and the Kilpatrick Hills loom especially close to the Wall, but it is unlikely that this would have caused the Romans any special concern. Perhaps the reason for the lack of troops in the eastern sector of the Wall is to be found in the presence of outpost forts to the north here, in Strathearn and Strathallan. As on Hadrian's Wall so on the Antonine Wall the barrier itself was not the provincial boundary, which presumably followed tribal borders rather than geographical features or military structures.

The fortlets also were constructed of the same materials as their predecessors on the turf section of Hadrian's Wall. Their ramparts were of turf, though on a stone base, and the internal barrack-block was of timber. It has only been possible in one case, Duntocher, to demonstrate the size of the barrack-block and there it measured 11m by 5m, rather larger than the smaller barrack-block found in certain milecastles on Hadrian's Wall. Fortlets were provided with a ditch, in some cases two, but, as on Hadrian's Wall, no provision seems to have been made for a causeway across the Wall ditch in front of the north gate. Causeways appear to have been provided at the primary forts – though not across all the three ditches at Old Kilpatrick – but not at all the secondary forts, where it may be presumed the Wall ditch had already been dug. There was a causeway outside the north gate at

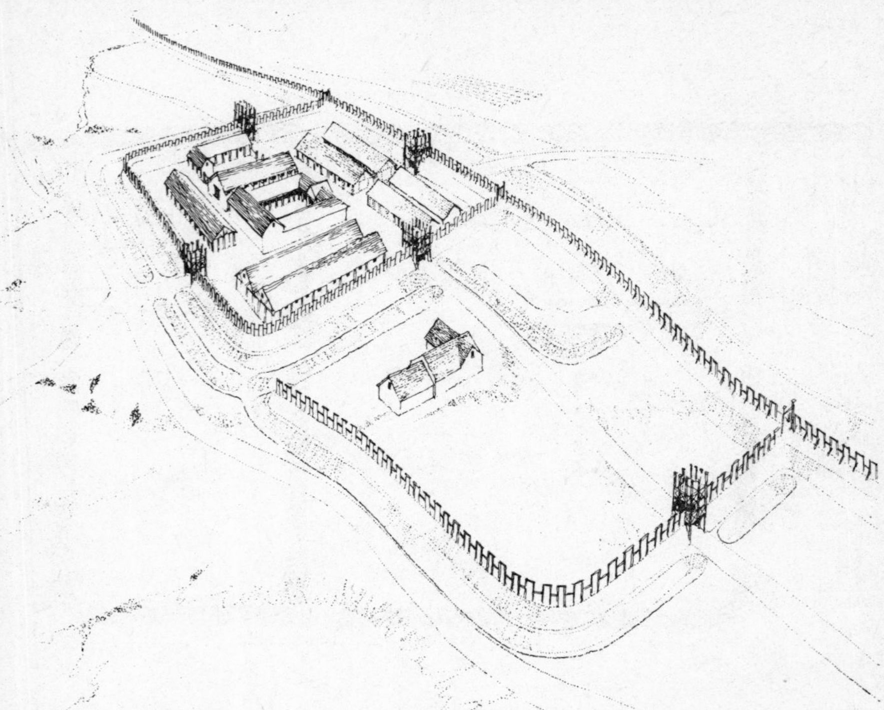

24 The fort at Rough Castle on the Antonine Wall, view from the south-east. Reconstruction showing the turf rampart, ditch and glacis, fort, annexe containing the bath-house, and the military way passing through the fort and by-passing it to the south. (Drawn by M. Moore)

Cadder and at Rough Castle while at Croy Hill the section of unexcavated ditch a few metres east of the fort appears to have been used as a causeway. But there was no causeway outside the forts at Westerwood, Duntocher and, it appears, Bearsden.

One final feature remains to be noted on the Antonine Wall, the 'expansion'. This is literally a rearward expansion of the Antonine Wall rampart. Excavation has demonstrated that the expansion is a turf platform placed on a stone base about 5m square and resting against the rear of the rampart. These platforms always appear in pairs. Two pairs are known on either side of Rough Castle and a third pair on the west brow of Croy Hill. It is presumed that the platforms were associated with signalling, the eastern four being concerned with signalling to the outpost forts to the north, while those on Croy Hill formed a connection with the garrison at Bothwellhaugh in the Clyde Valley. However, an element of doubt still surrounds these structures, not least because it is not clear how far fires lit on them might be seen and how messages might be sent using two fires.

The Antonine Wall, like Hadrian's Wall, was built by soldiers from the three legions of Britain. This is demonstrated by inscriptions, which also show that while *legio II Augusta* was present in full strength the other two legions only provided detachments. The size of these detachments is not known, but some of the camps occupied by them during construction work have been recognised through aerial photography. Many of the highly decorated inscriptions erected by these soldiers to record their labours have also been found. These reveal the distances constructed by each legionary gang and hence have been termed 'distance slabs' (pl. 17).

Together the distance slabs and the temporary camps show that all the Wall, with the exception of the four most westerly miles, were divided into major blocks of work, each subdivided in turn into three legionary blocks of 3, $3\frac{2}{3}$ or $4\frac{2}{3}$ Roman miles (4.3, 5.3, or 6.6km). Within each block, in at least two sectors, the legions were divided into four groups working from the ends towards the middle. This is perhaps clearest in the most easterly length, $4\frac{2}{3}$ miles long from Bridgeness, where a distance slab found in 1869 revealed that this was the length of *II Augusta*, to the River Avon at Inveravon where there was almost certainly a fortlet. Two temporary camps have been found at each end of this stretch. It is not known, of course, how the work was divided between the camps, though the fact that the turf does not appear to have been normally stripped from below the upcast mound for use in the rampart may point to separate rampart and ditch gangs. The provision of equal blocks of work for each legion suggests that part of *II Augusta* was engaged in other activities. Inscriptions from Balmuildy, a primary fort, demonstrate that it was working here and it is possible that all the primary forts, and possibly all the fortlets, were constructed by this legion.

That part of the Wall under discussion, all but the western four miles, was measured in paces on the distance slabs. Remarkably the unit of measurement was different on the slabs from the western four mile stretch; these legionary lengths were measured in feet. This may have been to allow apparent symmetry between the new and the old measurements. There were five feet to the pace and the new, smaller, distances measured in feet would appear, on superficial examination of the inscriptions, to be the same as the distances recorded on the easterly stones. There may, however, be further complications. It seems possible that the change in the unit of measurement on Castlehill was connected with the decision to build more forts on the Wall line. Castlehill lay within the area where the legions were working when they moved off to build the new forts, and it is tempting to assume that this was the very point they had reached when they left for their new task. When they returned to complete the western end of the Wall – after the construction of a fort at Duntocher – they were organised differently and took the opportunity to record their labours differently in order not to minimise their achievements.

The reason for the addition of the new forts to the Wall line is not known; nevertheless this action is consonant with other aspects of the occupation of Scotland at this time. On the Wall itself the close spacing of forts – on average about 3.5km – and the large garrison – proportionately almost twice as large as the garrison of Hadrian's Wall – reflects the close spacing of the small one-sixth mile enclosures. Behind the Wall is a similar pattern. The network of forts and fortlets is more dense now than either before or later in Scotland or in any other part of Britain. It seems unlikely that the Roman army was preoccupied with the local tribesmen, fearing attack from them at any time and therefore going out of their way to control them. A case might be made out for special defence from the Caledonians to the north. But again this threat would be met by moving the army out into the field, not by sheltering behind fort walls: the closer attachment of the forts to the Wall only gives a superficial impression of immobility. It seems better to connect this emphasis upon control, either of the people behind the Wall or of movement across it, with the reason for the advance into Scotland. If the advance had been merely in order to gain for Pius military prestige, prestige necessary to secure his position on the throne, it would be expected that his legate in Britain, Lollius Urbicus, and his successors, would do everything in their power to ensure that nothing soured that victory. This might account for the special measures taken at this time, not only on the Wall but also behind it in the territory of the Lowland tribes.

In spite of this apparent concern for control, the flanks of the Antonine Wall do not appear to have been protected in the same way as those on Hadrian's Wall. 17.5km to the east of Carriden, the easternmost fort on the Wall, lay a normal fort at Cramond and 14.5km on was Inveresk. Both these forts were placed beside river mouths and both estuaries may have been used as harbours. The west flank of the Wall was also protected by a fort, Whitemoss at Old Bishopton, on the south side of the Clyde with a wide panoramic view of the western end of the Wall. Further on two fortlets, Lurg Moor and Outerwards, both placed on the high ground overlooking the Clyde estuary, had wide views over the river and the land beyond. While the picture at present is of isolated flanking stations this picture could easily change. All three of the sites on the west flank of the Antonine Wall, and a fourth, first-century, site, have been found in the last thirty-five years: further sites, radically altering the above pattern, could be discovered at any time.

The Antonine Wall will have taken some years to complete. Most governors had a tenure of about three years so it is possible that Lollius Urbicus left Britain in 142. However, in view of the task allotted to him it is possible that he was given a slightly extended governorship, perhaps an extra year. Certainly work on the Wall had commenced before he left Britain for two inscriptions from Balmuildy record building under Urbicus, and as Pius does not appear to have been acclaimed as imperator until 142 this seems to be the earliest date for the commencement of building. Unlike on Hadrian's Wall there are no other dated inscriptions to help provide a chronological framework for the building activity. The chronology and time scale have to be estimated from the archaeological data.

Most of the Wall appears to have been divided into three-legion blocks of work. The relationship of the forts to the Wall suggests that building started in the east, for although Mumrills was planned and probably nearly completed before the rampart builders arrived on the site, Balmuildy and Old Kilpatrick further west, and also the fortlet at Duntocher, were completed before the arrival of the rampart, while the fact that both the fort and fortlet were constructed at Duntocher before the rampart suggests that some time had elapsed between the various building operations. The most easterly legionary length was $4\frac{2}{3}$ Roman miles long, close to the 5 miles generally apparently allotted to each legion on Hadrian's Wall, and this may not be coincidental. It may be therefore that it was expected that each three-legion length of Wall would take a year to complete.

If the above argument is accepted it would appear that the original proposal was to complete the construction of the whole of the Antonine Wall in three seasons, a similar period of time as initially planned for Hadrian's Wall. It seems unlikely that the Wall would be divided into three three-legion blocks if it was intended to complete all within one season, while various factors combine to suggest that it would not have been possible to work on all three sectors simultaneously. A start in 142 or 143 should have led to completion in 145 or 146. The distance of $4\frac{2}{3}$ miles constructed by *legio II Augusta* hints that the original intention may have been to divide the Wall into three three-legion blocks of 13 miles each. If so the proposal was altered after the first season, perhaps in view of the more difficult country in the centre of the Wall, which indeed was to give trouble, perhaps because work had been slower in the first season than expected. A reduction in the amount of work allotted to each legion in the second and third seasons – though it was increased slightly in the latter year – would have led to the gap of 4 miles at the west end of the Wall. However, before that could be completed it appears that many, perhaps all, the soldiers moved to the task of building new forts on the Wall line. This will have lengthened the building programme by an indeterminate period, at least another three years, if experience on Hadrian's Wall is a sound parallel. In that case the Antonine Wall may not have been completed until 147 or 148 at the earliest. Although several forts have produced legionary building inscriptions three have furnished auxiliary building stones, Rough Castle, Castlecary and Bar Hill: at the latter two sites both legionary and auxiliary building inscriptions have been found. The auxiliary stones are not dated within the reign of Antoninus Pius: they may date to either the original building of the Wall or a later phase. It may be, however, that auxiliary units were brought in to help construct some forts as the building operation was taking so long, just as auxiliaries had been brought in to help dig the Vallum on Hadrian's Wall and build the fort at Carvoran. It must be remembered too that the Wall was only one item that required to be constructed in these years. Forts and fortlets in the Scottish Lowlands were also built at this time.

The Antonine Wall in its final state was very different, superficially at least, from its predecessor. The main difference, and the reason why the Antonine Wall has not weathered the years as well as its southern neighbour, is that it was built of turf and not primarily of stone. In this, the Antonine Wall was the more usual, conforming to the norms established on other frontiers. The Antonine turf rampart was improved by the addition of a stone base not found on Hadrian's turf wall. A second, obvious, distinction to be drawn between the two Walls is that the forts were much closer together on the Antonine Wall and these forts were more closely related to the linear barrier. The original proposal for the Antonine Wall seems to have been for a frontier similar to the second scheme on Hadrian's Wall with forts at about half a day's march apart and fortlets at about Roman mile intervals between. While the fortlets seem to have been very similar to those on Hadrian's Wall the forts, all placed behind the rampart, give the impression of being more closely related to that rampart. The addition of more forts to the Antonine Wall brought more men to the frontier so that the number of troops based in the forts along the barrier was doubled from about 3,000 men to perhaps between 6,000 and 7,000 men, a high number in comparison to the 8,000 to 9,000 troops probably based in the forts on Hadrian's Wall. But it must not be assumed that the troops on the Antonine Wall were becoming frontier police. The linear barrier still served primarily as a base for these troops: if the province was threatened with invasion the army would move out into the field to deal with the invaders in the open, where it knew that its superior discipline, training and weapons gave it a better chance of victory.

Cavalrymen seem to have been even less common on the Antonine Wall than Hadrian's Wall. An *ala* was based at Mumrills and a mixed unit of infantry and cavalry at Castlehill, some cavalrymen from here possibly being outposted at Bearsden where cavalry-type barrack-blocks have been found. This lack of cavalry may be due to the terrain. The Campsie Fells and Kilpatrick Hills north of the Wall may not have been good cavalry country while between those hills and the Wall lay the marshy ground of the Kelvin and Carron valleys, also unattractive to cavalry.

Another, slightly less obvious, distinction between the two Walls is the greater flexibility and freedom displayed on the Antonine Wall. On Hadrian's Wall milecastles, turrets, bath-houses and to some extent forts, were built to set blueprints, but on the Antonine Wall no such regularity can be traced. Little can yet be said about the fortlets, but all the forts and their bath-houses seem to have been built to different plans with considerable variety in their dimensions, internal buildings and defences: even where it seems that two forts were built by the same legion this variety occurs.

In spite of these differences the two Walls hold several problems in common. How were the troops divided between forts and fortlets? How was the ditch crossed where no causeway appears to have been provided and no trace of bridges found? How did the command structure operate and the local commanding officers relate to the legionary legate at York and the provincial governor at London? These and many other problems remain to be solved.

The abandonment of Hadrian's Wall

The construction of a new Wall and of all the forts in the newly conquered territory led to the abandonment of Hadrian's Wall. The Wall itself does not appear to have been deliberately destroyed, but all the milecastles and turrets seem to have been abandoned and the gates of milecastles were forcibly removed from their sockets thus rendering them open to unimpeded traffic. An attempt was also made to slight the Vallum. In some areas the north and south mounds were backfilled into the ditch at regular intervals. However, this operation was not carried out along the whole length of the barrier. The position at the forts appears to have been different, at least in some cases. Although the Wall served no useful purpose once the frontier lay 160km to the north and a new Wall was constructed, the forts could continue to have an independent life of their own: they were, after all, only on the Wall for convenience. At Chesters two stones indicate building activity by *legio VI Victrix* during the reign of Antoninus Pius, while a legionary centurion dedicated an altar at Benwell. However, none need necessarily indicate a legionary garrison at this time. An auxiliary diploma dating to 146 has also been found at Chesters, which may imply that there was an auxiliary unit in garrison at that time. So many units are attested at Chesters as to make it more than likely that the fort was garrisoned during the years the Antonine Wall was occupied.

The actual date of the abandonment of Hadrian's Wall is not known, though it was probably late in the building programme for the Antonine Wall. Until their new buildings were ready to receive them the auxiliary soldiers presumably remained in residence in their old forts, at least in the winter when they were not out building or soldiering themselves. As their new forts became ready for occupation they will have marched north abandoning most of the forts in the Pennines and no doubt many on the Wall itself. It seems unlikely that caretaker garrisons were left in the forts, but on the other hand they do not appear to have been handed over to civilian use for many were reoccupied some years later when the Antonine Wall was abandoned. Some forts were still maintained in the Pennines and in certain areas arrangements were made to allow military operations to continue in spite of reduced strength. Thus the abandoned forts at Binchester and Ebchester appear to have been replaced now by a new site at Lanchester about half-way between them.

Antonine Scotland

The only known effects of the Roman advance of the 140s on the inhabitants of the

Scottish Lowlands are seen through the medium of archaeology. Excavation and field work have revealed a growth in native settlements at this time, the establishment of settlements outside forts and a drift of Roman goods northwards into barbary. It has been argued that the passage in the *Life of Antoninus Pius* recording the advance, that the barbarians were transported into another island, should be taken literally. The phrase was associated with the appearance of *numeri* (irregular army units) of *Brittones* on the Upper German frontier. Many of the ten or more of these low-grade units bore subsidiary titles taken from the river by which they were stationed. This is unusual and has been taken to imply that these were no ordinary military units but groups of soldiers accompanied by their wives and families. There is, however, no evidence for this and moreover it has now been discovered that the type of small fort occupied by these units had been in existence on the Upper German frontier for about forty years before the first appearance epigraphically of the units in 145–6.

It is still not impossible that men from the northern frontier region were drafted into the Roman army when southern Scotland was reoccupied in the 140s. Such recruitment may have taken place at any time, possibly as early as Agricola, and may have occurred even though the area from which the men were recruited was not part of the empire: the Roman army throughout its history attracted recruits from beyond the borders of the empire and there is no doubt that Britons from beyond the northern frontier would have joined the army even though they are not attested in any of our surviving sources. The early 140s would certainly have been an appropriate time for men from the newly reconquered tribes to join the army for they would have come more immediately under the attention of the recruiting officers and if any of the tribes had offered opposition to the Roman advance they would have lost their legal rights and thus been especially prone to the draft.

The tribes of southern Scotland would once more have been incorporated into the province, having their legal rights defined. There is no evidence that any of the tribes gained self governing powers either now or later, though presumably as before the Votadini held a special position. Authority over the tribes will have been the responsibility of the army, though special officers may have been appointed to help administer the civilians.

The returning Roman army will have brought in its wake taxation and other less welcome benefits. The army itself will have required servicing. Arms, armour, food, leather, clothing, pottery and horses, all were necessary to the proper working of the military machine. Many will have been imported from southern Britain or the continent. The Roman army in the fourth century had their own factories producing arms and armour: such factories may have existed in earlier years and some may have been located in Britain. Most goods, however, were purchased from civilians or were supplied as taxation.

The taxation was no doubt usually collected fairly, but Roman officials could be rapacious, harsh and cruel. The spark which ignited the rebellion of Boudica was the heavy-handedness of the Roman officials sent to the kingdom after the death of Prasutagus. Tacitus recorded that 'Agricola eased the levy of corn and the payment of tax by equalising the burden and abolished the devices invented by profiteers, which were more bitterly resented than the tax itself'. 'The provincials', Tacitus continues, 'had been compelled to wait outside locked granary doors and to buy back their own corn at farcical prices. They were forced to deliver it by devious routes and to distant locations even though there were permanent quarters for troops close by'. This passage should not be treated too seriously for Agricola's predecessor, Julius Frontinus, was a figure of great rectitude. Nevertheless, Tacitus would hardly invent a situation which did not exist somewhere and to some degree. He records a similar story elsewhere. The taxation of the Frisii, on the right bank of the Rhine, had been assessed by Drusus in ox-hides required for military purposes: the dimensions and quality of the individual hides were not specified. In AD 28 the officer in charge of the collection of the taxation interpreted the size of the hides as that of a wild ox, an auroch. Although these could be found in the forest, the size of domestic animals was small. The Frisians tried to meet the stipulation, in the process selling their cattle, lands and finally their wives and children into slavery. Eventually, their complaints having brought no relief, they rebelled and their revolt was only put down after considerable Roman loss. No such events are known in north Britain, but the two accounts do illustrate the type of burden placed on the native tribesmen as a result of their incorporation into the empire. And in addition to the perversion of the official system there was the private extortion of individual soldiers, the existence of which is amply testified by the edicts of various provincial governors banning such actions.

The main items required by the Roman army will have been corn and hides. Tents were not made of canvas, but leather and stocks would continually require to be replenished: a single tent for eight men would use the skins of about 38 calves. Leather would also be needed for clothing, shoes, bags, shields and shield covers and saddles, together creating an enormous requirement. Corn was the staple food, but the Roman soldier had a varied diet, including fish and shell fish, vegetables and fruit in addition to meat: cattle, sheep and pig bones are found at most Roman forts in some quantities as well as the bones of poultry and wild animals such as deer. Sour, or ordinary, wine was the common drink.

An important recent source of information on the Roman military diet has been the writing tablets found at Chesterholm-Vindolanda by Hadrian's Wall. One tablet is a list of food containing the following: spice, goat's milk, salt, young pig, ham, corn, venison and flour, all again pointing to a varied and sophisticated diet. Another list includes vintage wine, Celtic beer, ordinary wine, fish sauce and pork fat, while the site has yielded the physical remains of another variety of food, part of a cabbage. Another writing tablet from the site, incidentally, points to another requirement of the soldiers, clothing, for the letter mentions two pairs of sandals, woollen socks and two pairs of underpants.

The seasons will have affected the diet of the Roman soldier more than that of his modern counterpart. There will have been many times when meat, vegetables or fruit were unavailable. Recent excavations at Bearsden have emphasised that corn must at all times have been the basic item of food and also indicated that the soldiers' diet was more sophisticated than often realised. In a waterlogged deposit beside the latrine have been found the debris of both wheat and barley – the latter was fed to horses and used as punishment rations for soldiers – but in addition coriander and opium poppy, used to flavour bread. The seeds of figs, raspberry and wild strawberry survived in the deposit and also traces of hazel nuts and wild celery. Other remains, incidentally, suggest that peat may have been burnt in the fort, mosses may have been used instead of toilet paper, while foreign grain pest beetles indicate that the corn was not grown locally.

The remains indicate that soldiers would have eaten what was locally available as well as importing supplies. Some corn may have been acquired locally in addition to wild fruit, and presumably some animals were available from the immediate neighbourhood. Most cattle bones, for example, on Roman military sites in northern Britain were from adult and well-grown animals of the Celtic short-horn variety – the kind of beast that would have been found on the local farms. The soldiers made good use of these animals, often splitting or smashing the bones for marrow. The cattle bones from Newstead stand out in contrast for here many young animals were eaten and the marrow tended not to be extracted, while there were also indications of improved breeds: it seems probable that here cattle were in rather greater supply than in many areas, and also that local stocks had been improved.

The requirements of the Roman army in the staple item of food, wheat, were considerable. Each Roman soldier received about three pounds of corn a day. The units stationed north of Hadrian's Wall in the Antonine period will therefore have needed over 6,000 tons a year, the produce of at least 8,000 hectares. The impact of such requirements on the local population can scarcely be judged. In the western zone of the hinterland of Hadrian's Wall the construction of roads seems to have aided the growth of settlements in their vicinity, as if farmers were adapting themselves to supplying the military market: no such development can be detected in Scotland. Some of the Cumbrian farms, such as Ewe Close and Crosby Garret, grew to a considerable size, being surrounded by extensive field systems, and this can be paralleled in Scotland.

The Antonine advance appears to have heralded an era of peace and expansion in the frontier region. One tangible expression of the *pax Romana* appears to have been the change from timber to stone as the material used in domestic dwellings in large parts of the eastern half of the inter-mural zone (pl. 11). Stone had certainly been used before in houses, for over 3,000 years in some parts of northern Scotland, but it is only in the Roman period that this material became popular in the Borders. Datable artefacts from stone-built settlements range from the late first century to the mid-fourth century at least and the establishment of such a settlement at Milking Gap between the Wall and the Vallum, apparently before the construction of the Wall, emphasises that building in stone in this area had probably started early in the Roman period, if not before. However, the Roman era, and in particular the second century, appears to have witnessed a considerable growth in the number of these stone-built houses.

It is clear that on many sites the stone houses reflect continuing occupation of the settlement. However, in some instances the stone houses were built over the abandoned defences of earlier forts (fig. 32). Most houses had their own enclosures attached, though it is clear that these were essentially farmyards rather than defensive stockades. The average number of stone-built houses in each settlement was between four and five, though some contained only one house and others ten or more. The average size of the settlements in the coastal plain of Northumberland, where timber continued to be the material used in the construction of the houses, seems to have been the same. It is possible that all the huts in a settlement were not in occupation at the same time, and that some were used for animals rather than by humans. However, it has not been possible by excavation to demonstrate which, if any, were not used as dwellings, while the plans of many settlements argue for contemporaneity of occupation of all huts. Allowing five persons to each house, which may be on the low side, the average population of each average settlement may have been about 25 souls, though the full range in size of the social groups will have been from five to 50 persons.

Another phenomenon of these years appears to be the growth of both stone and timber settlements. It is immediately clear from the plans of many settlements that they grew from an original nucleus, with new houses being constructed both within the farm enclosure and outside it: in some cases the farmyard was extended to incorporate the latter houses. A small number of settlements grew into villages: that at Greaves Ash in Northumberland contained at least 30 houses with another ten less than 100m distant. It also seems probable, though this is as yet incapable of proof, that some folk left their ancestral homes to create new settlements for their families. It is certainly clear that this picture of growth and expansion in the Scottish Lowlands during the Roman period is at variance with the suggestion that families were transported wholesale to the continent.

Another form of settlement which grew during the Antonine period was the village outside the Roman fort. Merchants and traders will have accompanied the army into Scotland. Many will no doubt simply have moved with a unit on its way north from its old base in the Pennines or on Hadrian's Wall to its new fort in the Lowlands. A number of civilians are attested on inscriptions from the Antonine Wall but little is known about their dwellings. Recent excavations at Inveresk, however, have demonstrated that the civil settlement outside the fort there must have been extensive – it appears to have been larger than the fort – and contained both timber and stone houses which were rebuilt on at least one occasion. There seems to have been a main street leading from the east gate of the fort, and side streets branching off it. Analysis of the pottery from the site suggests that at least one potter moved north to Inveresk in order to improve his share of the lucrative northern market. Other discoveries point to the presence of at least four other potters working in Scotland at this time and selling their wares to the soldiers.

South-east of Inveresk a pattern of rectangular fields and enclosures have been revealed by aerial photographs and also in the vicinity at least five rectilinear settlements, possibly of the Roman period, are known: interestingly, and probably significantly, the only similar concentration of such sites lies around Traprain Law.

It is not possible to tell whether or not Inveresk was a typical civil settlement. Its position by the mouth of the River Esk, where there may have been a harbour, would give it a special importance. Cramond too, at the mouth of the Almond, appears to have been the site of an extensive settlement and one which continued in occupation, at least in part, beyond the withdrawal of its Roman garrison. Unfortunately recent excavations there have been unable to determine the layout of the settlement or even much about individual buildings, but they have demonstrated the presence of a variety of craftsmen at the site. Industrial activity appears to have taken place in open-ended timber sheds, and the trades practised included tanning, shoe-making, carpentry and iron working.

Practically nothing is known about the other settlements believed to exist outside forts on the Wall and in the Borders, with the exception of that at Carriden at the east end of the Antonine Wall. Here aerial photographs have revealed a complex pattern of boundaries and enclosures but these appear to relate more to agricultural activity than a town. However, this site has produced an inscription recording that the inhabitants of this town, called Velunia or Velunias, had gained self-governing rights. The acquisition of such powers suggests that the settlement was of some size, but its extent, even its position, is unknown. If one settlement on the Antonine Wall had achieved self-governing rights it might be expected that others also had.

Coincidentally the only civil settlement on the Antonine Wall extensively examined, that outside the fort on Croy Hill (fig. 25), has also kept its secret regarding its dwellings. Wide-ranging excavation has revealed traces of agricultural and small scale industrial activity, and a burial, but not the settlement

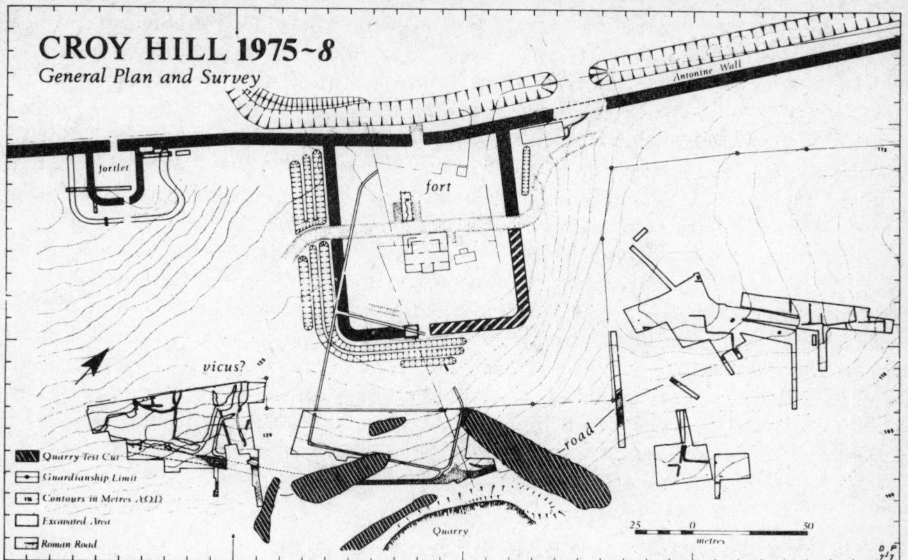

25 The fortlet and fort at Croy Hill on the Antonine Wall and the surrounding field boundaries. (Drawn by D. Powseland)

itself. At other sites, Westerwood and Bearsden, also examined recently, even less traces have been found, though clay and cobble foundations to the west of the fort at Bearsden were presumably part of civilian buildings.

The presence of the army in Scotland and the influx of many civilians from the south must have had an impact on the local population. The demand for food, leather, clothing might be expected to have led to a boom in farming, and indeed would help to account for the growth of native settlements at this time. The number of Roman objects reaching these settlements increased dramatically, but the total number of such objects found during archaeological excavations, or by chance, is still very small. Excavated settlements rarely produce more than the odd fragment of pottery from one or two Roman vessels, part of a rotary quern, an iron object, such as a brooch, a spindle-whorl also attesting the wearing of woollen clothes, occasionally a bone weaving comb and very rarely a coin: coins are rare no doubt partly because the local economy would have been mainly dependant upon barter. The standard of living of the inhabitants of such settlements, measured in terms of material possessions, would thus seem to have been low. But it is of course quite possible that their wealth was measured in different terms, in, for example, cattle. Certainly the rearing of cattle and sheep continued to be the main activity of the Border farmer, though goats and pigs would also have been found in the farms. Along the coast fish and shell fish were gathered while all would have supplemented their diet by hunting and gathering. There is no evidence for increased crop cultivation in these years.

There is some evidence for mining and smithing in the north by the native peoples. The iron ore of Redesdale and North Tynedale was probably already being exploited in the Iron Age and smelted in small bowl-furnaces, smithing continuing into the Roman period. Further north a smelting furnace for iron has been discovered in Constantine's cave on the Fife coast together with Antonine pottery. Some of the products of this 'cottage industry' will probably have found their way into Roman workshops: a large ingot, made up of small blooms of iron hammered together, was discovered at Corbridge. Stone moulds for casting small bars of copper alloy hint at bronze working in some settlements. Coal was also won, from outcrops rather than mining. This appears to have been put to little use by the natives, but it was put to good use by the army: a coal store was found at Housesteads. It is possible that the soldiers helped to exploit this and other local minerals as they did in certain parts of Wales and England.

The find spots of Roman objects on native sites in the second century, or as casual discoveries away from Roman forts, is closely restricted to the new provincial territory (fig. 26). The line of the provincial boundary across the north-west shoulder of Strathmore can almost be drawn from a distribution map of these finds, though of course the line also marks the edge of the Highlands. Relatively few objects found their way beyond that border. There was a drift of artefacts along the east coast, into the Moray Plain and as far north as Caithness, but a mere handful of objects occur in the west of Scotland and the northern Isles. As in earlier years the contact between Roman and barbarian appears to have been limited.

The abandonment of the Antonine Wall

The date of the abandonment of the Antonine Wall is one of the most vexed questions of the northern frontier. Over the last 100 years the suggested dates have ranged from the 160s through the 180s to 197 and 207, and finally back to the 160s. There is no guarantee that the date of about 163, which is the one now accepted by most scholars, is correct: it is merely the most probable in the light of the evidence available at the present time. However, before turning to the abandonment of the Wall it is necessary to consider its history.

Life for the soldiers on the Antonine Wall was not altogether uneventful. This is demonstrated by numismatic, epigraphic and archaeological evidence. In 154–5 a commemorative coin issue bore a portrait of *Britannia*, the personification of the province. It is usually assumed that this coin issue commemorates a particular event in Britain, on the basis of similar issues, a victorious campaign, in this case presumably on the northern frontier. Some time must have elapsed between the disturbance and the coin issue so whatever happened probably took place in 154, even 153 or 152. There is no corroborative evidence for trouble at that time – unless the garbled passage in Pausanias' *Description of Greece* is relevant. It is just possible that this coin issue is a repeat of the earlier commemorative issue of 142/3–4, with changes, as happened under Hadrian, though this seems unlikely. These coins of 154/5 are very rarely found on the continent, though they are common site finds in Britain. This has led to the suggestion that the coins were specially minted in Britain, and this receives some support from the fact that some of the coins are less well struck than usual.

Epigraphic material points to building activity on the northern frontier in the late 150s. An inscription from Hadrian's Wall, now unfortunately lost, records rebuilding activity in 158. A second inscription from Birrens in Dumfriesshire attests building there in 158 under the governor Julius Verus, while a third found at Brough-on-Noe at the southern end of the Pennines reveals that the fort there was rebuilt under the same governor. It seems probable that so much building activity reflects the implementation of a new policy in north Britain. The construction work on Hadrian's Wall implies that it was the intention to reoccupy that Wall and

26 The distribution of Roman finds on non-military sites in Scotland in the second century (after Robertson)

rebuild its outpost and hinterland forts: presumably this carried with it the intention to abandon the Antonine Wall.

Archaeological evidence points to a break in the occupation of the Antonine Wall sometime before its final abandonment, and also demonstrates that the fort at Birrens was destroyed before its rebuilding in 158. However, while archaeology can demonstrate that a fort was rebuilt, abandoned for a time or even destroyed, it can rarely prove the reason for such an event. The damaged armour, tools, personal ornaments and skulls found in pits of this date at Newstead may suggest destruction of the fort by the northern tribesmen, but different interpretations have been offered. Some artefacts may have come from votive deposits, others may have been equipment left by the army when they abandoned the fort peacefully; the skulls may have been trophies. Recent excavations at Birrens have been unable to prove conclusively the reason for the destruction of that fort. Hostile action may have been the cause, but equally the Roman army may have destroyed the fort itself preparatory to a change in garrison: such a practice was quite usual. Evidence from one fort recently excavated on the Antonine Wall, Bearsden, demonstrated that the fort there was demolished by the Roman army, presumably in connection with the rebuilding further south. It is tempting to connect these events and suggest that the army abandoned the Antonine Wall in favour of a return to Hadrian's Wall in 158.

The reason for such an event is, however, another matter. In the past it has been connected with a putative revolt in northern England by the Brigantes. The evidence for this event is open to more than one interpretation. The reference to the Brigantes by Pausanias is enigmatic, the archaeological evidence unclear, while the coin issue discussed above, appears to refer to events before 154 and the inscriptions to rebuilding in 158. If there had been an internal revolt in 154 the Roman reaction – if it did not occur until 158 – would appear to have been rather belated. However, one other inscription must be considered. A stone from Newcastle records the arrival of legionary reinforcements for the three legions of Britain from the army of the two provinces of Germany. Such reinforcements may suggest that the army had suffered reverses in Britain, but on the other hand they may have been required in order to supplement the normal recruiting patterns of the British legions.

It is perfectly possible that the events commemorated by the coin issue are not connected with the rebuilding of 158. A disturbance on the northern frontier, shortly before 154, may have been put down successfully, though at some expense, thus requiring reinforcements for the army to be brought in from outside. The same governor who received these reinforcements, Julius Verus, may then have decided to withdraw the army units from Scotland, abandon the Antonine Wall and reoccupy Hadrian's Wall and the forts in the Pennines. This would account for the building inscriptions.

There is some evidence to suggest that the abandonment of the Antonine Wall and the forts in southern Scotland was of short duration. Two forts, Newstead and Crawford, seem to have been reoccupied after the briefest gap, while there is nothing from the other excavated sites to oppose the possibility that the gap there was equally short. It is surprising that the army withdrew from Scotland only to return shortly afterwards. It seems unlikely that there was sufficient local military pressure to force the army to move: if there had been a revolt it would surely have been dealt with by the army in its usual way and not by the abandonment and destruction of all its forts. If the reconquest of Scotland in the early 140s had been merely in order to gain military prestige for Antoninus Pius then the decision by Julius Verus to abandon the Antonine Wall, taken without reference to the emperor, may have resulted in a counter order from Rome bringing troops back into Scotland and the rebuilding of the Wall. Such may seem a far-fetched scenario, but we are used to such policy changes today and imperial motives are a perhaps more likely reason for such moves than minor frontier disturbances.

The break in the occupation of Scotland in the late 150s was followed by the rebuilding and reoccupation of most of the forts on, behind and in front of the Antonine Wall. On the Wall itself several of the garrisons appear to have changed, and in a few instances it appears that the new force was slightly smaller than that in occupation earlier, but only one fort, Bearsden, does not appear to have been rebuilt. The garrison of at least two of the outpost forts seems to have changed, and Ardoch now contained a smaller garrison. In southern Scotland several forts and fortlets were abandoned. This is most noticeable in south-west Scotland, where the net of forts and fortlets was drawn most closely in the earlier Antonine period. In Nithsdale no military station can be shown to have been rebuilt at this time, while in Annandale and Clydesdale other fortlets were also not reoccupied. Elsewhere the fort at Lyne seems to have been replaced by a fortlet. It is possible that this process of disengagement commenced before the end of the previous period of occupation. The fortlet at Wandel in Upper Clydesdale does not appear to have even been completed, while the excavator of the small fort at Raeburnfoot considered that the occupation of this site was brief. However, it is difficult from archaeological evidence alone to judge the length of occupation of a single site, while the network in Antonine I seems to have been so integrated that it seems unlikely that many forts or fortlets were abandoned piecemeal. More likely, opportunity was taken of the brief disengagement about 158 to reorganise the forces occupying the Lowlands.

The pattern of occupation in the second Antonine period marks a return to the normal network of forts and fortlets (fig. 27). The close density of military stations found in the earlier Antonine occupation was abandoned and the normal spacing between forts returned to a day's march. If the advance into Scotland in the early 140s had been in response to hostile moves north of the frontier it might be expected that the reorganisation reflects increasing Roman confidence in controlling the Lowland tribes. If, on the other hand, the move north was in order to help smooth the succession of Antoninus Pius then the change in occupying forces might reflect the fact that the heat was now off the local situation in Britain and matters could be allowed to return to normal.

The reoccupation of the Antonine Wall and its ancillary forts appears to have been of short duration. Ceramic experts suggest that the abandonment of the Antonine system came in the mid-160s. However, although the Wall and forts in south Scotland may have been occupied for no more than five or six years, there is no evidence to suggest that the reoccupation was intended to be brief. The army moved back in force after 158, rebuilding the Wall and the forts and fortlets as if they were to be occupied permanently, as no doubt was the intention. In the second century as in the twentieth, defence policy could change radically in a short time.

A number of pieces of evidence combine to suggest a date for the abandonment of the Antonine Wall. The ceramic material points to a general date, but documentary and epigraphic sources can narrow this down. The documentary material, however, does not state that the Antonine Wall was abandoned, or even mention it, and, as usual, the actual events have to be pieced together from several fragments of evidence of differing quality.

Antoninus Pius, emperor for 23 years, the longest since Augustus, died on 7 March 161. He was succeeded, peacefully, by the long chosen Marcus Aurelius.

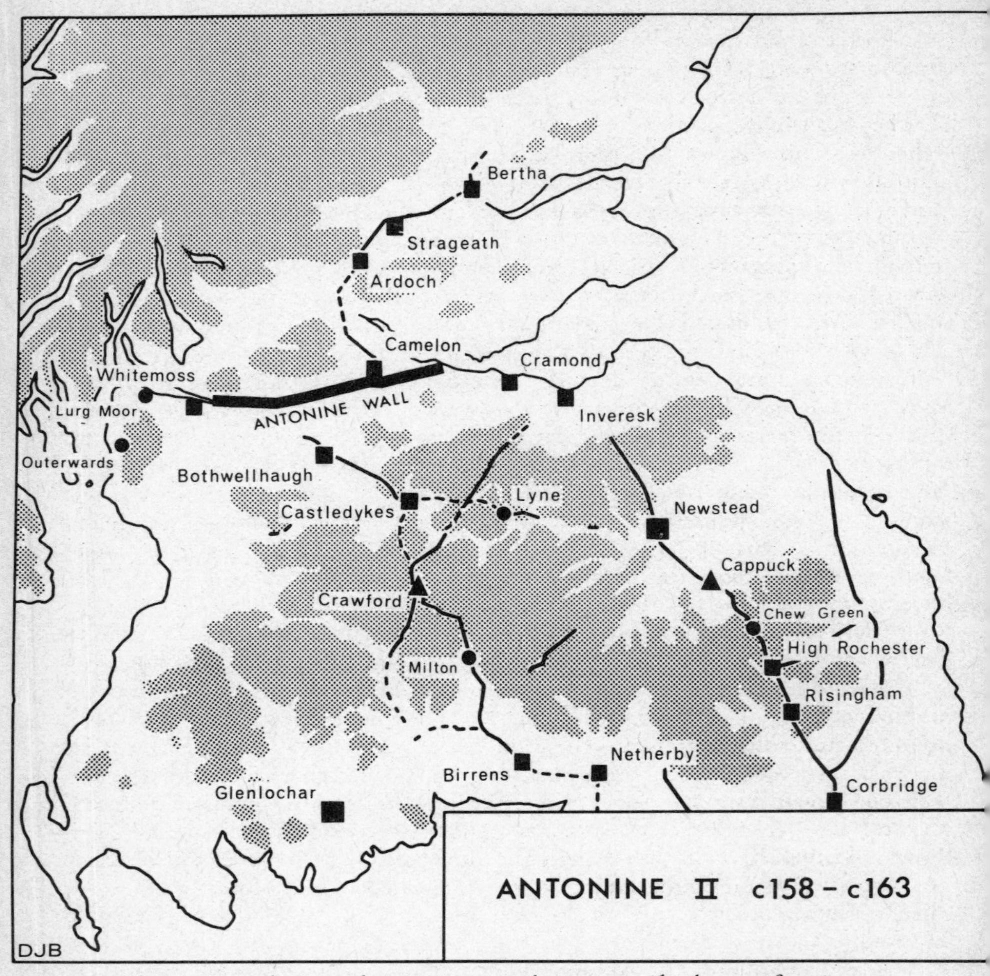

27 North Britain in the second Antonine period, c.158–63 (for key see fig. 4)

The first official action of the new emperor was to associate with him his adoptive brother Lucius Verus, and the senate agreed that the two would rule jointly. Ironically the reign of the stoic philosopher, Marcus Aurelius, began with invasions of the empire and was to continue in warfare through the nineteen years of his rule. In 161 the Parthians invaded the Roman protectorate of Armenia, while there was a threat of war in Britain and the Chatti invaded Germany and Raetia. Marcus' biographer goes on to record that Calpurnius Agricola was sent to deal with the Britons. Although this is a straightforward statement it is clear from other evidence that Agricola was not the first governor sent out to Britain by the new emperors to deal with the disturbing situation there. In the year of their accession they moved Statius Priscus from Upper Moesia on the Danube, where he had only recently been appointed governor, to Britain, only to send him to Cappadocia on the eastern frontier when a whole legion, just possibly *IX Hispana*, was massacred by the Parthians and the governor of Cappadocia committed suicide.

Sextus Calpurnius Agricola was their choice to replace Priscus. He probably arrived in 162. The nature of the trouble he had to deal with is unknown, though it may be presumed that it was on the northern frontier. Agricola may have campaigned against the northern tribes though there is no evidence for this. Building inscriptions from the Pennines, however, demonstrate that he was active there. Such records have been recovered from the forts at Carvoran, Chesterholm and Corbridge on the Stanegate, from Ribchester and possibly Ilkley. Although there are no inscriptions of his governorship from Hadrian's Wall it may be presumed that reoccupation of the forts further south would have carried with it reoccupation of the Wall. Building inscriptions dating to a few years following Agricola's governorship have been found at Stanwix and Greatchesters on the Wall and it may be that the task of recommissioning the forts and the Wall took several years to complete.

If warfare in Britain was imminent in 161 this might be considered an appropriate reason for the army to disengage from Scotland. On reflection, however, this is unlikely. Warfare on the northern frontier would be dealt with by the army in the field, or by diplomacy. It is improbable that in itself it would cause the army to abandon the Antonine Wall. As at the beginning of Pius' reign events in Britain cannot be examined in isolation. The serious situation on the eastern frontier led to major troop movements. Legionary detachments from the Danube and three entire legions from the Danube and Rhine provinces were sent to the east. As part of these arrangements it is possible that troops were withdrawn from Britain for service on the continent. As a result of these admittedly hypothetical withdrawals it may have been decided to abandon the recent conquests in Scotland and restore Hadrian's Wall as the frontier. A further possible reason can be found in political realms. If the advance in the 140s had been merely to allow Antoninus Pius to acquire military prestige it is possible that his adopted sons and successors, Marcus and Verus, decided to abandon his conquests, realising that they had served their purpose; if this would have released troops for service elsewhere, this might have helped their decision. It is interesting to note that 100 years before, after the death of Claudius, whose expedition to Britain had, according to Suetonius, merely been to obtain a triumph, his successor Nero toyed with the idea of abandoning Britain.

A totally different reason advanced for the abandonment of the Antonine Wall is that the holding of so many northerly forts caused serious problems of supply to the army. There is, in fact, little evidence that this was the case, though in the nature of the problem it would be difficult to prove the truth either way. Certainly the distribution of pottery vessels on the Antonine Wall demonstrates that it was possible to supply these goods to the troops in considerable quantities, and from all parts of the province, for pottery vessels have been found on the Wall from Colchester, Kent, Dorset, the west midlands, north-west England, south Yorkshire as well as southern Scotland. Nevertheless the apparent use of legionaries to garrison some of the forts on the Antonine Wall suggests that in one sphere the occupation of so much territory may have been causing difficulties. Whatever the reason it appears that the Wall was abandoned, the forts and fortlets destroyed by the withdrawing forces, and work started, yet again, on the repair of Hadrian's Wall and its outpost and hinterland forts.

The process of abandonment and rebuilding would take some time to complete and this may account for the discovery of coins later than 163, or thereabouts, on the Antonine Wall. Such coins have been found at Bar Hill and Mumrills and also possibly at Kirkintilloch. However, it is equally possible that although the new army bases were further south patrols continued to keep watch on the Lowland tribes and visit their former bases. Indeed some outposts may have continued to be held after the formal evacuation of the Antonine Wall. This might account for the erection of a temple at Castlecary, probably in the 170s or 180s. Certainly the army would not have lost all interest in the area to the north of Hadrian's Wall and would have maintained surveillance over the tribes beyond the province as they did on other frontiers. However, these new arrangements open up a new era on the northern frontier: from about 163 until well into the fourth century Rome was to control the northern frontier in a different way than during the previous forty years: now Walls were to become largely irrelevant.

7

War and Peace

The second century might in simplistic terms be called a century of war, the third century one of peace. This is certainly the impression provided by the contemporary sources. Through the second century references to warfare or disturbances on the northern frontier appear frequently, though usually as an aside, in the imperial biographies and other documents, but from 211 to 297 there is not a single such comment in the, admittedly sparse, literary sources. The difference between the two centuries may not merely reflect the different sources, or the change in imperial interest in Britain, but may accurately reflect the actual situation on the northern frontier for the picture which emerges from the literary sources is supported by the testimony of archaeology.

The unsettled state of the frontier in the first half of the second century continued into the early years of the third. The earlier years of the century had already seen remarkable vicissitudes. At the beginning of the century, it would appear, all or most forts north of the Tyne-Solway line were abandoned, though there is no mention of this in the literary sources. Epigraphy, however, suggests that there was warfare in Britain later in Trajan's reign, for an army unit based in the island was awarded decorations usually only given during warfare. At the opening of Hadrian's reign his biographer informs us that the Britons could not be kept under Roman control and, following the emperor's visit to the island, a Wall was built across the Tyne-Solway isthmus. Twenty years later this was abandoned for a return to Scotland, though Pius' biography makes no explicit mention of warfare at the time. Twenty years later, at the start of another reign, again war was threatening in Britain. The action initiated by the governor of the time, Calpurnius Agricola, presumably on imperial orders, was the abandonment of the Antonine system in Scotland and a return to Hadrian's Wall. Thereafter the units based on this Wall were to be the protectors of the province, and the literary sources demonstrate that this task was no sinecure.

There is a reference to Britain in a comment on the state of the empire in 169 following the death of the Emperor Lucius Verus. The biographer of his co-emperor Marcus Aurelius states that the Parthians and the Britons were on the verge of war. This bald statement is very similar to that made at the beginning of the reign and indeed may have been repeated in error. Such times – the death of an emperor and the succession of another – were often the occasion for a general resumé on the condition of the empire: they appear at the beginning of the reigns of Hadrian, Antoninus Pius, Marcus and Commodus, and at the death of Verus – and have consequently to be treated with care. It may be safer to ignore this particular comment.

The next reference to Britain is also rather enigmatic, though for very different reasons. In 175 Marcus Aurelius secured a temporary respite in his struggle on the Danube through making peace with the Sarmatian Iazyges. As a result of the alliance now concluded with this people, 100,000 Roman captives in their hands were surrendered and 8,000 cavalry was provided by the Iazyges for service in the Roman army, 5,500 being sent to Britain. It is possible that these cavalrymen were sent to Britain in order to help in warfare currently being fought there, or to strengthen the provincial army, but the fact that Britain was an island and far removed from the homeland of the Iazyges probably also played a part. It is not known where within Britain the Sarmatians were sent; the *ala Sarmatarum* later attested at Ribchester may or may not have been formed from the Sarmatian Iazyges.

It is probably to the reign of Marcus Aurelius that an inscription found at Kirksteads, three miles west of Carlisle, should be assigned. The altar was dedicated by Lucius Junius Victorinus Flav(ius) Caelianus, legate of *VI Victrix*, because of successful achievements beyond the Wall. This man may be identical with Junius Victorinus, governor of Upper Germany in the reign of Marcus. The brief statement on the altar does not allow the events in which the legate participated to be linked to any literary references to the northern frontier; indeed they may have no connection with any other known events.

This is certainly true of the event recorded on a late second or third century inscription from Corbridge. This records that Quintus Calpurnius Concessinius, prefect of cavalry, fulfilled his vow by dedicating an altar after slaughtering a band of Corionototae. This tribe, sect or group is otherwise unattested; nevertheless the inscription, and its fellow from Kirksteads, is eloquent testimony, of an unusual kind, of one type of activity which must have been fairly common on the northern frontier. A third inscription, also dated to the late second or third centuries, records the burial at Ambleside of two men, a retired centurion and an *actarius*, accounts clerk, probably father and son, the latter having been killed in the fort by the enemy. It is unfortunate that no further information is given about this enemy.

The beginning of the reign of the Emperor Commodus in 180 saw a more serious state of affairs. The main account survives in the *History of Rome* by the Greek Cassius Dio. He states that the greatest war of the reign was that in Britain and continues: 'the tribes in the island crossed the wall that separated them from the Roman forts, did a great deal of damage, and cut down a general and his troops, so Commodus in alarm sent against them Ulpius Marcellus, who inflicted a major defeat on the barbarians'. It was not until 184 that victory in Britain was celebrated by a commemorative coin issue and coins carrying the same message continued to be struck during the following two years. The date of the attack, however, is not known. There are three epigraphic reference to Ulpius Marcellus in Britain. Two are from Chesters on Hadrian's Wall, one clearly recording the construction of an aqueduct during his governorship, the other fragmentary. The third is also from Hadrian's Wall, in this case Benwell, a dedication in the governorship of Ulpius Marcellus by Tineius Longus who, while prefect of cavalry, had been adorned with the broad stripe of a senator and designated quaestor by the decree of the Emperors. The latter are not named, but they are certainly in the plural and therefore the inscription cannot refer to Commodus alone. It has been suggested that there was another, later Ulpius Marcellus governing Britain under Caracalla and Geta in the early third century under whom this inscription was erected.

It is perfectly possible that a governor is missing from the fragmentary provincial roll at this time and certainly the early third century was a period when extra facilities such as aqueducts appear to have been provided. However, it is also possible that Longus was designated as quaestor before the death of Marcus Aurelius, when he and Commodus were joint emperors, but did not make his dedication until some months later when a new governor had been appointed. Perhaps more likely is the possibility that the disaster on the British frontier occurred at the end of the joint reign of Marcus and Commodus and that Dio, in his summary of the state of the empire transferred to the beginning of the reign of Commodus events which had happened a few months before: such a transposition certainly can be demonstrated to have taken place in relation to another event of the time. The result of this plausible explanation would be to increase the length of the British war by about a year.

Much of the epitome of Dio's account of Ulpius Marcellus and his activities is concerned with anecdotes about his hero. It is thus doubly frustrating that he does not mention in his narrative the single most important fact to the present day historian: the precise Wall that was crossed. Archaeologists and historians have long argued about the identity of this Wall. The tortuous language employed has not helped: the wall which separated them from the Roman forts. In the past both Walls have been considered for this honour; it has even been suggested that the language employed by Dio could imply that it was the abandoned Antonine Wall, still somehow regarded as the frontier of the province, or at least separating the barbarians from the Roman forts, that was crossed. It seems, however, easier and simpler to assume that it was the Wall which was occupied at the time that was crossed and that Wall, at least on present theories, was Hadrian's Wall.

Archaeological evidence for the destruction of certain sites on Hadrian's Wall, dated on general archaeological grounds to the later second century, has been related to this disaster. In the past it has been considered that the Wall was destroyed wholesale during this invasion, but it now seems more probable that the effects were localised. At the forts at Halton Chesters and Rudchester destruction deposits have been assigned to this time and the burning of the military depot and town at Corbridge appears to be contemporary. However, investigations at other forts on the Wall line, and in particular at Carrawburgh, Housesteads, Wallsend and South Shields, have failed to furnish equivalent evidence. This seems to suggest that the barbarians moved south down Dere Street, using the Roman road against the Romans, and sacking the sites in their path, Halton Chesters, Corbridge and Rudchester. How far south they reached is, of course, unknown. The Roman officer killed was of senior rank and may have been the legate from York or even the provincial governor; the death of the latter might more easily account for the dispatch of a new governor to the province.

The measures taken by Ulpius Marcellus to protect the province are not known. There is but one hint: in 197 it is recorded that the Caledonians failed to honour their promises. This might suggest that the Caledonians had previously entered into a treaty with Rome and one suitable occasion for such an alliance might have been in the early 180s.

Although we hear of no more warfare on the northern frontier during the reign of Commodus the British army was in a ferment. The army tried to elevate two officers to the purple. At first they chose a legate, Priscus, but he refused. Then they sent a delegation of 1500 soldiers to Rome to protest against the praetorian prefect Perennis, an act which led directly to his downfall and death. The new governor of Britain, the later emperor Helvius Pertinax, was their next choice as usurper, but he also refused and although he managed to return most of the army to its loyalty to Commodus he did have to deal with a rebellion by one legion, during which he almost lost his life. His severity in putting down this mutiny caused resentment and as a result Pertinax asked to be relieved of his command. The reason for the turmoil in the army during these years is not known, though it may have partly resulted from the strict discipline of Ulpius Marcellus, a martinet of the old school, or possibly the sudden idleness of the army following years of activity.

The mutinous state of the British army in the late 180s is an interesting and unusual aside, an interlude, between the invasion of the first half of the decade and the civil war which began in 193 and which in Britain was followed by serious disturbances on the northern frontier culminating in the imperial expedition of 208–11. The position of the army on an island may have helped to create the conditions conducive for rebellion in the 180s; it certainly helped the governor in his bid for the throne in 193. On 31 December 192 the Emperor Commodus was assassinated. His successor, P. Helvius Pertinax, previously governor of Britain, did not enjoy his success for long before he too was murdered, as was his successor. In the ensuing struggle there were three main contenders for the empire, the governors commanding the main provincial armies. In the east Pescennius Niger was governor of Syria, in the west D. Clodius Albinus governed Britain, but in the centre, and commanding the only other three legion army, was L. Septimius Severus. Severus, the junior of the three governors and the least popular so far as the Senate was concerned, was well placed in Pannonia (modern Hungary) to reach Italy first. He won Rome in June 193 and on assuming the purple his first task was to deal with his rivals. Severus naturally chose to turn against Niger first: to move against Albinus was to risk being caught on an island while his other rival was still at large. Time was bought by recognising Albinus as consul for 194. The defeat of Niger in that year was followed by campaigns against the Parthians and other eastern nations while Severus' army was besieging the last stronghold of Niger's supporters, Byzantium. When that city fell at the end of 195 Severus returned to Rome and began preparations against Albinus. The decisive battle was fought at Lyons on 19 February 197 and after a hard fought engagement the forces of Severus were successful.

It seems probable that Clodius Albinus took measures to protect the province when he took the army to Gaul for the battle with Severus. It has been suggested that he made a treaty with the Caledonians, possibly implied by a statement by Dio that in 197 the Caledonians refused to honour their promises, and that he defended the towns of the province by the construction of walls. Neither suggestion can be proved. It may even be doubted that Albinus did much to protect the province: if he was successful he would have the full resources of the empire to repair any damage in Britain and if he failed such matters would no longer be his concern. At any rate the situation does not become clearer until after his defeat.

The new governor of Britain appointed by Severus was Virius Lupus. Dio records that Lupus found the northern frontier in an unsettled state: 'the Caledonians, instead of honouring their promises, prepared to assist the Maeatae. As Severus was at that time concentrating on the Parthian war, Lupus had to purchase peace from the Maeatae for a great sum, recovering a few prisoners'. Severus soon after the battle of Lyons had returned to Rome but the same summer set out for the east where he devoted himself to the Parthian war until 199. Although Lupus clearly had a difficult situation to deal with it would appear that it was not serious enough for it to interfere with the emperor's other plans.

The outline of the events on the northern frontier is straightforward and cannot be elaborated by reference to any other source. The Maeatae had been causing a disturbance, the nature of which is unknown but as it involved the capture of some Romans, possibly soldiers, it presumably included warfare. It would appear that

Lupus could keep this situation under control, but when the Caledonians, seemingly in treaty relationship with Rome, prepared to abandon their former position and help the Maeatae, Lupus changed his policy, and, preferring diplomacy to war, bribed the Maeatae in the time-honoured Roman tradition. The five coin hoards ending with Commodus and perhaps some of the four coin hoards ending with Severus found in central and eastern Scotland may reflect the payment of subsidies to these northern tribes. Thereafter no further trouble is recorded on the northern frontier for nearly ten years.

The Maeatae are an enigmatic people. They only appear in the record at this time and the precise location of their homeland is not known. Dio later states 'the two principal tribes of the [free] Britons are the Caledonians and the Maeatae, the names of the others having being merged in these two. The Maeatae live close to the wall which divides the island in two and the Caledonians beyond them.' Frustratingly again the name of the Wall is not stated as it would presumably have been obvious to the readers of the time. It seems almost certain that the Maeatae lived beyond the province: the names of the Lowland tribes continue through the Roman period with no hint of change while the names of the tribes beyond the frontier in eastern Scotland changed on at least two occasions.

Two place names appear to retain the name Maeatae: Dumyot Hill overlooking Stirling and Myot Hill south of the Forth at the east end of the Campsies. It seems probable that these places are so named because they lie on the edge of Maeatian territory and therefore that the tribe extended north from the Forth basin, presumably into Strathearn and Strathmore, possibly Fife as well (fig. 28). The apparent extension of this tribe south of the Forth is interesting. It seems probable that the Maeatae was an amalgamation of the tribes recorded by Ptolemy and reflects one of the regular impacts of Rome upon the barbarians: the coalescence of tribes beyond the frontier into ever larger units. Alternatively, this may be the 'lost' tribe of Ptolemy in Strathearn and Strathmore (cf. pages 29–31).

Dio's brief statement hints that the Romans treated the Maeatae and the Caledonians differently, though they were both presumably in treaty relationship with Rome. They were clearly two separate peoples and it might be that Rome, through her diplomacy, played one off against the other, losing this game in the late 190s when the tribes moved to combine against her.

The governorship of Virius Lupus saw the beginning of a long series of building inscriptions relating to forts on Hadrian's Wall and its hinterland. Over 30 inscriptions survive from the period 197–*c*.250. Several of the stones record the buildings erected or repaired: the gates and walls, granaries, headquarters building, armoury, exercise hall, bathhouse, aqueduct. It has been suggested that the earlier inscriptions at least relate to repairs carried out following an attack on the northern frontier while the army was away in Gaul with Albinus. Archaeological evidence from the forts, milecastles and turrets on Hadrian's Wall has been cited as support for the destruction of the frontier at this time. However, the destruction of those forts which more clearly suffered at the hand of the northern barbarians is now considered to date to the early 180s and not the late 190s, while the repair work at other sites may be better interpreted as part of a programme of rebuilding and improvement necessitated by the ravages of time rather than the ravages of an enemy.

The inscriptions seem to demonstrate that the intention of Severus was not to reconquer Scotland, but to repair Hadrian's Wall and its hinterland forts and maintain this Wall as the frontier. Thus Virius Lupus is recorded building at

28 The tribes of north Britain in the early third century

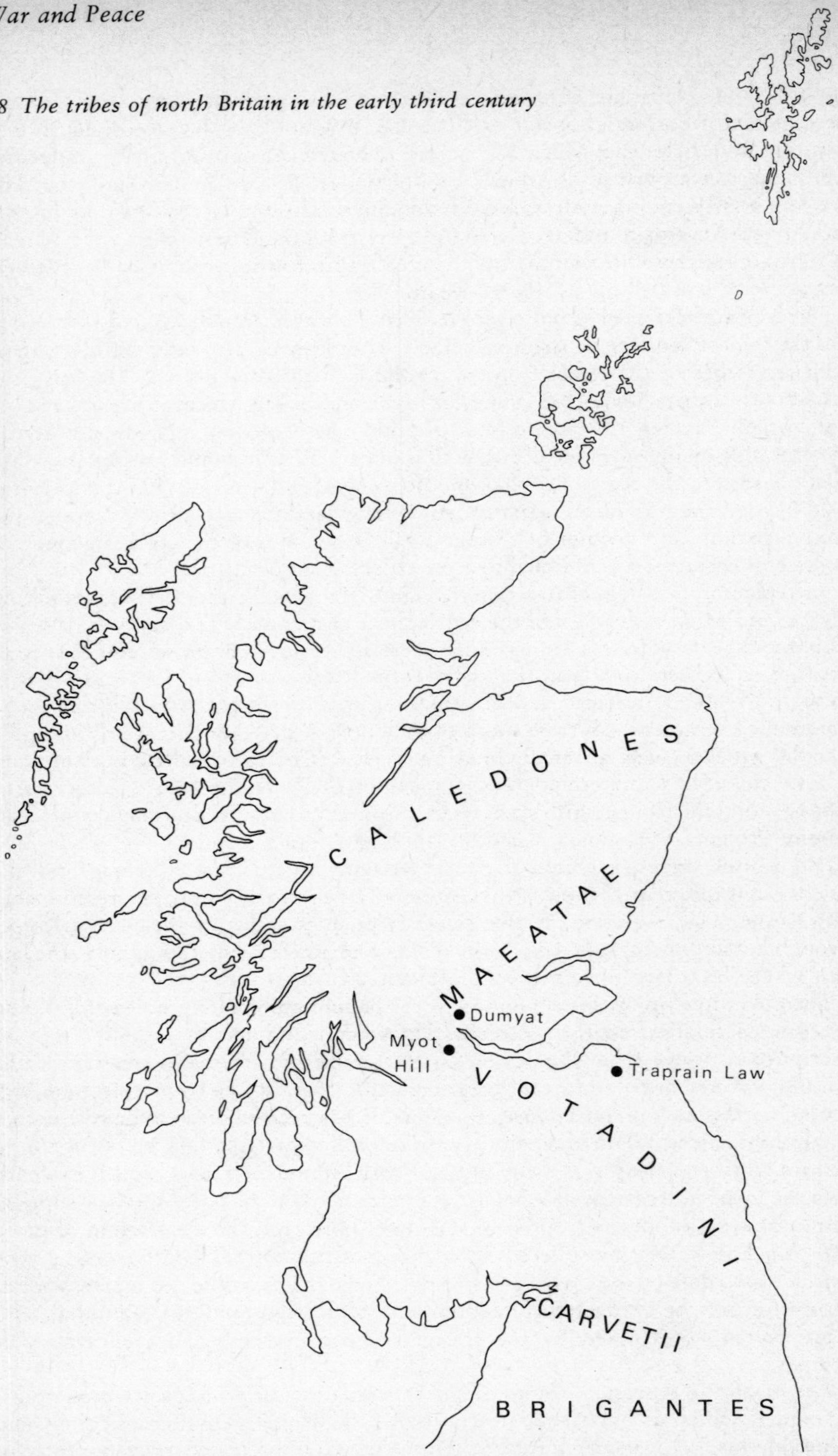

Brough under Stainmore, Bowes and Ilkley, his successor, Valerius Pudens, at Brough-by-Bainbridge and the next governor Alfenus Senecio at Bowes, Greta Bridge, Brough-by-Bainbridge, Corbridge, Chesters, Birdoswald and Risingham, the work extending over the ten years from 197. This work stopped at precisely the time that there was a major change in frontier policy in Britain and did not recommence until the 210s.

The events which led up to this change in frontier policy are tolerably well recorded by the contemporary historians Cassius Dio and Herodian. In 207 Dio recorded that Severus' generals were winning wars in Britain, yet in the following year he decided to come to the island to take command of the Roman forces himself. Herodian records that the governor of Britain wrote to the emperor informing him that the barbarians were overrunning the province, plundering and causing great destruction, and that for effective defence either more troops or the presence of the emperor was required. Severus was delighted with the chance of winning more victories and also, both Herodian and Dio assert, removing his sons from the decadent atmosphere of Rome. It has been pointed out that the Persian and German wars of Severus Alexander (222–35), Septimius Severus' great-nephew, were also prefaced, according to Herodian, by letters from governors reporting invasions and requesting the presence of the emperor. Although the invasions certainly took place, it seems possible in these cases that Herodian is just using stock phrases to elaborate an actual situation. It is therefore also possible that the British letter may have been engineered by Severus in order to give him an excuse to remove his sons from Rome and subject them to the discipline of military life as Dio and Herodian aver. Dio goes on to record that Severus' intention was to conquer the whole of the island.

The emperors – Severus and his elder son Caracalla – appear to have left Rome in 208, accompanied by members of their family, including Caracalla's younger brother Geta, and a large expeditionary force. The army included most, possibly all, of the praetorian guard and detachments from other legions: Dio states that a large sum of money was also taken. The expedition was marked by an issue of coins showing Severus and Caracalla on horseback accompanied by legionaries and by a coin with, on the reverse, a galley, in which are a flag and standards, indicating a military expedition by sea. Severus travelled quickly in spite of the fact that for most of the journey he was carried in a litter owing to his arthritis, the speed of his arrival together with the size of his army disconcerting the enemy who sued for peace. The envoys were, however, dismissed and Severus continued his preparations. Those put in hand now, or earlier, probably included the rebuilding of the granaries at Corbridge in order to aid with supply up Dere Street, which the evidence of temporary camps informs us was the main route taken by the army, and certainly included the construction of 20 new granaries within the fort at South Shields. This major undertaking at South Shields may in fact be more closely related to the planned occupation of Scotland rather than the campaigns, though the presence of detachments of the Rhine and Danube fleets in Britain at the time emphasises the concentration on transport by sea: this is reinforced by coins issued in 209 with Neptune and Oceanus on the reverse. Severus placed his younger son, Geta, supported by counsellors, in charge of affairs in the Roman part of the island while he and Caracalla took charge of the fighting.

Campaigning probably began in 209. Both surviving literary accounts concentrate more on the marshes, rivers, forests and hills which the Roman army had to cross, than furnish details of the route taken. Study of the surviving marching camps, however, suggests that the army marched up Dere Street and, after negotiating the Forth and the Tay, passed through Strathmore (fig. 29). Two series of camps have been assigned to the Severan period and the earlier camps, 25 hectares in size, appear to go no further than the northern end of Strathmore, the territory probably of the Maeatae. The later series – archaeological excavation has proved the relationship between the two series – are larger (44–52ha), and extend further north, passing round the Mounth and almost reaching the Moray Firth. It seems unlikely that the camps were built in the same season for at Ardoch one partially overlies the other; the two series presumably therefore reflect different campaigns or seasons. The smaller camps are almost exactly half the size of those in the other series. They march up Strathmore in two lines. This may indicate either two armies on the march, or simply a smaller force on a circuitous route.

The mention of the crossing of rivers by Dio and Herodian finds echo in coins. An *as* or small medallion of Caracalla dating to 209 shows a bridge of boats being crossed by soldiers. The location of this bridge is not known, but the Tay at Carpow, where there are defensive enclosures on both sides of the river, is generally the favourite choice for the stretch of water depicted on the coin. Other coins of this year show Caracalla galloping over a fallen barbarian and Caracalla accompanied by legionaries, indicating the campaigning.

The distribution of the few Severan coins found in Scotland, for what it is worth, also emphasises the concentration of army activity in eastern Scotland for with one exception they all lie along Dere Street or on the east coast (fig. 30). Nine coin hoards ending with Commodus or Severus may also point to Roman activity at this time, possibly even the payment of subsidies to the northern tribes, though a variety of reasons could have led to their deposition. Nevertheless the hoards do emphasise Severan activity in this area, not least because following the Falkirk hoard of 1900 coins, collected mainly under Severus but not deposited until twenty years later, there are no more coin hoards in Scotland until the fourth century.

The length of the campaign is not known. Although minor engagements did occur, there were no major battles for the Caledonians and Maeatae employed guerilla tactics, drawing the Romans on and attempting to wear them out. Dio even states that cattle and sheep were deliberately left as a lure. The sources give the impression that the Roman advance was slow but sure for in its progress the army provided causeways through the marshes, bridged rivers, levelled hills and cut paths through the forests. The Romans reportedly suffered heavy losses, 50,000 according to Dio – surely an exaggeration. Severus did not stop until he had almost reached the end of the island, a statement which suggests that more temporary camps remain to be discovered. In spite of the difficulties of coming to grips with the enemy he forced them to accept terms and cede a considerable part of their territory to Rome. Dio records an incident which took place while terms were being discussed, of no relevance here, but incidentally demonstrating that the peace negotiations were conducted by the emperors and their advisers and the Caledonians in front of the two assembled armies. On completion of the peace negotiations Severus and Caracalla returned south. The victory was celebrated by the adoption of the title Britannicus by Severus, Caracalla and Geta in 210. Early coins of this year do not include this title but the award is recorded on coins produced later in the year and victory in Britain was also celebrated on coins in the following year.

The only certain fact about the peace treaty is that the Britons – possibly a term used here to cover both the tribes involved – ceded a considerable part of their

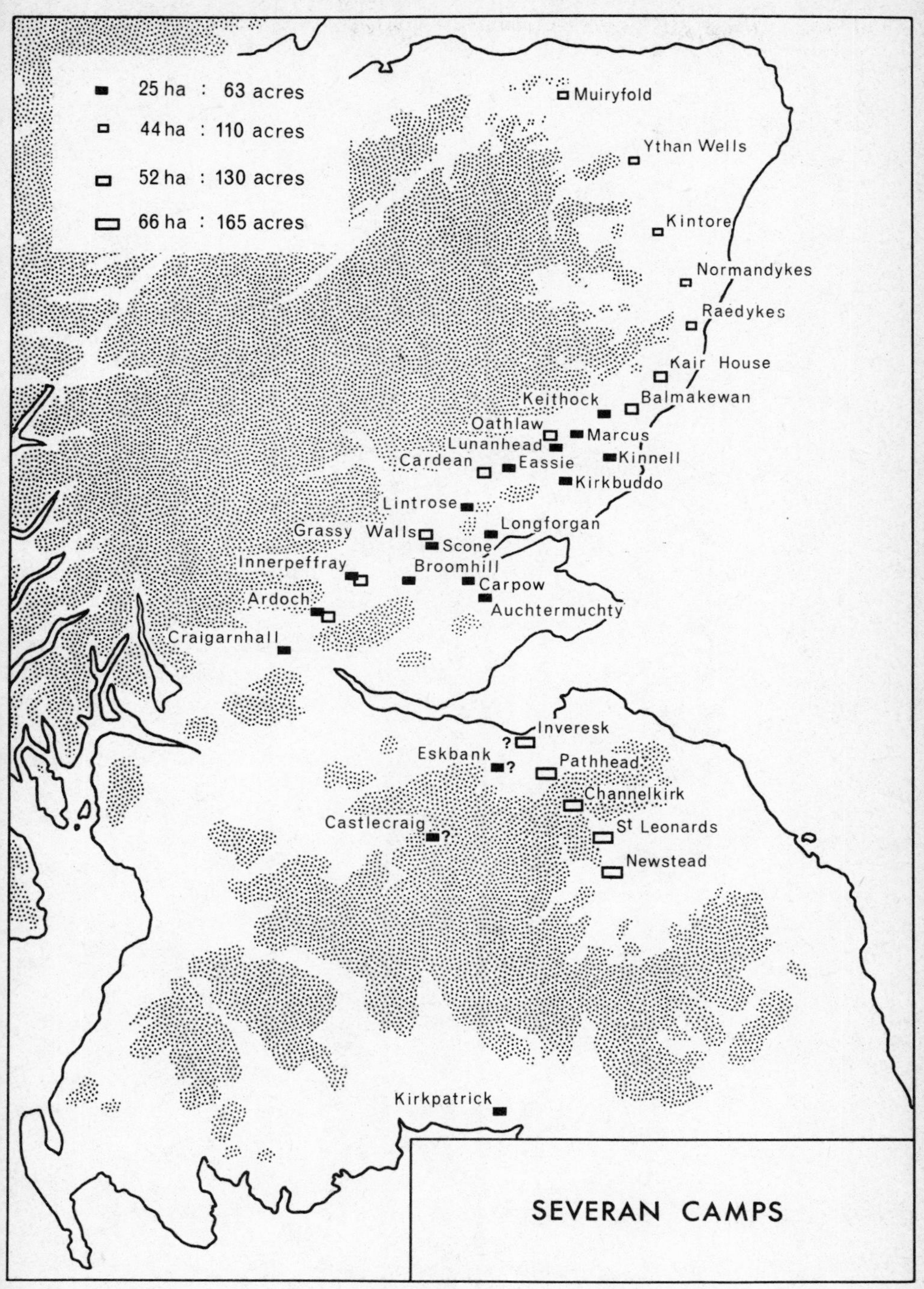

29 *Marching camps in Scotland considered to date to the Severan campaigns*

30 The distribution of Roman finds on non-military sites in Scotland in the Severan period (after Robertson)

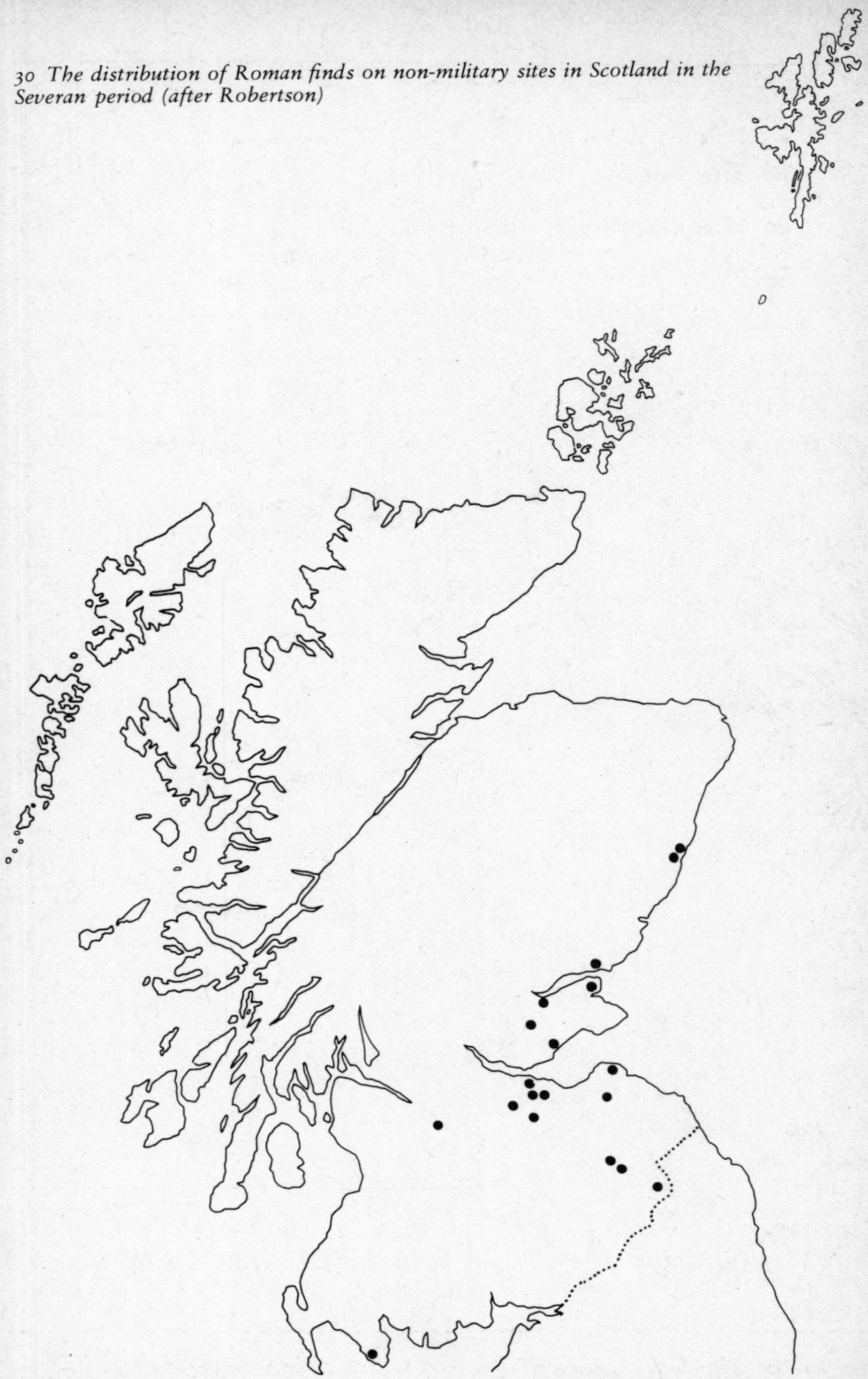

country to Rome. This will presumably have included all or part of Strathmore, once part of the province, but may have also extended to land beyond the Mounth, the territory of the Caledonians. In the third century, in 232, a unit, *Brittones dediticii Alexandriani*, is recorded in Upper Germany. The inclusion of the word *dediticii* in the title suggests that the soldiers were conscripted into the army from recently conquered tribes, such people being officially termed *dediticii*. The most appropriate occasion for the raising of such a unit in Britain at this time would be the extension of the province by Severus in 209. Even though this was not a permanent arrangement, there may well have been time before the abandonment of Roman pretensions so far north for the raising of new units from the new provincials.

In May 210 Severus was at York, for he and Caracalla issued a rescript on 5 May from there. However, that year the Maeatae broke out in revolt. Severus placed Caracalla in charge of the army and issued instructions to the soldiers to kill everyone they met. It is possible that the route taken by this force is reflected in the second series of third century marching camps in Scotland. After the invasion had taken place the Caledonians joined the revolt. Severus now, in spite of his illness, made preparations to join his army, but before he could do so he died at York on 4 February 211. Caracalla now had different priorities. In spite of the fact that he had been co-emperor for thirteen years his first concern would naturally be to return to Rome to ensure a smooth transference of power. It is not surprising therefore that he made peace with the barbarians, gave up the new conquests, abandoning forts, and, together with his brother and mother, returned to Rome with his father's ashes.

Only two forts in Scotland are known to have been occupied at this time (fig. 31). One was Cramond on the Forth. This may have served as a link in the supply chain up the east coast, though there is no definite evidence for this. The other is the legionary base at Carpow on the south shore of the Tay, a little downstream from modern Perth. Here a fortress was constructed, 11 hectares in size. At least two legions, *II Augusta* and *VI Victrix*, helped to build the base and it is possible that the garrison was furnished by these two units. The fortress, with ramparts of turf and gates of stone, contained headquarters building, palace for the commanding officer, and granary all in stone, with timber barrack-blocks.

The exact date of construction of the site is not known, though it has produced coins of the early third century and fragments of monumental building inscriptions. One inscription has been restored to record the titles of Caracalla after he became sole emperor in February 212 when he murdered his brother Geta. Unfortunately there is some controversy surrounding the interpretation of the inscription. There is further evidence to suggest that the occupation of the site may not have been too brief. In one area of the fortress at least there were two phases of building activity. The earlier, possibly temporary, timber buildings were dismantled at about the time that the adjacent stone headquarters and commanding officer's house were erected. The date of commencement of construction work at Carpow is not known. Building may have started as part of the preparations for the campaigns recorded by the literary authorities. On the other hand this would be unusual, if not most difficult in view of the position of the fortress in or on the very edge of Maeatian territory, while the stamped tiles from the site record that *legio VI Victrix* had been awarded the title *Britannica*, which would not have occured until after the proclamation of victory in 209 at the earliest, and more likely 210 or later. On all grounds a date of 210 for the commencement of building is the most likely.

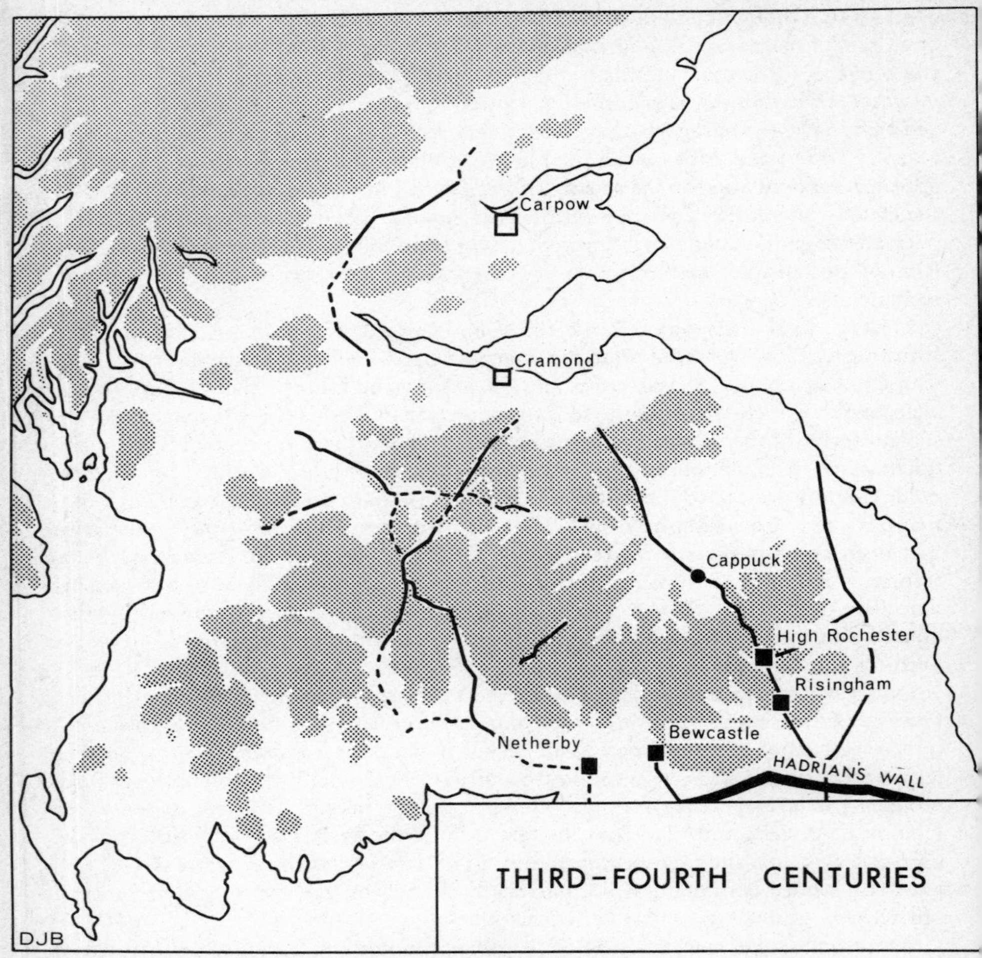

31 North Britain in the third and early fourth centuries

Whatever the date Carpow was certainly abandoned after a very short life and Cramond was presumably given up at the same time.

The reorganisation of the frontier in the late second century

It is now necessary to turn from the literary accounts of warfare in Britain to the archaeological and related material to examine the methods used by Rome to guard and patrol the northern frontier in the late second century and through the third. This evidence comes from a variety of sources, archaeological, epigraphic and documentary, and is piecemeal and sketchy. In broad outline it suggests that in the late second century important modifications were carried out to Hadrian's Wall while the outpost system north of the Wall was extended and strengthened. The effect of these changes appears to have been to reduce the importance of the Wall itself – though not the forts on the barrier – and push the real frontier northwards at least to the Cheviots. The size of the units based in the outpost forts was sufficient to patrol extensive areas north of the Wall, possibly even the whole area formerly within the province.

When the Roman army withdrew from Scotland in the 160s and reoccupied Hadrian's Wall and its hinterland forts the Wall appears to have been put back into commission with the minimum of change. The only important modification would appear to have been the addition of a road, which connected the forts, and was generally positioned between the Wall and the Vallum, though in places it ran along the north mound of the Vallum. Apart from this imposition the Vallum seems to have continued in use as before. The extra, or marginal, mound which can still be seen in places on the south lip of the ditch, between the ditch and the south mound, probably results from cleaning out the ditch at this time. However, there appears to have been no thorough attempt to dig out the rock and soil dumped at regular intervals to create crossings twenty years before. The milecastles and turrets were cleaned out and repaired and the forts regarrisoned. Where evidence survives it suggests that most forts were now occupied by units of similar size and type to those which had evacuated them on the occupation of the Antonine Wall: in one instance, Carvoran, the garrison was apparently the same.

Although the Wall was at first brought back to the state it was in when abandoned changes soon seem to have been made. Some turrets appear to have had short lives. One, 33b Coesike, seems to have had a brief period of reoccupation followed by blocking of the door and abandonment of the site. Some time later, probably in the late second century, or the early third, possibly at the time that Severus' governors carried out their repairs elsewhere, the turret was demolished down to its lowest courses and the recess into the thickness of the Wall built up. The history of other turrets seems to have been similar. The building-up of the recesses may have been necessary in order to make a walk along the top of the Wall safe through the replacement of rotting timber floors by a more substantial platform. In these years many turrets, mainly in the crags sector, were abandoned; most had been superfluous from the very beginning. Elsewhere the abandonment was more selective as if thought was given to the working of the Wall so that redundant turrets were given up while those serving a useful purpose were retained.

Milecastles too were modified, as a result of a more realistic reappraisal of their function. Excavation has revealed that many had either their north or south gate narrowed so that it could only be used for pedestrian traffic, while two (MCs 22 and 36) had their north gates blocked completely. However, only one milecastle, 27 Brunton, across the river from Chesters fort, is known to have been abandoned.

These changes extended to the structures on the Cumbrian Coast. Few milefortlets and towers seem to have been reoccupied in the 160s, though more than was once considered. However, only one of these sites appears to have survived in occupation till the later years of the second century, MF 5 Cardurnock, the largest milefortlet on the Coast, and a fortlet in its own right.

The major rethinking in fort garrisons appears to have been in the 180s, presumably by Ulpius Marcellus. In many cases the units garrisoning the Wall forts in the early third century were different in size and type from those recorded either by inscriptions, or, by implication, in the earlier years of the second century. The most important change was the strengthening of the cavalry component on the Wall. There were now apparently four cavalry units on the Wall line as opposed to two or three under Hadrian while at least seven of the remaining twelve forts now contained mixed units compared with four or five under Hadrian. The result would be to increase the mobility of the Wall garrison. It can be shown that three forts were provided with their new garrisons before the Severan campaigns, and in one case, Chesters, the unit was already in residence under Ulpius Marcellus. It is not impossible therefore that this governor was responsible for the complete overhaul and modification of all the fort garrisons.

These were not the only changes to fort garrisons on Hadrian's Wall. Inscriptions reveal that in the third century the normal garrison of three forts was supplemented by the addition of *numeri*. Four such *numeri* are known, garrisoning the three forts: at Housesteads the *cohors I Tungrorum* was strengthened by the addition of two units, the *cuneus Frisiorum* and the *numerus Hnaudifridi*. The date at which these units arrived is not known but it is not impossible that they were also introduced to the northern frontier by Ulpius Marcellus in the early 180s. It is possible also that Marcellus was responsible for the construction of the fort at Newcastle for recent excavation has suggested that the stone fort here may not have been built before the late second century.

The *numeri* on the Wall had their counterparts in the outpost forts to the north. However, before examining the garrisons of these forts it is necessary to examine the history of the sites from the abandonment of the Antonine system through into the third century. Most surviving archaeological evidence points to the abandonment of forts on and in front of the Antonine Wall in the 160s, *c.*163 being the preferred date. At this time not all forts behind the Wall were abandoned; on the contrary some were retained to serve as outpost forts for Hadrian's Wall. In the west all three Hadrianic outpost forts continued in occupation, or were reoccupied at this time: Birrens, Netherby and Bewcastle. In the east a line of forts appears to have been retained along Dere Street at least as far north as Newstead. There may also have been outposts beyond the Tweed, for several sites on the Antonine Wall have furnished evidence for occupation after the mid 160s. At Castlecary, an important fort on the watershed between the Forth and Clyde basins and apparently occupied at different times by milliary cohorts, the evidence comes in the form of an inscription. This altar, dedicated to Mercury, records the erection of a shrine or temple and a statuette by soldiers of *legio* VI Victrix who were citizens of Italy and Noricum. The most straightforward way in which these soldiers could have entered a British legion was by transfer from *legio II Italica*, raised in 165, almost certainly practically entirely in Italy, the normal area at this time for the recruitment of new legions. The inscription would have been erected within twenty-five years of 165, probably in the latter half of this period. The presence of a military establishment here receives some support from a sherd of late second-century samian ware, the only fragment of this date found on a military site north of Newstead. The other archaeological evidence for a military presence on the Forth-Clyde isthmus in the late second century is numismatic: two unstratified coins from former Antonine Wall forts, Mumrills and Kirkintilloch. No military structure of late second-century date is known at any of these sites.

The invasion of the early 180s seems to have resulted in a reappraisal of the outpost system. In the west Birrens appears to have been abandoned in the 180s and in the east Newstead: any outposts further north were presumably withdrawn at the same time if not before (fig. 31). Newstead may have been reoccupied briefly in the early third century when Roman armies were operating in Scotland, but otherwise the outpost system was now based upon the four forts at Netherby, Bewcastle, Risingham and High Rochester. These were not large forts – they varied in size from 1.6 to 2.4 hectares – but they appear to have been the bases for large forces, probably from the 180s into the third, possibly even fourth, century. Three units are attested at each of the eastern outpost forts: a 1,000-strong mixed unit, a *numerus* and a detachment of scouts. The garrisons of the western forts are not so clearly known, but Netherby, and probably also Bewcastle, was garrisoned by a thousand strong mixed cohort in the third century. According to the Antonine Itinerary the Roman name for Netherby was *Castra exploratorum*, which is certainly suggestive in relation to the garrison of the eastern outpost forts. Birrens, abandoned probably in the late 180s, was also the base for a thousand strong mixed unit in the second century. The total strength of the outpost forts in the third century will have been about 5,000 men, the equivalent in manpower of a legion.

The forts which were the nominal homes of these units were, in each instance, too small to hold even the milliary cohort alone, so it follows that many soldiers from the cohorts, *numeri* and *exploratores* must have been outposted elsewhere. Only one hint survives concerning the possible location of such an outpost. Two altars found at Jedburgh Abbey were dedicated by soldiers from the cohort and the *numerus* from High Rochester in the third century: it is possible that the stones were carried from Cappuck, 3km to the east, by the medieval masons.

The main duties of all the soldiers based in the outpost forts will have included long-range patrolling and surveillance of the tribes to the north of Hadrian's Wall as well as the protection of the province from attack. Documents from elsewhere in the empire demonstrate that such patrols could range widely in the pursuit of their duties. On the Eastern frontier of the empire one outpost, admittedly not the same as a mobile patrol, was permanently outstationed 250km from its parent unit at Dura Europos. If this was transferred to the north British frontier, it is almost exactly the distance from High Rochester to Stracathro, and suggests that Roman soldiers could have maintained watch over the whole of the territory of the former province north of Hadrian's Wall.

It has been suggested that the Ravenna Cosmography contained reference to places, *loca*, tribal meeting places, supervised by the army. However, it is possible that these are simply places north of Hadrian's Wall which did not fit into any other of the Cosmographer's categories. Nevertheless, it is probable, on the basis of parallels with other frontiers, that the army did closely supervise the activities of the tribes north of the Wall after the abandonment of the Antonine system. Cassius Dio records the arrangement made by the Roman authorities to control the tribes north of the Danube in the late second century when the Emperor Commodus (180–192) gave up the plans formulated by his father, Marcus Aurelius, to incorporate these peoples into the empire. Treaties defined the boundaries of the tribes, the size of the tribute to be paid to Rome and the tribal assemblies. The Marcomanni, for example, had to pay an annual tribute of corn and also supply weapons and soldiers, though rather less than the Quadi whose contribution was fixed at 15,000 men. They were allowed to assemble once a month under the supervision of a Roman centurion and were forbidden to make war on certain neighbouring tribes. The Buri and other tribes were forbidden to settle within 400 stades of the border of the province of Dacia. It seems probable that similar arrangements, though presumably not the restrictions on settlement, were introduced on the northern frontier as the army withdrew in the 160s.

The system of control established in the late second century, in part at least apparently as early as the 160s, seems to have lasted well into the fourth century. The historian Ammianus Marcellinus writing at that time records that in the Barbarian Conspiracy of 367 the *areani* (a term best interpreted as frontier scouts) had been bribed by the barbarian tribes to reveal the Roman positions to them. Ammianus asserts that the *areani* had been established in early times, and it seems possible that they are the descendants of the *exploratores*, and perhaps other units, placed in the outposts forts in the second and third centuries. Archaeological evidence supports the supposition arising from this, namely that the outpost forts continued in occupation into the fourth century.

Brochs, duns and souterrains

Before we move finally into the third century it is necessary to consider the intrusion of certain dwellings – brochs, duns and souterrains – more usually found north of the Forth-Clyde line, into southern Scotland. Brochs originated in the far north of Scotland in the second century BC, possible earlier. Their distribution is concentrated in the northern isles and the counties of Caithness and Sutherland, but spreading down the west coast to Skye and across to the Outer Hebrides. No brochs are known between the Firths of Moray and Tay, with the exception of three in the north shore of the Tay, but several, about a dozen, appear further south (fig. 33). Three of these southern brochs have been excavated. All have produced Roman artefacts: Torwoodlee in Tweedale samian and coarse pottery, glass, part of a glass armlet, a quern; Leckie in the Forth valley samian ware, glass, iron sword blade, quern, plough fragment, carbonised grain, sheep shears, brooch, beads, glass armlets, pins and finger rings; and at Buchlyvie a few miles west of Leckie, fragments of samian, coarse pottery, amphorae, mortaria and glass, a coin, four querns, a sickle blade, carbonised grain, whorls, pins and finger rings, brooches, lead ingots and iron slag. There is ample evidence here of contact with the Roman world; evidence too of farming communities. The farmers who lived in the brochs were not the first settlers on the site, for in all cases the broch succeeded a pre-existing structure. This is clearest at Buchlyvie where the stone tower followed a round timber house with no significant break in the occupation of the site. The occurrence of mid-second-century artefacts within the occupation levels at Torwoodlee and Leckie demonstrates that both were occupied in or after the Antonine period: at the former site pottery and glass were found beneath the broch wall. The occupation of both these brochs ended in destruction, at Torwoodlee apparently after only a short life.

The brochs probably entered southern Scotland from the west rather than the north: certainly the dun came from this direction. Two excavated duns, Castle Hill Wood in the valley of the Forth and Stanhope in Tweeddale, have produced Roman objects of second century date, including a brooch, glass and querns.

The final introduction to southern Scotland was the souterrain. This was an underground, or partially underground, passage which led off from a surface dwelling. Souterrains have been found attached to both timber and stone houses. Their function is uncertain and various possibilities have been suggested: store houses, byres, refuges, and temples. On the whole the former interpretation seems to be the best. Roman artefacts, usually of second or third century date, have been found in some souterrains in southern Scotland and one or two examples incorporated Roman stones. The main areas of distribution of souterrains in Scotland are Angus, Aberdeenshire and Caithness/Sutherland, though they also occur in the northern isles, Ireland, Cornwall and on the continent. They presumably spread south from Fife and Angus; a recently excavated example in this area, Newmill in Perthshire, was probably constructed in the first century AD and

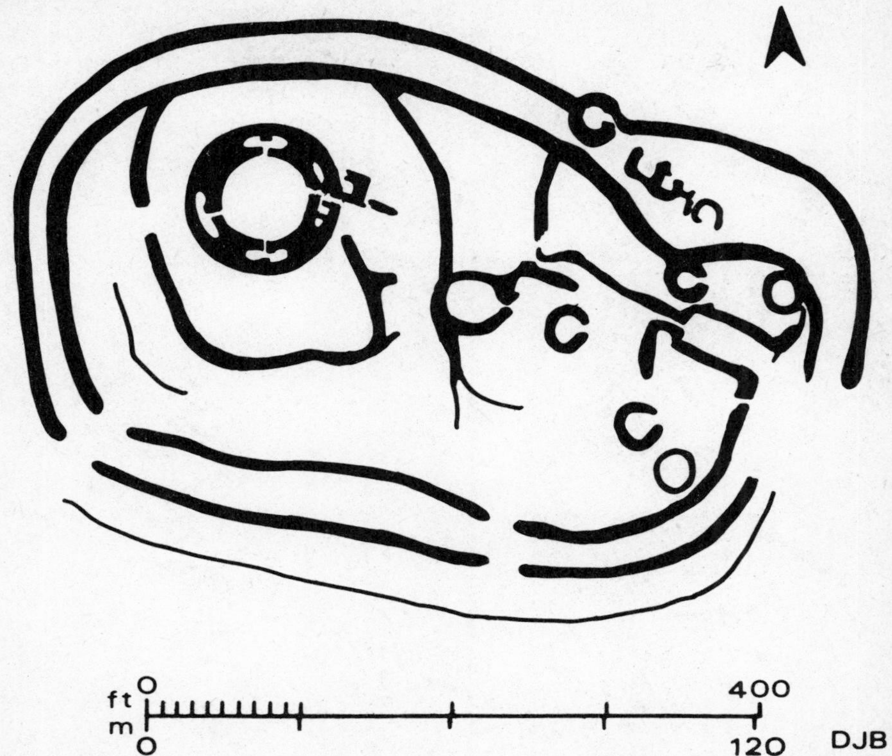

32 The broch and fort at Edinshall, Berwickshire (after RCAHMS*). The sequence appears to be: fort; broch, which lies in the W part of the enclosure; open (Romano-British?) settlement overlying the E part of the fort*

abandoned in the late second or early third century, though the site continued in occupation for several centuries.

The distribution of all these three structures in southern Scotland is similar. On the east they reach as far south as the Tweed, with several examples of brochs and souterrains on the north bank, but none on the south. In the west the brochs and duns extend further south, for their distribution is along the coast to Luce Bay, with a single outlier in Wigtown Bay to the east. It may or may not be significant that this pattern matches closely the spread of heavy armlets, snake bracelets and Donside terrets, whose manufacture and centre of distribution was clearly in Aberdeenshire. These objects, probably mainly in the second century AD, trickled down into southern Scotland though, interestingly, they stopped at the Tweed, with the exception of four outliers, two on the Tyne (fig. 34).

Although the distribution patterns of the structures and objects in southern Scotland may be similar, and fall within the same general period, they do not all have the same point of origin. The souterrains presumably spread south from Angus and Fife, while the metal objects emanated from north-east Scotland. The duns will have entered southern Scotland from the west, and it seems possible that the brochs moved in the same direction. It seems unlikely therefore that a single influence was at work. It is difficult to use the appearance of the structures and

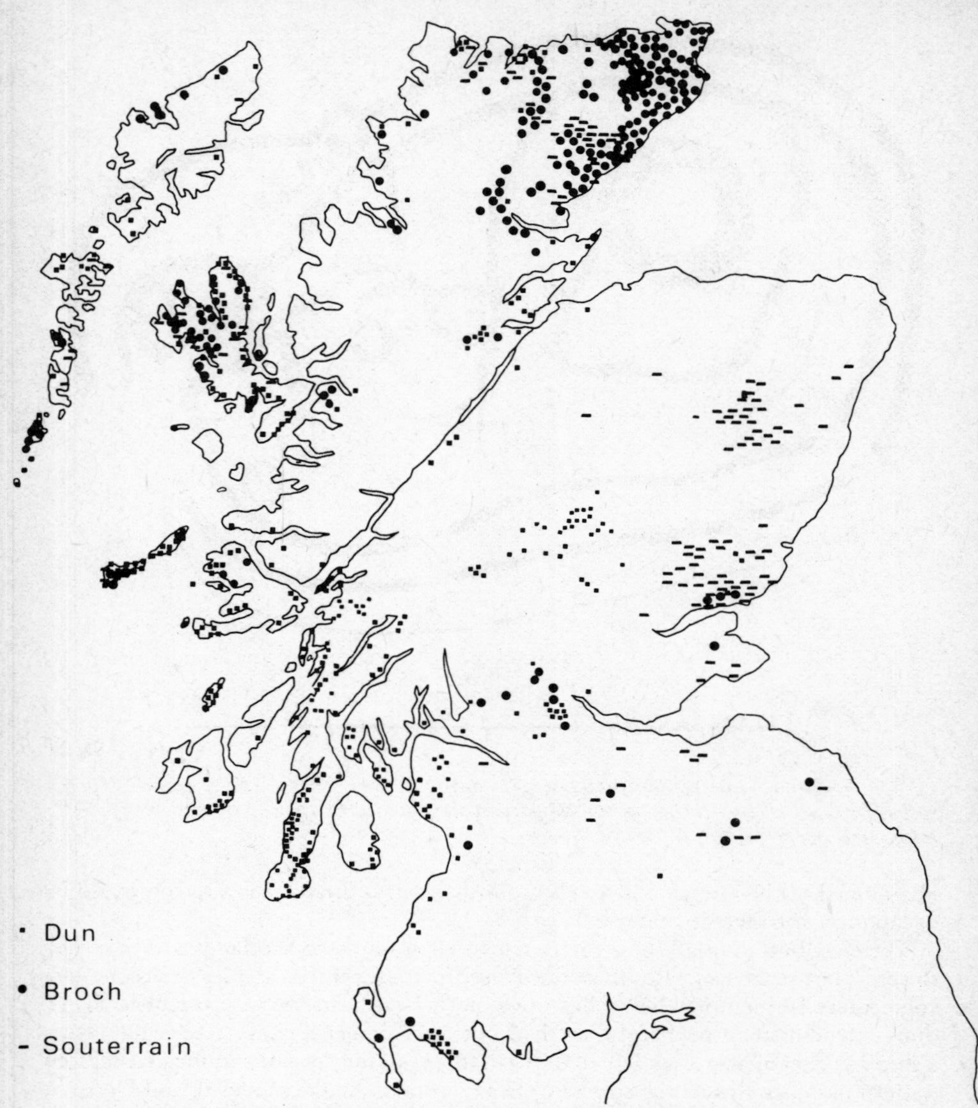

33 The distribution of brochs, duns and souterrains in north Britain

metalwork south of the Forth to support the hypothesis that they reflect an extension of Caledonian power, or at least influence, in the second century. The situation is complicated by the appearance of so much Roman material in the brochs and duns. It would appear that the inhabitants of these sites had close contacts with the Roman world and it seems more probable that the objects were gained through trade than plunder.

The people of the land between the Tweed and the Forth, former provincial territory, were, it seems, subject to influences from the south, north and west, probably over a period of years. However, when the archaeological material can be

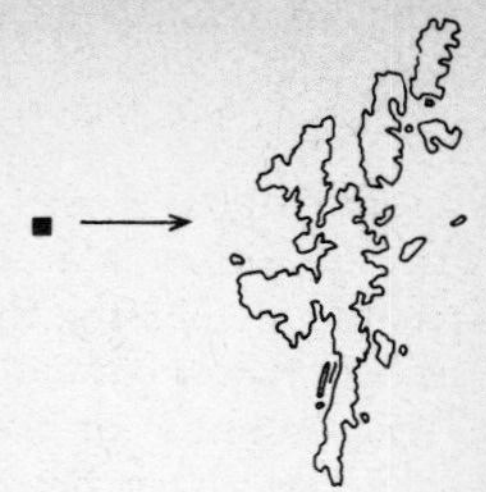

● MASSIVE ARMLETS

◆ SNAKE BRACELETS

■ 'DONSIDE' TERRETS

34 *The distribution of armlets, snake bracelets and 'Donside' terrets in north Britain*

closely dated most falls within the second half of the second century. For part of that period this area was, of course, part of the empire. But in the late second century, when the Roman army in Britain and the Roman empire was in turmoil, the army lost control over events in the north on at least two occasions. It may have been on either or both of these occasions, in the early 180s and the late 190s, that these southern brochs, duns and souterrains were erected and the metalwork trickled south. The new dwellings certainly seem to have been shortlived for no broch, dun nor souterrain has produced Roman artefacts of a date later than the second century. This may reflect the increased Roman control over southern Scotland from the Severan period through the third century, as seemingly recorded in the documentary sources. However, this is only a partial answer, and possibly not the correct one. The range of Roman objects found within the brochs is considerable. Buchlyvie and Leckie have each produced more finds than nearly any other native settlement in Scotland, the nearest comparison in range and number of objects being at Traprain Law. Indeed the wealth of Roman material at these two brochs is such as to hint that they were occupied while Roman forces still resided in Scotland, though it is difficult to see a context for their construction at such a time. Clearly in the present state of knowledge any definitive statement concerning the reasons and date of the construction of brochs, duns and souterrains in southern Scotland– and the entry of northern metalwork into this area – would be more than usually foolhardy.

The third century

The establishment of the system of supervision over the northern frontier in the later second century heralded an era of peace in the third. No war is known to have taken place on the north British frontier from that of Severus and Caracalla in 208–11 until the campaign of Constantius Chlorus against the Picts in 306. The reasons for this century of peace are not known. Certainly it cannot be claimed that the measures taken to control the frontier alone were responsible for they were the same as those that had not prevented the invasion of the early 180s nor the troubles of the late 190s. Perhaps events were moving in a cyclical manner: a century of disturbed conditions in north Britain was followed by a century of relative peace, a phenomenon which can be observed in other areas and at other times.

The Roman army of the early third century did not, of course, appreciate what was to come. They no doubt continued to train and prepare for war as they had done for centuries, so that, in the words of Josephus, their exercises were bloodless battles and their battles bloody exercises. Many of the training routines and exercises are known and there also survives part of the speech of the Emperor Hadrian (117–138) in which he commented on the military displays of certain units which he had just witnessed. No such evidence survives in Britain, though evidence of a different nature is preserved. A number of training areas in north Britain have been postulated. Two in particular are more certain than the others. Around the abandoned pre-Roman hill fort on Woden Law in Roxburghshire, immediately beside Dere Street, lie three lines of ramparts and ditches which have been interpreted as practice Roman siege works. More spectacular are the practice camps on either side of the long abandoned hill fort at Burnswark in Dumfriesshire, overlooking the road up Annandale (pl. 2). This seems to have been a training area for the army of north Britain. On top of the remains of the three south entrances of the hill fort targets were laid out for the soldiers to fire at. The missiles were arrows, ballista balls and sling shot. The latter are especially interesting, for they are made of lead and are thus a type of shot which went out of use elsewhere in the western provinces of the empire in the mid-first century. As many as 133 lead shot have been recovered from Burnswark and 28 from other military bases in north Britain: Housesteads, Birdoswald, Chesterholm, Corbridge and Ambleside. It would appear probable that troops came up from these sites to train at Burnswark. The date of use of Burnswark as a training area cannot be precisely determined. One practice camp, the southern, partly overlies the remains of an Antonine fortlet and the silting pattern of the fortlet ditch suggests that some time had elapsed between its construction and its infilling by the rampart of the camp. All the pottery from the site dates to the second century and the lead sling bullet from Birrens was found in a mid-second century layer. But two of the lead bullets, those from Chesterholm and Housesteads, came from levels tentatively dated to the third century, so it seems possible that the use of Burnswark as a Roman army training area may have continued from the mid-second century for some decades. It is not surprising therefore that traces of semi-permanent occupation have been discovered in one of the camps.

While the army, into the third century, no doubt continued training and patrolling, it also improved the facilities in its base forts as if realising that the days of large-scale troop movements were over. Many inscriptions record the maintenance of the fort or the improvement of its defences. Some inscriptions clearly state that rebuilding was necessary because the previous buildings had fallen down through old age. Thus in 205/7 at Risingham the south gate, with its walls, was restored from ground level because it had fallen in through age, while in 221 a similarly worded inscription records the restoration of an unnamed building at Chesters and another, a granary at Greatchesters in 225. This process continued throughout the third century being recorded on three other inscriptions, from Lanchester, where the headquarters and armoury was rebuilt in 238–44, Lancaster, where the baths were restored in 262/6 and in a slightly different formula at Birdoswald at the end of the century.

Other inscriptions adopt a variant wording: the building was built or restored from the ground level, or from its foundations. Thus baths were built at Chester-le-Street in 216 and at Lanchester in 238/44, while the *ballistaria*, or artillery platforms, were erected at High Rochester in 220 and restored 225/35 – perhaps a different platform. An inscription from Chesterholm specifically states that the (south) gate with its towers was restored from its foundations in 223. There is no reason to doubt the veracity of the carvers of these inscriptions. The Romans could be remarkably frank about the reasons for restoring buildings. Milestones from Cyrene record the restoration of a road which had been damaged during the Jewish revolt which broke out there in 115 while late second century inscriptions from Lower Pannonia (modern Hungary) state that the new defences were being constructed to afford better protection against bandits.

It is possible that some of the buildings which had collapsed through old age or were restored from the ground had previously lain abandoned for some years. But while that might be the case with Risingham in 205/7 it is unlikely, for example, that Greatchesters was abandoned prior to 225, or Chesterholm before 223. It may be that while certain inscriptions are recording the re-occupation of some forts or the restoration of parts of others, abandoned for perfectly acceptable reasons, others are bearing witness to the general round of maintenance carried out by the Roman army engineers.

The early third century saw not only the maintenance of existing defences and buildings but the improvement of facilities for the soldiers. Already under Commodus (180–92) an aqueduct had been constructed at Chesters. In 216 not only was the bath-house at Chester-le-Street rebuilt but a new aqueduct was laid as well and one for South Shields followed in 222. The soldiers may not altogether have approved of some of the facilities for they included the erection of a drill hall at Netherby.

This building activity, as recorded by inscriptions, continued unabated through the 220s. Thereafter it slowed in the 230s with a single later record at Lancaster in the 260s. This parallels the decline in the erection of inscriptions throughout the empire in the third century. However, it also parallels another development, the abandonment, partially or complete, of many forts in northern England in the late third century. There is considerable evidence, both literary and archaeological, for this abandonment. The 'literary' evidence lies in the pages of the *Notitia Dignitatum*. This document, probably prepared at the beginning of the fifth century, records the officials of the empire, listing in particular army units together with the rank of their commanding officer. In Britain there is a clear distinction between the names of the units on Hadrian's Wall and those behind the Wall (fig. 35). The former, with one exception, retain the form of titles found in the early empire and indeed many of the units were attested in these forts in the late second or third century. The latter, mainly, have the titles introduced in the late empire and in many cases these units replaced known third-century garrisons. It seems probable that the earlier units were withdrawn some time during the course of the third century, probably in the second half, while the new units arrived probably in the first quarter of the fourth century. Their distribution, generally on the two main roads leading north from York up the east coast and over Stainmore, suggests that their purpose was to act as a mobile reserve for the troops on the Wall.

Archaeology supports the suggestion that some forts in northern England were abandoned in the late third and early fourth centuries. However, recent excavations have emphasised that the pattern was not the same everywhere. Some forts appear to have been completely abandoned; others continued to be occupied but with a considerably reduced garrison; a third group continued in occupation seemingly at the same strength as before. Thus on Hadrian's Wall Housesteads seems to have been maintained with a full garrison through the third century, new buildings being constructed in the rampart backing apparently in an attempt to use all available space within the fort, while in the early fourth some or all of the barrack-blocks were rebuilt to a completely new design (fig. 36). At the eastern end of the Wall space was apparently not at a premium at Wallsend in the third century; and when, in the early fourth, the barrack-blocks were rebuilt to a new plan, not all the fort interior was utilised (fig. 37). Halton Chesters and Rudchester exhibit a different history. Here no barrack-blocks were built in the early fourth century; on the contrary, much of the area of the forts appears to have been abandoned for many years until buildings of a different form of construction were erected in the later fourth century. Yet the forts retained the same garrisons in the *Notitia Dignitatum* as they had in the early third century. This suggests that while the strength of the units was allowed to fall to minimal levels they were not permitted to die, but continued throughout the third and fourth centuries to be reinvigorated in the 360s. At South Shields, beyond the eastern end of the Wall, this process seems to have gone a stage further for archaeological excavations have suggested that the fort was abandoned in the late third and early fourth centuries while the *Notitia Dignitatum*

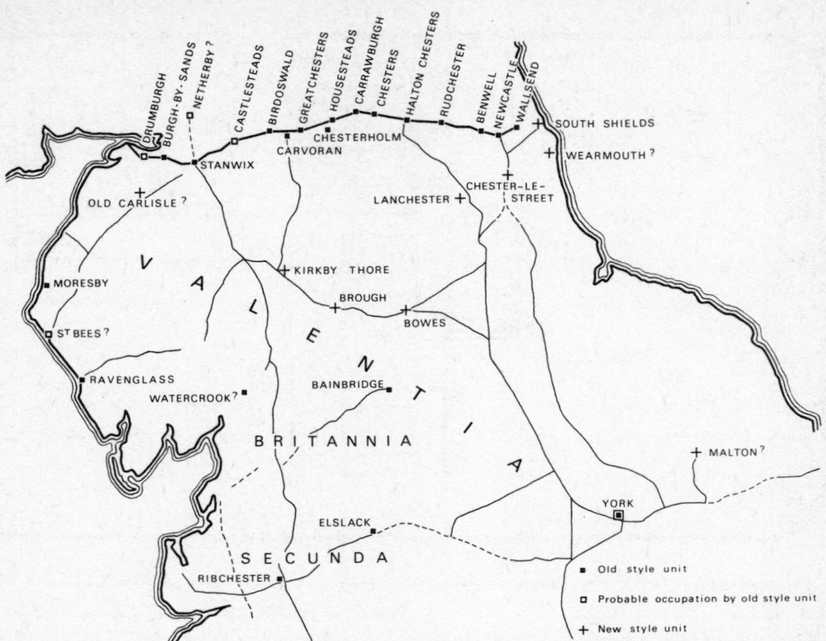

35 Forts in northern England listed in the Notitia Dignitatum. *A closed square denotes an old-style unit, an open square the probable site of such a unit, a cross a new-style unit. Forts considered, on archaeological evidence, to be occupied at the end of the fourth century are omitted*

records that the fort was later garrisoned by one of the new types of unit, the *numerus barcariorum*.

The differing history of these forts no doubt reflects changed conditions on the northern frontier in the third and fourth centuries. The strength of the garrisons of the outpost forts in particular, combined with the peaceful conditions apparently pertaining on the frontier during the third century, led to the withdrawal of units from many of the hinterland forts and the scaling down of the garrisons of certain forts on the Wall line. However, where strong garrisons were required these seem to have been maintained. Housesteads was such a fort, while in the west forts along the Cumbrian Coast continued to be occupied, probably to protect the west coast against raids from Ireland.

The peace of the third century appears to have led to the growth of a flourishing civil population. Little can be said concerning the rural native settlements north of the Wall, in addition to that discussed above, not least because so few have produced third- or fourth-century artefacts: this gap is a major problem in determining the relationship between Roman and native in the north at this time. Our knowledge of settlements south of the Wall is not much better. In the western zone of the hinterland the construction of roads aided the growth of the settlements in their vicinity, such farms no doubt profiting from the presence of the lucrative military market. Some of these farms, such as Ewe Close and Crosby Garret in Westmorland, grew to a considerable size, being surrounded by extensive field systems. Aerial photography in the southern part of the Solway basin has recently

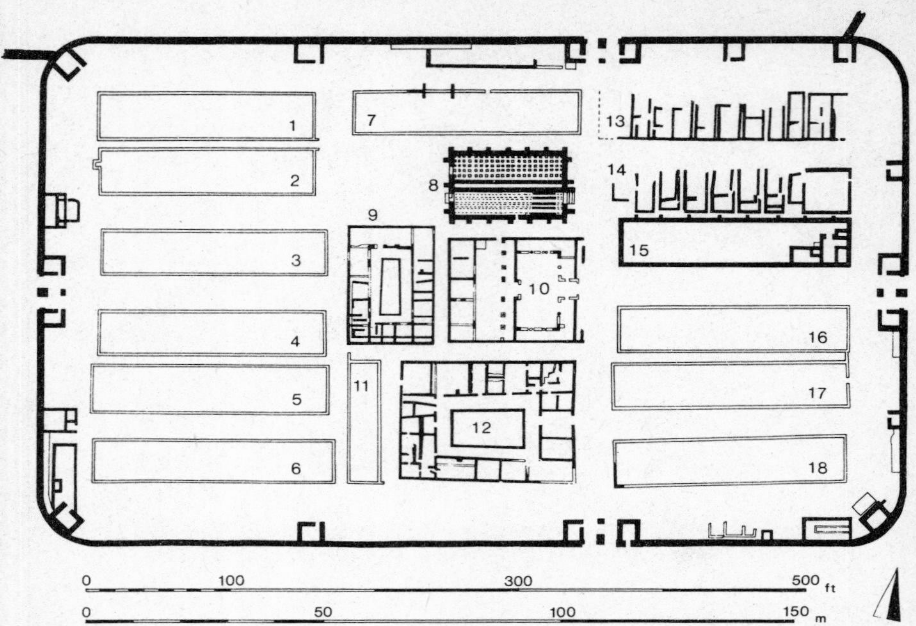

36 The fort at Housesteads in the early fourth century. 10 headquarters building, 12 commanding officer's house, 9 hospital, 8 granaries, 13 and 14 barrack-blocks, 15 ?store-house with baths at east end. The other buildings have not been re-excavated. (Drawn by C.M. Daniels)

emphasised the considerable number of settlements in this area, many associated with field systems, and while most are undated many no doubt are of the Roman period. There seems, on the other hand, to be rather fewer settlements on the north shore of the Solway, beyond the frontier. Taken at face value this would appear to support the view that the construction of the Wall aided the economic exploitation of the land to the south, but many factors must be taken into account in assessing this evidence and it is too soon to do more than note the possibility.

Civil settlements outside forts also continued to expand. On the Wall houses were allowed to encroach on the Vallum and spread round the forts, being constructed immediately outside fort gates. Some settlements grew to be even larger than the adjacent fort. Many must have acquired self-governing rights, though little is known of this. In addition to the inscription from Carriden on the Antonine Wall recording the existence of a *vicus* with self-governing powers there, such records survive only at Housesteads on the Wall and Old Carlisle in the western hinterland, while from Chesterholm comes a dedication erected by the *vicani Vindolandenses*. If settlements such as these were given powers to administer their own affairs, it may be presumed that similar authority was granted to the towns of Carlisle and Corbridge. Indeed the former may have been created a *civitas* in the third century, for the *civitas Carvetiorum* was then formed in the Eden valley (fig. 28). If not centred on Carlisle, then it seems almost certain that this town, the largest in the area, was established as a *civitas* in its own right. Corbridge too grew to a substantial town of about 12 hectares with walls, though it still remained a garrison town with legionaries being quartered immediately by its very centre.

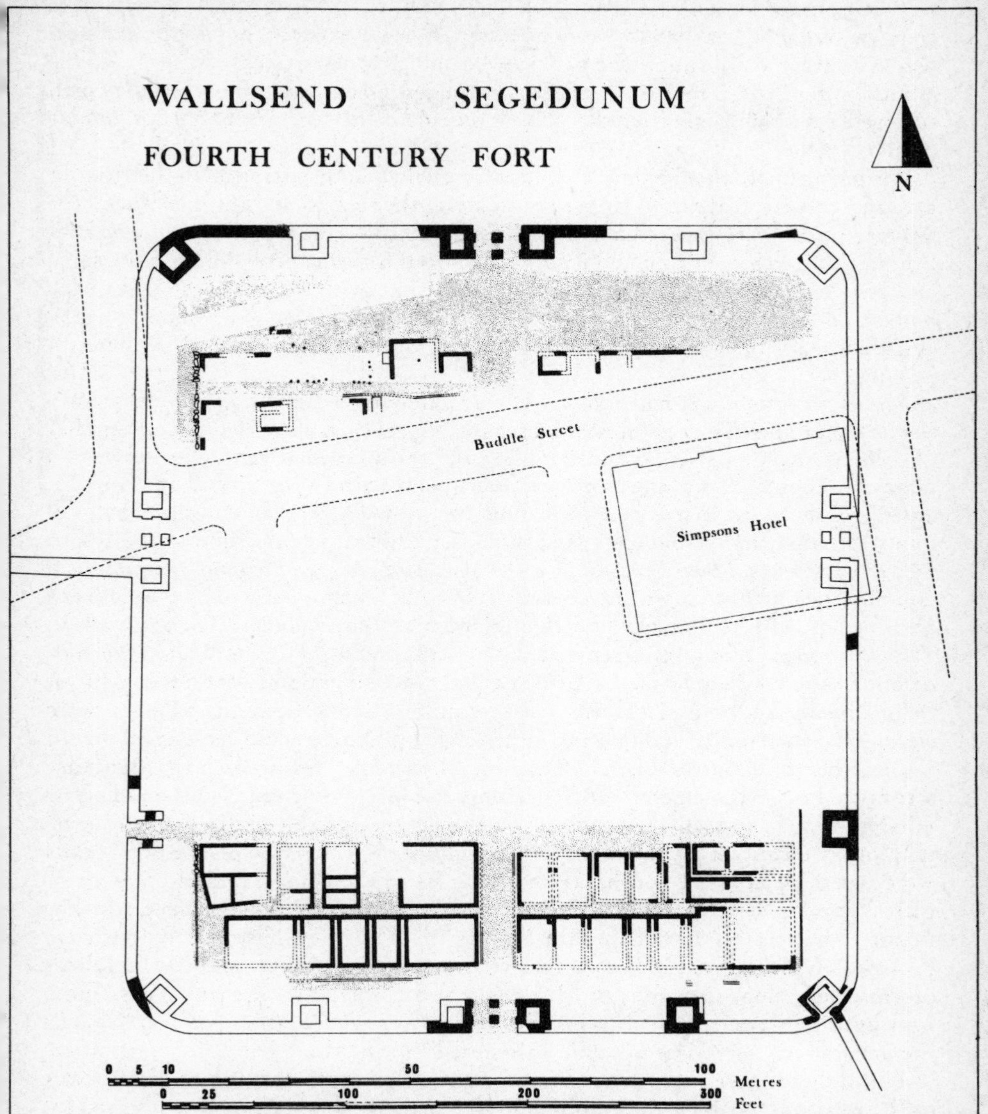

37 The fort at Wallsend in the early fourth century showing the new style barracks. (Drawn by C.M. Daniels)

There is a hint also at other administrative divisions in northern England: an inscription from the South Tyne valley points to the existence of the *curia Textoverdorum*, an otherwise unknown sept or administrative unit of the Brigantes, or just possibly the Votadini.

Sometimes it seems possible that the running down of the fort had an effect on the adjacent civil settlement. Thus the *vicus* at Chesterholm is now considered to have been abandoned in the 270s, possibly as a result of a similar event in the fort (pl. 12).

However, other settlements acquired a life of their own. What little evidence there is suggests that South Shields was not deserted by its townsfolk though the garrison was withdrawn: no doubt, the town owed much to its strategic position at the mouth of the Tyne. There is a hint too that the settlement at Cramond on the Forth survived for some time after the abandonment of the fort, probably for similar reasons.

It is unfortunate that so little evidence for civilian administration in the frontier area survives for Britain. In Upper Germany in the second and third centuries the military forces were reduced to a thin band stationed on the frontier, while the land behind was given over to civilian administration. It seems probable that the same process was happening in Britain at the same time, with the abandonment of the hinterland forts and the establishment of a *civitas* in the Eden valley and, one may confidently assume, another based on Corbridge, though detailed evidence is lacking.

The civil settlements had mostly, it may safely be assumed, started as shanty towns containing the dwellings of merchants and the unofficial wives and families of soldiers: Roman soldiers until at least the third century were not allowed to marry but there was nothing to prevent them contracting an unofficial union with a native woman, marrying her according to local custom, and inscriptions demonstrate that many soldiers availed themselves of this opportunity. Their sons were a valuable source of recruits for the army, which relied primarily upon local volunteers, from both town and country. This is best demonstrated by the career of Nectovelius, a Brigantian from north England who joined a unit raised originally in Thrace (modern Bulgaria), stationed at Mumrills on the Antonine Wall in the mid-second century, where he died. During the later second and third centuries many of these houses, shops and taverns were rebuilt in stone, and the villages were augmented by temples and possibly other civic buildings, while cemeteries spread beyond their boundaries (pl. 12). Sometimes the village grew to such an extent that it sprawled over the cemeteries of earlier inhabitants. While much of the life of the inhabitants of these villages centred on the activity of the soldiers in the forts, religious dedications in particular point to influences from elsewhere. Roman gods were worshipped in the fort and in the temples of the village, and in many cases these were equated with local Celtic gods. Foreign gods came from Germany, imported by soldiers drafted into the army of the Wall. New Eastern religions were brought by officers or soldiers transferred across the empire, and in the fourth century the potent mysteries of Mithraism and Christianity arrived. These must have added an element of variety to the households where father and son through the generations served in the unit garrisoned 'up the road'.

Throughout these years of peace, and on into the fourth century, little is known of the relations between the empire and its northern neighbours, as witnessed by artefacts. Few coins drifted north after the time of Severus. The Falkirk hoard of nearly 2000 coins buried in or soon after 230, though mainly collected in the Severan period, was the last known hoard of Roman coins in Scotland until the end of the century. Third century Roman pottery is scarce in barbary, but neither is it plentiful in the frontier installations. Its rarity in the north may accordingly reflect supply rather than demand. The small number of other artefacts cannot be closely dated and could fall within either the third or the fourth century: nevertheless these do not substantially affect the prevailing pattern.

Little can be said about life at, or the cultural affinities of, most settlements in southern Scotland in addition to that discussed above. However, the situation at

38 The distribution of Roman finds on non-military sites in Scotland in the late third and fourth centuries (after Robertson)

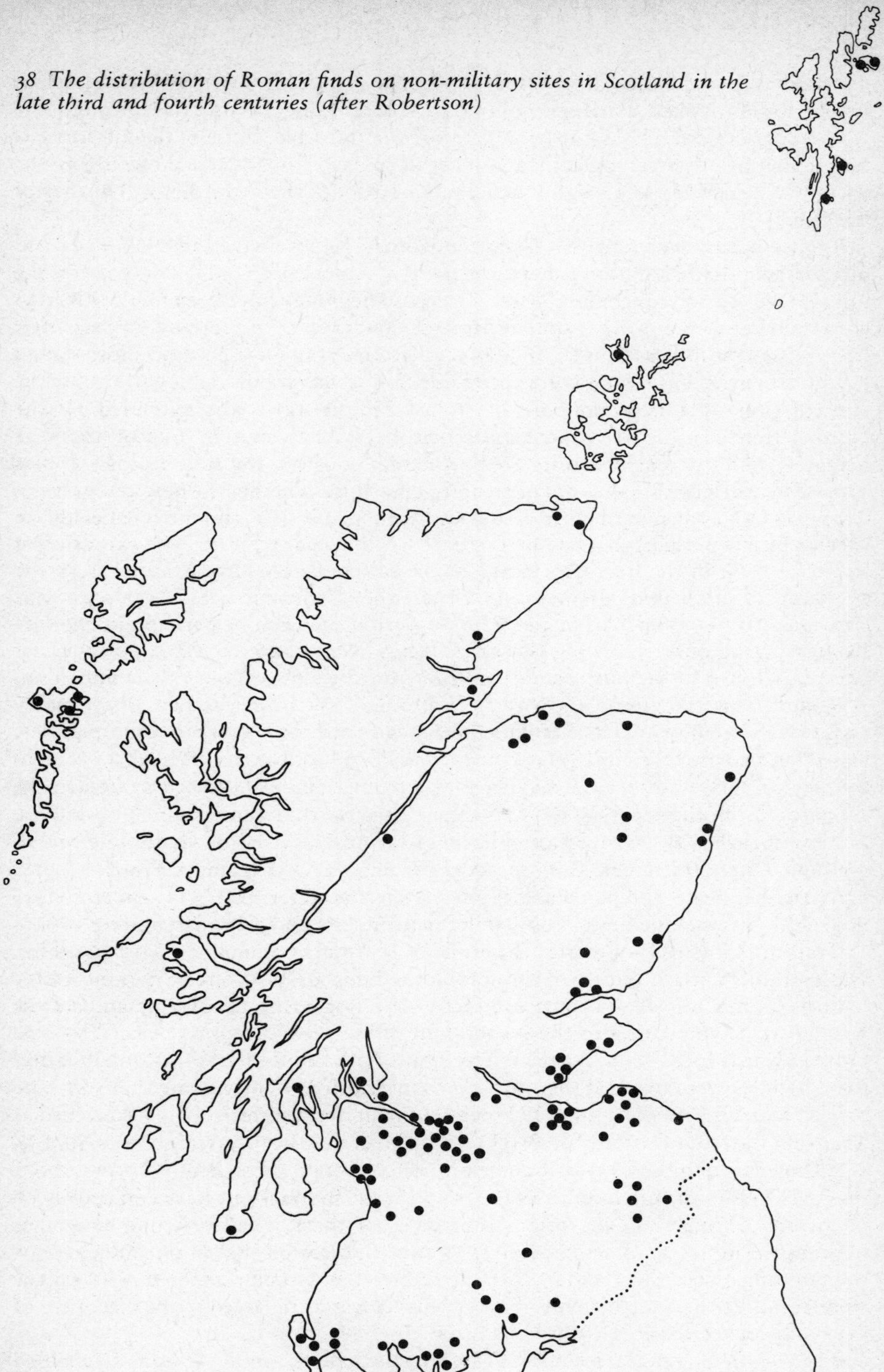

Traprain Law was very different. It is the only native site in southern Scotland which has furnished evidence not only of continuing occupation through the Roman period, but also occupation on a substantial scale. Little of the hill fort has been examined archaeologically and most of this work was carried out before the Second World War. As a result much doubt surrounds the chronological history of the site.

Traprain Law was a town. When the Roman forces arrived in the area it had already acquired a lengthy history, for there is evidence for human activity on the hill top over 2,000 years before AD80. The settlement may have been first fortified at the same time as many other similar, though smaller, sites in Scotland, in the earlier half of the first millennium BC. The first enclosure may have been no more than 4 hectares in area, but if so it seems probable that it was soon doubled in size by the construction of a new rampart of stone. This in turn was extended by the construction of a further stone rampart probably enclosing an area of about 12 hectares. The town achieved its greatest extent at about the time Roman armies arrived in north Britain. It is not possible to determine whether the new extension to Traprain Law took place before or after the Roman advance, though what evidence there is points perhaps to a late first or early second century date. The extension at this time took in the northern flanks of the hill and may have resulted from the pressure of increased population within the settlement. The rampart was subsequently repaired within the Roman period and again, perhaps in the late Roman period or in following centuries. It has been suggested that Traprain Law was abandoned in the late second and early third centuries, but this is uncertain.

Roman material found its way to Traprain Law from the late first century onwards. Samian ware from Gaul has been unearthed at the town in some quantity, as well as provincial pottery and crude locally produced wares. While late fourth-century pottery is absent the sequence of Roman coins continues through to the Emperor Honorius (395–423). The other objects from the site include knives, sickles, spearheads, bronze horse harness fittings, as well as items relating to clothing – dress fasteners, dragonesque, pennanular and trumpet brooches, pins and glass bangles – and personal ornaments such as finger rings and armlets. More unusual items include keys, locks, toilet instruments and a bronze folding spoon.

Traprain Law was not merely the home of a farming community. Metalworking was certainly carried out there for among the finds are portions of two-piece clay moulds for making small bronze artefacts, including a ring-headed pin and a dress fastener of a type dating to the second half of the second century. Crucibles also point towards local bronze-working at Traprain Law. It also seems possible that glass bangles were made at the town. Two inscriptions demonstrate that someone at least had a literacy of a kind. IRI on a fragment of pot was probably scratched at Traprain Law and the letters ABCD on a piece of mudstone certainly was (pl. 15).

Although much can be said about the artefacts from the site, little is known about the dwellings of the inhabitants of the town. Stone foundations have certainly been uncovered during the excavations, but whether these were for stone or timber buildings is not clear. There is, however, some indication that in one area at least the buildings were rectangular in shape rather than circular as the houses on the smaller native rural settlements. This sophistication is reflected in the discovery of keys and locks, possibly from houses, on the Law.

The wealth of material found at Traprain Law and its continuation as a defended town throughout the Roman period points to a special relationship between the Votadini and Rome. It is unfortunate that no other evidence survives to allow elaboration of this tantalising glimpse into frontier politics. Throughout the Roman period visitors from the south must have been a regular occurrence at Traprain Law. Merchants and traders certainly came there and, it may be presumed, soldiers also, though no carved name of a soldier has survived – as it has on a rock at Zinchecra, the hill fort capital of the Garamantes of the Fezzan in the Sahara desert. No matter what the strict treaty relationship between Rome and the Votadini, the army will have been concerned to keep almost as watchful an eye on their friendly northerly neighbour as on the other tribes of southern Scotland.

The Picts

If the theme of the third century was peace, that of the fourth was war. The changed situation was heralded by a chance comment at the end of the third century in a panegyric to the Caesar Constantius. The panegyricist, referring to events in 297, in passing mentioned that the Britons were only used to fighting the Picts and the Hibernians, both still half-naked enemies. This is the first reference to the Picts (and indeed to trouble from across the Irish Sea) but it is clear from later literary references that this nation was an amalgamation of earlier attested tribes. Already by the time of Septimius Severus some of the northern tribes recorded by Ptolemy had disappeared, probably incorporated into larger units. Now these tribes combined to form the Picts, a nation which, by the immediate post-Roman period, held sway over all or most of Scotland north of the Forth-Clyde isthmus (fig. 39; pl. 18–19). This process of coalescence took some time to achieve. Thus in the early fourth century a Roman writer could still speak of the Caledonians and other Picts, while the Verona list of 314 included the Caledoni and Picti (and Scotti); later in the century Ammianus Marcellinus mentioned the two divisions of the Picts, the Dicalydones and the Verturiones. This new unity may well have resulted from the adjacent presence of Rome: it was certainly a phenomenon which occurred along all the borders of the empire. The existence of a large and powerful state south of the Forth, occasionally interfering in their affairs, seems to have had the result of fusing the northern tribes together, eventually into one nation, consciously or subconsciously, in order to be able to resist the further expansion of Roman ambitions to the best of their ability.

The first known mention of the Picts in Roman sources was in 297 but it was not until 306 that war between Rome and the Picts was recorded. On 25 July of that year the Emperor Constantius Chlorus (305–6) died at York after defeating the Picts. The occasion for the war is not known, but in view of the general state of the empire and its frontiers elsewhere it is more likely to have resulted from the aggression of the Picts than the desire of the Romans to expand their empire. In 314 Constantius' son, Constantine the Great (306–37), took the title Britannicus Maximus and it seems possible that this followed a further campaign against the Picts.

The next disturbance was not for another thirty years. In the winter of 342/3 the Emperor Constans (337–50), son of Constantine, came urgently to Britain to deal with trouble apparently caused either by the Picts and Scots or by both. Then in 360 both nations, ignoring their treaty relationship with Rome, raided Britain, laying waste places near the frontier. The Emperor Julian (360–3), cousin of Constans, sent one of his generals, Lupicinus, with a small field army to the island to restore order. Four years later the writer Ammianus Marcellinus recorded further raids, this time by the Picts, Saxons, Scots and Attacotti, who were, Ammianus stated

39 The tribes of north Britain in the fourth century

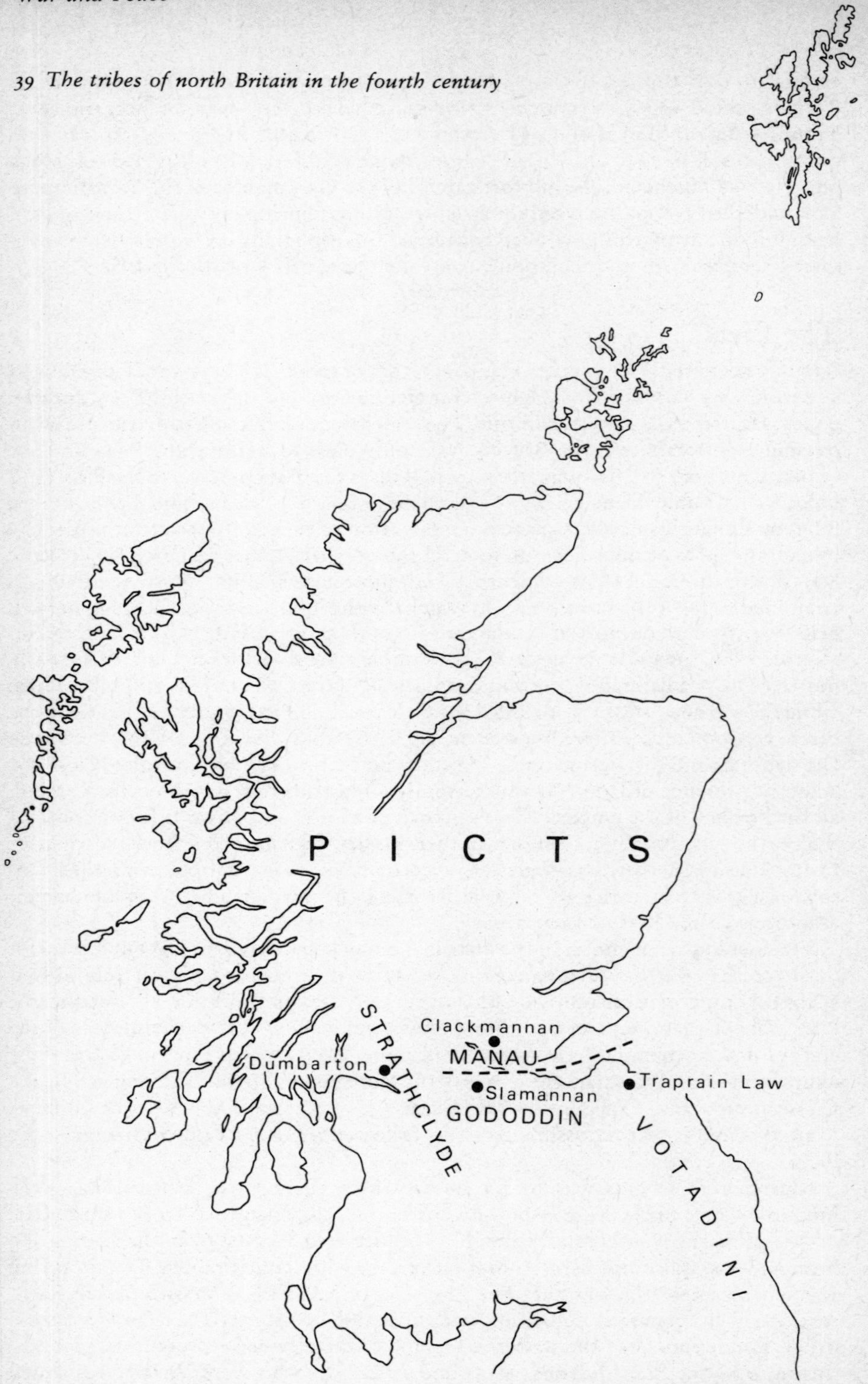

despairingly, harrassing Britain in a never-ending series of disasters. These attacks culminated in the 'Barbarian Conspiracy' of 367. In what appears to be a concerted invasion, the four tribes of 364 were joined by the Franks, who attacked the Channel coast, all the invaders, in the words of Ammianus, 'breaking in wherever they could, by land or sea, plundering and burning ruthlessly, and killing all their prisoners'. The frontier scouts were bribed by the enemy to reveal to them the disposition of the Roman forces. Nectaridus, Count of the Saxon Shore, was killed and Fullofaudes, commander of the army, surrounded. The Emperor Valentinian (364–75), at that time in Gaul, sent at first one of his leading generals, Severus, but quickly replaced him by another, Jovinus, who carried out a strategic withdrawal demanding a larger army, before Valentinian deciding to entrust the recovery of Britain to Theodosius.

Theodosius' campaigns against the invaders lasted into 368 and possibly 369. He at first made for London and restored order in that area. He attacked the marauding bands of the enemy, putting them to flight and recapturing their booty, including prisoners and cattle, which, after taking a percentage for his soldiers, he restored to its rightful owners. Before moving on Theodosius gathered intelligence concerning the enemy, planned his campaign, brought over two new generals from the continent and strengthened his army by issuing an edict summoning deserters back to the ranks without penalty, together with those absent on leave.

Thus with his army reinforced he left London, mopping up resistence as he moved north. Ammianus states that he restored cities and forts and protected the frontier with sentries and forts. The frontier scouts, who had gone over to the enemy, were disbanded. The historian, in passing, records their duties: 'they ranged backwards and forwards over great distances to obtain information about disturbances among neighbouring nations'. Thus they were clearly the descendants of the scouts established in the outpost forts in the late second or early third century. These are the only specific actions of Theodosius recorded in relation to the northern frontier. Nothing is known of the sentries established by him and no forts rebuilt or repaired at this time are recorded by name. It is possible that the general carried the war into the enemy's camp for the poet Claudian, writing at the time of Theodosius' grandson, the Emperor Honorius (393–423), states that he pitched camp among the Caledonian frosts.

Invasions by the Picts and Scots did not cease after the successful conclusion of the 'Barbarian Conspiracy'. In 382 they again invaded the empire and Magnus Maximus, later a usurper (383–8), conducted a vigorous campaign in order to defeat them. A few years later, at the very end of the century, Stilicho, ruler of the empire for Honorius, took measures to protect the island against the Picts, Scots and Saxons, though the nature of these activities is not known.

Throughout the fourth century Rome reacted to protect the provinces of Britain from their enemies – Picts, Scots, Saxons, Franks and Attacotti. Some of the defensive measures are known through literary references, documentary sources or archaeology. The strengthening of the army of Britain by the establishment of new units on the roads leading north from York to the Wall at the beginning of the fourth century has already been mentioned (fig. 35). Possibly at the same time, certainly before the death of Constantine in 337, all the army units in northern England came under the control of a newly created official, the *dux Britanniarum*. Previously the provincial governor had been responsible for both civil and military affairs within his province. Now this responsibility was divided, soldiers being appointed to the new military commands: this must have led to an improvement in the leadership of the army.

The *dux* commanded all the units of the province of northern England, Britannia Secunda, the new province created by Constantine, who subdivided both Upper and Lower Britain. The long struggle of Constantine for sole control of the empire also led to the creation of field armies. At first these remained with the emperor(s), but by the middle of the fourth century regional field armies under the command of *magistri* had been created. It was units of the field army based at Trier in Gaul which came to Britain in 360 and 367. The next step was the creation of more local field armies. Britain does not appear to have received its field army until the end of the fourth century, possibly shortly after 395 when Stilicho was active in Britain. This small force was under the command of the *comes Britanniae*, and may well have been stationed in the midlands within easy reach of both the northern frontier and the Saxon Shore.

Another army reform introduced by Diocletian was the institutionalisation of the family traditions of military service by making it hereditary and compulsory. Hitherto the army had mainly relied upon voluntary enlistment, though conscription was, at certain times and in certain areas, a not inconsiderable source of recruits: it is mentioned twice by Tacitus in relation to Britain. The new law was in theory a considerable change, but in practice it probably had little effect on matters in northern England where the sons of soldiers would continue to enter their father's unit in ready acceptance – and probably ignorance – of the law.

While the size, organisation and command structure of the army were being reformed, repairs and improvements to the defences of the province were also put in hand. Two inscriptions have survived to demonstrate that, in the years following the recovery of the island by the central authorities in 296, rebuilding was carried out at Birdoswald and Housesteads on Hadrian's Wall. At the former the ruined commanding officer's house was completely rebuilt and the headquarters building and the bathhouse repaired: the fragmentary inscription at Housesteads does not record the nature of the renovations there. At both forts archaeological investigation has revealed other modifications at about this time. These are particularly clear at Housesteads where some at least of the barrack-blocks initially built in the second century were completely remodelled. The previous arrangement of a centurion's block and ten rooms for the men in each barrack was swept away and replaced by a new centurion's block and several separate rooms for the men: six rooms in one of the two barracks so far examined and eight in the other. This arrangement of 'chalets' has been discovered at other forts, Greatchesters, Birdoswald and Wallsend on the Wall and also at the outpost forts at Risingham and High Rochester. It seems probable that these new arrangements reflect the reorganisation of the army that was taking place at the same time. However, it is impossible otherwise to relate the two events, not least because the size of the centuries at this time is not known, while the number of men who might be expected to live in one of the new barrack rooms is equally uncertain.

Elsewhere rebuilding was more drastic. Hadrian's Wall just west of Birdoswald was rebuilt from the foundations in the fourth century, while the fort at Chesterholm seems to have been completely rebuilt. Some of the milecastles on the Wall were also remodelled, probably at this time. In the area of the River Irthing milecastles and turrets seem to have been repaired. At two milecastles, 50 and 52, the normal round arch over the gateways was replaced by monolithic masonry doorposts, presumably carrying a flat lintel. However, these appear to be isolated repairs: there was certainly no attempt to restore all the turrets and milecastles, only a few of which can demonstrate occupation continuing into the fourth century.

It is not possible to date closely any of the repairs and rebuildings discussed above. Archaeology can point only to an approximate date within the later years of the third century or the early part of the fourth century, though it may be legitimate to link many with the re-establishment of central authority over Britain in 296 when affairs in the island must have been overhauled. There is no evidence to connect them with invasion from the north, which is not attested at this time.

An imperial visit to Britain may have been the occasion for further changes on the northern frontier. Constantius Chlorus was in the north in 306 while Constantine almost certainly came to Britain in 312 in order to gather troops in preparation for his struggle against his rival emperor Maxentius. It has been suggested that this latter visit led to the abandonment of the outpost fort at High Rochester, in spite of the extensive repairs which had taken place there just a few years before, for the coin series at this site ends in the early fourth century: this suggestion is, however, incapable of proof at the present time.

The putative visit of Constantine in 314, when he assumed the title *Britannicus Maximus*, probably following a successful campaign against the Picts, may have been the time when the new, mobile units were introduced into northern England in order to strengthen the northern frontier against attacks from the north. Possibly at the same time the military dispositions on the Cumbrian Coast were also strengthened, presumably following raiding by the Scots of Ireland, who appear to have menaced the whole of the west coast of Britain throughout the fourth century. A new fort was built at Burrow Walls sometime in the century and some of the milefortlets appear to have been reoccupied: none of these events are closely dated.

The final group of changes on the northern frontier are generally related to the events of 367 and their aftermath. There is little positive evidence for destruction in the Wall forts at this time, and it is possible that the Picts attacked by sea, sailing down the east coast and ignoring the Wall. However, renovations and rebuilding at several Wall forts, dated only approximately to the late fourth century, have been associated with the statement of Ammianus Marcellinus that Theodosius restored the forts, protecting the frontier with sentries and forts. New buildings were constructed at Birdoswald and Chesterholm and further minor modifications were carried out at the latter fort and at Housesteads. The work was more striking at Haltonchesters and Rudchester, forts which had been neglected through much of the preceding century. New buildings were erected over the accumulated debris of the previous 100 years. These buildings were not of the normal stone construction, but were of timber, the main uprights being set into large stones.

The strengthening of forts on the Wall, and in particular Haltonchesters and Rudchester, was accompanied by the abandonment of the system of scouting to the north which had operated for perhaps as long as 200 years. This event, recorded by Ammianus, is reflected in the archaeological record, for there is no evidence for any of the outpost forts continuing in occupation after about 367, though it is equally possible that some were abandoned earlier. After 367, for the first time in its entire history, Hadrian's Wall itself became the frontier of the province.

This frontier was strengthened by the addition of towers along the Yorkshire coast. Five of these towers are known and others may have existed along the coast of County Durham. The towers were placed on good vantage points and were presumably designed to maintain watch over the coastal approaches and possibly also communicate with Roman naval ships at sea. The construction of the towers emphasises the danger to the province from across the sea and supports the suggestion that the Picts in 367 sailed down the east coast to attack the Romans.

The attacks of the Picts, Scots and their allies in the fourth century must have had an important effect on the people of the frontier area, but that effect is impossible to measure. Practically no evidence survives from the rural sites to determine the history of even one such settlement during this century. There is more evidence from the villages outside the forts, but even that is difficult to interpret. There is evidence from only one village, Chesterholm, for occupation after 367, and this settlement appears to have been rebuilt after an abandonment of about 100 years. It is possible that the selective excavation carried out at other sites has failed to locate the remains of the late fourth century civilian occupation. On the other hand it is possible that in these years the civilians moved inside the forts to live with the soldiers, who were in any case fathers, brothers, husbands or sons to most of the civilians. This would account for the non-military objects found within forts in the later levels – infant burials at Chesters, trinkets at Housesteads – though it must be noted that most of these objects could have entered the forts after the end of Roman rule in 410.

The pattern of contact between Roman and barbarian, or rather lack of it, continued from the third century into the fourth. A small amount of pottery and glass found its way north, and also more exotic objects such as brooches of bronze, silver or gold as well as coins. However, all types of objects are few in number and most have a coastal distribution (fig. 38, pl. 13). Several of these objects were used as grave goods: glass vessels in Aberdeenshire (pl. 14) and Orkney, stone gaming counters in Aberdeenshire. Some of the objects, such as the pottery, are most likely to have entered Scotland by way of trade, but others, the brooches and the coins, may have been plundered. This is particular true of the seven fourth century coin hoards from Scotland, though it is difficult to see what use the northern tribes could make of Roman coins. One of the late fourth century is from Traprain Law and was found with a great collection of silver treasure (pl. 16). Some of the pieces in the hoard of treasure were cut up as if the collection was not to be used for its proper purpose, but as bullion, to be divided up among the tribesmen. The problem lies in the location of the treasure at Traprain Law, the capital for three centuries of a tribe supposedly friendly to Rome. Was the treasure plunder won by a tribe which had turned against its long standing friend, or was it a payment from Rome, aimed at supporting and continuing that friendship?

In trying to determine the answer to that question, and understand the late fourth century on the frontier, a new type of evidence comes into play, the genealogies of the British kings, written down in the medieval period but referring back even into the fourth century AD. These genealogies are partly garbled, not easy to interpret and are the subject of scholarly dispute. They demonstrate the existence of two, possibly four, native kingdoms in Lowland Scotland during the fourth century. One kingdom was centred on the Clyde and either now or later had its capital at Dumbarton Rock: this was known in later centuries as Strathclyde. Another lay in the east in the territory of the Votadini, known later as the Guotodin or Gododdin, and its main power base appears to have been in the Lothians and around the head of the Forth, the area termed the Manau of Gododdin. A third kingdom may have been in south-west Scotland, while the fourth is less easy to locate.

The genealogies suggest that these kingdoms were established in the late fourth century, possibly about the decade 370–80. Attention has been directed at the Roman names of many of the early kings and their immediate followers, and in particular to the name of the first king of the Manau Gododdin, Patern or Paternus Pesrut, Patern of the Red Cloak. This garment has been considered a symbol of office, Patern being invested with it by Theodosius. It has accordingly been proposed that Theodosius established two or more kingdoms in Lowland Scotland when he disbanded the scouting system and abandoned remaining outpost forts, to govern the people and act as buffer states between Rome and the Picts. Parallels have been drawn with the operation of a similar arrangement on the north African frontier in 371 when Ammianus Marcellinus, in a statement corroborated by St Augustine, reports that after Theodosius subdued the border tribes he placed over them reliable prefects, *praefecti gentium*. Two at least of the fourth-century kings in Britain, Cinhil of the Clyde and Patern Pasrut of the Manau Gododdin, appear to have come to their kingdoms from elsewhere, the former from the Mediterranean and the latter from Kent. One other is stated to have derived his authority from Magnus Maximus (383–8) and thus this emperor is sometimes seen as the designer of the northern settlement.

However, there are problems. Not all would agree, for example, that Cinhil is really Celtic for the Latin name Quintilius. Further, while Latin names may suggest Roman influence this may do no more than reflect the prestige of Rome among the tribes on its borders. It has also been suggested that the Roman names may merely indicate that these people had adopted Christianity, the Roman religion. Patern Pesrut, moreover, may have been so called because he liked to wear a red cloak! Certainly these kingdoms and their ruling dynasties were established by the early fifth century. What is less certain is that they can be extended backwards into the fourth and that they were established by Rome.

The end of Hadrian's Wall

Little can be said about the last days of Hadrian's Wall. We have already seen that Magnus Maximus (383–8) defeated the Picts and Scots who had invaded Britain in 382, the year before he left the island to claim, unsuccessfully, the empire. Maximus' name survived for long in folk memory and in several of the British genealogies, which implies that he did more than this, but the extent of his other deeds remains unknown. In 400 Stilicho is recorded as fortifying the British provinces against the Scots and Picts, but the exact nature of his activity is likewise uncertain. Then, in the latter part of the first decade of the fifth century the situation changed dramatically. On 31 December 406 hordes of barbarians crossed the Rhine and devasted Gaul. The British army appointed their own emperor, Marcus, who they murdered, then Gratian, who suffered in similar fashion, and finally Constantine (407–11). Constantine III appointed commanders for the troops in Britain and sailed for the continent, where he attempted to restore order. In his absence Britain suffered attack and in the absence of help from Constantine III, took measures to protect itself. Even on the death of Constantine III in 411 the central authority was not able to restore its rule in Britain owing to the more important threats from other quarters. Roman rule in Britain had officially ended.

There is no evidence that Hadrian's Wall in these last years was denuded of its garrison to help the British usurpers. No sources mention the exact origin, within Britain, of the armies of Magnus Maximus or Constantine III, or the 'legion' withdrawn by Stilicho in 401/2 to help protect Italy. Presumably the main body of troops was provided by the field army established on a permanent basis in Britain between 395 and 407, but no doubt this was augmented by soldiers withdrawn from the units in the forts of north Britain. Whole units, however, do not appear to have been withdrawn, for they survive to be listed in the *Notitia Dignitatum*, compiled in about 408. The *Notitia* does record units which had previously been stationed in Britain now serving on the continent, but none from Hadrian's Wall or its hinterland. Coins indicate the continuing occupation of sites on the Wall, though not necessarily by the army. Coins of 383–410 have been found at a number of forts on the frontier (Chesterholm, Birdoswald and Maryport), towns (Corbridge and Carlisle) as well at sites which might be either civilian or military (South Shields and Chesters) and as stray finds (Heddon and Walltown). There were also five coins of 387–96 in Coventina's Well at Carrawburgh, while in the adjacent fort a hoard of coins contained issues of the Emperors Valentinian (364–75) and Valens (364–78) so worn that the hoard may not have been buried until the early fifth century. Late fourth-century coins also found their way north of Hadrian's Wall. The hoard of four coins from Traprain Law, unearthed with the silver plate, has already been mentioned, but there are also records of another 20 coins, mostly stray finds. The army is the most likely source of all these coins, not only those found in forts, but in the towns and settlements inside and outside the province.

While Britain was still part of the Roman empire pay for these soldiers would continue to arrive at these forts, though much was now rendered in kind. Sometime between 407 and 411, however, these pay chests would have stopped arriving and it is probable that only then did the situation on the frontier change. At first the soldiers may not have understood what was happening, thinking that this was only a temporary break in payment, but as the position continued unchanged realisation must have set in. It seems unlikely that many soldiers immediately left the fort or its attendant village: most had probably lived there all their lives and stayed there, though presumably changing their occupation from soldier to farmer. Others may have turned to banditry. Quite simply no evidence survives. The only local inscription of later years is the fifth century tombstone of Brigomaglos at Chesterholm. But if the evidence for continuing occupation by the Romano-Britons is absent, evidence for the intrusion of Picts, Scots or Saxons into the frontier area is equally scarce, for only Corbridge has produced Saxon artefacts. It appears that the Roman frontiers had effectively done their job and defended the Roman province from foreign incursions to the very end.

8

Roman and Barbarian

The majestic remains of Hadrian's Wall, evocative survival of a long dead empire, can too easily obscure the fact that its life, so far as that empire was concerned, was short. A Roman state lasted in some form for over 2,000 years: Hadrian's Wall was occupied for less than three of those twenty centuries. Indeed the era of frontier building and experimentation may be considered to be even shorter, lasting in Britain from the late 80s for sixty years to the mid 140s, for thereafter no new frontier was built and the army merely modified the existing structures. The strength of Hadrian's Wall, even in decline, can also blind the onlooker to the fact that it is essentially a monument to failure: the failure of the Roman empire to expand and conquer the known world. The conquest of the Caledonians and their relatives would have eliminated the necessity for a frontier in Britain and, in the long run, have been cheaper than the maintenance of a large standing army in the island. The presence of a monolithic state in the southern part of the island, with well-defended frontiers, led to a reaction in the north and the creation of a nation capable of challenging, and occasionally defeating albeit briefly, the might of Rome. In the end sub-Roman Britain was to succumb to a different enemy, but this was only possible because the reaction against Rome on the continent had produced larger and more powerful foes who were able to triumph over the empire and thereby bring about the loss of limbs such as Britain. So far as Britain was concerned the empire had a hard shell in Hadrian's Wall, but a soft centre, and the collapse of that centre led to the abandonment of Hadrian's Wall, not the other way round.

Britain is singularly lucky in possessing the visible remains of two major Roman frontiers within a distance of little more than 160km. Further, archaeological research on these remains over the last century has produced a wealth of material allowing, usually, for greater understanding. The development of Rome's artificial frontiers can be traced here, perhaps more clearly than in any other province of the empire.

Little is known, ironically, of the only first-century frontier to be specifically attested in the literary sources, that established in 81 by Julius Agricola across the Forth-Clyde isthmus. Only one structure, a small fort of about 0.4 hectares, can be considered as a possible element in this frontier. The next frontier appears to be that built through Strathallan and Strathearn, probably in the late 80s, the 'Gask frontier'. This consisted of a series of timber watch-towers placed beside an existing road and between existing forts. The purpose of the soldiers stationed at these towers appears to have been to assist the units in the forts, whose main duty was to protect the province from attack, by improving the control of movement over the frontier. The slight archaeological dating evidence points to a late first century context for this frontier so it is mainly on historical, military and logical grounds that the towers are assigned to the late 80s.

Following the abandonment of most of the forts in Scotland in the late first and early second century no clear pattern can be determined until the construction of Hadrian's Wall. However, there was clearly an attempt to improve frontier control on the Tyne-Solway isthmus in the reign of Trajan (98–117). The existing forts between Corbridge and Carlisle, at either end of the Stanegate, were strengthened by the establishment of new forts, either now or early in the reign of Hadrian (122–38), so that the distance between each was reduced to about 11km, half the normal distance, which was approximately equivalent to a day's march. In addition two other forts of a different size are known: these 'small forts' were the same size as that built earlier on the Forth-Clyde isthmus and were clearly the bases for troops stationed elsewhere, presumably employed in frontier control duties. Archaeological evidence suggests that these elements were in existence some time before the construction of Hadrian's Wall. However, new elements appear, apparently shortly before work commenced on the Wall. One such element was the erection of watch-towers. Isolated towers were built, perhaps early in Hadrian's reign, on the line later taken by the Wall and also west of Carlisle, where one at least was soon superceded by an example of the second new element, a fort. At least two new forts were built in the west between Carlisle and Kirkbride, again seemingly early in Hadrian's reign, and the garrisons of some of the existing forts may have been changed at this time.

Whatever the improvements carried out on the northern frontier in the early years of Hadrian, they do not seem to have satisfied the emperor for he ordered, probably during his visit to the island in 122, the construction of the only effective method of control, a barrier. Initially this was to consist of merely a wall, punctured by gates defended by small fortlets and provided throughout its length with watch-towers. The troops to man the barrier and defend the province were to be those continuing to occupy their forts behind the Wall on the Stanegate and in northern England: some garrisons appear to have been changed at this time and new forts built. However, before the first scheme for the Wall was completed the forts immediately behind the Wall were abandoned and new forts were built on the line of the Wall itself, wherever possible astride the barrier. The main reason for this seems to have been that the Wall not only impeded the movement of the enemy, but it also hindered the free mobility of the Roman forces: placing the units on the Wall restored that mobility. Within a short period of this move forts began to be built not astride the Wall, but wholly south of it, though still attached. There was another experiment, the Vallum, an earthwork designed to protect the rear of the Wall installations.

The reasons for the advance north at the beginning of the reign of Antoninus Pius (138–61) do not concern us here. What is interesting is that the Wall now built was planned on similar lines to the redundant Hadrian's Wall: rampart and ditch, updated but otherwise hardly revolutionary; forts for whole units at 13km intervals, thus reflecting the length of the Wall; fortlets probably at every mile; and with the hint of a system of small enclosures only now being revealed. The main differences lay in the materials of construction, turf and timber predominating over stone. The experimental Vallum was not repeated, but a new feature was added, a road. This Wall, like its predecessor, was amended before it was completed, and again this was by the addition of forts. At least ten new forts were added, bringing the total to at least 16 and possible as many as 19, and reducing the distance between each to about 3.5km.

The artificial barrier had now reached its peak. With the completion of the Antonine Wall there were more men per mile stationed on the frontier than on any

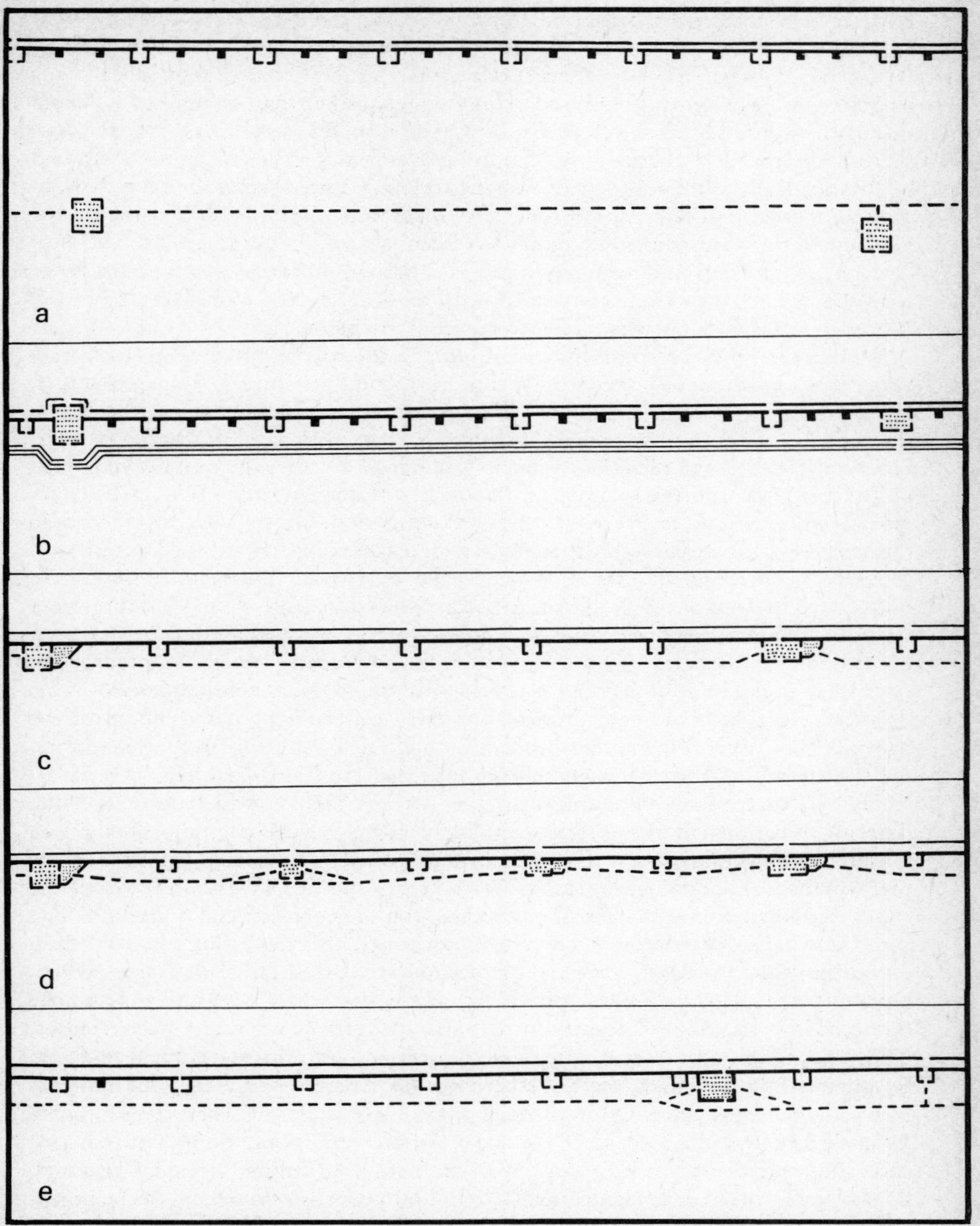

40 The development of Hadrian's Wall and the Antonine Wall in diagrammatic form: (a) Hadrian's Wall as planned; (b) Hadrian's Wall as completed; (c) The Antonine Wall as planned; (d) The Antonine Wall as completed; (e) Hadrian's Wall in the third century

frontier in Britain either before or after. The relationship between fort and Wall was close with the main axis of the former being related in all but one example to the barrier. Further, the later forts on the Antonine Wall were nearly all built for detachments, sometimes composed of legionaries, rather than complete units, and this also emphasised the close relationship between Wall and forts. Nevertheless there is no hint at a change in Roman military tactics. The Antonine Wall, and Hadrian's Wall, could not prevent a major attack on the province. It could slow up such an attack, it could help prevent petty local raiding and banditry and aid the Roman administration in controlling movement across the frontier but the defence of the province now, and for many years, lay with the units based in the forts on or near the Wall and the military issue would be decided in the field and not from behind fort walls, as it was on every recorded occasion.

Within the reign of Antoninus Pius himself there is a move away from this concentration of troops on the frontier line: the pendulum starts its return swing. In the second period on the Antonine Wall one fort was abandoned altogether while the garrison of another two can be shown to have been reduced. With the return to Hadrian's Wall in the 160s there was no attempt to increase the number of troops on the Wall line to bring this barrier into step with the Antonine Wall at either its most developed state or even during its second period. On the contrary there was the start of a process which reached its logical conclusion in the later second century. Then large, mobile units supported by smaller units and scouts were established in front of the Wall, while the garrisons of several of the Wall forts were strengthened. At the same time redundant turrets were abandoned, and even occasionally milecastles, while many remaining milecastles were adapted to the realities of their situation. A road was belatedly added to aid communication. This defence in depth, combined, presumably, with supervision of the affairs of the tribes to the north, was a more effective method of defence and was to last, apparently without major modification, into the late fourth century.

This defence in depth emphasises the various factors which governed the differing positions of the political, military and physical frontiers. Today we loosely refer to Hadrian's Wall or the Antonine Wall as a frontier, yet neither was the provincial boundary, the real frontier of the empire. The boundaries of the tribes in the frontier area controlled the position of the provincial boundary. The forts were placed in relation to this frontier, though also respecting the overriding topographical considerations. But if it was political, and military, factors which governed the position of the provincial boundary, then geography primarily ordained the location of the physical barrier. Agricola's Forth-Clyde frontier, Hadrian's Wall and the Antonine Wall all utilised natural geographical features, the great isthmuses which bisect northern Britain. These were the obvious 'natural' frontiers of the province within the island. It so happened that these geographical features largely coincided with the local tribal boundaries, though this is not surprising. However, on Hadrian's Wall the two, political and physical frontiers, do not appear to have coincided exactly, and outpost forts were held to the north. Outpost forts were also occupied north of the Antonine Wall, presumably because the provincial boundary lay further north, reaching up to the edge of the Highlands, and/or because the eastern end of the Wall did not make military sense and the army required more northerly posts to better protect the province. This leads to the final consideration. Two equal powers did not face each other across the provincial boundary. In spite of whatever treaties ordered the relationships between Rome and the barbarians, through most of the Roman period in Britain the empire was so powerful that she could intervene at will beyond the province and impose her views on the location of the frontier on the tribes beyond: the frontier was truly *Rome's* frontier.

The major developments on the frontier in the second century coincided with a century of warfare in north Britain. These years too saw the service in Britain of exceptionally able governors, men like Julius Severus sent by Hadrian from Britain to Judaea to deal with the Jewish revolt because he was the most able military man of his day, or Statius Priscus who in the early 160s moved in rapid succession from Upper Moesia on the Lower Danube to Britain and thence to Cappadocia, to organise the Roman reaction to the Parthian attacks on the Eastern frontier. Great care has, however, to be exercised in considering the literary sources: the relative wealth of the documentary sources for the second century, and indeed the fourth also, may artificially heighten the successive crises of these years at the expense of the third century.

The third century seems to have been a time of peace on the northern frontier, but for no obvious reason. The system of defence in depth was insufficient to prevent either the invasion of the early 180s or the troubles of the 190s, so there is no clear reason why it should have suddenly succeeded in the third century. Nor can it be seriously argued that the defeat of the Caledonians and Maeatae by Severus and Caracalla quelled those tribes for three or four generations. Remarkably, however, the apparently sharp change in the fortunes of the northern frontier coincided with a major administrative change in the province of Britain. Severus divided the single province which had existed since 43 into two, thus reducing the number of troops at the disposal of the governor of northern Britain. Furthermore, this province, Lower Britain, was not in the top group of provincial appointments so the northern frontier ceased to receive the attention of men of such high calibre as Julius Severus or Statius Priscus. If this area had been a continuing source of trouble through the third century the capacity of the Roman army to respond would have been seriously diminished.

The rise of the Picts in the fourth century and invasions from across both the Irish and North Seas brought about a changed situation. The creation of a unified military command in Britain under the *dux Britanniarum*, probably in the early fourth century, will have helped the army respond to these new threats, as did the stationing of new units in northern England. But as improvements in military architecture came to be introduced to the island during the fourth century, there seems to have been no attempt to strengthen the defences of the northern frontier by the addition of bastions, higher and thicker walls, etc, to the existing forts. In fact while new forts containing all these defensive devices came to be built in southern England, the north, in military architectural terms, became a backwater. Whether this reflected the nature of the enemy, it is difficult to determine.

It is unfortunate that all the literary source material for the northern frontier is one-sided, presenting only the Roman point of view. The speech of Calgacus before Mons Graupius is the only attempt to look at the situation from the other side, but even this of course is by a Roman intent on making a political point as much as presenting an alternative opinion. Almost the most that can be said about the barbarians' reaction to the Roman advance is that they resisted it in the only way they knew how, by military force. In this they showed guile and cunning, as demonstrated by their tactics against Agricola – in particular the night attack on the Ninth legion and the guerilla warfare employed against the might of Severus. However, in no war were the barbarians successful. True, the Highlands were never conquered, but this was due to Roman lassitude rather than Caledonian – or Pictish – might.

The progress of Roman arms in Britain, as indeed on any frontier of the empire, depended ultimately upon the will of the emperor. The sudden and major move forward of Roman arms in the 70s was due to the interest of the Emperor Vespasian (69–79), who had previously served in the island. This advance halted abruptly in 85 when the Rhine and Danube frontiers were assailed by more serious threats: the British frontier, on the edge of the empire, far away from the centre of power and the heartlands of the empire, could be safely left while more important, indeed vital, problems were dealt with. A new emperor, Trajan (98–117), was intent to expand the empire, but characteristically chose more exotic parts to achieve his ends. The progressive withdrawal of garrisons from Scotland over the twenty years following Mons Graupius had brought the northernmost line of forts in the province, by the early second century at the latest, to the Tyne-Solway isthmus. These were strengthened in Trajan's reign by the construction of new forts and this process continued into Hadrian's reign (117–38) when the Wall was built as an addition to an existing group of installations. The position of Hadrian's Wall was governed by the prior existence of these forts, and in turn they were related to a geographical feature, the Tyne-Solway isthmus. After the Forth-Clyde isthmus, this was the most convenient line on which to halt the creeping withdrawal, indeed almost the only line. It was also the northern boundary of the tribe of the Brigantes which, since they had accepted client status in the 40s, would have been regarded as part of the empire: to retreat further then would have been to relinquish territory 'Roman' for fifty years or more. Antoninus Pius (138–61) moved the frontier forward to the best line within the island, the Forth-Clyde isthmus, though the reasons for this are far from clear and the decision, sensible though it might be seen on many grounds, was reversed by his successors Marcus Aurelius (161–80) and Lucius Verus (161–9). This was the period when the empire could most easily have solved the running sore of the British frontier by moving towards the conquest of the whole island. Instead Pius decided on a limited operation, reconquering only those tribes formerly within the province.

Septimius Severus (193–211) in the early third century returned to the question of the northern frontier. Dio states, unmistakably, that he intended to conquer the whole island and Severus did achieve the defeat of the two major tribes of the north, the Caledonians and Maeatae. The subsequent revolt of these peoples is irrelevant, for Severus amply demonstrated his intention to deal with this rebellion and there is no reason to believe that he would not have succeeded. His purpose was frustrated by his death and Rome never again was in the position to take the offensive against the northern tribes and attempt to incorporate them into the empire. The absorption of an area as large as Britain was almost bound to be piecemeal, while the haphazard interest of the emperors ensured that the progress of Roman arms would be erratic. The conquest of Spain, a not unfair parallel especially in view of its mountainous fastnesses, in the unsettled conditions of the Republic took two centuries to achieve and was only completed under the single-minded directorship of Augustus. Conditions on the frontier in Britain for the first 150 years of the life of the province were almost equally unsettled, though in a different way, and two centuries after 43 Rome was no longer able to devote sufficient resources to the completion of the conquest of Britain. This, combined with the lack of interest shown in expansion through much of the second century, was to decide the issue. Furthermore, Britain suffered from its position on the edge of the empire. There was no particular need to press ahead because even if there was a major attack from the north Rome and the immediately adjacent provinces would not be affected. Yet there is every reason to believe that, given a series of emperors who viewed the British frontier through the same eyes as Vespasian, or even longer lives for certain emperors, or a lack of crises elsewhere, Rome would have proceeded north until she had reached the end of the island and then been able to reduce the garrison of the province to a token force, as she did, eventually, in Spain.

The main events on the northern frontier can be charted with a certain degree, sometimes a high degree, of accuracy and, at least on the Roman side, the main participants can be brought to life through the surviving literary or documentary records; but the more intimate details are less clear. Sometimes an occasional fragment, such as the negotiation of the treaty between Severus and the Caledonians, is preserved, but little else of the details of the relationships between the two armies. The Romans did not generally indulge in indiscriminate killing and it may be assumed that if they could take over a tribe without a fight they would. If the tribe resisted but then surrendered after defeat, they would be treated honourably. Trajan's Column reveals some of the actions undertaken by the army to achieve that surrender: not only hand-to-hand fighting but the burning of enemy villages and crops, the capture and enslavement of its people. If, after surrender, the enemy then rebelled, it was subject to harsher treatment, in theory extermination, though that can hardly having been carried out thoroughly. Nevertheless following the rebellion of the Ordovices, just before his arrival in Britain, Agricola led the ruthless suppression of the revolt and in 210 Severus, when the Maeatae revolted, ordered his soldiers to march against them and kill everyone they met.

Of embassies and personal communication between the Romans and the barbarians we know nearly nothing. The only recorded embassy was that sent by the northern tribes to Severus in 208 offering terms for surrender, which were refused. Nevertheless the accounts of the campaigns of Agricola and Severus demonstrate that there was more knowledge of the plans and movements of the other side – Roman or barbarian – than is often realised: there is a level of contact here of which we know little.

Our knowledge of the diplomatic relations between Roman and barbarian is much greater elsewhere, though still imperfect and patchy. Such records make clear that at all times and on all frontiers the Romans were prepared to stoop – in modern eyes – to immoral methods in order to secure their own ends: the imprisonment and murder of ambassadors, the assassination of foreign kings, the encouragement of inter-tribal feuding, if necessary by the payment of bribes. . . . The list is long and even otherwise honest and upright Romans indulged in such dealings. This picture was not one-sided and many similar deeds were perpetrated by the opponents of Rome, though retold by Romans to best effect. There is no reason to assume that the Romans and barbarians who acted out the events recorded briefly in the historical record for north Britain were any different, though little evidence for such dark deeds survive. One action may bear repeating: the treacherous deceit of the frontier scouts in 367 when they were bribed by the barbarians to reveal the Roman military dispositions. There is a record too of the payment of bribes by the Romans for Virius Lupus, governor of Britain 197–200, had to buy peace from the Maeatae for a considerable sum because he did not have the military strength to deal with them: in return Lupus also regained a few captives. There is even a hint in Dio's account of the troubles of 197 that Rome tried to play the Caledonians and Maeatae off against each other in the time honoured manner. Certainly the existence of a treaty relationship with the Caledonians in 197 demonstrates the extent of Roman influence in north Britain even when the frontier lay on Hadrian's Wall.

The Roman method of obtaining a *casus belli* is also worth examining, for in spite of their power and ability to intervene without having to justify their actions to anyone, they still liked to be able to say that they were fighting a just war. Thus, in considering intervention in Ireland in his fifth campaign, Agricola gained a justification by taking into his retinue a fugitive Irish prince. The following year the threatening activity of the Caledonians was given as the excuse for the Roman invasion of the tribes north of the Forth! The situation is not so clear at the beginning of the third century, but it seems probable that the intention of Severus to campaign in the grand manner in Scotland was occasioned more by personal desires than any real need so far as the safety of the British frontier was concerned. The garbled account of Pausanias concerning the appropriation of part of the territory of the Brigantes by Antoninus Pius might be an excuse for the action of that emperor in moving the frontier forward.

Yet all was not governed by dark events. Most Romans tried to rule fairly and when officials did misbehave, as for example, in the prelude to Boudica's rebellion, they were not applauded by the historians and writers. On the whole no doubt most governors and procurators were content to keep the peace. Tacitus waxes eloquently on the desire of Agricola to root out injustices and encourage the Britons adopt the manners and practices of Rome: how far he was representative of the normal governor is a matter of debate. Except during the great campaigns there is no record of provincial governors visiting the northern frontier. One provincial governor in the 130s, following its submission to Hadrian, published the report of his tour of inspection of the forts under his command on the Black Sea coast. While carrying out this tour Arrian, the governor, gave directions for the improvement of fort defences where necessary. Similar tours of inspection will presumably have been made on the north British frontier, though no reports survive. On a higher plane, Hadrian, during his visit to Britain in 122, will no doubt have inspected the provincial army as he did six years later in north Africa: the difference is that part of the record of that tour of inspection survives on inscriptions. In this whole area, which could be extended to the annual unit reports to provincial headquarters, or the relations between the auxiliary commanders on the frontier and the legionary legate in York, and his superior in London, no evidence from Britain survives. This major gap in our local knowledge has to be filled by evidence by analogy from the other frontiers of the empire.

One such area lies in the composition of the Roman army. Throughout the empire men from beyond the empire came willingly to join her army. Thus Arminius, the great enemy of Rome, had previously served in the Roman army, while his brother fought on the Roman side in the German revolt of AD 9. In the fourth century most of the field armies were composed of Germans from beyond the empire: Stilicho, virtual ruler of the empire in the late fourth century, was a Vandal. There are plentiful references to the service of Germans in the army of Britain from the Usipites at the end of the first century, through Notfried's regiment at Housesteads in the early third century to Fraomarius and his Alamanni in the late fourth century. In the second century there were also the Sarmatians sent to the island in 175 after their surrender to Marcus Aurelius. It seems probable that Caledonians, possibly even Hibernians, also joined the Roman army, though no undisputed record survives.

Yet even if this was the case it is unlikely that it would help to account for the

Roman artefacts found beyond the empire in both Scotland and Ireland from the first to the fifth century. The documents are uniform in stating that very few recruits from beyond the empire ever returned home, even after the completion of their term of service in the army. On retirement they would usually settle down, like other veterans, in the villages outside the fort in which they had served. These objects are mute testimony to contact of some nature between Roman and barbarian. The paucity of material of any century found beyond the Highland Line seems to point to relatively little contact. It may be assumed, on faith rather than firm evidence, that most objects found their way north through trade. Such might include the fine glass vessel from Aberdeenshire dating to the second century (pl. 14). Plunder must have accounted for some at least of the artefacts, while the payment of subsidies or bribes will have brought not a few of the Roman coins into Scotland. What is remarkable, however, is not the paucity of material in the north, but the few objects of third or fourth century date in the Lowlands. Nearly every Roman period farmstead between Tyne and Forth, on excavation, produces at least one object of second century date, but very rarely one of the succeeding years.

Nevertheless certain objects particularly emphasise the close relationship between Roman and native in southern Scotland. Glass bangles, mainly dating to the late first and second centuries, are common to both military and civil sites in the Borders, and stretch down into northern England, with few found either north of the Forth or south of the Mersey. The significance of this object, however, would be greater if it were known who wore it and how it was worn; whether it was manufactured locally before the Romans arrived or whether it was a southern import. Another such object is the so-called dress fastener, more usually found on Roman and native sites in the military north than further south. This did have pre-Roman antecedents but, like the glass bangle, its function is still uncertain. The number of finds of fasteners at military installations suggests that they were items of military equipment, but their manufacture at Traprain Law and discovery elsewhere points to another, uncertain dimension.

Such gaps in our knowledge, on the military, civil and native sides, and in the relationship between all three, can only be solved, if at all, by further excavation. Over the last decade archaeological research has made great strides on the northern frontier. The first Agricolan fort on the Forth-Clyde line has been discovered. An important new dimension has been added to Hadrian's Wall by the detection of Hadrianic and pre-Hadrianic frontier works behind and beyond the west end of the Wall. The implications for the Antonine Wall of the discovery of five new fortlets and three examples of a wholly new structure, the one-sixth of a mile enclosure, are considerable. Also on the Antonine Wall much of a complete fort has been examined archaeologically for the first time in over forty years, while on Hadrian's Wall almost the whole of Wallsend fort is being excavated in a rescue operation, revealing important information concerning, in particular, the layout of the fort in the second and fourth centuries and the history of the site. At Chesterholm large-scale excavation has uncovered, for the first time, almost a complete civil settlement with most important results and implications far beyond that particular site, while the chance discovery of the writing tablets has brought into existence a wholly new strand of evidence for northern Britain, while revealing the large element of luck which plays such an important part in archaeology. Further north, also for the first time, the existence of civil settlements outside forts in Scotland has been confirmed by excavation, while two brochs with important Roman connections have been examined. In a different field judicious small-scale excavation has allowed the elaboration of theories concerning the function of the camps at Burnswark with more confidence. In many areas methodical work has produced no wide implications, but has rather added a little flesh to the still very bare bones of the history and life of the northern frontier and its people.

This more eye-catching work in the field has been accompanied throughout by its counterpart, examination and analysis in the study. The range of new books, articles, papers and lectures is too numerous to enumerate there, but attention may be directed to the date of publication of many of the works cited in the bibliography. There is no doubt that excavation and research will continue and will result in fresh discoveries and the solving of old problems as well as the creation of new.

References and Bibliography

General

A.R. Birley, 'The Roman governors of Britain', *Epigraphische Studien* 4, (1967) 163–202

A.R. Birley, *The People of Roman Britain*, London, 1979

E. Birley, *Roman Britain and the Roman Army*, Kendal, 1953

D.J. Breeze, *Roman Scotland: A guide to the visible remains*, Newcastle upon Tyne, 1979

D.J. Breeze and B. Dobson, *Hadrian's Wall*, Harmondsworth, 1978

R.G. Collingwood and J.N.L. Myres, *Roman Britain and the English Settlements*, Oxford, 1937

C.M. Daniels, 'Problems of the Roman northern frontier', *Scottish Archaeological Forum* 2, 1970, 91–101

B. Dobson (ed) The Tenth Pilgrimage of Hadrian's Wall, Kendal, 1979

S.S. Frere, *Britannia*, London, 1974

J.P. Gillam, 'The frontier after Hadrian – a history of the problem', *Archaeologia Aeliana* 5 ser. 2 (1974) 1–15

B.R. Hartley, 'Some problems of the military occupation of the north of England', *Northern History* 1 (1966) 7–20

B.R. Hartley, 'Roman York and the northern military command', in R.M. Butler (ed), *Soldier and Civilian in Roman Yorkshire*, Leicester, 1971, 55–69

E.N. Luttwack, *The Grand Strategy of the Roman Empire from the First Century AD to the Third*, Baltimore and London, 1976

J.C. Mann (ed), *The Northern Frontier in Britain from Hadrian to Honorius: Literary and Epigraphic Sources*, Newcastle upon Tyne, nd. [1971]

J.C. Mann, 'The frontiers of the principate', in H. Temporini (ed), *Aufstieg und Niedergang der Römischen Welt* II, i, Berlin, 1974, 508–33

J.C. Mann, 'Power, force and the frontiers of the empire', review of E. Luttwack, *The Grand Strategy of the Roman Empire from the First Century AD to the Third*, Baltimore and London, 1976, in *J. Roman Studies* 69 (1979) 175–83

J.C. Mann and R.G. Penman, *Literary Sources for Roman Britain* (= Lactor II), 1977

S.N. Miller, *The Roman Occupation of South-western Scotland*, Glasgow, 1952

T.W. Potter, *Romans in North-West England*, Kendal, 1979

I.A. Richmond, *Roman Britain*, London, 1963

I.A. Richmond (ed), *Roman and Native in North Britain*, London, 1958

A.L.F. Rivet and C. Smith, *The Place-Names of Roman Britain*, London, 1979

A.S. Robertson, 'Roman Finds from non-Roman sites in Scotland', *Britannia* 1 (1970) 198–226

A.S. Robertson, 'The Romans in North Britain: The Coin Evidence', in H. Temporini and

W. Haase (edd), *Aufstieg und Niedergang der Römischen Welt* II, iii, Berlin, 1975, 364–426

A.S. Robertson, 'The circulation of Roman coins in North Britain: the evidence of hoards and site-finds from Scotland', in R.A.G. Carson and C.M. Kraay (edd) *Essays presented to Humphrey Sutherland*, 1978, 186–216

P. Salway, *The Frontier People of Roman Britain*, Cambridge, 1965

J.K. St Joseph, 'Air Reconnaissance in Roman Britain, 1969–72', *J. Roman Studies* 63 (1973) 214–46

J.K. St Joseph, 'Air Reconnaissance of Roman Scotland, 1939–75', *Glasgow Archaeological J.* 4 (1976) 1–28

J.K. St Joseph, 'Air Reconnaissance in Roman Britain, 1973–76', *J. Roman Studies* 67 (1977) 125–61

L. Thoms (ed), *Scottish Archaeological Forum* 7 1975, Edinburgh, 1976

D. Young, *Romanisation in Scotland, an essay in perspective*, Tayport, n.d. [1955?]

1 Romans

Ancient sources

Caesar, *The Gallic War*

Cassius Dio, *History of Rome*, 19–23; 62

Florus, *Epitome of Roman History*, 4, 12

Velleius Paterculus, *Compendium of Roman History*, 2, 90–131

Tacitus, *The Annals of Imperial Rome*

Tacitus, *Agricola*

Modern works

H. Schönberger, 'The Roman Frontier in Germany: an archaeological survey', *J. Roman Studies* 59 (1969) 144–97

G. Webster, *The Roman Imperial Army*, London, 1969

C.M. Wells, *The German Policy of Augustus*, Oxford, 1973

2 Barbarians

Ancient sources

Bede, *A History of the English Church and People*, 1

Caesar, *The Gallic War*

Cassius Dio, *History of Rome*, 76

Herodian, *History of Rome*, 3

Ptolemy, *Geography*

Tacitus, *Agricola*

Modern references

L. Alcock, 'Was there an Irish Sea Province in the Dark Ages?' in D. Moore (ed), *The Irish Sea Province in Archaeology and History*, Cardiff, 1970, 55–65

B. Cunliffe, *Iron Age Communities in Britain*, London, 1978

J.G. Evans, *The Environment of Early Man in the British Isles*, London, 1975

K. Jackson, *Language and History in Early Britain*, Edinburgh, 1953

G. Jobey, 'Homesteads and settlements of the frontier area', in C. Thomas (ed), *Rural Settlement in Roman Britain*, London, 1966, 1–14

M. MacGregor, *Early Celtic Art in North Britain*, Leicester, 1976

V. Megaw and D.D.A. Simpson, *British Prehistory*, Leicester, 1979

G. and A. Ritchie, *Edinburgh and South-east Scotland*, London, 1972

G. and A. Ritchie, *Scotland, Archaeology and Early History*, London, 1981

A.L.F. Rivet (ed), *The Iron Age in Northern Britain*, Edinburgh, 1966

A.L.F. Rivet and C. Smith, *The Place-names of Roman Britain*, London, 1979

A. Ross, *Pagan Celtic Britain*, London, 1967

A. Ross, *Everyday Life of the Pagan Celts*, London, 1970

3 Agricola and the first frontier in Britain

Ancient sources

The basic text, with commentary, of the *Agricola* is:

R.M. Ogilvie and I.A. Richmond (ed.), *Cornelii Taciti, de vita Agricolae*, Oxford, 1967

There is also a translation in the Penguin classics series.

Modern works

Two fundamental, though differing, discussions of Agricola's career and achievements are:

E. Birley, 'Britain under the Flavians: Agricola and his predecessors', in *Roman Britain and the Roman Army*, Kendal, 1953, 10–19

I.A. Richmond, 'Gnaeus Julius Agricola', *J. Roman Studies*, 34 (1944) 34–45

Scottish Archaeological Forum 12, 1980, forthcoming, will be devoted to Agricola, containing papers by D.J. Breeze, B. Dobson, S.S. Frere, W.S. Hanson, V.A. Maxfield and G.S. Maxwell

A.R. Birley, 'Agricola, the Flavian Dynasty, and Tacitus', in B. Levick (ed), *The Ancient Historian and his Materials*, Farnborough, 1975, 139–54

A.R. Birley, 'The date of Mons Graupius', *Liverpool Classical Monthly* 1, No. 2 (1976) 11–4

D.J. Breeze and B. Dobson, 'A view of Roman Scotland in 1975', *Glasgow Archaeological J.* 4 (1976) 124–43

J. Clarke, 'Roman and Native, AD 80–122', in I.A. Richmond, *Roman and Native in North Britain*, Edinburgh, 1958, 28–59

R.W. Davies, 'The investigation of some crimes in Roman Egypt', *Ancient Society* 4 (1973) 199–212

W.S. Hanson, 'The first Roman occupation of Scotland', in W.S. Hanson and L.J.F. Keppie (edd), *Roman Frontier Studies 1979* (= BAR International Series 71), Oxford, 1980, 15–43

W.S. Hanson and G.S. Maxwell, 'An Agricolan *Praesidium* on the Forth-Clyde Isthmus (Mollins, Strathclyde)', *Britannia* 11 (1980) 43–9

J.C. Mann, review of R.M. Ogilvie and I.A. Richmond (edd), *Cornelii Taciti, de vita Agricolae*, Oxford, 1967, in *Archaeologia Aeliana* 4 ser. 46 (1968) 306–8

N. Reed, 'The fifth year of Agricola's Campaigns', *Britannia* 2 (1971) 143–8

4 The retreat from total conquest

The Gask Frontier

Ancient sources

Tacitus, *Histories*, 4, 64 (Tencteri)

Tacitus, *Germania*, 41 (Hermanduri)

Modern works

D. Christison, 'Excavation undertaken by the Society of Antiquaries of Scotland of earthworks adjoining the "Roman Road" between Ardoch and Dupplin, Perthshire', *Proc. Soc. Antiq. Scot.* 35 (1900–1) 15–43

C.M. Daniels, 'Problems of the Roman northern frontier', *Scottish Archaeological Forum* 2, 1970, 91–101

A.S. Robertson, 'Roman "Signal Stations" on the Gask Ridge', *Trans. Perthshire Society of Natural Science*, Special Issue (1973) 14–29

E. Ritterling, 'Legio', in Pauly-Wissowa, *Real-Encyclopödie der Classischen Altertumswissenschaft* XII, 2

J.K. St. Joseph, 'Air reconnaissance in Roman Britain, 1969–72', *J. Roman Studies* 63 (1973) 218

J.K. St. Joseph, 'Air reconnaissance in Roman Britain, 1973–76', *J. Roman Studies* 67 (1977) 135–9

H. Schönberger, 'The Roman frontier in Germany: an archaeological survey', *J. Roman Studies* 59 (1969) 144–97

The abandonment of Scotland

E.B. Birley, 'The fate of the Ninth Legion', in R.M. Butler (ed), *Soldier and Civilian in Roman Yorkshire*, Leicester, 1971, 70–80

D.J. Breeze and B. Dobson, 'A view of Roman Scotland in 1975', *Glasgow Archaeological J.* 4 (1976) 124–43

J. Clarke, 'Roman and Native, A.D. 80–122', in I.A. Richmond (ed), *Roman and Native in North Britain*, Edinburgh, 1958, 28–59

B.M. Dickinson and K.F. Hartley, 'The evidence of potters' stamps on samian ware and on mortaria for the trading connections of Roman York', in R.M. Butler (ed), *Soldier and Civilian in Roman Yorkshire*, Leicester, 1971, 128–42

W. Eck, 'Zum Ende der *legio IX Hispana*', *Chiron* 2 (1972) 459–62

B.R. Hartley, 'The Roman occupation of Scotland: the evidence of samian ware', *Britannia* 3 (1972) 1–44

The Stanegate 'frontier'

E. Birley, *Research on Hadrian's Wall*, Kendal, 1961, 132–50

R. Birley, *Vindolanda*, London, 1977

C.M. Daniels, 'Problems of the Roman northern frontier'. *Scottish Archaeological Forum* 2, 1970, 91–101

G.D.B. Jones, 'The western Stanegate', in B. Dobson (ed), *The Tenth Pilgrimage of Hadrian's Wall*, Kendal, 1979, 27

G.D.B. Jones, 'The hidden frontier', *Popular Archaeology* 2, 1 (July 1980) 14–7

5 Hadrian's Wall

Ancient sources

Scriptores Historiae Augustae, Hadrian, 5 and 11

Cornelius Fronto, *Letter to Marcus on the Parthian War*

Modern works

General

E. Birley, *Research on Hadrian's Wall*, Kendal, 1961

D.J. Breeze and B. Dobson, *Hadrian's Wall*, Harmondsworth, 1978

J.C. Bruce, *Handbook to the Roman Wall*, 13th edition by C.M. Daniels, Newcastle, 1978. This contains a detailed bibliography of each structure on the Wall

D. Charlesworth, 'The turrets on Hadrian's Wall', in M.P. Apted, R. Gilyard-Beer and A.D. Saunders (edd), *Ancient Monuments and their interpretation*, London, 1977, 13–26

Ordnance Survey, *Map of Hadrian's Wall*, 1st edition 1964; 2nd edition 1972, Chessington

G. Simpson (ed), *Watermills and Military Works on Hadrian's Wall: Excavations in Northumberland 1907–1913 by F.G. Simpson*, Kendal, 1976

Cumbrian coast

See the series of papers by R.L. Bellhouse in the *Trans. Cumberland Westmorland Antiquarian and Archaeological Soc.* 2 ser. from 54 (1954) to 70 (1970)

N.J. Higham and G.D.B. Jones, 'Frontier, forts and farmers: Cumbrian aerial survey', *Archaeological J.* 132 (1975) 16–53

G.D.B. Jones, 'The western extension of Hadrian's Wall: Bowness to Cardurnock' *Britannia* 7 (1976) 236–43

G.D.B. Jones, 'The development of the coastal frontier', in B. Dobson (ed), *The Tenth Pilgrimage of Hadrian's Wall*, Kendal, 1979, 28–9

G.D.B. Jones, 'The hidden frontier', *Popular Archaeology* 2, 1 (July 1980) 14–7

T.W. Potter, *Romans in North-West England*, Kendal, 1979

T.W. Potter, 'The Cumbrian coast defences and Ravenglass', in B. Dobson (ed), *The Tenth Pilgrimage of Hadrian's Wall*, Kendal, 1979, 24–8

T.W. Potter, 'The Roman frontier in Cumbria', in W.S. Hanson and L.J.F. Keppie (edd), *Roman Frontier Studies 1979* (=BAR International Series 71), Oxford, 1980, 195–200

The function of Hadrian's Wall

E. Birley, 'Hadrianic frontier policy', *Carnuntina* 3 (1956) 25–33

D.J. Breeze and B. Dobson, 'Hadrian's Wall: some problems', *Britannia* 3 (1972) 182–93

R.G. Collingwood, 'The purpose of the Roman Wall', *Vasculum* 8 (1921)

The building of the Wall

P.S. Austen and D.J. Breeze, 'A new inscription from Chesters on Hadrian's Wall', *Archaeologia Aeliana* 5 ser. 7 (1979) 115–26

B. Dobson and D.J. Breeze, *The Building of Hadrian's Wall*, Newcastle upon Tyne, 1970

B. Heywood, 'The Vallum – its problems restated', in M.G. Jarrett and B. Dobson (edd) *Britain and Rome*, Kendal, 1966, 85–94

J. Hooley and D.J. Breeze, 'The building of Hadrian's Wall: a reconsideration', *Archaeologia Aeliana* 4 ser. 46 (1968) 97–114

R. Hunneysett, 'The milecastles of Hadrian's Wall: an alternative explanation', *Archaeologia Aeliana* 5 ser. 8 (1980) 95–107

V.A. Maxfield and R. Miket, 'The excavation of turret 33b (Coesike)', *Archaeologia Aeliana* 4 ser. 50 (1972) 145–78

C.E. Stevens, *The Building of Hadrian's Wall*, Kendal, 1966

B. Swinbank and J.E.H. Spaul, 'The spacing of the forts on Hadrian's Wall', *Archaeologia Aeliana* 4 ser. 29 (1951) 221–38

6 The Antonine Wall

The move north

Ancient sources

Scriptores Historiae Augustae, Antoninus Pius, 5

Pausanias, *Description of Greece*, 8, 43

Eumenius, *Panegyric Constantio Caesari*, 14

Modern references

A.R. Birley, *Marcus Aurelius*, London, 1966

A.R. Birley, 'Roman Frontiers and Roman Frontier Policy. Some Reflections on Roman Imperialism', *Trans. Architect. Archaeol. Soc. Durham Northumberland* 3 (1974) 13–25

D.J. Breeze, 'The abandonment of the Antonine Wall: its date and implications', *Scottish Archaeological Forum* 7, 1975, 67–80

J.G.F. Hind, 'The "Genounian" part of Britain', *Britannia* 8 (1977) 299–34

B. Swinbank, 'The activities of Lollius Urbicus as evidenced by inscriptions', *Trans. Architect. Archael. Soc. Durham Northumberland* 10, Pt 4 (1953) 382–403

The Antonine Wall

General

G. Macdonald, *The Roman Wall in Scotland*, Oxford, 1934

Ordnance Survey, *Map of the Antonine Wall*, Chessington, 1969

A.S. Robertson, *The Antonine Wall*, Glasgow, 1979. This contains a detailed bibliography of all structures on the Wall.

R. Feachem, 'Six Roman Camps near the Antonine Wall', *Proc. Soc. Antiq. Scot.* 89 (1955–6) 329–39

J.P. Gillam, 'Possible changes in plan in the course of the construction of the Antonine Wall, *Scottish Archaeological Forum* 7, 1975, 51–6

L.J.F. Keppie, 'The Building of the Antonine Wall: Archaeological and Epigraphic Evidence', *Proc. Soc. Antiq. Scot.* 105 (1972–4) 151–65

L.J.F. Keppie, 'Some rescue excavation on the line of the Antonine Wall, 1973–6', *Proc. Soc. Antiq. Scot.* 107 (1975–6) 61–80

L.J.F. Keppie, *Roman Distance Slabs from the Antonine Wall*, Glasgow, 1979

G.S. Maxwell, 'The building of the Antonine Wall', *Actes du IXe Congrès international d'etudes sur les frontières Romaines*, Bucharest, 1974, 327–32

I.A. Richmond, 'The Roman frontier in Scotland', *J. Roman Studies* 26 (1936) 190–4

A.S. Robertson, *An Antonine Fort: Golden Hill, Duntocher*, Glasgow, 1957

RCAHMS, *An Inventory of the Prehistoric and Roman Monuments in Lanarkshire*, Edinburgh, 1978

K.A. Steer, 'The Antonine Wall 1934–1959', *J. Roman Studies* 50 (1960) 84–93

K.A. Steer, 'The nature and purpose of the expansions on the Antonine Wall', *Proc. Soc. Antiq. Scot.* 90 (1956–7) 161–9

Antonine Scotland

Ancient sources

Tacitus, *Agricola*, 19

Tacitus, *Annals*, IV, 72: Frisii.

Modern Works

D. Baatz, *Kastell Hesselbach (Limesforchungen 12)*, Berlin, 1973

A.K. Bowman, 'Roman Military Records from Vindolanda', *Britannia* 5 (1974) 360–73

R.W. Davies, 'The Roman Military Diet', *Britannia* 2 (1971) 122–42

J.H. Dickson, C.A. Dickson and D.J. Breeze, 'Flour or bread in a Roman military ditch at Bearsden, Scotland', *Antiquity* 53 (1979) 47–51

J.H. Dickson, 'Exotic Food and Drink in Ancient Scotland', *Glasgow Naturalist* 19, pt 6 (1979) 437–42

J.C. Ewart, 'Animal Bones', in J. Curle, *A Roman Frontier Post and its People, The Fort of Newstead*, Glasgow, 1911, 362–77

W.S. Hanson, 'Croy Hill', in D.J. Breeze (ed.), *Roman Scotland: Some Recent Excavations*, Edinburgh, 1979, 19–20

N.M. McQ. Holmes, 'Excavations at Cramond, Edinburgh 1975–78', in D.J. Breeze (ed.), *Roman Scotland: Some Recent Excavations*, Edinburgh 1979, 11–4

C. Jobey, 'Homesteads and settlements of the frontier area', in C. Thomas (ed), *Rural Settlement in Roman Britain*, London, 1966, 1–14

C. Jobey, 'Notes on some population problems in the area between the two Roman Walls, I', *Archaeologia Aeliana* 5 ser. 2 (1974) 17–26

W.H. Manning, 'Economic influences on land use in the military areas of the Highland Zone during the Roman period', in J.G. Evans, S. Limbrey and H. Cleere (edd), *The Effect of Man on the Landscape: The Highland Zone*, London, 1975, 112–6

G.S. Maxwell, 'Early rectilinear enclosures in the Lothians', *Scottish Archaeological Forum* 2, 1970, 86–90

G. Thomas, 'Inveresk Vicus, Excavations 1976–77', in D.J. Breeze (ed), *Roman Scotland: Some Recent Excavations*, Edinburgh, 1979, 8–10

S.N. Miller (ed), *The Roman occupation of south-western Scotland*, Glasgow, 1952

I.A. Richmond and K.A. Steer, '*Castellum Veluniate* and Civilians on a Roman Frontier', *Proc. Soc. Antiq. Scot.* 90 (1956–7) 1–6

The abandonment of the Antonine Wall

D.J. Breeze, 'The abandonment of the Antonine Wall: its date and implications', *Scottish Archaeological Forum* 7, 1975, 67–80

J.P. Gillam, 'Sources of Pottery found in Northern Military Sites', in A. Detsicas (ed), *Current Research in Romano-British Coarse Pottery*, London, 1973, 53–62

B.R. Hartley, 'The Roman occupation of Scotland: the evidence of samian ware', *Britannia* 3 (1972) 1–55

G.S. Maxwell, 'Excavations at the Roman fort of Crawford, Lanarkshire', *Proc. Soc. Antiq. Scot.* 104 (1971–2) 147–200

I.A. Richmond, 'Excavations at the Roman Fort of Newstead, 1947', *Proc. Soc. Antiq. Scot.* 84 (1949–50) 1–37

7 War and Peace

Ancient sources

Scriptores Historiae Augustae, Marcus Aurelius, 8 and 22

Scriptores Historiae Augustae, Commodus, 6 and 81

Scriptores Historiae Augustae, Pertinax, 2 and 3

Scriptores Historiae Augustae, Severus, 19, 22 and 23

Cassius Dio, *History of Rome*, 71–77

Herodian, *History of Rome*, 3

Modern Works

A.R. Birley, *Septimius Severus*, London, 1971

A.R. Birley, 'Virius Lupus', *Archaeologia Aeliana* 4 ser. 50 (1972) 179–89

M. Brassington, 'Ulpius Marcellus', *Britannia* 11 (1980) 314–5

B. Dobson and D.J. Breeze, 'Hadrian's Wall: some problems', *Britannia* 3 (1972) 200–6

J.D. Leach and J.J. Wilkes, 'The Roman military base at Carpow, Perthshire, Scotland; summary of recent investigations (1964–70, 1975)', in J. Fitz (ed), *Limes: Akten des XI Internationalen Limeskongresses*, Budapest, 1977, 47–62

R. Reece, 'Coins and frontiers: The Falkirk hoard reconsidered', in W.S. Hanson and L.J.F. Keppie (edd), *Roman Frontier Studies 1979* (= BAR International Series 71), Oxford, 1980, 119–29

N. Reed, 'The Scottish campaigns of Septimius Severus', *Proc. Soc. Antiq. Scot.* 107 (1975–6) 92–102

A.S. Robertson, 'The bridges on Severan coins of AD 208 and 209', in W.S. Hanson and L.J.F. Keppie (edd), *Roman Frontier Studies 1979* (= BAR International Series 71), Oxford, 1980, 131–9

C.J. Simpson, 'Ulpius Marcellus again', *Britannia* 11 (1980) 338–9

R.P. Wright, 'Carpow and Caracalla', *Britannia* 5 (1974) 289–92

The reorganisation of the frontier in the late second century

J.P. Gillam, 'Calpurnius Agricola and the northern frontier', *Trans. Architect. Archaeol. Soc. Durham Northumberland* 10, pt 4 (1953) 359–75

J.P. Gillam, 'The frontier after Hadrian – a history of the problem', *Archaeologia Aeliana* 5 ser. 2 (1974) 1–12

J.P. Gillam and J.C. Mann, 'The northern British frontier from Antoninus Pius to Caracalla', *Archaeologia Aeliana* 4 ser. 8 (1970) 1–44

M.G. Jarrett and J.C. Mann, 'Britain from Agricola to Gallienus', *Bonner Jahrbucher* 170 (1970) 178–210

I.A. Richmond, 'The Romans in Redesdale', *Northumberland County History* 15 (1940) 82–106

A.S. Robertson, *Birrens (Blatobulgium)*, Edinburgh, 1975

K.A. Steer, 'The Severan reorganisation', in I.A. Richmond (ed), *Roman and Native in North Britain*, Edinburgh, 1958, 91–111

Brochs, duns and souterrains

E. Mackie, 'Excavations at Leckie, Stirlingshire', in D.J. Breeze (ed), *Roman Scotland: Some Recent Excavations*, Edinburgh, 1979, 52–5

L. Main, 'Excavations at the Fairy Knowe, Buchlyvie, Stirlingshire', in D.J. Breeze (ed), *Roman Scotland: Some Recent Excavations*, Edinburgh, 1979, 47–51

S. Piggott, 'Excavations in the broch and hill-fort of Torwoodlee, Selkirkshire, 1950', *Proc. Soc. Antiq. Scot.* 85 (1950–51) 91–117

R.B.K. Stevenson, 'Metal-work and some other objects in Scotland and their cultural affinities', in A.L.F. Rivet (ed), *The Iron Age in Northern Britain*, Edinburgh, 1966, 17–44

F.T. Wainwright, *The Souterrains of Southern Pictland*, Edinburgh, 1963

T. Watkins, 'Excavation of a settlement and souterrain at Newmill, near Bankfoot, Perthshire', *Proc. Soc. Antiq. Scot.* 110 (1980), 165–208

The third century

R.E. Birley, *Civilians on the Roman Frontier*, Newcastle upon Tyne, 1973

R.E. Birley, *Vindolanda*, London, 1977

C.M. Daniels, 'Excavations at Wallsend and the fourth-century barracks on Hadrian's Wall', in W.S. Hanson and L.J.F. Keppie (edd), *Roman Frontier Studies 1979* (=BAR International Series 71) Oxford, 1980, 173–93

J. Dore and J.P. Gillam, *The Roman Fort at South Shields*, Newcastle upon Tyne, 1979

J.P. Gillam, 'Excavations at Halton Chesters, 1961', *University of Durham Gazette*, n. ser. 9, no 2.

J.P. Gillam, R.M. Harrison and T.G. Newman, 'Interim Report on Excavations at the Roman fort of Rudchester', *Archaeologia Aeliana* 5 ser. 1 (1973) 81–5

G. Jobey, 'Traprain Law: a summary', in D.W. Harding (ed), *Hillforts*, London, 1976, 191–204

G. Jobey, 'Burnswark Hill', *Trans. Dumfriesshire Galloway Natural History and Antiq. Soc.* 53 (1977–8) 57–104

G.D.B. Jones, 'Invasion and Response in Roman Britain', in B.C. Burnham and H.B. Johnson (edd), *Invasion and Response, The case of Roman Britain* (=BAR British Series 73), Oxford, 1979, 57–70

J.C. Mann, 'The northern frontier after AD 369', *Glasgow Archaeological J.* 3 (1974) 34–42

P. Salway, *The Frontier People of Roman Britain*, Cambridge, 1965

D.A. Welsby, 'Roman building inscriptions, recording buildings collapsed through age or destroyed by the enemy?', *Archaeologia Aeliana* 5 ser. 8 (1980) 89–94

The Picts

Ancient sources

Panegyric Constantio Caesari

Panegyric Constantino Augusti

Anonymous Valesianus, 2.4

Ammianus Marcellinus, *History of Rome*, 20; 26–28

Claudian, *On the fourth consulship of Honorius*

Claudian, *On the first consulship of Stilicho* 2

Modern Works

P.J. Casey, 'Constantine the Great in Britain – the evidence of the coinage of the London mint, AD 312–14', in J. Bird *et al* (edd), *Collectanea Londiniensia: studies in London archaeology and history presented to Ralph Merrifield*, London, 1978, 181–93

P.J. Casey and M. Savage, 'The coins from the excavations at High Rochester in 1852 and 1855', *Archaeologia Aeliana* 5 ser. 8 (1980) 75–87

D.V. Clarke, D.J. Breeze and G. MacKay, *The Romans in Scotland*, Edinburgh, 1980

K. Jackson, 'The Britons in southern Scotland', *Antiquity* 114 (June 1955) 77–88

J.C. Mann, 'The northern frontier after AD 369', *Glasgow Archaeological J.* 3 (1974) 34–42

J.C. Mann, 'What was the Notitia Dignitatum for?' in R. Goodburn and P. Bartholomew (edd), *Aspects of the Notitia Dignitatum* (= BAR Supplementary Series 15) Oxford, 1976, 1–9

J.C. Mann, '*Duces* and *comites* in the fourth century', in D.E. Johnston (ed), *The Saxon Shore*, London, 1977, 11–15

J. Morris, *The Age of Arthur*, London, 1973

F.T. Wainwright, 'The Picts and the problem', in F.T. Wainwright (ed), *The Problem of the Picts*, Edinburgh, 1955, 1–53

The end of Hadrian's Wall

Ancient Sources

Claudian, *On the first consulship of Stilicho*

Claudian, *On the Gothic War*

Notitia Dignitatum Occ. XL

Modern works

J.P.C. Kent, 'Coin evidence and the evacuation of Hadrian's Wall', *Trans. Cumberland Westmorland Antiq. Archaeol. Soc.* 2 ser 51 (1951) 4–15

8 Roman and Barbarian

A. Alföldi, 'The moral barrier on Rhine and Danube', in E. Birley (ed), *The Congress of Roman Frontier Studies 1949*, Durham, 1952, 1–16

D.J. Breeze and B. Dobson, 'The development of the mural frontier in Britain from Hadrian to Caracalla', *Proc. Soc. Antiq. Scot.* 102 (1969–70) 109–21

D.J. Breeze and B. Dobson, 'The development of the northern frontier in Britain from Hadrian to Caracalla', *Actes du IXe Congrès international d'etudes sur les frontières Romaines*, Bucharest, 1974, 321–6

J.P. Gillam, 'Roman and Native, AD 122–197', in I.A. Richmond (ed), *Roman and Native in North Britain*, Edinburgh, 1958, 60–90

J.C. Mann, 'The frontiers of the principate', in H. Temporini (ed), *Aufstieg and Niedergang der römischen Welt II*, i, Berlin, 1974, 508–33

R.B.K. Stevenson, 'Romano-British Glass Bangles', *Glasgow Archaeological J.* 4 (1976), 45–54

Index

Index

D1436403

STUDIES IN REVOLUTION

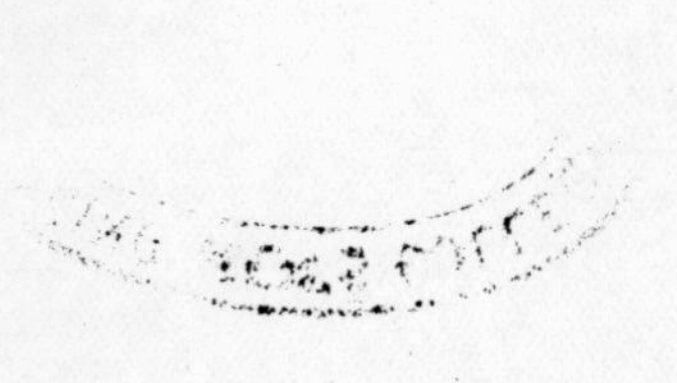

STUDIES IN REVOLUTION

BY

EDWARD HALLETT CARR

LONDON
MACMILLAN & CO. LTD
1950

PRINTED IN GREAT BRITAIN

PREFACE

THE articles out of which this book has been made appeared in the *Literary Supplement* of *The Times* and I am indebted to the Editor of the *Supplement* for kind permission to republish them: I have also incorporated in "The Revolution that Failed" some passages from a talk given in the Third Programme of the British Broadcasting Corporation. A few topical references have been adjusted, a few cases of overlapping removed, and a few corrections made to meet criticisms, public or private. Otherwise the articles appear substantially unchanged; the year of original publication is appended to each in the list of contents. Of the two articles on Stalin with which the volume ends, the first was the earliest item in the collection to be written, the second the last.

E. H. CARR

CONTENTS

1
SAINT-SIMON: THE PRECURSOR

HENRI DE SAINT-SIMON was an intellectual eccentric. He was a member of an aristocratic family who abandoned his title of *Comte* with a dramatic gesture in the French Revolution and spent most of his life in penury; a rationalist and a moralist; a man of letters who never succeeded in writing or completing any coherent exposition of his ideas; and, after his death, the eponymous father of a sect devoted to the propagation of his teaching, which enjoyed a European reputation. Saint-Simon lacked most of the traditional attributes of the great man. It is never easy to distinguish between what he himself thought and the much more coherent body of doctrine, some of it astonishingly penetrating, some not less astonishingly silly, which the sect built up round his name. It is certain that posterity has read back into some of his aphorisms a greater clarity and a greater significance than he himself gave to them. But the study of Saint-Simon often seems to suggest that the great French Revolution, not content with the ideas which inspired its leaders and which it spread over the contemporary world, also projected into the future a fresh ferment of ideas which, working beneath the surface, were to be the main agents of the social and political revolutions of one hundred years to come.

Of these ideas Saint-Simon provided the first precipitation on the printed page. No one who writes about him can avoid applying to him the word " precursor ". He was the precursor of socialism, the precursor of the technocrats, the precursor of totalitarianism — all these labels fit, not perfectly, but, considering the distance of time and the originality of the conceptions as first formulated, with amazing appositeness. Saint-Simon died at the age of sixty-five in 1825, on the eve of a period of unprecedented material progress and sweeping social and political change; and his writings again and again gave an uncanny impression of one who has had a hurried preview of the next hundred years of history and, excited, confused and only half understanding, tried to set down disjointed fragments of what he had seen. He is the type of the great man as the reflector, rather than the maker, of history.

The approach of Saint-Simon to the phenomenon of man in society already has the modern stamp. In 1783, at the age of twenty-three, he had recorded his life's ambition: " Faire un travail scientifique utile à l'humanité ". Saint-Simon marks the transition from the deductive rationalism of the eighteenth to the inductive rationalism of the nineteenth century — from metaphysics to science. He inaugurates the cult of science and of the scientific method. He rejects equally the " divine order " of the theologians and the " natural order " of Adam Smith and the physiocrats. In his first published writing, *Lettres d'un habitant de Genève*, he enunciated the principle that " social relations must be considered as physiological phenomena ". Or again: " The question of social organization must be treated absolutely in the same way as any other scientific question ". The term " sociology " was apparently the invention of Saint-Simon's most famous pupil, once his secretary, Auguste Comte. But the idea came from the master himself and was the essence of his philosophy.

Another of Saint-Simon's pupils, Augustin Thierry, was to become a famous historian; and there is in Saint-Simon not only an embryonic sociology, but an embryonic theory of history which looks forward to a whole school from Buckle to Spengler. History is a study of the scientific laws governing human development, which is divided into " époques organiques " and into " époques critiques "; and the continuity of past, present and future is clearly established. " History is social physics." No doubt later nineteenth-century and twentieth-century theories of history owe more to Hegel than to Saint-Simon. But they owe most of all to Karl Marx, who combined the metaphysical historicism of Hegel with Saint-Simon's sociological utilitarianism.

But perhaps Saint-Simon's most original insight — original enough at a moment when the French Revolution had consecrated the emancipation and enthronement of the individual after a struggle of three centuries — was his vision of the coming resubordination of the individual to society. Saint-Simon, though no partisan of revolution in principle (he once said flatly that dictatorship was preferable to revolution), never abated his enthusiasm for the revolution which had overthrown the *ancien régime*. " La féodalité " was always the enemy ; incidentally, it may well be due, directly or indirectly, to Saint-Simon that " feudalism " became Marx's chosen label for the pre-bourgeois order of society. Nearly all Saint-Simon's contemporaries, and most western European thinkers for at least two generations to come, took it for granted that liberalism was the natural antithesis, and therefore the predestined successor, of " feudalism ". Saint-Simon saw no reason for the assumption. He was not a reactionary, nor even a conservative ; but he was not a liberal either. He was something different — and new.

It was clear to Saint-Simon that, after Descartes and Kant, after Rousseau and the Declaration of the Rights of Man, the cult of individual liberty, of the individual as an end in himself, could go no farther. There are some astonishingly modern echoes in a collection of essays under the title *L'Industrie*, dating from 1816 :

> The Declaration of the Rights of Man which has been regarded as the solution of the problem of social liberty was in reality only the statement of the problem.

A passage of *Du système industriel*, in which Saint-Simon a few years later sought to establish the new historical perspective, is worth quoting in full :

The maintenance of liberty was bound to be an object of primary attention so long as the feudal and theological system still had some power, because then liberty was exposed to serious and continuous attacks. But to-day one can no longer have the same anxiety in establishing the industrial and scientific system, since this system must necessarily, and without any direct concern in the matter, bring with it the highest degree of liberty in the temporal and in the social sphere.

Or again, and more emphatically:

The vague and metaphysical idea of liberty in circulation to-day, if it continues to be taken as the basis of political doctrines, would tend pre-eminently to hamper the action of the mass on the individual. From this point of view it would be contrary to the development of civilization and to the organization of an ordered system which demands that the parties should be firmly bound to the whole and dependent on it.

The individual, as Saint-Simon puts it elsewhere, depends on " the mass ", and it is the relations of each individual with this " progressively active, expanding and overwhelming mass " which have to be " studied and organized ". Even the word " liberty ", in the first two passages quoted above, has the question-begging adjective " social " quietly appended to it. The proper study of mankind is no longer man, but the masses.

In short, Saint-Simon stood at the point of transition from " feudal " to industrial civilization. He perceived the nature of the transition more clearly than his contemporaries, and read more of its implications. How far he himself foresaw the practical application of science to industry cannot be ascertained. It was his disciples who hailed the building of railways with an almost religious fervour as the symbol and instrument of social progress (one recalls Lenin's definition of socialism as "the Soviets plus electrification"), and other disciples who in the 1840s founded the Société d'Études du Canal de Suez. But Saint-Simon insisted — it became more and more the *leitmotiv* of everything he wrote — that industrial production was henceforth the main function of society. "Industry", "production", "organization" — these were the key words in the Saint-Simonist vocabulary.

Logically enough, therefore, Saint-Simon appears as one of the founders of the nineteenth-century cult of work. The beginnings of it are in Rousseau and Babeuf; but it was Saint-Simon who placed it in the very centre of his system. The conception of leisure and contemplation as the highest state of mankind died with the last vestiges of the medieval order. "All men will work," wrote Saint-Simon in the *Lettres d'un habitant de Genève*, where so many of his ideas appear in their primary and simplest form; "the obligation is imposed on every man to give constantly to his personal powers a direction useful to society". Indeed, in a later "Declaration of Principles", he defines society "as the sum total and union of men engaged in useful work". Work is no longer a necessity but a virtue. The new principle of morality is "man must work"; and "the happiest nation is the nation in which there are the fewest unemployed". Saint-Simon provided the moral foundation for the labour theory of value which was being worked out at the same period in England by Ricardo. He also looked forward to the prominence given one hundred years later in the new Soviet gospel to the precept: " He that does not work neither shall he eat ".

The generation which followed Saint-Simon was fruitful in the creation of Utopias; and his views on the organization of society and the State, though there is no systematic exposition of them, were among the most popular of his speculations. It need hardly be said that the liberal conception of politics and economics, introduced into France by Adam Smith's disciple J. B. Say, was anathema to Saint-Simon, for whom " politics is the science of production ". But the identification is achieved by the subordination of politics to economics, not of economics to politics. This is logical; for since " society rests wholly on industry ", which is " the sole source of all riches and all prosperity ", it follows that " the state of things most favourable to industry is for that very reason most favourable to society ". Government in the old sense is a necessary evil. Its sole purpose is to put and keep men at work; for, unhappily, there are "*fainéants*, that is to say, thieves ". But this is a minor and subsidiary function. The supreme authority will be an " economic parliament " (a notion which still had its attractions more than a century later), divided into three chambers concerned respectively with invention, examination and execution.

But Saint-Simon's city of the future presents

other features still more curious. The division of functions is precise. The artists will appeal to the imagination of the worker and excite the appropriate passions. The men of learning " will establish the laws of health of the body social ". (Incidentally these provisions show that the marshalling of art and science in the service of the State is neither new nor peculiar to any one part of Europe.) The " industrials " (in which term Saint-Simon includes producers of all kinds and even traders) will legislate and issue administrative orders. Finally the executive — it is an unexpected climax — will be composed of bankers. It was the age of the great private banks; and the power of credit in the affairs of government and of business was just becoming a current topic. For Saint-Simon, as for Lenin nearly a century later, the banks were the hidden hand that made the wheels of production go round. It was as logical for Saint-Simon to give them a central place in his administrative scheme as for Lenin to treat the nationalization of the banks as the key measure necessary to destroy the economic stranglehold of the bourgeoisie. But what is interesting is to find an embryonic philosophy of planning built up by Saint-Simon round this central executive function of the banks:

The present anarchy of production, which corresponds to the fact that economic relations are being developed without uniform regulation, must give way to the organization of production. Production will not be directed by isolated *entrepreneurs* independent of each other and ignorant of the needs of the people; this task

> will be entrusted to a specific social institution. A central committee of administration, being able to review a broad field of social economy from a higher point of vantage, will regulate it in a manner useful to the whole society, will transfer the means of production into hands appropriate for this purpose, and will be specially concerned to maintain a constant harmony between production and demand. There are institutions which include among their functions a certain degree of organization of economic work: the banks.

Lenin, who quotes this passage at second-hand and is, perhaps, a little jealous for Marx's priority, calls it "a guess of genius, but still only a guess".

More directly fruitful than these visions of a distant future was the conception, running through Saint-Simon's writing about the State, of a distinction between "government" and "administration". It recurs in many shapes. Formerly there were spiritual and temporal "powers"; to-day these have given place to scientific and industrial "capacities". Power, which is an absolute of government, is an oppressive force exercised by men over men; and "the action of man on man is in itself always harmful to the species". On the other hand, "the only useful action exercised by man is the action of man on things". This is administration; and "an enlightened society needs only to be administered". Society is "destined to pass from the governmental or military regime to the administrative or industrial regime after having made sufficient progress in positive sciences and in industry". Saint-Simon does not, like Engels, say that the State will die away. Even Engels's phrase that " the government of men will be replaced by the administration of things " has not been traced textually to the works of Saint-Simon and his disciples. But the idea is borrowed direct from him. The influence of Saint-Simon on Proudhon and on the development of French syndicalist thought with its contempt for the politics of government is not less obvious.

How far should Saint-Simon be called, not merely a precursor of socialism, but himself a " Socialist " ? The word had apparently not been coined in his lifetime. It cannot be traced back farther than 1827, when it appeared in England in an Owenite publication. Its first recorded use in French is in an article of 1832 in *Le Globe*, a newspaper edited by Saint-Simon's disciples after his death. " Nous ne voulons pas sacrifier ", remarks the article, " la *personnalité* au *socialisme*, pas plus que ce dernier à la personnalité." In this sense of placing the stress on society rather than on the individual, Saint-Simon was a Socialist. But in the more political modern sense many doubts arise. The only occasion when Saint-Simon placed a label on his own political opinions was when he said that he belonged neither to the Conservative Party nor to the Liberal Party but to the *parti industriel* ; and while it may be misleading to translate *industriel* by " industrial ", it can hardly be made to mean " Socialist " or even " Labour ". His legislature of *industriels* and executive of bankers came nearer to a benevolent despotism of technocrats or to the managerial society of later speculations.

On the other hand, Saint-Simon was constantly preoccupied with the well-being of those whom he called, in a much-quoted phrase, " la classe la plus nombreuse et la plus pauvre ". He stood in principle for equality of distribution (" luxury will become useful and moral when the whole nation enjoys it "), though he did not make this square with his desire to adjust rewards to capacities. He believed that " the existence of society depends on the conservation of the right of property ". But he added that every society must decide for itself what things could become objects of private property and on what conditions they might be held; for " the individual right of property can be based only on the common and general utility of the exercise of this right — a utility which may vary with the period ". Not only is the priority of the claims of society over those of the individual once more unequivocally asserted, but the idea of historical relativism is introduced to bar any absolute right. Rejection of the feudal conception of property as the absolute right on which society rests is fundamental to Saint-Simon's thought. The society of the future will be not a society of proprietors but a society of producers.

After Saint-Simon's death his disciples systematized his vague and inchoate pronouncements on this question as on others; and current opinion moved more decisively along lines which he had dimly adumbrated. *Le Globe* carried for some time at the head of each number a set of aphorisms which were supposed to sum up the essentials of the master's teaching:

> All social institutions should have as their aim the moral, intellectual and physical improvement of the most numerous and poorest class.
>
> All privileges of birth are abolished without exception.
>
> From each according to his capacity, to each capacity according to its works.

The *Communist Manifesto* sets Saint-Simon side by side with Fourier and Owen as " critical-Utopian Socialists ", who attacked existing society on valid grounds but prescribed Utopian remedies. More specifically, they are accused of failing to appreciate the role of the proletariat in the class struggle or to countenance violent methods of changing the established order. Yet it is fair to recall Engels's handsome tribute — though Saint-Simon would not have liked to be excluded from the " scientific " thinkers — nearly thirty years later :

> German theoretical Socialism will never forget that it stands on the shoulders of Saint-Simon, Fourier and Owen — three thinkers who, however fantastic and Utopian their teachings, belong to the great minds of all times and by the intuition of genius anticipated an incalculable number of the truths which we now demonstrate scientifically.

It was at the very end of his life, and after the failure of an attempt at suicide, that Saint-Simon wrote a book under the title *Le Nouveau Christianisme*, which was the first of several nineteenth-century attempts to create a secular religion on a basis of Christian ethics. At an early stage in his career, while professing belief in God, he had declared that

" the idea of God cannot be employed in the physical sciences " (in which the social sciences were for Saint-Simon included), adding, however, a little enigmatically that " it is the best method yet found to motivate high legislative decisions ". This pragmatic basis was evidently not lacking in *Le Nouveau Christianisme*, though it purported to be the expression of certain moral absolutes, including the brotherhood of man and the universal obligation to work. The " Catholic system ", Saint-Simon had discovered, was " in contradiction with the system of the sciences and of modern industry ". Its downfall was inevitable. Saint-Simon's ambition was nothing less than to provide a substitute for it.

It is not, however, quite fair to lay at Saint-Simon's door all the absurdities afterwards perpetrated in his name by the Saint-Simonist sect. The literary propagation of his doctrines led to the investment of the master with a spurious halo of sanctity; and from this it was a short step to the creation of a church with priesthood and ritual and of a secular monastery at Ménilmontant, in the suburbs of Paris, in which forty of the faithful at one moment secluded themselves. The high priest of the order, Enfantin, was a colourful and masterful figure whose writings were admitted into the canon, but whose unorthodox indulgences led to the dissolution of the order by the authorities. After serving a prison sentence Enfantin migrated to Egypt. But the sect survived for thirty or forty years in France and had some following even in foreign countries, though in England it was soon to be eclipsed by the more sober and reputable ritual of Comte and the Positivists ; and it is an odd irony of history that this posthumous apotheosis should have awaited one who strove so earnestly to establish a secular science of society.

2

THE *COMMUNIST MANIFESTO*

THE winter of 1847–48 (it is difficult to fix a more precise date for the celebration of the centenary) saw the birth of one of the capital documents of the nineteenth century—the *Communist Manifesto*. In the summer of 1847 a group consisting mainly of German craftsmen in London held the first congress of a new " Communist League ". They had been in touch with Marx, then living in Brussels, for some time; and Engels attended the congress, which adjourned to a future congress the drafting of a programme for the League. Inspired by this prospect, Engels tried his hand and produced a catechism in twenty-five questions, which Marx and he took with them to the second League congress in London at the end of November. The congress thereupon charged Marx and Engels to draft their programme for them: it was to take the form of a manifesto. Marx worked away in Brussels through December and January. The " Manifesto of the Communist Party " was published in London in German in February 1848, a few days before the revolution broke out in Paris.

The *Communist Manifesto* is divided into four parts.

The first reviews the rise of the bourgeoisie on the ruins of the feudal system of property relations, government and morality which it destroyed; shows how " the powerful and colossal productive forces " which the bourgeoisie itself created have now grown to a point where they are no longer compatible with bourgeois property relations and bourgeois supremacy; and finally demonstrates that the proletariat is the new revolutionary class which can alone master the forces of modern industry and end the exploitation of man by man. The second part proclaims the policy of the Communist Party, as " the most progressive and resolute section of the working class of all countries ", to promote the proletarian revolution which will destroy bourgeois power and " raise the proletariat to the position of the ruling class ". The third part surveys and condemns other recent and existing schools of socialism; and the fourth is a brief tactical postscript on the relations of Communists to other left-wing parties.

A historic document like the *Communist Manifesto* invites examination from the point of view both of its antecedents and of its consequences. On the former count the *Manifesto* owes as much to predecessors and contemporaries as most great pronouncements; and the worst that can be said is that Marx's sweeping denunciations of predecessors and contemporaries sometimes mask the nature of the debt. Babeuf, who also called his proclamation a " manifesto ", had announced the final struggle between rich and poor, between " a tiny minority " and " the huge majority ". Blanqui had anticipated the class interpretation of history and the idea of the dictatorship of the proletariat (the phrase was not used by Marx himself till 1850). Lorenz von Stein had written that the history of freedom, society and political order was essentially dependent on the distribution of economic goods among the classes of the population. Proudhon also knew that " the laws of political economy are the laws of history " and measured the progress of society " by the development of industry and the perfection of its instruments " ; and Pecqueur had predicted that, with the spread of commerce, " the barriers between nation and nation will be broken down " until the day when " every man becomes a citizen of the world ". Such ideas were current coin in advanced circles when Marx wrote. But neither such borrowings, nor Marx's overriding debt to Hegel's immense synthesis, detract from the power of the conception presented to the world in the *Communist Manifesto.*

To-day it is more appropriate to study the famous manifesto in the light of its hundred-year influence on posterity. Though written when Marx was in his thirtieth year and Engels two years younger, it already contains the quintessence of Marxism. Beginning with a broad historical generalization (" the history of all hitherto existing society is the history of class struggles ") and ending with an inflammatory appeal to the workers of all countries to unite for " the forcible overthrow of all existing social conditions ", it presents Marxist methodology in its fully developed form — an interpretation of history which is at the same time a call to action. Some passages in Marx's writings, especially at the revolutionary crises of 1848 and 1871, appear to commend revolutionary action as a good thing in itself. Some passages, both earlier and later, appear to dwell on the iron laws of historical development in such a way as to leave little place for the initiative of the human will. But these momentary shifts of emphasis cannot be taken to impair the dual orthodoxy established by the *Communist Manifesto*, where interpretation and action, predestination and free will, revolutionary theory and revolutionary practice march triumphantly hand in hand. It propounds a philosophy of history, a dogma of revolution, belief in which will take the spontaneous form of appropriate action in the believer.

The *Communist Manifesto* is thus no broadsheet for the hoardings or the hustings. Marx — and many others who are not Marxists — would deny the possibility of any rigid separation of emotion and intellect; but using the terms in a popular sense, it is to the intellect rather than to the emotions that the *Manifesto* makes its primary appeal. The overwhelming impression which it leaves on the reader's mind is not so much that the revolution is desirable (that, like the injustice of capitalism in *Das Kapital*, is taken for granted as something not requiring argument) but that the revolution is inevitable. For successive generations of Marxists the *Manifesto* was not a plea for revolution — that they did not need — but a prediction about the way in which the revolution would inevitably happen combined with a prescription for the action required of revolutionaries to make it happen. The controversies of a hundred years ranged round the questions as to what Marx actually said or meant and how what he said should be applied to conditions diverging widely from those of his own time and place. Only the bold offered openly to " revise " Marx ; the sagacious interpreted him. The *Communist Manifesto* has thus remained a living document. The centenary of the *Communist Manifesto* cannot be celebrated otherwise than in the light, and in the shadow, of the Russian revolution which was its culminating embodiment in history.

The *Communist Manifesto* sets out a coherent scheme of revolution. " The history of all hitherto existing society is the history of class struggles." In modern times Marx detects two such struggles — the struggle between feudalism and the bourgeoisie, ending in the victorious bourgeois revolution, and the struggle between the bourgeoisie and the proletariat, destined to end in the victorious proletarian revolution. In the first struggle a nascent proletariat is mobilized by the bourgeoisie in support of bourgeois aims, but is incapable of pursuing independent aims of its own : " every victory so obtained is a victory for the bourgeoisie ". In the second struggle Marx recognizes the presence of the lower middle class — " the small manufacturer, the shopkeeper, the artisan, the peasant " — which plays a fluctuating role between bourgeoisie and proletariat, and a " slum proletariat " which is liable to " sell itself to reactionary forces ". But these complications do not seriously affect the ordered simplicity of the main pattern of revolution.

The pattern had been framed in the light of Marx's reading in modern English and French history and in the works of French and British economists, and of Engels's study of factory conditions in England. The English bourgeois revolution, winning its victory in the seventeenth century, had fully consolidated itself by 1832. The French bourgeois revolution, more suddenly and dramatically triumphant after 1789, had succumbed to reaction only to re-emerge once more in 1830. In both countries the first revolutionary struggle of the modern age, the struggle between feudalism and bourgeoisie, was virtually over; the stage was set for the second struggle, between bourgeoisie and proletariat.

The events of 1848, coming hard on the heels of the *Manifesto*, did much to confirm its diagnosis and nothing to refute it. In England the collapse of Chartism was a set-back which none the less marked a stage in the consolidation of a class-conscious workers' movement. In France the proletariat marched shoulder to shoulder with the bourgeoisie in February 1848, as the *Manifesto* had said it would, so long as the aim was to consolidate and extend the bourgeois revolution. But once the proletariat raised its own banner of social revolution the line was crossed. Bourgeoisie and proletariat, allies until the bourgeois revolution had been completed and made secure, were now divided on opposite sides of the barricades by the call for proletarian revolution.

The first revolutionary struggle was thus over: the second was impending. In Paris, in the June days of 1848, Cavaignac saved the bourgeoisie and staved off the proletarian revolution by massacring, executing and transporting the class-conscious workers. The pattern of the *Communist Manifesto* had been precisely followed. As Professor Namier, who is no Marxist, puts it: " The working classes touched off, and the middle classes cashed in on it ".

> The June revolution [as Marx wrote at the time] for the first time split the whole of society into two hostile camps — east and west Paris. The unity of the February revolution no longer exists. The February fighters are now warring against each other — something that has never happened before; the former indifference has vanished and every man capable of bearing arms is fighting on one side or other of the barricades.

The events of February and June 1848 had provided a classic illustration of the great gulf fixed between bourgeois and proletarian revolutions.

Farther east the pattern of England and France did not fully apply, as the concluding section of the *Manifesto* admitted — almost by way of an after-thought. In Germany the bourgeois revolution had not yet begun. The German bourgeoisie had not yet won the fundamental political rights which the English bourgeoisie had achieved in 1689 and the French a hundred years later. The task of the German proletariat was still therefore to support the bourgeoisie in the first revolutionary struggle against feudalism; in Germany, in the words of the *Manifesto*, " the Communist Party fights with the bourgeoisie whenever it acts in a revolutionary manner against the absolute monarchy, the feudal landlords and the petty bourgeoisie ". But it could not be argued that Germany would simply follow the same path as England and France at a greater or less distance of time. The German revolution would occur " under the most advanced conditions of European civilization " which would give it a special character. Where the proletariat was already so advanced, thought Marx, the bourgeois revolution " can only be the immediate prelude to the proletarian revolution ".

When Marx, in the brief concluding section of the *Manifesto*, devoted to Communist Party tactics, thus announced the prospect in Germany of an immediate transition from bourgeois to proletarian revolution without the intervening period of bourgeois rule, he showed a keen historical perception, even at the expense of undermining the validity of his own theoretical analysis. The events of 1848 in the German-speaking lands confirmed Marx's intuition of the impossibility in Germany of a period of established bourgeois supremacy comparable with that which has set so strong a mark on English and French history. This impossibility was due not so much to the strength of the German proletariat, which Marx perhaps exaggerated, as to the weakness of the German bourgeoisie. Whatever the prospects of an eventual proletarian revolution in mid-nineteenth-century Germany, the material for a bourgeois revolution such as England and France had long ago achieved was still conspicuously absent.

Indeed, the bourgeoisie, far from bidding for power for itself, was plainly ready to ally itself with the surviving elements of feudalism for defence against the proletarian menace. It need hardly be added that the same symptoms, in a still more pronounced form, repeated themselves in Russia more than half a century afterwards.

The problem, therefore, which Germany presented in 1848 to the authors of the *Communist Manifesto* was the same which Russia would one day present to the theorists of her revolution. According to the revolutionary pattern of the *Communist Manifesto*, the function of the bourgeoisie was to destroy feudal society root and branch preparatory to its own destruction in the final phase of the revolutionary struggle by the proletariat. But what was to happen if the bourgeoisie through weakness or cowardice — or perhaps through some untimely premonition of its own eventual fate — was unable or unwilling to perform its essential function? Marx never provided a categorical answer to this question. But his answer was implicit in the doctrine of " permanent revolution ", which he propounded in an address to the Communist League in 1850:

> While the democratic petty bourgeoisie wants to end the revolution as rapidly as possible . . . our interests and our task consist in making the revolution permanent until all the more or less possessing classes are removed from authority, until the proletariat wins State power.

The responsibility was thus placed on the proletariat to complete the task, which the bourgeoisie had failed to perform, of liquidating feudalism.

What form the liquidation was to take when the proletariat found itself directly confronted by a feudal society without any effective and independent bourgeoisie was not altogether clear. But if one insisted — as Marx apparently did, and Engels continued to do down to the end of his life — that " our party can come to power only under some such form as a democratic republic ", then the conclusion followed that the immediate aim of the proletariat must be limited to the establishment of a political democracy in which it was interested only as a necessary stepping-stone to the proletarian social revolution. This was, however, a theoretical construction unlikely to be realized in practice — as the experience of both the German and the Russian revolutions was one day to show. Marx never really fitted his analysis of revolution to countries where the bourgeoisie was incapable of making its own revolution ; and acrimonious controversy about the relation between bourgeois and proletarian revolutions continued to divide the Russian revolutionaries for several decades.

The economic corollary of this conclusion was still more startling. If the establishment of a democratic republic was a prerequisite of the proletarian revolution, so also was the full development of capitalism ; for capitalism was the essential expression of bourgeois society and inseparable from it. Marx certainly held this view as late as 1859 when he wrote in the preface to the *Critique of Political Economy* : " No social form perishes until all the productive forces for which it provides scope have been developed ". It appeared to follow, paradoxically enough, that in backward countries the interest of the nascent proletariat was to promote the most rapid development of capitalism and capitalist exploitation at its own expense.

Such was the view seriously propounded by Russian Marxists, Bolshevik and Menshevik alike, down to 1905 — perhaps even down to 1917. Meanwhile, however, in the spring of 1905, Lenin's practical mind worked out a new scheme under which the proletariat was to seize power in conjunction with the peasantry, creating a " democratic dictatorship " of workers and peasants; and this became the official doctrine of the October revolution. The Mensheviks stuck to their guns, and their survivors and successors to-day attribute the shortcomings of the Russian revolution to its failure to pass through the bourgeois-democratic, bourgeois-capitalist phase on its way to the achievement of socialism. The issue is not to be settled by reference to Marx, who can hardly be acquitted of inconsistency on this point. Either he made a mistake in suggesting, in the last section of the *Communist Manifesto*, that Germany might pass immediately from the bourgeois to the proletarian revolution; or he failed to fit this new conception into the revolutionary framework of the earlier part of the *Manifesto*.

Marx was to encounter similar difficulties in applying the generalizations of the *Communist Manifesto* about nationalism, which were also based on British and French experience, to central and eastern

Europe. The charge often brought against Marx of ignoring or depreciating national sentiment rests indeed on a misunderstanding. The famous remark that " the workers have no country ", read in its context, is neither a boast nor a programme; it is a complaint which had long been a commonplace among socialist writers. Babeuf had declared that the multitude " sees in society only an enemy, and loses even the possibility of having a country "; and Weitling had connected the notion of country with the notion of property:

> He alone has a country who is a property owner or at any rate has the liberty and the means of becoming one. He who has not that, has no country.

In order to remedy this state of affairs (to quote once more from the *Manifesto*) " the proletariat must first conquer political power, must rise to be the dominant class of the nation, must constitute itself the nation, so that the proletariat is so far national itself, though not in the bourgeois sense ".

The passage of the *Manifesto* in which these sentences occur is not free from ambiguities. But the thought behind it is clear. In Marx's view, which corresponded to the facts of English and French history, nationalism grew up as an attribute of bourgeois society at a time when the bourgeoisie was a revolutionary and progressive force. Both in England and in France the bourgeoisie, invoking the national spirit to destroy a feudalism which was at once particularist and cosmopolitan, had through a period of centuries built up a centralized State on a national basis. But the advance of capitalism was already making nations obsolete.

> National differences and antagonisms are to-day vanishing ever more and more with the development of the bourgeoisie, free trade in the world market, the uniformity of industrial production and the conditions of life corresponding thereto.
>
> With the victory of the proletariat they will vanish still faster. . . . With the disappearance of classes within the nation the state of enmity between nations will come to an end.

Hence the first step was for the proletariat of every country to " settle accounts with its own bourgeoisie ". The way would then be open for a true international communist order. Like Mazzini and other nineteenth-century thinkers, Marx thought of nationalism as a natural stepping-stone to internationalism.

Unfortunately the national pattern of the *Manifesto*, far from being universal, proved difficult to extend beyond the narrow limits of the place (western Europe) or the time (the age of Cobden) in which it was designed. Beyond western Europe the same conditions which prevented the rise of a powerful bourgeoisie also prevented the development of an orderly bourgeois nationalism. In central Europe (the Hapsburg Empire, Prussia) as well as in Russia the centralized State had been brought into being under pressure of military necessity by feudal overlords indifferent to national feeling; and when in the nineteenth century, under the impetus of the French revolution, nationalism became for the first time a force to be reckoned with in central and eastern Europe, it appeared not — as in England and France — as an attribute and complement of the State but as a sentiment independent of any existing State organization.

Moreover, the relation of nation to State worked itself out in different ways and sometimes involved even the same national group in inconsistent attitudes. This was particularly true of the Hapsburg Empire. The growing national consciousness of the German-Austrian bourgeoisie did not diminish its support of imperial unity; the bourgeoisie of the other constituent national groups sought to destroy that unity or at least to dissolve it into a federation. The Hungarians asserted the rights of the Magyar nation against the German-Austrians, but denied the national rights of Croats and Slovaks.

In these circumstances it is not surprising that Marx and Engels never succeeded in working out, even for their own day and generation, a consistent theory of nationalism which would hold good throughout Europe. They supported the Polish claim to national independence; no revolutionary, no liberal, of the nineteenth century could have done otherwise. But Engels, at any rate, seemed mainly concerned that this claim should be satisfied at the expense of Russia rather than of Prussia, proposing on one occasion to offer the Poles Riga and Mitau in exchange for Danzig and Elbing; and in the candid outburst of a private letter to Marx he referred to the Poles as "*une nation foutue*, a serviceable instrument only until Russia herself is swept into the agrarian revolution ". In the same spirit he rejected outright the national aspirations of the Slavs of the Hapsburg Empire, whose triumph would be, in his eyes, a subjugation " of the civilized west by the barbaric east ".

In these judgments, from which Marx is not known to have dissented, Engels was indubitably swayed by national prejudice and in particular by hostility to Russia as the most reactionary Power of the day. But he was also moved by the recognition that these nationalisms of central and eastern Europe, whose economic basis was agrarian, had little or nothing to do with the bourgeois nationalism of which Marx and he had taken cognizance in the *Communist Manifesto*. It was not only a question of " the civilized west " and " the barbaric east " : it was a question of the subjugation " of town by the country, of trade, manufacture and intelligence by the primitive agriculture of Slavonic serfs ". On the presuppositions of the *Manifesto*, this seemed necessarily a retrograde step. The failure of Marx and Engels to take account of agrarian nationalism was one aspect of the other great lacuna of the *Manifesto* — the question of the peasant.

If, however, the theory of nationalism propounded in the *Communist Manifesto* could not be transplanted from western to central and eastern Europe, it equally failed to stand the test of time. The *Manifesto* contains indeed one reference to " the exploitation of one nation by another " and declares, by what seems a tautology in one sense and a *non sequitur* in another, that it will end when the exploitation of one individual by another ends. But Marx has little to say (nothing at all in the *Manifesto* itself) about the colonial question, touching on it in detail only in the case of Ireland; and here it is perhaps significant that, while in 1848 he was prepared to sacrifice the Irish in the same way as the Austrian Slavs, he had become convinced by 1869 that " the direct absolute interest of the English working class demands a rupture of the present connexion with Ireland ". Marx did not, however, live to see the full development of the process by which the great nations, already victims of the contradictions of capitalism, vied with one another in bringing the whole world under their yoke in a desperate attempt to save themselves and the capitalist system — the process which Lenin was afterwards to analyse in his famous work on *Imperialism as the Highest Stage of Capitalism*; nor could he foresee that rise to national consciousness of innumerable " unhistorical " nations of which the Austrian Slavs had been the harbingers. The Soviet theory of nationality, in which the colonial question and the question of small nations divide the honours between them, can derive only a pale and faltering light from the simple and far-away formulation of the *Communist Manifesto.* But critics of the national theories, whether of Marx or of the Bolsheviks, may do well to reflect that bourgeois thinkers and statesmen have also not been able to formulate, and still less to apply, a consistent doctrine of national rights.

Marx's attitude to the tiller of the soil is more seriously open to criticism. Here too there is a foretaste of subsequent controversy — both the Mensheviks and Trotsky were accused, rightly from Lenin's point of view, of " underestimating " the peasant; and here too Marx ran into trouble because his initial theories had been primarily framed to fit western conditions. The *Communist Manifesto* praised the bourgeoisie for having, through its development of factories and towns, " delivered a great part of the population from the idiocy of country life " ; and it classed peasant or peasant proprietor with handicraftsmen, small traders and shopkeepers as members of the " petty bourgeoisie " — an unstable and reactionary class, since it struggled against the greater bourgeoisie, not for revolutionary ends, but only in order to maintain its own bourgeois status. In England, in France (which in revolutionary circles was generally thought of as Paris writ large) and in Germany, the *Communist Manifesto* upheld the strict pattern of successive revolutions of which the bourgeoisie and the proletariat would be the respective driving forces, and reserved no independent place for the peasant.

Events were soon to show up the lacuna left by this scheme of things even in western Europe. The French peasants were unmoved when the revolutionary workers of Paris were shot down in June 1848 by the agents of the bourgeoisie, and voted solidly for the bourgeois dictatorship of Louis Napoleon. In fact they behaved exactly as the *Communist Manifesto* expected them to behave (which did not save them from incurring some of Marx's fiercest invective in *The Eighteenth Brumaire of Louis Napoleon*) ;

but in so doing they showed how far things would have to travel before the French proletariat would be able to make another French revolution.

In Prussia and throughout Germany the revolution of 1848 was in the hands of intellectuals who thought as little of the peasants as Marx himself; and the peasants failed to move. In Austria the peasants did move. They rose in Galicia against the landlords and would have risen elsewhere with the right leadership. They formed a large and vocal group in the new democratic Reichstag. But the claims of the peasant encountered the hostility of the bourgeoisie and the indifference of the urban workers. Peasantry and proletariat were crushed separately in the absence of a leader and a programme to unite them; and in central Europe the surest moral of 1848 was that no revolution could succeed which did not win the peasant and give a high priority to his concerns.

In eastern Europe this was still more abundantly clear. As regards Poland, even the *Communist Manifesto* declared that " the Communists support the party that sees in agrarian revolution the means to national freedom, the party which caused the Cracow insurrection of 1846 ". But this passage, which occurs in the tactical postscript, is the only incursion of the *Manifesto* into eastern Europe and the only reference to agrarian revolution; and even here agrarian revolution is regarded as the ally of a bourgeois revolution leading to " national freedom ", not of a proletarian revolution.

Spending the rest of his years in England, where

there was no peasantry and no agrarian question, Marx never felt any strong impulse to fill this lacuna in the *Communist Manifesto.* In 1856, drawing a moral from the failure of 1848 in Germany, he spoke casually of the importance of backing up the future proletarian German revolution " with some second edition of the Peasants' War ". But even here only a subsidiary role was assigned to the peasantry. It was towards the end of his life that Marx was called on to pass judgment on a controversy just opening in far-away Russia. The leading Russian revolutionaries, the Narodniks, regarded the Russian peasant commune with its system of common tenure of land as the seed-bed of the future Russian Socialist order. On the other hand, the first Russian Marxists were already beginning to argue that the way to socialism could only lie, in Russia as elsewhere, through a development of capitalism and the proletariat.

Four times did the Marx-Engels partnership attack this ticklish issue. In 1874, before the Russian Marxists had raised their head, Engels had recognized the possibility in favourable conditions of the direct transformation of the communal system into a higher form, " avoiding the intermediate stage of individualized bourgeois property ". In 1877, in reply to an attack in a Russian journal, Marx confined himself to a doubtful admission that Russia had " the finest chance which history ever presented to a nation of avoiding the up-and-downs of the capitalist order ". In 1881 Marx gave a more positive response to a direct personal inquiry from

Vera Zasulich; and in the following year the last and most authoritative pronouncement appeared in the preface to a Russian translation of the *Communist Manifesto*, signed jointly by both its authors:

> If the Russian revolution is the signal for a workers' revolution in the west so that these complement each other, then the contemporary Russian system of communal ownership can serve as the starting-point for a Communist development.

Russian Social-Democrats of a later generation, both Bolshevik and Menshevik, looked askance at this quasi-Narodnik deviation, and returned to the purer theoretical pattern of the *Manifesto* with its clear-cut dialectic of bourgeois and proletarian revolutions; and Lenin himself, not less than the Mensheviks, sternly maintained the paradox that the further development of capitalism in Russia was a necessary prelude to social revolution. Nevertheless, Lenin, like Marx in his later years, recognized that no revolution, and no revolutionary, in eastern Europe could afford to ignore the peasant and his demands. After 1905 — and before and after 1917 — the Bolsheviks were obliged to devote an immense amount of energy and controversy to the task of fitting the Russian peasant into the western formulae of the *Communist Manifesto*.

Franz Mehring, Marx's best and most sympathetic biographer, remarks of the *Communist Manifesto* that "in many respects historical development has proceeded otherwise, and above all has proceeded more slowly, than its authors expected". This is true of the expectations of the two young men who composed the *Manifesto*. But how far were these expectations modified? As regards pace, Marx in later life certainly no longer believed in the imminence of the proletarian revolution with all the eager confidence of 1848. But even the *Manifesto* in one of its more cautious passages had predicted temporary successes followed by set-backs and a slow process of " growing unity " among the workers before the goal was achieved. Marx came, with advancing years, to accept the necessity of a long course of education for the proletariat in revolutionary principles; and there is the famous *obiter dictum* in a speech of the 1870s, which admits that in certain advanced countries the victory of the proletariat may be achieved without revolutionary violence.

As regards the scheme of historical development, it would be difficult to prove that Marx, speaking theoretically and *ex cathedra*, ever abandoned the strict analysis of revolution which he had worked out in the *Communist Manifesto*. But he was not a pure theorist. He was willy-nilly the leader of a political party; and it was when he found himself compelled to make pronouncements in this capacity that he sometimes appeared to derogate from his principles. Thus in the last section of the *Manifesto* itself he had already foreseen that in Germany the bourgeois revolution would be the " immediate prelude " of the proletarian revolution, thus skipping over the period of bourgeois supremacy; in the next few years he was drawn into some uncomfortable compromises and inconsistencies on the national question; and towards the end of his life he was constrained to admit that a predominantly peasant country like Russia had the chance of achieving the social revolution without passing through the bourgeois capitalist phase at all, thus not merely modifying but side-tracking altogether the revolutionary analysis of the *Manifesto*.

It is curious and significant of the vitality of Marx's thought to watch how accurately this evolution was repeated in the Russian Social-Democratic Party. Its first leaders — Plekhanov and Axelrod, Lenin and Martov — accepted without question the scheme of the *Communist Manifesto*. After 1903 the Mensheviks, remaining consistent with themselves and with the Marxist scheme, ended in bankruptcy because they could find no way of applying it to Russian conditions. The more flexible Lenin took the scheme and brilliantly adapted it to those conditions; and the adaptations which he made followed — in broad outline, though not in every detail — those which Marx himself had admitted in his later years. The process can be justified. Marxism was never offered to the world as a static body of doctrine; Marx himself once confessed that he was no Marxist; and the constant evolution of doctrine in response to changing conditions is itself a canon of Marxism.

It is on such grounds that the Russian revolution can claim to be a legitimate child of the *Communist Manifesto*. The *Manifesto* challenged bourgeois society and offered a revaluation of bourgeois values. The Bolshevik revolution, with all its deviations, all its adaptations to specifically Russian conditions and all the impurities which always disfigure practice as opposed to theory, has driven home the challenge and sought to apply the revaluation. That bourgeois society has been put progressively on the defensive in the past hundred years, that its fate still hangs in the balance, few to-day will deny; and until that fate is settled, until some new synthesis has been achieved, the *Communist Manifesto* will not have said its last word.

3

PROUDHON: ROBINSON CRUSOE OF SOCIALISM

"A MAN of paradoxes" Proudhon called himself in one of his earliest extant letters in that challenging, defiant manner which is characteristic of his personality and of his style. It was no empty boast. It is the same man who can proclaim that "God is Evil" and that "Christianity has no ethic and cannot have one", but that "atheism is even less logical than faith" and that Catholicism is "the unique refuge of morality and beacon of conscience". It is the same man who declared that he voted against the constitution of 1848 not because it was a good or bad constitution, but because it was a constitution, and who praised the Vienna settlement of 1814–15 as "the real starting-point of the constitutional era in Europe". It is the same man who argued that war was irrelevant because it did nothing to solve essential economic problems, but declared that "man is above all else a warrior animal" and that "it is through war that his sublime nature becomes manifest".

Proudhon's writings are difficult of access owing both to their incoherence and to their enormous extent. Editors and publishers have, on the whole, been kind, and most of his major works are readily available, though a mammoth complete edition remains unfinished. The fourteen volumes of the far-from-complete collection of his correspondence have been conveniently reduced for the ordinary reader to a single volume of selections; [1] but the mass has received a fresh accretion from the recent publication of a series of important and characteristic letters from the last years of his life to his friend Rolland.[2]

There is thus ample evidence that Proudhon has retained his fascination for his countrymen, if only as a vast storehouse of ideas from which nuggets of any quality and complexion can be drawn. Many years ago Bouglé, who remains the most satisfactory of a host of commentators, neatly but inadequately ticketed him as an analyst of the social forces of revolution. To-day a volume of carefully chosen extracts from his works,[3] the tendency of which is indicated by the interlarding of the text with passages from Péguy and by a quotation from General de Gaulle on the title-page, calls for a " return to Proudhon " as the antidote to the poisons of capitalism, democracy *and* socialism, and as the symbol of a recall to religion. Meanwhile an ingenious American professor, using many of the same texts and taking the hint from a eulogy of Proudhon which appeared in the French collaborationist Press under

[1] P. J. Proudhon, *Lettres choisies et annotées*, par Daniel Halévy et Louis Guilloux.

[2] P. J. Proudhon, *Lettres au citoyen Rolland.*

[3] Proudhon, *Textes choisis*, par Alexandre Marc.

the German occupation, depicts him with skill and plausibility as the first progenitor of Hitlerism.[1] More judicial than either of these, Mlle. Amoudruz has produced a scholarly monograph [2] which, while professedly confined to Proudhon's views on international affairs, necessarily touches on the wider ground of his whole political creed.

The element of incoherence in Proudhon derives largely from the character of the man. He had a passion for contradiction, and contradicted himself almost as readily as he contradicted others. Sometimes, especially in the letters, one suspects the practical joker. When he explains his hostility to the North in the American civil war by his dislike of "so-called liberal and democratic states" he may be nine-tenths serious (though that was not the fundamental reason for his attitude). When he adds, "J'ai en horreur la liberté", he is manifestly putting out his tongue at his correspondent and at himself. But there was in Proudhon a profound and unresolved contradiction between revolutionary opinions which expressed, in part, at any rate, his resentments against a cramped, poverty-stricken and persecuted life and the passion of the self-educated peasant for bourgeois respectability. He might, in theory, reject Church and State, authority and property. But anything that touched the sanctity of the family aroused his instinctive fury. It was this that led him into his last and most

[1] J. Selwyn Schapiro, "Pierre Joseph Proudhon, Harbinger of Fascism" (*American Historical Review*, Vol. L, No. 4, July 1945.)

[2] Madeleine Amoudruz, *Proudhon et l'Europe*.

grotesque self-contradiction. The man who had started his career (and made his name) by declaring that property is theft, ended it by denouncing a tax on inheritance on the ground that it destroyed the family by transferring its property to the State.

The question of the influence of the Hegelian doctrine of thesis and antithesis in forming Proudhon's thought has been frequently canvassed. No thinker of the day could escape Hegel; and Herzen tells a pleasant story of Bakunin expounding to Proudhon through the whole of one night, by the embers of a dying fire, the mysteries of the Hegelian dialectic. Proudhon even wrote a long and complicated work entitled *Système des contradictions économiques ou philosophie de la misère*, in which he proved that the soundest economic principles had the most evil consequences, though all led ultimately to the goal of equality. But Marx, who indited an angry retort entitled *La Misère de la philosophie*, was probably right in alleging that Proudhon never understood Hegel. A superficial dabbling in the dialectic provided a respectable cloak for the Proudhonian passion for paradox — but little more.

There is, however, another element in Proudhon's self-contradiction which is missed by those editors and critics — unfortunately, a majority of them — who fail to place him against the rapidly changing background of his period. "I mistrust an author who pretends to be consistent with himself after twenty-five years' interval", wrote Proudhon; and the plea is incontestably valid for the generation

(Proudhon's dates are 1809–65) whose careers were split in two by the historical watershed of 1848. His first prolific years as a writer were passed amid the generous revolutionary enthusiasms of the 1840s — a period fertile in ideas so simple, so noble and so Utopian that it seems difficult to take them seriously to-day, yet the seed-bed of nearly all political thought for the rest of the century. Everything that was radical and subversive in Proudhon's thought grew out of this congenial soil. " Destruam et Aedificabo " was the motto which he prefixed to one of his early works. It would have been representative of his attitude at this time if he had been content to plead, like Bakunin, that " the passion for destruction is also a creative passion ".

For the visionaries of the 1840s, the year 1848 came as a bitter disillusionment. The great upheaval which was to complete the work of the French Revolution and usher in the age of social equality and the brotherhood of man had ended, in the very capital of revolution, with the shooting down of the workers by Cavaignac amid the approbation of the self-satisfied bourgeoisie and its representative assembly. The split had come between the middle class and the workers, between bourgeois democracy and " social democracy ", alias Communism. This was the lesson and the consequence of 1848. Marx drew the necessary conclusion and invented the doctrines of " the dictatorship of the proletariat " and " permanent revolution ". The proletariat must now take matters into their own hands and bring to full fruition the revolution which the bourgeoisie had failed to consummate. From this time forward the bourgeoisie became the target of all the worst insults of the revolutionaries. The revolt against bourgeois democracy, due to the disillusionments of 1848 and after, still determined the anti-political bias of the French syndicalist movement fifty years later.

The reaction against 1848, intersecting the Utopian idealism of his earlier years, governed the self-frustrating course of all Proudhon's subsequent thought. Like Marx, he turned violently against bourgeois democracy, and pursued its leaders into exile — Louis Blanc, Ledru-Rollin and the rest — with some of his most venomous sallies. "Democracy", he writes in *La Solution du problème social*, "composes its ruling class (*son patriciat*) of mediocrities." Pages might be filled with arguments — or sheer abuse — from his later writings against universal suffrage, "the surest means of making the people lie". An extract from *Les Confessions d'un révolutionnaire* echoes precisely the familiar Marxist thesis:

> How could universal suffrage reveal the thought, the real thought, of the people, when the people is divided by inequality of fortunes into classes subordinate one to the other and voting either through servility or through hate; when this same people, held in restraint by authority, is incapable notwithstanding its sovereignty of expressing its ideas on anything; and when the exercise of its rights is limited to choosing, every three or four years, its chiefs and its impostors?

But Marx was, after all, right in describing Proudhon as a *petit bourgeois*; and he had all the *petit bourgeois* fear of, and contempt for, the proletariat (a noteworthy anticipation here of the ideological foundations of National Socialism). Picking up Saint-Simon's formula of " la classe la plus nombreuse et la plus pauvre ", he declared that this class is, " by the very fact of its poverty, the most ungrateful, the most envious, the most immoral and the most cowardly " ; and later he was to speak of " the stupidity of the proletariat content to work, to hunger and to serve, provided its princes grow fat and glorious ".

For Proudhon, therefore, there was no escape after 1848, as there was for Marx, into the ideology of the proletariat as the bearer of the revolutionary faith. Proudhon became a revolutionary without a party, without a class, without a creed, " the Robinson Crusoe of Socialism ", as Trotsky called him ; and the position suited, and intensified, the wayward individualism of his temperament. The most significant analogies that can be found for his development are the Russian revolutionaries, Herzen and Bakunin. Several curious letters to Herzen appear in Proudhon's correspondence of the eighteen-fifties. Like him, Herzen had lost faith in western democracy without acquiring faith in the proletariat ; and after 1855 Herzen sought to build his hopes — short-lived, indeed — on the liberal aspirations of the young Tsar Alexander II. Meanwhile Bakunin had written from a Russian prison his famous *Confessions* to Nicholas I ; and in Siberia he toyed with the potentialities of enlightened despotism in the person of the Governor-General,

Muraviev. It can hardly be mere coincidence that Proudhon should have followed the same path. His one contact with the Legitimists permits of a fairly innocent explanation, which is given at length in one of the newly published letters to Rolland. But his enthusiastic welcome of the *coup d'état* of December 2, 1851, as the embodiment of social revolution, his appeal to all republicans and socialists to rally to the banner of the Prince-President, and his subsequent flirtations with the Second Empire — punctuated, after Proudhon's usual manner, by periods of vituperation — cannot be so lightly dismissed. These political romantics of the 1840s, nourished on visions of a better world of the future, but disillusioned after 1848 both about the means of attaining this better world and about the human beings who were to inhabit it, strayed along some strange by-ways in the attempt to recapture their lost ideal.

Such were the conditions in which Proudhon became the founder of the political doctrine of anarchism, if anything so inchoate as anarchism — not a programme, it has been aptly said, but a *critique* of society — can be held to constitute a doctrine, and if so radical an iconoclast as Proudhon can be said to have founded anything. In the theory of anarchism Proudhon had William Godwin for his ancestor; in its practical advocacy he was preceded by Wilhelm Weitling, the wandering tailor from Magdeburg who, though only a few years older than Proudhon, started his missionary career at an earlier age. But it was Proudhon who first gave anarchism its place and its influence in nineteenth-century thought; for Bakunin, who might have ranked as a co-founder, gallantly awarded him the priority. Proudhon and Bakunin stand side by side as men who seem to have believed in revolution as a good in itself (though Proudhon, as usual, sometimes denounced even revolution), and felt it unnecessary, perhaps because they felt themselves unable, to furnish any positive definition of their goal. In this respect the successor who stands nearest to them is the syndicalist Sorel, who held that the business of doctrine is to provide an appropriate myth, whether true or not, to inspire and stimulate the forces of revolution.

Yet, notwithstanding all that has been said — and rightly said — about the self-contradictions of Proudhon and about the mood of frustration and disillusionment in which his teaching was rooted, the immense impression which he made on his contemporaries and on posterity bears witness to the vitality and sincerity of his thought. He gave to nineteenth-century political thinkers and political programme-makers something which they needed and which they greedily devoured. Out of the welter of Proudhon's writings there remain two fixed points round which he gravitates and to which he returns again and again with all his wonted pertinacity and with an unwonted consistency. These are his rejection of the State and of political power as a principle of evil, and his advocacy of " federalism " (whatever precisely that might mean) as a form of common organization for social and national groups.

The conception of political power as a necessary evil called into existence by man's sinful nature is rooted in the Christian tradition; and the belief in an era of primitive bliss before the formation of States is common, among other thinkers, to Rousseau and Engels. But nineteenth-century anarchism, which first received form and content from Proudhon, is no mere vision of a golden age in the past or in the future. It is a creed of active rebellion against the State, which it seeks to destroy, if necessary by force. Proudhon begins in 1847 by demanding "la République, anarchie positive"; and in the last year of his life he defines anarchy more concretely as

> a form of government or constitution in which the public and private conscience, formed by the development of science and right, is sufficient by itself for the maintenance of order and the guarantee of all liberties, and where consequently the principle of authority, police institutions, the means of prevention or repression, bureaucracy, taxation, etc., are reduced to their simplest expression.

Between these dates Proudhon's pages pullulate with denunciations of the State. It is "the constitutional muzzling of the people, the legal alienation of its thoughts and its initiative". It is "that fictitious being, without intelligence, without passion, without morality, which we call the State"; and "whoever lays hands on me to govern me is a usurper and a tyrant". Proudhon rejects altogether "this fatal theory of the competence of the State".

But what is to be put into the void thus created? Proudhon has two answers to this question. The first derives from a fruitful inspiration of that queer genius Saint-Simon. Here was a man who was not an anarchist but — to use an anachronistic piece of jargon — a technocrat, believing that " les industriels " (by which he meant all concerned in the productive or distributive processes) were destined to control the State, that political power would be succeeded by economic power and " government " be replaced by " administration ". In a phrase apparently not used by Saint-Simon himself, but by his disciples, the State would become " an association of workers ". This vision, like Auguste Comte's surrealist plan for the management of " the human planet " by 14,000 bankers, seemed to presage the eventual elimination of the State; and it had the fortune to be adopted by both Proudhon and Engels, by both syndicalists and Bolsheviks. Proudhon attempted to give shape to the tempting prospect by outlining a scheme for a free credit bank based on the principle of " mutualism "; but neither contemporaries nor posterity have been induced to treat this seriously. It is only necessary to record on Proudhon's behalf this further claim to originality as one of the first crank financial reformers.

Proudhon's second answer, given in the last work published in his lifetime, which he called *Du principe fédérateur et de la nécessité de reconstituer le parti de la Révolution*, is that sovereignty rests with " the commune " — the local unit which has, in Proudhon's eyes, as natural a basis as the family. This unit he would allow to govern itself, to impose taxes on itself and perhaps even to legislate for itself. If Dr. Thomson, in his book on *Democracy in France*, is right in describing the French political ideal as "ranging from an extreme individualism which is tantamount to anarchism to a respect for small and intense human communities which are but the individual writ large", then Proudhon was the very embodiment of the French ideal.

The Paris Commune reflected Proudhon's ideas and terminology; and the anarchists continued to uphold the tradition of the small community. Bakunin thought in terms of the Russian peasant commune, Kropotkin of the village community of the Middle Ages. Anarchism thus became a protest against the mass civilization of the industrial age. Its strength lay among the small craftsmen in countries where large-scale industry had not yet made important inroads — in Italy, in France, and above all, in Spain. In the First International it was the delegates from the Latin countries who were Proudhonists or Bakuninists and a constant thorn in Marx's side. Marx and the Marxists were, on the whole, right in affixing to anarchism and "anarcho-syndicalism" what was to them the derogatory *petit bourgeois* label.

If the commune bears the weight of Proudhon's protest against the centralized State, it also opens the way to his other principle — federalism. He predicted that the twentieth century would be the age of federations. What precisely he meant by the term remains more than ordinarily vague. Bakunin regarded a "free federation of communes" as the only legitimate form of political organization. Proudhon, with his usual inconsistency, took existing States as his starting-point and approached the issue from the angle of current international affairs. He wanted federation as the basis of relations between States. But he perceived that one of the difficulties was the existing inequality between States, and thought that this, too, might be got over by the application of the federal principle, namely, by an "interior distribution of sovereignty and government". Federalism, in both senses, was "the alpha and omega of my policy".

Here it becomes necessary to say something on the vexed question of Proudhon's attitude to nationality and nationalism. In his earlier life he was influenced by the flaming patriotism of Michelet. But he afterwards reacted strongly both against the man and against his work, and denounced the fashionable advocacy of self-determination and of the rights of nations to unity and independence. "Those who speak so much of re-establishing these national unities", he wrote with a certain amount of prescience, "have little taste for individual liberties." The South in the American civil war had his enthusiastic support against the North because the Southerners were federalists seeking to break up an artificial Union. Alone among advanced thinkers of the period, Proudhon was bitterly opposed both to the liberation of Poland and to the unification of Italy. Poland has always been "the most corrupt of aristocracies and the most indisciplined of states"; what she needs is a

" radical revolution which will abolish, with the great States, all distinctions of nationality, which will henceforth have no foundation ". As for " the *present* emancipation of Italy by the Cavours, the Victor-Emmanuels, the Bonapartes, the Saint-Simonians, the Jews, the Garibaldis and the Mazzinis " (a characteristic Proudhonian catalogue of anathemas), it is nothing but a " hideous mystification ". Writing in 1861, Proudhon breaks a lance with Herzen on the subject:

Do you suppose that it is through French egoism, hatred of liberty, or contempt for the Poles and Italians that I despise and distrust this commonplace of *nationality* which is going the rounds and makes so many rascals and so many honest men talk so much nonsense? For heaven's sake, my dear Bell [the name of Herzen's journal], don't be so touchy. Otherwise I shall be obliged to say of you what I said six months ago of your friend Garibaldi: great heart, but no head. . . . Don't talk to us of these reconstitutions of nationalities which are at bottom pure retrogression and, in their present form, a plaything used by a party of intriguers to divert attention from the social revolution.

Yet the charge of " French egoism " which Herzen had evidently brought against him is not altogether easy to refute. Proudhon's applications of his principles, if not the principles themselves, are always capricious; and his applications of the federal principle are not above suspicion. Proudhon had as large a measure as most Frenchmen of local patriotism: to the end of his days he liked to remember, and to remind the world, that he was a Franc-Comtois. But the suggestion of distributing French sovereignty in the name of federalism does not occur to him. On the contrary, Proudhon sometimes gave offence to foreigners — including his Belgian hosts during his period of exile in Brussels — by speaking too freely of the advantage of federation between France and her smaller neighbours. His desire to prevent the unification of Italy and to bring about the federalization of Austria-Hungary fitted in too comfortably with French national interests and French national prejudices to inspire undue confidence in the objectivity of his argument.

The case of Poland is less straightforward. It would be unfair to doubt the sincerity of Proudhon's conviction that an independent Poland would be a bulwark of opposition to the social revolution. "Poland has never had anything to offer the world but her Catholicism and her aristocracy." He can hardly have foreseen Russia's future role as an ally of France; for he died without having become conscious of the menacing prospect of German unity. But he had an illogically persistent sympathy for Russia, which may perhaps be explained by his temperamental leaning towards autocracy or by a common hatred of democratic liberalism.

Be that as it may, and even if one dismisses as a passing aberration, or explains away as a confusion of thought, his panegyric on war in *La Guerre et la paix*, a disconcerting streak of self-assertive nationalism is constantly getting in the way of Proudhon's federalism. Though an enemy of the State, one whose loyalties should in theory have been bounded by the limits of his own Franche-Comté, Proudhon was a good French patriot. He was one of the first socialists to illustrate in his person the impossibility, at any rate in western Europe, of a consistently international socialism. Marx constantly complained of the national prejudices of the English trade unionists and the French Proudhonists in the First International; and in Germany Lassalle had already laid the foundations of a German national socialism. " All my faith, all my hope, all my love ", wrote Proudhon, " are in Liberty and *la Patrie* "; and there is a paean of praise addressed to " la patrie, patrie française, patrie de la liberté ", which must not be exposed to the ordeal of translation, but goes far to explain why Proudhon has had admirers on the extreme Right of French politics as well as on the extreme Left:

> Commence ta nouvelle vie, ô la première des immortelles; montre-toi dans ta beauté, Vénus Uranie; répands tes parfums, fleur de l'humanité!
>
> Et l'humanité sera rajeunie, et son unité sera créée par toi: car l'unité du genre humain, c'est l'unité de ma patrie, comme l'esprit du genre humain n'est que l'esprit de ma patrie.

It is a sobering thought that these words were penned to celebrate Louis Napoleon's *coup d'état* which extinguished the Second Republic.

It is as difficult to assess the influence of Proudhon as to define the content of his thought. He poured out ideas in an unceasing flow; many of them were original, many of them were silly, some of them were brilliantly inspired. Though he had disciples, he cannot be said to have founded a school; for anarchism is, in Burke's phrase, " the dissidence of dissent ", and is, in its nature, recalcitrant to the idea of a school. Bakunin committed the superficial inconsistency of combining anarchist doctrine with the fruitful idea of a conspiratorial party, highly organized and disciplined from above; and from that moment anarchism and terrorism came to be associated in the public mind. This combination was perhaps defensible so long as the targets of attack were the agents of the detested State. But, later on, the anarchists in the Spanish civil war were to prove just as ruthless as other parties in their denial of liberty to any political opinion other than their own, and just as confident of their right and duty to eliminate opponents with the knife or the bullet. As Dostoevsky once said, the end of unlimited liberty is unlimited despotism.

Yet it was not so much this inner inconsistency as the whole social and industrial development of the period which condemned anarchism to sterility. Nineteenth-century anarchism was the philosophy of the isolated intellectual or of the small group, peasant or artisan, not of the industrial masses. At its best it was a noble and salutary protest against the centralizing and standardizing tendencies of mass civilization with its progressive encroachments on individual freedom and individual eccentricity. At its worst it was a futile and aimless quest for desperate remedies against symptoms which it failed to diagnose or understand. Both these elements, nobility and futility alike, were present in Proudhon's career and in Proudhon's thought. In the history of ideas, as in his own life, Proudhon remains a lonely figure — an isolated eccentric. His vision of a world of independent self-assertive individuals, each seeking and striving in perfect liberty to realize his own conception of justice, belonged to an age which was rapidly passing away. The big battalions of the industrial revolution were on the side of Marx.

4

HERZEN: AN INTELLECTUAL REVOLUTIONARY

ALEXANDER HERZEN claims attention in many capacities. He is not one of the major figures of world literature, but certainly a distinguished minor figure — one of the select company of diarists and memoir writers who continue to be read long after their own time. His autobiography and the abundant store of his surviving correspondence reveal him as a slightly incongruous and uncomfortable member of the generation of nineteenth-century romantics who worshipped at the shrine of George Sand. But his main title to fame must be as a publicist in the broad sense, a significant figure in the development both of Russian and of European political thought, a link between western Europe and the Russian revolution. Though he foreshadowed much that was to come, Herzen himself remained essentially a nineteenth-century intellectual. Born in Moscow in the year of Napoleon I's invasion of Russia, he died in Paris in the year of Napoleon III's downfall. The dividing-line in his life was the year 1847, when he left Russia with his family, never to return. The dividing-line in his thought, as in that of so many of his contemporaries, was the year of revolution, 1848.

Herzen was the illegitimate son of a Russian aristocrat and a bourgeois German mother, though his upbringing was less unconventional than the bare statement of his origin suggests. From his mother he may have derived his understanding of western thought and idiom. He remains the most western and in many respects, notwithstanding his detestation of the western bourgeoisie, the most bourgeois of distinguished Russian writers. His paternal origin made him the first and most distinguished representative of the class known in Russian revolutionary history as "the conscience-stricken gentry". Herzen was thirteen at the time of the so-called "Decembrist conspiracy" — the first chapter in the long story of revolutionary movements in nineteenth-century Russia. The work of a handful of officers and small land-owners, it was crushed without difficulty and five of the ringleaders were executed. Herzen relates how, when the news of the execution reached Moscow, he stood with his friend Nick Ogarev, two years his junior, on Sparrow Hills, and the pair swore to devote their lives to the cause in which the Decembrists had suffered. Not every oath taken by schoolboys has been so accurately fulfilled.

Alexander Herzen's father, like most Russian aristocrats of his day, was a good "Voltairean", a rationalist in the French eighteenth-century mould. Alexander kept throughout life the strong stamp of his father's influence. He continued to profess himself a rationalist, even a cynic; and the profession was perfectly sincere. But this stratum was overlaid in him by a characteristic nineteenth-century vein of sentimental romanticism, both personal and political. This dual outlook made him a complex character. He was incapable of those straightforward enthusiasms which came so naturally and easily to his friend Ogarev or to Bakunin. He was capable — though he never quite recognized it himself — of a naïve political romanticism. But the approach to it always lay through disillusionment with current reality; and with Herzen the disillusionment generally seemed stronger than the belief. The history of his development may be read as a series of disillusionments.

The first of these disillusionments was with the Russia of Nicholas I. When Herzen entered the University of Moscow in 1829 the dreary and iron-handed repression of Nicholas's regime was at its height, and the university was one of the few places where hot-headed and intelligent young men still found an opportunity to indulge in dangerous thoughts. Advanced circles among the students fell into two groups — those who drew their revolutionary sustenance from German metaphysics and the teachings of Hegel, and those who sat at the feet of French political thinkers from Rousseau to the Utopian Socialists. Herzen, though he afterwards coined the famous aphorism which described Hegel as "the algebra of revolution", was never a good Hegelian. The political influences that moulded him were predominantly French: he was the political offspring of the ideas of 1789.

These ideas made young Herzen a political radical rather than a social reformer. It was the political oppression of the regime of Nicholas I, not the inequalities of the social and economic system, which shocked and disillusioned him and led him to idealize the liberal institutions of the west. From the vantage ground of Moscow it was not so difficult to see in the bourgeois monarchy of Louis-Philippe an exemplar of freedom and democracy. Herzen's disillusionment with his native land was completed when the Tsarist police pounced on the group of politically minded students of which he was a member and expelled them from the university and from Moscow. He spent the next three years in the provincial town of Vladimir. It was during this time that he married his first cousin Natalie, the illegitimate child of one of his father's brothers.

Through his father's influence, Alexander was eventually reinstated in the favour of the authorities and obtained a post in the Ministry of the Interior. But his political inclinations and freedom of speech again proved his undoing. In 1841 he was dismissed from his post and exiled from the capital for a year — this time to Novgorod. This experience was Herzen's final break with Russian reality. In 1846 his father's death left him the possessor of an ample fortune. In January 1847 he collected his wife and three children, his mother and several nurses, retainers and dependants — a party of thirteen in all — and left Moscow for Paris.

He travelled as fast as two post-chaises carrying

thirteen people could be expected to travel, and was in Paris by the middle of March, after seven weeks on the road. The spirit of 1789 lived on in the Paris of Louis-Philippe. It was still the home of revolution and the Mecca of advanced political thinkers from all over Europe; it played much the same role as Moscow played in the 1920s and 1930s for the intellectuals of western Europe. Herzen has left in his memoirs an account of his emotions when he first stood on this holy ground:

> We had been accustomed to connect the word Paris with memories of the great events, the great masses, the great men of 1789 and 1793, memories of a colossal struggle for an idea, for rights, for human dignity. . . . The name of Paris was closely bound up with all the noblest enthusiasms of contemporary humanity. I entered it with reverence, as men used to enter Jerusalem and Rome.

It was the first, and not the last, enthusiasm in Herzen's career bred by rejection of a repellent reality.

It did not take Herzen many weeks to become disillusioned with the bourgeois monarchy. In the place of revolutionary ardour and passion for liberty he found in it only " a seventeen-year-old creed of crude egoism, of the unclean worship of material gain and tranquillity ". Even before leaving Russia he had described the " mercantilism and industrialism " of western Europe as " a syphilitic growth infecting the blood and bone of society ". There was now an open clash between the spacious traditions of Russian life as lived by the well-to-do Russian gentry and the narrow, commercial, self-seeking habits of the liberal bourgeoisie; and this clash cut right across the neat picture which Herzen brought with him in his mind of western freedom as the antithesis of Russian despotism. It was at this moment of his first contact with the west that Herzen conceived that hatred and contempt of bourgeois democracy which played so capital a part not only in his own development, but in the whole development of Russian revolutionary thought.

But it was the revolution of 1848 which finally shaped Herzen's political course. He was in Italy when it began; and the despair of the past twelve months gave way to a short-lived mood of enthusiasm. By the time he got back to Paris early in May, however, the laurels of the revolution were already bedraggled. On May 15 a demonstration of workers at the Hôtel-de-Ville was dispersed and its leaders, including Blanqui and Barbès, arrested. "France", commented Herzen bitterly, "is already asking for slavery. Liberty is burdensome." He was the first observer to diagnose that strange political malady which Erich Fromm has analysed under the title *The Fear of Freedom* and described as the psychological foundation of Fascism. It is significant that the country in which Herzen diagnosed it was on the way to what may well be called the first Fascist dictatorship — the empire of Napoleon III.

On June 23 riots occurred in Paris. The Assembly proclaimed martial law, and Cavaignac crushed the workers. The sequel provoked the most famous passage in Herzen's memoirs:

> On the evening of June 26, after the victory over Paris, we heard regular volleys at short intervals. . . . We all looked at one another, our faces were green. . . . " Those are the execution squads " we said with one voice and turned away from one another. I pressed my forehead to the window-pane and was silent: such minutes deserve ten years of hate, a life-time of vengeance.

The year 1848 was the dividing-line in more than Herzen's life and thought. It was the moment when the bourgeoisie, having, in alliance with the nascent proletariat, got what it wanted, turned in fear against its allies, and passed over from the revolutionary to the conservative side of the barricades. It was the same story which was repeated, though with a different ending, in that other February revolution of 1917.

This was the turning-point which was responsible for Herzen's last great political disillusionment and last great act of faith. After 1848 he shed altogether his belief in the political institutions of the west. Democratic liberties were a sham, universal suffrage a trick to deceive and cajole the masses. Western society was rotten to the core. " The last word o civilization ", he wrote to Mazzini, " is revolution." So far Herzen, after 1848, followed the same road as Marx, Proudhon and Bakunin. All four shared the same attitude towards bourgeois democracy; none of them had any words for it other than those of hatred or contempt.

But what was to fill the void? Herzen, coming from a country where industry scarcely yet existed, could not take refuge with Marx in an all-sufficient and all-conquering faith in the proletariat. He was too rational and too critical, too orderly and too sensible, to travel the anarchist path with Proudhon and Bakunin. He could thus find no positive hope, and fell into a mood of sincere, though rather melodramatic, despair of civilization. He reverted to his discovery that men do not really want freedom, and offered a pungent comment on Rousseau's dictum that " man is born to be free — and he is everywhere in chains ":

> What would you say to a man who sadly shook his head and remarked that " fishes are born to fly and yet they eternally swim "?

These were the years of Herzen's bitterest and profoundest disillusionment. They coincided with the years of his great personal tragedy — the unfaithfulness of his wife, the quarrel with Herwegh, the death of his wife — the period of storm and stress which ended only with his migration to England in the summer of 1852. But, though capable of nursing a romantic melancholy, he still needed a romantic faith in the future. In a vision which a century later has a prophetic ring he saw the torch of civilization being taken over by two young nations:

> I do not believe that the destinies of humanity and its future are fixed and nailed to western Europe. If Europe does not succeed in recovering herself by a

social transformation, other countries will transform themselves. There are some already prepared for this movement, others which are preparing. One is known — I mean the States of North America; the other, full of vigour, also full of barbarity, is known little and badly.

Herzen's thoughts turned often at this time to the United States:

> This young and enterprising people, more active than intelligent, is so much occupied with the material ordering of its life that it knows none of our torturing pains. . . . The sturdy race of English colonists multiplies exceedingly; and if it comes to the top, the people belonging to it will be, I will not say happier, but more contented. Their contentment will be poorer, more commonplace, more sapless than that which was dreamed of in the ideals of romantic Europe; but it will bring with it no Tsars, no centralization, perhaps no hunger. He who can put off the old European Adam and put on the new Jonathan, let him take the first steamer to — somewhere in Wisconsin or Kansas. He will be better off there than in decaying Europe.

But in the end it was not to America but to his own country that Herzen turned for salvation. "I have never felt more clearly than now", he writes to his Russian friends in 1851, "how Russian I am." And, looking back many years later, he records that "faith in Russia saved me when I was on the verge of moral ruin". This belief in Russia did not take the place of the old belief in revolution: it blended harmoniously with it. Russia, like the United States, was a country without a history (all the Slavs, except the Poles, "belong to geography rather than to history"); and nations without a history are potentially revolutionary. Moreover, Russia is not only revolutionary but essentially socialist. The two pledges of her future greatness are " her socialism and her youth ". Herzen is not disturbed by the fact that " social revolution is a European idea ".

> It does not follow that the western peoples alone are destined to realize it. Christianity was only *crucified* in Jerusalem.

And there is an odd *obiter dictum* about " communism " — a word which Marx was just bringing into use for the more systematic and authoritarian brand of socialism :

> I think there is a certain basis of truth in the fear which the Russian Government is beginning to have of communism ; communism is Russian autocracy turned upside down.

Such was the position which Herzen had reached when Nicholas I died in 1855, in the middle of the Crimean War. In Russia the restraints and repressions of the thirty years' reign of an unimaginative and bureaucratic despot seemed suddenly relaxed. The first task of Alexander II was to wind up a disastrous and discreditable war. Defeat in war has often bred ambition for reform. This was the mood which prevailed in Russia during the first years of the new reign ; this was the mood in which Herzen launched his new journalistic venture in London. Those who reproach Herzen — as he was afterwards reproached — with having believed in the possibility of a reforming Tsar might recall how Proudhon hailed the empire of Napoleon III as the harbinger of social revolution; how Bakunin in captivity saw, or professed to see, visions of an enlightened and progressive despotism even under Nicholas I; and how Lassalle was later to make terms with Bismarck. Herzen's illusion that Alexander II could be impelled by public opinion to inaugurate in Russia an era of what he called " peaceful human progress ", though equally vain, was on the whole less ignoble.

The Bell was a monthly, or later a fortnightly, journal published in London in Russian, price sixpence, under the joint editorship of Herzen and Ogarev, Herzen being throughout the dominant partner and the driving force of the concern. Its first number appeared on July 1, 1857; and its circulation in its best period sometimes reached from 4000 to 5000, a phenomenal success at that time. It was the first uncensored Russian journal that had ever been published. Lenin, when he wrote a laudatory article on the centenary of Herzen's birth in 1912, praised Herzen for having been " the first to raise the standard of battle by turning to the masses with the free Russian word ". It sounds odd to suggest that *The Bell* was addressed to the masses. Herzen was, and always remained, an intellectual speaking to intellectuals, and he belonged to an age when politics were still the prerogative and monopoly of the well-to-do. But he was the first Russian public man to use the appeal to public opinion and the weapon of propaganda as instruments of political reform. That was the permanent significance of *The Bell* in Russian history.

For a time *The Bell* succeeded in pleasing nearly everyone. It pleased the westerners — the radicals of Herzen's own generation — who saw in it a striking example of progress along western lines and of the successful introduction of democratic methods of publicity and agitation into Russian political life. It pleased the Slavophils by its profession of faith in the Russian people. It pleased the now influential reformist wing of the official classes in Russia by strengthening their hand against the reactionaries; and by that kind of unavowed toleration which sometimes mitigated the absurdities of the Russian bureaucracy, copies of *The Bell* found their way through the censorship into high places in Russia itself. It even pleased the Emperor, who was flattered by the portrait of himself as an ardent reformer endeavouring to carry out an enlightened programme in the teeth of obstruction from old-fashioned bureaucrats.

The creation of *The Bell* was Herzen's major achievement. It would be agreeable to attribute some share in it to the country where he had taken up his abode. But the evidence reveals little trace of English influence in Herzen's life and thought. Victorian England treated the political refugee from Europe with complete toleration so long as he did not break the law, but also with complete indifference. Herzen appreciated the toleration, and was even able to praise what he called the " rude strength " and " unbending obstinacy " of the English character. He liked Colman's mustard and English pickles; and a recent Russian writer on Herzen notes his admiration for *Punch* as a satirist of English bourgeois life, and records some hitherto undetected borrowings.

But he found nothing to stimulate him, and never revised the verdict, penned three years after his arrival in London, that " life here is about as boring as that of worms in a cheese ". In a period of thirteen years he made one or two English political acquaintances — Carlyle among them — but no English friends. The role of England in his political development was purely negative. As in his youth he had lived in Russia and believed passionately in the freedom and democracy of the west, so now, in his maturity, residence in England nourished a fervent faith in the political destinies of a regenerated Russia. Herzen's enthusiasms always flourished in isolation from the realities to which they related.

The liberation of the serfs in 1861 was a Russian landmark comparable to the landmark of 1848 in western Europe, and had similar results. By liquidating the system of feudal ownership it brought Russia ostensibly into line with the west and paved the way for industrialization. By satisfying the aspirations of the Russian liberals, it turned them into conservatives; and it created a new generation of irreconcilable revolutionaries who would have no truck with mere reformers. *The Bell* could no longer hold a middle course. Herzen faltered and was caught between the two fires. Both extremes seemed to him wrong; he became, as Marx said of the Prussian bourgeoisie, " revolutionary against the conservatives, but conservative against the revolutionaries". Stultified by this uncertainty, *The Bell* declined rapidly from the high-water mark of 1861. The Polish insurrection of 1863 was its death-blow. Herzen had already antagonized the revolutionaries. He now antagonized the remaining moderates by espousing the Polish cause. In 1865 he moved *The Bell* to Geneva without reviving its fortunes; and it expired in 1868. Herzen himself died in Paris, a tired and — for the last time — disillusioned man, in January 1870.

If it is necessary to define in a single phrase Herzen's place in the history of the Russian revolution, he may be called "the first Narodnik". The Narodniks formed the first generation of active Russian revolutionaries who, before Marx had made any impact on Russia, proclaimed the revolutionary potentialities of the downtrodden Russian peasant and sought salvation in the movement which came to be known as "going to the people"; and they were the direct ancestors of the Social-Revolutionaries who became the revolutionary rivals of the Marxist Social-Democrats. Herzen was the inventor of the Narodnik belief that the traditional Russian peasant community, with its undivided communal property, was a proof of the socialist character of the Russian tradition. As early as 1850 he attacked the view of the Prussian traveller Haxthausen, who had described the commune as being despotically ruled by its president and as an instrument of the imperial authority.

It was this allegedly democratic and socialist character of the Russian commune which helped

Herzen to rationalize his faith in Russia as the pioneer of social revolution. Thanks to this, Russia could achieve socialism without having to pass through the repulsive stage of bourgeois capitalism which had wrought such havoc in western Europe. Herzen was the progenitor of the whole Narodnik (and afterwards Social-Revolutionary) doctrine, of which the cult of the Russian people, hatred of the western bourgeoisie and contempt for the western proletariat were the distinguishing features. Even Marx towards the end of his life cautiously admitted, under pressure from the Narodniks, that the existence of the Russian commune might, in certain circumstances, enable Russia to make the direct transition from feudalism to socialism without the intervening capitalist stage.

If, however, the Narodniks owed much to Herzen in the shaping of their doctrine, they emphatically rejected his belief in the possibility of peaceful evolution. This belief Herzen also justified on the ground of the socialist character of the Russian commune; for " what in the west can be achieved only through a series of catastrophes can develop in Russia on a basis of what already exists ". His last political utterance is a series of open letters *To an Old Comrade*, written in 1869. The " old comrade " was Bakunin. Bakunin in his later years idealized the Russian peasant as romantically as Herzen himself and believed as firmly as Herzen in the socialist tradition of the Russian peasant commune. But Bakunin was a lifelong believer in revolution by violence; and it is on this ground that Herzen now takes him to task. Herzen's condemnation of violence and terrorism was the dividing-line which separated him from the younger revolutionary generation and ranged him more and more during his last years in the conservative camp.

Before Herzen died, the cause which he had so brilliantly sustained in *The Bell* was irretrievably lost. In his own country the prospects of the revolution by persuasion which had seemed possible in the first years of Alexander II had faded away; the revolutionaries and the government were equally committed to policies of violence. The ineffectual conclusion of Herzen's career reflected, as Lenin said, " that world historical epoch when the revolutionism of bourgeois democracy was already dying and the revolutionism of the socialist proletariat had not yet ripened ". The revolution of the intellectuals in which Herzen believed had already exhausted itself; the revolution of the masses which was about to begin was one that he neither believed in nor understood. He was a revolutionary only in ideas, not in action. But his thought was a necessary step in the development of the Russian revolution; and it is pleasant to record that his qualities have lately received full and wide recognition in his own country, where the seventy-fifth anniversary of his death was commemorated by a spate of articles and other publications in 1945.

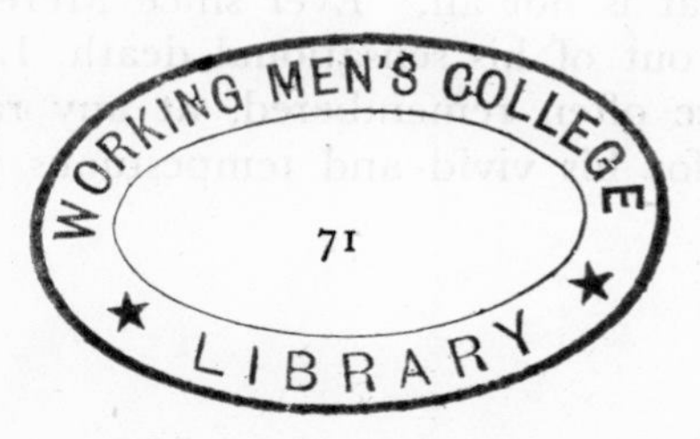

5

LASSALLE MEETS BISMARCK

GEORG BRANDES opens his essay on Lassalle, originally published in the 1870s, with some reflections on the " surprise and astonishment " provoked by " the process by which the Germany of Hegel was transformed into the Germany of Bismarck ", and notes the " strongly marked " figure of Lassalle as one of the significant features of the transformation. Ferdinand Lassalle lived for less than forty years; of his writings only the letters and diaries now possess more than an antiquarian interest; and the General German Workers' Association, which he founded, was reshaped after his death by rivals eager to consign his name and tradition to oblivion. Yet his career touched history at so many points, reflected and transmitted so many influences and foreshadowed so much that lay in the future that it remains one of the most rewarding quarries for the student of nineteenth-century political and social evolution in western Europe.

But that is not all. Ever since Meredith made a drama out of his sensational death, Lassalle has been more often remembered, at any rate in this country, for his vivid and tempestuous personality than for his political achievement. Mr. Footman's book, as its needlessly banal title suggests,[1] belongs to the personal rather than to the political school of biography. It is more concerned to portray Lassalle the man than to determine his place in history. It is none the less a scholarly work, written with scrupulous regard to the evidence and with a restraint which enhances its interest. It is also the first English life of Lassalle, though there is an English translation of the standard German biography by Oncken, unfortunately abridged as well as made from an early and now out-dated edition.

Born in Breslau in 1825, son of a fairly prosperous Jewish merchant one generation removed from the Polish ghetto, Ferdinand Lassal (the longer form of the name was an elegant invention of his own, dating from a visit to Paris) entered the University of Berlin at the age of nineteen, soon after Marx, Engels and Bakunin had left it. It was still in the full glow of that remarkable period when philosophy was the only study for an intelligent and ambitious young man, and Hegel (who had died in 1830) the only philosopher. Already at Breslau young Ferdinand had become a Hegelian. By this conversion he had been " born again " ; and, as he explained in a long epistle to his father, " this second birth gave me everything, gave me clarity, self-assurance . . . made of me self-containing intellect, that is self-conscious God ".

The hyperbole is characteristic of the writer's

[1] David Footman, *The Primrose Path.* A Life of Ferdinand Lassalle. The Cresset Press. 15s.

temperament. But it is characteristic also of the age. If the standard of measurement be the weight, the breadth and the duration of the influence which he exercised, Hegel was beyond question the most important of modern philosophers. He moulded the thought of more than one generation, and his teaching was the philosophical cradle of every significant political theory for a century to come. It was his astonishing achievement to provide within the limits of a single coherent system both a creed of State worship and an " algebra of revolution ". From 1840 onwards the " Hegelian Left " had taken the bit between its teeth and, by a strictly logical process of interpretation, made of " the master " — what he himself had certainly never dreamed of — a revolutionary standard-bearer. It was primarily in this sense that the young Lassalle became a Hegelian. But he lacked Marx's rigid consistency and (after his early student years) Marx's application; he was an agitator and pamphleteer rather than a thinker; and, as his later development showed, he had imbibed elements of the Hegelian doctrine which were anathema both to Marx and to Bakunin.

" Man's temperament is his fate ", quotes Mr. Footman from his hero on the title-page; and beyond doubt Lassalle's career owed more to his temperament than to his philosophy. At the beginning of 1846 he fell in love with the beautiful but impecunious Countess Sophie von Hatzfeldt, long separated from a wealthy but mean husband and in the throes of a perennial dispute with him about money matters. Lassalle was twenty, and she was just twice his age. He became her mentor, legal adviser, knight errant and lover; for, even if documentary evidence is lacking, it is surely pedantic to observe Mr. Footman's cautious suspension of judgment on this last point. The Countess Hatzfeldt was the main formative and stabilizing influence in Lassalle's life, and emerges as perhaps the one wholly sympathetic figure in his biography. "She is my own re-embodied Ego", he wrote fifteen years later to one of his many mistresses; "she is part of all my triumphs and perils, fears and toil, sorrows, strains and victories, part of all the emotions I have ever had. She is the first and essential condition of my happiness."

The course of the Hatzfeldt affair was oddly intertwined with the 1848 revolution. At the moment when Louis-Philippe was being driven from France, Lassalle was arrested on the charge of instigating the theft of a casket supposed to contain vital papers belonging to the Count, and remained in prison till his trial in August. He used the dock for an eloquent recital of the Countess's grievances against her husband. By skilfully identifying her cause with that of liberty and democracy he won from a politically minded jury his own acquittal, which was not unjustly hailed as a triumph of the Left. He plunged into political agitation, and was arrested in November on a charge of inciting to violence. He did not emerge again until July 1849 (this time after a six months' sentence); and by then the revolution was over.

The indirect result of Lassalle's prison experiences was to keep him out of any direct participation in revolutionary disturbances. He was the one Prussian revolutionary of any consequence who was not seriously compromised, and was able to remain on Prussian soil after the *débâcle* of 1849. Thus, through the reactionary period of the 1850s, he was uncontested leader of what remained in Germany of a workers' movement. When the political ice began to melt in the next decade, he became the founder in 1863 of the first embryonic German Labour Party — the General German Workers' Association. The last two years of his life made Lassalle a political figure of the first importance.

That such a man should clash with Marx for the headship of the German workers' movement was inevitable. Personal rivalries and temperamental incompatibility counted for much. Here sympathies will not be wholly on the side of Marx. Marx was an intensely jealous man, and Lassalle's relative affluence, his eloquence and the magnetic personality which won him so large a personal following, were all more than his rival could stomach. Lassalle was capable of an impulsive generosity of thought and deed which was not in Marx's nature; and he never bore malice or nourished personal enmities. That Lassalle found time for wide human and intellectual interests — including the writing of a five-act historical drama in blank verse — was not as serious a blemish on his character as it seemed to Marx's one-track mind.

On the other hand, it could not be denied that,

as a leader of the workers, Lassalle was highly vulnerable and that many of Marx's shafts were well aimed. The intimate connexion between the wrongs of the proletariat and the Hatzfeldt *cause célèbre* was less apparent to others than to Lassalle and the Countess. When at last in 1854, through Lassalle's persistence, the Count was partly browbeaten, partly blackmailed, into making a favourable settlement on the Countess, Lassalle received out of the proceeds the tidy pension of 4000 thalers a year, and thereafter, with a sumptuous flat in Berlin, combined the life of a proletarian leader with that of a Don Juan and man about town. The second role often seemed nearer to his heart than the first. He confessed to "a horror of workers' deputations where I always hear the same speeches and have to shake hard, hot and moist hands". Marx might have said the same; but what would have been intellectual fastidiousness in Marx was a cultivated social snobbishness in Lassalle. The crowning tragedy in which, in his fortieth year and at the height of his political reputation, he was killed in a duel at Geneva by a young Wallachian count, his rival for the hand of a girl of 17, was the culminating instance of this constant intrusion of disreputable melodrama into his political ambitions. Others besides Marx found Lassalle's behaviour incongruous and distasteful; the reader of Mr. Footman's unimpeachably impartial story will have ample material on which to base his own judgment.

It may, of course, be said that Lassalle's flamboyant temperament, for all its restlessness and rebelliousness, had in it a marked conservative streak. Certainly he had a sense of personal property and of the value of money (he was a constant speculator on the stock exchange) which was unthinkable to Marx or Bakunin. In the affair with the Countess Hatzfeldt he revealed both a keen eye to the main chance and an unconcealed liking for high society; and neither of these tastes altered with advancing years. These things are not commonly associated with a revolutionary outlook. Few of those with whom he associated in his later years shared his proletarian sympathies. More important was the dictatorial strain in Lassalle's character. His self-assurance, his amazing vitality, his lust for power and fame, his contempt for the common man — all these seemed, at the period of history to which he belonged, to deny him any natural affinity with the political Left.

It would, however, be superficial to dismiss the rift between Marx and Lassalle as an affair of personal or political rivals between whom temperament and circumstance had fixed an unbridgeable gulf of incompatibility. To take such a view would be to underestimate Lassalle's influence and significance — a mistake which, incidentally, Marx himself did not make. It may well be argued that in the history of nineteenth- and twentieth-century Germany Lassalle proved eventually a more potent force than Marx; and the conceptions for which he stood made their way, even in countries where he exercised no direct influence at all. He was one of the first protagonists and instruments of a historical process which has not yet fully worked itself out — the alliance between socialism and nationalism.

Any serious analysis of the clash between Lassalle and Marx or of the ultimate significance of Lassalle as a representative historical figure must start from the divergent strands in the Hegelian system, which, from the earliest moment, appear side by side in Lassalle's thought. The historical process, ever in flux and continually advancing through a dialectical series of contradictions resolving themselves in a new synthesis — all this young Lassalle eagerly digested and, like his contemporaries, made it the basis of a passionate belief in the social revolution. Already as a student in Berlin he was exposing the " formal " and " individual " character of the liberties won by the French revolution and asserting the necessity of a new revolution to overthrow capitalism and the competitive system as the road to the liberation of the working class. This path he travelled as whole-heartedly, and as early, as Marx himself.

But, equally at this early stage, we find in Lassalle unmistakable traces of the Hegelian doctrine of the State as the foreordained institution through which alone the individual can achieve the rational development of personality and freedom. The socialist tradition, handed down from More through Godwin to Saint-Simon, and thence to Marx as well as to Proudhon and Bakunin, to Lenin as well as to Kropotkin, was fundamentally hostile to the State. The only difference on this point between Marx and Lenin on the one hand and the anarchists on the other was that the former accepted the State (in the form of the dictatorship of the proletariat) as a temporary, but necessary, evil until the communist society had been fully established, while the anarchists would not agree to palter even temporarily with the iniquities of State power.

For this tradition, with its belief in the dying away of the State as the ultimate goal, Lassalle was too good a Hegelian to have any sympathy whatever; and as the years went on he came more and more to regard the State as the potential instrument through which the wrongs of the workers could be redressed and the aims of socialism attained. He attacked the bourgeois State not, like Marx, because it was strong and oppressive, but because it was weak and futile. His was the famous phrase of contempt for the "night-watchman State", coined in a speech of 1862 which he published as *The Workers' Programme*:

> Thus the middle class conceives the moral object of the State. This object consists simply and solely in securing the personal freedom of the individual and his property. This is the night-watchman theory, for this conception can regard the State only under the form of a night-watchman whose duties are confined to preventing burglary and theft.

And a little later he was informing an audience of working men in terms which were the very negation of all that Marx had ever taught: "The State belongs to you, the needy classes, not to us the well-to-do, for the State consists of you".

Lassalle's view of the State is reflected in his

view of law, to which he devoted intensive, though intermittent, study. He defined law in Hegelian terms as an expression of the national consciousness of right. Since that consciousness varies from time to time, so also the law must vary; and on this thesis Lassalle founded a somewhat perverse argument to justify retroactive legislation. But national consciousness also varies from nation to nation, and this consideration brings Lassalle near in spirit and intention to the famous German school of jurisprudence. Indeed, the most significant aspect of Lassalle's acceptance of the State was that it involved him, perhaps unwittingly at first, in the acceptance of orthodox national patriotism, of loyalty to the national State. It is not without importance that Lassalle, almost alone among the revolutionary leaders of the nineteenth century, was never an exile and spent the whole of his working life in his own country.

Be this as it may, Lassalle by the last few years of his life had achieved an unexpected, and at this time highly original, synthesis between his socialism and his feelings as a good Prussian. The war of 1859 between France and Austria had led him to demand that Prussia should seek compensation by annexing Schleswig-Holstein. In the early 1860s he " hoped and believed " that " external factors, *e.g.* war ", would bring about the " national-political revolution " of the unification of Germany; but he added that the bourgeoisie was incapable of realizing this revolution, which would " only be effective if driven on by a solid and class-conscious workers' party". In 1862 he delivered in Berlin, at the celebration of the Fichte centenary, a laudatory lecture on Fichte as a great German patriot and the prophet of German unity.

The stage was now set for the final episode of Lassalle's political career — his meetings with Bismarck. A certain piquancy is added to the situation by a letter of some two years earlier to the Countess Hatzfeldt, in which Lassalle had called Bismarck "a reactionary Junker from whom one can only expect reactionary measures", a man who would "rattle his sword to get the military budget through on the pretence that war is imminent". Until the 1920s the principal authority for these meetings was a statement made in 1878 by Bismarck himself in response to an interrogation in the Reichstag. This statement left it in doubt exactly when they took place and on whose initiative. Letters and other documents now available date the first meeting in May 1863, at the moment when the General German Workers' Association was being constituted, and show that the invitation came direct, without any preliminary contacts, from Bismarck himself. This discovery partially relieves Lassalle of the charge afterwards levelled at his memory by his rivals of having deliberately sought to ingratiate himself with the ruling powers. But it also assigns to Bismarck rather than to Lassalle the stroke of genius which perceived a bond of common interest between them capable of being exploited to their mutual advantage. It may also be recalled that when, some years later, Marx received similar, though less direct, approaches from Bismarck, he refused to be drawn into the net.

The outward link between Bismarck and Lassalle was their common hostility to the Progressives — the Prussian Liberal Party. Bismarck, who still feared them as his chief opponents, would gladly have seen their more radical elements attracted away from them by a new party of the Left; Lassalle nourished the same ambition. But the more intimate link of a common outlook on political realities drew the two men together and gave them at any rate an intellectual respect for each other. Both despised the flabby idealism and constitutional word-spinning of the Progressives; both understood that politics mean power, and they could measure their forces against each other in the same terms. Both had a fundamental contempt for democratic methods, and believed firmly in efficient dictatorship as a principle and in their own capacity to exercise it. A letter from Lassalle in the last year of his life on the affairs of the General German Workers' Association shows that he had nothing to learn from Bismarck about the imposition of his will on his subordinates:

> Branch representatives are there to direct their branches as instructed by headquarters — not to take orders from the branches. . . . Whenever I attended branch meetings there was never any idea of the branch passing a resolution unless I myself took the initiative. . . . Why is it being allowed to happen otherwise in Berlin? I suppose because there one is nearer to the heart of parliamentarianism.

Out of the soil prepared by these coincidences of interest and outlook grew that working alliance between Bismarck's nationalism and Lassalle's socialism — the " social-service State " or " State socialism " — which was Bismarck's specific contribution to domestic policy. Exactly what passed between them when they met, exactly how much Bismarck was influenced by what did pass, cannot be known. Even the number of meetings is a matter of guesswork : Bismarck himself, fifteen years later, mentioned " three or four ", the Countess Hatzfeldt " twenty ". The records show that Lassalle pressed for universal suffrage ; and Bismarck's subsequent adoption of it can hardly be dissociated altogether from his pleadings. It is certain that, at Lassalle's instigation, Bismarck caused the King to receive a deputation of Silesian weavers and to promise them consideration of their grievances. Lassalle was acute enough to guess that Bismarck " wanted to put through the social part of our programme, but not the political part ". What he did not foresee was that Bismarck, having been astute enough to " dish " the socialists by stealing the more harmless and practical trappings of their programme, would one day be strong enough to take repressive measures against the party itself.

Whatever their immediate influence, the meetings were a historical landmark. The coming together of the masterful Prussian Prime Minister and the headstrong socialist agitator symbolized the new and pregnant alliance between nationalism and socialism.

Lassalle was by this time a patriotic Prussian as well as a sincere socialist; and it was a result of his policy that henceforth — and not in Prussia alone — a man could profess himself a good socialist and a good patriot. The national State was to become an instrument promoting, within the limits of the capitalist system, the welfare of the masses; in return the masses would become imbued with patriotic loyalty to the national State. Both these unspoken terms of the alliance were significant. If the Bismarck-Lassalle conversations foreshadowed the social-service State, they also foreshadowed the birth of "jingoism" (the word was coined in the 1870s) and sharpened the edge of nationalism by making it an interest of the masses as well as of the middle class. The field of international discord was now conterminous with the whole nation. The way was open for the coming not only of the totalitarian State, but of total war.

The creation of national, as opposed to international, socialism was, whether he consciously sought it or not, Lassalle's main historical achievement. But other striking pointers to the future may be found scattered throughout his writings and speeches. In one of his early letters to his father he foretold that the growth of industry must entail "the negation of the principle of property" and the "merging of man's subjective individuality" in the organized State. He may well have been the first to use — at any rate, he used it in the early 'sixties — the now well-worn argument that, since the State knows no financial limit to what it can spend in war, it can afford to spend without limit for social purposes in peace. His proposal to organize, in the place of trade unions, " productive unions " supported by the State, was a foretaste of the almost exactly similar proposal which was made by Trotsky in the early 1920s and which, though then rejected, helped to mould the future shape of the Soviet trade unions — and perhaps of others. Lassalle was not a profound or systematic thinker. His treatises on law and economics, for all their pretentiousness, are the work of a clever dilettante, not of a master of his subjects. But he had an uncanny aptitude for discerning the significant development or the significant idea — or rather the development or idea which would one day become significant. In many respects it is easier to-day than it would have been fifty years ago to recognize how far he was in advance of his time.

The period following Lassalle's death seemed to spell the defeat of nearly everything for which he stood. Six weeks after the fatal duel in Geneva, Marx brought to birth in London the International Working Men's Association — the First International. In Germany Marx's followers steadily undermined the Lassallean tradition; and when the United Social Democratic Party was at length founded in 1875, Lassalle's General German Workers' Association was merged in it without leaving more than superficial traces on its programme and leadership. Socialism had been established on a solid international basis; and Bismarck's legislation against the socialists seemed to mark the final breakdown of the alliance which he and Lassalle had once conspired to forge. Yet the sequel showed that, beneath all these appearances, Lassalle had builded better than he knew and that history was on his side. In 1914 it was national, not international, socialism which emerged triumphant in every European country except Russia. In Germany it was not only Bernstein the " revisionist " but Kautsky the " renegade " who showed, when the test came, that they were successors of Lassalle rather than of Marx ; and without seeking to saddle the Jew from Breslau with responsibility for Hitler's particular brand of " national socialism ", the curious may still speculate how far " socialism in one country " is not, in another context, an unconscious tribute to the vitality of the Lassallean conception.

6

SOME NINETEENTH-CENTURY RUSSIAN THINKERS

RUSSIAN social and political thought in the nineteenth century is of high interest and importance on two counts. It inspired one of the great creative periods of modern literature; and it forms the background of the Russian revolution of 1917. Its significance in the second context has been increased by the recent tendency to dwell on the continuity of Russian history before and after the revolution rather than on the break in continuity which was the theme of the first revolutionary writers and historians.

Shortly before the first world war T. G. Masaryk, the future president of the Czechoslovak Republic, published a detailed survey of Russian nineteenth-century thought which was translated into English in 1919 under the title *The Spirit of Russia*. But, while numerous articles have been written about individuals or particular movements, no further synoptic view of the whole field seems to have been attempted in any language till the publication in Paris in 1946 of Berdyaev's *The Russian Idea*, which has since appeared in a welcome English translation. Berdyaev was one of a group of young Russian intellectuals who, having passed through the school and discipline of Russian Marxism, went over about 1908 to the Orthodox Church. Some time after the Bolshevik revolution he emigrated to Paris where he died in 1948. His book is slighter, more personal and more dogmatic than that of the liberal Masaryk. But, like all his work, it displays an always fresh and acute, though sometimes rather wilfully one-sided, insight into Russian conditions and ways of thought, past and present.

Russian nineteenth-century thought revolves unceasingly round the central idea of revolution. It was Nicholas I — so far as responsibility can be assigned to any one person — who, by virtually proscribing all forms of political, social and philosophical speculation, threw the whole intellectual movement of three generations into a revolutionary mould. The first overt act was the trivial " Decembrist conspiracy " of 1825 — a sort of officers' mutiny; its promoters were the first representatives of the so-called " conscience-stricken gentry ", who illustrated the perennial truth that the seeds of revolution are sown when a ruling class loses its belief in its right to rule. This stage of the movement developed under the predominant influence of Hegel. It culminated in the 'forties in the brilliant figures of Bakunin and Herzen, the first Russian revolutionary *émigrés*, who not only mediated western ideas to Russia, but also, though somewhat later, broke fresh ground by introducing Russian ideas to the revolutionary movements of western Europe.

In Russia itself Belinsky was the most significant representative of the "men of the 'forties". Belinsky shifted the focus of the revolutionary movement from the "conscience-stricken gentry" to the middle-class intelligentsia of which he was the forerunner and creator. Though much of his comparatively brief period of literary activity was occupied by incessant controversy about the interpretation of Hegel (one of the guises in which political speculation might still hope to escape the censor's vigilance), he made the transition from the idealism of Hegel to the materialism of Feuerbach. Himself dying in 1848 in his thirty-seventh year, he paved the way for the new generation of the 'sixties and set the revolutionary movement on a materialist basis which was not thereafter challenged.

It was the "men of the 'sixties" — Chernyshevsky, Dobrolyubov and Pisarev are generally named as the most important and typical of them — who began to give to the revolution the shape in which it ultimately triumphed. Like Belinsky, they were obliged to couch their ideas in the form of philosophical or literary criticism, and were contributors to those solid "advanced" periodicals to which the relaxed censorship of Alexander II offered a temporary and much qualified licence of opinion. Chernyshevsky, who won laudatory appraisals both from Marx and from Lenin, has been much studied in revolutionary Russia. A collected edition of his works in ten volumes appeared before the war; and his novel *What is to be Done?* published in 1864, the year in which he was condemned for subversive activities and sent to Siberia, is still a revolutionary classic. Dobrolyubov, a collaborator of Chernyshevsky who died prematurely in 1861, was noted for his attacks on the liberal bourgeoisie, who hoped that reform might provide an alternative to revolution (Chernyshevsky and his followers afterwards had a famous quarrel with Herzen on this issue). Pisarev, the third and most daring of the trio, won his spurs by a striking review of Turgenev's *Fathers and Sons*. While other advanced critics denounced its "nihilist" hero Bazarov as a malicious caricature, Pisarev hailed him as the true prototype of the modern revolutionary materialist. A vigorous and — considering that more than four of his twenty-eight years were spent in prison — incredibly prolific publicist, Pisarev has been made the subject of an immensely detailed monograph by a French critic, M. Armand Coquart. This is one of those meritorious and valuable works which, being devoted to a minor writer, will henceforth save all but the most meticulous from the labour of consulting the original texts, and which, once done, need never be repeated.

The "men of the 'sixties" opened the way for the active revolutionaries of the following decade. Chernyshevsky was the first revolutionary publicist to participate actively in one of the new secret societies just beginning to spring up. In the 'seventies the movement passed from the sphere of philosophy and literature to that of action, whether in the form of missionary work among the peasants (the so-called "going to the people") or of terrorist conspiracies. The latter policy reached its climax with the assassination of Alexander II by Zhelyabov and his group in 1881.

The revolutionary movement was now ripe for its last stage. Hitherto every Russian revolutionary had assumed that, in an agricultural country like Russia, the peasantry must ultimately be the backbone of the revolution. But by the beginning of the 1880s the campaign of " going to the people " had failed to stir the peasant, and terrorism had been defeated by popular apathy and police repression. A new start was required. It was twenty years since the emancipation of the serfs had started the process of the industrialization of Russia with foreign capital. In 1883 Plekhanov founded the first Russian Marxist group and planted the roots of Marxism in the new industrial proletariat of Russia. The last considerable social and economic essay of the century was Lenin's maiden work, *On the Development of Capitalism in Russia*, which set out to prove that Russia was treading the western path of bourgeois capitalism on the way to proletarian revolution.

" Independent Russian thought ", writes Berdyaev, " was awakened by the problem of the philosophy of history. It had reflected deeply upon what the thoughts of the Creator were about Russia, about what Russia is and about what sort of destiny it has." Such passages, as well as the very title of his book, show that Berdyaev embraces a kind of national mysticism — a sense of the destiny of Russia as the explanation of her history — which seems to be bound up with his acceptance of Orthodox Christianity. He does not even eschew the cruder forms of national determinism, as when he describes Lenin as " a characteristically Russian man with an admixture of Tartar traits ". This approach will invalidate some of his conclusions for those who do not share it, but does little to detract from the value of his searching analysis of the main issues which exercised Russian nineteenth-century thought.

The issue which lay beneath all others and was, in some sense, the distillation of them all was the question of Russia and Europe, of east and west, of Slavophils and westerners. After Peter the Great no Russian thinker could evade this issue. In its nineteenth-century form it was posed by Chaadaev, who declared that Russia had neither history nor tradition nor civilization of her own. Russia formed a blank in the " moral world order ".

> We belong to the number of nations who so to speak do not enter into the framework of mankind and exist only in order to give the world some serious lesson.

The " men of the 'forties " all assumed without question that salvation could be found by Russia only through borrowing and assimilating from the west; nor did the " men of the 'sixties " differ from them on this vital point.

The Slavophil movement started in the 'forties as a reaction against the prevailing orthodoxy of the westerners. It indulged in an unhistorical idealization of the past, and had puerilities and affectations, extending even to matters of dress. But in the hands of Kireevsky and Khomyakov, its ablest and most consistent expositors, it became a powerful body of doctrine. Its essential tenets were that Russia had a tradition and civilization of her own entirely independent of those of the west; that Russia was called on to follow her own line of development, not to borrow from the west; and that the future belonged not to decadent Europe but to young and unspoiled Russia, what was commonly referred to as Russia's " backwardness " thus becoming a positive asset.

A mistake commonly made about the controversy between westerners and Slavophils is to equate westerners with radicals and revolutionaries and Slavophils with conservatives and reactionaries. There was a western conservative, as well as a western radical, tradition: Chaadaev, for example, though an out-and-out westerner, was not in any sense a radical. Nor did those Russians who looked for enlightenment to the west necessarily accept existing western institutions. Herzen, a professed westerner and democratic, had little use for the democratic institutions which he found at work in western Europe; and the Russian Marxists, who must be classified as westerners, none the less denounced the bourgeois democracy of the west.

On the other hand, the first Slavophils, scarcely less than the westerners, were in revolt against the repressive officialdom of Nicholas I. It is true that they purported to seek their ideal in an imaginary Russian past. But Slavophilism (which Pisarev called " a psychological phenomenon due to unsatisfied needs ") had even less to do with the facts of that past than had the ideal of the westerners with the existing facts in western Europe. The original Slavophils were not champions of the Romanov autocracy; nor, when they spoke of Russia's mission to Europe, were they thinking in terms of political power. It was only in the second Slavophil generation of the eighteen-seventies, marked by Danilevsky's *Russia and Europe* and the later political essays of Dostoevsky, that Slavophilism degenerated into a crude form of Russian nationalism and provoked the challenge of the philosopher Soloviev: "What East do you want to be, the East of Xerxes or the East of Christ?"

Nor did the dichotomy of east and west wholly coincide with the other vital issues which tormented Russian nineteenth-century thinkers. In the grand debate between society and the individual, between authority and freedom, between the "eternal harmony" and the sacrifice of the innocent, which was pursued in one form or another throughout the great literature of the period, it would be misleading to assign the conflicting roles to the protagonists of east and west. It is true that westerners like Belinsky, Herzen and Mikhailovsky were particularly prone to assert the claims of the individual, and that Khomyakov the Slavophil imported into the debate the ecclesiastical word *Sobornost* (notoriously untranslatable, but meaning something rather more precise and more authoritative than "community-mindedness"). But it was Turgenev's nihilist Bazarov — a westerner if ever there was one — who maintained that it was as unscientific to study individual men and women as to study individual birch trees. The typical westerner Belinsky was as conscious of the underlying dilemma as the typical Slavophil (so far as concerns his later years) Dostoevsky and expresses it in strikingly similar terms.

Hegel opened the debate. His immense influence in Russia was beyond doubt due to the fact that he represented a reaction against the individualism of the Enlightenment, a victory, in Berdyaev's words, " of the general over the particular, of the universal over the individual, of society over personality ". In the Russian argument over Hegel, Belinsky came to occupy the central place. He ran through the whole gamut of experience and changed his attitude to the extent of 180 degrees between the article on Griboedov, in which he exclaimed that " society is always juster and higher than the private person ", and the letter to Botkin in which he declared that " the fate of the subject, of the individual, of the personality is more important than the fate of the whole world ". The second position was that in which he ultimately found anchor. It was as a disciple of Belinsky that Ivan Karamazov was presently to say: " I renounce altogether the higher harmony; it is not worth the smallest tear of one tormented child ".

Belinsky found his way out of the dilemma in the conception of a new society based on respect for the individual personality, on truth and justice — that is to say, in a socialism which was Utopian not so much in its organization as in its major premise. Dostoevsky sought his solution in a new synthesis of freedom and authority through Orthodox Christianity: the Catholic synthesis he rejected as incompatible with freedom. But some critics have felt that Dostoevsky was more convinced of the logical necessity of his solution than of its cogency, and that he remained to the end a dual and divided personality. It will be readily conceded that Russian thinkers of the nineteenth century have plumbed these deep waters more profoundly than any of their predecessors; it will be less readily conceded that they have found firm ground on which their successors can build.

An outcrop of this controversy was the struggle to find a rational, utilitarian basis for morality and for art. Rationalism, said Khomyakov the Slavophil, was " the mortal sin of the west ", and had infected Catholicism as much as other forms of western life. Dostoevsky's *Man from Underground* wanted to free humanity from the tyranny of two plus two equals four; and the Slavophil poet Tyutchev declared, in a couplet which remained famous, that it was impossible to comprehend Russia with the mind, it was possible only to believe in her. The conception that faith, and therefore morality, lay altogether beyond reason was rooted in Orthodox Christianity and in Russian thought.

The first westerners believed, by implication, in a rational morality. But it was Chernyshevsky who, substituting Feuerbach and Comte for Hegel as his masters in philosophy, imported into Russia the utilitarian philosophy of Bentham and Mill, whose *Principles of Political Economy* he translated into Russian.

His enormously popular novel *What is to be Done?* depicted a set of young people actuated by what were supposed to be the purest principles of rational egoism — which, illogically enough, did not exclude the duty, eagerly recognized and accepted, of sacrificing one's immediate interest to those ultimate principles.

Pisarev, as usual, was responsible for the systematization and *reductio ad extremum* of the doctrine:

> The morality of men does not depend on their qualities of heart or nature, on abundance of virtue or absence of vice: words of this kind have no tangible meaning. The morality of this or that society depends exclusively on the question to what degree the members of the society are conscious of their own interests.

Moreover:

> In order to be a moral man it is indispensable to be to a certain degree a thinking man: but the faculty of thinking only becomes strong and well developed when the individual succeeds in escaping from the yoke of material necessity.

Here already are the solid foundations of class morality on which Engels was presently to build.

But more interest was excited by the controversy about art in which Pisarev was once more the protagonist. As Berdyaev points out, the west has never been conscious of a need to justify culture as such. The western world, including western Catholicism, has assimilated without question Greco-Roman culture and Greco-Roman humanism and combined it with the Christian tradition. The Orthodox Church, primarily eschatological in outlook and severed from the traditions both of the Roman Empire and of the Renaissance, has always been implicitly hostile to the culture of this world. It was long before Russia acquired a secular literature or a secular art. In the nineteenth century two great writers, as far removed from each other in time and in point of view as Gogol and Tolstoy, both renounced and condemned their own artistic creation — a scarcely thinkable phenomenon in any western country.

Russian tradition was, then, less openly affronted than western tradition would have been when the young materialists of the 'sixties raised the question of the utility of art. Chernyshevsky, like Belinsky before him, frankly judged literary works by their content and was unconcerned with style. But his primary interest was not in literary criticism, and he formulated no very clear aesthetic theories. Dobrolyubov more boldly called literature " a subordinate force ", declaring that " its importance resides in propaganda, and its merit is determined by the content of this propaganda and the manner in which it is done ". Pisarev and a colleague named Zaitsev carried these views to their logical conclusion. Zaitsev, who seems to have anticipated Housman's discovery that artistic creation is accompanied by the physical symptom of a titillation of the spine, declared that " any artisan is more useful than any poet to the extent to which any positive number, however small, is greater than zero ". In an essay called *The Annihilation of Aesthetics*, which appeared in 1865, Pisarev described a famous

Petersburg chef as a more useful member of society than Raphael, and added that he himself would rather be a Russian cobbler than a Russian Raphael.

Stated in this extreme form, such views ended by refuting themselves. But it would be rash to pretend that the utilitarian view of art was ever seriously supplanted by the opposition which Pisarev's challenge excited. The glorification of Pushkin by the Slavophils was an answer to Pisarev. But it was an answer on his own ground. Pushkin was not, as Pisarev had pretended, useless to society: on the contrary, he was highly valuable to it because he inculcated and encouraged a right view of man's place in it. Neither side denied that content was what ultimately mattered, or had any truck with anything that smacked of art for art's sake; not until the symbolist movement appeared at the turn of the century was this view seriously contested. Nor did anything happen to shake the conviction of the 'sixties that art was an essentially aristocratic and conservative phenomenon, while science was democratic and progressive. Such prejudices died hard in nineteenth-century Russia. It is not certain that they are dead to-day.

It remains to consider Russian nineteenth-century thought in its relation to the State. Berdyaev is hardly correct in claiming anarchism as "the creation of Russians". The genealogy of anarchism goes back to William Godwin, if not farther: it was firmly embedded in the incipient socialist movements of western Europe before it established itself in Russia. But the significant point is that a doctrine, which in western Europe was specifically socialist and revolutionary, coloured in Russia the thinking of the whole intelligentsia of whatever political complexion.

Political thought in nineteenth-century Russia, whether of westerners or of Slavophils, began in opposition to the bureaucratic State of Nicholas I. The first westerners, such as Herzen, were at best grudging advocates of the western democratic State; from the first, as Berdyaev says, the Russian idea of freedom was bound up, not with liberalism but with anarchism. The first Slavophils unreservedly treated the State — any State — as an evil. Dostoevsky passed, in his later years, for a fervent upholder of the autocracy. Yet the "Legend of the Grand Inquisitor", though ostensibly directed against the secular arm of Catholicism, is in fact valid against any attempt to set up a "kingdom of this world". Tolstoy, in theory, rejected not only the State but every exercise of power.

The struggle between Marx and Bakunin thus acquires fresh significance as a struggle between western and eastern conceptions of revolution, between the Jacobin conception of revolution through the State by seizing and using State power and the anarchist conception of revolution through the people by destroying the power of the State. Marx, it is true, paid tribute to socialist freedom by postulating the eventual dying away of the State. But his immediate concern was with the dictatorship of the proletariat. The essence of Bakunin's case against Marx was that Marx was a believer in State power — which the Russian anarchist regarded as a characteristically German trait.

When Lenin, steeped as he was in Russian as well as in Marxist thought, came to expound his view of the State in *State and Revolution*, at the critical moment of 1917, what he did was to refurbish the old western socialist tradition of hostility to the State, which remained embedded and half buried in classical Marxism, in order to convict the German Social-Democrats of a State worship incompatible with the fundamental tenets of Marx. Beelzebub was invoked to cast out Beelzebub. *State and Revolution*, with its double insistence on the immediate dictatorship of the proletariat and ultimate dying away of the State, is a characteristic synthesis of west and east, of Jacobinism and anarchism. It is a striking example of Lenin's superlative skill in rooting western revolutionary doctrines in congenial Russian soil.

Masaryk, the western liberal, who completed his survey of Russian thought before the revolution at a time when many western observers still believed in the prospect of a liberal and democratic evolution of Russian society, regarded the choice before Russia as one between theocracy and democracy. Berdyaev, the Orthodox philosopher, has a double advantage of standpoint. He writes as a Russian who understands — as no western liberal, however acute his perceptions, could ever understand — the lack of any foundation in Russian thought and tradition which could have carried the elaborate and delicate structure of liberal democracy; and he writes after a revolution which, while it has provided no final synthesis for the contradictions of Russian nineteenth-century thought, has carried the debate a stage farther and, so to speak, shifted it on to another plane.

Whatever else may have changed, the fundamental theme of east and west has not ceased to play its customary part in the Russian politics and Russian thought of the last thirty years. Bolshevism is primarily a creation of western thought and experience. But the eastern element in it, and the growth of that influence in recent years, will not be seriously contested. It is possible to read the whole story of the defeat of Trotsky and the "old Bolsheviks", who had spent their formative years in Europe and whose revolutionary outlook was predominantly western, by Stalin and a group whose background and training were mainly Russian and non-European, as a re-emergence in Russian history of the eastern factor temporarily eclipsed by its western counterpart.

Indeed, no understanding is possible of many of the outstanding characteristics of the Soviet regime without some study of the background of nineteenth-century Russia. The combination of a rigidly materialist outlook with a call, widely and fervently accepted, for self-sacrifice in the revolutionary cause; the demand for the liberation of human beings from exploitation through the pursuit of collective good, which in its turn threatens to become a new source of oppression; the demand for a philosophy which embraces politics, society and art and uses them as the expression of its purpose — all these are the direct legacy to Bolshevism of Russian radical thinkers of the nineteenth century.

The debt to the Slavophils, though in some respects paradoxical, is unmistakable. The rejection of bourgeois democracy, of bourgeois individualism, of bourgeois notions of property (Berdyaev himself remarks that "the Soviet constitution of 1936 enacted the best legislation in the world about property") links Soviet theory and practice with a long line of Russian thinkers. The Russian messianism of the Slavophils, philosophical rather than political in its origin but susceptible of political perversions, reappears in the form of a messianism of the proletariat. "Communism", writes Berdyaev, "is a Russian phenomenon in spite of its Marxist ideology. Communism is Russian destiny; it is a moment in the inner destiny of the Russian people." This is an exaggeration of the specifically Russian aspects of Bolshevism, which may be dangerous if it induces the belief that Communism has no more than an external and episodic interest for other nations. But no student of Russian history will be tempted to ignore the grain of truth which it contains.

7

PLEKHANOV: FATHER OF RUSSIAN MARXISM

JUST thirty years after George Plekhanov's death, which occurred in Finland on June 12, 1918, an English translation of his principal philosophical essay has appeared under the title *In Defence of Materialism.*[1] Plekhanov was a prolific writer. But the twenty-four volume edition of his works, published in Moscow in the nineteen-twenties, is no longer easy to come by; and only a few of his essays and articles had hitherto been available in English. The present translation has been entrusted to the safe hands of Mr. Andrew Rothstein. It is preceded by an introductory sketch which is as accurate and masterly an account as could be desired of Plekhanov's career and significance.

The text-book label for Plekhanov is " the father of Russian Marxism ". In the words of one enthusiast, he " brought down the ten commandments of Marx from Sinai and delivered them to the youth of Russia ". He was Lenin's acknowledged teacher in

[1] G. V. Plekhanov, *In Defence of Materialism.* The Development of the Monist View of History. Translated by Andrew Rothstein. Lawrence and Wishart. 18s.

Marxism, and laid the foundations of Russian Social-Democracy. Born in 1856, he graduated as a revolutionary in the Narodnik movement, breaking with it in 1879 on the issue of individual terrorism, which he rejected as futile and irrelevant. The assassination of Alexander II in 1881 led to a general round-up of revolutionaries; and Plekhanov fled abroad.

The next two years were decisive. The break with the Narodniks on the policy of terrorism, and the manifest bankruptcy of that policy after 1881, led Plekhanov to re-examine the basic tenets of the Narodnik philosophy — the belief that the peasantry was the coming revolutionary force in Russia. This belief, attested by a long tradition of peasant revolts and revolutionary peasant leaders, from Stenka Razin to Pugachev, was universally held in the west as in the east. Marx himself had encouraged the favourite Narodnik speculation that the Russian peasant commune was destined to evolve into a socialist society without an intervening capitalist stage.

Plekhanov's claim to an outstanding place among the makers of the October revolution is the insight, brilliantly original in the early eighteen-eighties, that capitalism was already in the process of striking roots in Russia, that its development would create a Russian proletariat, and that it was this Russian proletariat, and not the Russian peasantry, which would provide the driving-force and the ideological justification of the Russian revolution. There was thus no reason to place Russia outside the orthodox Marxist scheme. The trend of Plekhanov's thinking was apparent in 1882 when he published a Russian translation of the *Communist Manifesto*, though the preface shows that he was not yet a Marxist. In the following year, with two of his close associates in exile, Paul Axelrod and Vera Zasulich, he founded a group under the name "The Liberation of Labour" with a Marxist programme. Plekhanov was the undisputed ancestor of Russian Social-Democracy, both as a doctrine and as an organization.

The ten years that followed were occupied by incessant controversy with the Narodniks. Plekhanov's position was defined in two essays dating from 1883 and 1884 respectively, *Socialism and the Political Struggle* and *Our Differences*; and the broad lines of policy here laid down were not seriously amended or added to for twenty years. Plekhanov asserted that the Russian peasantry was fundamentally non-revolutionary; that the peasant commune could evolve only into petty bourgeois capitalism, not into socialism; that the revolution would culminate in the seizure of power by the industrial workers; but that this final step could be taken only under conditions of bourgeois democracy, the achievement of which was therefore the first and immediate revolutionary goal. To count on a peasant revolt as the source of revolution was tantamount to anarchism; to advocate an immediate seizure of power by the workers was "Blanquism". But these ideas made such slow headway that, when Plekhanov appeared in Paris in 1889 at the founding congress of the Second International and announced that "the Russian revolution will triumph as a proletarian revolution, or it will not triumph at all ", he was uttering a bold paradox.

Such was the picture when Lenin entered the lists with a vigorous polemic against the Narodniks in 1894. By this time Russian capitalism, under the powerful impulse of Witte, was growing by leaps and bounds; the first serious strikes and demonstrations of workers had occurred in Petrograd; and the views of Plekhanov were coming into their own. Small Marxist groups sprang up in the principal Russian cities. On the other hand, the authorities still saw revolution in terms of Narodniks and terrorists; and they were not displeased with the appearance of this new sect which was splitting the revolutionary movement, which did not appear to be preaching immediate action and which was mainly occupied in analysing the growth of Russian capitalism. For a few years the writings of the Marxists, provided they were couched in learned and not openly provocative language, received the *imprimatur* of the censors. It was the period of what came to be known as " legal Marxism ".

This curious circumstance explains why Plekhanov's chief philosophical work was also the only one of his writings legally published in Russia before the revolution. He completed it in London in 1894. It was copied out by an enthusiastic young Russian Marxist named Potresov, who carried the manuscript back with him to Petrograd and secured a publisher for it. The conditions of its publication also explain why the title originally chosen for it by Plekhanov (which has been restored in the present translation) was abandoned in favour of the meaningless and therefore harmless circumlocution, *On the Question of the Development of the Monist View of History*. It appeared in the last days of 1894, bearing the date 1895, and was at once read by Lenin, who expounded it with enthusiastic approval to the Marxist circle in Petrograd. It had an immediate and lasting success. Lenin afterwards said that it had " reared a whole generation of Russian Marxists ".

In Defence of Materialism (followed a year later by *Essays in the History of Materialism*, of which an English version is available) is a systematic, orderly and effective presentation in an historical setting of the Marxist doctrine of dialectical materialism. Starting from French eighteenth-century materialism, which he traces back to Locke, Plekhanov then illustrates how the idea of the class struggle passed into French thought in the half-century after 1789, turns from this to the Utopian socialists and to German idealist philosophy, and finally shows how the " modern materialism " of Marx springs from all these diverse sources. Apart from some unduly lengthy polemics against contemporary Russian " subjectivists ", all this wears remarkably well. There is no better exposition available of what Marx (and Lenin) meant by dialectical materialism.

The essence of dialectical, as opposed to " metaphysical ", or static, materialism is to introduce the element of opposition, struggle and movement into the explanation of reality. This relieves materialism of the determinism implicit in the more rigid forms of the doctrine, but puts a question mark against the nature of the forces generating the dialectical process. In postulating that the ultimate source is to be found in changes in material conditions of production, Marx does not pretend that these operate automatically or without the conscious intervention of free human will. In a famous letter written in the last years of his life, Engels goes so far as to admit that he and Marx may sometimes have overstated the role of the " economic factor " and neglected the " other factors in the reciprocal interactions of the historical process ". The doctrine of dialectical materialism thus gains in subtlety what it loses in the false simplicity sometimes attributed to it.

Translated (as all Marxist philosophy must be) into concrete political terms, the Marxist doctrine of man and matter raises the issue of the respective roles in revolutionary policy of the " spontaneous " action of the masses, which is dependent on objective material situations, and of " conscious " leadership, which is based on a study and grasp of revolutionary theory. The balance is so nice that writers and actors in the revolutionary drama are in constant danger of tipping it over on one side or the other. Plekhanov, while stating the doctrine fairly enough, leans on the whole towards those who count on the ripening of objective conditions to produce spontaneous action as the main revolutionary force. " History is made by the masses ", he wrote in a famous passage. " . . . While we are preparing the leaders of the revolutionary army, the officers and non-commissioned officers of the revolutionary army, that army itself is being created by the irreversible march of social developments."

Lenin, on the other hand, sometimes — notably in his famous pamphlet of 1902, *What is to be Done?* — went rather uncomfortably far in preaching the need of conscious leadership working " from without " on the otherwise inert masses. This idea dictated Lenin's conception of the Russian Social-Democratic Party as a small highly disciplined group of professional revolutionaries. Only thus could the masses be made ripe for revolution: " There is no conscious activity of the workers without social democracy ". It was this attitude which exposed Lenin from time to time to charges of " Blanquism " and " Bakuninism ". According to present interpretations, Lenin's and Stalin's main contribution to the theory of dialectical materialism has been " to reveal the active role of consciousness."

This divergence was the basis of the rift, doctrinal and temperamental, which was presently to open between Plekhanov and Lenin. But for the moment all was well. When Lenin visited the older man in Geneva on his first journey abroad in the summer of 1895 the relations were still those of revered master and brilliant disciple. On Lenin's return to Russia he was arrested in December 1895, and spent the next four years in prison or in Siberia. He was, however, able to follow and applaud Plekhanov's vigorous polemics against the " legal Marxists " and the " economists ", who were trying to empty Marxism of its revolutionary content by treating it as a pure theory of economic evolution; and he hailed with enthusiasm the first attempt in 1898 to create a Russian Social-Democratic Party.

When Lenin emerged from exile in 1900 he met Potresov and another young revolutionary called Martov, and between them the three hatched a project to found a popular revolutionary journal and a solid Marxist periodical, to be called *Iskra* (" The Spark ") and *Zarya* (" The Dawn ") respectively, and to be issued somewhere in Europe. It was Potresov who, having well-to-do relations, furnished the funds and seems at the outset to have been the moving spirit in the enterprise. Mr. Rothstein, who oddly refers to Potresov as Plekhanov's " publisher ", ignores altogether Potresov's role in the foundation of *Iskra*, which he ascribes to Lenin alone. It is true that Potresov became a Menshevik in 1903, a " defencist " in 1914 and a bitter enemy of the Bolshevik revolution after 1917. But these subsequent falls from grace need not depose him from his distinguished niche in the pre-history of the revolution. Be this as it may, the three young men proceeded, one by one, to Switzerland to lay the scheme before Plekhanov and his group. Not without difficulty, agreement was reached. The journals were to be published with an editorial board consisting of Plekhanov, Axelrod and Zasulich, Lenin, Potresov and Martov.

The possibilities of friction were soon apparent. Plekhanov, the senior member and undisputed doyen of the group, remained in his own eyes and in those of others the presiding genius of the enterprise. Lenin quickly emerged head and shoulders above his fellow editors by his energy, by the clarity of his ideas, and by his determination to establish both a body of revolutionary doctrine and an organized revolutionary party. The first of these aims required, in addition to filling the columns of *Iskra*, the promulgation of a party programme; the second, the summoning of a party congress to take up the work begun and abandoned in 1898.

Plekhanov sympathized with both these aims. He drafted a programme on the lines of those prepared fifteen and twenty years ago for the "Liberation of Labour" group. This was criticized by Lenin, and out of the subsequent discussions came the draft programme which was published in *Iskra* in the summer of 1902. Plekhanov's prestige was still great; and almost for the last time in his life Lenin was prepared to bow to superior authority, or at any rate to compromise with it. A significant "concession" secured by Lenin in these discussions was the inclusion in the programme of the Marxist doctrine of the "dictatorship of the proletariat", which had characteristically found no place in Plekhanov's draft. One of the charges brought by Lenin against Plekhanov many years later was his failure to deal with the relation of the revolution to the State.

The party congress, which met in Brussels and then in London in the summer of 1903, was more troublesome. It adopted the programme without difficulty, but split on the party rules. Here Lenin proposed a formula for party membership designed to cover his conception of the party as a disciplined army of trained and active revolutionaries. The prestige of the master had hitherto weighed with the disciple; but now the determination and forcefulness of the disciple carried away the master himself. Plekhanov supported Lenin throughout the congress. This did not save Lenin from being defeated on the issue of the rules. But by a turn of the wheel, his group secured a majority in the elections of party officers. This victory had two results. Lenin and his supporters are known to posterity as "Bolsheviks" or majority-men, leaving the title of "Mensheviks" to the minority; and Lenin and Plekhanov were left in undisputed control of *Iskra*, the organ of party policy.

Plekhanov had now reached the summit and turning-point of his career. Many explanations might be suggested of the next phase. Though he was not yet fifty, complaints about his health began to be heard at this time; he may have lacked the physical strength and endurance to cope with the younger rival who was driving him where he did not want to go. Plekhanov was by character a mild man — a man of the pen rather than of action. In words he could be trenchant enough. At the congress he had shocked the delegates, and provoked some hisses, by proclaiming, with a logic less faulty (unless the reporters have traduced him) than his Latin: *salus revolutiae suprema lex*. But in practice the cloak and dagger were antipathetic to him. Nature had fitted him to theorize about revolution, not to make it. Stalin rather unkindly lumps him with Kautsky among the "theorists" whose role is finished as soon as revolution actually begins.

Another cause of the split was diagnosed by

Krupskaya when she remarked that " after the turn of the century Plekhanov had lost the capacity for understanding Russia ". Like all the early revolutionaries he had always been a " westerner " in terms of Russian nineteenth-century thought; and by 1901 he had lived continuously in western Europe for twenty years. He had imbibed the softer, as well as some of the more arid, traits of western rationalism and western radicalism — its humanitarianism, its belief in ordered progress, its dislike of violence and of abrupt or catastrophic change. He had incapacitated himself to understand the Russian revolution — or to understand Lenin.

In essence the rift between Plekhanov and Lenin was the same which divided Mensheviks from Bolsheviks. Both accepted the ordered sequence laid down in the *Communist Manifesto* according to which bourgeois democratic revolution was to be followed by proletarian socialist revolution. Both agreed that Russia was as yet only on the threshold of the bourgeois revolution, whose advent was being inevitably hastened by the development of Russian capitalism. Plekhanov, the theorist, in common with the Mensheviks, remained content with this tidy scheme. Lenin, the practical revolutionary, became from 1901 onwards increasingly impatient of a policy which, until some undefined date in the future, left the proletariat with little to hope for and little to do — except, perhaps, to further the progress of capitalism, its own greatest enemy and oppressor. It was when Lenin tried to escape from this dilemma, to hasten the bourgeois revolution by an alliance between the proletariat and the peasantry and to carry it forward at the earliest moment to the socialist stage, that he encountered the stern opposition, in the name of Marxist orthodoxy, of Plekhanov and the Mensheviks.

Psychologically and politically the break was overdue when Plekhanov and Lenin celebrated their joint victory at the 1903 congress. Plekhanov was quickly shocked by the ruthless consistency with which Lenin proposed to exploit the victory. The Mensheviks, whom Lenin wished to excommunicate, included most of Plekhanov's old friends and associates. The rigid party discipline in matters of opinion as well as of organization which Lenin wished to enforce was alien to Plekhanov's western notions of political organization and agitation. Unthinkably for Lenin, Plekhanov began to advocate reconciliation with the dissidents. Before the end of 1903 Lenin had resigned from the editorial board of *Iskra*; Plekhanov had co-opted on to it the former members rejected by the congress, Mensheviks all; *Iskra* had become a Menshevik organ; and Lenin had been left to organize his Bolsheviks as an independent faction.

The next twelve months saw a series of scathing articles from Plekhanov's pen against Lenin and the Bolsheviks. Lenin's *What is to be Done?* was answered by Plekhanov's *What not to Do.* Lenin was declared guilty of fostering a "sectarian spirit of exclusion", of claiming to act "in obedience to an infallible class instinct", of "confusing the dictatorship of the proletariat with the dictatorship over the proletariat ". Plekhanov was a learned controversialist. With a wealth of quotation he proved that Lenin, by his insistence on " consciousness ", was reviving the idealistic heresy of the Bauer brothers which Marx had denounced in the eighteen-forties, and that, by his advocacy of an army of professional revolutionaries, he was a disciple not of Marx but of Bakunin. It is perhaps significant (though there was provocation for this on the other side) that Plekhanov's arguments turn always on the issue of conformity with Marx, never on that of the practical utility of the courses of action proposed. Plekhanov remained to the end doctrinaire and academic.

The rest of his career was one of wavering and frustration. He never became an orthodox Menshevik, and in the party controversies of the following years occasionally even found himself in Lenin's camp. The last meeting between the two men happened after the outbreak of war in 1914. Plekhanov, ten years earlier, at the time of the Russo-Japanese war, had ardently preached " defeatism " and the class war, and had written that " international social-democracy cannot help rising in revolt against international wars ". He now appeared as an advocate of national defence on a Socialist platform at Lausanne, and found himself suddenly and unexpectedly confronted by an angry Lenin. Krupskaya, who relates the incident, admits that a majority of the audience was on the side of Plekhanov.

In the spring of 1917 the February revolution

allowed Plekhanov to return to Russia after an interval of thirty-six years. He took part in the famous " democratic conference " in Moscow in August, and denounced the Bolsheviks both before and after the October revolution. For a reissue of his thirty-four-year-old essay on *Socialism and the Political Struggle* he wrote a postscript (it has not been reprinted in the collected edition), in which he accused Lenin of reviving an old Narodnik heresy by supposing that the introduction of socialism could be made to coincide with the overthrow of the old regime, and predicted " fearful harm " from the attempt to telescope the bourgeois and proletariat revolutions. When over-zealous Red Guards ransacked the house in Tsarskoe Selo where Plekhanov lay sick, his friends protested to Lenin ; and an order was issued in the name of the Council of People's Commissars " to protect the person and property of citizen Plekhanov ". The material guarantee was thus accompanied by a verbal insult. Plekhanov was no longer a socialist " comrade " but a bourgeois " citizen ".

Plekhanov was now in an advanced stage of tuberculosis, and died before the revolution was a year old. At his own request he was buried in Petrograd near the grave of Belinsky. The request was significant of Plekhanov's political affinities in his later years. Belinsky — the typical " man of the 'forties " — had evolved from the position of a Hegelian conservative to that of a Hegelian political radical. He ended where Marx began, and, dying young, was always in the vanguard of his own contemporaries. Plekhanov's main work of providing a Marxist foundation for the revolutionary cause of Russia was done by the time he was forty; and though he lived on to recede to a position not far from that where Belinsky had ended, his achievement gives him a lasting place among Russian thinkers. He is perhaps the only man who, having crossed swords with Lenin in bitter controversy, is to-day quoted with respect in the Soviet Union.

8

THE CRADLE OF BOLSHEVISM

What became the " All-Russian (afterwards All-Union) Communist Party (Bolsheviks) " was founded at Minsk fifty years ago, under the name of the " Russian Social-Democratic Workers' Party ", by a tiny congress of nine men. They represented local organizations at Petersburg, Moscow, Kiev and Ekaterinoslav, and the " Jewish General Workers' Union in Russia and Poland ", commonly called the " Bund ". The congress lasted three days — March 13-15 (March 1-3, O.S.), 1898. It authorized the publication of a manifesto (which was drafted by Peter Struve, a Marxist intellectual), appointed a central committee and decided to issue a party organ. But before anything else could be done, the police arrested all the principal participants, so that virtually nothing remained of this initial effort save a common name shared by a number of local committees and organizations which had no central rallying point and no other connexions with one another.

The manifesto, after referring to the " life-giving hurricane of the 1848 revolution ", which had blown over Europe fifty years before, noted that the

Russian working-class was " entirely deprived of what its foreign comrades freely and peacefully enjoy — a share in the administration of the State, freedom of the spoken and written word, freedom of organization and assembly ". These were necessary instruments in the struggle " for its final liberation, against private property, for socialism ". In the west the bourgeoisie had won these freedoms. In Russia conditions were different.

The farther east one goes in Europe, the weaker, meaner and more cowardly becomes the bourgeoisie in the political sense, and the greater the cultural and political tasks which fall to the lot of the proletariat. On its strong shoulders the Russian working class must and will carry the work of conquering political liberty. This is an essential step, but only the first step, to the realization of the great historic mission of the proletariat, to the foundation of a social order in which there will be no place for the exploitation of man by man.

In western democratic terms, the programme was extreme but constitutional. In Tsarist Russia it was unconditionally revolutionary; the intention to " throw off the yoke of the autocracy " was specifically proclaimed.

Nearly three years later a fresh start was made when the three young revolutionary Marxists — Lenin, Potresov and Martov — who had just served sentences in Siberia for illegal activities met the " Liberation of Labour " group in Switzerland. Lenin was then thirty. Since 1894, when his first political writing had been circulated in hectograph form, he had been known as an able and vigorous disciple of Plekhanov; and he had been, before his arrest in December 1895, a leading spirit in one of the groups represented at the 1898 congress. He now showed himself the most energetic member of the *Iskra* board. It was he who drafted the manifesto announcing the new journal, and who was its steadiest and most prolific contributor. It was he who led the agitation for a second party congress to take up again the work begun and interrupted at Minsk. The congress, which opened in July 1903, was the real founding congress of the party — not the less because its concluding stage also produced the epoch-making split between Bolsheviks and Mensheviks. The breach was intensified when, three months after the congress, the wavering Plekhanov went over to the Mensheviks, Lenin resigned from the board and *Iskra* became a Menshevik organ.

The party thus founded in 1898, refounded in 1903 and (so far as its Bolshevik wing was concerned) remodelled by Lenin after the split, became the directing instrument of the revolution of October 1917. The congress of 1903 was the crucial turning-point in its history, the focus round which all the main party controversies, both earlier and later, revolved. Some understanding of these controversies is essential to any judgment on the revolution itself and on the events which issued from it. The English reader can find an account of them in the unsatisfactory official short *History of the Communist Party of the Soviet Union*, published in 1938, or in Popov's less cursory *Outline History of the Communist*

Party of the Soviet Union, published five years earlier. The Russian reader is embarrassed only by the mass of often indigestible and unreliable material. An important recent accession to the Russian sources of party history is *The Origin of Bolshevism*, by F. I. Dan,[1] the former Menshevik leader, who died almost at the moment of its publication in New York. The last chapter contains what is virtually a recantation of Dan's previous attitude, and the book represents a sincere, though not uncritical, acceptance of Lenin's views. It bears some of the marks of a work of old age, but is full both of knowledge and of penetration. No more objective account of early party history has been written by any of those who participated in it.

When the 1903 congress met, three ideological battles had been fought and won; and these three victories formed the basis of the party programme unanimously adopted by the congress. As against the Narodniks, the Russian Social-Democratic Workers' Party regarded the proletariat and not the peasant as the bearer of the coming revolution; as against the " legal Marxists ", it preached revolutionary action and no compromise with the bourgeoisie; as against the " economists ", it emphasized the essentially political character of the party programme.

The campaign against the Narodniks had been conducted by Plekhanov in the 'eighties and early 'nineties. " The Russian revolution ", ran Plekhanov's famous aphorism, " will triumph as

[1] F. I. Dan, *Proiskhozhdenie Bolshevizma*.

a proletarian revolution, or it will not triumph at all." This clearly meant that the way to revolution in Russia would be paved by industrial development; and in the last decade of the century Witte and foreign capitalists were busy fulfilling this requirement. Lenin, in the writings against the Narodniks which opened his polemical career, had little to do but to drive home Plekhanov's arguments and to point tellingly to what was happening in Russia before the eyes of all. The star of the industrial worker was rising, the star of the backward peasant waning, in the revolutionary firmament. It was not until 1905 that the problem of fitting the Russian peasant into the revolutionary scheme again became a burning party issue.

The struggle against the "legal Marxists", whose views, expressed in slightly cryptic language, were allowed by the censorship to appear in learned journals, was more complicated. The ablest member of the group was Peter Struve, author of the manifesto of the Minsk congress; and Bulgakov and Berdyaev, who later joined the Orthodox Church, were at one time members of it. Lenin welcomed the temporary alliance of the "legal Marxists" against the Narodniks. They accepted without qualification the Marxist view of the development of capitalism as a first step towards the eventual achievement of socialism, and believed that in this respect Russia must tread the western path. So far Lenin agreed with them. But insistence on the necessity of the capitalist stage led them to treat this development as an end in itself and to substitute reform for revolution as the process out of which socialism would eventually grow; and it was on this point that Lenin attacked " legal Marxism " as tantamount to democratic liberalism and the enemy of the proletariat.

This attitude towards the " legal Marxists " was symptomatic of a dilemma which pursued the party for many years. Marxist theory from the *Communist Manifesto* onwards made it clear that, so long as political freedom had not been achieved, the proletariat shared with the bourgeoisie the same interest in winning it. In pursuance of this theory the party programme adopted by the second congress laid it down that the party " supports every opposition and revolutionary movement directed against the existing social and political order in Russia ". It was a rather undistinguished delegate to the congress who pointed out that only two contemporary movements answered to this description — the Social-Revolutionaries (who were the heirs of the Narodniks) and the " legal Marxists " — and that the congress had passed resolutions specifically condemning both of them. No ready reply was forthcoming. Whatever Marxist theory required, co-operation between the proletariat and the bourgeoisie for a specific end, common to both, could never be free from embarrassment so long as the destruction of the bourgeoisie remained the ultimate goal of the proletarian revolution. This inherent contradiction, and not the intolerance of Lenin or his successors, was responsible for a long-standing crux.

The " economists ", against whom the third

ideological battle of these years was fought, were a group of Marxist intellectuals who in the autumn of 1897 started in Petersburg a journal called *The Workers' Thought.* Like the " legal Marxists ", they remained within the constitutional framework, eschewed revolution and treated socialism as a distant ideal. Unlike the " legal Marxists ", who confined themselves to theory, they had a programme of action. The advance to socialism must be by stages. At the present stage in Russia, the class-consciousness of the worker could be stimulated by encouraging him to concentrate on economic demands for economic ends, to better his condition by trade-union organization, mutual aid, self-education and so forth.

Meanwhile, political action must be reserved for the intellectuals; and, since there was as yet no basis for a Marxist political programme, that action could only take the form of supporting the liberal bourgeoisie in their demand for political freedom. In the words of the document which served as the manifesto of the group:

> Discussions about an independent workers' political party are nothing but the result of transferring foreign problems and foreign solutions to our soil. . . . For the Russian Marxist there is one way out: to help the economic struggle of the proletariat and to participate in the activity of the liberal opposition.

In other words, the immediate objective in Russia could only be to reach the position long ago established in the west by the bourgeois revolution.

"Economism" received a forceful impulse from the

wave of industrial strikes which began to sweep over Russia in 1896, and it was for five years an influential movement, perhaps the most influential movement, among Russian Marxists. But it was at once denounced by Plekhanov in Switzerland and by Lenin and his fellow-exiles in Siberia as a denial of the essence of Social-Democracy. The controversy was carried on into the *Iskra* period; and a good part of Lenin's first major work, *What is to be Done?* published in 1902, was devoted to a polemic against the "economists". Political as well as economic agitation was needed to arouse the class-consciousness of the masses.

The ideal of the Social-Democrat must be not a trade-union secretary, but *a tribune of the people*. . . . A trade-union policy for the working class is simply a *bourgeois policy* for the working class.

When the second party congress met in 1903, the three tendencies represented by the Narodniks, the "legal Marxists" and the "economists" appeared to have received their death-blow, being almost unanimously denounced by the delegates — by future Mensheviks as well as by future Bolsheviks. Yet it was a Pyrrhic victory. The Social-Revolutionaries took up the unanswered challenge of the Narodniks; and the Mensheviks came to occupy positions scarcely distinguishable from those of the "legal Marxists" and of the "economists". Nor was this an accidental perversity. The issue of fitting the Russian peasant into the Marxist scheme of proletarian revolution had not yet been faced; and the tragic contradictions of the attempt to make a socialist revolution in a country where no bourgeois revolution had yet occurred to win political freedom, had not been resolved.

It was against the background of these controversies that Lenin built up the future " All-Union Communist Party (Bolsheviks) ". He accused the Mensheviks, as he had once accused the " economists ", of lack of principle ; " opportunism " meant for Lenin not a shifting of ground for tactical reasons (this he admitted and advocated freely enough) but a postponement of revolutionary work on the pretext that conditions were not ripe. But most of all he accused them of lack of organization, of amateurishness, of " small-scale craftsmanship ". The most significant division at the second congress was not the critical vote or the elections but the division on the party statute. Was the party, like western political parties, to be a mass organization of supporters and sympathizers ? Or was it to be a disciplined army of active revolutionaries ?

The question of organization thus raised a vital question of principle. Everything that has been most controversial in the history of the Russian revolution was involved in it. In the Menshevik view, the socialist revolution could be achieved only as the sequel of a bourgeois revolution and through a political party of the kind which had emerged from the bourgeois revolutions of the west. In the Bolshevik view, the Russian socialist revolution must carry within itself the bourgeois revolution which the Russian bourgeoisie had failed to achieve ;

and this called for a special form of party organization unknown to the west. In a sense both were right. Lenin, with his unerring perception of realities, knew the only way in which the Russian revolution could be led to victory. But if the survivors of Menshevism were to-day to retort that this is not the socialist revolution as understood by them or by the world in the early 1900s it would be difficult to prove them wrong. History disappoints the programme-makers as often as it refutes the prophets.

It must then be confessed, if justice is to be done, that Lenin's conception of the party, which he drove home after 1903 with all the ruthlessness of extreme consistency and unshakable conviction, owed much less to theory than to his own intuition of Russian requirements. If he accused the " economists " of exaggerating the case for " spontaneity " in the workers' movement, and declared that the class-consciousness of the workers could be developed only " from without " by an organized party of revolutionary intellectuals, the argument, however theoretical and general in form, was a faithful record of particular observed facts of Russian society. Lenin's conception of the party had at least the empirical justification that it was the kind of party required to make the revolution triumph in Russia. His opponents were prescribing for conditions which did not exist.

Lenin had two essential prerequisites for a revolutionary party: it must be small in numbers and disciplined and conspiratorial in character.

While Plekhanov and Lenin both preached that " history is made by the masses ", both recognized that the main business of the party was to train the " officers and non-commissioned officers of the revolutionary army ". Social conditions would provide the rank and file when the moment arrived. For Lenin the party was always a minority and its backbone would always be a group of professional revolutionaries. The 1905 revolution for the first time brought a significant number of workers into the party; and from that time Lenin began, for tactical reasons, to emphasize the importance of the role of the workers in the party. But it was not until some years after 1917 that workers began to form more than a small minority of the delegates to party congresses or of the members of party committees.

Lenin's second prerequisite for the party — its disciplined and conspiratorial character — derived even more directly from Russian conditions. Isolated revolutionary groups of workers and students in Russia, well-meaning amateurs, quickly fell victims to the police, as Lenin himself had done. In order to maintain secret revolutionary groups and conduct secret revolutionary propaganda in Russia itself, organization and discipline were paramount. While the principles of democracy were professed within the party, the necessities of the case precluded, as Lenin explicitly recognized, anything like public and open discussion or the election of leaders. Russian conditions dictated a form of organization utterly alien to the political parties of the west.

The attempt to execute a western political

programme — for such Marxism essentially was — in the conditions of the autocratic police State of the Romanovs created a series of contradictions which were the tragic dilemma of the Communist Party and of the Bolshevik revolution. It was impossible to attain a congruence of means and ends where the indispensable means belonged to a different order of society from that in and for which the ends had been conceived. It was impossible to establish a stable or rational relation with the bourgeoisie, domestic or foreign, since the doctrine appeared to impose two contradictory attitudes, alliance being alternately sought and spurned. Finally it was impossible to create in terms of men and women that basis of democratic administration on which socialism of the kind contemplated in the Marxist tradition could alone rest.

All these dilemmas emerge clearly from the bitter debates which accompanied the founding of the party and its initial steps in organization forty and fifty years ago. The party moved forward on the course set by Lenin inexorably, in spite of every set-back, through an ever-tightening discipline and an ever-narrowing circle of authority and power. In the 1890s it had already been established that the proletariat must lead the revolution; the dictatorship of the proletariat was naturalized in Russia. In 1903 it became accepted doctrine that the party must lead the proletariat; and the "dictatorship of the party" was a phrase long in use. Then came the phase of the leadership of the party by its central committee; this was the period of the revolution itself. After the introduction of the New Economic Policy in 1921 Lenin himself tightened the reins once more; and for a time the Politbureau of the party was the decisive organ, taking precedence over all other party and State institutions. Finally, when the restraint of Lenin's personal prestige was withdrawn, leadership passed to an inner group whose composition was never certainly known and which had no constitutional standing even within the party. The process had been precisely foreseen by Trotsky (of all people — since none was more dictatorial than he by temperament and ambition), who in a brilliant pamphlet published in 1904 predicted a situation in which " the party is replaced by the organization of the party, the organization by the central committee, and finally the central committee by the dictator ".

It would be difficult to pretend that Lenin in these early years of the party's history saw clearly whither the demand for rigid organization and discipline would lead. It would be even more difficult to pretend that, had he seen, he would have recoiled from the choice. His mind and heart were set on the revolution, in which he saw the crowning necessity for Russia and for the world. He would reject or neglect nothing that could contribute to its consummation.

Yet the unresolved dilemma remains. Dan brilliantly diagnoses the " immanent contradiction " in Russia's social development: its " retarded character ", which had brought it to the point of revolution only when socialism was already knocking at the door and democracy could no longer be realized without socialism, and its " backwardness ", which prevented the " realization of socialism in free democratic forms ". The words come from Dan's concluding chapter, which is, in effect, a renunciation of his former Menshevism and an acceptance of Lenin's conclusions and policy. Precisely because he recognizes the tragedy and the contradictions which, however inescapable they may have been, lay behind that policy, Dan's book constitutes a more powerful apologia for the party and for the revolution than the stereotyped official histories.

9

LENIN: THE MASTER BUILDER

FEW great men have so quickly won so secure and uncontested a place in history as Lenin. Even those who most hated Lenin's work have praised his comparative moderation and statesmanship as a foil to the blacker villainy, first of his colleagues, then of his successors. Death removed him at a moment when the clouds of contemporary calumny had begun to disperse and before he had time to become involved in the embittered controversies which generally attend the consolidation of a revolution. For his own generation he stood out head and shoulders from his contemporaries by the length and devotion of his service to the cause, by the clarity and forcefulness of his ideas, and by his practical leadership in the critical moments of 1917. For the next generation he became the embodiment of the victorious revolution, his writings its sacred text.

Lenin, for all his fame as a revolutionary leader, was a creator rather than a destroyer. He played no personal part in the events of 1905 or in the February revolution of 1917; nor were Bolshevik ideas an important contributory factor. What

Lenin achieved in October 1917 was not the overthrow of the provisional government — that followed logically from all that had gone before, and was bound to happen — but the construction of something to take its place. The decisive moment of the revolution came when, at the first congress of Soviets in June 1917, an orator remarked from the platform that there was no revolutionary party willing to take over the responsibilities of government, and Lenin, amid mocking laughter, retorted from his place in the hall, " There is such a party ". Only when the new regime had taken over did Lenin rise to his full stature as administrator, head of government, organizer and supreme political tactician.

Lenin was also a builder, or re-builder, of his country's international status and authority. The great Russian Empire, when the Bolsheviks took possession of it and for some time after, was in a process of rapid disintegration — the result of internal turmoil and of defeat in war. The Brest-Litovsk treaty of March 1918 lopped off not only those western appendages of the former Tsarist realm whose independence the Soviet Government had spontaneously recognized, but a large slice of predominantly Russian territory. The summer of 1918 saw the beginning of civil war and British, French, Japanese and American intervention, which long outlasted the German collapse, and for more than two years forcibly divided the country between several conflicting authorities. Meanwhile Bolshevik acceptance of the right of self-determination and secession for all nations and national groups appeared to favour the process of dispersal and to rule out anything like a reconstitution of former unity.

Yet by the end of 1922, little more than two years after the victorious conclusion of the civil war, the diverse units had been gathered into the fold of the newly established Union of Soviet Socialist Republics (the formal incorporation of the two Central Asian republics was delayed till 1924); and the cohesion of the new federation was destined to prove at least as strong and enduring as that of the defunct empire. This consummation, which few could have foreseen in the dark days of 1918 or 1920, was not the least remarkable of Lenin's achievements. In the eyes of history he appears not only as a great revolutionary, but as a great Russian.

Public interest in Lenin, in his own country and elsewhere, shows no signs of abating. The second and third editions of his complete works (really two issues in different format of the same edition) were published between 1926 and 1932. Shortly before the war a fourth edition was decided on, and its publication is now in progress. The copious additional material appearing in these volumes had for the most part been published in the *Leninskii Sbornik* or other periodical publications, so that it is not, strictly speaking, new; but its inclusion in a new edition of the works makes it, for the first time, conveniently accessible.

On the other hand, the lengthy and valuable expository notes and the appendices of documents (often convenient, even if the documents could be found elsewhere) have disappeared. An official pronouncement of 1938 had already condemned " crude political errors of a damaging character in the appendices, notes and commentaries to some volumes of the works of Lenin " ; and the Marx-Engels-Lenin Institute has evidently shrunk from the task of revising them in the light of more recent information and a more up-to-date orthodoxy. The new edition appears with a slender and quite inadequate apparatus of notes ; for this purpose the student will still have to use the earlier editions.

Meanwhile English students of Lenin will be assisted by two new publications. A complete English translation of Lenin's works, started in the 'thirties, has apparently been abandoned. But *The Essentials of Lenin*, translated from a Russian two-volume edition of his principal works, includes some which have not before appeared in English.[1] The volumes are large, the price low ; and, while there are omissions to be regretted (including all but a few of Lenin's speeches and reports to congresses), the main corpus of Lenin's writings is now easily accessible to the English reader. The other new book is a short popular biography by Mr. Christopher Hill[2] which easily outdistances any of its predecessors except that of D. S. Mirsky, now nearly twenty years old.

Mr. Hill, whose mandate from the series in which the book appears is " to open up a significant theme

[1] *The Essentials of Lenin.* In two volumes. Lawrence and Wishart. 12s. 6d. each.

[2] Christopher Hill, *Lenin and the Russian Revolution.* Hodder and Stoughton. 5s.

by way of a biography of a great man", has obviously been cramped by limitations of space. Apart from the usual biographical details and a concluding chapter of appreciation, he has chosen to concentrate on a few essential topics — Lenin's conception of the party, his agrarian policy, his philosophy of the State, his view of the relations of the revolutionary republic with the outside world and his economic policy. The choice of topics is judicious, and the handling sensible and accurate. The non-specialist reader, for whom the book is designed, will obtain from it a very fair and readable presentation of the main problems Lenin had to face and of his methods of solving them.

The central focus of Lenin's thought and action was his theory of the State, which found its most mature expression in *State and Revolution*, written on the eve of the October revolution and published in the spring of 1918. The socialist tradition from Godwin onwards had been almost unreservedly hostile to the State. Marx, especially in his early works, repeatedly denounces the State — "the form of organization adopted by the bourgeoisie for the guarantee of its property and interests". The *Communist Manifesto*, true to this tradition, looked forward to the day when, differences between classes having been wiped out, "social power will lose its political character". But the *Manifesto* also concerned itself with the more immediate practical step of winning the revolution; and for this purpose it was necessary that the proletariat should "establish its supremacy by overthrowing the bourgeoisie " and the State become identical with " the proletariat organized as the ruling class ". This was the idea which Marx crystallized a few years later into the famous slogan of " the dictatorship of the proletariat ".

The doctrine of the State, as it emerged from the writings of Marx and Engels, was twofold. In the long run the State, being a product of class contradictions and an instrument of oppression, would die away and have no place in the communist order of the future. In the short run, the proletariat, having destroyed the bourgeois State instrument by revolution, would have to set up a temporary State instrument of its own — the dictatorship of the proletariat — until such time as the classless society had been achieved. The reconciliation of the two points of view was not always easy. Orthodoxy, when Lenin first began to consider the matter, had to steer a careful course between the Scylla of anarchism, which rejected the State so vehemently as to exclude also the dictatorship of the proletariat, and the Charybdis of State socialism, especially dangerous in Germany, where the Lassallean tradition encouraged the belief that socialism might triumph, not by destroying the bourgeois State, but by allying itself with the existing State power.

Lenin, when he wrote *State and Revolution*, was still smarting from the " treachery " of the German Social-Democrats in embracing the national cause in 1914, and was therefore more impressed by the dangers of State worship than by those of anarchism. This makes the work a little one-sided. The argument against the anarchists in defence of the dictatorship of the proletariat occupies only a few hurried paragraphs; the bulk of the pamphlet is an assault on those pseudo-Marxists who refuse to recognize, first, that the State is a product of class antagonisms and an instrument of class domination, doomed to disappear with the disappearance of the classes themselves, and secondly, that the immediate goal is not the taking over of the bourgeois State machine, but its destruction and the substitution of the dictatorship of the proletariat.

For the student of history the most important passages in *State and Revolution* are those which show how Lenin at this time conceived the dictatorship of the proletariat. It is " something which is no longer properly a State "; it is " already a transitional State, no longer a State in the proper sense ". It will " begin to die away immediately after its victory ". Marx and Engels believed themselves to have discovered the prototype of the dictatorship of the proletariat in the Paris commune of 1871; in April 1917 Lenin eagerly transferred the discovery to the Soviets. The point of the discovery was that neither the commune nor the Soviets were " a State in the proper sense ". Both had the same exclusively working-class representation and the same basis of voluntary self-organization, and stood for the same kind of loose federation of like-minded autonomous units in place of the sovereign authority of the bourgeois State. Both were to exercise administrative as well as legislative functions, and the evils both of regular armies and of a regular bureaucracy were to be superseded. A militia of workers was to displace the army. Most of the administration would be managed by the workers themselves in their spare time.

> Under socialism [wrote Lenin] much of " primitive " democracy will inevitably revive, since for the first time in the history of civilized societies the *mass* of the population will be raised to independent participation not only in voting and elections, *but in day-to-day administration.* Under socialism *all* will administer in turn and will quickly become accustomed to nobody administering.

It is often said that these somewhat Utopian projects applied only to the coercive organs of administration, not to the economic and financial apparatus. But this is not altogether true. Lenin at first believed that the tasks of business management and accounting, like those of administration, could be carried out by ordinary citizens. He observed that these tasks have been " extraordinarily simplified " by capitalism and reduced " to uncommonly simple operations of checking and registration within the reach of every literate person, to a knowledge of the four rules of arithmetic and to the handing out of correct receipts ". What was wrong about these aspirations was in part, no doubt, an over-optimistic estimate of human nature, but most of all a failure to understand that the dictatorship of the proletariat, or any form of socialist society, would involve not a reduction, but an immense increase, both in the numbers of those engaged in administration and in the complexity of their work.

In three years Lenin learned much. On the eve of the introduction of NEP in the spring of 1921 he dismissed as a "fairy tale" the idea that every worker could "know how to administer the State". Harsh necessity forced the Soviet administration into the traditional State mould which Lenin had never intended for it. Yet, so long as Lenin lived, something remained of the large-minded distrust of the State which he had expressed in *State and Revolution*. The Soviets, and especially the local Soviets, retained a wide measure of autonomy and initiative, even if their competence did not stray far from the parish pump; and Lenin continued with his last official breath to preach the need for untiring vigilance in curbing and controlling bureaucracy. Not till many years after Lenin's death did the inexorable tide of events re-establish a degree of State worship which would have seemed unthinkable to the men who made the revolution.

Lenin's personal share in moulding the foreign policy of the new regime was even more important and decisive than in shaping its domestic policy; and here, too, the same flexibility, the same readiness to study and follow the dynamic of events, is equally conspicuous. The foreign policy of the young Soviet Government was made up of three distinct strands — of radical pacifism, of world revolution and of national or State interest. The three strands sprang from different origins and could rarely be isolated in practice: the subtle web into which they were deftly woven was mainly Lenin's own work.

The *motif* of radical pacifism was particularly

strong during the first weeks and months of the revolution for two reasons. In the first place the Bolshevists were still vitally dependent, in the Soviets and elsewhere, on the support of the peasants and of their Social-Revolutionary leaders. The peasant masses, including the mobilized masses, were wholly indifferent, after more than three years of war, either to the defence of national interests or to the spread of world revolution. Their unconditional demand for peace was reflected in the ideology of those radical democrats who proclaimed without qualification or analysis that peace was always in the interest of the people everywhere, and that to follow and carry out the will of the people was the sure way to peace. Secondly, this radical pacifism was the basis of the political thinking of Woodrow Wilson and of those Left-wing circles in other countries where alone the Soviet regime might still hope to find friends. It was thus essential to dwell on the one point of view which seemed to provide a bridge between the regime and these potential supporters rather than on those aspects of Soviet policy which would inevitably divide them.

Such was the principal inspiration of the famous " decree on peace " which was the first public act of Soviet foreign policy. Its language is not Marxist but Wilsonian. It must be interpreted, not as some remote descendant of the *Communist Manifesto*, but as the forerunner of the Fourteen Points issued just two months later. What is demanded is not a socialist but a " just, democratic " peace — a peace " without annexations or indemnities ", a peace based on the right of self-determination for all nations by " a free vote ". The decree declares secret diplomacy abolished and announces the intention — which was promptly carried out — to publish the secret treaties of the past : future negotiations were to be conducted — and this too was carried out at Brest-Litovsk — " completely openly before the whole people ".

Nothing is said, in the decree, of capitalism as the cause of war or of socialism as its cure. The one hint of world revolution occurs in the final injunction to the workers of England, France and Germany to assist their Russian comrades " to bring to successful conclusion the work of peace and also the work of liberating the labouring and exploited masses of the population from every kind of slavery and exploitation ". The decree reflects, above all, that radical belief in the rightness and efficacy of mass opinion which was so deeply rooted in nineteenth-century democratic doctrine — the appeal from wicked governments to enlightened people, which had been a commonplace of Wilson's utterances. This note was echoed much later, though with rapidly diminishing sincerity, in Soviet pronouncements about disarmament.

The second strand in Soviet foreign policy — the promotion of world revolution — did not, however, long remain in the background. Peace at any price, however deep the psychological roots of its appeal and however great its political expediency at this juncture, was difficult to reconcile with fundamental Bolshevik doctrine ; and the policy of transforming the imperialist war in all belligerent countries into civil war for the overthrow of capitalism had been too assiduously proclaimed to be discarded overnight. During the first weeks of the revolution enormous importance was attached to the spread of propaganda in the German armies by fraternization and by the distribution of literature; and less successful attempts were made to set propaganda on foot in the allied countries. For a brief moment this mood was all-powerful and all-pervading. Trotsky, on the testimony of his autobiography, went to the Commissariat of Foreign Affairs believing that his task was to publish the secret treaties, "issue a few revolutionary proclamations" and then shut up shop. World revolution would take care of the rest. Foreign affairs in the accepted sense would cease to exist.

But the third strand in Soviet foreign policy — national interest — was not slow to assert itself. Lenin, with his sense of realism, was the first to perceive that a Soviet republic, living even for a limited period in a world of States, would be compelled in many respects to behave like any other State. In an article in 1915, which afterwards did manful service in the controversy about "socialism in one country", Lenin had pointed out that the country or countries in which socialism was first victorious would have to stand up for a time against an agglomeration of hostile capitalist States; and in 1917, when some stalwart internationalist put up the slogan "Down with frontiers", Lenin sensibly replied that the Soviet republic, coming into existence in a capitalist world, would necessarily have

State frontiers, as well as other State interests, to defend. If the rest of the world was organized on a system of States, it was not open to a single region to contract out of the system by an act of will.

It would, however, be rash to deduce from all this either a theoretical or a practical clash in Soviet foreign policy between the claims of world revolution and those of national interest. It was this clash, and the priority given to national interest, which had in Lenin's view destroyed the Second International. No such clash could occur in Soviet policy for the simple reason that all the Soviet leaders were agreed in believing that the survival of the Soviet regime in Russia was bound up with the success of the revolution in the rest of the world, or at any rate in Europe.

Mr. Hill, in common with most recent writers, exaggerates the difference between Lenin and Trotsky on this point, and makes one of his few serious mistakes when, having quoted Trotsky's remark that " either the Russian revolution will cause a revolution in the west, or the capitalists of all countries will strangle our revolution ", he adds that Lenin would never have committed himself to such a statement. Half a dozen statements of the same tenor can be found in Lenin's works, of which one, precisely contemporaneous with that of Trotsky, may be quoted as a sample :

> Anglo-French and American imperialism will *inevitably* strangle the independence and freedom of Russia *unless* world-wide socialism, world-wide Bolshevism triumphs.

And in the purely hypothetical event of a clash, Lenin gave the same answer as Trotsky and in no less categorical terms. " He is no socialist ", Lenin wrote after Brest-Litovsk, " who will not sacrifice his fatherland for the triumph of the social revolution."

The debate between Lenin and Trotsky over Brest-Litovsk turned therefore on a question of timing and tactics rather than of principle, since the same premise was common to both. Bitterly as it was contested, it led imperceptibly to a kind of synthesis between national and international aspects of Soviet policy; for while Trotsky supported his case for staking everything on world revolution (or, more specifically, on revolution in Germany) by the argument, which Lenin at this time fully accepted, that without such a revolution the Soviet regime in Russia could not survive, Lenin, on his side, argued that nothing would be so certainly fatal to the cause of revolution in Germany as the overthrow of the Soviet republic by German imperialism, and that to defend and strengthen the Soviet regime by a prudent national policy was the surest ultimate guarantee of international revolution. Lenin was right. But the irony of the situation is that he was right for a reason which contradicted the premise accepted both by Trotsky and by himself — namely, the dependence of the survival of the regime in Russia on revolution elsewhere.

The synthesis established at the time of Brest-Litovsk between national and international policy, between the interests of the Soviet republic and those of world revolution, proved lasting. A whole generation of communists — Russian and foreign — was nurtured on the dual conception of the promotion of world revolution as the ultimate and necessary crown and reinforcement of the Soviet republic, and of the strengthening of Soviet power as the immediate and necessary spearhead of world revolution. The attempt to drive a wedge between these two facets of policy and exalt Lenin's realism in foreign policy at the expense of his loyalty to world revolution is misleading and mistaken. After Lenin's retirement from the scene, when it became clear that the prospects of the world revolution were, to say the least, far more remote than Lenin or any of his colleagues had dreamed, fresh strains were put on the synthesis. But though the balance was disturbed it was never broken. It remained reasonably possible nearly thirty years later to argue, as Lenin had argued over Brest-Litovsk, that the survival and strength of the Soviet State were the best pledge for the socialist revolution in other countries.

It has become a commonplace to praise Lenin's realism, his flexibility, his practical common sense in judging what could and what could not be done at the given moment; and all these qualities he possessed in a pre-eminent degree. But perhaps the most vivid impression left by a re-reading of his major works is of the amazing intellectual power and consistency of purpose which runs through them. His tactical readiness to compromise, to tack, to retreat when it became necessary was an enormous asset to the politician. But what is infinitely more striking is that he seems to have known from the first where he was going and how he intended to get there, and that when he died in 1924 the revolution was firmly established on foundations which he had begun to dig thirty years before.

Lenin was clear from the outset that to make the revolution it was necessary to make a party. Virtually the whole of his active life before 1917 was devoted to this task. " There can be no revolutionary action ", he wrote in *What is to be Done?* " without a revolutionary theory " ; and revolutionary theory dictated the character of the revolutionary party. As against the Narodniks the party was conceived by Lenin as a party of the proletariat; as against the " legal Marxists " as a party of action as well as of theory; as against the " economists " (the Russian counterpart of the " syndicalists " in the west) as a party with a political as well as an economic programme. Above all, it must be a party with a single mind and purpose: " if unity of view collapses, the party collapses ".

It was in the light of this doctrine that Lenin split the party, almost at the moment of its birth, by separating " Bolsheviks " from " Mensheviks ", and was prepared again and again during the next twenty years to sacrifice numbers to rigid discipline and unity. The only important compromise admitted by Lenin — his concession to the peasants — was dictated by the need of adapting what was originally a western doctrine to an eastern country where the peasantry formed more than 80 per cent of the population. But even this policy bore the marks of a strict and unbending consistency. It first took shape at the Stockholm congress of the party in 1906, when Lenin found it tactically necessary to retreat from the logical programme of nationalization and large-scale cultivation of the land. It continued in 1917, when Lenin took over the programme of the Social-Revolutionaries and made it the basis of the agrarian decree of the Soviet Government. It was carried to its logical conclusion in 1921, with the New Economic Policy. But, for all these compromises, Lenin never abandoned the two essential points that the leadership of the revolution rested with the proletariat (and this, among other reasons, presupposed a policy of industrialization as the *sine qua non* of a socialist order), and that the revolution could be carried into the countryside only by splitting the peasantry and raising the potentially revolutionary "poor peasant" against the petty bourgeois *kulak*. Collectivization was the logical and ultimate triumph of Lenin's agrarian policy, which he did not live to see.

Of the founder of every great religion, philosophy or political movement it is customary to say that he would have been horrified by much that was done by his disciples in his name. The statement is usually made meaningless in its application to a dynamic world by the assumption that the ideas of the founder remain static at the point where he left them. The curious compound of consistency and flexibility — or, as the critic might put it, of dogmatism and of opportunism — which marks Soviet history is already inherent in the thoughts and writings of Lenin. But much has happened since Lenin died in 1924 in his fifty-fourth year and with his work only half done; and when Mr. Hill says, in his concluding chapter, "it is Lenin's words, Lenin's ideas, which are really authoritative in the Soviet Union to-day", he raises the whole controversy that centres round the name and achievement of Stalin.

10

SOREL: PHILOSOPHER OF SYNDICALISM

BORN at Cherbourg on November 2, 1847, Georges Sorel was, from the early twenties to the age of forty-five, a blameless *ingénieur des ponts-et-chaussées*. Then in 1892 he abandoned his profession to devote himself to his newly found hobby of writing about socialism. He helped to found two reviews and contributed to many more, wrote several books (of which one, *Reflections on Violence* — the only one of his works to be translated into English — enjoyed a *succès de scandale*) and became the recognized philosopher of the French trade-union or "syndicalist" movement. He died in August 1922 at Boulogne-sur-Seine, where he had spent the last twenty-five years of his uneventful life.

Sorel wrote — or at any rate published — nothing till he was in the forties; his masterpiece was written at fifty-nine, and he wrote with undiminished vigour till well on in his sixties. His late maturity gives a peculiar shape to his career. His formative years covered two intellectual generations; he wrote primarily for a third. He stands, a solitary and daring pioneer, at the most important cross-roads of modern social and political thought. Born a few weeks before the *Communist Manifesto* and living on till the eve of the " march on Rome ", he looks back to Marx and Nietzsche (of the great thinkers who, more than anyone, undermined the foundations of bourgeois society and bourgeois morality — Marx, Nietzsche and Dostoevsky — Sorel missed only the third) and forward to Lenin, to the neo-Catholicism of Bloy and Péguy, and to Mussolini. There is no conceivable parallel in any other country to Sorel, except perhaps Bernard Shaw, ten years his junior in age, his contemporary in literary apprenticeship. But this parallel breaks down in at least one respect: Sorel was no artist and not even a very good writer.

Marx was Sorel's first master. He states in his *Confessions* that he was an orthodox Marxist till 1897; and this is as nearly true as it could be of one who was temperamentally incapable of bowing the knee to any orthodoxy. His starting-point, according to his own statement, was to discover " how the essential of the Marxist doctrines could be realized ". He drew largely from Nietzsche, in part directly, in part through Bergson, the philosopher of *L'Evolution créatrice* and the *élan vital*. The other, though less important, literary influence was Renan. Sorel wittily describes Renan as one of those French writers — he also counts Molière and Racine among them — who have eschewed profundity for fear of being excluded from the *salons* of their female admirers. But it was from Renan's belief in religious dogma as " a necessary imposture " that he derived his famous conception of the socialist " myth ".

The study of Sorel reveals unexpectedly numerous points of contact between Marx and Nietzsche. It is often puzzling whether Sorel's thought should be described as Marx reflected through a Nietzschean prism, or vice versa. But the dual influence, blended with an extreme subtlety, is always there, and colours all Sorel's fundamental beliefs.

The first article in Sorel's corrosive creed is derived equally from both his masters — his conviction of the decadence of bourgeois society. Sorel, one of his commentators has said, was literally haunted with the idea of decadence. *La Ruine du monde antique* was his first major work. The persistent attraction of Christianity for him is its dogma of original sin. The " princes of secular thought ", from Diderot onwards, are " philistines " ; they bear (like Marx's " vulgar economists ") the hallmark of bourgeois culture — the belief in progress. *Les Illusions du progrès*, published in the same year as *Réflexions sur la violence*, is the most clearly and closely reasoned of his books.

Secondly, the rejection of the bourgeoisie and of bourgeois philosophy carries with it a revolt against the intellect. Sorel's earliest literary essay, *Le Procès de Socrate*, denounces Socrates for having corrupted civilization through the false doctrine that history moves forward through a process of intellectual inquiry and persuasion. This is the essence of the bourgeois heresy : " Est bourgeois ", in Alain's well-known aphorism, " tout ce qui vit de persuader." Like Marx, Sorel believes in

Nietzsche's (or rather, Pindar's) "eternal strife, father of all things". Struggle and pain are the realities of life. Violence is the only cure for the evils of bourgeois civilization.

Thirdly, Sorel shares the common contempt of Nietzsche and Marx for bourgeois pacifism. In his specific glorification of war he harks back to Proudhon rather than to Marx (though Marx, in preaching class war, did not condemn national wars provided they were the right ones). Never, he remarks in *La Ruine du monde antique*, was there a great State so averse from war as the Roman Empire in its decadence. "In England the pacifist movement is closely connected with the chronic intellectual decadence which has overtaken that country." The surest symptom of the decay of the English bourgeoisie is its inability to take war seriously; English officers in South Africa (the date is 1900–01) "go to war like gentlemen to a football match". The only alternative to a proletarian revolution as the creator of a new and healthy society would be a great European war; and this seemed to Sorel in the early 1900s a solution scarcely to be hoped for.

The fourth target of Sorel's animosity is bourgeois democracy. The case against bourgeois democracy has been so amply developed by others from the original Marxist premises that Sorel's contributions, though copious, are no longer specially significant:

> Government by the mass of the citizens has never yet been anything but a fiction: yet this fiction was the

last word of democratic science. No attempt has ever been made to justify this singular paradox by which the vote of a chaotic majority is supposed to produce what Rousseau calls the " general will " which is infallible.

Sorel's bitterness against democratic politics and democratic politicians was further sharpened by the *affaire Dreyfus*, when what had started as a noble campaign to vindicate justice was exploited for the mean ends of party or personal ambition. It was an error to look for noble aims in the masses. The majority, he had already declared in *Le Procès de Socrate*, " cannot in general accept great upheavals " ; they " cling to their traditions ". The audacious minority is always the instrument of change.

Sorel does not, however, remain merely destructive. His pessimism, he insists, is not the barren pessimism of the disillusioned optimist but the pessimism which, by accepting the decadence of the existing order, already constitutes " a step towards deliverance ". Yet while the goal is the goal of Marx, the voice is the voice of Nietzsche :

> Socialism is a moral question in the sense that it brings into the world a new way of judging all human actions or, following a famous expression of Nietzsche, a transvaluation of all values. . . . The middle classes cannot find in their conditions of life any source of ideas which stand in direct opposition to bourgeois ideas ; the notion of catastrophe [Nietzsche called it " tragedy "] escapes them entirely. The proletariat, on the contrary, finds in its conditions of life something to nourish sentiments of solidarity and revolt ; it is in daily warfare with hierarchy and with property ; it can thus conceive moral values opposed to those consecrated by

tradition. In this transvaluation of all values by the militant proletariat lies the high originality of contemporary socialism.

The two moralities of Marx (proletarian morality and bourgeois morality) have oddly blended with the two moralities (" master " and " slave " morality) of Nietzsche. Sorel preached a " morality of producers " (among whom intellectuals were apparently not included); and in a further echo of the German philosopher he branded Christian morality as a " morality of mendicants ". Curiously enough it was Jaurès, a favourite target of Sorel's ridicule, who made the apt remark that the proletarian was the contemporary superman.

Such is the basis of Sorel's cult of " revolutionary syndicalism ". Syndicalism is, in Sorel's eyes, the true heir of Marxism. It is anti-political in two senses, both of them Marxist. In the first place it rejects the State, as Marx did and as most contemporary Marxists did not; it seeks not to capture the machinery of the State — much less to find places for socialist ministers in bourgeois governments — but to destroy it. Secondly, it asserts, as Marx did, the essential primacy of economics over politics. Political action is not class action: only economic action can be truly revolutionary. The *syndicats*, the trade unions, being not political parties but organizations of the workers, are alone capable of such action.

Revolutionary syndicalism, the economic action of the workers, can take the form only of the strike, and of the most absolute form of strike, the general strike, which had been a central point in the French syndicalist programme since 1892. A sworn enemy of all Utopias, Sorel refuses to draw any picture at all of the social order which will follow this health-giving outburst of proletarian violence. He borrows a phrase from Bernstein, the German " revisionist " who, from a different point of view, also laboured to purge Marxism of its Utopian ingredients: " The end is nothing, the movement is all ". And if critics drew attention to the motivelessness of the general strike so conceived, Sorel boldly rejected this excursion into rationalism. The general strike was not a rational construction, but the " myth " of socialism, necessary like the dogmas of the Christian Church and, like them, above rational criticism.

This famous Sorelian concept of the myth involves two significant consequences. The first is a purely relativist and pragmatic view of truth which in his earlier writings he had vigorously rejected. The myth is not something which is true in any abstract sense, but something in which it is useful to believe: this is indeed the meaning of truth. From the implied pragmatism of Bergson Sorel went on to the avowed pragmatism of William James and the American school. The last of all his writings was *De l'utilité du pragmatisme*, published in 1921.

The other consequence, which Sorel faced less clearly, was an " aristocratic " view of the movement which was asked to accept this philosophy. The syndicalist movement was to be based on a myth devised and propagated by an *élite* of leaders and enthusiastically accepted by the rank and file.

Such a view accorded well with Sorel's long-standing rejection of democracy and belief in " audacious minorities ". But it was not an easy view to fit into the principles and programmes of the CGT. The rift between the syndicalist movement in France and syndicalist philosophy elaborated for it by Sorel and his disciples was never really bridged.

It was perhaps some dim consciousness of the unreality of his position which brought Sorel to an intellectual crisis in 1910. It was a lean year in the history of socialism. It marked the nadir of the fortunes of Bolshevism; and even Lenin fell a prey to some discouragement. What is more to the present point, it was in this year that Benedetto Croce, who had hailed syndicalism as " a new form of Marx's great dream, dreamed a second time by Georges Sorel ", declared that socialism, whether in its old Marxist or its new Sorelian form, was " dead ". Sorel, in his sixty-third year but still at the height of his powers, was too restless a spirit to resign himself to defeat. His main work had been done. But the turn which he now took is of immense significance in assessing his ultimate influence. Of the three paths which led forward from the cross-roads at which Sorel stood — Neo-Catholicism, Bolshevism and Fascism — all were tentatively explored by Sorel himself. But he followed none of them to the end.

One of the more baffling by-products of the *affaire Dreyfus* had been the formation of a tiny group of which the moving spirit was a young Dreyfusard, the self-taught son of a peasant, Charles Péguy. It centred round a modest periodical, *Les Cahiers de la Quinzaine*, edited, and for the most part written, by Péguy himself. Contrary to all the traditions of the *affaire*, Péguy was strongly nationalist, pro-Catholic, anti-democratic and a hater of the bourgeoisie. Since 1902 Sorel had written occasional papers for the *Cahiers*, had attended the weekly Thursdays of the group, and had been accepted as its " elder statesman " and mentor. Through this group Sorel elaborated the idea of a reconciliation between French syndicalism and French nationalism. His first contribution to the *Cahiers* had borne the significant title, " Socialismes nationaux " : its theme was that " there are at least as many socialisms as there are great nations ".

French nationalism was at this time scarcely thinkable outside the framework of Catholicism, and it was therefore logical, though surprising, that Sorel and his syndicalist disciple Berth should in 1910 have formed, in alliance with three members of the *Action Française*, a group which they called *La Cité Française*, to publish a periodical under the title *L'Indépendance Française* ; and in the same year Sorel wrote in *Action Française* (his sole contribution to the journal) an appreciation of Péguy's *Mystère de la charité de Jeanne d'Arc*. The whole enterprise, the form of which changed in 1912 to a " Cercle Proudhon ", was short-lived ; the cohabitation was never easy. But the break came in 1913, not from Sorel but from Péguy.

The causes of the rupture are obscure, and Péguy may have suffered from persecution mania. But it seems clear that Péguy, young, devout and austere, could not in the long run accommodate himself to a philosophy which enthusiastically hailed the dogmas of the Church as necessary myths. Nevertheless, when Péguy died on the Marne in September 1914, it was in that firm faith in war as the means of salvation for a decadent French society which Sorel had held from the outset of his career. No study either of the movement represented by the *Cahiers de la Quinzaine* or of the revival of French nationalism in general in the decade before 1914 can ignore the author of *Réflexions sur la violence*. It is these years which have led Sorel's able German biographer, Michael Freund, to give his book the inept sub-title, " Revolutionary Conservatism ".

The story of Sorel's affinities with Bolshevism is less complex and probably less important. The documents are at least unequivocal. Lenin was a sworn enemy of syndicalism, which he regarded as tantamount to anarchism. He had no faith in the all-sufficiency of the general strike. He believed firmly in political as well as economic action; and, though he was more deeply committed before 1917 than after to the ultimate denial of the State, he was convinced that a political dictatorship of the proletariat was the immediate goal of revolution. He seems to have mentioned Sorel only once in his published works, dismissing him curtly as " muddle-headed " and his writings as " senseless ". Nobody familiar with the clear logic of Lenin's own thought will find the verdict surprising.

Sorel, on the other hand, welcomed the October

revolution with open arms. For five years he had written scarcely anything. The war, begun as a war for the French nation, which he loved, was being more and more widely hailed as a war for democracy, which he loathed. Here was a long-awaited breath of fresh air — a revolution which preached and practised a salutary violence, spat on bourgeois democracy, exalted the " morality of the producer ", *alias* the proletariat, and installed Soviets as autonomous organs of self-government. Moreover, the Bolshevik Party — had Sorel cared to note the fact — was built up precisely on the Sorelian premises of an " audacious minority " leading the instinctive proletarian mass.

Sorel made no formal declaration of adhesion to the new cause and creed. But he wrote several articles for the French *Revue Communiste*; and in 1920, when Bolshevism was at the height of its unpopularity in France, he added to the fourth edition of *Réflexions sur la violence* a " plaidoyer pour Lénine " in which he hailed the Russian revolution as " the red dawn of a new epoch ".

> Before descending into the tomb [concluded the " plaidoyer "] may I see the humiliation of the arrogant bourgeois democracies, to-day so cynically triumphant.

Bolshevism was not yet prosperous enough to ignore its few distinguished friends, even if they were not wholly orthodox. After Sorel died the *Communist International*, the official journal of Comintern, opened its columns to a lengthy, if critical, appreciation of this " reactionary petty-bourgeois Proudhonist and anarcho-syndicalist " who had rallied to the defence of the proletarian revolution.

> Sorel [concluded the article] for all his mistakes has helped, and will continue to help, the development of the will to revolution, rightly understood, and of proletarian activity in the struggle for Communism.

The facts of Sorel's relations with Fascism are also beyond dispute. Italy always held a special place in his affections; in no other foreign country were his works so widely read, admired and translated. The shabby treatment of Italy by the peacemakers at Versailles had deepened his resentment at the triumph of bourgeois democracy. His writings teem with anticipations of Fascist doctrine. " What I am ", said Mussolini himself, " I owe neither to Nietzsche nor to William James, but to Georges Sorel." Georges Valois, one of the *Action Française* group which collaborated with Sorel in 1910, called him admiringly the " intellectual father of Fascism "; and his first biographer was Lanzillo, the Italian Fascist. He praised the first achievements of Fascism. But when the Fascist revolution brought Mussolini to Rome, Sorel was already dead.

What Sorel would have thought of the Fascist regime in power is an unprofitable, though inevitable, speculation. When he praised the first Fascists in a letter to Croce it was because " their violence is an advantageous substitute for the might of the State " — a modern equivalent of the Mafia and the Camorra, whose extra-legal activities and organization had always fascinated him. He saw in

Fascism a realization of the syndicalist dream of an administrative power independent of the State. The question which Sorel died without having to answer was that of his attitude to the totalitarian State. All his life he had been a strong, almost violent, individualist; all his life he had fought, not for the concentration of power but for its dispersal and decentralization to the very limit of anarchism. At the very end of his life he argued against any absolute religious belief on the ground that it could not be successfully propagated without restoring the Inquisition. It would have been disconcerting — to say the least — to find Sorel as a prophet of totalitarianism. But his thought contains too many inconsistencies, his career too many unexpected turns, for anyone to pronounce with assurance on this hypothetical question.

But the most interesting point raised by Sorel's career is that of the resemblances and differences between Bolshevism and Fascism. If Sorel stands on the common ground where Marx and Nietzsche meet, this is also the common ground from which Bolshevism and Fascism diverge. Marx and Nietzsche, Bolshevism and Fascism, both deny bourgeois democracy with its bourgeois interpretations of liberty and equality; both reject the bourgeois doctrines of persuasion and compromise; both (though this is where Sorel held aloof from both) proclaim absolutes which command the obedience of the individual at the cost of all else.

There was, however, an essential difference. The absolute of Nietzsche and of Fascism ends with the super-man or the super-nation or simply with power as a good in itself and for its own sake. Marx and Bolshevism propound a universal end in the form of the good of the proletariat of all countries, in which the whole of mankind is ultimately merged; and the ideal stands, whatever shortcomings may be encountered in the pursuit of it. Sorel, while clear enough about what he rejected, never committed himself on the positive side. That, among other reasons, is why he has left no school or party, even among the syndicalists whom he sought to serve and teach. He cannot be assigned either to Bolshevism or to Fascism (and still less to the Catholics). Sorel's thought is not a beacon — or even a candle — throwing a steady beam within a defined radius; it is rather a prism reflecting, fitfully but brilliantly, the most penetrating political insights of his day and of our own.

11

MR. GALLACHER AND THE CPGB

DESERT and accident have combined to make Mr. William Gallacher the most representative British Communist. He was in the thick of all the frays out of which the Communist Party of Great Britain (CPGB) was born; he was a delegate at the second congress of the Communist International in Moscow in the summer of 1920, when the main lines of guidance for the then embryonic CPGB were laid down; he has been a regular member of the central committee of the party and of its Politbureau; and he was an M.P. for three or four times as long as any other member of the party, having sat for West Fife as a Communist for 15 years. It is not, therefore, surprising that he should have been invited to write a companion volume in the "Penguin" series to the recent volumes on the Labour and Conservative Parties, *The Case for Communism.* His previous writings consist of two volumes of reminiscences, *Revolt on the Clyde*, published in the 1930s, and *The Rolling of the Thunder*, published in 1947.[1]

[1] William Gallacher, *The Case for Communism.* (Penguin Special.) Penguin Books. 1s. 6d. *The Rolling of the Thunder.* Second Impression. Lawrence and Wishart. 5s.

Mr. Gallacher and the CPGB

The CPGB was the product of a marriage between haphazard British initiative and strict Leninist discipline. The first world war multiplied and stimulated the various groups of the extreme Left, especially on the Clyde, always the home both of Left-wingisms and of stubborn and unruly labour movements. The first Russian revolution of February 1917 evoked a wave of enthusiasm. Ramsay MacDonald and Philip Snowden were among the sponsors of a famous meeting at Leeds in the summer of 1917, which decided to establish Workers' and Soldiers' Councils throughout Great Britain and appointed a committee to carry out the decision. The October revolution further stimulated the left wing of the Labour movement, but drove a wedge between it and the centre, especially as the anti-war attitude of the Left became more pronounced, agitation for social revolution to stop the war took the place of the vague pacifist idealism of earlier pronouncements. Reality was given to this agitation by industrial unrest, of which the Clyde was once more the centre. After the armistice it flared up on "Red Friday", January 31, 1919, when there was a battle between strikers and police in George Square, Glasgow, and a red flag was run up on the city flag-pole. Mr. Gallacher and Mr. Shinwell were among those who were arrested and received sentences of imprisonment for their share in these proceedings.

Out of the anti-war movement two main parties with more or less openly revolutionary programmes had emerged — the British Socialist Party and the

Socialist Labour Party; other groups of a similar character flourished in particular localities. The strongly pacifist Left wing of the ILP contained many fellow-travellers; and the Plebs League, a group of intellectuals interested in the education of the workers in Marxist doctrine, formed the theoretical spearhead of the movement. On another front the rapidly developing shop-stewards' movement had a marked revolutionary colour. It was opposed both to the old trade-union leadership and to parliamentary action in general; though varying in outlook from place to place and from time to time, it was syndicalist in character and tended to advocate "direct action" without any very clear definition of political purposes. It was with this movement, collectively known as the Workers' Committee Movement, that Mr. Gallacher was at this time primarily associated.

The founding of the Third or Communist International in Moscow in March 1919 had little immediate impact on these groups. It was the second congress of Comintern in July 1920 which proved the decisive force in the creation of the British party. The party was officially founded in London on July 31, 1920, while the Moscow congress was actually in progress. But the real arguments which moulded its shape and destiny were conducted in Moscow, where Lenin presided over a commission to advise on the affairs of the new party. The British Left was more amply represented at this than at any other congress of Comintern; and in those formative years a latitude and diversity of opinion was still tolerated. Quelch and MacLaine, both of the British Socialist Party, represented a "joint provisional committee" for the creation of a British Communist Party; Murphy, the Socialist Labour Party; Gallacher, Tanner and Ramsay, the shop-stewards' movement; and Sylvia Pankhurst a small independent group which had tried to get in first by appropriating the name of "British Communist Party".

Lenin's policy at this time was to rally all the forces of the extreme Left against the orthodox parties of Social-Democratic or Labour complexion which had supported their respective national Governments during the war, and could therefore be considered as having sold themselves irretrievably to the bourgeoisie. Thus, while opposed to any co-operation with such parties, he was tolerant of the many differences dividing the extreme Left and anxious only to bring them together in united Communist parties. Mr. Gallacher begins the second instalment of his autobiography with the story how, on arriving in Petrograd on his way to the second congress of the Communist International, he had thrust into his hand the English edition of Lenin's newly published pamphlet, *The Infantile Disorder of "Leftism" in Communism*, and found himself indicted by name as a victim of this disease on the ground of his opposition to parliamentary action.

At the congress itself Lenin was ranged with the two delegates of the British Socialist Party, who formed the Right wing of the British group, against Mr. Gallacher and the other British delegates in support of the thesis that the future Communist Party of Great Britain should take part in parliamentary elections and seek affiliation to the Labour Party. It is piquant that Britain's future Communist M.P. should have gone on record as declaring that Communists " have something better to do than waste time over parliamentary elections ". But Mr. Gallacher, having been out-voted, allowed himself to be won over by Lenin's persuasive personality, and went home promising not only to carry out the majority policy but to dissuade his Scottish friends from indulging their nationalist feelings so far as to found a separate Scottish Communist Party. The news of the foundation of the CPGB reached Moscow while the congress was in progress. It was due in part to Mr. Gallacher's efforts that it secured the adhesion of all the main Left-wing groups north and south of the Border. The formal constitution of the party was approved at a conference at Leeds in January 1921. Arthur McManus was elected president (a post which has long since disappeared); Mr. Gallacher was the runner-up.

The history of the first years of the CPGB has yet to be written. In the 1930s an attempt was made by one of its founders and its first national organizer, Tom Bell. But his work was subjected in party circles to charges, not unfounded, of inaccuracy and distortion; and nobody has since been bold enough to repeat the experiment. The author of *The Rolling of the Thunder* has no claim to be a historian. But as a participant in every stage of party history he is an important witness. His particular contribution is to fit party affairs into the framework of British Labour and trade-union history during this period, and thus to rebut the stereotyped charge that party policies were dictated from Moscow. Mr. Gallacher is a sturdy Scot, and nobody will suspect him of taking orders or of allowing himself to be persuaded against his will. But the founding of the party in 1920 was not the only occasion on which the casting vote of Moscow was decisive in divisions and disputes between British Communists. The very weakness of the party made the tutelage of Moscow inevitable, even where it was not deliberately imposed or consciously accepted.

The initial dilemma which faced the CPGB faced virtually every other Communist party throughout the twenty years after 1919, and was indeed the fundamental problem of Comintern. Was the party to remain small, highly organized and disciplined, and doctrinally impeccable — as Lenin's Bolsheviks had been before 1917 — even at the cost of exercising no present influence on national affairs and becoming, if necessary, an illegal and persecuted sect? Or was it to seek to become a mass party playing an active role in national politics, even at the cost of loosened discipline and organization and a certain measure of doctrinal eclecticism or, at any rate, toleration? Neither Lenin nor the other Bolshevik leaders ever fully understood the dilemma confronting the Communists in the western democracies — a dilemma which had no counterpart in Russia. Thus the Comintern resolutions of 1920 enjoined the nascent

British Communist Party to play an active part in British parliamentary democracy and to seek affiliation to the Labour Party. But they also imposed on it, in common with other Communist parties, a rigid organization subject to " iron discipline " and periodical purges of the unruly, as well as to acceptance of all decisions of the Communist International; and they required it not only to conduct propaganda for the establishment of the dictatorship of the proletariat but to create an underground organization in preparation for civil war. Nobody in Moscow seems to have realized that these were incompatible alternatives.

Of all the Communist parties the CPGB was the only one which, thanks in part to peculiar British conditions, in part perhaps to its share of the famous British genius for compromise, seriously attempted the impossible. The membership of the CPGB after its congress of January 1921 amounted to not more than 2000 or 2500; the total of 10,000 announced at the third congress of Comintern that year and repeated by Mr. Gallacher was obtained, as Bell admits, by adding up the wishful estimates of half-organized branches. On the other hand, the " Hands off Russia " movement and the Councils of Action in the last stages of the Russian civil war had revealed a vast mass of vague sympathy with Soviet Russia and her institutions. This sympathy was strongly tinged with pacifism and hostility to war in general, and did not betoken revolutionary convictions. But few — and, least of all, the Communists — recognized these limitations; and to create a disciplined Communist Party on Moscow lines with a mass following did not seem a hopeless task.

The first blow was the blank rejection by the Labour Party of the application for affiliation — a rejection three times repeated and endorsed by an enormous majority at the annual conference in 1921. The CPGB showed apparently sincere surprise at the decision, and expressed a keen sense of grievance, which is reflected in Mr. Gallacher's pages, at the unfriendly Labour attitude. But this was surely an inevitable result of the equivocal position of the Communists themselves. It was at the second congress of the Communist International that Lenin coined the famous recommendation to "support the Labour Party as the rope supports the man who is being hanged" — an aphorism which an English Communist is said to have translated as "taking them by the hand as a preliminary to taking them by the throat". Alliance with the Labour Party could never be more than a tactical device, a stage on the road to the dictatorship of the proletariat. At the moment when the alliance was being offered, the Communists were already seeking to undermine Labour authority in the trade unions through such organizations as the Minority Movement and the National Unemployed Workers' Movement; and it was not surprising that the alliance should have been consistently rejected by the Labour Party leadership. Indeed, the Communist assault from the Left was one of the factors which drove moderate Labour parties to seek an open or covert bourgeois alliance.

These inconsistencies within the CPGB were, however, complicated by violent zigzags of policy in Comintern itself. Delays in the realization of European revolution, the introduction of NEP, the opening up of trade relations with the capitalist world, all brought a certain mitigation of Moscow's uncompromising hostility to the non-communist world. In December 1921 the Executive Committee of Comintern (ECCI) for the first time issued the slogan of a " united front " with other working-class parties and support for " Labour Governments " ; and three months later the CPGB was specifically instructed to " establish relations " with the General Council of the TUC and to apply once more for admission to the Labour Party. This blind persistence merely courted another snub. The 1922 conference of the Labour Party at Edinburgh produced more plain speaking at the expense of the Communists than ever before. This time the party could not fail to perceive that something was seriously wrong. On Mr. Gallacher's proposal a committee of three non-official members of the party — Mr. Harry Pollitt, a trade unionist, Mr. Palme Dutt, an intellectual, and Harry Inkpin, brother of the secretary of the party — was appointed to report on its affairs.

The results of this report were far-reaching. The party was reorganized on the model of the Russian party, discipline was tightened, and it was decided to refrain from electoral attacks on the Labour Party. These changes yielded some dividends. In 1923 two Communists, Newbold and Saklatvala, standing for constituencies where there was no Labour candidate, were elected to Parliament with unofficial Labour support.

This tacit alliance was, however, never welcomed or sanctioned by the Labour leaders, and its artificiality was quickly demonstrated. What proved fatal to it was the accession of Labour to power in January 1924. The CPGB could, at the cost of some mutual embarrassment, support a Labour Opposition; it could not conceivably support a Labour Government. Relations were soon worse than ever. The London conference of the Labour Party in 1924 took steps to exclude Communists from individual membership of any branch of the party, though they could still come into it as members of affiliated trade unions. The ultimate crisis arose, logically enough, out of the British general strike. This was the parting of the ways between those who wanted revolution and those who rejected revolution. It quickly became clear that the majority of those who had embarked on the general strike were not prepared to cross the Rubicon which separates strike from revolution, even if by holding back they brought about the defeat of the strikers.

The Communists, applauded and backed up by Moscow, denounced the retreat as treachery to the working class, but thereby only revealed their own isolation. The prestige of the CPGB, as well as that of the Soviet Government, underwent a severe slump. In the early 1920s sympathy with Soviet Russia among the Labour rank-and-file had not only tempered official Labour hostility to the Communists but had put an effective brake on official action against Soviet Russia. Now only the feeblest of protests followed the Arcos raid and the breaking off of relations with the Soviet Union in 1927. Under the first Baldwin Government, with Joynson Hicks as Home Secretary, anti-Communist feeling reached its height. According to the figures quoted by Mr. Gallacher, the party membership fell from 11,000–12,000 after the general strike to 5000 in the following year.

These disasters led to a second reorganization of the CPGB in the winter of 1927–28. The policy of supporting the Labour Party against the bourgeois parties, equivocal though it was, and inconsistently as it had been pursued, had been an official plank in the party platform ever since its foundation and rested on the mandate given to the party by Lenin himself. The majority of the central committee, including Mr. Gallacher himself, saw no reason to change this policy. But a minority, led by Mr. Palme Dutt and Mr. Pollitt, now challenged it as wrong in principle. They argued that the situation in Great Britain had changed radically since Lenin made his recommendations of 1920. The economic position of Great Britain was deteriorating and therefore bringing nearer the objective conditions for a mass revolutionary movement; the Labour Party had been in office and had revealed itself as "a third bourgeois party"; and it had in effect abandoned the loose and undogmatic federal structure, which had made it seem possible for Communists to seek admission to it, in favour of a centralized organization which was being used to impose the views of the leadership and to ban the Communists. On these grounds open opposition to Labour as to other parties was recommended as the right tactics for the CPGB.

The split in the central committee was taken to Moscow for settlement at a moment when Comintern was being rocked by a major crisis over the affairs of China. The occasion provided an admirable illustration of the results of the assumption, habitually made at Comintern headquarters, of a doctrinal and tactical uniformity applicable to all Communist parties. The collapse of the Anglo-Russian Joint Trade Union Council in 1926, after little more than a year of life, had already caused perturbation in Comintern circles and prepared the way for a swing to the Left. When, however, ECCI met in February 1928 to consider the British issue, many other things had happened. Trotsky had just been expelled from the party and banished to Alma Ata; and, after six months of embittered debate, the new "Left" policy in China of out-and-out opposition to Chiang Kai-shek had just been put in operation. Thus the views of Mr. Dutt and Mr. Pollitt, and not those of the majority, fitted in with the prevailing temper at headquarters. The ruling went in their favour. For tactical reasons, the CPGB was to maintain "the slogan of affiliation to the Labour Party". In all other respects the break was to be complete.

This decision, which was general rather than particular, marked a fateful new turn in Comintern policy as a whole. From 1928 onwards, and especially after the sixth congress held in August of that year, it became the fashion to treat Labour and Social-Democrat Parties not merely as declared enemies, but as the worst enemies, of the workers; and this line, pursued to its logical conclusion, had fatal consequences in Germany during the period of Hitler's ascent to power. Mr. Gallacher, who is too good a party man to defend his own stand in 1927-28 (he does not even refer to it), admits the error of the German Communists in the early 1930s, though he makes out a case for assigning an equal share of blame to the Social-Democrats. The dilemma which had dogged the steps of the CPGB from the outset proved an equally insuperable obstacle to the unity of the German Left.

In Britain the chief result of the 1928 decision was the retirement of Albert Inkpin, the secretary of the party since its inception. He was succeeded by Mr. Pollitt, who has been its virtual leader for the past twenty years. The history of the CPGB under Mr. Pollitt's leadership has been less turbulent and less eventful than in the preceding eight years of its existence. Technically the party has been much more efficiently run. The *Daily Worker* dates from 1930. Sharp changes of policy, even sudden changes, have occurred. But the party line, however vulnerable, has always been clear and precise, and has always responded to directives from Moscow. On the other hand, thoughts of a mass party have been abandoned or relegated to an indeterminate future. The influx of members into the party in the " united front " period of the middle 1930s was largely unsolicited. This was no longer the " united front " with Labour in the old sense, but a diplomatic alliance, irrespective of opinions, between all who were willing to fight Hitler. What was wanted was not primarily converts to Communism, but converts to a policy of active resistance to German aggression. The same was true of the period after 1941, when the party received another substantial but transient accession of membership.

Mr. Gallacher's autobiography does not throw much light on events within the party after 1928; and, though he remained a member of the central committee and of its Politbureau, it may be inferred that he took little part in shaping policy. He had already on several occasions stood as a candidate for Scottish constituencies and come out at the bottom of the poll; the first was the Dundee election of 1922 when Mr. Churchill ran third to E. D. Morel and Scrymgeour, the prohibitionist. In 1935 Mr. Gallacher was elected as a Communist for the mining constituency of West Fife, and re-elected ten years later. In the House of Commons he won popularity and respect as a good parliamentarian. In the CPGB he represents, not the esoteric side of party life but its link with the masses; he has been for the past ten years its most important " public face ". He continues, within the limits of party discipline, to stand for the conception of the party as an extreme Left wing within the British parliamentary system rather than as an entity standing outside, and in unqualified opposition to, that system.

Something of this attitude tinges even the cautious and carefully balanced pages of *The Case for Communism*. As a popular exposition of Marxist theory and of the economic aims, immediate and ultimate, of Socialism and Communism, this could not be bettered either in matter or in style. But when it comes to the political instruments for translating theory into practice and realizing economic ends, everything is suddenly vague and blurred. The dictatorship of the proletariat is lost altogether in the haze, and does not seem to be mentioned at all. The haze thickens to a fog in the last chapter, in which Mr. Gallacher returns some bewildering answers to questions from an imaginary critic. Here and there the reader even catches glimpses of an independent version of Communist doctrine and Communist tactics adapted to the demands of British politics. But this is surely a lost cause. Its development is inhibited by the slavish imitation of Soviet methods and of Soviet policies which has become endemic in the CPGB. The vicious circle cannot be broken. A more independent party would have shown greater health and strength; a healthier and stronger party would have achieved greater independence. The growth of the child has been fatally stunted by too successful and too masterful a parent.

12

THE REVOLUTION THAT FAILED

THE German Communist Party was one of the very few Communist parties other than the Russian which had independent roots of its own and was not a product of the Russian revolution or a child of the Communist International. Its pre-history began with the outbreak of the first world war. In August 1914 the German Social-Democrats, the largest, most powerful and best organized Marxist party in the world, were guilty of the great betrayal by voting for the German war budget — the symbol of support for the German national cause. A tiny handful of the party leaders, and perhaps a larger proportion of the rank and file, were against the decision. But party discipline demanded that the minority should accept the decision of the majority; it was not till December 1914 that Karl Liebknecht, and he alone, broke the party unity by voting against the war credits in the Reichstag.

As the war dragged on, opposition grew beneath the surface; and in 1916 there was a big break-away ending in the formation of the Independent Social-Democratic Party — the USPD, to use its German initials — which was against the war. Even the USPD was not really a revolutionary party. It wanted primarily to end the war, and found room for elements which were pacifist rather than Marxist. But it was within the USPD that there arose a group calling itself the *Spartakusbund*, which was out-and-out Marxist and revolutionary as well as anti-war, and came nearer than any other group in Germany to acceptance of Lenin's slogan of turning the imperialist war into a civil war of the proletariat against the bourgeois ruling class. The intellectual driving force of the *Spartakusbund* was Rosa Luxemburg; Karl Liebknecht, who was a leader and agitator rather than a theorist, was also one of the leaders of the group. The *Spartakusbund* and all its publications and activities were, of course, highly illegal in war-time Germany; both Liebknecht and Luxemburg spent the last months of the war in prison.

The *Spartakusbund* came into existence before the Russian revolution. But events in Russia gave its work a fresh impetus. At the end of December 1918, in the midst of the turmoil and upheaval which followed the armistice in Germany, a congress was held in Berlin. It was attended by Radek as a fraternal delegate from the central committee of the All-Russian Congress of Soviets: Zinoviev and Bukharin were also to have come, but were refused admission by the German Government. The congress decided to found a German Communist Party (KPD); and for old time's sake the name *Spartakusbund* was kept in brackets at the end of its name, just as the Russians afterwards called themselves " Russian Communist Party (Bolsheviks) ".

The *Spartakusbund* had been a small group composed mainly of intellectuals and engaged in propaganda, but not in active preparation for revolutionary action, which would indeed have been scarcely practicable during the war. When the KPD was created, the question arose whether it was to remain a small and highly concentrated party for the revolutionary indoctrination of the masses, or whether it was at once to go out for a mass membership and seek to become a mass revolutionary party. Liebknecht wanted the second course. Out of the chaos of post-armistice Berlin there had appeared a genuine workers' revolutionary movement, the shop-stewards' organization. It had, as yet, not spread beyond the capital. Its positive aims were not defined in very articulate terms. But it wanted social revolution and the overthrow of Ebert's Left coalition government, did not believe in parliamentary action and was prepared and organized to use force to attain its ends. If this group could be married to the *Spartakusbund*, a mass Communist Party, equally qualified for theory and for practice, was in sight.

This alliance was, however, opposed by Rosa Luxemburg, who believed that the masses were not yet ripe for a proletarian revolution, that a period of education and indoctrination was required, and that for this purpose a small party of agitators and propagandists on the model of the *Spartakusbund* was the right instrument; and the division among the leaders stultified the negotiations which Liebknecht carried on with the shop-stewards' movement during the founding congress of the KPD. The shop-stewards would have come in on terms, including parity of representation in the organs of the new party, which, considering the numbers they had behind them, was not unreasonable. But the old stalwarts of the *Spartakusbund* were obdurate and negotiations broke down. It was a decisive moment. Within a fortnight the Independent Social-Democrats had been ousted from the Ebert Government. Noske had become Minister of War with a mandate to use the Reichswehr to restore order in Berlin, and Liebknecht and Rosa Luxemburg had both been arrested and " shot while trying to escape " — apparently the first use of this famous euphemism for the official assassination of political opponents. Tragedy dogged the steps of German communism from the very outset.

Just two months after the foundation of the KPD in Berlin, the Communist International — Comintern — was born in Moscow. Rosa Luxemburg, who had regarded the creation of a mass Communist Party in Germany as premature, took the same view of the creation of a Communist International with world-wide pretensions; and this view was reinforced in German minds by the well-grounded fear that, if a Communist International were brought into being at a time when the German party was still a puling infant and the Russian party was the only one with a successful revolution to its credit, the centre of gravity would inevitably be in Moscow and not in Berlin. Thus the German delegate, one Eberlein, appeared in Moscow in March 1919 with instructions to oppose the founding of the International. He found himself completely isolated among the delegates of the very real and active Russian Communist Party and of rudimentary and sometimes mythical communist organizations in such countries as the United States, Switzerland, Holland, Sweden, Norway, Hungary and Austria; and in the end, having stated his objections, he abstained from voting in order not to mar the universal harmony. But the fact remained that the Communist International had been created without the vote of the one potentially powerful Communist Party outside Russia, and of the one great industrial country where Marxist doctrine had a real hold on proletarian consciousness — a country on which all good Bolsheviks, from Lenin downwards, still pinned their confident hopes of a European revolution.

For the first eighteen months of its existence the KPD remained what the *Spartakusbund* had been during the war, a small, illegal, persecuted sect without any overt influence on events. Its outstanding figure at this time was Paul Levi, a brilliant and highly cultivated intellectual, but not in the least a political leader of the masses. The period after the foundation of Comintern in March 1919 was the time when contacts between Russian and German communists were at their lowest point. The year 1919 saw Soviet Russia almost entirely cut off from the rest of the world, and her leaders too preoccupied with the desperate struggle of the civil war to have much time or thought for anything not directly concerned with it. In Germany Radek had been arrested and imprisoned by the German authorities; no other leading Bolshevik came to take his place.

The KPD played no role in the famous Bavarian revolution of April 1919, though some communists joined the short-lived Soviet Government which was set up in Munich. It had only a walking-on part in the first attempted nationalist come-back after the humiliation of November 1918 — the so-called "Kapp putsch" of March 1920 — which was defeated, not by the communists but by a general strike organized by the old trade unions. But in the autumn of 1920, partly under Russian pressure, a split occurred among the German Independent Social-Democrats — the USPD. Under the combined influence of the prestige of Comintern and the eloquence of Zinoviev, who addressed a party congress at Halle for four hours on end, a majority of the USPD decided to join the communists to form the United Communist Party of Germany. There was thus, at the end of 1920, a mass German Communist Party with an effective membership of over 300,000 and a much larger number of fellow-travellers. But the unreality of the union between the intellectuals of the KPD and the workers of the USPD has been brilliantly portrayed by an eye-witness of the Berlin convention which ratified it:

There was an artistic frame of classical music and revolutionary poetry. The USPD delegates, mostly workers from the bench, were disgusted by the new official pomp: they had looked forward to a sober analysis of the German situation, concrete proposals on what to do next. Paul Levi gave them instead a speech on the economic situation of the world, in which a wealth of statistics was combined with varied news of events in Asia and in the Anglo-American world, and which ended with the bombast, "Enter, ye workers of Germany, enter, for here are thy [*sic*] gods". I watched workers from Essen and Hamburg leaving the conference hall: they could express their disgust with this rhetoric only by despoiling some of the nice decorations with their plebeian spit.

For all the spitefulness of this account, there is truth in the picture of failure to unite the masses with the party leadership.

The book from which this quotation comes was published in the United States in 1948 under the rather misleading title, *Stalin and German Communism*. Its author, Ruth Fischer, is an Austrian who joined the KPD in 1919 and remained one of its leading members till her expulsion in 1926. For the story of the party during that time it is a primary source of great importance. It is, however, a source which the historian will have to handle with some care. Mrs. Fischer was in a position to know nearly everything that went on at this time in the inner counsels of the German Communist Party, and something — though not by any means all — of what went on in the Communist International. Her narrative is packed with detail; but, except where it is actually documented (as many of her statements are), it is often difficult to disentangle what rests on personal knowledge from hearsay and, even more, conjecture.

Some of Mrs. Fischer's political speculations are not particularly convincing. One can rarely prove a negative. But it does not seem at all likely that Trotsky failed to return to Moscow in time for Lenin's funeral as the result of " a secret understanding with the Politburo "; or that the famous " Zinoviev letter " which played a part in the British general election of 1924 was a forgery of the GPU; or that J. D. Gregory, the British civil servant involved in the case, was in the pay of the GPU; or that Dimitrov's defence in the Reichstag fire trial was a put-up job after a bargain for his release had been struck with his own cognizance between the GPU and the Gestapo.

The other qualification that must be made concerns Mrs. Fischer's political attitude. At first sight her reminiscences invite comparison with those of another woman who worked in Comintern in the early days and was bitterly disillusioned by the experience, Angelica Balabanoff. But they belong to different worlds. Balabanoff was a disappointed idealist who apparently did not know that Communist parties, like other political organizations, are not run without a great deal of wire-pulling, manipulation and sordid calculation of expediency. Mrs. Fischer was, from the outset, a politician to the finger-tips. If she became embittered, it was because she lost the last move in the game, not because she did not understand the game that was being played. In German party affairs she belonged to the Left, that is to say, to those communists who were opposed to temporary tactical co-operation with the Social-Democrats, and believed that the workers could be directly organized for revolution. Writing twenty-five years later on the other side of the Atlantic, after her opinions have undergone a complete transformation, it can hardly be expected that she will have done full justice to her own position at the time — and still less to that of adversaries, who ousted her from the party leadership and against whom she has many old scores to work off.

The split between Right and Left in the KPD really dates from the so-called " March action " of 1921. In March of that year a spontaneous rising in the mining area of central Germany was followed by an attempted rising organized by the Communists in the great industrial centres. It seems to have been poorly prepared, and ended in defeat. The reprisals undertaken by the police and the Reichswehr were harsh, and left the party crippled, discredited and discouraged. Recriminations followed. According to one account, the " March action " was forced on reluctant leaders by the enthusiastic new recruits who had come into the party in the previous autumn. It is certainly true that Paul Levi had been forced to resign from the leadership a few weeks earlier on another issue; and his resignation had been widely interpreted as a signal for a more active policy. According to the account favoured by Mrs. Fischer, who, as a good German, has the habit of blaming German failures on the Russians, the " March action " was dictated from Moscow by Zinoviev and Bela Kun who, on the eve of the Kronstadt mutiny, were desperately anxious to score a German success to counterbalance troubles at home. Whatever the background of the attempt, its failure made a change of leadership inevitable. Paul Levi was succeeded as leader of the Right first by Ernst Meyer, another intellectual, and later by Heinrich Brandler, a worker from Saxony, who had all the caution of the old trade-union tradition; Mrs. Fischer together with her close associate Maslow soon emerged as the leaders of the Left.

The fiasco of the March rising in Germany discredited not only the German communist leaders, but Comintern itself and Zinoviev as its presiding genius. This resounding defeat for the cause of revolution in the country where, by every token, its prospects were most favourable, forced on Moscow a reconsideration of the whole time-table of world revolution; and it came at a time when Lenin had just announced the forced retreat on the home front embodied in NEP — the New Economic Policy of limited toleration and encouragement for private enterprise. It had become clear that Soviet Russia would have to go on living in a world of capitalist states for a much longer time than had at first been foreseen. The idea of marching straight forward to a world-wide victory of socialism had to be discarded. Strategic manœuvres, temporary retreats, political expedients of all kinds would be required to maintain and increase Soviet power until such time as the final goal was in sight. And this was just as true of foreign as of domestic policy. In international terms it meant that the star of Narkomindel was in the ascendant, the star of Comintern on the wane. Chicherin began to eclipse Zinoviev.

This change raised an issue which has never ceased to be a source of embarrassment for the communist parties of the great countries other than Russia. Were these parties to pursue policies calculated to promote revolution at the earliest moment in their countries? Or were they, taking a broader view, to argue that the power of Soviet Russia, the one communist State, was the major asset of communism all over the world, and must therefore be maintained and supported even at the cost of temporary local sacrifices? This question took a particularly acute form in Germany, because Germany and Russia were linked by a common interest as the two great dissatisfied powers (though dissatisfied for different reasons) of the post-war settlement, the two pariah nations of European society. So long as Russia saw prospects of salvation in an imminent German revolution, the role of German communists was clear. But once the German revolution was not imminent and Soviet Russia had her back to the wall, the prudent course for Moscow might well be to stand shoulder to shoulder with the German Government against a world equally hostile to both. In this case the role of German communists must be, not to overthrow the German Government but to come to terms with it on the basis of a policy of friendship with the Soviet Government; and such a policy could perfectly well be defended, even from the standpoint of German communism.

According to Ruth Fischer, whose testimony does not stand alone, this idea was first conceived by Radek when he was in prison in Berlin in the year 1919, and was then laughed out of court in Moscow. But after 1921, when NEP was in full swing and optimism about world revolution was no longer in fashion, things looked very different. In the next year the bargain was sealed by the famous Rapallo Treaty signed by Chicherin and Rathenau during the Genoa conference. It was about this time that the secret arrangements were started between the German Reichswehr and the Red Army for the purpose of evading the military provisions of the Versailles Treaty. In brief, the Reichswehr was to get facilities in Russia to carry out certain processes of manufacture and training, and the Red Army got in return technical training and equipment. But this new partnership between governments cast something of a blight on the German Communist Party. Radek, now chief agent of Comintern for Germany, cast the mantle of Moscow over Brandler, who wanted no rash revolutionary ventures and was prepared for temporary compromises with the Social-Democrats, and worked to oust Maslow and Ruth Fischer as the leaders of the Left. Naturally enough, Ruth Fischer has no love for Radek, and still less for Brandler, as every turn of her narrative shows. But the main facts here cannot be challenged. Radek was prepared to coquet even with the extreme German nationalists, just as they were prepared to coquet with Russia, on the ground of a common hatred of the western allies. Many later patterns of policy can be traced in outline at this period.

At this point the destiny of the German Communist Party became involved not only in the changes of Soviet foreign policy, but in the feuds between Soviet leaders. By the late summer of 1923 the German workers were feeling the desperate pinch of the French occupation of the Ruhr and the German passive resistance policy; and the German Communist Party decided that the time was ripe for action. According to Mrs. Fischer, it was Stresemann's accession to power in August 1923 on a declared policy of coming to terms with the western Powers which caused a flurry of alarm in Moscow and prompted a decision by the Russian leaders that a German communist revolt against the Stresemann government was urgent. But this version, which fits in neatly with Mrs. Fischer's desire to lay every German failure at the door of Moscow, does not square with the facts. In Moscow the project of a German revolution was enthusiastically applauded only by Trotsky. Zinoviev, as usual, shilly-shallied; and Stalin preached caution. These divisions in Moscow meant that Russian assistance was half-hearted, and encouraged divisions and hesitations within the German party itself. Brandler, an excellent party organizer in ordinary times, was useless as a leader of armed insurrection. Elaborate preparations were going quietly forward when, in October, the Berlin Government struck first, sending the Reichswehr to depose the government of Saxony in which Brandler and two other communists had seats. This should have been the signal for a general rising. But the leaders were not ready; and, except for an unpremeditated outbreak at Hamburg which was suppressed with much bloodshed, nobody moved. The great project of a German communist revolution was snuffed out before it could start. "Seen from the inside", writes Mrs. Fischer of this experience, "the communists were an insufficiently organized group of panic-stricken people, torn by factional quarrels, unable to come to a decision, and unclear about their own aims." That seems a not unfair epitaph on the largest Communist Party outside Russia.

The German defeat, like every other failure of a militant revolutionary policy, discredited Trotsky and Zinoviev and, by the same token, helped Stalin; and since it also meant the downfall of Brandler in Germany, Stalin paradoxically became, for the moment, the patron of the German Left. Manuilsky, who was a Stalin man, replaced Radek as principal Comintern agent in Germany. Mrs. Fischer passes rather lightly over the period when the Left communists in Germany hitched their waggon to Stalin's rising star. A relic of this period is a vivid and revealing description of Stalin in the summer of 1924, when he was just emerging into prominence among Bolshevist leaders:

At this Fifth World Congress Stalin became known to Comintern delegates for the first time. He glided silently, almost furtively, into the salons and corridors around St. Andrew's Hall. Smoking his pipe, wearing the characteristic tunic and Wellington boots, he spoke softly and politely with small groups, assisted by an inconspicuous interpreter, presenting himself as the new type of Russian leader. The younger delegates were impressed by this pose as the revolutionary who despises revolutionary rhetoric, the down-to-earth organizer, whose quick decision and modernized methods would solve the problems in a changed world. The men around Zinoviev were old, fussy, out-moded.

Mrs. Fischer's narrative becomes a little confusing at this point; for, in her anxiety to exonerate her patron Zinoviev and herself of too-prolonged collaboration with the now hated Stalin, she has pushed back the split between Zinoviev and Stalin a good deal earlier than either evidence or probability allows.

At any rate, Zinoviev and Stalin were still on terms of friendship and co-operation, and Maslow and Mrs. Fischer, now the effective leaders of the KPD, were still in good standing at Moscow, when in April 1925 the Right in Germany decided to put forward Hindenburg as presidential candidate. The view of Comintern, supported by Maslow and Mrs. Fischer, was that the Communist candidate, Thälmann, should be withdrawn in order not to split the anti-Hindenburg vote. A majority of the KPD, inspired by Thälmann, decided otherwise, with the result that Hindenburg was elected. Neither of Mrs. Fischer's favourite generalizations — that the mistaken policies of the KPD were imposed on it from Moscow, and that she herself was a champion o the party against the domination of Moscow — held good on this occasion. It was only at the end of 1925 that Mrs. Fischer joined the Zinoviev opposition against Stalin. But by this time her popularity in the German party had been eclipsed by that of Thälmann, and in the following year Manuilsky had not much difficulty in bringing about her expulsion from the party as a Trotskyite. It is not a particularly edifying story. But it is not so simple, nor are the rights and wrongs so clear, as Mrs. Fischer's narrative might suggest to the uninitiated reader.

The party was now in a tragic decline, numerically, intellectually and as a political force. During the spurious prosperity of the Dawes period there could be no thought of a communist coup; and in the great depression which set in in 1929 the German Communist Party fell between two stools. It allowed the Nazis and the nationalists to make the pace in the campaign against the ineffective Weimar republic. On the other hand, the principle of non-co-operation with Social-Democrats, which had held ever since the debacle of 1923, prevented the communists from forming a common front against the Nazis. It is these years rather than the earlier period which justify one of the morals drawn by Mrs. Fischer: the difficulty which any Communist Party outside Russia has in standing up to the Russian party. A weak opposition party, often persecuted in its own country, is clearly no match for a party which has a victorious revolution behind it, and controls the affairs of a great nation. According to Mrs. Fischer, the influence of Moscow in the

German party was largely explicable by the number of jobs which Comintern with its large funds was able to offer to those who followed its line. This no doubt happened. But there is also the subtler influence of prestige, of rating in the scale of communist values. The weak, unsuccessful foreign party inevitably tends to take its cue from the strong successful Russian party; whenever a difference of view, or a difference of interest, manifests itself, the weaker yields to the stronger. Hence, it is only the exceptionally strong communist parties abroad which can hope to achieve some independence of Moscow. On a long view, it may well seem a disaster that the German communist movement after 1918 failed to develop its expected strength: had it done so, the one-sided identification of Russia and Communism which dominates world history to-day would have been avoided.

The failure of German communism is a phenomenon which deserves a more profound analysis than it has yet received, or than it receives from Mrs. Fischer, who is for the most part content to evoke the personal equation or the baneful influence of Comintern. Lenin, when he looked eagerly to the German revolution to save the revolution in Russia, believed — as Marxist doctrine entitled him to believe — that German communism was potentially a far more powerful, effective and earth-shaking force than Russian communism. Why did this not happen? One of the factors was obviously the unexpected strength of the nationalist come-back after the humiliation of Versailles. What seemed crushed had only been scotched. Moscow was not alone in the miscalculation of supposing that German national resentment could be encouraged up to a point, utilized and kept within safe bounds. Both Moscow and the western Powers from their different points of view overestimated the strength of German social-democracy. Both failed to take account of the absence in Germany of any of the conditions or traditions of western liberal democracy. The attempt to create a liberal democracy in Germany failed in 1848 and again after 1918; the attempt to create a social-democracy on the western pattern failed equally; and extreme Right and extreme Left confronted one another, just as they did in the Russia of 1917.

But in Germany, more than in any other country, the old pre-bourgeois ruling class, the feudal order of society with its military tradition, had succeeded in capturing and harnessing to its purposes the modern power of organized large-scale heavy industry. This was the achievement of Bismarck who, by his brilliant invention of the social services, also roped an influential section of the workers and the trade unions into a new power complex. This combination went into action in 1914; and, after the military disaster of 1918 and the political fiasco of the Weimar republic, it was still strong enough for Hitler to furbish it up once again in a rather more up-to-date and ostensibly popular guise. The strongest impression which the reading of Mrs. Fischer's book leaves on the mind is the terrifying power which the old forces in Germany continued to exercise after 1918; and the chief reason of all for calling it a gloomy book is that it raises the question how far, in circumstances presenting so many analogies to the post-1918 period, these old forces are still alive and at work in Germany to-day.

13

STALIN: (1) THE ROAD TO POWER

In the Soviet Union the name of Stalin has long been ranged with those of Marx, Engels and Lenin as an authoritative source, or at any rate an authoritative interpreter, of Bolshevik doctrine; and a collected edition of his works, now in course of publication in Moscow, was therefore overdue. It is being issued under the auspices of the Marx-Engels-Lenin Institute and will be complete in sixteen volumes, the last being devoted to his war-time speeches. The first volume covers the period 1901–1907, when Stalin — not yet generally known by this name — was an active revolutionary organizer in the Caucasus in the intervals of imprisonment and exile to Siberia. Most of the articles it contains were originally published in Georgian in fugitive underground periodicals and are now made accessible for the first time to the Russian reader. The editor explains that not all of Stalin's writings of this period have even now been re-discovered.

It has been customary among Stalin's enemies and detractors, beginning with Trotsky, to speak with contempt of his talents as a theorist. Compared with many of the others of his generation of Bolsheviks

— not merely Lenin and Trotsky, but such men as Bukharin, Zinoviev and Radek — he has not been a fluent or prolific writer. No doubt the later volumes of this edition will be swelled by official pronouncements, the drafting of which may be attributed in part to his secretaries and advisers; it is even proposed to include the official Short History of the Russian Communist Party published in 1938 which, though prepared under Stalin's direction, certainly did not come from his pen. The pretension that Stalin ranks with Marx or Lenin as a thinker is exaggerated to the point of absurdity. Nevertheless the first volume of his works goes a long way to refute the legend fostered by Souvarine and others that the Soviet leader is a semi-literate ignoramus who repeats and distorts the already hackneyed ideas of others — a politician or a bureaucrat or an administrator unconcerned with theories and incapable of understanding them.

Nearly all the articles in this first volume are inspired by local controversies, mainly with the Mensheviks, who in Stalin's native Georgia always formed the more powerful wing of the party. The major items are an article of 1904 on the national question which foreshadows the famous article of 1912, both in its general conception and in its empirical conclusions, and invalidates the suggestion sometimes made that the later article was merely a transcription of Lenin's views; two articles on the party differences between Bolsheviks and Mensheviks; and a rather crude exposition of dialectical materialism in the form of a defence of Marxist socialism against anarchism. These writings reveal Stalin, not indeed as an original thinker, but as an active and competent propagandist and popularizer and as a faithful disciple of the Bolshevik creed. Lenin is mentioned by name only a few times (Stalin's first meeting with him occurred at the end of 1905, but is not referred to here); and, on the only two noteworthy occasions during this period in which Lenin's personal opinion was rejected and overruled by the majority of the party, Stalin supported the majority. He wrote in favour of boycotting the elections to the first Duma, where Lenin was for participation; and he voted at the fourth party congress in 1906 for the distribution of land to the peasants, where Lenin was for nationalization.

It is, however, apparent that even at this early period Stalin was, consciously or unconsciously, moulded by Lenin and by a particular aspect of Lenin. The acute and bitter controversies which marked the formative years of the party all turned in one way or another on an issue which involved both ideas and organization. Was the workers' movement to be supplied with its philosophy, its leadership and its initiative by a small and highly organized group of determined revolutionaries, who must, in the nature of things, be drawn mainly from the intellectuals? Or was the party to regard itself as the servant and follower of the workers and rely for its initiative on the "spontaneous" urge to revolution which intolerable conditions would sooner or later breed among them? Lenin, the passionate protagonist of the first view, contemptuously dubbed the supporters of the alternative view " tail-enders ", and amid many backslidings built up the Bolshevik party almost single-handed on his own narrow but powerful conception of the way in which revolutions are made.

Stalin emerged from the ruck as one of those who stood without hesitation for Lenin's policy. It was not for nothing that Lenin in a much-quoted letter referred to him as the " wonderful Georgian " and made him, in 1912, a member of the central committee of the party. From the first, Stalin accepted, perhaps with even less reservation than Lenin himself, the obligation of the party to lead, to organize and to fight. " Our party ", he says in one of these early articles, " is not a collection of individual chatterers, but an organization of leaders." And again: " Only *unity* of opinion can unite the members of the party into one centralized party. If unity of opinion collapses, the party collapses." Lenin's pamphlet *What is to be Done?* which expresses these ideas in their clearest and most forcible form becomes his bible, and the writings of his early period bristle with praise of organization and scorn for those who depend on the efficacy of " spontaneous " forces within the working class. " The spontaneous workers' movement ", he quotes from Lenin, " so long as it remains spontaneous, so long as it is not united with socialist consciousness, submits itself to bourgeois ideology and is inevitably drawn to such submission." The formula is a " union of the workers' movement with socialism ";

and this can be achieved only by a small organized party of high intellectual as well as moral quality, imbued with complete mastery of the intricacies of revolutionary socialist doctrine.

The danger plainly inherent in this doctrine is the temptation to exalt organization as a necessary means to revolution, and revolution as an end in itself. Formally speaking, the Bolshevik theorists — Stalin perhaps less than Lenin — guard themselves against this danger. One passage in these early writings oddly recalls the optimistic conviction of pious Victorians that the good, by some ultimate law of progress, will prevail over the bad.

> If the teaching of the anarchists represents the truth, it will, of course, necessarily make its own way and gather the masses round it. If it is unsubstantial and built on a false foundation, then it will not hold for long and will vanish into the air.

This optimism is supported elsewhere by a reference to the famous Hegelian doctrine — in view of the recent attitude of the Russian philosophical schools to German philosophy in general and Hegel in particular, it is interesting to find Stalin defending Hegel — of the identity of the real and the rational. Marxism will triumph, says Stalin explicitly, because it is rational: what is irrational is doomed to perish. Yet the first critics of Hegel perceived clearly the dilemma of finding any criterion of what is rational other than what, in fact, succeeds; and the youthful Stalin is no more successful than they in resolving it. The cause of revolution is the rational, and therefore the good, cause, because its inevitability can be scientifically proved. But the validity of the proof can only be tested by the event; and if your calculations should turn out to be wrong, it would mean, not that the science was false but that your application of it was faulty. The door is thus thrown wide open for sheer empiricism.

Beyond doubt some distinction, at any rate of emphasis, can be drawn between the empiricism of Lenin and the empiricism of Stalin. "Proletarian socialism", writes Stalin at this time, "is built not on sentimental feelings, not on abstract 'justice', not on love for the proletariat, but on scientific principles." Stalin in his maturity might have expressed himself more cautiously. Yet the impression remains that Lenin's dryness concealed a certain degree of humanity, perhaps of sincere "love for the proletariat", which was absent from the make-up of his more ruthless disciple. Lenin's earlier writings are marked by a strong tinge of Utopianism, which was shed slowly and reluctantly when he was brought into contact with the stern realities and responsibilities entailed by the exercise of power. In *State and Revolution*, written on the eve of October 1917, Lenin strongly denounced those who regarded the State as anything but a necessary evil or sought to obscure the Marxist doctrine of the dying away of the State as a condition of the communist order. Even when this dream had to be relegated to the comparatively remote future, Lenin continued to insist on the need for "direct democracy", for self-government from below, for the ordinary citizen himself learning to administer and control, as the antidote to State bureaucracy. Of such visions, unsubstantial as they proved to be, there is little or no trace in Stalin's speeches or writings.

Such differences of doctrine and emphasis as may be detected between Lenin and Stalin can, however, be plausibly attributed not so much to personal divergences of outlook or temperament as to differences in the historical situation which confronted them. Lenin, for all his insistence on the leadership of a highly trained and organized group of professional revolutionaries, knew that revolutions are made by the masses and that to win the active, or even the passive, support of the masses something more than organization and leadership was required. He knew that even discontent with existing conditions, indispensable though that was as a starting-point, was not enough to sustain a revolutionary ardour. The vision of a new world — in which men, freed from the oppression of bourgeois capitalism and of the bourgeois State, would learn to govern themselves and to organize the processes of production and distribution for the common good — was necessary to fire the revolutionary imagination. Lenin inherited the splendid vision from a long line of nineteenth-century socialists. He accepted it, sincerely believed in it, and justified his policies by the prospect of its realization. If, after the first few months of power, the prospect seemed to recede into a remote future and the difficulties of its realization became increasingly apparent, there is no evidence that Lenin ever abandoned his faith in it.

Stalin's career was different. Lenin appraised his merits as a professional revolutionary. His function was to organize; and in this he was supreme. He never sought to kindle the enthusiasm of the masses; for he lacked altogether the temperament, and perhaps the convictions, necessary for such an achievement. His stepping-stone to power was an appointment that required exactly those gifts of organization which he possessed — the secretaryship of the party; and he rose to power because, after 1922, it was no longer revolutionary enthusiasm but capacity to organize which the historical situation demanded. In this sense Stalin was a product of the revolution in its later phase. He inherited it from its chief progenitor, and for more than twenty years he directed and tamed and moulded it. To inquire how far he shaped its course by his personal intervention and initiative, and how far he was the agent of inevitable forces working themselves out to a predestined end, is merely to raise the eternal question of the position of the great man in history.

One of the most marked features which distinguishes Stalin's outlook from Lenin's and gives Stalin a crucial place in revolutionary history is the shift from the international to the national standpoint. Here, too, differences of background played their part. Lenin spent the most formative years of his life abroad, and spoke the principal European languages; and his revolutionary doctrine was international to the core. Stalin knows no language but Russian and Georgian and has never left Russia except for visits to three or four party conferences before 1914 and for his recent excursions to Teheran and Potsdam. His Georgian origin accounted for his early special studies of nationalism and for his choice as People's Commissar for Nationalities in 1917; but it does not seem to have had any important influence on him — unless it was to give an almost fanatical intensity to his Soviet patriotism. It was thus no accident that made him the sponsor of "socialism in one country" in the 1920s, the antagonist of the internationally minded Trotsky, and the protagonist of the revival of Russian national sentiment, after its revolutionary eclipse, in the 1930s. When war came in 1941 he was already the national rather than the revolutionary hero. His relations with the army seem from the outset to have been easy. He had done much, even before the war, to restore its prestige and to bring it back to its former place of honour in the national life. The war brought his finest qualities and capacities to their full fruition; and his designation as Marshal of the Soviet Union in March 1943 could be regarded as a natural culmination of his career rather than as a mere concession to the exigencies of war.

It is no doubt a paradox that one who appeared on the scene as a revolutionary conspirator should be acclaimed to-day principally for his patriotic devotion to his country and for his unflinching leadership in time of war. The frontispiece to his collected works significantly shows him in his marshal's uniform. But such paradoxes are not without precedent in the history of revolutions; and Lenin, though his revolutionary convictions were far more deep-rooted than Stalin's, might well have undergone some such transformation, had he lived long enough. The criticisms which will have to be taken into account in the ultimate assessment of Stalin's record relate not so much to the ends which he pursued and achieved as to the means by which he pursued and achieved them. Lenin, in his so-called testament, described Stalin as "too rough" and referred to him as deficient in "loyalty". His rise to power was beyond doubt marked by an unusual skill in the less amiable arts of political intrigue. He worked beneath the surface, undermined established reputations, held back while others committed themselves to untenable positions and then struck, and struck hard. He was a cunning, vindictive and ruthless antagonist; and the indignities and brutalities which he heaped on his fallen adversaries while they had many precedents in the Russian tradition, were shocking to western minds.

Yet, if Stalin introduced or reintroduced into Russian history a narrow and systematically ruthless intolerance which the first enthusiasm of the revolution seemed to have expelled or mitigated, this was in the character of the time as much as of the man. The Bolshevik revolution, like other revolutions, began in an atmosphere of idealism which bordered on Utopia. But soon opposition from within and from without provoked repression, and violence bred violence. Terror was soon being applied not only against survivors of the *ancien régime* and of the bourgeoisie but against other revolutionary parties which attempted to maintain an independent existence. Even Lenin's prestige and his genius for persuasion did not suffice in his later years to maintain party unity without threats of expulsion and limitations on the freedom of speech and opinion of its members. When Lenin disappeared from the scene, profound rifts quickly revealed themselves, and the weapons of repression hitherto used only against dissentients outside the party were, logically and almost inevitably, turned against dissentients within it.

The judgment of history on Stalin's role will depend in part on the wider judgment which it passes on the Bolshevik revolution. The claim of that revolution to have inaugurated a "new civilization" has been asserted and contested. But, on any view, it was one of the great turning-points in history, comparable with the French revolution and perhaps surpassing it in significance. No country in the world has remained indifferent to it, no form of government has been able to evade its challenge, no political or economic theory has escaped its searching criticism; nor, according to all signs and portents, has its influence yet reached a peak. The collected edition of Stalin's writings and speeches, while it will probably add little that is specific to existing knowledge of the man or his work, will help to place it in perspective, and will constitute a historical document of the first importance.

14

STALIN: (2) THE DIALECTICS OF STALINISM

EVERY biography of Stalin is necessarily a "political biography"; for Stalin is a politician to his finger-tips, and there is no other capacity in which either contemporaries or posterity are likely to interest themselves in him. What Mr. Deutscher means by giving his new biography of Stalin[1] this sub-title is, perhaps, not so much that he has wasted less time than the hagiographers of Moscow or than hostile biographers like Souvarine and Trotsky on more or less mythical episodes, creditable or discreditable, of Stalin's youth and personal life, but rather that he intends his book as an analysis of his hero's political achievement. This is, in fact, what it is; and the intention has been brilliantly executed. The usual difficulty of political biography, the difficulty of separating the record of the man from the history of his time, scarcely arises in dealing with Stalin. Since Lenin's death Stalin's career and the history of Soviet Russia have been inseparable. Nothing that belongs to the one can be regarded as

[1] I. Deutscher, *Stalin*. A Political Biography. Oxford University Press. London: Cumberlege. 25s.

irrelevant to the other. A story so dramatic as Stalin's cannot be dull. Mr. Deutscher has missed none of the points and has written a book which, among its other merits, is absorbing to read. But it is absorbing in part because, in all the excitement of the external detail, he has never lost sight of his central theme of the nature of Stalin's achievement and his place in the history of the revolution.

It need hardly be said that this, like everything else about Stalin, is highly controversial. It raises many questions which, like most of the profound questions of history, cannot be readily answered with a simple yes or no. Is Stalin the disciple of Marx or an Oriental despot? Has he fulfilled or renounced the heritage of Lenin? Has he built "socialism in one country" or blighted the prospects of socialism throughout the world for a generation to come? Has he — a second Peter the Great — Europeanized Russia, or — a second Genghis Khan — made Russia part of a vast Asiatic empire? Is he a nationalist assiduously seeking to increase the prestige and power of Russia, or an internationalist concerned to bring about the universal triumph of a revolutionary creed? These questions are susceptible of many different answers. Mr. Deutscher's book will enable the reader, if not to answer them, at any rate to ask them with greater understanding.

History never stands still — least of all in the middle of a revolution. What Lenin created and what Stalin inherited from him was a constantly changing entity, not a static system, but a process of development. It was a process in which, to borrow the Hegelian idiom, thesis was continually begetting antithesis, so that the question whether Stalin continued or negated the work of Lenin may reflect a distinction of language rather than of substance. Put less abstractly, the truth seems to be that every revolution is succeeded by its own reaction and that, when Lenin was withdrawn from the scene, the Russian revolution had already entered this secondary stage of its course. The once current slogan, "Stalin is the Lenin of to-day", did not assert that Stalin was the Lenin of 1917, but that he was performing the function which Lenin himself would have had to perform if he had remained the leader of the revolution ten years later. Even so, it was not wholly true. But it contained some elements of the truth.

The early Bolsheviks were students of history and knew what happens to revolutions: they feared that their revolution, too, would meet its Thermidor. But the spell of Bonaparte made them assume that the source of danger was a dictator in shining armour. It was this assumption which proved fatal to Trotsky and smoothed Stalin's path to power. In Mr. Deutscher's words:

> It had always been admitted that history might repeat itself, and that a directory or a single usurper might once again climb to power on the back of the revolution. It was taken for granted that the Russian usurper would, like his French prototype, have a personality possessed of brilliance and legendary fame won in battles. The mask of Bonaparte seemed to fit Trotsky only too well.

Indeed, it might have fitted any personality with the exception of Stalin. In this lay part of his strength.

Thus it was that Stalin became, if not " the Lenin of to-day ", the Bonaparte of to-day, the heir of Lenin as Bonaparte was the heir of Robespierre, the man who chained and disciplined the revolution, and consolidated its achievements, and garbled its doctrines, and wedded it to a great national power, and spread its influence throughout the world.

Yet this, too, was not the whole truth. For, while history sometimes repeats itself in unexpected disguises, every historical situation is none the less unique. The odd thing is that Stalin, unpredictably and seemingly in spite of himself, became, unlike Bonaparte, a revolutionary in his own right. More than ten years after Lenin's revolution, Stalin made a second revolution without which Lenin's revolution would have run out into the sand. In this sense Stalin continued and fulfilled Leninism, though the slogan of " socialism in one country ", under which he made his revolution, was the rejection of what Lenin believed (the efforts of Stalin's theorists to father it on Lenin were childishly disingenuous) and Lenin would have recoiled in horror from some of the methods by which the second revolution was made.

Intellectually, as Mr. Deutscher is careful to point out, " socialism in one country " made no new and original contribution to doctrine. It was not even very coherent, since Stalin himself, clinging firmly to the ill-fitting garments of Marxist orthodoxy, admitted that socialism could never be completely and securely realized in one country isolated in a capitalist world. But psychologically and politically it was a brilliant discovery; and it does not seriously detract from Stalin's political genius to say that, like other great discoveries, its author stumbled on it unawares. It happened in 1924, the year in which Lenin died, at the height of the controversy with Trotsky and between two editions of Stalin's *Foundations of Leninism*. The first edition contained a passage which read too much like an endorsement of Trotsky's "permanent revolution". In the second edition this gave place to a clear and unequivocal statement that socialism could be built in one country — even in backward, peasant Russia.

When Lenin died, orthodox Bolshevism had run into a blind alley. All agreed that the first task in 1917 had been to complete the unfinished bourgeois revolution in Russia; and this, it could fairly be said, had been done. All Bolsheviks agreed (as against the Mensheviks) that, in completing the bourgeois revolution, they would pass over directly into the stage of the socialist revolution; this, too, had happened. But at this point all Bolsheviks, from Lenin downwards, had confidently assumed that the torch kindled in Russia would ignite the socialist revolution in western Europe, and that the European proletariat would take up the burden of completing the socialist revolution and building a socialist society. This task — Lenin had said it again and again — was too heavy for backward Russia to carry out alone.

Unfortunately this time-table had not been realized. Revolution in Europe, which seemed certain in 1919 and imminent in 1920 when the Red Army was outside Warsaw, still unaccountably tarried. In the autumn of 1923, when the German proletariat for the third or fourth time since 1918 suffered a crushing defeat (recriminations about who was to blame did not help), it came to be gradually understood in Moscow that the European revolution was still a long way off. But what, on this new hypothesis, was the role of the Russian Bolsheviks? Nobody denied, it was true, that one of their tasks was to proceed with the building of socialism in Russia: Trotsky was pressing the case for intensive planning and industrialization long before it had been taken up by Stalin. But, none the less, since it seemed to follow from the orthodox doctrine that it was not possible to get very far in Russia in the absence of revolution elsewhere, a sense of unreality and frustration could hardly be avoided. The rank and file, if not the party *intelligentsia*, needed the stimulus and inspiration of a finite goal set in a not too remote future, and dependent for its realization, not on incalculable events in far-away Europe but on their own efforts.

This need was brilliantly met by "socialism in one country". Mr. Deutscher's imaginative reconstruction of what the new slogan meant to Stalin's followers cannot be bettered:

Of course we are looking forward to international revolution. Of course we have been brought up in the school of Marxism; and we know that contemporary social and political struggles are, by their very nature, international. Of course we still believe the victory of the proletariat in the west to be near; and we are bound in honour to do what we can to speed it up. But — and this was a very big, a highly suggestive "but" — do not worry so much about all that international revolution. Even if it were to be delayed indefinitely, even if it were never to occur, we in this country are capable of developing into a fully fledged classless society. Let us then concentrate on our great constructive task.

An English empiricist might have said: "Let the theory take care of itself, and get on with the job". Stalin the Marxist had to wrap it up in a tiresome paraphernalia of doctrine. But it came to much the same thing.

On the slogan of "socialism in one country" Stalin rode to power — to become the prisoner of the spirits he had conjured up. For there was, it turned out, something to be said for the older, more cautious, less empirical Marxism of an earlier generation, however inconvenient its application might be to the Russia of the later nineteen-twenties. The hard core of reality behind the division of Europe into east and west was the frontier running approximately from Danzig to Trieste, the frontier between developed capitalist Europe, where the proletariat was already a force, and undeveloped peasant Europe, where the hold of feudalism had hardly yet been broken. Perhaps, after all, Lenin and Trotsky — and Stalin himself down to the autumn of 1924 — had been right when they argued that the victory of socialism could not be achieved in backward Russia without a socialist revolution in the proletarian countries of western Europe. Perhaps even — though nobody dared to hint this in Russia — the Mensheviks had not been altogether wrong when they maintained that it was not possible to pass over direct from the bourgeois to the socialist stage of the revolution and that socialism could be built only on an established foundation of bourgeois capitalism.

Naturally the answer to these questions turned partly on what was meant by socialism. Stalin had undertaken to produce " socialism in one country ". Whatever he produced must clearly be called " socialism "; moreover, the Five-year Plan and the collectivization of agriculture were unimpeachable items in a revolutionary socialist programme. Nevertheless it would be a mistake to assume that these measures were imposed on Stalin, or imposed by Stalin on Russia, on the strength of any slogan or programme, whether " socialism in one country " or another. They were imposed by the objective situation which Soviet Russia in the later nineteen-twenties had to face.

The Leninist revolution had by this time run its course. The key industries had been nationalized and, in a superficial and fragmentary way, " planned ", but not fitted into an economy designed as a single unit. The land had been given to the peasants. Every device had been tried to step up agricultural production — the key to the whole structure. The *kulak* had been first terrorized for the benefit of the poor peasant, then encouraged to fend for himself under NEP; Bukharin had even told him that he was fulfilling the highest purposes of socialism by enriching himself. But none of these devices had more than a momentary success. Since any substantial assistance from the capitalist countries had to be ruled out, the economy could not advance on socialist lines, or on any other lines, without an increased yield from agriculture; and this was conceivable only through the restoration of large-scale farming and the introduction of mechanization. Short of a relapse into conditions more primitive than those destroyed by the revolution, or of an unconditional surrender to foreign capitalism — and neither was a conceivable solution — there was no road open save the hard road which Russia was to travel under Stalin's leadership and the banner of "socialism in one country".

The most baffling feature of Stalin's career is that he carried out a revolution which was no less far-reaching than the revolution of 1917, and was in many senses its logical and necessary completion, at a time when the popular tide of revolutionary enthusiasm had ebbed away, and to the accompaniment of many "Thermidorean" symptoms of counter-revolution. It was thus that Trotsky could find ground for denouncing Stalin as a counter-revolutionary and as the destroyer of the revolution. Mr. Deutscher sums up the difference between the Leninist and Stalinist revolutions by calling the first a revolution "from below" and the second a revolution "from above". The distinction must not be pressed too far. Lenin specifically rejected the idea that revolutions are made by the spontaneous enthusiasm of the masses; he believed in, and imposed, strict revolutionary discipline. Stalin, whose theory on this point did not differ from Lenin's, could not have executed his colossal task unless he had been able to rely on a broad base of popular support. Yet it is clear that Stalin had to contend with far more apathy and disillusionment in the masses, far more opposition and intrigue in the party *élite*, than Lenin had ever known, and was driven to apply correspondingly harsher and more ruthless measures of discipline. It is also significant that most of the appeals by which Stalin justified his revolution were to instincts normally the reverse of revolutionary — to law and order, to the sanctity of the family, to the defence of the fatherland and to the virtue of cultivating one's own garden: it was as a restless international adventurer, a man who cared nothing for his country, a champion of "permanent revolution", that Trotsky was pilloried.

Stalin thus presents two faces to the world — a revolutionary-Marxist face and a national-Russian face — two aspects which are partly conflicting and partly complementary. And if the gradation from the Leninist to the Stalinist revolution is expressed in these terms, it may perhaps be said that the one was essentially designed as an international revolution occurring in Russia and to that extent adapting itself to Russian conditions, and the other as a national revolution which no doubt carried with it its international demands and its international implications, but was primarily concerned with establishing itself. Mr. Deutscher quotes somewhere the retort of Dostoevsky's Grand Inquisitor to Christ: " We have corrected Thy deed ". One of the ways in which Stalin corrected Lenin's deed was to root it firmly and tenaciously in the national soil. This was, after all, the central tenet of Stalin's philosophy. He believed, what Lenin doubted or denied, that socialism could be built in an isolated Russian State.

The marriage of the international ideals of the revolution to national sentiment was bound to occur. It had happened in the French revolution. It had begun to happen in Soviet Russia long before Stalin took charge of her destinies: the first occasion on which patriotic and revolutionary feelings were conspicuously blended and intertwined was the war against Poland in 1920. The long isolation of Soviet Russia, the persistent hostility of the greater part of the capitalist world were bound to reinforce the trend. When Stalin in 1924 proclaimed the possibility of " socialism in one country " he was, without knowing it, appealing to the deep springs of a national pride which for ten years had been not only dead but damned. He told his followers that Russians could do precisely what Lenin and all other Bolsheviks had hitherto believed them incapable of doing. " Russia will do it for herself ", he might have said, parodying Cavour. The five-year plans were launched under the slogans of " catching up " and " overtaking " the capitalist countries, of beating them at their own game.

It was thus that Stalin became the reviver of Russian patriotism, the first leader explicitly to reverse the international or anti-national attitude which had dominated the early stages of the revolution. The first Bolshevik historians had depicted previous Russian history in the main as a long series of barbarities and scandals. " Backward " was the standard epithet to attach to the name " Russia ". Stalin changed all that. He put out of business altogether the " Marxist " school of historians headed by Pokrovsky (whom Lenin had highly praised and valued), and rehabilitated the Russian past. A new drive was required in place of the cooling revolutionary ardour in order to render tolerable the hardships of industrialization and to steel resistance to potential enemies. Stalin found it in nationalism. New-found enthusiasms tend to exaggeration; and victory over Hitler was an intoxicating achievement. Soviet nationalism since the war has taken some forms which western observers have thought sinister and others which they have thought absurd. But it has, perhaps, not differed as much as is sometimes supposed from that of other great Powers at the moment of their ascent to greatness.

Other aspects of Stalin's return to a national tradition may weigh more heavily against him in the scales of history. The real charge against Stalinism is that it abandoned those fruitful elements of the western tradition which were embodied in the original Marxism, and substituted for them retrograde and oppressive elements drawn from the Russian tradition. Marxism stood on the shoulders of western bourgeois liberal democracy, and, while ultimately rejecting it, assumed and adopted many of its achievements. This is the meaning of the insistence in the *Communist Manifesto* that bourgeois democracy had been in its day a progressive liberating force and that the proletarian revolution could come only as a second step after the consummation of the bourgeois revolution; and many of the first legislative acts and declarations of the Soviet regime in Russia were inspired as much by the ideals of bourgeois democracy as by those of socialism. When the moment came to pass on to the realization of socialism, this meant, not that democratic ideals would be abandoned, but that they would be fulfilled, as the degenerate bourgeois democracies of the west were no longer capable of fulfilling them.

Such was Lenin's dream in 1917. But it was from the Marxist standpoint an anomaly, and from the standpoint of socialism a tragedy, that the first victorious socialist revolution should have occurred in what was economically, socially and politically the most backward of the great countries of Europe. The workers who were called on to build the first socialist order had been for generations the victims of economic poverty, social inequality and political repression more extreme than those prevailing in any other great country. The socialist order in Russia could draw neither on the wealth created by past capitalist enterprise nor on the political experience fostered by bourgeois democracy. At the very end of his life Lenin began to realize to the full the handicaps imposed by these shortcomings. A passage quoted by Mr. Deutscher from his speech at the last party congress he attended penetrates to the taproots of " Stalinism ":

> If the conquering nation is more cultured than the vanquished nation, the former imposes its culture on the latter; but if the opposite is the case, the vanquished nation imposes its culture on the conqueror.

Something of the same sort, Lenin continued, could happen between classes. In the RSFSR the culture of the vanquished classes, " miserable and low as it is, is higher than that of our responsible Communist administrators "; the old Russian bureaucracy, in virtue of this relatively higher level of culture, was vanquishing the victorious, but ignorant and inexperienced, Communists.

This was the danger which Lenin, with the clear-sightedness of genius, diagnosed in what he saw around him in the fifth year of the revolution. It was implicit in the continued isolation of socialist Russia from the rest of the world and in the necessity of building " socialism in one country ". International Marxism and international socialism, planted in Russian soil and left to themselves, found their international character exposed to the constant sapping and mining of the Russian national tradition which they had supposedly vanquished in 1917. Ten years later, when Lenin was dead, the leaders who had most conspicuously represented the international and western elements in Bolshevism, — Trotsky, Zinoviev and Kamenev, not to mention minor figures like Radek, Krasin and Rakovsky — had all disappeared; the mild and pliable Bukharin was soon to follow. The hidden forces of the Russian past — autocracy, bureaucracy, political and cultural conformity — took their revenge, not by destroying the revolution but by harnessing it to themselves in order to fulfil it in a narrow national framework. These forces carried Stalin to power and made him what he remains to-day, the enigmatic protagonist both of international revolution and of national tradition.

The reader of Stalin's biography, holding this thread in his hand, will be able to pick his way through a maze whose intricacies appear at first sight infinite, but whose general pattern gradually reveals itself. It is not perhaps an issue which lends itself profitably to discussion in terms of praise and blame. The isolation of the Russian revolution compelled it to rely on its own resources; in turning its back on the outside world it increased its own isolation. Each step drove Russia farther back into her past. When Stalin determined to drive the revolution to its logical conclusion at all costs through industrialization and collectivization, the least fanciful observers were reminded of Peter the Great. When he resolved to protect himself against the potential dangers of treachery in the event of foreign attack by eliminating every possible rival, men thought of Ivan the Terrible. Party orthodoxy came to play the same constricting role as ecclesiastical orthodoxy had played in medieval Russia, with its claim to a monopoly over all philosophy and literature and art. Yet it would be unfair to suppose that Stalin deliberately and consciously sought isolation. Again and again gestures of approach were made to the western world. But only under the stress of war could the barriers be overcome. Once it was over, the iron curtain again descended. The rift between the Russian revolution and the west was too wide to be bridged.

At the end of 1949 Stalin celebrated his seventieth birthday. He has led his country victoriously through its greatest war and surmounted the immediate difficulties of demobilization and reconstruction as smoothly as any of the belligerents. To all outward seeming he stands at the pinnacle of his own and his nation's power. In spite of the familiar injunction to call no man happy till he is dead, the temptation is strong to assume that the shape of Stalin's career is fixed and will not be substantially modified by anything yet to come. Even, however, if this assumption is correct, it does not mean that Stalin's place in history is already fixed — or will be for a generation to come. We can still only begin to see, " through a glass, darkly ", what has been happening in the last thirty years. We dimly perceive that the revolution of 1917, itself the product of the upheaval of 1914, was a turning-point in world history certainly comparable in magnitude with the French revolution a century and a quarter earlier, and perhaps surpassing it. The significance of Lenin's work is just coming into focus.

But of Stalin it is still too early to speak ; Stalin's work is still too plainly subject to the distorting lens of excessive propinquity. How far has he generalized the experience of the revolution of 1917 and how far particularized it? Has he carried it forward to its triumphant conclusion, or destroyed it altogether, or twisted it out of shape? The answer — and one which to some extent begs the question — can for the present be given only in terms of the concluding sentences of Mr. Deutscher's biography:

> The better part of Stalin's work is as certain to outlast Stalin himself as the better parts of the works of Cromwell and Napoleon have outlasted them. But in order to save it for the future and to give it its full value, history may yet have to cleanse and reshape Stalin's work as sternly as it once cleansed and reshaped the work of the English revolution after Cromwell and of the French after Napoleon.

THE END

PRINTED BY R. & R. CLARK, LTD., EDINBURGH

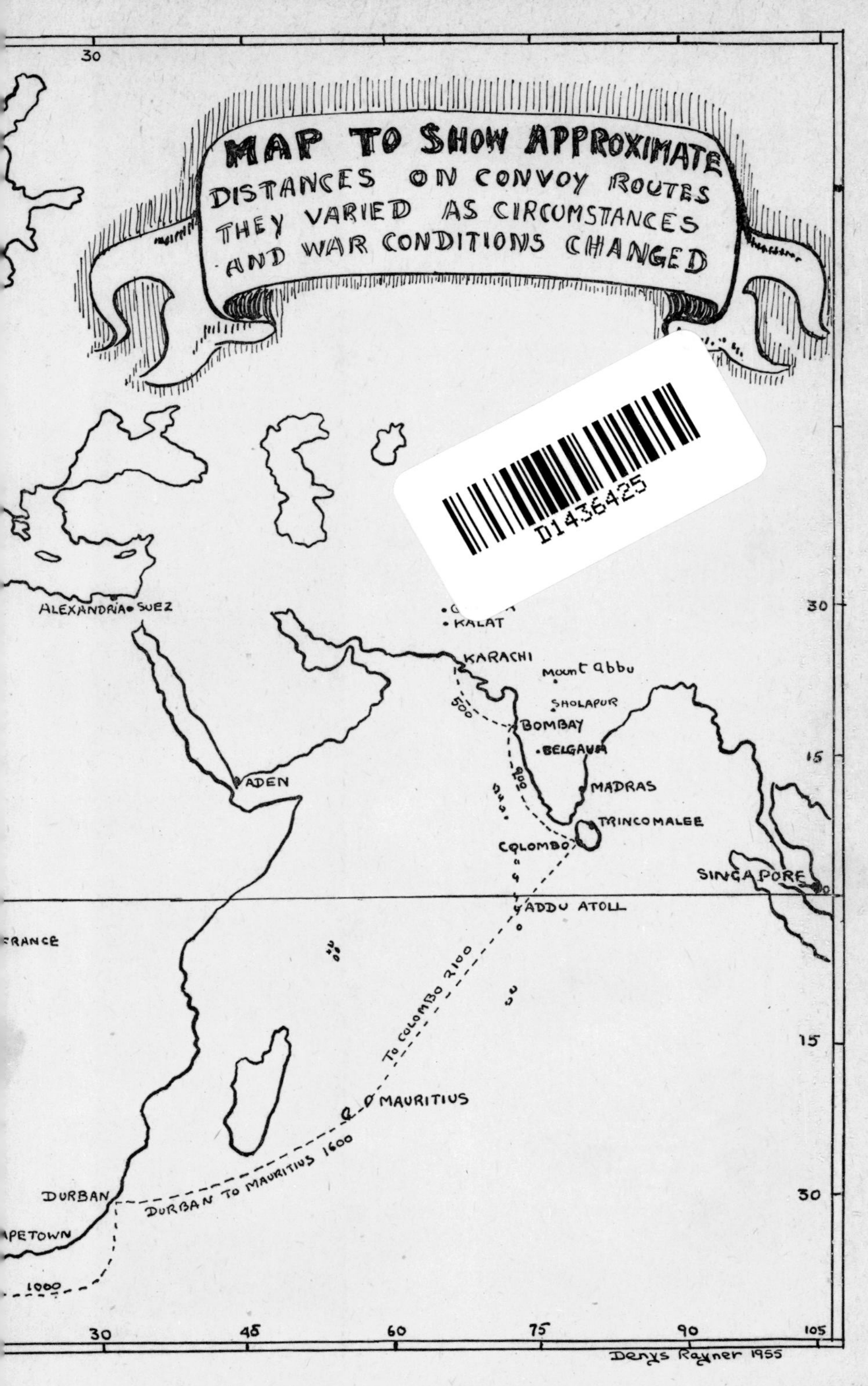
MAP TO SHOW APPROXIMATE
DISTANCES ON CONVOY ROUTES
THEY VARIED AS CIRCUMSTANCES
AND WAR CONDITIONS CHANGED
ALEXANDRIA
SUEZ
KALAT
KARACHI
Mount abbu
SHOLAPUR
500
BOMBAY
BELGAUM
900
ADEN
MADRAS
TRINCOMALEE
COLOMBO
SINGAPORE
ADDU ATOLL
TO COLOMBO 2100
MAURITIUS
DURBAN TO MAURITIUS 1600
DURBAN
1000
30
45
60
75
90
105
15
Denys Rayner 1955

ESCORT

THE BATTLE OF THE ATLANTIC

ESCORT

THE BATTLE OF THE ATLANTIC

by

COMMANDER D. A. RAYNER

D.S.C. and Bar, V.R.D., R.N.V.R.

Edited by

CAPTAIN S. W. ROSKILL, D.S.C., R.N.

Author of the Official History of 'The War at Sea 1939–1945'

WILLIAM KIMBER

LONDON

First published in 1955 by
WILLIAM KIMBER AND CO. LIMITED
46 Wilton Place, London, S.W.1

MADE AND PRINTED IN GREAT BRITAIN BY PURNELL AND SONS, LTD.
PAULTON (SOMERSET AND LONDON

EDITOR'S FOREWORD

By Captain S. W. Roskill. D.S.C., R.N.
Author of the Official History of the War at Sea

Commander Rayner's story came to me in snatches at various times when we met after the end of the war. Not until quite recently did it occur to either of us that in it lay the material for a book. When men have lived through periods of great strain there often is, I fancy, a strong reluctance to commit their experiences to paper, at any rate until the passage of time has assimilated them into the whole pattern of their lives. The scars then still remain, but the wounds themselves are no longer raw, and by a process of healing relaxation the mind no longer shrinks from memories that for long could only hurt. It was at my suggestion that Commander Rayner began to write about the war at sea as he saw it, and it may have been mere chance that I made the proposal at the time when, at last, he felt able and prepared to record his experiences.

I do not for one moment suggest that this true story of one man's part in the Atlantic battle is unique in all, or even in many respects; for there were Escort Commanders who brought in more convoys than Rayner, and who also sank more U-Boats. Some men also certainly fought for as long as he did, or even longer, in that protracted struggle. But I do believe that in one respect this story, if not unique, is very nearly so. I know of no other officer, let alone one of the Royal Naval Volunteer Reserve, who served continuously for more than five years in command of escort vessels; nor of any other who graduated from a trawler at the very beginning to a corvette, then to a small destroyer, to several larger destroyers or groups of destroyers, and finally to command of a group of the new and greatly improved war-built escort vessels. This astonishing continuity of experience and, if I may say so, of endurance gives to Commander Rayner an authority to speak on his subject which can hardly be questioned. Furthermore, the discerning reader will, for all the modesty with which the story is told, have no difficulty in detecting the deep confidence which Rayner inspired in the minds of the senior officers under whom he served. He was for a long time in Commander Howard-Johnston's redoubtable 12th Escort Group; his ships came through the severe tests imposed by Commodore (Vice-Admiral, Retired) G. O. Stephenson at Tobermory with flying colours; and he won the high regard, even affection, of that great leader and shrewd judge of character, Admiral Sir Max Horton.

But I have other reasons for feeling glad that the public will be able to read this story. We British do not like to be reminded of how narrowly, through our own negligences and follies, we have escaped disaster; nor of how in our thoughtless selfishness we have often left our safety in the hands of very small bands of men who had the vision to see what was needed, and the devotion to fulfil the needs themselves. It cannot be doubted that the pre-war R.N.V.R. officers, of whom Rayner was one, come within the latter category. They were prominent among the first properly trained reserves available to man the small ships; and to a considerable extent it was that tiny nucleus which made possible the enormous expansion of the R.N.V.R. as the war progressed. If it serves no other purpose than to remind us of these simple facts, this book will have been well worth writing.

I have neither added anything significant to, nor subtracted anything from, Commander Rayner's account. I have verified matters of time and place, and such suggestions as I have made have mostly been concerned with the manner of presenting the story. In its details as well as in its broad relation to the war at sea as a whole, I believe this story to be accurate; but it does, of course, view tremendous events through the comparatively narrow lens of one man's vision. I would emphasise that where matters of opinion are expressed they are Commander Rayner's and not necessarily mine. I have not thought it a proper part of an editor's functions to modify or alter sincerely held opinions on such matters as anti-submarine tactics and weapon development, on pre-war naval policy, or on the design of some of our ships. Though I would not always accept Rayner's views,

I feel that his long experience at sea fully justifies his expressing them; and that they will therefore command respect, if they are unlikely to receive universal agreement.

Where I believe the book may have lasting value is that, at least to my mind, it rings absolutely true in its picture of the men who manned the little ships. Their endurance under conditions of appalling discomfort, their unflagging persistence in carrying out the tasks allotted to them, their ribald humour and unfailing good nature, and, above all, their great-hearted humanity, are all recorded here. Of course they grumbled. British sailors always have done so. But they rarely complained, and never whined. Perhaps it was these qualities, of which Commander Rayner's narrative will vividly remind all who took part in the Atlantic struggle, which contributed most to bringing the nation through to victory.

It has been a privilege to be asked to edit this contribution to the story of the Royal Navy from 1939 to 1945.

S. W. Roskill

PREFACE

I have long wished to write a book on the Western Approaches, but the subject is so vast, and the people who served there were so many that it has been very difficult to see how this could be done.

As I saw it there were three possible alternatives—a fictional tale, a story of the war in those seas embracing everybody, and lastly an autobiography. Fiction I think always reads as fiction; it can never quite be believed, and one never knows where truth ends and imagination begins. To write the story of the Western Approaches as a serious war book would be to invade the preserves of the official historian to the Admiralty: and even so there would be many people left out who should have been mentioned. I have therefore very reluctantly chosen the third alternative. I say very reluctantly because I would rather have written about anybody other than myself; yet to attribute my experiences to another person would at once produce the illusion that I was writing fiction.

Here it is then—the story of the war at sea *as it affected me.* I emphasise this most particularly because I have been throughout most careful to include no single incident that did not actually happen to me. If I had included all the events that to my knowledge happened to other people I could fill twenty books. If I were to include just one thing which did not happen I should be untrue to myself, and untrue to all those less fortunate than I who perished by wind, by wave, and by enemy action.

Throughout I have used the names and ranks of people as I would have used them had I been speaking of them at the time. I have nearly always refrained from interrupting the narrative by inserting after the name of Commander Blank, for instance, the words 'now Admiral Sir John Blank, K.C.V.O., D.S.O.' It can be assumed that age and experience have added to the rank and honours of all the officers of Her Majesty's Navy who figure in these pages.

It is also, in more official writings, the custom to place after the name of every ship when first mentioned the name of her captain. Once again, and for the same reason, I have refrained from doing so, unless the name was necessary to my story.

I write only of ships and of men, both of whom have character, and change from one generation to another. These I would try to fix in a moment of time as I knew them. I do not write of the sea, which has no personality of its own and does not change. The sea is neither cruel nor kind. It is supremely indifferent, and wholly lacks sensibility. Confined by the great land masses its surface is moved only by the wind. The greatest ship ever built by man is no more than a fly on the wall of its immutability. Although its face may appear different in the Atlantic to that which it presents in the Indian Ocean, it is the same element. Any apparent virtues it may have, and all its vices, are seen only in relation to the spirit of man who pits himself, in ships of his own building, against its insensate power. To conclude otherwise is to diminish its majesty.

This book is dedicated to the memory of all those who lost their lives or their health in the Western Approaches, and in particular to the officers and men who were lost in H.M.S. *Warwick*, 20th February 1944.

D. A. RAYNER

Burghclere,
June 1955

ACKNOWLEDGMENTS

I acknowledge with a deep sense of gratitude the help that I have received from Captain S. W. Roskill, D.S.C., R.N., without whose encouragement this book would surely never have been printed. To him, too, I am greatly indebted for much valuable advice and for a great many suggestions.

I would also express my gratitude for the help that my wife has given me; and to Miss Joan Waldron, who has had the thankless task of turning my handwriting into typescript.

CONTENTS

ILLUSTRATIONS

ILLUSTRATIONS

MAPS

AUTHOR'S NOTE

It is the fashion to place a glossary at the end of a book, with the result that many people do not discover what they have been reading about until it is all over.

In writing this book I have found cases where abbreviations entirely intelligible to the specialist would yet mean nothing at all to the layman. To describe each one as they occur would unduly interrupt the narrative, and as the abbreviations are really very few I have placed this 'glossary' in the front of the book in the hope that the reader will see it before he embarks on the story itself.

C.-in-C.	Commander-in-Chief. Followed by the Sea Area or Fleet commanded.
F.O.I.C.	Flag Officer in Charge. Followed by the port which he commanded.
N.O.I.C.	Naval Officer in Charge. Followed by the port which he administered.
Captain (D).	Captain administering one or more flotillas of destroyers. In wartime in the Western Approaches he also had the administration of frigates, corvettes, and trawlers. In the case of Londonderry after Commodore G. W. G. Simpson had been appointed for this purpose he was known as Commodore (D).
First Lieutenant Number One Jimmy Jimmy-the-One	The officer next in seniority to the Captain in any warship up to the size of and including a destroyer. This officer is responsible to the Captain for the appearance, and day-to-day organisation, of the ship.
Coxswain.	The Senior Chief Petty Officer who takes the wheel in action and when entering and leaving harbour. He is also the ship's 'policeman', and is responsible for the

	victualling in a small ship. He is very much a confidential servant to both the Captain and First Lieutenant.
Yeoman of Signals.	The senior Signalman. Again very much in the confidence of the Captain, particularly in wartime, when a number of signals are received and sent whose contents should not be divulged to all and sundry.
Quartermaster.	A rating who steers the ship at sea and who keeps watch at the gangway in harbour. There will always be one for each watch.
Bosun's Mate.	Bridge messenger at sea and companion of the quartermaster at the gangway in harbour.
H.A. Gun.	High Angle Gun (capable of firing at aircraft).
L.A. Gun.	Low Angle Gun (for use against surface targets or for bombardment of shore objectives).

Chapter I

PREPARATION

How very difficult it is to see where any particular matter starts, especially when the subject is one which has filled so great a part of your life. Delving into the depths of memory, you may follow the roots of a particular experience while they change from strong growth to the minutest tendrils of memory no thicker than a hair. When I do this to myself I find I lose the thread where, as an inky schoolboy eight years of age, I first seriously considered sinking U-Boats. This was in the First World War, and my drawing of the machine by which the enemy was to be destroyed earned me a beating for defiling the pages of the geometry book which I had misused, presumably because it was the largest sheet of comparatively white paper on which I could lay my hands at the time. The infernal machine which brought me such uncomfortable consequences was nothing more than a bottle of petrol inserted, by a gentleman suitably clad in a cloak and provided with a dagger, into the pocket of the U-Boat Commander. When a lighted pipe was placed in the pocket the U-Boat blew up. Diagrammatically portrayed, this spoilt the page—I can see that now. At the time I was bitterly disappointed that what I considered an excellent idea should earn such payment.

Next I remember that an uncle by marriage, who was a real First Lieutenant of a real destroyer, was the cause of an almost continuous border of destroyers appearing round the pages of my school books. This was followed in later years by an endless stream of model destroyers, some so small that a flotilla of eight could be carried in a matchbox and others of grander proportions which really floated, and were fitted with systems of propulsion varying from elastic to electric motors.

Leaving preparatory school for public school did not reduce the destroyer output, although I had suffered a severe set-back when I was rejected for the Navy on the score of flat feet. However, unkind fate did offer a loophole. At the Wembley Exhibition there was a most realistic reproduction of the attack on Zeebrugge, and afterwards an officer climbed on the stage and gave a lecture about the work of the Royal Naval Volunteer Reserve. I decided at once that as soon as I left school I would join—flat feet or no. On return to school I refused to take the Certificate A examination in the Officers' Training Corps; told the Corps Commander that I was going to join the R.N.V.R. as soon as I left school, and firmly declared that I was not going to have any army label on me whatever.

Within a month of leaving school I was knocking at the door of the Captain's cabin in H.M.S. *Eaglet*, the drill ship of the Mersey Divison R.N.V.R. The establishment of officers was full and there were no vacancies. I went back the next month, and I called during the first week of every month from March to June 1925. By the end of that time Captain Maples was getting to know me quite well.

In those days it was extremely difficult to enter the R.N.V.R. as an officer. The applications far outnumbered the vacancies and it had become the practice, at any rate in the Mersey Division, that when a vacancy did occur the Captain would ask the gunroom officers to nominate two or three of their friends, and from these he would make the final choice. Unfortunately my family had only recently moved to the district, and I had no friends amongst the junior officers who might have helped me. However, my pertinacity was finally rewarded, and when I called in July it was to be told that there was a vacancy, and that, provided I passed the doctor, I could consider myself a Probationary Midshipman.

Such was the start of my twenty-four years' service with the R.N.V.R. By 1939 length of service and the passing of a few examinations had brought me to the rank of Lieutenant-Commander. Throughout those pre-war years I had to attend drill on at least one night every week, and preferably on both the drill nights. I had to give up firstly one month and then fourteen days of my yearly holiday to service with the Navy. But it did not seem very much to pay for the good fellowship and all the social functions we enjoyed in return; nor was it very onerous while we remained unmarried. After marriage it became for many a burden too great to be borne. Those of us who carried on after we had found ourselves a wife did so only by the grace of our ladies. To the R.N.V.R. wives who found themselves grass widows on one or two evenings a week, and who had their holidays with their husbands cut short, should go much of the credit for the efficiency of the force at the outbreak of the war.

In every generation there are ships which by some happy choice of name, by particular beauty of appearance or by some individual action, have won popular regard above that of their less fortunate sisters. Once this has been achieved they seem to gather further fame unasked. They become the crack or 'tiddly' ships of the Navy. The appointments office of the Second Sea Lord sends to these lucky ships the best officers at its disposal. The drafting depots of Portsmouth, Plymouth, or Chatham send them picked ratings. They become at once the testing ground to promotion for both officers and men. A young officer appointed to one of them would already feel a tenuous halo forming round his head. A halo which might with the passage of years become changed into a 'brass hat' and commander's rank.

I call to mind five such ships, *Queen Elizabeth*, *Warspite*, *Tiger*, *Ark Royal*, and the mightiest of all—that ship which to my eyes was the most beautiful steamship that ever man devised—the incomparable *Hood*.

I was fortunate enough to serve in two of these five. For one month as a midshipman in the *Tiger* in 1926, and for three months in the *Hood* in 1932. In those ships I saw the Navy at its very best. It was efficient yet gay, strictly bound with the panoply of age-old custom, but warm with the benevolence which only perfect discipline can afford to bestow. One day in 1945 I picked up a Navy list. Nearly all the surviving midshipmen of the *Tiger's* gunroom and all the lieutenants of *Hood's* 1932 commission were then commanders. Even allowing for the expansion of war this was a remarkable verdict on the efficiency of those two ships.

Throughout the R.N.V.R. it had been generally supposed that Gunnery was the branch in which it was most worthwhile to specialise. This had come about not only because the gun was so obviously the weapon of the Navy, but because it was the easiest weapon in which to train in a drill ship. In the *Eaglet* we had an excellent gun battery fitted with all the manually operated guns from the big 6-inch to the 4-inch breech-loading and quick-firing guns. These were controlled by a director tower which was coupled to an ingenious device for teaching officers the principles of gunnery control. Gunnery was a branch in which both officers and men could reach a high state or proficiency, in spite of the inevitable limitations of a drill ship.

To be confirmed in the rank of Lieutenant it was necessary not only to pass an examination but also to undergo a qualifying course in some specialist branch, such as Gunnery, Navigation, Signals, or Torpedo. I dare say that at the outbreak of war 97 per cent of the officers on the active list of the R.N.V.R. had qualified in Gunnery. I was one of the few exceptions.

Early in 1932 I had asked the Captain of the Mersey Division (then Captain E. Elgood, as Captain Maples had retired some years previously) for permission to take a specialist Navigator's course. He explained to me, at first kindly, and then more emphatically as he saw my obstinacy growing, that I had much better devote my time to gunnery; that the Navy would never allow a ship to be navigated by an R.N.V.R. officer; that I should end up as nothing better than a 'tanky' (navigator's assistant); that in any case I was a bloody fool; and finally that if I wanted to spend the whole of the next war correcting charts I was going the right way to do so.

However, it was rather like asking the Captain's permission to grow a beard. The request to grow 'a set' is a formality laid down to prevent the lazily unshaven from claiming that their condition is only the start of a bigger operation. The commanding officer could only note the fact, he could not really prevent its happening. I took my navigator's exam.

I have never worked so hard before or since. To everyone's surprise, no less than to my own, I passed with the percentages of 94 and 98 in the two papers. The Admiral Commanding Reserves wrote a complimentary letter to Captain Elgood and thus spiked the Captain's guns. He now had to accept that he possessed an embryo navigator in his Mersey Division. Later, as war came nearer, the Admiralty began to offer more and more exciting courses. The new twin 4 in. high angle gun was mounted in the *Eaglet*, and training was begun to ensure that R.N.V.R. gunnery officers would be mobilised with the guns' crews whom they had trained in peace time, and that they would all be sent to the same ship to take over a complete 4 in. A/A turret.

Out of the hundreds of R.N.V.R. officers only a handful had specialised in navigation, but even these were not forgotten. In 1936 the anti-submarine school at Portland required officers to act as Unit Commanders in the fleet of trawlers which would be formed from the big Icelandic and White Sea trawlers in the event of war. For each group of five trawlers one trained Group Commander and two Unit Commanders were to be provided. The Group Commanders were to be retired Navy officers, while the Unit Commanders would come from the Royal Naval Reserve and, if any chose to volunteer, from those few Volunteer Reserve officers who had specialized in navigation.

This seemed to me to be too good an opportunity to miss. Once again I went to see Elgood. Again he told me I was crazy. War would—so he said—almost certainly come, and even at this late hour I could still qualify in gunnery, and would then almost certainly become gunnery officer of a destroyer, perhaps even of a cruiser. To this I replied that I wanted to get command of an anti-submarine vessel, for I had heard that when the war construction programme got under way they would have to use the Group and Unit Commanders to provide commanding officers for the new ships.

'You'll never get command, Rayner—the Navy won't give R.N.V.R.s command of a ship, no matter how long the war lasts.'

He tried hard, but could not shake my resolution. In 1937 I took the first part of the course. I was to have completed this in the autumn of 1938, but the Munich Crisis intervened.

I received a telegram ordering me to report to Naval Officer in Charge, Kirkwall. All the other officers of the Mersey Division were going off to join the fleet, or to man ships of the Reserve Fleet. The only difference between their telegrams and mine was that mine instructed me to join 'with all despatch' whereas theirs only carried the words 'forthwith'. Now there is a subtle difference between the two. 'Forthwith' in naval language means without wasting time. The meaning of 'with all despatch' is peculiar. It is stronger than 'forthwith'.

It tells you that you must get there whatever happens. If you are in a ship and are told to 'proceed with all despatch', it allows you to take risks beyond what normal prudence might dictate. It indicates that you are expected to arrive as fast as you can; and in some measure the officer who gives such an order accepts responsibility for what follows. I explain all this because it was to have unexpected results.

On the way north I fell in with another R.N.V.R. officer, Lieutenant J. Black, also a navigator, and also bound for the same destination with a telegram worded the same as mine. We travelled together from Glasgow to Perth and on to Inverness, where we hoped to get a train northward to Thurso, in which port a fleet minesweeper was said to be lying to ferry us across to Scapa.

Arrived at Inverness we heard that Chamberlain had flown to Munich, that the last train to Thurso had already left, and that there would be no further train that night. Inverness station was a seething mass of officers and men. There was no chance of getting a bed, and very little chance of food.

Black then displayed a most competent knowledge of the railway system. He found a man who answered to the title of Controller, and having showed him our telegrams we asked him if it was quite impossible to go on northwards. He assured us that if we really wanted to go north we could do so if we took a local train to Helmsdale where a trainload of A/A ammunition was waiting. He would arrange for a carriage to be hitched to the back of the goods train, but of course it would be unheated. Even this appeared to be a better fate than Inverness at that moment and we were at least complying with instructions. Collecting a warrant officer whom we had met and who seemed likely to prove a good travelling companion, the three of us set off in the local train. In due course we steamed into the little wayside station of Helmsdale, only to find that the ammunition train had already gone on. We seemed to be in a worse mess than ever. I went to talk to the engine driver. He telephoned to some authority, and was told to take us on himself. On we went—three officers in a three-carriage train. Two of us, Black and myself, were becoming a little apprehensive, but the warrant officer was still full of cheer. However there was nothing we could do, so we waved to the children gathered at the little stations to see the 'special' go by, and bided our time. Soon it was dark, but the train rumbled on. At last it stopped. I got out and went to see the engine driver again, since wherever we were, it obviously was not Thurso. A bitter wind whipped across the open moors, and there was no shelter at all in all that waste of heather except a small brick station hut.

'I'm sorry, Sir, this is as far as I can take you. My ticket only covers the line to Wick.'

No argument, no expostulation, would make him change his mind. Here the line divided. To Wick he would take us. Nearer than this to Thurso he could not go.

We unpacked ourselves and stood shivering in the wind. A human form appeared out of the shadows of the hut.

'Somebody on the phone to speak to the senior officer of the special.'

I looked at the others.

'That's me,' I said, 'I'll answer it, and if there's trouble you two can take to the heather for the night.'

I went to the telephone.

'Hallo.'

'This is Movements Officer Thurso speaking. Is that the Senior Officer of the special?'

'Yes, Sir.'

'You've two hundred men there haven't you?'

'No, Sir.'

'What have you got?'

'One Lieutenant R.N.V.R. and one Warrant Officer.' It sounded a very inadequate cargo for a whole train.

'Good heavens, is that all?'

'Yes, Sir.'

'What's your name?'

'Rayner, Sir.'

'What, the one from Mersey Division?'

'Yes, Sir.' There was heartfelt relief in that answer. The owner of the voice obviously knew me, and had become much more friendly.

'What the hell are you doing in the middle of the night with a special train and one Lieutenant and one Warrant Officer?'

'It's a long story, Sir. . . . Who are you, Sir?'

'Crick of the *Hussar*.' I knew him of course. Only a few months before the First Minesweeping Flotilla had visited Liverpool. Lieutenant-Commander T. G. P. Crick had then been in command of H.M.S. *Hussar*.

'What are you doing as Movements Officer Thurso?' It was my turn to ask a question.

'I'm running the ferry over to Scapa—you'd better spend the night aboard, there's a bunk or two free.'

'Thank you very much, but how do I get on from here?'

'There's a little branch-line train I've got working for me. I'd already sent it down the line before I got through to you. Bring it straight back won't you?'

He sounded apprehensive.

Shortly it hove in sight, we bundled ourselves in and set off for Thurso.

'Well,' I said as we stretched ourselves out in the warm carriage, 'we may be the subject of the first court martial of the war, but at least we travel in style.'

We spent the night in warmth and peace, and decided the next morning to go by civil aircraft from Thurso to Kirkwall. We felt that it might be healthier to by-pass Scapa. It was as well that we did so, for we heard afterwards that enquiries were being made. Crick did not give us away, and no one thought of bothering about making enquiries in Kirkwall. Very soon Chamberlain flew back from Munich, and we all went home. But Crick remembered me, and when the real war had come and in 1941 he had to choose a number of corvettes for a special purpose, he chose mine.

The reason for our appointment to Kirkwall was, we discovered, concerned with establishing a contraband control base. Being navigators we were to be used as boarding officers, a prospect which filled me with gloom. I determined that as soon as possible I would complete my anti-submarine course.

As I was one of the first two officers to arrive I was given the job of billeting the men on a population willing enough to receive them, but justifiably indignant at being offered only three shillings and sixpence a day to do so. In vain I pointed out that this was a sum fixed by Government in about the year 1870 and that nobody, least of all the base Paymaster, could do anything about it. They were only silenced when I told them that by law this sum was supposed to pay for an armed man and his horse, and added that they were very lucky not to be asked to keep the horse as well.

When I got back to the *Eaglet*, Captain Elgood proceeded to point out just what a fool I was. I was the only officer who had not had an interesting appointment. He begged me to change before it was too late; but I still remained firm to my convictions, and rushed down to complete my anti-submarine training at Portland.

It was a busy winter for us in the R.N.V.R. The Admiralty had given approval to increase the strength of the division above the eleven hundred men we were allowed. Our numbers rose steadily until we had sixteen hundred men, and sometimes as many as four hundred men in uniform drilling on a single night.

The R.N.V.R. had, between the wars, and contrary to the generally accepted opinion of the public, made remarkably little impression on the yachtsmen of the nation. To join the R.N.V.R. meant giving up so much leisure that it was almost impossible to combine the two. I did so myself, but only with the greatest difficulty. Now in a last minute attempt to sweep the yachtsmen into the fold, the Admiralty created the Supplementary Reserve, or R.N.V.S.R. Many of them took a fortnight's holiday with the fleet and an attempt was made to teach them navigation and gunnery in the drill ship on nights when the R.N.V.R. was not using her. But it was not much more than a list of names. Elgood seized on me and placed me in charge of their navigational instruction, so that often I went down to the ship three nights in a week. I had already been teaching our own junior officers for the last three or four years, and therefore found this new job easy enough; but nothing short of the imminent prospect of war would have made me give up so much of my time. Now there was an urgency about our preparations that had been lacking before. Training went on apace, and when mobilization came Captain Elgood had the satisfaction of sending off more than forty officers and sixteen hundred trained men from Merseyside.

Chapter II

SO THIS IS IT

Four days before the outbreak of war I received my telegram ordering me to report to the Sparrows' Nest Trawler Base at Lowestoft, to which I was sent, in the Admiralty's polite phrase, 'for disposal' as Unit Commander of anti-submarine trawlers.

I had already packed my bags, set my affairs in order and seen to the laying up of my yacht. As I was one of the last to be mobilized I had time to get myself ready. In that I was luckier than many others.

When I joined the Sparrows' Nest there was no cause to wonder why my mobilization had been delayed. As a base it simply did not exist. Even the taxi driver at Lowestoft station did not know of it, except in its pre-war guise as a park with a pierrot show. He told me that he thought he knew of a house which the Navy had taken over and I agreed that we might as well go there to see if they knew anything about a base for His Majesty's Trawlers.

When I arrived at the house, which was in fact to be the base, I met Commander Gardiner on the doorstep. He and I were, as yet, the only staff. The Captain was due to arrive at four o'clock that afternoon, and we would receive the first draft of men on the following day. We had twenty-four hours to get the base working. I dumped my bags in the house and we walked together down the road to the tree-lined park. Passing inside the gates we came to a large concert hall. Sounds of music and singing could be heard. We went round to the stage end of the building, and came upon some of the artists sunning themselves in deck chairs and drinking coffee. Others were on the stage rehearsing. Gently but firmly we told them that there would be no show that night. We had come to take over the building.

By lunch time two more unit commanders had joined, as had the base Paymaster and his staff. Early in the afternoon lorries arrived from Chatham bringing stationery, mess tables, forms, a small working party and a few writers, stewards and cooks.

We might be getting off to a late start, but the organisation behind the Paymaster's side of the base was obviously superb, and the cases had been packed with great intelligence. The first to be unpacked contained twelve waste-paper baskets. The whole operation had been planned in that sort of detail. All we lacked in that first twenty-four hours was man power, and executive officers. Obviously someone had said, 'Oh, the trawlers will not be ready for a week or two. Those unit commanders we are sending there can turn to and run the base until their ships are ready.'

During that night and the next day a dozen or so officers and a like number of ratings working with their coats off, man for man and without distinction of rank, had created a working base out of absolutely nothing. We were dog tired, but we were ready for the first incoming draft on the evening of the second day. To my lot had fallen the key position of Drafting Officer, and I sent off the first crew to join their ship at eight o'clock on the second morning. As assistant I had Lieutenant Lord Churston, R.N.V.R. For a week we drafted crews to the minesweeping trawlers. At the end of that time the base was a flourishing concern. We had accommodated over six hundred Patrol Service ratings, had manned over eighty minesweeping trawlers, and had built enough air raid shelters from sand-filled fish boxes, commandeered from Lowestoft fishing harbour, to house our men while they were awaiting draft. They were more than usually odoriferous shelters, and their architecture was unique. It was perhaps fortunate that they were never tested.

Soon we began to hear rumours that the first anti-submarine trawlers would be ready. It took considerably longer to fit a trawler for A/S work than for minesweeping. The vessels chosen for the former purpose were the big modern 900 ton Arctic trawlers sailing mainly out of Hull, whereas the minesweeping trawlers had been drawn from the smaller Fleetwood and Grimsby boats and were 600 ton vessels. Even so there was a great difference between individual ships—an individuality that was well known to the men, a great number of whom had actually sailed in or knew intimately the ships whose names were now beginning to appear on the list of A/S trawlers which had completion dates beside them.

Lord Churston and I would have shown the character and self-denial of saints had we not taken advantage of our peculiar position. We set about collecting five good ships' companies for our own group intending, when the time was ripe, to choose our ships in the light of the knowledge we had gained from the men, and then to draft ourselves and them together. After all we had come to fight a war, not to be Drafting Officer and Assistant Drafting Officer of the Royal Naval Patrol Service Base Lowestoft. There were, we felt, plenty of officers who, for one reason or another, would be more suited to carry out those duties.

We each chose the skippers for our own ships. Fate led me to make a supremely good choice. Skipper Lang was a perfect example of the Devon trawler skipper. Although he had not often handled ships as big as the 900 ton *Loch Tulla* to which we eventually drafted ourselves, he had risen from boy to become master of a sailing trawler out of Brixham; and then, after a period in steam trawlers, he had been appointed harbour master of that port at a remarkably early age. A harbour master must have a great deal of tact; and a tactful man Lang certainly was. He could get men to work because he knew just how far they could be driven, and everyone in the ship knew that he could do any job better than they could do it themselves.

He was a first rate seaman and knew things about the way of a ship at sea which no one not trained in sail could have understood. He would have made a great sailing master in any earlier age. His tall figure, topped by a head of short and crisp grey hair, for he rarely wore a cap, could easily be visualized in trunk hose on the decks of one of the English ships which chased the Armada up-Channel, or in white breeches and blue coat on the deck of a privateer running down upon one of Napoleon's fat supply craft. He gave me an enormous store of weather lore, whose accuracy astonished me. Later it was put to very good use, when I had to decide such questions as whether to let the escorts of a convoy go on oiling or wait for better weather.

'Wind'll freshen from the south'ard before midnight, Sir.'

'How so Skipper?'

'See those gulls Sir, throwing water over their backs—sure sign of a southerly wind that Sir.'

'Thick weather or clear Skipper?' I'd ask.

'Oh thick Sir, with a mizzel of rain. Did you not notice how red was the rust on that buoy we passed a while back—blood red it was. 'Twill be thick as the Earl o' Hell's riding boots tonight.'

Probably this conversation would take place at noon in bright, clear weather with no sign of the approaching 'warm front' beloved of the meteorological men. Later as I peered with strained eyes into a driving mist that formed into drops on my eyelashes, I would remember the conversation only too plainly, as I strove to make out the dark and unlighted headland which was the northerly limit of our night patrol line.

He had a hundred more such sayings, and all equally true. They were important enough to me then with a thousand horse power in a steam kettle below me, but how much more valuable they would have been a hundred and forty years earlier!

Lang had a great mistrust of all aids to navigation, and to him even the compass was more of a convenience than a necessity. In all the twelve months we served together I never remember seeing him fix the ship's position by navigational methods. He found his way about the sea as much by instinct as by knowledge. I well remember once, when I was teasing him about this while I was fixing the ship, he said, 'But you don't really need that Sir! We are here,' and he pointed with a large and slightly spatulate finger to a particular spot on the chart. My 'fix' proved him to be as correct as made no matter. He must have had a three-legged station pointer built into his brain.

On another occasion I was a good deal worried because our compass had developed quite extraordinary errors after a depth charge attack in narrow waters. I thought this would mean having the compass re-corrected and re-swung, but Lang remarked: 'But why bother about correcting it so long as we know the error? Lor' bless you Sir, in my old trawler we used to go down-Channel nor'-nor'-west and come home nor'-nor'-east. It's just a question of knowing how wrong it is.'

We got to know each other very well indeed, for of course we had our meals together in my cabin. I thus came to know his wife as well, although I never actually met her. He was very much a family man, and all his comments on the food, which was not always as well cooked as it might have been, were delivered as from her tongue. From this I gathered an impression of a very kindly house-proud woman, and an excellent cook. How we longed for her pasties!

So Churston and I let two or three groups of trawlers go by, until at last our men gave us the green light.

'That *Loch Tulla* Sir—that's a fine ship for us Sir. Built special she was, Sir, for an Icelander—a very big man he was—and everything about her of the best—and the *Regal*, *Brontes* and *Istria*, Sir—there's three good sound ships—not as you might say extra modern Sir, but real good seaboats that any man would go fishing in. The *Davy* Sir? Never heard tell of her—reckon she's a new boat.'

Churston and I drafted ourselves. There was no lack of unit commanders waiting to step into our shoes. We fixed our own reliefs, and went to say good-bye to Commander Gardiner and the Captain. 'But you can't do that—not yet.' Apparently it had occurred to no one that two young men in our position would help themselves. But it was too late, the signal had already been made. We handed over to our grinning reliefs and left. We heard later that Lieutenant-Commander Bruford, R.N.V.R., who had taken over from me, had found a ship to his own liking within twenty-four hours. After that they got a proper Drafting Commander, and the racket closed down.

The fine weather which had set in with the start of the war still held—and mercifully so; for the conditions aboard the ships when we arrived in Birkenhead were indescribable. There were ninety-two men working on *Loch Tulla's* upper deck, and more than half of them had in their hands some tool to which either an electric cable or a high-pressure air pipe was attached. The upper deck looked as if an enormous spider, possessed of a sense of humour and slightly inebriated, had attempted to spin a gigantic camouflage net. The remaining forty-five men, carrying brushes and pots of grey paint, went solemnly round the ship, repainting wherever the tool men had blistered the previous application with their oxy-acetylene welders, or had riveted on some new fitting since last the painter had passed that way.

There had been no one to meet us; nor was there any organization to cater for our wants, which were many. If a ship had been declared ready to receive her crew on a certain day—well, she was ready and the crew must live in her. Luckily the firm of Camell Laird came to our rescue. They threw open their canteen to us and fed us for three days; then they put a large moulding loft at our disposal, and we used that as a mess deck. There were a hundred and one things to see to. Watch and quarter bills had to be drawn up so that every man would know what watch he was in, what was his action station, and in which mess he would eat and sleep. There were standing orders to write and get typed, ammunition and Naval and Victualling stores had to be embarked. And all the time these duties were interrupted by tests on gun mountings and depth charge throwers; tests on the water tightness of the asdic fittings; on the magazine flooding arrangements, and on many other of the new machines that were being put aboard. Each one of these tests must be attended by a ship's officer; and there were only two of us, Lang and myself. It is true we had a petty officer, called a 'mate', who was supposed to be a watch-keeper and more of an officer than a rating. This rank was never a success, and as soon as the Patrol Service got properly under way it was dropped and the mates were replaced by young Sub-Lieutenants. Very few of the mates had actually served as such in fishing trawlers; for the only qualification needed was the possession of a Board of Trade fishing mate's ticket. The mate of an Arctic trawler would almost certainly have had his Skipper's ticket, and could then have been a Skipper in the Patrol Service, receiving quite a useful yearly retainer through the R.N.R. grant. Ours, who looked better than most, was a sorry sight when the first days of seasickness had taken the curl out of his hair. Both Lang and I considered him quite unsuitable as a watch-keeper, and thus began our long months of 'watch and watch'.

Lying astern of us in the fitting-out dock was a big Cunard liner being converted to an Armed Merchant Cruiser. Beside her the piles of first class mattresses grew, as her passenger accommodation was ripped out and made into mess decks.

Returning one night to the ship I paused to talk to our quartermaster.

'It do seem a shame to see all they mattresses going into store where the rats will nest in 'em Sir.'

'It does that Quartermaster.'

'How would it be Sir——?'

'I'll have nothing to do with your sinful thoughts Quartermaster.' I made my way to the companion hatch that led down to my own accommodation. As I was half way down I paused:

'Quartermaster.'

'Sir?'

'You realize I shall not inspect the mess decks until after we have left Liverpool. Goodnight.'

My cabin was in the after end of the old fish hold, separated from the new mess decks by a bulkhead. For the next half hour sounds of men handling bulky and awkward bundles reached me through the thin partition, and there was a constant shuffle of feet on the deck above my head.

In the morning one corner of the pile appeared to be lower, and some of the mattresses looked very rough to have come from the staterooms of a liner. I could only imagine that the local rats had been quick to seize the opportunity to provide for their own nests.

As soon as the ships were ready we went down the Mersey River for compass swinging and gun trials. We returned to a berth in Birkenhead docks. For one night we lay in the dock which was just inside the main lock. We then received orders to go alongside a shed in another dock to embark our Naval Stores. As this was some distance away I telephoned to Flag Officer Liverpool's staff, and asked for a dock pilot. I was told that all were too busy, and that anyway trawlers were expected to find their way about without recourse to dock pilots.

We started. I thought I knew Birkenhead docks fairly well, as they were so near my own home. 'It doesn't really matter,' I had said to Lang, 'I know it well. I'll act as pilot if they won't give us one.' All we had by way of a plan of the docks was the rather small one on the chart of the Mersey. This showed a certain opening between two docks, and feeling proud of ourselves we took her towards this place with reasonable speed on her. We came round the corner of the dock to find a brick wall barring our path. The Harbour Board had decided to close this particular passage between one dock and the next. We came to a grinding stop, and *Loch Tulla* was ten feet shorter than she had been a moment before.

Fortunately she was what is known in trawler phraseology as 'a soft-nosed ship'; that is to say the real stem of the ship was the forward watertight bulkhead. The idea was that if, when fishing in the White Sea or off Bear Island she should run into pack ice, the bows would crumple rather than split. So, although we had spoilt her looks and her immediate readiness for war, we had not done any great structural damage.

We were dry-docked the next day for repairs. They took only four days to fit us with a new stem and bow plates. I had feared that the shock might have cracked the engine bearers, and such damage would have taken a long time to repair. Fortunately our soft bow had taken the jolt out of the crash, so that the only damage was to the bow itself.

During those four days I was summoned to a Board of Enquiry at the office of the Flag Officer in Charge in the Liver Building.

Addressing me the President of the Board asked:

'You are in command of H.M. Trawler *Loch Tulla*?'

'No Sir.'

He looked over his spectacles at me.

'What do you mean, "No Sir"?—of course you are.'

'No Sir. I am in charge, not in command—Skipper Lang is the commanding officer.'

'How can he be? So long as you're there, you're the senior.'

'I'm the Unit Commander Sir—in charge of the operational conduct of one unit of anti-submarine trawlers. I live in *Loch Tulla* because she is fitted as a unit commander's ship, the other trawler of my unit is not so fitted; but I can, if occasion demands, equally well go to sea in her.'

'Well, how did it happen?'

'We'd asked for a dock pilot and been refused one. We are a 900 ton ship Sir—I don't think the staff realize just how big these Arctic trawlers are; people think we are no bigger than a drifter of 120 tons. With that gun up forward and all the fishing gear out of her she is riding two foot above her normal trim forward. You've got to handle her fairly fast or her bows will blow off down-wind. As unit commander I'm entirely satisfied with Skipper Lang's conduct. It was in my opinion an accident that could hardly have been avoided once we had taken the wrong turning.' I felt that I was now no longer the prisoner in the dock, but counsel arguing a defence.

However the Paymaster Commander, who was acting as Secretary, intervened. Speaking to the President he said:

'You know I think we'll have to adjourn until we've seen the Admiral on this, the board was to be held on Lieutenant-Commander Rayner, I don't think we can switch it to Skipper Lang just like that Sir.'

'When does the Admiral get back?'

'Tomorrow night.'

'We're sailing for Portland tomorrow morning. Sir,' I informed him.

The President looked up at me and smiled. 'Aren't you lucky!' he said.

We sailed, and we never heard anything more about that episode; but for weeks I scanned the mail anxiously and looked at every buff coloured envelope to see if it had come from the Flag Officer Liverpool.

On the afternoon after the enquiry I had been down to the *Eaglet* to see Captain Elgood. He was still in command of her although she was now flying the flag of F.O.I.C. Liverpool, and was being used as a training ship for the Defensively Equipped Merchant Ships (D.E.M.S.). When a gun had been fitted to a merchantman, crews would be sent to the *Eaglet* for training in its use. The gun deck was loud with the slamming of breech mechanisms and the sharp orders of the gunnery drill, as three or more crews were put through their paces. It was all much the same as when she had been our own drill ship, less than one month ago, and yet it seemed that an age had passed during the thirteen days we had been at war.

Elgood's command was titular more than executive. His war work had been completed when the division had been mobilised; but he was a man of action, and hated the backwater into which he had fallen. But I think that illness had already laid cold fingers upon him. He was pleased to see me, and pleased that I had called, and when I bemoaned my invidious position as 'in charge but not in command' he answered me:

'Rayner, I have always told you so, but you'd never listen. The Navy cannot give command to an R.N.V.R. officer. Your experience today proves what I've always said. The discipline of the Court Martial means nothing to us. If you were dismissed the service tomorrow Elizabeth and your kids would not starve, you'd just go back to your shoreside job. Now with the R.N. it's entirely different. A severe reprimand will lose them the chance of promotion, and an R.N.R. could lose his Board of Trade certificate.'

'Oh well, it's too late to change now, and you know Sir I wouldn't anyway.'

'You always were a bloody fool,' he said as he shook my hand.

Words which were so typical of the man's sincerity. Although he always succeeded in conveying just what he meant, his thoughts were never as fierce as the words that clothed them. He had been a good master to serve, so long as one stood up to meet him sure of one's own ground. The training he gave me in dealing with senior officers was to prove most useful to me when, in later days, I was serving under Admiral Sir Max Horton in the Western Approaches; for the two men were singularly alike. Alas they were the last words I ever heard Elgood speak.

Chapter III

LOCH TULLA AND SENIOR OFFICER 14TH ANTI-SUBMARINE GROUP

As the rest of the group had gone ahead while we were having the new stem fitted, we sailed alone from Liverpool to Portland. The plan had been that we should go there for a week or so to 'work up' and receive a final training before going on to our war stations. However, after the *Athenia* sinking, Mr. Churchill, speaking as First Lord, had promised the country that eighty anti-submarine vessels would be on their stations within a fortnight. The rush that followed killed the 'work up' plan. We arrived at Portland at 5 p.m. one night and sailed at noon the next day—a certified operational anti-submarine vessel.

Because his ship had developed some defect and remained behind, our own senior officer was not present. It therefore fell to *Loch Tulla* to lead the 14th Anti-Submarine Group through the breakwaters of Portland harbour. From the yardarm fluttered a string of flags, new and brilliant in the bright sun. 'Order one, George ten,' form line ahead, speed ten knots. It was the first order I had ever made to a group of ships, and I was proud of myself and my command. As the three ships took up their stations astern of me, perhaps a little uncertainly, I leant over the after end of the bridge and watched. Astern of me *Istria* was shuffling into station, her high bow slicing the short channel seas, astern of her was *Regal* with Churston as unit commander leading the second division of the group. The last ship in the line was the unknown quantity *Davy*.

Loch Tulla was unique amongst trawlers. If I was to say that she was the most handsome trawler ever built the commanding officers of all the other trawlers would rise up and tear me limb from limb. Let us leave it that she was different. She had been specially built for an unusual man. *Regal*, *Istria* and *Brontes* were as much alike as three pins. It was not until they developed little idiosyncracies of their own under their new commanding officers that you could tell them apart at a distance of a mile. The *Davy* again was different. As we had guessed she was a new ship taken fresh from the builders. Looking at her one had the impression that her designer had tried to do something special, but the arrow of his thought seemed to have missed the target. To a seaman it did not appear that the bow matched the stern. Somehow or other the lines of her hull did not flow evenly along the length of her. As a ship she had a lean and hungry look; and she was to prove light-headed and irresponsible. This is not to belittle the officers and men who manned her. Her commanding officer, Skipper Mackintosh, was as good in his way as my own Skipper Lang. Mackintosh came from the Moray Firth. His men were always both smart and happy, and he ran an excellent ship. But I know the *Davy* nearly drove him to despair. She was a nightmare to take alongside. Without warning her high thin bow would suddenly blow down-wind, and there was nothing for it but to go astern and try again. Although she had two foot more freeboard forward than any other ship in the group, she was the wettest sea boat of the five; and in a steep head sea such as often fell to her lot on patrol in the Pentland Firth with wind against tide, she would take fantastic quantities of water over her bow. As befitted one who came from the north-east coast Mackintosh was a good Presbyterian. He was never heard to swear aloud, but the *Davy* must have tried his patience hard.

The 14th Anti-Submarine Group was bound for Rosyth, where we would be used to patrol the entrance to the Firth of Forth. Our one evening at Portland had been a hectic one. The camber where the anti-submarine trawlers lay was crowded with ships, moored four and five deep. Most of the group and unit commanders knew each other, and we were all eager to find out where our friends were going. The groups were bound to so many ports; patrol groups to Alexandria, Malta, Gibraltar, Rosyth, Portsmouth, Plymouth, Liverpool, Belfast and the Clyde; groups specially selected for coastal convoy work to Harwich, Rosyth and Plymouth. We might have picked anything out of the hat.

We rounded the North Foreland as it was getting dark, threaded our way through the maze of swept channels and sandbanks which marks the entrance to the great port of London, and hurried on northward. The fine weather which had lasted since the day war was declared had gone with the sun, and a stiff easterly gale was rising. About ten o'clock that night one of the pins holding the compass bowl in the wheelhouse worked itself loose, and could not be found. Without a steering compass I could not lead the group up the narrow war channel, so I sent Churston on ahead, but it proved impossible to follow the last ship in the line with no compass for the quartermaster to steer by, so I hove to until dawn.

When dawn came we found the missing pin on the wheelhouse floor, and I was able to refit it to the compass. The steering compass was the original one which had been in the ship before conversion. It was a merchant service pattern, and not a proper Admiralty fitting like the new binnacle on the upper bridge, which had been built above the wheelhouse when she was converted to a warship.

When we had mended ourselves we hurried on northward alone, passing the Humber as night fell. The previous night's wind had eased considerably. The sea was littered with the lights of fishing vessels, and this gave us an idea. Why be a darkened shape, and so an obvious war vessel when if we had lights and looked like a fisherman we would actually be less conspicuous? There was always the possibility of a U-Boat. We switched on our navigation lights. An hour later the asdic operator reported a strong echo bearing north seventy degrees west, at a range of one thousand yards.

Looking along the bearing I could see no surface vessel. I rang down for dead slow on the engines and went into the asdic hut. It was true enough—it was just such an echo as a U-Boat might be expected to give. While I was considering the matter, I wearing one pair of headphones and the operator the other, we both heard a very definite clanging noise followed by the steady beat of engines. The propeller noise stopped, and shortly afterwards there came another distinct clap. I went to action stations, and *Loch Tulla* ran in at full speed to fire her first pattern of depth charges.

We circled round afterwards. There was a strong smell of

oil, a piece of grey painted wood floated in the water disturbed by the explosion of our charges. With the knowledge we then had it looked pretty conclusive. Later in the war we would have known better. It could have been a minelaying U-Boat and we could have killed it, but in those early days we did not realize just how close a depth charge must be to a U-Boat to cause lethal damage. We heard later that when two mine-sweeping trawlers were sent to investigate the area one was herself mined, which was an indication but not a proof that we had attacked our first enemy.

The next morning we arrived at Rosyth. I had to go ashore and report. The rest of the group were already on patrol, and before nightfall—so were we. There was, we soon found, to be absolutely no rest, no let-up at all, for the next six months.

Long lines of ships in convoy wound their way up the east coast. Destroyers of the east coast escort force fussed round them. One or two anti-submarine trawlers would be there, and we cast envious glances at them. At least they went from one port to another, whereas we flogged the same bit of sea, day in and day out. We began to feel the boredom of war. So it was not going to be all fun, and action was going to be a rarity. Were we not the Patrol Service? Patrol, patrol, and more patrol. Up and down the line. Ping, ping, ping on the asdic for days without number, until you knew every aspect of the coast bordering your beat. In fog it had peered at you dimly, and sometimes unexpectedly close. At night it would recede until you longed to catch a glimpse of landmarks which by day you hated because of their familiarity.

We were not left long at Rosyth, which had appeared to be a friendly base with the enchantment of the city of Edinburgh within reach—if ever we should be so lucky as to have a night ashore. Urgent orders sent us hurrying northwards. Captain Prien had taken his U-Boat into Scapa Flow, and had there torpedoed the battleship *Royal Oak*. There was then no anti-submarine group defending Scapa. It is not for me to question the decisions of authority. It is always unwise for junior officers to do so, because they cannot know all the facts on which decisions are made. Perhaps there were not enough groups to go round, possibly the protection of a hundred merchantmen in the Firth of Forth was considered more important than that of Scapa Flow. Such a one as I should make no comment.

I was on patrol when our sailing signal came. *Loch Tulla*, *Istria*, *Regal* and *Davy* met and formed up. For the first time for a week we had all been in sight of one another. Already we were becoming a team, and we felt a warmer glow when a dark blur answered our signal lamp and we knew that it was one of our own group. We arrived off the eastern entrance to the Pentland Firth about four in the morning, and settled down to patrol until we could enter by daylight. As dawn came we sighted another anti-submarine trawler coming up from the south. It was our group commander in *Brontes*. He led the group into Scapa, and at once developed another defect.

The truth had best be told. Our group commander was a man who I am sure was as brave as a lion, but his health was simply not strong enough for war in a trawler. He would spend long hours brewing and drinking some herbal tea in his cabin, and it seemed almost impossible to winkle H.M.T. *Brontes* from her anchorage. It was hardly a week before he was invalided south, and the mantle of senior officer 14th Anti-Submarine Group fell upon me.

To patrol the approaches to the windswept and tidebound fleet anchorage of Scapa Flow was one of the most difficult and arduous tasks that could have fallen to any group. On the few days when there was no gale there was fog; and always there was a sluicing tide running first one way and then the other through the rock-encumbered Pentland Firth at eight knots. When the wind was against the tide the sea was indescribable; and when the wind and the tide were going the same way together it was almost impossible to make headway against their combined onslaught. We were not encouraged to ask for the shore lights except in an emergency, and it became a point of honour not to do so. As a matter of fact I do not remember any of the group ever asking for the lights.

The conditions of work were arduous in the extreme. With five ships I had to keep three patrol lines manned; and the two ships off duty were expected to anchor in strategic places within the Flow as a further guard against any U-Boat which got through the outer patrols, evaded the booms across the entrances, or was not noticed by the 'loops'. These last were electric cables laid on the sea bed which, connected to a galvanometer ashore, would detect the passage of any large metal object. With all these defences it might seem a little unnecessary to anchor anti-submarine vessels inside, but the truth was that half were still only in an embryo state.

To anchor the trawlers inside at instant readiness for steam was just as arduous as being on patrol. With the high windage forward caused by their being out of trim, and the extra windage of the 4-inch gun and its platform, they would have ridden to anchor very badly indeed even if the bottom had been good holding ground—which it was not. They were only too liable to drag their anchors, and a constant watch both on deck and in the engine-room had to be maintained. All of us preferred the days of patrol to the days at anchor, probably because the ship herself seemed to feel happier steaming into the sea than when yawing and snubbing at her cable.

Fresh food was almost unobtainable. There was no leave for the ship's company, and nowhere to go if there had been. Later Lyness was to become a great base with canteens for the men, 'Ensa' parties, and surfaced roads. When we arrived it comprised only a few first-war huts in a poor state of repair, an old seaplane hanger, and miles of unsurfaced road. My first call on Admiral French, Admiral Commanding Orkneys and Shetlands, was to find him in a hut which was strangely reminiscent of a potting shed, or even of one of those other sheds which used to stand in farmhouse gardens before interior sanitation became common. The Admiral and his staff were supposed to be accommodated in H.M.S. *Iron Duke*; but a German aircraft had seriously damaged her, and she was now beached off Lyness and barely usable even as a home. Later she was raised and taken round to Long Hope where, beached again, she became a houseboat for the auxiliary patrol craft.

From October 1939 to January 1940 with five vessels I kept the same patrols for which in the following winter fifteen ships were used. Of the first hundred days at Scapa I spent ninety-six on patrol. Only on four occasions did we have a night lying at anchor doing nothing. When we were out, Lang and I were watch and watch. Four hours for me, four hours for him. He who was off watch in the morning must work the hands. When I was not on watch in the afternoon I must do the paper work for the group. When we were in harbour for an hour or two for coal or water I would have to go by boat to see the Admiral, the Chief of Staff, or Commander J. M. ('Lampy') Heath in the defence office. I slept either from eight at night until midnight and from four o'clock in the morning until seven, or from midnight to four in the morning and took my chance whether I could get some sleep in the forenoon or not. The group never missed a patrol. I don't know how the men stood it. The devotion to duty of the seaman can be quite incredible. On the whole, morale was excellent. I only saw it crack once, and then for so short a time, and the mend was so good, that I could hardly believe it had happened.

Because one of the ships had developed a defect and we were out of step with our routine, we had had a particularly vile patrol—four days at the western end of the Pentland Firth instead of our usual two days on that hated patrol line. We entered harbour just as it was getting dark, the ship short of coal and the men short of rest. One hundred days and only four nights' peace. We were just slipping into Long Hope to anchor when Flotta signal tower called us, 'Coal from *Hekla* in Gutta Sound and be prepared to escort S.S. —— to Loch Ewe. Sailing orders will be sent.'

We turned round and went to Gutta Sound. Lang berthed her alongside the dusty collier. Even as we tied up I sensed the men were grumbling. It was not that anyone said anything. It was just the way they threw the heaving lines. I always think that you can tell the morale of a ship's company from the way heaving lines are thrown. Heaving lines smartly thrown, and another ready at once to back it up if the first one falls short, then all is well. Heaving lines slackly thrown, in a 'take it or leave it' fashion—there is something wrong. There was something wrong with us. Lang went down to his cabin below the bridge as the first grab-load of coal descended on our deck. I went to my cabin below the forward deck. The men were standing round looking at the coal—just looking. The coaling shovels were stacked along the ship's side. No one moved to take them up. I looked at the men, I knew I had trouble on my hands.

I had to think quickly. I felt no anger towards the men. They were all fishermen, born and bred under trade union rules and regulations. Any leader of the Seaman's Union would have had a fit if he had served a month in any ship of the group—let alone one hundred days.

We were in sight of Flotta signal station, in sight also of two or three fleet destroyers. I had only to send a signal asking for an armed guard, and arrest the whole ship's company. But what purpose would that serve? To put my ship out of action for want of a crew? Surely that was not the way. I went into Lang's cabin.

'Sorry, Skipper, to turn you out, but the men won't handle the coal. Will you come and give me a hand? We'll start in, and my bet is that they'll join in too. Don't say anything—just take a shovel and pretend nothing has happened.'

Tired as he was he rose at once, heaving his long legs from the bunk in which he had already fallen fast asleep; for in those days to lie down was to go out like a lamp.

We each took a shovel and started. The men watched us. We were not working alone for long. First to come was a foul-mouthed red-headed little stoker. His exact words cannot be written, but they were to the effect that something very unnatural could happen to himself before he would let a couple of brass-bound Don Juans do his work for him. Five minutes later the storm in the teacup was over, and coaling was going with its normal swing.

In that instant of time when I had decided to deal with the matter in my own way I had climbed a further step up the ladder towards maturity. Now I felt that if I had the chance I could command a ship, because I would never again have any fear of men.

Clothing too was a great trouble. The men had come to war with only their uniform. There were no 'comforts' yet for Scapa, or at least not on an adequate scale. My mother, in London, had tapped a source of stockings and sweaters; but when these arrived we found they were so badly knitted as to be almost unwearable. A tiny foot, into which no seaman could force more than his toes, would be topped by a long leg that could have reached to his armpits. Two men could insert themselves into one sweater, or alternatively the garment clung to one like a corset.

By comparison my wife's aunts, of which she seemed to have an inexhaustible supply, sent us some beautiful garments; but they could not get enough wool. One night when we were lying anchored inside the gate I took all our useless garments down to the messdeck and set the whole ship's company to unravelling wool. Twenty-eight men unravelling twenty-eight garments. Quickly the number of balls of wool mounted. 'The aunts' were set up in wool for months. Soon well shaped sweaters and stockings began to arrive in a steady stream from their active needles. The *Loch Tulla's* men were at last warm, and we could spare some for the rest of the group.

Life in an anti-submarine trawler was not of course always one long fight with the weather and the patrol lines. There is always, in any ship's company, the man who can raise a laugh however bad the conditions; and we had a first class crowd. We laughed a lot, and on the messdecks they sang a lot. Someone had a banjo, and someone a mouth organ and everyone had a voice.

I was most sorry for the signalman. He was a nice lad from the London Division R.N.V.R., for they had no signalmen in the Patrol Service. In private life he was clerk in a London office. On each and every night of his working life he had taken the public transport to his home along brightly lit streets. His first view of Scapa depressed him enormously.

'Oh Sir—no trams—not even a lamp-post,' he had said when I asked him what he thought of our new base.

He was quite a good signalman, but absolutely unable to recognize one ship from another even after some weeks at sea during which he had often seen units of the fleet coming and going on their way through the Pentland Firth. Anything that was grey and floated was a ship, and might be the one to which he was supposed to be sending a signal. All he wanted was the answering flash of light at the end of each word, and he was quite happy.

On one occasion when the group had been hurriedly assembled from their patrol lines in order to hunt the area where a U-Boat had been reported, I told him to make a signal to the *Brontes*:

'You really must keep better station.' I had my head in the chart table as I was plotting our search scheme, and realized suddenly that he was passing the signal to some ship on the starboard side whereas *Brontes*, however badly out of station, should have been somewhere on the port side. Hastily raising my head I saw with horror that my signal had been passed to a 'Town' class (10,000 ton) cruiser which was rapidly coming up over the horizon.

'And what sort of reply do you expect from that?' I asked.

It came 'Your signal not understood.' In the circumstances I considered it remarkably lenient. I made back.

'Sorry. Case of mistaken identity. My signalman cannot distinguish an acorn from an oak tree.'

On another occasion when patrolling off Hoy Sound in a dense fog, a fleet destroyer showed suddenly through the mist.

'Quick' I said to the signalman, 'make to him—"can you tell me where I am?"'

He took up the lamp and passed the signal. Almost at once I could see the reply coming back from the destroyer which was already disappearing from view in the fog. I spelt it out for myself. 'Regret-have-not-known-you-long-enough-to-venture-an-opinion.'

'That's a very curious reply. What on earth did you make to him?'

It turned out that the signalman had made 'can you tell me *what* I am?' Their signal made sense even if it did not help me much.

In some measure we solved the food problem by indenting for a 'harness' cask. I cannot remember in what book I discovered that ships on certain stations where fresh meat was not available could demand such a thing from the Naval Stores. It is a large butt of teak or oak, in which meat can be salted down with common salt and saltpetre. This seemed to be an excellent idea for us so I went to the Paymaster Commander at Lyness Base.

'Please Sir, I want a harness cask.'

'Good God, I don't suppose anyone's asked for a harness cask since the last sailing ship went out of commission.'

'Well there's no harm in just trying Sir.'

What a wonderful organization the Navy is, and particularly the Naval Stores Department! Within a month *Loch Tulla's* harness cask arrived, and enough saltpetre to last us for years. Thereafter we could salt down a week's supply of fresh meat, when we could get it. All it meant at that time was that we could take in all the meat we could get without fear of it going bad.

Christmas 1939 looked as if it was going to be a particularly lean time. We had our Christmas dinner at anchor inside Hoxa gate. Much to my surprise I heard that we had been successful in getting some liver, and when I went down to the decorated messdecks I was amazed to find heaped plates of liver and bacon. I was even more surprised when my steward brought down liver and bacon for breakfast the following morning, instead of the usual bacon and elongated tinned tomato which was our normal breakfast dish. When liver again appeared on the menu at lunch time I said to Lang that we really must investigate the origin of all this liver. It seemed unlikely that honest means had been used to acquire what must have amounted to a couple of hundredweight of a delicacy which our wives told us was no longer part of the body of any animal used for food.

As I feared we were receivers of stolen goods. It transpired that a working party from a battleship had been sent to Lyness base to collect three wicker 'skips' full of liver for the twelve hundred odd men of her company. The jetty at Lyness was made of large planks, with a good two inches between one plank and the next. The battleship's party had put down the skips just above the place where *Loch Tulla's* boat lay waiting for her supply party, who had gone ashore to draw our usual bully beef. It was more than human nature could stand, particularly when it had sharp knives. Holes had been cut in the wickerwork placed so temptingly above the heads of the boat's crew, and the succulent meat was abstracted until only a thin layer covered the bottom of each skip.

Although we had many alarms no alleged sighting of a U-Boat was confirmed. Perhaps they considered the area too unhealthy, or perhaps some of our supposed contacts really were U-Boats and they escaped us, having at any rate learnt that we were on the look-out for them. It had always intrigued

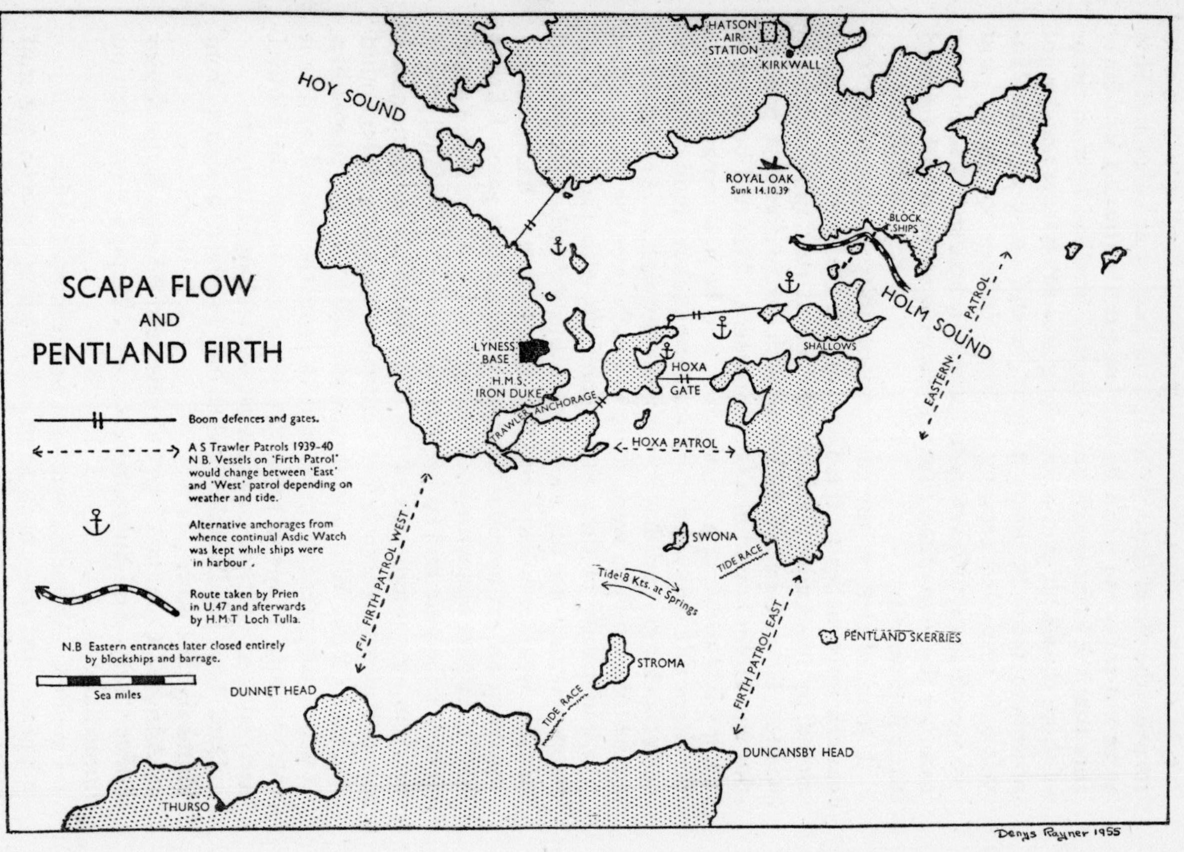
SCAPA FLOW
AND
PENTLAND FIRTH
Boom defences and gates.
A S Trawler Patrols 1939-40
N.B. Vessels on 'Firth Patrol' would change between 'East' and 'West' patrol depending on weather and tide.
Alternative anchorages from whence continual Asdic Watch was kept while ships were in harbour.
Route taken by Prien in U.47 and afterwards by H.M.T Loch Tulla.
N.B Eastern entrances later closed entirely by blockships and barrage.
Sea miles
HOY SOUND
HATSON AIR STATION
KIRKWALL
ROYAL OAK Sunk 14.10.39
BLOCK SHIPS
HOLM SOUND
EASTERN PATROL
SHALLOWS
LYNESS BASE
H.M.S. IRON DUKE
TRAWLER ANCHORAGE
HOXA GATE
HOXA PATROL
SWONA
TIDE RACE
Tide 8 Kts. at Springs
FIRTH PATROL WEST
FIRTH PATROL EAST
PENTLAND SKERRIES
STROMA
TIDE RACE
DUNNET HEAD
DUNCANSBY HEAD
THURSO
Denys Rayner 1955

me to discover how Prien did get his U-Boat into Scapa to torpedo the *Royal Oak*. Although the booms at Hoxa and Hoy were not complete when he carried out his attack I was fairly sure that the loops would have detected him had he used either of those routes. If ever a patrolling anti-submarine trawler got anywhere near the loops a signal would come at once 'Investigate suspected crossing on loop Number so and so' and we would have to investigate ourselves, and spend some time assuring the loop officers that it was only we who had agitated their instruments.

I took, therefore, an early opportunity of inspecting the eastern approaches to the Flow, which had supposedly been closed by blockships. I had with me at that time an article written by a German Admiral which describes his passage through Holm Sound in a German yacht. This had been quite a big yacht drawing a lot of water, and he had remarked that the fierce tide had worn a deep water channel round one end of each blockship; and that if you went through, as he had done, against the tide you were going so slowly over the ground that you had plenty of time to go carefully with the lead. It so happened that on the morning of the day when I first had suitable weather to explore these approaches, I had been involved in an acrimonious discussion with Hoxa gate. I forget now the rights and wrongs of the matter, but I was in the mood to damn the gate and its keepers to eternity. The flood would be running strongly out of the Flow in the afternoon, and I decided about an hour before high water to go into Holm Sound and take a look. With a leadsman sounding we went in steadily. It was so easy, that as it was time to leave this patrol, and as it was our turn to spend the night at anchor inside the Flow, I decided to go in that way instead of tackling Hoxa gate.

Dark had hardly fallen when we received a signal from Flotta signal tower.

'Admiral Commanding Orkneys and Shetlands to Senior Officer 14th Anti-Submarine Group. Report your position immediately.'

I replied, 'At anchor one mile north Hoxa Gate.'

There must have been some telephoning between the staff office and the boom gate for it was an hour before the next signal came.

'By what route did you enter?'

'By Holm Sound.'

'My barge is being sent for you.'

It may have been a crazy thing to do, but I was convinced it was the way Prien took. We were just about the same length as a U-Boat and drew the same amount of water. *Loch Tulla* could be expected to steer more easily, and we had daylight. Prien of course did it at night, and with enemy territory all round him.

Needless to say this escapade caused something of a sensation. It may have hastened the proper blocking of the eastern approach, because very shortly afterwards the channel was completely blocked. At any rate I did not receive quite the dressing-down I had expected.

Much to my surprise I found myself included in the first honours list of the war, but had no idea for what reason the D.S.C. had been given to me. I would like to have thought it was for our action south of Flamborough Head on our way north, and perhaps at the time I did think so. Later experience was to prove how very difficult it was to destroy a modern U-Boat. There can be no doubt that we in the anti-submarine branch had not made sufficient allowance for the advances in the technique of welded construction. The pressure hull of a U-Boat was believed to be far weaker than in fact it was. We had thought that a well carried out attack by an anti-submarine vessel in coastal waters would certainly effect a kill. At first it had been estimated that a depth charge exploding twenty yards from a submarine's hull would kill it. Later experience was to prove that this distance should be very much reduced.

But whatever may have been Their Lordships' reason for decorating me, nothing that I had done would have been possible without the willing co-operation of the men. The temperament of the men was peculiar. They were all volunteers and so showed to the full that typically British willingness to endure, no matter what hardships, so long as they felt they were doing so of their own free will. Once conscription is introduced much, if not all of this valuable quality is inevitably lost. The men were drawn entirely from the fishing fleets, and already their old comrades were earning very large sums of money for the food they gathered for the nation. By and large the fishermen who stayed at home were not working so hard as the men in H.M. Trawlers. Their innate morale could be placed on the credit side of the ledger, but on the debit side was a most curious refusal to service the ships properly. Until I realized the basic reason for this it caused me considerable worry. I discovered that this apparent reluctance to take care of weapons and engines on which their lives might at any moment depend, was the result of the custom by which the crew of a fishing vessel left their ship the moment she docked, and only rejoined her when she was in the sea-lock ready to sail on her next fishing trip. During her time in harbour the ship would be taken over by a gang of men known by the delightful name of 'ships'-husbandmen', and they would go over her completely, refitting and renewing where necessary. The fishermen were, therefore, quite unused to servicing anything, and their natural inclination, when machinery became out of order, was to leave it to the shore staff to put right. Unfortunately for them there was practically no base staff available in those early months, and our only hope of repairing machinery lay in the workshops of Messrs. Cox and Danks, who had been salvaging the German warships scuttled after World War One. In keeping the patrols going my greatest difficulty had been to teach the ships to be self reliant. There were of course some technical matters which were beyond our own immediate control—in particular the asdic machines. But at Scapa we were blessed with a most hardworking anti-submarine officer, Lieutenant M. F. Isaac, R.N., who slaved without respite to keep our asdics going. It was nothing for him to arrive alongside in a motor boat at two o'clock in the morning, when we were at anchor six miles from the base. Such men have an influence far beyond the scope of their own work. If we were important enough for him to come out on a vile night across the Flow to service our asdic, then encouragement is given to the whole ship's company—for the men are no fools. The gunnery ratings will start to keep their guns just that much cleaner, and the engineers will see that their engines receive the little extra attention which prevents a breakdown. The efficiency of a ship, or of a group is extremely sensitive to the attention of the base staff. Throughout the war I was always to admire the unselfish, and so often unthanked, efforts of those who, living ashore and often in much worse conditions than ours, yet managed to keep our ships fit for sea. To us fell the thrill of action, and the feeling that what we did was of real use; to them the long hours struggling with defective electrical circuits while others slept.

By the middle of January 1940 we were getting some relief from the wretched watch at anchor within the gates. The *Iron Duke* had been converted into a base ship for the auxiliary patrol, which was composed of small drifters, officered often by the R.N.V.S.R., and manned by 'hostilities only' ratings. The drifters were equipped with an immature asdic, and were employed to steam back and forth within the booms. They intrepidly strapped a couple of depth charges to their sterns, and we often wondered what would happen if they ever had to fire one. Commander C. A. R. Shillington of the Belfast Division R.N.V.R. was their Godmother, and he reigned benevolently over their comings and goings from the one-time Captain's cabin in the *Iron Duke*.

Their arrival released us to perform our proper duties and now, when off patrol, we could look forward to an escort job. Unbounded was our joy when we could actually steam for more than six miles in a straight line, after months of constantly retracing our steps. One of our favourite jobs was to escort the Trinity House ship round the outlying lighthouses, and it was on one of these trips that *Loch Tulla* came across and attacked what was almost certainly a U-Boat, although the staff ashore were inclined to suggest it was a whale. However, it had broken surface half way between ourselves and the Trinity House vessel, and was clearly seen by both ships to be on her side. Unfortunately an asdic defect prevented our continuing the attack, and by the time we had mended ourselves she could no longer be found.

To this period too belongs a hunt for a reported U-Boat when an extremely ill-matched pair of ships were ordered to investigate an aircraft sighting to the west of Hoy Sound. H.M.S. *Kelly* (Captain Lord Louis Mountbatten) and H.M. Trawler *Loch Tulla* were sent off together, presumably because we were the only two asdic-fitted ships available. Of course we found nothing, for the scent was more than a little cold when we got to the position. Then, as always until we learnt to develop proper air to surface vessel co-operation, the delay between an aircraft sighting and the arrival of the ships was so great that the chances of the latter obtaining contact were absolutely negligible. In this particular case no less than twenty-four hours had elapsed.

Let us consider the case of a U-Boat observed by aircraft to be in position X. We will, for the moment, overlook the fact that the aircraft, because of its relatively poor navigational facilities and its high speed, might have been anything up to ten miles wrong in its estimate of the geographical position. Even if it had reported the position correctly it is certain that the U-Boat, knowing himself observed, would move on at about four knots, so long as he was kept submerged by further aircraft patrols. Of course if the U-Boat was allowed to surface during darkness and get away using his diesel engines the position at once became hopeless. Assuming, however, that he could be kept down and that the hunting ships arrived one hour after the sighting report, then it was necessary to sweep fifty square miles of sea surrounding the sighting position. An hour later the area had increased to two hundred square miles; and two hours later the area was over eight hundred square miles. It will be seen therefore that theoretically it was almost useless to go to a sighting report unless you could arrive within an hour or two. In one hour a group of anti-submarine trawlers could sweep an area ten miles long and eight miles wide, but almost at once the zone to be investigated started to increase faster than they could search. Fortunately practice was rather more in favour of the hunting craft than theory. In coastal waters the land would often cut down the space to be searched, or there would be definite arcs of the circle which could be put outside the 'probability area'. After all the U-Boat was not merely engaged in avoiding the hunting craft. He was there for his own nefarious purposes, and could be expected to hang around convoy routes or, if sighted on passage to or from his operational area, it could be assumed that he would continue on his outward or homeward course. Even so, to go a-hunting twenty-four hours late was little more than a gesture of defiance. It was extremely unlikely to find the enemy. Successes were rare until later in the war when air and sea forces were put under joint operational control, and the aircraft which sighted the U-Boat had been provided with equipment to enable it to circle the position, and 'home' to it the ships of the escort group.

However, there was certainly a U-Boat nosing its way round Scapa Flow during the second week of January 1940, for the night before our search with the *Kelly* he had been over one of the outlying loops, and a day or two previously *Davy* had attacked a suspected contact to the eastward of the islands. By the time *Kelly* gave up our particular search and made the signal 'proceed independently', I had been without sleep for seventy hours. This experience interested me a good deal, because I found the period from twenty-four to thirty-six hours by far the worst. Thereafter I had felt peculiarly well, and quite recovered the competence which I had almost lost in the bad period.

Returning to Scapa we berthed alongside *Kelly* and I was invited by Lord Louis to dinner. Better even than that was the fact that Lang was also invited. For me it was a fairly common occurrence to be asked aboard a destroyer for a bath, dinner, or drinks, or for all three. *Kelly's* captain was the first to ask my skipper as well. Lang made his excuses, but he was terribly pleased none the less.

In February it was arranged that the group should go, one at a time, to Aberdeen to have 'de-gaussing' fitted as a protection against the magnetic mine. Fortunately when the first berth fell vacant, I took *Loch Tulla* down and went on to attend the first investiture of the war in Buckingham Palace. I was the only R.N.V.R. there, and so the last naval officer in the line. When it came to my turn His Majesty said conversationally, 'I'm so pleased to see one of you here today.' I was so surprised that I muffed my going astern and turn to starboard, so that the very senior Army officer who was behind me had to do a quick shuffle to avoid a collision.

In London I had two nights with my wife and then went back to Aberdeen to take *Loch Tulla* north once more.

One ship constantly away, meant more work for the remaining four, and by mid-March 1940 all the officers were in danger of going 'round the bend'. At the end of the month I went to see the doctor because I was having difficulty in seeing lights at night, and even such well known objects as the buoys on the booms appeared to be double. I was given three weeks' sick leave, and a junior watchkeeper was provided to help Lang with *Loch Tulla*.

Arrived home, my own doctor took one look at me and put me to sleep with tablets for three consecutive days. Two days later my father-in-law returned from London with the news that there would almost certainly be trouble in Norway. I could not let my ships be taken into action by anyone else, so hurried back after only one week's leave. As I went north Hitler's legions went to Norway. I had sent a telegram to Lang telling him by hook or by crook to get *Loch Tulla* on the western patrol, and to have a boat in Thurso harbour to meet me. I had no intention of going near Lyness base in case someone should prevent my going aboard. My plan worked smoothly. As the rest of the officers and ratings hurried aboard the Scapa ferry, I stepped into *Loch Tulla's* seaboat and was rowed off to my ship. There I sent a signal to A.C.O.S., 'Have resumed command of my group'. I don't suppose anyone cared a tuppenny damn what I was up to. They were all far too busy.

Groups of anti-submarine trawlers were coming in every day, fuelling and going on to Norway. We were desperate with envy. We badgered all and sundry to be allowed to go too, but we were kept just where we were.

A month later they were coming back—what was left of them. By ones and twos they came through, paused to off-load the most curious assortment of army gear salvaged from the wreck, and went on southward. I spoke to many whom I knew. They all told the same tale. Airpower had defeated them—not the weather, not Hitler's surface forces—just air-power. They had learnt a thing or two about the German air-men. They were deadly—if you did nothing. They had no fear of the Lewis guns which were all the anti-aircraft defence we carried; but they would not stand a 4-inch gun. It did not matter that it was only a low-angle gun. The Hun could not know that fact for certain. So long as it was pointing in the right general direction and went off with a satisfactory puff of smoke, he would go away to bother some less excitable target. These officers also told me that in order to survive they had found it necessary to abrogate the age-old custom whereby fire was held until the Commanding Officer gave the order. They told me that things happened far too quickly, with German aircraft coming suddenly out of the clouds. Guns' crews must be allowed the initiative to open fire as soon as an aircraft was identified as hostile. What I learnt convinced me of the wisdom of their decisions. I at once issued orders that any aircraft that was obviously hostile could be engaged without waiting for an order from me. I continued this practice in every ship which I afterwards commanded. On three occasions in later years my ship was saved by this order. On no occasion was it abused.

Norway saw the end of the group commander and unit commander system. It had functioned well enough when we had more men than ships. It was wasteful of men capable of command. A group of five ships would have one group commander and two unit commanders in addition to the five Commanding Officers. Three officers capable of command were spare numbers. As soon as the new ships started to come along, the group and unit commanders R.N.R. were taken to command the new corvettes. Large numbers of war-trained officers were coming forward. A junior officer arrived for each of the trawlers. The old 'watch-and-watch' life was over. We should now be in three watches. The break-up of the old groups enabled reinforcements to be sent to those still functioning as groups. We received two ships, and were promised two more for July, and another group of five for the next winter. At the same time there was a definite shift of emphasis in anti-submarine tactics. So far we had patrolled the approaches to ports. Now the loops, booms, and auxiliary patrols had made the ports safe, and the emphasis slowly but surely shifted to escort work; for where would we be more likely to find a U-boat than round a convoy? The convoy was at once our charge and our bait.

Now that the group consisted of seven ships, several of which were bound to be always at sea, I could not look after them all properly if I stayed in *Loch Tulla*. Gradually I was squeezed out of the ship. I had a small group office in the new depot ship *Dunluce Castle*. I was given a seat in the Extended Defence Office (X.D.O.) ashore at Lyness, and I had a staff title of Staff

Officer Anti-U-Boats. It was arranged that in the event of a hunt developing I should go to sea in whichever of the group happened to be the emergency ship at the time. Dunkirk came and went without causing any difference to our routine. In July the other group arrived with Lieutenant-Commander I. J. Tyson, R.N.R., in command. Although he was senior to me, by virtue of my staff title, I still continued to operate the patrols. There was now no need for me ever to go to sea. Tyson was more than capable of taking charge of the ships. Force of circumstances had driven me from my beloved ships into what was virtually an office job ashore. I began to plan moves to extricate myself from the position. I wrote a letter to the Admiral. Somehow it came back to me for my remarks. I minuted it 'I think he ought to go' and signed it; but it must have got lost.

As it was I was more than fully employed. I always had two ships in harbour and I persuaded the X.D.O., under whose authority we had been placed when our only job was the patrol lines, and who still retained a lien on us, to inspect each ship during her rest period. My own group had been at Scapa for ten months, and no staff officer had ever visited them. I felt that an official visit would help them to feel that they were part of the show. The inspections went very well indeed. The ships turned themselves out smartly, and Commander 'Lampy' Heath was an excellent inspecting officer. Inspecting officers vary a great deal. It is easy to be pernickety; to make caustic comment, and so do more harm than good. 'Lampy' was such a charming personality that he was a great success. We only had one disaster, perhaps because I only had one ship which, if not bad, was certainly always in trouble. It is a curious thing that in any group there is always one ship which is best in every way, a number which reach a high level of adequacy, and one bad boy. *Istria* was our bad boy and I had looked forward to her inspection with little expectation of a happy outcome. It started badly. As the inspecting officer's boat with Commander Heath and myself aboard, came alongside, there was nobody ready to receive us. They had somehow taken down the signal wrongly, and expected us an hour later. Worse was to follow, the ship was not over-clean, and a naked man was discovered shut in a cupboard where he had been bundled because they could not muster sufficient uniforms to clothe the whole crew. He was fast asleep and snoring when Commander Heath opened the cupboard door, and we peered with horrified faces into the dark interior. Slowly closing the door Heath turned to me. 'More ready for inspection by the Doctor than by me,' he said.

I wrote another letter to the Admiral asking to be recommended for command of a corvette. This time I was sent for and told quite plainly 'No.'

Lord Churston had left just before Dunkirk to take command of a trawler. I suppose I could have got out then, but I wanted a corvette and they were still too few and far between for an R.N.V.R. to hope to get one. I saw Churston occasionally as he was coming and going between the north-east ports and Iceland. After the fall of Norway it had been vitally necessary to secure the Faroes and Iceland for our use, and even more important to deny them to the enemy. It always seems to me that the German High Command made a fundamental error in not immediately following up their success in Norway by a determined raid on Iceland. A U-Boat base in Iceland would almost certainly have brought disaster on us in the Atlantic struggle. One can only assume that the German is mainly a land-based animal, and hesitates to leap into a boat to cross the water. The indecision which he displayed over those northern islands was to be repeated when he reached the Channel coast two months later. There he vacillated, demanded the impossible of his air force—and lost the initiative. The same was true of the northern islands. The German fights best with the odds heavily in his favour. It is fortunate that with us it is the other way round.

The supply of goods and services to the garrison in Iceland was intermittent, and consisted usually of one supply ship with one or more trawlers as ocean escort. I tried hard to get my trawlers a chance on this run, but already there was a notable tendency to use the trawlers commanded by patrol service skippers for the coastal work, and to employ those commanded by R.N.R. and the few R.N.V.R.s for the ocean escort.

One of these trawlers, a member of the class named after famous football teams, and rejoicing in the peculiar name of H.M.T. *Preston North End* had a pet as strange as her name.

There are few things more complimentary to the human than the unwavering devotion of a dumb animal. In this case the human concerned was the First Lieutenant of the *Preston North End,* and the dumb animal a young bullock which this officer had encountered on a walk over the hills behind Lyness. They must have enjoyed their walk together, for the bullock came down to the water's edge and mooed softly as its friend was rowed off to his ship. It continued to call in bovine language all night and was still there in the morning gazing, with longing eyes, at the trawler. The First Lieutenant, who had spent a night punctuated by the faint roarings of his walking companion, approached his Captain. What cajolery was used I do not know, but that afternoon the First Lieutenant bought his friend and this time they were rowed off together to the ship. The bullock was duly taken on the books as Able Seaman Bullock, and drew rations as fitted an able seaman—and what is more he waxed fat and sleek on a cannibalistic diet that consisted largely of bully beef. The animal developed a remarkable dexterity in getting about the deck even in a seaway, and appeared thoroughly to enjoy his new environment.

The expression 'I could hardly believe my eyes' was fully justified when, on my first visiting the ship, I saw a large bovine posterior, fitted with a tail and supported on cloven feet, disappear round the engine-room casing as I climbed aboard. This was some months after A.B. Bullock joined the Navy, and he was already causing concern because he was now far too heavy to be taken ashore easily in the ship's boat. In what way he met his end I never discovered, for I only made his acquaintance as *Preston North End* was going to Iceland. By the time she returned I had left Scapa.

In August and September the corvettes were coming forward in increasing numbers. I wrote to Lieutenant-Commander Manning, R.N.V.R., whom I knew to be in the Second Sea Lord's office and largely concerned with drafting officers to the new corvettes. I pointed out that I was one of the first unit commanders to get command of a group, that I was now fast becoming a staff officer, and that my job could be done by somebody who had less experience of anti-submarine vessels at sea.

There was no reply for a week, nor during the week following. I knew Manning was a very busy man, and that in any case he would probably send a query to the Admiral, and I would then get a 'rocket' for going behind the Admiral's back. I went to sea for a week's patrol in my old ship. On my return I found a buff envelope. Hastily I tore it open. 'Appointed *Violet* in command. Date to be reported.' I left that night for Middlesbrough after handing over the groups to Tyson.

I arrived the following night and having found from the office of the Naval Officer in Charge that the *Violet* was completing in Smiths' Docks, I took a room in an hotel for the night.

Early the next morning I called at the firm's office to make enquiries. I was taken down the yard. All around me corvette hulls reared their red painted skeletons to the sky. In the wet docks the launched hulls were tied up. *Violet* was one of these. She would be ready perhaps in six weeks, perhaps two months. Who could say? They advised me that I had better go back and ask for a month's leave, as I could do no good in Middlesbrough until then. I asked the manager to show me a corvette nearly completed. We went down to the river wall. There in the river lay a corvette almost ready. She was the first long fo'c'sle corvette, *Verbena.*

'Who's her Captain?' I asked.

'Well as a matter of fact it's a most extraordinary thing but they haven't sent anyone yet.'

'Get me a taxi—quick.'

He got me a taxi. I was back in N.O.I.C.'s office six miles away in Middlesbrough within half an hour.

I telephoned to Manning.

'Do you know *Verbena* hasn't got a captain and *Violet* won't be ready for months?'

'Are you asking me to change your appointment?'

'Yes of course.'

There was a pause while I could hear papers being flicked over.

'You're quite right. No one has been appointed to her. Thanks for letting me know, I'll make the signal right away.'

I took the taxi back again to Smiths' Docks. I was going to step aboard my first command. I would see the manager afterwards, just at the moment I wanted to be alone. I hurried down to her. She was lying alongside the fitting-out jetty. A shimmering haze above the funnel told me that at least one of her boilers was lit. There were wires and pipes all over the place. The smell of fresh paint mingled with the smell of fuel oil. The sharp rattle of riveting machines rose in a never ending cacophony. But I could only see her as she would be, slipping quietly out of the northern mists with only the hiss of her bow wave to disturb the sea birds, and the steady throb of her propeller beating like a heart. She was quite perfect.

CHAPTER IV

VERBENA IN THE WESTERN OCEAN

FEW things could have been more exciting to watch than the metamorphosis of my command from a mass of metal into a warship. Gradually the grey paintwork of manhood crept over the red paint of adolescence. The long lines of electric cables and air pipes grew less as day followed day. Much as I would have liked to spend all the hours of each day aboard, it was out of the question to do so. There were too many other things to be done. But to go away from her even for an hour was to add zest to my return, for I always wondered what I would find completed when I came back. Things happened with remarkable suddenness, for corvettes enjoyed a very high priority. Naval uniforms other than my own began to be seen aboard. The Fitting Out Gunnery Officer might be found inspecting the gun mechanisms, or an officer of the torpedo branch checking the clearance of the depth-charge rails. One learnt to be careful how one addressed people. Strange figures in boiler suits emerged from unexpected places, and an engineer captain who has crawled on hands and knees through a shaft tunnel would look as much like a dockyard matey as he would dislike being addressed as one.

Already she smelt and felt like a ship. Commissioning day was advancing upon us at a gallop. There was not enough time for all I had to do, and never enough time to gloat over her as I would have liked. Standing on her deck in the gathering dusk it needed little imagination to see her as the finished ship, and I realised suddenly that as soon as she was commissioned I would be piped over the side whenever I went ashore on official business, and piped aboard again on my return. There is no sound that means more to a naval officer than the shrill fluttering notes of the bosun's call. They link him for ever to all those captains of warships who have gone before, and to all who will follow after him. The tradition is not only stimulating—but just a little frightening. A new boy on his first day at his public school may wonder if he will make the grade or let his side down. There are few new captains who can feel such self confidence that, in their inmost thoughts, there does not lie a fear that they may prove unworthy of their charge. It is remarkable how the customs of the Navy aid one. When you come to think of it the surest way to help a man is to remind him continually of his position, and of what the men whom he has been called to join expect of him. The psychology of the Navy is excellent.

I had brought my wife and children from Liverpool to stay in an hotel at Redcar for the fourteen days before we actually commissioned. It was the first time I had really seen the children for a year, and except for one brief visit of *Verbena* to Liverpool I was not to see them for another year. At that time we thought that the ship would be based on Liverpool, and that I would see my family every time she was in harbour. As it turned out we were sent to work from Londonderry. My wife and I then had to decide whether she and the children should move over there, or whether it was not better to stay in our own home so that the children's schooling would not be disturbed. We chose the latter course, and I am sure it was the right one. Several captains did bring their wives to Londonderry, but I cannot think that at a time when ships never knew where they would be tomorrow, it was fair to place the wife in such a position of doubt and uncertainty. I well remember that when *Petunia* was detached from the group to act as a special escort and did not rejoin for some six weeks, her captain's wife suffered great anxiety, and that none of us could do anything to ease her mind because we had not the slightest idea where *Petunia* had gone.

On the morning of commissioning day the officers arrived. Two Sub-Lieutenants R.N.V.R. and a Midshipman R.N.V.R. They had come straight from H.M.S. *King Alfred*, the officers' training establishment, and not one of them had a watch-keeping certificate. They had all three been 'hostilities only' ratings, who had been selected from their fellows and made officers overnight. *Verbena* was the first ship in which they had served as officers. I had expected at least one Lieutenant

H.M.T. *Loch Tulla.*

North Atlantic in winter. The ice forming on the bow and bridge superstructure can be clearly seen.

A North Atlantic convoy. Two escort vessels can be seen zig-zagging ahead of the convoy and two more on the starboard beam. This is a small convoy of forty-five ships. Many convoys contain double this number.

R.N.R. or long-service R.N.V.R. who would have been my First Lieutenant. I went ashore and telephoned to Manning.

'Awfully sorry, but I've had to provide an extra officer for all the trawlers in the Western Approaches. The bag is quite empty. I'll send you a First Lieutenant as soon as I can. Possibly Liverpool base will find you one when you get there. If they do let me know.'

I went back to the ship. The Captain of *Verbena* and the Number One were evidently going to be the same person. At any rate they had known each other for thirty years, and were not likely to quarrel.

I cannot say that I viewed the immediate prospect with much pleasure. The Captain and the First Lieutenant are complementary one to the other. However good the former may be, his ship cannot be a success unless the latter is efficient. If the Captain is responsible for the ship's body, to the First Lieutenant falls the charge of her soul. He is at once the translator of the Captain's authority to the men and their own ambassador at the court of that authority. In many ways it is more difficult to be a good First Lieutenant than a good Commanding Officer, for the Captain looks only one way, while Number One must look both fore and aft.

Fortunately the staff of the Second Sea Lord's office well knew from their own experience afloat the difficulty of finding good First Lieutenants. They were remarkably eager to help, and once assured that you would help them by recommending officers for promotion, they would replace those who proved unsatisfactory very promptly. There were two kinds of Captain whom they would not help—the man who selfishly kept back a promising officer because he did not wish to lose his services, and the man who recommended unsatisfactory officers just to get them removed from his own ship. Throughout the war I found that the more one tried to help the Admiralty Staff, the more they tried to help you.

There was little I could do about my present position. I only hoped that I should get *Verbena* safely through the training base at Tobermory. Terrible tales were already beginning to be passed round the anti-submarine world about the standards of efficiency demanded there. It was rumoured that Captains had been taken out of ships, junior officers relieved and ships almost recommissioned by the ruthless, eccentric, but essentially fair autocrat who ruled the training base—Commodore 'Puggy' (Vice-Admiral retired) G. O. Stephenson. Realising that training and still more training was the basis of efficiency Admiral Dunbar-Nasmith the Commander-in-Chief Western Approaches had set up this base in the quiet waters of Tobermory. With its unerring gift for producing the right man for the job, the Navy had put in charge there a martinet of truly fierce aspect, who was a master of the small ship trade. Although he could be very frightening—and meant to be so—and many ships failed to reach the high standard he demanded, I do not believe that he ever rejected any officer who threw his heart and soul into the job; and it was not long before we found that the tyrant really had the kindest of hearts.

If we had commissioned when the bag of officers was absolutely empty, the men at least were promising material. Unlike the trawlers, which were manned by the Patrol Service from their base at the Sparrows' Nest, the corvettes were major war vessels, and were manned by the Navy proper from the main depots of Devonport, Portsmouth or Chatham. *Verbena* was a west country ship manned from Devonport. The barracks had sent her a crew in which long-service ratings and 'hostilities only' men were mixed more or less evenly. At once it was obvious that they had sent me a first-rate coxswain, and for this I was truly grateful. In a small ship the coxswain is the third most important man, as far as the happiness of the ship is concerned; and without a First Lieutenant I was going to need him badly. Fortunately I had a nominal list of the crew, so that I was able to prepare a watch and quarter bill before their train arrived. At any rate the men would at once see that *Verbena* was going to be run properly. As a matter of fact the ship's company never gave me a moment's concern, from the minute they began to file aboard at five o'clock in the evening. All my officers were there with me, and the men were shown straight to their messes. We were able to pipe 'Liberty men' half an hour after the crew came aboard. Naturally not many men wished to go ashore the first night. It was just a gesture that the ship was a real ship. It was the 4th of December, 1940.

We began our acceptance trials the next day. She moved—she really moved! My own ship going down the river! A bitter wind blew from the north-east, but I was warm inside. I was desperate too to get my hands on her, to make her obey me; but the pilot had her all the time. She would not be mine to handle until she had proved herself, and I had signed the receipt. On three consecutive days we went to sea, for compass swinging, steaming trials, and gunnery trials. Owing to the danger from magnetic and acoustic mines we were not allowed to steam at more than eight knots, so the engines were never run at any speed. This caused some concern both to the Chief Engine Room Artificer and myself, because our engines had one peculiarity which I must explain.

In a reciprocating engine perhaps the most important gland is that through which the connecting rod rises and falls as it is carried up and down by the piston. In most 'push-and-pull' engines this gland is made up of pieces of special metal held in place by 'coil' springs. *Verbena* had been fitted experimentally with segmental pieces of metal held in place by a garter spring. It was supposed to be a more efficient gland packing, and so it was. But like so many small experimental alterations it was never properly followed up by those who thought of it. The result was that when running continuously at high speed we always suffered from the disease known as 'hot rods'. This can only be kept in check by the engine room artificer continually swabbing down the rods with an oily rag. Our work in the Western Approaches rarely called for long spells of high speed, but once we had gone to the Eastern Fleet we nearly always had to steam at our maximum speed. It was there that so much 'swabbing down the rods' had to be done that oil worked its way into the feed water and caused boiler trouble; and it was this that finally laid up the ship for nine months in Bombay dockyard.

The trouble with the engine, however, still lay in the future. In the present I had a much more pressing worry, for our charts had not arrived from the chart depot. Hectic signals back and forth had disclosed the fact that they had been destroyed in a bombed train. In desperation I took the chart folios which had been sent for *Violet*; but I had not got the up-to-date corrections which were so necessary in war time, and the best I could do was hastily to correct what charts I needed for the passage round to Tobermory from those kept in the Naval office.

We were ready to sail. I signed the receipt, and said 'good-bye' to the manager of the dockyard. *Verbena* was mine, and next morning I would take her to sea.

When I awoke I could hear the howl of the wind, and felt the short, fierce movements of the ship against the jetty. No need to go on deck to know that it was blowing a full gale from the north-east. I was faced with my first major decision—to sail, or not to sail. I had a ship whose engines were virtually untried, because of the restrictions imposed while she was in the builders' hands, and there would be a lee shore all the way up to Peterhead. Not for one moment in such weather could I stop the engines to make any adjustment.

I went ashore to the Naval officer in charge of the port. He was surprised to see me. I explained the position.

He was a busy man, anxious only to get rid of the ships that were building in the port. 'If you can't take your ship to sea I'll get someone who can,' he told me. I insisted on putting the matter up to Chief of Staff, Western Approaches. N.O.I.C. and I glowered at each other while we waited for the call to come through. Though I was sure that I was right, I felt distinctly uneasy about the outcome. There seemed to be no doubt in the Chief of Staff's mind. 'We want you badly, but we want you whole. Use your own judgment and get round to Tobermory as soon as you can.' I went back to the ship with a light heart.

The gale moderated with the turn of the tide in the afternoon, and we sailed at three. We put the pilot into his boat at the mouth of the river, and then she was entirely mine. As I turned her away northward into the war channel no man could have been happier.

She was obviously a first-class sea-boat. I had enough experience to recognise that as soon as she met the sea. She was the first long fo'c's'le corvette to be built. All the earlier corvettes, some fifty in number, had a break between the fo'c's'le and the bridge. This meant that a man going from the bridge to the mess decks must cross the low deck forward of the bridge before he gained the sanctuary of the mess decks. In *Verbena* the fo'c's'le had been carried right aft as far as the funnel, giving us a covered space in which the whole ship's company of seventy-odd men could easily be mustered. This arrangement allowed men to come on watch without being soaked through and, still more important, the cooks could carry the food down to the mess decks from the galley, which was between the bridge and the funnel, without the risk of losing it overboard. The earlier corvettes were very lively indeed in a seaway. In fact it was commonly said that it was impossible to get your legs into your trousers aboard one. The extra weight of the long fo'c's'le actually steadied them a great deal, and made them much better sea-boats. It improved their trim by putting them slightly down by the head, so that its weight detracted nothing from their speed—rather the reverse. *Verbena* actually exceeded her designed speed, and other corvettes, when altered, reported that they too had similarly benefited.

Originally the corvette had been designed as an off-shore anti-submarine vessel. It had never been thought that they would be used for long distance ocean convoy work. Now that we had realised that the best way to sink U-Boats and to protect the convoys was to build up the escorts, they were being used for a purpose for which they were not designed. None the less after the long fo'c's'le had been added they were wonderful little ships. They hardly ever took green seas aboard, and although their movements were lively they suffered very little weather damage of any sort. Within the limits of the equipment that they could carry they were excellent warships, and their contribution to the battle of the Atlantic was a vital one.

I may have been a happy man, but I soon had my troubles.

Soon after settling to our course I fetched myself a cigar from my cabin and jamming myself in a corner of the bridge settled down to enjoy it. To my surprise I soon found everyone looking very glum. The asdic rating had turned a curious pea-green. The signalman was draped over the lee side of the bridge. The officer of the watch was gulping like a goldfish in a bowl. I took over the watch in all directions. Fixing the asdic head-phones over my own head, I called the wheelhouse.

'Coxswain, are you all right?'

'Perfectly Sir.'

'Thank God. They're all sick as dogs up here.'

His words came back to me disembodied by the voice-pipe between us, but still carrying the respectful tone of the trusted chief petty officer.

'Your cigar Sir. Not used to it I expect.'

'Oh, thank you Coxswain—you're probably right. How thoughtless of me.'

Later when the watchkeepers had recovered a little and Farne Island light was coming up, I told the officer of the watch to fix the ship's position. It was hopeless. Lessons learnt on the shore compasses in the *King Alfred* had not taught these officers how to take a bearing at sea. Obviously I must teach them everything. I started. I spent all the watch teaching. How lucky I had spent so much time teaching junior officers before this war started! Came the last dog watch, and another officer to teach. It was dark by then. Obviously I could never leave the bridge until they were proficient, so I had my first dinner in the asdic hut. I had no sleep that night. Not until the next afternoon, when we had rounded Cape Wrath and had the long run down the Minches ahead of us, was I able to sleep. Then I sent for my Lilo mattress and sleeping bag, and made up a bed in the asdic hut within reach of all the voice pipes, the alarm bell, and the officer of the watch. This was such a success that I used the asdic hut as my sea cabin all the time I commanded the ship. It gave my officers great confidence, because they felt that they could get instant help if they wanted it; and the men too seemed to prefer their Captain always to be at hand. Neither knew how totally inadequate he himself frequently felt.

In a glorious winter dawn five days before Christmas 1940 we slid gently into Tobermory harbour. Four corvettes were lying at anchor there. Two more and a submarine had been sighted going off to the exercise area before we entered. The old inter-island passenger ship *Western Isles*, now painted grey, swung at anchor in the centre of the harbour. We were told exactly where to anchor. As our anchor cable rattled out I took up the binoculars and looked at the *Western Isles*. From an upper deck scuttle peered an avuncular face, with tufts of grey hair sprouting below eyes which, so I learnt later, were of a brilliant blue and quite the most piercing I have ever encountered. So that was the 'Terror of Tobermory', the new Lord of the Western Isles. I felt sure that we had brought him something to chew on.

We had. We were beaten into bruised efficiency. At any time of the day or night the lash might fall. 'Send away a boat! Let go a second anchor! Rig sheer-legs, and hoist your boat clear of the water! Prepare to tow forward! Prepare to take a merchant ship in tow! Send a boarding party to *Western Isles*! Your ship is dragging her anchor, weigh and proceed!' Anything might happen—almost everything did. Crack went the whip and jump went the *Verbenas*. At first we squealed as we leapt. Later we learned to achieve the leap without the squeal.

We were a very broken reed when we arrived. After a ten days' ordeal came our inspection, when the Commodore and all his staff came aboard. It was the final test. Afterwards in my cabin he said to me, 'Well, you'll do—but you must have a First Lieutenant. You can't carry the whole thing yourself. I've made a signal to C.-in-C., Western Approaches, and you'll get one in Liverpool when you arrive. You'll also get your evaporators put right. As far as I'm concerned you're an ocean escort now. Come and have dinner with me tonight.'

We sailed for Liverpool in the morning, still without our proper Notices to Mariners—those essential weekly publications by which charts are kept up to date. I had corrected such as I would need for the passage to Liverpool from the charts in the *Western Isles*. Perhaps I had not quite realized that we 'were an ocean escort now', certified as such by Tobermory, and that we might therefore be sent anywhere.

We left Tobermory full of confidence. We knew we were a long way from being perfect; but everything worked. Time would oil the wheels, and with luck we would be an efficient unit. We steamed on to the southward.

Passing the Mull of Kintyre we received a signal from Commander-in-Chief, Western Approaches. 'Fuel at Greenock and join outward-bound convoy estimated to pass Mull of Kintyre noon tomorrow as additional escort. Senior Officer in *Velox*.' So there would be no First Lieutenant this trip anyway; and no corrected charts either. I altered course for the Clyde. The morning's sun had now gone, and before we passed the boom gate at the entrance to the Clyde the night was dark and full of rain.

We asked the signal tower where the oiler was. They gave me a berth number, but it meant little to me. I had the tide under me, and the darkened shapes of anchored merchantmen were suddenly looming out of the murk. My only hope was to feel my way through the anchorage until I found the two blue lights that marked the oiler. To have lost my 'night sight' by looking into the lighted chart table would have been fatal. Oh why did I not take Elgood's advice and become a gunnery officer? At least it would not be my worry to look for one particular ship in a crowded anchorage, when I could not even see my own bows. When I did find the oiler—if I ever did—I would have to turn the ship and make my first 'alongside'. It was impossible. No one could find the oiler in that.

Was there a light? Yes I could see it—two little blue lights one above the other. I had to turn her.

'Coxswain.'

'Sir.'

'Have special sea dutymen piped. Lively there—we're very close. Port fifteen.'

'Port fifteen on, Sir.'

I see her bow start to swing—not fast enough.

'Increase to twenty.'

'Port twenty on, Sir.'

'Check revolutions.'

'Seventy revolutions, Sir.'

'One one O revolutions.'

'One one O revolutions on, Sir.'

'Ease to ten.'

'Port ten on, Sir.'

'Slow ahead.'

'Slow ahead on, Sir.'

'Midships.'

'Midships, Sir.'

'Coxswain.'

'Sir.'

'Can you see her now?'

'Plainly, Sir.'

'I'm going to put her bow just on that second fender.'

'Second fender, Sir.'

The slap-slap of water between the two closing hulls—heaving lines snaking through the night——

'Port twenty. Half astern.'

'Port twenty, half astern on, Sir.'

'Stop engines.'

'Stop engines, Sir.'

The ship lurched slightly as her shoulder nudged the fender. Lines were passed rapidly. We were made fast.

'Finished with engines, Coxswain. Thank you.'

I breathed a sigh of relief, and patted the wet rail of the bridge with my hand. The ship had done me proud. She had spun round like a top when I asked her to.

Received signal, 'On completion of oiling anchor in position——'

Hell and damnation! I had hoped they would leave us alongside for the night.

I went down to my cabin to lie down. The extending of the fo'c's'le had only one disadvantage. It completely enclosed the captain's cabin below decks, and the only means of ventilation was through scuttles opening on to the covered flat outside the mess decks. I could not help hearing remarks by the men that were not intended for my ears. As I lay down that night I heard a rich west country voice saying: 'Cor—and don't e' ever tell me the wavy navy can't handle a ship. We wasn't more'n five minutes out in the bleeding rain.' It was balm to my spirit. As I drifted off to sleep I felt sure *Verbena* would be quite a ship.

We moved to our anchor berth at three in the morning, and sailed again to meet our first convoy at eight. We met them off the Mull of Kintyre. A long line of ships in two columns extending for nearly ten miles. Ahead of them was a 'V and W Class' destroyer—*Velox*. Signal lamps flashed from her. We were being given our stationing signal. A corvette bucketing cheerfully over the seas and looking, to our eyes, quite indecently efficient gave us a résumé of all the signals made since leaving Liverpool on the previous afternoon, and particulars of *Velox's* own group orders for use in the event of an attack on the convoy. By the time she had passed all the signals it was getting dark. We were bound up the Minches, and until past the Butt of Lewis the convoy would stay in two columns. Once clear of the coast it would form up on a broad front. The two columns would then become eight, ten, or even more, with four or five merchant ships in each column. As this was a slow convoy, and probably made not much more than six knots, it took a long time to form up on the following morning. Some of the ships could not make more than seven knots, even if the leaders reduced to four, and it would be four hours before the rearmost ones had covered the twelve miles necessary to take up their stations. The morning was spent in getting the convoy into its ocean-going formation. *Velox* was zig-zagging across the front of the merchantmen; astern of the convoy was another destroyer, and there was a corvette at each corner. *Verbena* had been given the position on the starboard quarter.

Our first night was uneventful. We stopped zig-zagging at dusk and hung close to the nearest merchantman. No lights were of course shown; and in those days there was no radar. It was more important to remain with the convoy than to continue the zig-zag. In any case the U-Boats generally attacked on the surface, and in such conditions a visual look-out was a better protection to the convoy than the asdic. One senses that there had been a certain lack of realistic thinking about what would happen in war if the U-Boats should attempt to cut our sea communications in the Atlantic. Before the war we had beaten our chests with pride in our new asdic, and had confidently announced to all the services that we had the answer to the U-Boat peril. And so we had—so long as the U-Boat stayed submerged. But in the darkness of the winter nights he nearly always attacked on the surface, and until we could detect his presence with radar we fought him with our eyes, with seamanship, and with bluff. We had no other effective weapons against the surfaced raider.

On the second morning *Verbena* sighted a Focke-Wulf long-range bomber, coming in low from the north-east. The Germans had stationed a number of these nuisances at Stavanger in Norway. Until our own Coastal Command got busy and chased them away for good they were a confounded pest. If they could get over the convoy they would bomb some luckless merchantman. In any case they reported our position so that the U-Boats should find us.

Hastily turning out the gun's crew of the watch *Verbena* fired a star shell. At night one was always kept loaded in the gun, and time was too precious to reload with high explosive. The burst of the star shell, bright even by day, hung in the sky in front of him. He banked steeply, probably wondering what it was, so we fired again. He went away into the mist that hid the northern horizon. *Verbena* had shown her teeth, even though they may have been false ones.

Although the officers on joining had been a disappointment to me because of their inexperience, I was already beginning to appreciate their qualities. They were terribly young and very earnest; and they tried so hard. Besides we had a reputation to keep up, or more correctly to make. We were the first corvette to be commanded by a Volunteer Reserve Officer, and it was many months before another corvette entirely officered by the R.N.V.R. was to join us. If we could make *Verbena* a success the way would be open for a flood of R.N.V.R.'s to pour through on their way to command. It was a responsibility that I had pointed out to them. Before the war Sub-Lieutenants P. M. Whittaker and R. F. E. Pettifer had been clerks in an office, and Midshipman C. S. Edwards had been a schoolboy. They had each served nine months on the lower deck, and then three months at *King Alfred*; now they were keeping watch over twenty or thirty merchantmen. It was a transformation which the mind can hardly appreciate. On this our first trip, the midshipman was more sea-sick than anyone I have ever seen before or since. At last he collapsed entirely, and ate nothing solid for twelve whole days. We kept him alive on lime juice and sugar. On our return I offered to put him ashore, but he was determined to try again. Happily he was quite all right on our second trip.

The sea was too rough. We were not molested by the enemy. For eight days the convoy staggered on until it reached the longitude of 20° West, which was as far as we then could provide escorts. We would then leave it, and either go to meet an inward-bound convoy or return home to take out another outward one.

Our defective evaporator had allowed salt water to get into

the fresh water tank, so tea, cocoa, and everything else tasted of salt. We sent all the available stock of wardroom drinks—beer, lime juice, and orangeade to the mess decks to try to help the men. There was nothing more we could do about it. As I had expected the coxswain proved a tower of strength. Tall, fair and good-looking, he was a representative of the very best type of pre-war chief petty officer. He was always immaculately dressed, even in the middle of the Atlantic. This was a point of great importance in those days of hard work and little play, for it was very easy to let the men slide into slipshod ways; and once started on that road it was desperately difficult to stop. All through the war I insisted on certain standards of uniform and shaving for the bridge watchkeepers and as they included the look-outs, who changed round every two hours, it virtually meant that the whole ship's company kept themselves smart. I do not say that if a ship accepted a low standard in this respect she became inefficient in action. All that I do declare is that it was much easier to keep up efficiency if a high standard was rigorously maintained. In this the coxswain was an invaluable ally, for he was himself so smart a man. As a matter of fact he was one of the last men to carry the rank of Chief Coxswain. Most of those junior to him were Chief Gunners' Mates transferred to the new role. I was therefore all the more lucky to have him appointed to such a very small 'major war vessel' as my *Verbena*. Somehow or other he managed to keep the grumbles over the water situation within bounds at a time when they might have boiled up into serious trouble.

The escorts swept back to the Minches after we had left the convoy. With Cape Wrath just coming up over the horizon, and *Verbena* as usual the port wing corvette, we sighted a merchantman to the northward obviously sinking.

We reported to *Velox*.

Signal from *Velox* to *Verbena*, 'Investigate.'

Report, 'Dutch merchantman sinking. Propose to pick up survivors.'

Reply, 'Proceed, but your attention is called to Notices to Mariners Number——'

We picked up one boatload of survivors. The rest of the group was still visible on the southern horizon, steaming back and forth waiting for us. *Velox* was signalling again, 'Your attention is called to Notices to Mariners——'

All right—our Notices to Mariners are lying blasted all over some midland railway station. We waited until the nearest corvette was out of line with *Velox* so that the senior officer could not read our lamp and then made, 'What is Notice to Mariners—please.'

Back came the reply.

'Minefield—you are in it—we are not.'

'Newnes,' I said to the yeoman, 'don't you tell anyone about that—we can't steam away and leave the second boatload.'

'No Sir—no—we couldn't do that.' He crumpled up the signal and tossed it over the side.

We got the second boatload and signalled to *Velox*, 'Have picked up master and all ship's company, including ship's dog.'

Reply, 'Well done—I'm glad it was not my decision.'

What could we say but, 'Thank you', and make a resolution never to sail again without our Notices to Mariners.

We went down to Liverpool. There we would get a First Lieutenant, our Notices to Mariners and our evaporators mended. We got our repairs and our Notices to Mariners; we did not get our First Lieutenant. Liverpool base was out to a clinch in every respect, and we were going to be based on Londonderry. Londonderry would fix us up with a Number One.

As we were the first of the new corvettes everyone wanted to see us. Admiral Dunbar-Nasmith was aboard almost before we had finished berthing, and as a constant stream of people came up our gangway; I could neither get home to my wife, nor could I see Elgood. I telephoned to the Admiral's office as soon as we arrived, only to be told that Captain Elgood was on sick leave. Alas he was very sick. How proud he would have been of *Verbena*, and how nothing on earth would have permitted him to show it!

We went to Londonderry. Leaving the dispassionate sea behind as you go up the River Foyle, the friendly, green land enfolds you. Further and further your ship noses her way up the tortuous channel, until an S bend at Lisahally entirely shuts out all sign of the sea. Your ship steams on between the walls of woodland, so that her salt-encrusted sides are almost brushed by the overhanging branches; and your bow wave and wash, which for weeks have been lost in the immensity of the ocean, now slip-slop amongst tree roots, and stir the long tendrils of seaweed on half-tide ledges. Another S turn, and there before you lies the enchanted city, silhouetted against the light of the noon-day sun. In the shadow of the wharf would be lying a long single line of escorts, mostly destroyers in those days—and many of them in need of repair. In later years the line became four or five deep, and ninety per cent of them were ready for sea. But the approach to 'Derry never lost its magic.

We tied up alongside an 'S Class' destroyer whose long lean lines captivated me. What covetous eyes I cast on her! But she was as far outside my reach as if she had been a battleship—or so I thought then. Perhaps there are still magicians in Ireland, for two years later I was to find myself appointed to *Shikari* and to have, as Senior Officer, 21st Escort Group, all the six surviving 'S Class' destroyers under my command.

Captain Ruck-Keene and his deputy Commander 'Jacky' Slaughter were creating a great Naval Base out of nothing. How they drove everybody, and themselves as well! Stores and services appeared from nowhere, and even jetties which had been falling to pieces, were repaired overnight. I had hoped to find 'B 12' Group, which *Verbena* had been ordered to join, in harbour; but unfortunately they were at sea. In those days no escort capable of going to sea could be allowed to remain in harbour. I was told I would not immediately join the group, but must do one convoy trip to Gibraltar with another group. I was also told that there were no spare First Lieutenants in Londonderry. As Liverpool was only willing to look after its own chickens, that base took no interest in me once I had been sent to Londonderry; and the latter had no officers to spare, nor anywhere to accommodate them if they had appeared. I must sail without.

We joined an outward-bound convoy.

To be sent to another group was always difficult for the commanding officer. The Senior Officers of the groups were all busy inventing special tactics for their groups, and they gave these operations code words of their own. Later when Admiral Max Horton had become Commander-in-Chief, Western

Approaches, with Captain Gilbert Roberts as his tactical adviser, all the various orders and manoeuvres were tried out on the floor of the tactical school. Those found to be most successful were then adopted and a general manual of operations was published. But in January 1941 to be attached to a strange group was to find oneself submerged by a flood of code words which meant just nothing to you. If you joined in the middle of the day perhaps you would get details of the more intricate manoeuvres passed to you by flash lamp. Sometimes, you would receive by rocket line a nice folder, parcelled in waterproof cloth, and containing all the group orders properly typed. But such an easy introduction was very rare, because you might be taken away as suddenly as you had joined, and then the Senior Officer would lose his orders as well as you. More often than not you would join at dusk, when all but 'Immediate' visual signals were forbidden. Then you would probably be awakened by the yeoman of signals in the middle of the night with some such ominous words as:—

'Krakatoa Sir.'

'Krakatoa Yeoman? What on earth's that?' you would say raising yourself from your couch.

'Seems to be a code word Sir. Starshell on the other side of the convoy now, Sir—and rockets too. Funny group this, Sir. Wish we could get back to our own group—do at least speak English there, Sir. What the hell can you make of "Krakatoa", Sir?'

'Sorry Yeoman, I just don't know. Better go to action stations and be on our toes. Press the alarm for me while I get this oilskin buttoned up.'

But what would you have? The attack by more than one U-Boat at the same time was then so novel. A number of intelligent men were independently striving to find some general tactics which, when carried out simultaneously by all ships of the group, would force the Hun to submerge. Once driven below the surface they would be targets for our only anti-submarine weapon—the asdic. Each group was working on different lines to achieve the same object. Each group developed remarkably similar manoeuvres, but they all differed in the code words which set them in motion. Each Senior Officer naturally thought his own solution the best, and it needed a very strong hand indeed to persuade 'Commander Blank' that his operation 'Krakatoa' was really just the same as the official operation 'Buttercup', and that if he would only use 'Buttercup', any additional escort sent to him from time to time would know exactly what was required of her.

We met the convoy off Inistrahull. This one was not going north through the Minches and then to Canada and America, as our previous convoy had done. It was bound to the southward. It would go out to the longitude of 20° West and then turn south to a position south and west of the Azores, where it would be dispersed. Some ships would then go on to Africa, some westward to Brazil and the Argentine, and some would stay with the escorts and steam eastward to Gibraltar.

The ships were already forming on to a broad front when we met the convoy. The Senior Officer was not like kindly *Velox*, who had shepherded the obvious new boy. The weather was vile, the convoy difficult, and whatever we did seemed to be wrong. It must be remembered that Senior Officers were often tired and exasperated. For them time in harbour was taken up by attending conferences, writing reports, and organizing the group. It could be just as tiring as a spell at sea, and in any case all men are not alike.

It blew almost a gale, with rain from the south-west. Now we were to discover the different character of each convoy. In the previous slow one all ships had been of approximately the same speed; but this convoy contained ships destined for many different ports, and their capabilities differed widely. Instead of a convoy speed of seven knots, we were trying to make nine. This was desperately slow for ships capable of sixteen knots or more, but was too fast for many of the others. They shuffled and jostled each other like strange horses in the same stall. Some carrying supplies for the Army in Egypt were deep laden, others were flying light. The beam sea and wind drove the lighter ships out of their columns. Striving to get back into position they called for so much effort from their own engines that they inevitably cast long wisps of black smoke into the wind —the chief bugbear of every escort commander. The convoy was more like a herd of cattle than an organized team. While the Senior Officer of the escort tore his hair and steamed back and forth across the front of the convoy, *Verbena* stationed

The corvette H.M.S. *Verbena* leaving Smith's Docks, Middlesbrough, December 1940.

H.M.S. *Churchill*. One of the ex-American destroyers taken over by the Royal Navy in 1941.

H.M.S. *Shikari*.

H.M.S. *Warwick* preparing to oil at sea.

astern, tried desperately to push back the babies as they fell out of the bed. A continuous stream of signals flicked back to us from the Senior Officer. Signals which were difficult to read because his ship was always passing out of sight behind merchantmen, and his harassed signal staff would continue their signal whether we could read it or not.

'Number 14 is making smoke—stop her.'

'Number 23 is out of station.'

'Number 35 is out of station.'

'Why are you so slow in answering my signals?'

'Regain your correct station.'

So it went on for three days. I was up all day attending to the stream of signals; and at night when the Senior Officer was mercifully quiet (for it was before the days of the short-range radio telephones) I had to stay on watch for the safety of the ship. I had no experienced officers, and the weather was such that it really needed experience to keep station on what was nothing more than an occasional dark grey flurry in the blackness, visible only when the last ship of the centre column lifted her propeller half out of the water in a burst of throbbing foam.

I had had three hours sleep in three days when at last we turned south. I really did not know for how much longer I could keep it up. Then to complete the débâcle we ran into fog. Thick impenetrable fog. We settled down to the convoy course and speed. We could see little more than the bare outline of our own wash. We saw nothing all night, and when the dawn at last came, there was no sign of the convoy.

I had not attended the convoy conference in Liverpool, and no one had thought of telling me that this particular Commodore always signalled his convoy rendezvous (where ships would reassemble if they got scattered) no less than twenty-five miles astern of where he actually intended to be. I had received by light his convoy rendezvous for the next three days so naturally I went, as well as I was able, to each of them in turn. The weather was thick all the time and I had taken no sights. Indeed I had been running on dead reckoning ever since we left Inistrahull. Owing to the many jobs that had been given me it had been impossible to keep an exact track of my ship's comings and goings. In fact my dead reckoning was based on a guess at the convoy's speed. Before the days of radar, to keep in touch with the convoy in bad visibility was a nightmare for all commanding officers. Many escorts lost touch with their convoys, but given a chance of a sight, and if you knew the rendezvous, you could generally find them again. It thus happened that, in visibility which never exceeded a couple of miles, we went to a position twenty-five miles astern of where the convoy actually was, and found it not.

At the end of three days I decided to go down the track of the convoy to Gibraltar, keeping more or less at convoy speed. I thought that once I got a sight I would report my position by wireless to the Senior Officer, and ask for a course that would enable me to rejoin. But for a week I had no sight. It was the season of the 'Portuguese Trades'—south westerly winds which carried with them low cloud shrouding both the horizon and the sun. We plugged on to the southward until we had been two weeks without a sight, and then, at six o'clock one evening we suddenly ran out of the murk into glorious sub-tropical sunlight.

Hastily I got the sight I had longed for, but at that late hour it gave me only one position line—the longitude. I was now about one hundred miles west of Gibraltar with my latitude very uncertain. I decided to steer in for the coast, and get a star sight at dusk. I had by then had plenty of sleep, and was feeling fine. The ship's company were really beginning to work together, and the officers to gain confidence. It had been a wonderful 'shake down' cruise, and we had exercised everything that we would ever be asked to do.

I prepared for my star sight, choosing stars to the north and east of us. I had the sextant in my hand when I noticed that the horizon appeared to be doing peculiar things. It was. All round us to north and east lay a thick bank of fog. We plunged into it as if it had been cotton wool. The fog eddied round the bridge. It was something palpable and solid, catching at your throat. From the bridge the ship seemed to be cut off by the fog just abaft the funnel, and one could only dimly discern the look-out who had been sent to the eyes of the ship. It was even thicker above us, and the man in the crow's nest could be heard but not seen. Never before or since have I seen a fog as thick as that one. Fortunately the sea was dead calm, and in those perfect conditions our asdic would warn us of the approach of a surface vessel. So we steamed on.

At eight the next morning we should by my reckoning have been in sight of Gibraltar, or at any rate we should have seen one of the headlands north or south of the entrance to the straits. As we were still enveloped in fog I rang down for slow on the engines. Promptly we ran into a lane in the fog. Looking down this lane we could see land about six miles away. Obviously it was a headland—but which? The top of the headland I was seeking had a lighthouse on it, and I could have identified it from its shape—could I but see the lighthouse. But the top was hidden in the fog.

I could not go any closer until either I had recognized it, or had rigged my sounding boom. While we rigged the sounding boom the fog closed in again. All we knew was that we were near the land. I assumed it was the south-west corner of the straits, and put her head to the northward, sounding all the time and going slowly. Another lane in the fog, and we glimpsed a low, red-cliffed coast. It seemed to be lying east and west, and across my path. I turned and retraced my steps. We saw nothing. We continuously found no bottom at thirty fathoms, which was as deep as my sounding machine would go. Two years later I would have had the whole position plain before me on my radar scan; but then I was completely lost. Just before noon the fog was thinning, and the sun came out. On our port hand as we steamed slowly south we could see the coast—high empty hills, a sandy beach on which the long Atlantic swell was breaking, and something was moving on the beach. It couldn't be, but it was—a camel! It must be the coast of Africa, but how far down it we did not know. We turned the ship and hurried north. There was the same headland we had first sighted, but the fog still shrouded its summit. A destroyer suddenly came out of the fog ahead, and turned southward. I looked at her through the binoculars.

She was at sea with her quarter-deck awning spread. No British ship ever did that. She must be a Spaniard, and I was too proud to ask a Spaniard where I was. We waved to each other as we passed, and rather surprisingly she dipped her ensign to us as she swept by. With Spaniards to the north and camels to the south we could not be far away from our objective. In the log we entered the noon position, 'Fixed ship by camel and sombrero 260° Europa Point 20 miles.'

Gingerly we approached the fog bank from which the destroyer had come. The fog began to roll back and there, blessed sight, was an anti-submarine trawler on patrol. I called him up to ask where I was. He was just about to take the message when the fog rolled clean away, and there ahead of us was the Rock of Gibraltar. I changed the signal just in time to read 'Good afternoon.'

Gibraltar was very short of anti-submarine patrols, and borrowed our services for a month. In exchange for this they did provide me with a First Lieutenant, but insisted in return on removing one of my subs. Which should it be? There seemed nothing to do but toss for it. Pettifer went, and I was sorry to see him go. I would have been just as sorry to lose Whittaker. The new Number One was an R.N.V.R. liuetenant who had been in Mediterranean destroyers since the outbreak of war. He was an entirely competent officer, but as he knew he was only coming with us to make sure of a passage home he never threw himself fully into the ship's life, nor did she take him to her heart.

In Gibraltar our paragon of a coxswain suffered his one fall from grace. I was disturbed one night in harbour by the quartermaster who dived into my cabin and announced, 'Please Sir, Coxswain's fallen down and hurt hisself.' He then rushed out again. I followed. There by the gangway lay the coxswain, stretching his long length upon the deck, his eyes closed and his face a deathly white.

'Quick—go and get the sick berth attendant,' I told the quartermaster. As he went forrard, I knelt beside the fallen man and gently raised his head to see if it was seriously damaged.

As I touched him his eyelids fluttered.

'Are you all right Coxswain?' I asked.

His eyes opened. 'Yes Sir. Just some "old ships" of mine I met ashore, and too much brandy Sir. Thought this was the best way Sir. Can you have me put in my bunk Sir?'

'Certainly Coxswain, gently as a baby. Ssh—they're coming now with the stretcher.'

Solemnly he was rolled on to the canvas. The sick berth attendant having diagnosed the skull as still sound, the party bore the coxswain away to his bunk.

They gave us a boiler clean too at Gibraltar, and we persuaded the Naval Stores to give us enough paint to make the ship look really nice. When we had finished boiler cleaning we were going home, but first we must do one more patrol in the straits.

All night we beat back and forth and then, just as it was dawn, we sighted to the west of Tangier a Vichy French destroyer and two merchantmen. She was coming up inside territorial waters. A glance at the chart showed that she would certainly pass outside the three mile limit in the middle of the deep bay of Tangier if she held on her present course. The recognition manual showed her to be rather larger than a destroyer. The French had a class of super-destroyers called 'Contre-Torpilleurs' and this vessel was *Le Malin*, the name ship of the class.

She could see me as plainly as I could see her. She had five 5.5-inch guns. It infuriated me that she should sail by without altering course. I decided that if she came outside territorial waters I would stop her. Carefully timing our arrival to coincide with her coming outside the limit, *Verbena* ambled slowly across the straits with her men at action stations, but out of sight. Leaning over the bridge I called to Whittaker who was jammed tightly inside the shield of the 4-inch gun along with its crew:

'Mr. Whittaker, when you hear the signal lamp telling this Frenchman to stop I want you to bring your gun to the ready and keep it trained on his bridge all the time. If he tries any nonsense you may use your own judgment.'

The two ships were not two cables apart. I checked the position. We were outside territorial waters, and so was she. I turned on to a parallel course; the international code flag K for 'Stop instantly' broke from our signal halliards. Our ten- inch signal lamp repeated the order, and the guns swung round to cover her bridge.

The consternation on board was delightful. Her men were all closed up at the guns but they were trained fore and aft. Mine was pointing at his bridge at a distance of little more than fifty yards, and as the two ships rolled my gun rose and fell as it was kept laid on its target. The gun's crew grinning like codfish, held fresh charges.

I leant over the bridge and opened up in my best French. For once the 'loud hailer' worked perfectly.

'Pardon messieurs. Je vous prie de ne pas toucher un de vos canons, et je désire que vous arrêtez votre vaisseau tout suite. Je vais vous rapporter a mon Amiral et peutêtre qu'il me demandera de vous prendre au contraband control.'

It was the longest and most singular remark I have ever made in the French language.

There was complete silence from his bridge, but there was obviously a very heated argument going on. The turbulence under her stern died away. She stopped. We flashed 'stop' at her convoy. They also stopped.

I made an immediate signal to Gibraltar 'Have intercepted contre-torpilleur *Le Malin* and two merchantmen outside territorial waters. Request immediate assistance to bring in to contraband control.'

The reply came.

'Emergency destroyer will join you. Await instructions.'

We waited. Half an hour later a destroyer could be seen leaving Gibraltar like a man getting out of bed in the morning. Puffs of black smoke rose first from one funnel then from the other. Soon she was racing towards us, the bow wave springing like wings from her stem.

Signals flashed.

'I will assume control of situation. You are not, repeat not, to hurt him.'

We returned to Gibraltar. That night someone somewhere woke up, and realized that those ships were carrying nine million pounds of Polish gold that had been left in Dakar when France fell; and the gold might be on its way to Germany. A general order to apprehend at all costs went forth; but it was too late. *Le Malin* and her charges had disappeared in the mist towards Oran, and could not be found. We were on our way back to England as additional escort to a fast convoy and could not take part in the chase. It was the nearest I've ever been to a gold mine.

The convoy home was uneventful, and we arrived back to find the group about to sail from Londonderry. We fuelled and joined them. From the mail I learnt that a First Lieutenant had been appointed to *Verbena*, and also another officer to replace Pettifer. When they arrived I should have a strong team.

It was a delight to join our own B.12 group at last, and to be able to speak the same language as the corvette ahead and astern—to be one of a team instead of the odd man out. To have a senior officer whom you knew well, and who relied on you; who never, never fussed you with unnecessary signals, whom you regarded as the finest senior officer in the Western Approaches, and who so obviously had the best group. It is perhaps worth mentioning that probably all the western ocean escort groups felt the same about their own senior officers. The point I make is that these very mixed groups of ships were held together by a team spirit that neither wind, weather nor the enemy could break, and which more than cancelled out any disparity between the ships. I still consider Commander Howard-Johnston (now Rear-Admiral C. D. Howard-Johnston D.S.O., D.S.C.) senior officer of B.12 group, to have been a master of tactics. In all those terrible summer months of 1941 we escorted convoy after convoy without one single loss, once the protective screen of the group had been spread around the convoy. It is true we sank only one U-Boat, but as our Escort Commander said, 'Our business is to bring home the merchantmen. The sinking of the enemy is only a secondary consideration at this stage of the war. Our turn will come later.'

I am sure that until we had perfected our radar, Commander Howard-Johnston was right. To other groups might go the glory of submarine kills—B.12 brought home the bacon.

Unfortunately *Verbena* was boiler cleaning when on the 29th June the group did slay U.651. This was a lucky meeting, as the U-Boat was found across the course of the convoy by daylight. She was not, I think, actually engaged in attacking the convoy rather was she, so to speak, overlaid in bed. *Malcolm* attacked as the convoy overran the U-Boat, but after firing once she had to break off the attack because the enemy was passing under the convoy. When the U-Boat came out at the back it was met by a hunting party comprising *Malcolm*, *Violet*, *Arabis*, *Speedwell* and *Scimitar*, and was blown to the surface. The next few minutes were hectic in the extreme, as every gun opened fire and shells went ricocheting all over the ocean. It was not without interest that the U-Boat's engineer officer, who was the last to leave, said that no damage had been done to the pressure hull by gunfire. As a means of damaging strongly constructed, circular sectioned hulls, 4-inch gunfire is indeed virtually useless. It may spoil their looks but can do no material harm.

What makes the achievement of Commander Howard-Johnston's group all the more remarkable is that throughout this period we were working from Hvalfiord in Iceland to escort outward and homeward-bound convoys between 20° and 40° West. This mid-ocean stretch was the most dangerous to the convoys, and the most fruitful to the U-Boats; for we could expect no help from aircraft. There were I believe some Catalinas in Greenland, but owing to weather conditions we saw very little of them. For years those waters, where air cover was impracticable, were known as 'the gap'. It is no wonder that with such a successful record Commander Howard-Johnston was eventually taken from us to serve as Anti-U-Boat officer in the Admiralty.

In the middle of May the group was lying in Hvalfiord, when I saw a boat coming alongside, and a tall officer with a grin leapt aboard. There was something about the way he spoke to the quartermaster, something about the nonchalant way in which he left his luggage to find its own way aboard that appealed to me. I was standing inside the screen door and went out to meet him. The grin increased in dimensions. My memories of Jack Hunter are overlaid with memories of his wonderful grin. The worse the conditions the broader the grin. As he saluted me and said, 'Lieutenant Hunter. Come aboard to join Sir', I knew that I had been lucky. Here was a trained officer sure of himself, and using the correct expression.

Hunter was a Scot from the East Scottish Division R.N.V.R. He had the physique of a Rugby forward, the modulated voice of a barrister (he was a Writer to the Signet in Edinburgh in private life), and a puckish sense of humour. He could always rely on his charm to get him out of the appalling scrapes into which the sense of humour would lead him. What could not be acquired by legal logic was secured by use of that formidable grin. The ship's company were enslaved from the first moment. Even now I am unable to think of him without beginning to smile. As one of my brother corvette captains remarked to me rather plaintively, 'It's all right for you and your bloody

Verbenas. With a barrister for First Lieutenant any of you can get away with murder.'

The important words of course were 'any of you *Verbenas*'. We were no longer officers, petty officers, and men. This commanding officer of another ship had paid us the supreme compliment of classing us all together as '*Verbenas*'. This unity was Jack Hunter's contribution to my ship. He was the catalyst which changed the parts into one corporate whole, so that anything which affected anyone of us was felt by all. The sensation of being 'one' with the 'whole' gave me a feeling of deep satisfaction—a satisfaction which once I had left *Verbena*, I was not to recapture, until another First Lieutenant did exactly the same for me in the destroyer *Highlander*.

The commanding officer of even so small a war vessel as *Verbena* tended to be a very lonely man. Assumed by his officers and men to know far more than he usually did about future movements, he had at all times to keep a very close watch on his tongue. As the fountain head of the ship's discipline, and the ultimate arbiter of their fate at the 'defaulters'' or 'requestmen's' table the crew were only too ready to suspect the Captain of having tyrannical tendencies; while the officers, feeling that his exalted state might interfere with their more light-hearted moments, were inclined to indicate that it might be better if he kept away from some of their parties.

Hunter was able to charm away all these fears. Perhaps his experience as a barrister had given him a particular understanding of the frailty of human nature. The men would confide their troubles to him with absolute confidence, while if I should stay away from a wardroom party because I thought that the weight of my rank would damage the effervescence of their spirits, Hunter would be sure to follow me to my cabin and persuade me to return. I cannot recall that he ever had to use much persuasion.

He was equal to any occasion, even to extracting suspected malefactors from the clutches of the local police. Late one night in Londonderry we heard that one of our very ordinary seamen had been taken in charge for being in possession of articles for which he could not give a satisfactory explanation. The 'article' in this particular case was an immense marble clock of repellently ugly design. He had been taken up by the police as he staggered shipward very late at night, and the best tale that he could produce was that he had bought this incredible timepiece for the sum of five shillings from a civilian whom he had met in a public urinal.

The tale was so unlikely that no one could have believed it. Hunter, however, was for getting him out if humanly possible. The pair of us went ashore right away, but without the Inspector's permission the police would not release their captive. Next morning found us back again in the police station to meet the Inspector. I forget what legal quibble our counsel used to convince this officer that there was absolutely no case to answer, and that if he were not very careful he would find himself involved in a matter of wrongful arrest. Having thus carried the war well into the enemy camp, we departed with our retrieved seamen, who followed us back along the jetty to the ship, staggering under the sixty pound weight of the ghastly clock.

It was May 1941 when Hunter joined. We went to sea almost at once to meet the homeward-bound convoy SC.31 in 42° west, which is about the longitude of Greenland. The convoy route crossed the fortieth meridian about one hundred and fifty miles south of Cape Farewell, the south-easterly point of the land. This time we were ordered to meet the convoy two degrees further west than usual, as U-boats had been found to be working a patrol line as far west as the fortieth meridian. There is no doubt that had the ships been available the Admiralty would have provided anti-submarine escort for the whole passage of the Atlantic; but at this time we simply had not got the ships and even escorting beyond twenty degrees west had only been introduced in the last three months. Generally speaking the Hun liked his meat easy to kill. As soon as we had enough escorts to give reasonable protection as far as twenty degrees he withdrew further to the westward, and at once found more easily-slaughtered targets. Early in 1941 the escorts had received very important reinforcements from two sources. Our own yards were turning out corvettes, of which nearly eighty were in service, and the Prime Minister had obtained fifty old destroyers from America. These latter were nothing like ideal escort vessels; but they were ships manned by British sailors, and that was what mattered most.

Each Atlantic convoy had with it an armed merchant cruiser or an old 'R Class' battleship as protection against surface raiders. SC.31 was to have been taken as far as the meeting place with our group by the armed merchant cruiser *Salopian*, but on the 22nd of May early in the afternoon she was torpedoed in convoy.

Actually the group was early at the rendezvous, although neither the Commodore of the convoy nor the Captain of the *Salopian* were to know this; for we did not lightly break wireless silence. The *Salopian* was sunk when the group were only just below the horizon, and the Commodore gave the order to scatter the convoy. Why this order was given we could not tell. The Commodore may have been sent warning that exceptional enemy surface ships' movements were afoot. In which case he was justified.

The position of the Commodore of a convoy vis-à-vis the Senior Officer of the escort should perhaps be explained. The Commodore of the convoy was responsible for the safety of the merchant ships against all enemies, and for their control. The Senior Officer of the escort was responsible for the safety of the convoy from U-Boat attack. It was a divided command which worked well enough in practice while there was only the U-Boat to be considered; for the Commodore always, as far as I know, acceded to the requests of the Senior Officer of the escort, if he was asked to alter the course of the convoy.

In this case the Commodore, having seen his ocean escort sunk, and having no anti-submarine escort with him, may have expected more U-Boat attacks to follow quickly; he may therefore have decided to scatter the convoy so as to spread the target over the widest possible area. As soon as we in B.12 group heard the order given to scatter, Commander Howard-Johnston in *Malcolm* and the four other destroyers of the group went off at full speed to try to deal with the situation. Behind them the four corvettes plugged along as fast as they were able, and behind us again came the two anti-submarine trawlers.

The night was spent in a desperate effort to reassemble the scattered convoy. It was incredible how far away from each other the ships had got in the two hours before our arrival. When we did collect one or two together they had to be escorted back to the fold, where the *Malcolm* was dashing back and forth like a worried sheep dog. By midnight we had collected over half, and had driven them into some sort of order. Away to the northward Commander J. Bostock R.N., in the ex-American destroyer *Churchill* had another ten merchantmen under his wing and, with the help of a trawler, was bringing them down to join the main body. Then, shortly after midnight, the *Elusa* a big Dutch tanker was torpedoed. At once she became a flaming pillar of fire as, with engines stopped, she lay beam on to the sea. Clouds of smoke and lurid bursts of flame drifted down-wind. The burning oil spread from her torn side in a blazing arc.

Taking the *Churchill* up-wind of the burning vessel Commander Bostock brought his ship in with her bows at right angles to the tanker. Then, with as much coolness as if he had been exercising in harbour, and not in very close proximity to a vessel which might disintegrate at any moment in one huge explosion, he rigged a breeches buoy and took off every man of the crew and her master's wireless set as well. This last was given as a personal present to the rescuer of the *Elusa's* crew.

In a British destroyer the feat would have called for superb seamanship, for there was quite a sea running. In an ex-American destroyer it was almost incredible, and this for a purely technical reason. The Americans for some reason best known to themselves had built these destroyers with both propellers turning the same way. Although this peculiarity had little effect on the ships' speed, it did mean that they were just as difficult to handle as a single-screw ship. Having taken off the crew Commander Bostock returned to his charges.

Early on the morning of the following day the 23rd May, *Verbena* was ordered by *Malcolm* to return to the wreck of the *Elusa* and, if still afloat, to take her in tow until the arrival of the ocean tugs. At this period of the war we were salvaging anything which might again be made seaworthy.

As we approached the wreck we were astonished to see a surfaced U-Boat also going to inspect the result of the night's work. It was fully surfaced about four miles away, and coming directly towards us. We went to action stations and waited. He seemed to be taking absolutely no evasive action, and I could only assume that having found himself in that position her commanding officer preferred to fight it out with the gun, rather than submerge and face the inevitable depth charging. Alternatively if he chose to stay 'on top' and run away he could run much faster than *Verbena.* In his position I would have done the same. He was a very difficult target to damage, whereas *Verbena* was much larger and much more vulnerable to gunfire. I made a signal to *Malcolm*, 'Am engaging surfaced U-Boat with gunfire close to wreck,' and heard over the radio telephone *Malcolm* calling the *Churchill.* '*Verbena* is having a gun battle with a U-Boat. Go to her support with all despatch, and be prepared to pick up her survivors.'

I gave the order to fire when the range was about 2,000 yards. The spray from the shot must have wetted his conning tower. He turned swiftly into the sea and began to dive. Our second shot fell just astern of him. Closing watertight doors we went in to ram; but we had not the speed. As we passed ahead of his diving position depth charges flew from our stern. It was a gesture only, but we might have been lucky. He had dived at speed, and might then have been at any depth. He would have difficulty in getting his boat in trim, and because he must go fast to keep control, and use his pumps to adjust his ballast tanks, we would have a good chance with the asdic.

We gained asdic contact—loud and clear. He was making to pass under the *Elusa.* I tried to carry out an attack but had to break off to avoid hitting the wreck. I took *Verbena* round the stern of the *Elusa* and picked him up the other side. We attacked him, and opened him up. He was leaking oil now and steering up-wind. We went in for another attack, but he must have turned right round just as we lost contact ahead, because when we regained contact he was heading back for the wreck. Possibly he knew he was leaking, and wanted to get down-wind into the oil slick that covered the sea for miles down-wind of the wrecked tanker. We attacked him again. By certain signs I considered that he had gone very deep; and we had then not been issued with the special heavy depth charges for use against deep U-Boats. We were now short of depth charges, because at that time we had only stowage for fifty.

However, as *Churchill* was already in sight hurrying towards us, I decided to wait and put her in contact. Unfortunately the obsolete type of American asdic with which she was fitted was nothing like as efficient as our own British machines, particularly with deep U-Boats. By passing to her the range and bearing we were able to guide her over the target and she carried out one attack. This was a technique later to be developed to a fine art. If two ships could be used together, and all ships were fitted with radar so that the constantly shifting range could be ascertained accurately, it was remarkably effective. At that time *Verbena* fired a 'pattern' of five depth charges. Later when converted for the use of heavy charges she fired a pattern of ten at a time—five light and five heavy, hoping that the U-Boat would be the jam in the sandwich between the heavy charges exploding below the light ones.

After this attack we lost contact, and hoped we had sunk our U-Boat. But as we could not be certain we stayed in the neighbourhood until dawn next day (the 24th May). Then, with our fuel reserves getting very low, we began, in company with the *Churchill*, the long trip of over 400 miles back to Reykjavik.

Shortly after ten we intercepted a report that the *Hood* had been sunk, but did not immediately know how or where. Soon any amount of signals were being received and we learned that she had fought and been blown up by the enemy battleship *Bismarck* in the Denmark straight between Iceland and Greenland, and no more than two hundred miles away. It was soon obvious from the reports of the shadowing cruisers, *Norfolk* and *Suffolk*, that the enemy were going to pass very close to us. I made a signal to *Churchill*, 'Any comments?' and received back the reply, 'Only watch and pray.'

Just before lunch we could see a big ship on the horizon hurrying to the southward; but she was hull down and difficult to identify. I made to *Churchill*, 'Are you reporting what I think I see?' and got back the reply, 'Better not—identification by no means certain. Might cause confusion. Gather *Suffolk* has the situation in hand.'

So the chase sped away to the south-east and we went on to our destination. There we rejoined Commander Howard-Johnston, who in the *Malcolm* had been sent to search for survivors in the area where the *Hood* had sunk. He later showed me an attaché case full of little strips of wood. They were all that he could find of the lovely *Hood*.

In the middle of June we went back to Londonderry for a boiler clean. We had been sending back one or two ships of the group with each homeward-bound convoy, for there were no facilities in Reykjavik. Thus we missed the group's U-Boat sunk on the 29th June.

At Londonderry we were told that when our next boiler clean was due we would be sent to refit. This meant that the very detailed 'refit list' must be prepared and typed in quintuplet. As corvettes did not carry a typewriter, and in any case we had no one aboard who was able to type, there was nothing ahead of us but a seemingly endless period of operating with one finger upon a typewriter borrowed from the base.

We were saved by Chief Wren Mackintosh. She really was a wonderful girl. She was an invention of Jack Hunter's fertile brain, for he was an excellent mimic.

On the first occasion when she helped us, the refit papers were left at Captain D's office. Half an hour later Chief Wren Mackintosh rang up and said that *Verbena's* defect list was to be typed at once. We collected it the next afternoon, making a passing reference to the kindness of the Chief Wren and how we really must buy her some chocolates.

The next day, emboldened by our success with the defect list, we took up a number of other letters and papers. The Chief Wren was just as efficient as before. We began to think that Aladdin's lamp was only a little better than our dear friend.

That night I was called to the telephone during dinner. It was a First Officer W.R.N.S. Very haughty she sounded at the other end of the line.

'Who is Chief Wren Mackintosh?' she asked me.

I replied that the poor girl had been drowned in a hole in the River Foyle—so sad.

There was an ominous silence and the line went dead. I returned to the wardroom.

'Number One, we must hold a "wake" for Chief Wren Mackintosh—she's been drowned.'

We held the wake. Considering we had no body we felt it was a very good wake.

The next morning I was sent for by Captain Ruck-Keene.

'About Chief Wren Mackintosh.'

'Yes Sir, I am sorry Sir.'

'Sorry she was drowned, or sorry she ever happened?'

'Both Sir.'

'The base will be an easier place for me to run when you and your *Verbena* have gone to refit. Go away, and don't you or your First Lieutenant play these tricks on my staff.'

'Thank you Sir.'

I was almost through the door.

'Rayner.'

'Yes Sir.'

'I hate to tell you just at this moment, but I have to congratulate you.'

My head swam. Did this mean that the Admiralty had confirmed my claimed U-Boat by the wreck of the *Elusa*? Apparently not, that was still classed as 'doubtful'.

The news was something almost as good. I had been granted 'qualified status'. This unromantic promotion meant a lot to a Reserve Officer, for it made his position in the Navy's hierarchy of command the same as his seniority in his rank. Instead of my precious *Verbena* being the 'dog's body' of the Western Approaches corvettes she would be second senior corvette in her own group, and even ships commanded by Royal Navy officers who were junior to her captain would be junior to her. *Verbena* had grown up.

Captain Ruck-Keene recalled me to the present. 'You're getting on now Rayner, and that's another reason why you should not indulge in these pranks.'

'Yes Sir.'

Good advice, yes, but as his own Chief of Staff, 'Jacky' Slaughter, indulged in more pranks than anyone I have ever met before or since, I gathered that it somewhat depended on who had been 'pranked'.

We had one more sojourn in Iceland, and then in August returned to Londonderry with the whole group. We were going to refit in the middle of the month at Grangemouth near Edinburgh, but before we left we wanted to give a farewell party to the group. It was a little difficult to hold a party that would have just that touch of difference which we felt was

Verbena's due. Number One and I had a conference in my cabin. We emerged with smiles on our faces and went to see a stationer from whom we ordered invitation cards, printed in silver. We then went back to lunch in the wardroom.

A new officer, Lieutenant Cook, had just joined. He sat with his mouth open and a drink in his hand, while he heard our explanation. I am convinced he thought he had joined H.M.S. Madhouse.

'Edwards,' I said to the midshipman, 'prepare to assume the feminine gender.'

'Me Sir!'

'Yes, you're going to be the blushing bride. Don't look so worried man, we've borrowed some feminine garments. Whittaker, on Saturday morning you are marrying Miss Joyce Edwards, and the reception will be held aboard this ship. The cards are being rushed through the printers, and will be distributed tonight. Number One is going to order the taxis. We'll invite all the group and Captain D's staff.'

As a matter of fact we nearly came unstuck over the taxis, because they had already been booked for a funeral. However, Hunter and his grin were able to persuade them that a wedding was much more important than a funeral, and succeeded in getting the interment put off until the Monday.

In clothes borrowed from a friend of mine in Londonderry, the midshipman made a wonderful girl. She had what I believe is called a boyish figure, and so the midshipman needed very little padding to fill the bill.

The ship's company of course got wind of our scheme, and were lining the ship's side, perched on every vantage point, when our guests started to arrive. Sharp on time the two white-ribboned taxis arrived, bearing Whittaker and 'Miss' Edwards in the first, and Hunter and Cook in the second. For myself I had decided to be the photographer, with a bootbox fixed to a theodolite that we had borrowed from a surveyor. The whole contraption was camouflaged with a large black flag.

Captain D and the party from the base arrived just at the right moment when the bride, desperately trying to manage high-heeled shoes, was almost carried aboard. Number One met Captain D and led him round the far side of the engine room screen while I, hastily getting rid of my photographic impedimenta, doubled round the other side to greet him officially.

Of course once in our wardroom the game was up—but not entirely, because we were determined to carry it through properly, and were going to see them to the train. When we came to leave after the reception, hundreds of ratings from the other ships had joined our own ship's company. A way was cleared with some difficulty, and down the lane ahead of the happy pair went the First Lieutenant handing out bags of confetti to the men. It was a wonderful send off.

There were quite a lot of people at the station too. And then, just as the train was starting Number One, who had secured from somewhere a train key, locked them in. As the train started to move the poor bride almost showed signs of hysteria and Jack Hunter, suddenly realising that they had no money, handed them a ten shilling note. Then they went off. We had expected them to get out at Lisahally, but the train did not stop there. It did not stop until it got to Coleraine.

There was still no news of them at dinner time.

Nor was there any news until ten o'clock when the dockyard police rang up to say that an officer was trying to bring a girl aboard *Verbena*. We had to send the First Lieutenant down to the gate to recover the two of them.

It transpired that the money was just enough to pay for the fares and a beer each—and not a penny over. That was the trouble. 'Miss' Edwards discovered with horror just before the first return train that a penny was essential to her. As then dressed the 'Gentlemen's' was obviously out of bounds to her, and as she had no penny they must go outside the station to look for a bush. By the time the bush was found the train had come and gone; and there are not very many trains on the small branch lines.

It had been a wonderful party, but not all our time in harbour was spent in frivolities. There was training, and more training of asdic and depth-charge crews; and the continual chase round the base to repair defects, or to get little additions carried out for the efficiency of the ship or comfort of the men, was continual. Mostly it was the men themselves that provided the problems that kept the officers so busy.

The great majority of the defaulters who appear cap in hand

before the Captain's table arrive in that situation from sheer carelessness—from the misfortune of a missed bus, or quite frequently from not having even bothered to look at the timetable at all. Just occasionally you meet a special brand of malefactor—the man who just does not care. Something has turned him against the Service; perhaps some unfair punishment in his early years, or perhaps some matter which was not investigated thoroughly enough, has cast a blight upon him. These men are old by comparison with others of their own rating, and are often the best seamen in the ship. Sometimes they hold back from a definite desire to avoid promotion, because they feel themselves lacking in the ability to take command. At sea these men carry the whole weight of the ship. In harbour they are a confounded nuisance.

Verbena had two of these—an able seaman and a stoker. Regularly these two appeared at my defaulter's table, for they were 'chummy ships' and hung together. Each time the charge was the same, 'Absent over leave so many hours so many minutes; aggravated offence, ship under sailing orders.' It so happened that the seaman was a really first-class man, and the stoker more than pulled his weight in the boiler room. They knew that not to get back would let me down and let the ship down, for I had told them so often enough. They made great efforts to get back. The stoker was discovered one morning progressing on hands and knees along the dockside, with his finger in one railway line while the seaman used the other line as a guide. 'And keeping perfect station they was Sir, one singing out to the other every few minutes. Very keen to get back to the ship they was Sir, so instead or taking them along to the station we brought 'em down here to see if you'd really be wanting them Sir.'

Having signified our appreciation of the perspicacity of the local police, we duly accepted two human bundles and steamed off down the river.

But this was too much.

I gave them two days to recover and then, when we were comfortably at sea, I sent for the two of them to see me privately in my cabin. There, putting on what I hoped was a 'pained parent' expression, I addressed them. It was soon after our return from Gibraltar.

'First I suppose I must thank you for getting back to the ship. You know as well as I do the strength of the ship's company, and you both know you are carrying more than your fair share of work when we are at sea. But this last escapade of yours goes quite beyond reason. What can I do with you? What appeal can I make to you? I gather you want to stay in the ship or you'd have missed her long ago.'

'Oh we do Sir. Never been so happy Sir.'

They were like a chime going off together.

'What you mean is that you've never met such a bloody fool as I am who'll put up with you.'

'Not quite that Sir,' from the seaman, 'you've treated us decent.'

'Now look, I want you to go for Leading Hand, and you for Leading Stoker. You can both pass easily.'

'No good Sir. We'll only drop the "hook" next time in Sir.'

'Oh no you wouldn't—not with extra pay; and besides haven't you got a girl? Surely you want to marry? Won't she be pleased to hear you've picked up a leading rate?'

'A girl Sir!' The seaman answered me in much the same tone of voice he might have used if I'd suggested to him that he kept a tame elephant. As I knew he was no mean performer as a ladies' man I was a little surprised.

'Yes, a *Girl*—one of those pretty things on the beach. Haven't you one you want to marry?'

'Marry Sir—not me Sir. Why should I buy a book if I can go to the library?'

I gave it up as hopeless.

I was rather surprised therefore when, just before we returned to harbour, Jack Hunter came to me with a broad grin on his face.

'Something to please you Sir. I've two requestmen. One to take the board for Leading Seaman and one for Leading Stoker.'

Their examinations took place on the same day, and of course they both passed.

Thereafter whatever they did ashore, they behaved perfectly within the ship, returning aboard with extreme regularity, and full of as much beer as they could conveniently carry—just one minute before leave expired.

A month or two later we returned to harbour to find amongst the mail a draft chit for both. Devonport barracks, always short of leading rates, had seized them for another ship. However our own crew was stronger by then, and although I hated to see them go I had no real cause to try to alter things. On their last morning aboard two rather sheepish faces appeared at the door of my cabin.

'Just come to say "Goodbye" Sir.'

'Oh I hadn't forgotten. I was going to see you before you left.'

We said our goodbyes and then self-consciously they pressed three photographs upon me—one of each separately and one of the pair of them together.

'Taken special for you they was Sir.'

I valued those photographs enormously.

In the second week of August we sailed from Londonderry to Grangemouth to refit, and after the conference I rushed down to my home in Liverpool, for I had not seen my wife and family, except for one day, since the previous December. We took the children away for a fortnight's glorious holiday at Ambleside in the Lake District.

But fate intervened again. Four days before the end of my leave I was telephoned by Hunter from Edinburgh.

'Things are happening to her—strange things. I can't tell you over the telephone, but I think you'd like to know about them.'

'All right Number One, I'll be back.'

We packed up, took the children home, and my wife and I went up to Edinburgh together.

Chapter V

VERBENA GOES EAST

Hunter met me at the station at Grangemouth, and we walked down to the ship together. I stood looking across the dock to where she lay, and could hardly recognize her. In ten days her appearance had been transformed. Now a huge structure resembling a gigantic pepper pot rose from the back of the bridge. It was higher than the funnel, and to my eyes, looked just about as unseamanlike a contraption as could be devised. To make matters worse it was not even on the centre-line of the ship, but was offset to port by at least ten feet.

No one knew what it was for. All we could learn was that Rosyth Dockyard was to fit whatever went inside it. But the pepper pot was not all. Awning stanchions were being fitted, and already the sailmaker who was to make the awnings had been aboard to measure the ship.

I went back to Liverpool to see the Chief of Staff to the C-in-C, Western Approaches. He told me that six of those corvettes which had been fitted for minesweeping were to be used for a very special purpose, and that we had been chosen by Commander Crick who was to be Senior Officer of the party; that for this operation we would need radar, and that as we were such very high priority the radar set would be supplied to us from the battle cruiser *Renown*. Naturally I begged for more information, but the Chief of Staff told me that the less I knew the better. I countered this by saying that the men would talk, and that we had best think up some tale. He suggested that I tell them that we were being lent to Freetown. The U-Boats were already working in the southern half of the Atlantic ocean, even down to Ascension Island and St. Paul's Rock off the Brazilian coast.

As that was all that he would tell me I went back to my ship.

As I journeyed northward I cursed the luck that had put my

ship into Commander Crick's mind. Had it not been for that madcap episode with the special trains he would probably have forgotten all about me. Now, told to pick out six corvettes, he must have run his eye down the list, and recognized my name. Thus I and my *Verbena* were taken. It was not that I objected to the chance of what promised to be an unusual operation. I had simply fallen in love with the job that we had been doing. It was so obviously one which was worth while; and there could be few sights more thrilling to see than an Atlantic convoy. The great concourse of ships, held together by the encircling fringe of escorts, would crawl home before the prevailing westerly winds. Rolling heavily, the deep-laden merchantmen, who held in their capacious bellies the food and armaments for a beleaguered Britain, would spew white water from their scuppers. Poised on the Atlantic swell they would for a short moment be borne steadily forward on the crest, only to sink into the hollows with surprising grace as they waited for the next wave to overtake them. A few weeks later those same ships would be outward-bound again, butting bluff bows into the advancing waves. Still rolling, but more jerkily, and every now and then flinging a sheet of spray from their sterns as their propellers came half out of the water.

We had learned to think with genuine affection of our charges. We remembered them from one convoy to another, and sometimes formed real friendships with them. They too had characters as distinct as those of the individual escorts. Often they earned themselves nick-names. There was 'Smokey Joe', a great ugly surly brute of a ship, who was for ever making smoke. At the change of the watch the first thing the new officer would ask was, 'How's Smokey Joe behaving?' and receive the answer, 'Not so good. He was blowing tubes half an hour ago, and I had to tick him off again. But it's no use telling Smokey anything.' When you had steamed for a week within sight of him you felt you had a special interest in him. When you found him in the next outward-bound convoy but one, you would feel a warm glow of friendship, you might even go alongside to greet him by loud hailer, knowing full well that within a few hours you would receive a signal telling you that Number 34 in the convoy was making smoke, and that the next time you addressed him your remarks would be far from polite.

Consider for a moment the men in those ships. In mid-1941 the U-Boats were sinking as many as sixty ships in a single month, as many as there were in one whole convoy—all lost. Yet there was no lack of men to man the ships. No British ship ever stayed in harbour because she could not find a crew. Was there ever a finer testimonial to our nation?

The bravest ship I ever met was one whom we christened 'Sinbad the Sailor'. We met him first on a homeward-bound convoy. He was immediately noticeable, and would have stood out in any company. From what junk heap of worn-out ships had he been rescued to fight in the most terrible of all wars? 'Sinbad' was a very, very old ship. Almost everything about him went straight up—straight bow, tall slender masts, a very tall and extremely thin funnel. Only his counter was as fine and delicate as that of a steam yacht. When we first met him smoke was pouring from his slim funnel. We had tried commands, arguments, cajolery—all to no purpose. Sinbad was smoking his pipe. That was only the start of it. Very soon he was falling out of bed repeatedly. We put him back time after time. He was so good-humoured about it all that we could not be really cross with him. His captain would come to the rail and wave to me as I called to him over the loud hailer. He was as old as the ship herself. He would stand, a short stocky figure wearing a bowler hat, swaying on the bridge of his ship. The wind fluttered his white mutton chop whiskers, and his red face was always split in a grin of welcome. One imagined that he was the owner as well as the Captain of his crazy charge.

But one day he could not get back to the convoy. Some defect in his aged machinery had reduced his speed to walking pace. I stayed with him as long as I could. At last as dark was coming I received a signal from *Malcolm*.

'Leave your straggler and resume your station.'

I knew why—there were six U-Boats shadowing the convoy.

I went very close alongside.

'Can you not get her going any faster?'

'Nay—Mister——' the words came slowly. I could just hear them above the whistle of the wind and the roar of waters between the ships. 'Nay—we—be—launched—over—fifty—years—ago. It's—an—engineer shop—I—be—needing.'

'I am sorry I must leave you—very sorry. We expect attack on the convoy. Goodnight and good luck.'

'Ay—you—get—off—to—the—convoy—Mister. We'll—be—all—right—you'll—see.'

If I ever prayed for anything it was that the U-Boats would not find our Sinbad that night. Next morning he was out of sight astern. There had been no S.O.S. in the night, and we had kept a special wireless watch for him.

Three weeks later we had taken some ships down to Liverpool. Coming out of the Mersey was a convoy and in the middle of it was Sinbad. Even as we watched a long trail of smoke spread from his high funnel. We could see a watchful corvette leap towards him. We laughed. We knew that one. She would have to do that many times. As we had left our own ships we went over to have a word with him.

He was delighted to see us. They'd almost rebuilt his engines for him. His ship was as good as new, so he said. As we left him we flung out from our yardarm in international code the signal 'Good luck'. In reply a puff of sooty smoke burst from his funnel, and a shower of ashes fell on our decks.

To go to sea in such a crate was to play with death. Yet he went—and had found a crew to go with him. No men could have been braver; and I was now to leave these men and this work which I knew and loved, to go elsewhere.

We took *Verbena* alongside the *Renown* in Rosyth Dockyard, and the complicated radar set was taken out of her and put into us. We felt very important that so vast a ship should be stripped of a new machine for our benefit, and I wondered more and more for what operation we were to be used. We were to sail to Londonderry to await instructions. Letters had told us that our own group would be in harbour, and that a group dance was to be held on the Friday night.

There were now many new faces in the ship's company. My years spent in training officers and men had given me a deep pleasure in seeing them advance. We had been six months at sea, and many men were now passing for leading seamen. Two of our leading seamen had passed for petty officer. The midshipman, recommended for sub-lieutenant, had been taken away and Midshipman A. D. Townsend had his berth. Anyone in *Verbena* who wanted promotion was encouraged to try. This did not result in a lowering of efficiency. New people came up to take the place of old, and friendly relations having been established with the drafting officer at the Barracks, he sent us promising young ratings. Sub-Lieutenant Whittaker had been promoted to Lieutenant, but remained in the ship.

How greatly things had changed since I had taken her up the north-east coast ten months before! Then I was the only officer with any sea experience. Now I had three Lieutenants, all with watch-keeping certificates.

It was a Wednesday night when we left Rosyth, and by Thursday afternoon we were off Cape Wrath, the north-westerly corner of Scotland, and had every chance of making Londonderry in plenty of time for the dance. Rounding the headland we could see into the Minches, that stretch of tide-swept water between the mainland of Scotland and the Outer Hebrides. At once we ran into a gale, with driving rain and fog. This was a special brand of Minch weather. It was surprising how often it could be clear outside and absolutely foul inside the Minches. There appeared to be nothing to do but 'heave to', or proceed very slowly. I thought then of our new radar. If it really did what it was supposed to do we might yet make Londonderry in time. I sent for its operator. Yes he could pick up the land. We tried it. It was wonderful. I asked the operator if he was game to work it for six hours at a stretch himself, because at that time he was the only rating in the ship trained in its use. We started off down the Minches at full speed, and I was amazed at the efficiency of the instrument. No more searching for a convoy in thick weather. Half the worry and strain of a commanding officer's life would be taken away by this wonderful invention. I even forgave it for its terrible outward appearance. In six hours we were through the narrows, and heading for Londonderry river.

It was a wonderful dance. Our friends had the same weather at Londonderry, and knowing when we had sailed they had never expected us to make the passage in time. We were kept very busy for the next few days, showing off our new toy.

And then suddenly, without warning, Hunter went sick. He must have an operation—and *Verbena* a new First Lieutenant. The good that Hunter had done was not easily undone. All that he had built stood firm, and showed no signs of cracking for many months.

A commanding officer is remarkably impotent to tackle many of the problems that arise. Service tradition assumes that both Captain and First Lieutenant are of the first class, as in peace time they usually are. In war this can not always be so. A good commanding officer may have an efficient ship, but he cannot also have a happy one unless he has a good First Lieutenant. Looked at from below the Captain may appear as a deity, benevolent or otherwise according to his nature; but his powers are actually very restricted. He can function only through an efficient body of officers. It is the First Lieutenant in a small ship, the Commander in a big one, who brings to the Captain all the contentious matters, all the problems that arise. It is he who translates the Captain's decisions to the men. In this endless matter of go-between he must tread warily. His first loyalty is of course to his captain, but he must advise him tactfully. His second loyalty is to the men, whose viewpoint he must learn to understand, and often to represent. It is very much of a full time job, for he has his own duties as a ship's officer as well.

Very soon after Hunter had left it became plain that trouble was brewing amongst the crew. I went to see Captain (D) Londonderry, and he decided to replace the new First Lieutenant at once. Two days later we slipped down the river on a wonderful golden morning, bound for adventure we knew not where.

All we knew was that we were being sent as additional escort to join a convoy going to the southward, and that we and the five other specially fitted corvettes were to be detached with those ships of the convoy which were bound for Freetown, Sierra Leone. It was a forty ship convoy, which was small compared with those to which we were accustomed. The escort consisted of six corvettes and two ex-American coastguard cutters. These last were Lease-Lend craft. They were big, unhandy brutes, and except for their long endurance they were not at all suitable for escort work. Even so we should have been able to give the convoy adequate protection. We steamed off westward at nine knots and turned to the south in 15° West. Nothing happened until we reached the latitude of Brest, when we were attacked by Focke-Wulfs. Although no damage was done they would obviously report our position, and I was not surprised when the following night a ship was torpedoed in the convoy. She was carrying ammunition, and blew up with a terrific explosion. Oh for B.12 group! There had been no evening deployment to put down a shadowing U-Boat. We waited for orders that never came. The team had not played together before, and indeed we had no proper Senior Officer of Escorts with us. As the wind was moderate from the north, it was fairly obvious that the attack had come from astern. *Verbena* ran across the wake of the convoy dropping depth charges every five hundred yards. Whether this had any effect I do not know, but the U-Boat was content with his one victim.

The next morning found a large ship straggling. *Verbena* was told to guard her until she had mended herself. We steamed round her for twelve hours. The convoy was then one hundred and eight miles ahead of us. Although our straggler was a fast ship, and when mended could make thirteen knots we only had a speed of four knots in excess of the convoy. It would take us twenty-two hours to catch up. One day at full speed would reduce our oil reserves considerably. Already two corvettes had been sent to the Azores for fuel. By the time we caught up we also were running short of fuel, and had to go there too.

We arrived off Punta Delgada, only to find that the port was closed because of an onshore gale. The seas were enormous. We hove to and waited throughout the night. The next day was just as bad, and although the one after that was a little better, the port was still closed. The position was now desperate. Either we could try to make the harbour, or go and drift about in the Atlantic a prey to any U-Boat. I decided to take her into harbour. Going in was thrilling in the extreme. A huge wave lifted us up and carried us towards the harbour mouth. It raced ahead of us, and we slid down its back. Another came up astern. The entrance of the harbour seemed to be rushing towards us with the speed of an express train. We were surf riding in a vessel weighing twelve hundred tons. The wave on which we travelled burst on the harbour walls, and sent up a huge plume of spray to a hundred feet. As soon as my bow was level with the tower on the end of the breakwater I ordered the wheel hard a-port and the engines full ahead. She lay over as she spun round on her heel and shot into the protected harbour. A pilot boarded us. He was gesticulating madly and talking nineteen to the dozen—a very excitable gentleman, and all in Portuguese. At last he ran out of breath and said in English, 'You very lucky man Sah.'

'I'm much less trouble inside than being a wreck outside,' I told him.

We took in fuel, water, sherry and a quantity of chickens, and left at dawn the next day. They would not let us out that night.

The convoy was now more than three hundred miles ahead, and we received a signal 'Rejoin with all despatch'. We knew why, for the Admiralty had signalled that U-Boats were in the vicinity of the convoy. I had to comply, although it meant using up fuel at a prodigious rate. Four days later we had almost caught up the convoy. Then the escort signalled to us, 'Your friend straggling again. Please do the necessary.'

By using our radar we found her in the night; but it was morning before she got herself going again, and by that time the convoy was one hundred miles ahead once more. There seemed to be no end to it. During the day we heard the escorts that were bound for Freetown being detached, but we still had half a day's steaming to put our straggler back to bed. Early the following morning we pushed him in, said 'au revoir' to the senior of the ex-American cutters and went off to find Freetown.

At full speed we had each day been using more than twice as much fuel as we would have used at cruising speed. We had been at full speed for a week, the equivalent of more than two weeks' steaming at ten knots, and we still had a long way to go. I wondered if we would make it. I had the fire drawn in the second boiler and continued on one. I did not know what there might be in Freetown, but had heard that there was practically nothing. It was unlikely that they would have an ocean tug. I had no fancy for spending any time drifting oil-less in the Atlantic, for when the engines stopped the electrics would stop also. There would then be no radar, and no asdic. I felt it would be better to be going somewhere, even if only very slowly. Besides to have to sail the ship would greatly encourage the men. There are few things so disheartening and so disruptive of morale as lying helpless at sea with the engine stopped. As soon as the steady beat of the propeller dies away and the ship, no longer answering her rudder, begins to drift aimlessly, a sensation of being utterly helpless and lost comes over all on board. It is as if the iron heart of the ship has been in some way connected with your own body. I can think of no punishment more vile for dishonest seamen than that they should be cast adrift in ships whose engines are destined to break down, so that they will drift aimlessly around the great oceans for all eternity.

We spent an amusing and quite profitable morning rigging the corvette for sailing.

The griping spars of the boats, each fourteen foot long, made two yards secured three-quarters of the way up the mast. These were fitted with slings, guys and lifts and stood out at right angles to the mast. They were capable of being trimmed to any required position. On the yard on the weather side we prepared to set the quarter-deck awning, and on the lee side yard to use the bridge awning. The fo'c's'le awning, which was triangular in shape, would serve as a jib. At midday the engineer officer reported that there was virtually no oil left. If we were to make harbour, we had to keep going for another four hours. On the wireless we could hear the other corvettes hunting a U-Boat to the southward, so we could not expect them to come to tow us in. We made a signal for a tug and, as we expected, the answer came back that no tug was available. A most curious smoke was now coming from the funnel, as the stokers burnt the sludge in the bottom of the tanks. The seamen were facetiously sending down to ask which of the stokers was being burnt!

At last the high land behind Freetown came in sight. Slowly our speed dropped. With the anchor ready for slipping we crept into harbour, and anchored as soon as we were inside the boom. After waiting there an hour or more a small tug appeared and towed us to the oiler.

Freetown anchorage was large. Except for the prominent hill behind the town it was curiously like the Solent. The red roofs peeping from the trees on the south side might well have been the village of Lee before it was quite so much built-up. The north shore was a long way across the mud flats, and showed only as a line of green trees on the horizon.

Lying in the anchorage was the most curious collection of

shipping we had ever seen. There were landing craft with strange square bows and big ramps, and an assault ship hung round with dozens of motor launches.

The crews of the fleet oilers were the scandal-mongers of the Navy. Much of their life was spent in secluded anchorages, and the one break in the monotony of their lives was the arrival of ships wanting fuel. They acquired a nice taste in rumour and, subtle as a taster of wine, they could distinguish the genuine from the spurious. If they ran out of facts they were not too particular about spreading fiction. From the oiler we learnt that the strange shipping was an amphibious force intended for a landing on the French African coast. There could be only one objective—Dakar.

Naturally in such an operation they would want the minesweeping corvettes to sweep ahead of the landing ships. It was also now possible to hazard a guess regarding the purpose for which forty large and second-hand lorry tyres had been delivered to the ship before we left England. Up till now we had thought these rather a joke. But taken with an order we had received to practice getting out our minesweeping gear without stopping engines, they suggested that on our projected trip to the shore we should have barge loads of soldiers lashed alongside; and presuming that the 9.2 inch guns had not blown us out of the water first, our radar would enable us to arrive at the correct assault point.

The next day I discovered what I had suspected the evening before. I was one of those people who could not sweat enough to keep going in the tropics. I swelled. By noon my cap was two sizes too small for me, and my shoes were too tight. Men had been flown home who could not sweat. I sent for a carpenter's saw and a large block of wood, and started sawing after lunch. By four o'clock I had sawn that block all ways, and was sweating nicely and feeling a lot better. In the evening Commander Crick and the submarine hunting party returned, and I went with him to call on the Commander-in-Chief, Admiral Willis. Apparently the rumour we had heard from the oiler was right. It was to have been Dakar, but the operation had been postponed indefinitely. We were to be used for ocean escort work until a decision regarding our future was made. The assault craft hung about in Freetown until the following

July, when they were used for the attack on Madagascar. *Verbena* unfortunately missed that action, because by then she had broken down and was in Bombay harbour.

It was in Freetown that I first ran up against serious trouble over my seniority. Commander Crick had picked a good team without realising the implications of 'qualified status'. When sweeping for moored mines the ships work in two sub-divisions; the second senior ship is the sub-divisional leader, and carries quite heavy responsibilities. Commander Crick had brought with him from the fleet minesweepers a Lieutenant-Commander, Royal Navy, whom he had expected to be his sub-divisional leader. However, all the other commanding officers of the corvettes were 'qualified officers'; and I was the senior of the four. To me therefore would fall the duties of sub-divisional leader. I was left in no doubt about the feelings of the R.N. Lieutenant-Commander. I could indeed sympathise with him, for although in the Western Approaches we were by then thoroughly used to commanding officers who were reservists, the main fleets had not yet met us in that capacity.

Commander Crick told me that before he left no one had warned him about the 'qualified officer' status, but that he had no objection at all to *Verbena* leading the second sub-division. Even so I thought the whole position was more than awkward; for I was not only the second senior commanding officer, I was also the youngest. I went to Captain (D) Freetown, Captain Rupert Sherbrooke, now Vice-Admiral R. St. V. Sherbrooke, V.C., C.B., D.S.O. (he won his Victoria Cross in the Arctic on New Year's Eve 1942 when his flotilla fought off the *Lützow*, *Hipper*, and six German destroyers). After explaining the position to him I suggested that my qualified status should not be considered while I was working from Freetown. He replied that I was talking nonsense, and told me that he had just had my most difficult colleague calling on him to complain about the situation. He had told that officer that when his ship was as efficient as *Verbena* he would talk to him. Until that time he would not even meet him socially.

Partly to escape from so difficult a situation, and partly because we were not going to be used as minesweepers, I suggested that *Verbena* be detached to carry out a patrol off St. Paul's Rock on the other side of the Atlantic, where U-Boats were known to replenish from the special tanker submarines called 'milch cows'. We could have fuelled in Brazil, carried out another patrol and then returned to Freetown. Captain Sherbrooke promised to put the suggestion before the Commander-in-Chief; but before the reply was received a U-Boat was reported south of Freetown, and I was ordered to take the three corvettes commanded by the R.N.R. officers and search for it. We never found the enemy, but I did have a conversation with one of her officers over the radio telephone, and he very nearly tricked me into giving away the plan of my hunt. For a time the Germans did try the dodge of fitting their boats with a radio telephone working on the same wave-length as our own, and supplying them with an English-speaking officer. They would break into our conversation in an attempt either to mislead the hunt, or to discover what we were up to. In this particular case I had sent two ships to one end of the 'probability area' while I, with the fourth, worked inwards towards the spot where the enemy had been reported. The U-Boat would therefore have ships to the north and south of him, the pairs of ships being out of sight of each other.

We were using as call signs the nicknames of the commanding officers, my own being 'Ben'. When 'Possum' was heard to call 'Ben' on the R/T and ask for my intentions, I might well have given him the plan of my hunt had the German not added, 'and what is your geographical position now?' As 'Possum' was the ship hunting with me it was a rather peculiar question, because he knew the whereabouts of the pair of us as well as I did. I called to him by light, 'Did you make that signal asking for my position?' and got back the reply, 'Not me.'

Had we been able to use visual signals to the other ships it might perhaps have been possible to double-bluff the Hun. With the ships out of sight I had to signal to the group, 'There is a Hun butting in on our conversation. All future signals to be coded.'

It was I think the first occasion that they tried to catch us in this way. An immediate signal was made to the Commander-in-Chief telling him of this new trick.

Only luck would have enabled us to catch that U-Boat, since it was one of those many hunts when the delay between the first sighting and the arrival of the hunters really made the position hopeless.

After this the four of us were ordered to take a fast convoy down to the Cape of Good Hope, refuel in Capetown and then bring another one north.

These ships were not like the merchantmen that we were used to escorting. They were big passenger liners, and they were full of soldiers going to join the armies in Egypt and the Far East. The speed of the convoy was fifteen knots, the same as our own best speed. It was a nerve-racking job because, if we lost station on the convoy it was impossible to regain it; and we could carry out no anti-U-Boat manoeuvres at all for the safety of our charges. An anti-submarine escort can only be fully effective when the escorting ships have a big excess of speed over that of the convoy.

On the way down to Capetown on the 7th December came news of the Japanese attack on Pearl Harbour, and on the 9th we heard of the German and Italian declarations of war on America. The United States were now in it up to the hilt. Not only was it nice to feel that we were no longer alone; but from our experience in the Western Approaches we well knew what a vast difference it would make to the convoy system in the Atlantic. Now perhaps we would really have a chance to take the offensive against the U-Boats. We longed to be back there to see that fight out rather than go eastward, for I had very little expectation of seeing Freetown again. Personally I had little to complain of. I found myself senior officer of four efficient corvettes, and so long as we were used for anti-submarine work I felt confident of our ability to do our job.

One by one the escorts were detached to refuel at Port au France in French Equatorial Africa. When our turn came I felt quite excited at the prospect of seeing a tropical port. In my imagination I had pictured a sheltered harbour, with great trees hanging over a land-locked bay; enormous creepers, draped like writhing snakes would be festooned from the heavy branches; while monkeys, parrots and strange butterflies would be much in evidence.

I felt that the glamour of the tropics would be all the more impressive if I were to come suddenly upon the scene I had visualised; so I fixed the ship's position from the morning stars, and then went below to my cabin having told the officer of the watch that I was not to be called to the bridge again until the detail of the trees could be seen.

In due course I was told that land had been sighted; that the lighthouse on the harbour entrance was in sight; that the radar range of the nearest land was one mile.

'But surely you can see the trees now?'

'No Sir—sorry Sir.'

Damn it—I'd have to go up. I went on to the bridge. The land ahead of me was quite bare, and strikingly like the Berkshire Downs. There were no trees, and no monkeys. It was one of the most bitter disappointments of my life.

We were to oil from a pipe line on the jetty. The previous corvette had not yet finished. It was four o'clock in the afternoon before we started to take in the oil, which was fed by gravity from a tank on the hill. At that rate it would take us four hours to fuel.

We decided to call on the local Governor, of whom rumour said that he was rather inclined to side with the Vichy French. The First Lieutenant and I started off to walk the two miles to Government House. When we got there we were told that he was away; but we did not quite believe this as we thought we saw somebody slipping quickly away from a window. We had no option but to retrace our steps, but we had quite overlooked the suddenness with which a tropic night descends. One moment there was the sun, low but bright in the sky. The next it was pitch dark.

The road back to the port was entirely deserted. Hardly had darkness fallen when we heard something patter across the road very fast behind us. We spun round, and something about the size of a small dog crossed quickly. We turned again, and once more there was a dry rustle and a curious clicking behind us. It was all very eerie.

'Land crabs,' I said.

'Are they friendly, Sir?'

'Frankly I'm damned if I know.'

We had stopped and they were coming closer.

'I wish they wouldn't make that noise Sir.'

'Number One,' I said, 'I'm going to run for it. It may be cowardly, but I'd feel happier.'

We pounded down that road as if the devil himself was after us.

We escorted our convoy well south of the Cape, and then were ordered to Simonstown to refuel. There we were told that we would not be going back to Freetown. We were to remain at the Cape to await instructions.

The state of the war in the Pacific was critical in the extreme. The Japs, using a striking force of carrier-borne bombers, had temporarily wiped out the American Pacific Fleet at Pearl Harbour on the 7th December; and a few days later we had lost the old battle cruiser *Repulse* and the new battleship *Prince of Wales*. Except for a few destroyers of the Eastern Fleet we were the most readily available escort ships, and it seemed only too probable that within a matter of days we should be going on eastward.

As senior officer of the four ships I was now faced with a very serious problem. All the ships needed boiler cleaning. We ourselves had 1,500 hours on our boilers when we arrived. Any advance eastward to the theatre of war would mean at least another 500 hours steaming. When we arrived we would have to boiler-clean before we could be used for operations. It therefore seemed obvious to me that we should do so in Capetown, and at once. I could get nothing done. We were told to remain at four hours' notice, and to await instructions. In vain I pointed out that to keep these ships, which had fire tube boilers, at four hours' notice was exactly the same as keeping them at sea; because one boiler must be alight all the time. In spite of all I could do the ships lay there adding hours to their boiler time. We were there for one month 'awaiting orders'.

But it was a month that brought us a great deal of fun. The hospitality committee at Capetown gave us all, officers and men, a wonderful time. We were the first visitors from the real war who had stayed for any length of time, and the local hostesses vied with each other for our company. I found myself lent a powerful American saloon car the better to drive to see my hosts, or to reach the stables where the horses were kept. We organized a wonderful telephone system for recalling the ships' companies in the event of our being given sailing orders, and this system was responsible one day for an urgent recall for me.

Going to the telephone I was told by a horrified Lieutenant Whittaker that he had lost overboard the keys of the confidential safe. He had been inspecting liberty men, and afterwards had walked along the deck spinning the keys round his finger, when they had flown off and over the side. What should he do? Should he report the loss to the Admiralty as was laid down? I told him to do nothing, and hurried back to the ship which was lying in the new tidal dock in Capetown. I knew that the bottom was clean sand. If only we had possessed a magnet we might, so I thought, perhaps have been able to recover them. I suddenly had a brainwave and took all the magnets from the magnetic compass. I tied them together in a bundle until they looked like a bunch of asparagus, and when we had attached these to a line we began dragging the bottom of the dock. Whittaker and the quartermaster of the watch kept it up all night. Not I—I slept. As I was having breakfast the following morning Whittaker came to me.

'It's no use, Sir. We'll never find them. We'll have to report the loss and get a diver.'

'Go on,' I told him, 'until after I have finished my breakfast. If you haven't got them by then I'll telephone to Simonstown and see if they can send us a diver.'

I had hardly started my second cup of coffee when Whittaker burst into my cabin with the keys in his hand. A board of enquiry had been avoided. Now I had to put back all those magnets in the compass, and re-swing the ship. Fortunately I still had my notebooks from the days when I had taken my navigation examination nine years before. With that help it proved quite simple.

We kept *Verbena's* second Christmas in Simonstown Dockyard. On Christmas Eve I had made a signal to the Naval Store Officer asking for a new boat to replace the one that had been smashed in the gale off the Azores, and had added, 'It would be a nice Christmas present if this boat should be fitted with sails and a centreboard.' But the Captain of the Dockyard had answered that no such boats were available at Simonstown.

On Christmas morning the quartermaster reported that a tug was coming alongside with a boat. The boat had both sails and a centreboard, and on the centreboard case was a note tied with red ribbon 'With the compliments of the Naval Store Officer—A Merry Christmas.'

One sensed a certain coolness between the Naval Store Officer and the Captain of the Dockyard.

At last our signal came. I was recalled and told, 'You are to sail tomorrow afternoon for Singapore.' It was then the 28th of January, 1942. All the ships had over 1,500 hours on their boilers, and *Verbena* had nearly two thousand. I refused to sail unless all the facts were reported to Commander-in-Chief, Western Approaches, as we still considered we belonged to his command. Other authorities were only too ready to use us, but not to look after us.

It was not a pleasant interview. At last when we had reached a deadlock I was told 'Very well, I must tell you in strict confidence—you are going to evacuate Singapore. Now will you sail?'

'Yes Sir' I said and left the room.

We prepared to sail and were unexpectedly joined by a fifth corvette, the *Aster* (Commander E. Hewitt R.N.R.). He had been sent down to take over as Senior Officer of the Group. With the difficulties facing us over maintenance I was only too pleased to hand over to him.

We fuelled at Durban and at Mauritius.

Mauritius is a fantastic island. It lies in the middle of the Indian Ocean, and in this the clearest of all seas, the masts of ships whose hulls are below the horizon can easily be seen. The high ridge of mountains down the middle of the island appeared above the rim of the ocean like the spined back of some prehistoric monster; and the tree-covered hills were, at that great distance, an olive green colour such as one would expect from the skin of some giant reptile.

While the ships fuelled their Captains and First Lieutenants were invited to dinner by the Governor and his charming American wife. There, sitting at a long table under the open colonnade of a great porch that ran the whole length of Government House, it was difficult to realise that the war was so near. As I looked down the long line of officers and of ladies, the candles in their little glass bowls cast a warm glow over the diners, who all sat at one side of the table. On the other side, across a lighted fountain in which goldfish swam there was a floodlit gazebo; and beyond it was the dark backcloth of the star-filled tropic night. After dinner there was dancing, and we returned very late to the ships.

At Durban we had been asked to take to Mauritius some soldiers who had been wounded in North Africa, and had been waiting many weeks for a ship to take them home. We had agreed to give them passage. They were black, and proved to be lousy. They were, however, charming fellows, and from what they told us we gathered that the lice were their misfortune rather than their fault. We were able to buy enough sulphur candles to fumigate the mess decks as soon as we got to Colombo, and so the harm they did was not lasting.

We sailed from Mauritius on the 8th February 1942. Singapore fell on the 13th when we were south of Ceylon. As no signal had reached us amending our instructions Commander Hewitt broke wireless silence, and signalled to Colombo for orders. The reply came almost at once. My guess was that our pin had fallen out of the map. We were to go to Colombo. Commander Hewitt and I went to call on Commander-in-Chief, East Indies, Admiral Arbuthnot. Hewitt found himself immediately taken out of his ship, and given a station appointment to a sloop whose captain was sick. He went off at once to pack his things. His own First Lieutenant was put in command of the *Aster*. Once again I was left to deal with a base which had never heard of corvettes, and had no time to spare to come and see for themselves. The staff which had been adequate in the old days was quite unable to cope, if only numerically, with the many big new problems forced upon it. On entering the harbour we had been instructed to secure ourselves in berths which were only suitable for a ship half our size —indeed we should have been aground before we even got to them. They would treat us either as trawlers or what was almost worse, would give us jobs beyond our capacity. A complete new staff was on its way out from England, but they were not expected until May. In the meantime, the few officers shouldered fantastic burdens, and did the best they could.

Once again I was begging for boiler-cleans; but the ships must run till they burst. During March the Jap carrier force, which had done the damage at Pearl Harbour, appeared south of Java, and in the first week of April they struck at a convoy coming down from Calcutta; and ever since we had been there they had kept a submarine at sea off the coast of Ceylon. Our job was to escort convoys from Trincomalee on the east coast, round the southern tip of Ceylon to Colombo, and thence up to Bombay. For this and the many special escort jobs I had only the four corvettes and a little Greek destroyer.

The *Aetos* was a marvellous little ship. At a distance she looked like a modern 'D Class' destroyer; but she was really only a tiny model of one, and displaced little more than 600 tons. She had been built before the first world war and modernized between the wars by Samuel White of Cowes. She was absolutely full of fight, and I had great difficulty with her one night coming southward from Trincomalee when we came across a Jap cruiser. She badly wanted to go in and fight, but we were escorting a very valuable oil tanker which was to fuel our battleships at Addu Atoll. I knew that no other oil was immediately available, and therefore refused *Aetos*' request. Hastily steaming inshore we sought the shelter of the dark hills, while *Verbena* kept between the cruiser and the tanker and made white smoke.

We took our charge to Addu Atoll, which is a wonderful picture-book coral atoll about six hundred miles south-west of Colombo. The four 'R Class' battleships arrived, and while they fuelled from the tanker *Aetos* and *Verbena* kept asdic watch outside the entrance. Round the atoll we experienced the most fantastic ocean currents, and it was nothing to be swept twenty miles off our patrol line between the evening star sight and the morning one. The 'R Class' battleships then left for Mombasa. That was the best place for them, as they were far too old to be used against the Jap aircraft carrier force.

We got back to Colombo just three days before Easter 1942, and were told to prepare ourselves for a boiler clean. Half the ship's company were sent up to the rest camp in the hills. The boilers were opened up on the Saturday night, and I went ashore to enjoy an evening with friends. We had been very fortunate to reach Colombo before the war got too big for the local population to cope with. There was still a hospitality committee when we first arrived, and we had been given introductions and already had friends ashore. Later Colombo was flooded with naval officers, and the small white colony then rather drew into its shell.

In the middle of a very pleasant dinner I was called to the telephone. It was my yeoman Newnes speaking. There was a general recall. Excusing myself I jumped into a rick-shaw and was soon aboard. Newnes showed me the signal. 'Anticipate attack by air-borne carrier force a.m. tomorrow. All ships should be prepared to counter possible sea-borne attack.'

It was not much later than nine o'clock. I mustered all the ship's company left aboard, and we spent two hours exercising action stations. We had not enough men for the ammunition supply parties, so we brought up as much ammunition as we thought necessary and stowed it near the guns. The attack would be short and sharp anyway. Then, as the ship was not berthed parallel with the harbour wall, we laid out a warp so that we would be able to haul her round and allow the 4-inch gun to cover the sea approach. I went to sleep in my sea-berth on the bridge.

At six o'clock we went to action stations, and then sent the men to breakfast in the galley, four at a time. Nothing happened. The sun rose and a great bank of cloud lay to the south of the town. It was this cloud which interfered with the radar defences. At 8.15 we got a general signal from the tower saying that the ships' companies could be sent to breakfast. Newnes showed me the signal. 'We've had our breakfast, Newnes. The men are quite happy, so we'll stay as we are for a bit longer; but I'm going down to get myself a book from my cabin.'

I was half-way down the second ladder when both the bridge Oerlikons and the four-barrel heavy machine gun began firing. By the time I got back to the bridge it was all over, but I did just see the bullets from the port Oerlikon going straght into the nose of a Jap plane. We claimed three shot down. The Jap planes came out of that cloud in sections of three planes each. Each section chose a target, and attacked it from three separate directions.

We looked round the anchorage. The *Hector*, an armed merchant cruiser, was on fire. A bomb had exploded inside the depot ship *Lucia*. An 'S Class' destroyer was under water, with only her funnels and bridge showing, and a fleet auxiliary was on her side. We were the only warship in harbour still afloat. The multiple machine gun was manned by its own gunlayer. One bridge Oerlikon was manned by signalman Reeves, and the other by an asdic rating. Each of our attackers took it full on the nose. Two ended up in the sea, and one outside the Galle Face Hotel.

We made a signal reporting three enemy aircraft destroyed, and as we had nothing better to do we stayed at action stations, in case the enemy should return. An hour later the signal tower was calling us. I had expected a congratulatory signal. What I got was, 'Why have I not received your return of church parties for Sunday, 29th March?'

Newnes' remarks almost burnt up the signal lamp. On the previous Sunday we had been playing 'tick' with the Jap cruiser.

'No—you're wrong yeoman,' I told him. 'Don't you see it's the most wonderful signal in the world? It's just the same as those little notices we've seen stuck on the bombed shops at home. It means "business as usual". It's quite true I haven't sent the ruddy form, and I ought to have done so.'

The ensuing scramble on the part of the population had to be seen to be believed. It was estimated that the crowd outside the railway station was over a hundred thousand. The Singhalese were not going to stay if the Japs got busy. They ran for the mountains; but rice was rationed, and their ration cards could only be cashed in their own home town. Hunger, and relations indignant at sharing their rice, drove them slowly back to Colombo.

On that same Easter Day the *Dorsetshire* and *Cornwall* were intercepted by the Jap striking force and sunk south of Ceylon. Four days later the aircraft carrier *Hermes* and one of our corvettes the *Hollyhock*, who was her anti-submarine escort, were sunk together off Trincomalee with very heavy loss of life. *Hermes* had been in Simonstown with us in January, and we knew her officers well. We were particularly 'chummy' ships with the *Hollyhock* whose commanding officer, Lieutenant-Commander T. E. Davies R.N.R., had been a very good friend of mine.

Those of our crew who were in the rest camp were sent down to us, and we were told to close up the still uncleaned boilers and raise steam immediately. The same night the quartermaster came down to my cabin, where I was having a talk with my new First Lieutenant, and told us that a barge had drifted alongside. That night Colombo harbour was full of strange things. I was just about to tell the quartermaster to give it a push and get rid of it, when my new officer suggested we look inside it first. We did. Under the cover were Oerlikon guns. We turned out the ship's company, and we had two of those hoisted aboard within half an hour. Then we gave the barge a push and sent it clear of us. We had only two breast drills to pierce the necessary holes in the steel deck, and they blunted very quickly. Every man in the ship, officers included, took a fifteen minute spell on the drills and we had those two guns bolted down by sunrise. After a lick of paint no one would know that they had not been there for months. We now needed ammunition for our new trophies, and as the chief had reported steam available for the engines we took the ship over to the ammunition store. There was still a considerable panic ashore, and we filled ourselves up with ammunition for the asking. We even had it stowed in my cabin and under the wardroom table.

The new Number One whom I have just introduced had come to me through a 'station appointment'. He had been at Singapore when it fell. If the reader blames us for thieving, he should hear the tales of the Singapore disaster; how after using the ammunition to the last round they were unable to draw any more, although there was plenty in the Fortress. Riches did not intend the same thing to happen twice in a lifetime if he could prevent it.

He was quite a different type of man to his immediate predecessor. Before the war he had been in business in Singapore, and was used to the East. He was a Lieutenant in the Singapore Division of the R.N.V.R., and was well grounded in service customs. He was a real go-getter, and knew just how to go about the East getting things. As a matter of fact that was the one point on which we did not quite see eye to eye. His limit of how far it was allowable to go in order to get something for the ship was considerably in advance even of mine. He acquired a real motor boat from Bombay Dockyard by means which can only be described as dubious; but perhaps he reached his high water mark of devilry a week or two later.

I had always disliked the plain iron hand-rails on the ladders leading from the wardroom to the flat where my cabin was, and thence upward to the deck. We had tried to cover them with canvas on which neat 'turks-heads' had been worked, but there was too much traffic up and down those ladders for the canvas to last. I had often asked various bases for teak rails to be fitted, but always without result.

At this particular time we were lying in Bombay outside the big fleet destroyer *Nubian* (Commander D. E. Holland-Martin R.N.) I came aboard one night, and as I was passing over her deck the captain met me and asked me into his cabin for a drink. There amongst other things he talked about the awful thieving that went on in the dockyard.

'Damn it, Rayner, this afternoon my First Lieutenant put the new teak accommodation ladder ashore right alongside the ship—within full view of my quartermasters; and do you know it's gone—and no one knows where or how? It's just been spirited away, and the dockyard can't make me another in time.'

Naturally I expressed my sorrow at this disaster, because I knew how terribly difficult it was to get anything nice for your ship in war time.

It was dark when I crossed over to *Verbena*. As I went in through the blackout screen, I put out my hand to grasp the well known iron rail—but my fingers closed on substantial wood. I struck a match, and there was a teak rail. I looked upward at the other ladder. It too had miraculously grown a similar rail since tea time. The match burnt my fingers.

'Number One,' I called out to the dimly lit flat below, 'Come out you bloody thief.'

He came out grinning and stood looking up at me.

'Number One I presume that these are all that are mortal of *Nubian's* new accommodation ladder.'

'That's right Sir—very careless ship that, Sir. Leaves her gear all over the jetty.'

'Careless or not, her captain's coming to drink with me tomorrow night.'

'That's fine Sir,' (he sounded really pleased) 'He's never been aboard us before. He'll not know Sir.'

'Perhaps not—but it's devilish awkward for me. I wish you'd learn where to stop.'

I started for my own cabin, and then curiosity got the better of me. I went back.

'How did you do it?'

'I gave some Indian "dockyard maties" a couple of tins of tobacco. They picked it up quite easily as if they were taking it away, put it on a barge and brought it round to our starboard side.'

An over-zealous First Lieutenant can be a nightmare, but he did my ship a power of good; for he was a first-class officer, and the men liked him.

We did not get our boiler-clean at Colombo after all. We went to sea again to take a convoy round to Trincomalee with three thousand hours on our boilers. On the way back to Colombo we received a signal.

'Embark one hundred sheep, one hundred goats for Addu Atoll.'

The First Lieutenant looked at it dubiously. I laughed.

'Don't worry it can't mean what it says. It's some silly code. Sheep for soldiers, goats for marines. They can't really be turning us into a Noah's Ark.'

But they were. Apparently units of the Indian Army had been put on the island with anti-aircraft guns. Being Mohammedan they needed fresh killed meat. We delivered the goods, but we stank to high heaven.

A fortnight later we were taking a convoy up to Karachi. It was a big convoy, and for once we had one of the other corvettes, the *Heliotrope* with us.

Passing Bombay the engineer came on the bridge. 'Sorry Sir, I've had to draw the fire in Number 2 boiler. The water's running out of the firebox doors.'

'What is it, chief. Tubes gone?'

'Afraid so, Sir.'

I made a signal to *Heliotrope*.

'Take over convoy; I have serious boiler defect and must go into Bombay.'

It was quite impossible to keep up with the convoy on only

one boiler. It was the constant high speed work as much as the lack of boiler cleaning which had proved *Verbena's* undoing.

We limped into Bombay. As we manoeuvred the ship to go alongside the jetty in the Naval dockyard the telephone from the engine-room rang on the bridge. I picked up the hand-set. The engineer was telling me that the other boiler had gone too, and that he must stop the engines. 'Just five minutes chief,' I begged.

'I dur's'n't, Sir.'

'All right we'll anchor.'

I leant over the fore side of the bridge.

'Number One, I'm going to anchor. The chief's bust his second kettle.'

I never handled *Verbena* again. We were towed the remaining two hundred yards.

Examination proved that we needed eight hundred and sixty-four new tubes. They could not be made in India, but must be shipped out from home. The first consignment was in a ship that was torpedoed. We put into Bombay in May, and in August we were still there. My lovely *Verbena* was only an anti-aircraft guard-ship lying off the Taj Mahal Hotel.

I did not waste my time. I arranged as well as I could for the comfort of the men. We kept two-thirds of the ship's company up country in a rest camp, and one-third aboard. I took leave as often as I could. I explored India from the jungles south of Belgaum, through the fantastic Mount Abu that rises sheer from the plain of Rajputana, to the North-West Frontier where I made a trip of two hundred miles on horseback into the Harboi hills; and I stayed at Kalat as a guest of the Khan. There, as I was the first naval officer ever to visit Kalat, I was pressed into inspecting the whole of the Kalat state force—all 2,000 of them. I arrived on the parade ground after a ride of some thirty miles on a lovely chestnut mare wearing my number one white uniform, which by the grace of heaven I had with me, and surrounded by an escort of hill tribesmen on their ponies. It was magnificent fun—but it was not war.

I longed for the North Atlantic convoys, and there was still no news of *Verbena's* boiler tubes.

The trouncing which the United States Navy had given to the Jap aircraft carrier force at the Battle of Midway Island in

June 1942, had removed the threat to India of a sea-borne invasion direct from Rangoon and Singapore across to the Madras coast. The Japanese U-Boats were obviously of very inferior calibre to the German craft, and had shown a very different spirit to that of the Jap airmen. As there could be no general advance into the eastern Indian Ocean until Germany had been dealt with, it was plain to me that advancement in my chosen anti-submarine profession could only come from service in the Western Approaches.

A chest complaint could turn to anything, and as the doctors wanted to invalid me home, I allowed them to do so. I stepped on board a troopship early in September 1942.

The ship docked in Liverpool on Christmas Eve. I went straight home, and then immediately after Christmas up to London to see the Admiralty. To my surprise I was asked if I could handle a destroyer. Naturally I said that I could, and I walked out of the Admiralty with an appointment to command the 'S Class' destroyer *Shikari*. I could hardly believe my own senses, for I was the first R.N.V.R. in the history of the Navy to be appointed to a destroyer.

I went back to Liverpool to call on the new Commander-in-Chief, Western Approaches, Admiral Max Horton. I had heard all sorts of things about this new Admiral. Some people swore by him, other people swore at him.

It is impossible to be a very efficient senior officer, and at the same time to be universally popular. The actions which such officers must take for the good of the service will almost certainly cause trouble and heartburning to a number of perfectly decent human beings, who do not happen to measure up to their standards of super-efficiency; and to climb in any service sometimes involves treading on the toes of one's contemporaries. It is enough that Max Horton's own staff regarded him as something less than God but more than Man. If they had not done so they would have found themselves relieved.

The staff that he had built up was very good indeed, for he certainly had a flair for picking men. He had more personal charm than any man I have ever met, but he could be unbelievably cruel to those who fell by the wayside. There is a picture by Goya of a 'Grand Inquisitor' which suggests much the same characteristics. Quite by chance I was later to discover the key to his character. He loved, and I really mean loved, the things which he himself had built; the Northern Patrol Command which he held from the outbreak of war to December 1939; the Submarine Command from January 1940 to November 1942, and the Western Approaches from November 1942 to the end of the war.

These great commands, in all of which he was outstandingly successful, were wife and children to him. Is it too much to suppose that when the last closed down the man himself could no longer live? At any rate he only survived his last command by six years. No one seeing him on the eve of victory would have believed that he would last for such a short time in the retirement that he sought as soon as the Western Approaches ceased to exist.

Max Horton's achievement in Western Approaches was tremendous, but he was more than fortunate in those who had gone before him. He took command at a time when a great many vital reforms initiated by his brilliant, if less well known, predecessors were coming to fruition. By any standards the Western Approaches command was already extremely efficient. Admiral Sir Percy Noble had succeeded in creating a first-class organization before ever Max Horton arrived, and before him Admiral Dunbar-Nasmith had started from nothing to build the broad foundation on which the whole edifice was to rest. It is profitless to venture an opinion as to what the ultimate position would have been if these three great officers had taken over the command in a different sequence. For what it is worth my guess is that the final outcome would have been much the same under any one of them. If I came to know Max Horton better than the other two, it was only because in their day I was very small fry indeed.

There had been great changes in the Western Approaches in the fifteen months that I had been away. All the old Escort Commanders had been replaced by new, for there was a limit to the point to which flesh and blood could be driven. Howard-Johnston was now Anti-U-Boat Officer at the Admiralty, and had been promoted Captain. The new Commander-in-Chief brought in a number of new officers, many of them ex-submariners like himself. His new tactical school, under the direction of Captain G. H. Roberts R.N., had already set about evolving a general tactical system for dealing with the U-Boats. At this time of the war they were hunting in packs, and had been doing enormous damage if they succeeded in breaking through the escort screen. I believe that Max's secret was no more and no less than this. He saw that some groups whose team work was excellent achieved results, and that others were less effective. Being himself strongly biassed towards the offensive, he concluded that it was in the tactics of offensive-defence that success would be gained.

Here we should note that the lack of trained ships would have prevented either of his predecessors from passing from the defensive to the offensive, however much they may have wished to do so. Basically Max's achievement was, with the help of his tactical school, to co-ordinate the best of each group's tactics, and to provide the punch to get his new 'Convoy Instructions' carried out. When he had done this and protected his convoys, he could then organize the destruction of the enemy by creating from the new ships coming forward the Support Groups, whose work reached its zenith in the hands of the greatest of all Escort Group Commanders—Captain F. J. Walker R.N.

I went to call on Admiral Max Horton. He told me that *Shikari* was in Belfast refitting, and that I was to do a tactical course and join her in a month. He told me also that he was collecting all the 'S Class' destroyers into one fast escort group. Naturally I was interested, for I wondered who the Senior Officer would be. I had opportunity for wondering, because my interview was interrupted by an officer of the Free French Navy. This officer had produced a chart, and there had been a certain amount of leaning over tables looking at it. When he left the Admiral turned to me.

'Rayner, had that man really a revolver in his hip pocket?'

'Yes Sir', I answered. 'He obviously hasn't learnt the difference between British and French Admirals.'

The interview continued, and I was kept wondering just when I should take my leave. I can only assume that Max was sizing me up, for when I did see a chance to go he said, as I got up from the chair, 'You realize that you will be Senior Officer of the 21st Escort Group.'

I left him in a complete daze. This was something that was

beyond even my wildest dreams. I would have not one 'S Class' destroyer, but all six under my command. I could see them already—six long pencils of ships—the bow waves level with the fo'c's'le as they manoeuvred at speed. I tried them in line abreast, and I tried them in line ahead. They looked wonderful whichever way I tried to see them. I fell down the stairs on the way out, and was picked up by an astonished Wren officer who obviously thought that I was drunk.

CHAPTER VI

SHIKARI AND THE ROSEGARDEN

I JOINED *Shikari* in Belfast. She was lying in the dry dock, the beautiful hull a delight to the eye. Before going aboard I walked around her admiring the cunning of the draughtsman who put her lines on paper. It was only a pity that she had not been built on a bigger scale, for then she would have been the perfect escort vessel. It appeared to a seaman's eye that she was carrying far too much gear on the upper deck—as indeed she was; for she had been designed in the first world war as a small fleet destroyer to deal with German torpedo-boats in the North Sea. It had never been intended that she should work in the wilder weather and much bigger waves of the North Atlantic, and certainly her designer had never meant her to carry 110 depth-charges on the upper deck, with all their heavy throwing gear. Looking at her in the graving dock I could see that her present waterline was eighteen inches higher than the designer had planned.

It is almost an inevitable fate that the Navy should ruin the plans of any ship designer. During the comparatively long life of a ship, the weapons she carries are bound to develop and change; but her hull remains the same as when it was built. This is no new problem. Henry VIII had exactly the same trouble with the *Great Harry*, when he had hopelessly overgunned her. Pepys mentions similar problems, and we find Captain Cochrane in the Napoleonic Wars complaining bitterly that his ship was 'crank' because the Admiralty had replaced his 32-pounder carronades with the new long gun.

The changes in armament nearly always mean added top weight, and so reduce stability. I daresay that there are few commanding officers, at any rate of the smaller ships, who have not on some occasion had their hearts in their mouths for this reason. *Shikari's* designed metacentric height was eleven inches.

This meant that her centre of gravity should have been eleven inches below her centre of buoyancy. I had a stability test taken before we left dock, and found that alterations and additions had reduced the metacentric height to four inches, which was far too little for a ship of her size.

As I was walking round the dock I noticed the officer of the day keeping an eye on me. I could imagine the poor man's feelings, waiting for his new commanding officer and wondering when the fellow was going to come over the gangway.

I went aboard. The sub-lieutenant who was officer of the day showed me round. A new after funnel had just been lowered into position by a gigantic crane.

'You lost the funnel overboard?'

'Yes Sir.'

'Do you often lose a funnel over the side?'

'Not often Sir—not funnels.'

We went on along the upper deck.

'Where's the motor boat?'

'Don't carry one Sir.'

'Why ever not?'

'Not worth it Sir; we lose 'em. N.S.O. got fed up with replacing them, so we have two whalers now instead. We don't often lose both, and you can get whalers off the hook.'

We went on forward.

'What happened to the bridge, Sub?'

'She stuck her nose into a big one and it flattened the Captain's sea cabin—just like that, Sir. Luckily the Captain wasn't in his bunk at the time.'

I agreed.

'We'd have needed a tin-opener to get him out.'

In bad weather I never slept very soundly in that sea cabin.

It appeared that my latest pride and joy was going to be a 'problem child'—and so she turned out to be. A few pertinent questions revealed the astonishing fact that she had not recommissioned since 1938. At least sixty per cent of the ship's company were long-service ratings, and there were Petty Officers in the ship who had joined her as able seamen. Enquiries as to why this party of old shellbacks remained year after year in an old, not too seaworthy and terribly congested ship (for the asdic, radar, and depth-charge crews added nearly forty men to the number for which the messdecks had been designed) elicited the opinion that the men liked her because she spent so much time in harbour having weather damage repaired! Such a reason for staying in an uncomfortable ship did not sound too promising from my point of view. As Senior Officer of the group it was absolutely essential for the ship to go to sea whenever she was ordered to do so. The attitude of the officers and the ship's company can make a great difference in this respect. Defects of a marginal nature can either be overstated or understated. In war time in the Western Approaches the commanding officers had a good deal of control over this problem. I had always taken the view that even a half efficient escort was better than no escort at all.

Her First Lieutenant came back from leave that night. It was my first experience of having regular officers of the Royal Navy serving under me, and I was disappointed in the extreme when he appeared to be of the opinion that *Shikari* was a good appointment because one got so much leave. The next day I took a car from Belfast Naval Base and motored the sixty odd miles to Londonderry to see the new Commodore (D). If *Shikari's* views were to be altered I wanted a First Lieutenant whose outlook was the same as mine.

To ask for a new First Lieutenant on a first call on your new Flag Officer is not an easy matter. It is never an easy matter. However great your justification in your own eyes, there is the danger that you may be damning yourself as one of those men with whom it is impossible to get on. I had never met Commodore G. W. G. Simpson, and had no idea what I should find.

I was fortunate. I found a sympathetic ear, and as a result three days later a new First Lieutenant arrived aboard—Lieutenant G. Blackwood, R.N. There was never any question about him from the moment his stocky figure appeared in my cabin. He was a terrific worker, a first class seaman and came from a family which had the Navy in its blood for generations. Nelson had a Captain Blackwood amongst his 'band of brothers' and if he was anything like our 'Blacky' I am sure his ship was both happy and efficient.

All the time we had her *Shikari* went to sea exactly when she was ordered to do so. It was true that on one occasion she nearly let us down when the dynamo failed to 'excite'. It went round and round perfectly, but no current came from it. The base engineer officers were called in and a galaxy of talent was fiddling with the machine, trying this and that. I joined the party in the engine-room to ask how much longer they would be. When I got a vague reply I remembered the old stoker's precept for dealing with recalcitrant machinery, 'Give it one with the sledge, mate.' So I picked up a heavy hammer and gave that dynamo three sharp blows. Immediately it sprang to 'life' and we sailed on time.

We left Belfast for Londonderry at the end of February. Twenty thousand horse-power in two steam turbines was a joy to handle after *Verbena's* twelve hundred horse-power.

We went down Belfast Lough at ten knots, with the engines turning at one hundred revolutions each minute. As soon as we were at sea I rang down for two hundred and thirty revolutions and was amazed at the way she leapt forward. The powerful engines seemed to thrust the very deck from under my feet.

It was blowing hard from the north-west, but the sea was calm under the land; and even when we got to Rathlin Island sound the wind and tide were going the same way, so that the seas were remarkably small.

On our way round we took in a signal from the Commander-in-Chief, Western Approaches, 'Fuel at Moville and proceed to a position 200 miles south-west of Iceland where a tank-landing craft with survivors has been reported by aircraft.' The position was about five hundred miles from the north-west corner of Scotland.

Moville was the name of the anchorage at the seaward end of the River Foyle, which leads to Londonderry. The tide was approaching the turn as we neared the oiler, and the strong westerly wind had swung her stern towards the shallow sandbank on the east side. There was barely room to turn up to the oiler and, to make matters worse, I had to berth on her downtide side. Finally, and just to round off the problem, a destroyer was already lying alongside, and her commanding officer was *Shikari's* previous captain!

As I made my approach I could see the new commanding officer of the *Duncan* leaning over his rail, watching his old ship approach. To the uninitiated bringing a ship alongside in a sluicing tide often appears far more difficult than it is. So long as the tide is steady and flowing parallel with the jetty or stage it is a simple matter, because one has plenty of steerage way even though the speed of the ship over the ground is small. *Shikari* with two propellers and her enormous horse-power was much easier to handle than the single-screw *Verbena*.

After fuelling we got away to sea just as it was getting dark. It was blowing nearly a full gale from the west, and there was a big sea running. I was at once reminded of what I had thought when I first saw her in dry dock. She was terribly wet, and her motion, on a course that was forty-five degrees from the direction of the waves, was awful. She just was not big enough for the weight she was being asked to carry. Head-on to the sea she did very well; and beam-on to it she rode quite nicely, even if she rolled like a log. It was obvious that humouring her would greatly reduce the weather damage she would suffer.

My course to the position of the aircraft's report was north-west, and that was the course she did not like. If I went up through the Minches where I could use my speed, and then went out into the Atlantic, I would be going a long way round but I would get there faster. Our course from the Butt of Lewis to our destination would then be almost straight into the sea.

So up through the Minches we went, doing twenty-five knots in the smooth water inside the Hebrides. The sensation of power was terrific. She vibrated all the time like a live thing. I began to forgive her for her failings and I was reminded of the remark of that great horse-lover John Jorrocks, 'Be to their faults a little blind and to their failings ever kind.'

I made a signal to Commander-in-Chief, Western Approaches, to tell him what I was doing and got back the reply, 'Is your journey really necessary?' To that I answered, 'For the continuance of my funnels, yes.'

We shot round the Butt of Lewis before dawn, and had to reduce speed to fifteen knots. All that day we ploughed into the lonely green waves that rolled out of the west beneath a heavy layer of grey cloud. After the hard light and the brilliant, sun-flecked waves of the Indian Ocean, I felt at home once more. This was the Western Approaches, and it was here that the U-Boat battle was being fought and won. It was not a great fleet action like Jutland or Trafalgar. It could not suddenly produce spectacular results as happened after the battle of Midway. It was a long, cold, hard death-grapple, fought against the most cunning of all enemies, under an almost continuous waterfall of salt spray. I still do not think that the nation realizes what went on in those vast wastes of sea when, from mess decks in which six inches of water washed from side to side as the ship rolled, the watch would come on deck in wet clothing only to go back at the end of four weary hours wetter still—and like as not find that their dinner had been flung from their mess table. Nor were the officers in better case. The Navy has always stowed its officers aft, and to get forward to the bridge to stand their watch they had to cross the long slippery length of the destroyer's main deck, across which the seas would often be swirling two or three feet deep. True, life lines were always rigged and if one kept a tight grasp on them one was unlikely to be washed overboard. It was not however good to start a watch soaked to the skin. Yet even in such conditions a ship was always ready to attack a U-Boat, or to rescue survivors.

I was the only man in the ship who had a fair chance of staying dry. I had a sea cabin—a small slit just big enough for a bunk—under the bridge, and from it I could get directly up to the bridge. I only got wet if I could not duck my head quickly enough when she put her nose into a sea and sent the spray flying in sheets over the bridge. As I did not leave the bridge at sea, all my food had to be carried along the upper deck by my poor steward in a sling made from a dish-cloth held at the four corners. It could be quite exciting to see it coming. Coming?—would he?—he's going to be caught—he has been. Damn! there goes my lunch!

At dawn the next day we reached the eastern edge of the area of sea I intended to search. It was then forty-eight hours since the aircraft had reported the tank-landing craft. Assuming that such a machine—for it can hardly be called a ship—would blow down wind at four knots, I had reckoned its position to be no less than 192 miles from the place in which it had been reported. I had been told that aircraft from Iceland would co-operate, but I had heard nothing from them; nor was I surprised, for they could hardly have flown in that weather, or seen anything if they had done so.

I started the search on a line two hundred miles from the sighting position. It was like looking for a needle in a haystack. The only thing in our favour was that the wind had remained steady for the past two days. On the second leg of the thirty mile zig-zag which I had plotted, and at ten o'clock in the forenoon watch, a look-out raised the cry 'Submarine on the surface!'

At first glance his report seemed to be correct, and I hastily pressed the alarm bell for action stations. Through my binoculars I could see the object plainly. It certainly had the characteristic outline of a U-Boat—the long bow parallel with the water, and the conning tower. But it rode the seas too buoyantly. Whatever it was it was no U-Boat. I realized that it was the tank-landing craft!

We closed it rapidly, but could make out no sign of life. As we got closer we could see that it was much smaller than we had expected, and afterwards learnt that it had been part of the deck cargo of a torpedoed American merchantman. At its after end was the armoured conning tower below which would be its engine. It was closed with a heavy hatch. Before laying off to sink it by gunfire, we thought we had best knock on the door by firing at it with a rifle. A very astonished face appeared as the hatch was flung back. We apologized through the loud hailer for disturbing them, and asked if we could be of any assistance. We got them aboard quickly, and then lay off while the gunnery department had a good practice. Then we started for home.

As each 'S Class' destroyer came in from sea she was ordered to join the new 21st Escort Group. Very smart we considered ourselves too, for were we not the fastest group in the Western Ocean? All the other ships were commanded by senior Lieutenants, Royal Navy. They had been put into these craft to learn their trade before taking over the new 'Hunt Class' destroyers which were now coming forward in numbers. We therefore had a strong Navy (as distinct from Western Approaches) bias, and would go everywhere very fast and in close order, carrying out manoeuvres that could not be carried out by the escort groups, because of the wide differences of speed and turning circle between their individual ships. High speed manoeuvres are only safe when all ships have a similar performance. With destroyers, frigates, corvettes and trawlers all serving in the same group one could only carry out the simplest of movements.

As soon as we were formed into a group we were put to work escorting the fast convoys of big troopships which were bringing the American soldiers from their training grounds in Iceland to the build up for D Day in England. It was certainly a fairly responsible job, but as the convoy speed was only fifteen knots we had plenty of excess speed in weather when a submerged attack was probable, and could give the troopships good protection. A surfaced attack on a fifteen-knot convoy was not very likely. If a surfaced U-Boat came in from before the beam he would be detected by the radar of one of the escorts, while if he came in abaft the beam his own maximum speed was so little in excess of the convoy's that he would certainly 'lose bearing' (i.e. drop behind) his target and never get into a firing position. For the Senior Officer of the escort these fast convoys were fairly simple and, as I always had at least four destroyers to escort three troopships, the asdic screen could be really effective. By comparison with an ocean convoy of anything from sixty to a hundred merchantmen our closely packed little party, carrying out a permanent zig-zag would have deterred any but the most determined of U-Boat commanders. We never saw the enemy. Satisfactory it is true, as our job was to deliver the soldiers; but we badly wanted a U-Boat for the group. Often, talking it over in harbour, we would plan methods of enticing one into our net. But we always had our convoy with us, and for weeks we never got an opportunity.

At last our chance came—at least to lay the bait we hoped the fish would take. The group was due to sail on a Saturday with a convoy to Iceland, but when *Shikari* was 'duty destroyer' on the day before, an urgent job took us down to Liverpool. This was no less than the delivery of a new type of German magnetic mine, which someone had discovered when Bizerta fell. It had been rushed home in a frigate, and the wooden box in which it was packed was only to be spoken of in a hushed voice as 'Parcel A'. Unfortunately for us, the frigate had returned home so fast with its precious parcel that her engines had developed a defect, and she had crept into Londonderry. *Shikari* was then told to take the package on to Liverpool. There we could expect to be met by a lorry specially sent from London, with a party of very experienced mine-disposal officers. We duly lashed the beastly box down, and started off gingerly for Liverpool. We had been warned not to shake it, because the mine people in Bizerta only 'thought' that it had been rendered safe. We arrived in Gladstone dock, Liverpool, at one o'clock on the Saturday. Everyone had gone to lunch. When it was time for them to come back we discovered that it was 'Saturday afternoon', and no one knew about 'Parcel A'. Nor did they want to find out about it until Monday morning.

It was, of course, nothing to do with Western Approaches. They knew nothing about the matter at all. It was purely the business of Flag Officer, Liverpool. All Western Approaches wanted was that *Shikari* should go back to her job of escorting as soon as possible. We landed the wretched parcel ourselves, and put it on the dock wall, telling the crane man who had helped us that the case contained the embalmed body of a houri who had been the favourite concubine of the Bey of Tunis.

At last I got through to the Flag Officer himself.

'It's about "Parcel A" Sir.'

'I don't know anything about "Parcel A". What's in it anyway?'

'It's a mine Sir, a new German magnetic mine. And no one knows whether it's really safe . . .'

'Where is it now?' he interrupted me.

'On the jetty by the dock gates at Gladstone dock Sir.'

'Good God! I'll see to it.'

And he did. There was a bomb-disposal lorry alongside within an hour. But *Shikari* had missed her convoy, and we went up alone to join the group in Iceland.

All the U-Boats coming from Germany to work in the North Atlantic, and all the U-Boats at Brest going back to Germany to refit, had to make the passage between the Faroes and Iceland. As we were on our own for once, without a convoy, we decided to bait our trap. In the old days B.12 Group had used barrels of tar to decoy the enemy, and the Naval Store officer at Londonderry had been only too pleased for us to clear what he now considered redundant stock. All the other groups were slaughtering U-Boats, and we had never been given a chance. On the way north we prepared our decoy. We buoyed the barrel to make certain it would float and fitted an ignition system to set it alight. On the second night out when we were just about in the right position to find a U-Boat if one were about, we set fire to our toy, and set it adrift. At the same time we fired a few rockets into the air to entice any customers who might be below the horizon. Then we lay off to await results. We watched it burn right out and then as no inquisitive U-Boat appeared, we turned towards Iceland. But we had overlooked the efficiency of Coastal Command. They reported our tar barrel as a ship on fire and sinking, but they reported it twenty miles south of where it really was. Commander-in-Chief, Western Approaches, sent us to investigate, and of course we had to go. As we expected there was nothing there and I had to report, 'Reference aircraft report, nothing found, suspect it was tar barrel fired by me in position ——.'

On our return to Londonderry I was told to go over to Liverpool to see the Commander-in-Chief.

I must admit that I was frightened. Max had a certain reputation.

As I was ushered into his office he looked up from the pile of reports on his desk.

'What the hell do you think you are doing setting my ocean on fire, Rayner?'

'Trying to catch some flaming U-Boats for you Sir.'

He grunted and getting up from his desk led me into the big operations room.

'See that bit of sea between the Faroes and Iceland, where the minefields are. The Germans call that the Rosegarden. All deep mines there. Coastal Command are putting the U-Boats down. We hoped the mines would catch them, but they don't—at least not often enough. I'm going to put your group in the Faroes. When the 'Met' people say its going to be fine, you'll stay at sea on patrol. When the weather's bad you'll lie in Halfiord at two hours' notice. As soon as there's a sighting report you'll go to the position at full speed and sink the U-Boat. Coastal Command damage more than they sink. Captain Walker's doing wonders on that system—you can do the same. Commander-in-Chief, Home Fleet, will provide three fleet destroyers to help, and I'm basing the 10th Escort Group on Iceland to support you that end. You've the same chance as Walker.'

'Not quite Sir.'

'What do you mean "not quite?"'

'The weather Sir—it's terrible. Captain Walker has got smoother water and wonderful air co-operation, and he picks them up much nearer to the coast of France than I can get to the coast of Norway. But I'm terribly grateful for the chance Sir.'

'Don't forget I commanded the Northern Patrol. I know all about the weather there. Do your best.' He led the way back to his own office.

'That's all I can promise you Sir.'

As I was going I said, 'I hope Sir that the three fleet destroyers will be picked with regard to my seniority.'

He looked at me. 'You can leave that to me. You've one more trip to Iceland haven't you?'

'Yes Sir.'

We took a convoy to Iceland and were lying in Reykjavik waiting for the merchantmen to load their cargoes of soldiers. As usual in that harbour the fish were plentiful, and the sailors were fishing over the side for a 'fry' for tea.

The officers had been discussing the question of fishing over lunch, and the gunnery officer had put forward the theory that the proper way to catch fish was to use a demolition charge fired from the surface by an electrical contact and immured in a basket of fish guts which would act as bait.

So as not to spoil the sailors' fishing the officers took the motor boat some distance away from the ship. The charge was now in the wardroom waste paper basket, and securely packed with fish guts. I had insisted on carrying a motor boat in *Shikari*, not only because it was necessary for me to visit the other ships of the group, but because I felt that now we were all 'S' boats together the chances of looking after them in heavy weather were better. They would no longer be at the beck and call of a Senior Officer of an ocean escort group, who was probably in a larger and very much more modern destroyer.

When the motor boat had gone some distance from the ship, we lowered our noisome basket over the side. We were just about to 'touch it off' when someone, I think it was the doctor, noticed that *Shikari* was flying the motor boat's pennants, indicating that she was recalled. Glancing towards the ship, and cursing the luck that had interfered with our fishing, we could see much activity on the upper deck. Then a signalman jumped on to the top of the bridge and began to semaphore.

'Number One, read it if you will, while I fire this basket of guts. Guns,'—addressing the gunnery officer—'what do I do? Touch this end on the battery?'

'Yes Sir.'

I did so. There was a muffled explosion below the surface, anxious faces peered over the side. For a moment nothing happened then, with a hurrush, a huge bubble broke surface—bringing back the fish guts.

Four filthy faces were raised to the First Lieutenant who was still reading the signal from the destroyer, and the doctor was desperately trying to catch the one small dab which was all we had to show for the officers' fishing party.

'Well Blacky,' I asked as I washed my face with water, 'what is it this time?'

'You've been promoted. Half-yearly promotions Sir.'

'Promoted what?'

'I presume Commander Sir.'

'Nonsense I'm only thirty-five. Even if I was R.N. I'd still have to serve another year before I would be in the zone; and as far as the R.N.V.R.'s concerned there's a very small establishment of Commanders and I haven't heard of any of them dying. If it's the half-yearly promotions it can't be acting rank.'

We got the motor going and the doctor having retrieved his fish we went back to the ship. The ship's company started to cheer as we came alongside—filthy and dirty, and with only our one small fish. But it was true. The seniority problem for Operation Rosegarden had been solved, for it was most unlikely that the Commander-in-Chief, Home Fleet, would detach a flotilla leader carrying a commander for such an operation.

A little more than a month later I was sitting in the heather on a shoulder between two mountains in the Faroes. Below me the fiord, never more than three-quarters of a mile wide, stretched its six mile length. The half which was to the south shimmered golden with the reflection of the midday sun. The northern half was vividly blue, and reflected the brilliantly clear northern sky. There was absolutely no sound but the wind in the heather; for as usual it was blowing hard. Every now and then a cumulus cloud, torn by the north-west gale would flick over the mountains on the other side of the fiord, and drift in long streamers across the sky, throwing bars of shadow on the water below.

Far below me my ships lay at anchor. *Shikari* was at the head of the line, then the three fleet destroyers, *Meteor*, *Oribi*, *Opportune*, followed by the remainder of the 'S Class' *Sardonyx*, *Sabre*, *Saladin*, *Scimitar*. These were the eight destroyers taking part in Operation Rosegarden. Probably nearly one thousand eight hundred men—what a command! But my heart was heavy. Operation Rosegarden was a failure, and it was my duty to tell the Commander-in-Chief, Western Approaches, that no further effort should be wasted upon it. I had climbed the mountain the better to find the seclusion I needed. The weather had beaten us, not the enemy. How to tell the Admiral that I had failed? Before getting out the pencil and paper to draft my letter, I lit a pipe and allowed myself to think over the events of the last few weeks.

Three weeks ago we had entered Halfiord, five destroyers slipping confidently into harbour, sure that they could do the job that had been given to them.

As we swept in line ahead through the narrow entrance we could see the three fleet destroyers already lying at anchor, and my yeoman of signals was bending on a small blue and white flag. This was a flag, or more correctly a burgee, not normally used in the Western Approaches. It brought back nostalgic memories of pre-war training, when the sea had been all fun, and U-Boats did not lurk within its clean waters.

'What's that you've got Yeoman?' I had asked.

'Senior Officer's pennant Sir.'

'But you know we don't use that in the Western Approaches.'

'The "fleets" won't know that Sir. Made it myself last night, seeing we haven't one aboard.'

'All right Yeoman, we'll wear it while we're here.'

It made me think. The 'fleets' would not know that in the Western Approaches it was usual to allow ships to anchor independently. Not only were our anchorages so crowded that only rarely could a clear enough stretch of water be found for a whole group in line ahead, but the different size of ship, and their different anchors and cables, made it a rather hazardous operation. In addition there was a technical reason against anchoring as a flotilla, because when the anchors were let go simultaneously the ships would still have a little headway on them, and the cable running out might have caught the delicate dome in which the asdic was housed. Unlike the frigates, corvettes, and trawlers, the destroyers could haul the asdic machine within the hull. With our retractable domes there was no reason why we should not anchor as a flotilla, so long as our domes were housed.

'Yeoman, I'll anchor the group as a flotilla. Pass it down the line, and tell them to check that their domes are up. Better send the bosun's mate to get another signalman on the bridge. You'll need him.'

Soon the bright coloured flags were climbing up to our yard-arm—the signal on ours, the answering pennants on the ships astern. In addition to the anchoring signals, the signalmen were busy with equal speed signals, telling the ships astern *Shikari's* speed, so that they would keep perfect station. We swept round and approached our chosen anchorage. Slow now. Hardly a ripple spread from our bows. Stop engines. It was strange how quiet everything seemed. There was only the steady hum of the big fans that supplied air to the boiler-rooms, and to that one was so accustomed that it remained unheard. At a sign from me the signal flags dropped to the deck, and five anchors fell simultaneously into the deep, clear water.

'Yeoman, make a signal to *Meteor* and ask her how tall her Captain is.'

Reply: 'About six foot.'

'May I borrow your cabin for conference? Headroom in mine is only five foot nine inches below the beams.'

'With pleasure and relief.'

That day was the last which had given me any pleasure. The very next day had come our first aircraft sighting report of a

U-Boat, and as we had ourselves intercepted the aircraft's report *Shikari* had led the group to sea even before we had received the signal from Commander-in-Chief, Western Approaches. In the smooth water under the land we had been steaming at twenty-five knots. Astern of *Shikari* was *Meteor*, looking to our eyes enormously big. Rounding the headland *Shikari* almost drowned herself in the first wave from the open Atlantic. We had to reduce speed immediately, fearful lest the *Meteor* should run into us. But she too was easing down already. As she lolloped over a big wave, I could see her keel plates almost as far aft as her bridge. The eight destroyers, which a moment before had been a compact orderly force in perfect station, were now spread out. Their masts swayed dizzily as they rolled and plunged, throwing sheets of solid water over their backs. When they were in the troughs of the waves you could only see their masts, and perhaps the top of a bridge and the funnels. Then suddenly they would climb into view, dragging themselves from the sea until their whole fore part was as naked as in dry dock, and solid water poured from their decks in arched lines of foam.

The position where the aircraft had sighted the U-Boat was a hundred miles away. We should have been there within five hours from the aircraft's signal, and we could still hear him homing us on to him with his wireless. It took us twelve hours to get there. I had told the 'fleets' to go on and leave us to follow, but they could go no faster than we could. After six hours the aircraft could stay no longer. We had searched fruitlessly for twenty-four hours in a gale, and then returned to Halfiord.

And so it had gone on; or rather it had got worse, because on that first day communications with the aircraft had been quite good, and they were never good again. For some reason wireless communication in that part of the world was deplorably bad.

It had, I thought, best be a personal letter.

'Dear Admiral Horton,

'I am very sorry to tell you, Sir, that bad weather and bad communications prevent me obtaining any success with Operation Rosegarden. All I have achieved in three weeks is, in spite of taking the greatest care of them, to reduce all five Western Approaches destroyers to a state where not one of them is seaworthy. I have sent details of weather damage to Commodore (D) Londonderry.

'I have considered transferring to one of the fleet destroyers, leaving Lieutenant Blackwood in command of *Shikari*; but although the big destroyers are more comfortable for the men, they cannot really go much faster than the "S Class". Besides it is our Western Approaches ships that we must get to the enemy. The "fleets" only fire a five charge pattern of depth-charges, they have no heavy charges (for deep U-Boats), and they do not handle well in the heavy seas at hunting speeds.

'The officers of the fleet have given me magnificent co-operation and the "S Class" destroyers have been beyond praise. We have nearly a foot of water in the mess decks every time we go to sea; but never a grumble.

'All this would be more bearable if only the wireless communication were better. There seems to be something peculiar in the atmosphere here. Quite frequently we have been unable to establish wireless contact with an aircraft flying overhead, but must pass messages to it via Iceland. Two days ago we had to ask Quebec (Canada) to pass a message to an aircraft six miles away; and my last signal to you, Sir, was routed via New York, as we could raise no station in U.K.

'It is my considered opinion that with these ships and in the prevailing conditions, the continuance of Operation Rosegarden cannot be justified.

'Naturally I am terribly sorry and disappointed that I must make such a report.'

I put down my pencil and looked at the ships. *Shikari* caught by a different air stream had swung round and, by reason of the drift of her cable, looked out of station and apart from the others. The local soldiers had asked us to co-operate in a field day, and we had landed a number of men from each ship that morning. The boats had just returned and were lying alongside the ships. *Oribi* had taken the opportunity to paint her topsides, and had men over the side on the painting stages.

A sudden roar of powerful engines made me look up. A Heinkel passed over me. As he shot between the hill tops the German plane was so low that I could have hit him with a twelve-bore gun. I could see his nose go down following the slope of the land. Almost at once he was below me going down —going down to the ships. I could tell the exact moment when he made up his mind to attack. His wings dipped as he turned away to give a longer run to his bomb aimer. Now his other wing dipped, and he turned to run in down the line of ships. He would bomb *Shikari* and strafe the others. I prayed and cursed alternately. The decks were crowded with men. As our own ships' radars were useless under the high land, we had been relying on the local radar for air raid warnings. The plane was going in fast. 'Oh God!—Oh *Shikari*! Do something.' It came—dear God it came! First one red ball of a tracer bullet rising from *Shikari's* port Oerlikon, then a burst. Now the starboard Oerlikon—a steady stream poured from both guns. How slowly the little red dots climbed to meet the black plane! I could see the Hun pull up, as a pheasant will do when a charge of shot passes ahead of it. His bombing run was spoilt. He banked steeply, his wings intensely black against the golden water. A puff of white smoke showed abaft *Shikari's* after funnel. Oh lovely! Someone had brought the 3-inch high-angle gun into action. The plane was pulling out, it was climbing, turning away, going. Only then the rattle of the first shots reached me. The 'fleets' opened up with their two-pounder pom-poms. A long triangle of scarlet tracer bullets tore after the retreating plane from the whole line of ships. I shall never forget the way the shadow of the plane swept up the mountain on the opposite side of the fiord. He was gone in a burst of gunfire, and then silence dropped like a pall over the lovely scene. But if *Shikari* had not been just in time there would have been men swimming down there, and men dying.

I knelt in the heather and thanked God—and the men who had died in Norway, that we should learn.

So now we were observed. That Hun would certainly have photographed the anchorage. Even if it meant nothing to the pilot, the German staff would see from our camouflage, white and green, that an escort group lay in wait for their U-Boats.

Only the Western Approaches groups carried the light camouflage, and it was as definite a sign as writing 'Beware' in white letters on a blue ground. The boats would make the passage of the Rosegarden submerged. Sighting reports would be fewer, and autumn was only just round the corner.

In the month of June Captain Walker had slain three U-Boats off Brest, and in July a further two. In the Rosegarden none had been accounted for. I folded up the letter and put it in my pocket. Then I went down to where the motor boat waited for me.

It was a very peculiar team that had fired *Shikari's* guns—cooks, sick berth attendant, and a stoker. The stoker had been the gunlayer of the first Oerlikon to open fire. Cookie had rushed out of his galley and laid the 3-inch high-angle. When the proper gunlayer arrived he was very upset to find that pastry had been smeared all over the trigger.

I sent Max Horton my letter. A week later we were withdrawn. The fleet destroyers were ordered to Scapa. *Sardonyx*, *Saladin*, *Sabre* and *Scimitar* were sent to Londonderry to be patched up, and I was ordered to take *Shikari* to Scapa where a plane would be waiting at Hatston to take me to a conference at Rosyth.

It was then August 1943. In the three years since I had left Scapa there had been fantastic changes. Where there had been miles of muddy roads and open fields there were now hard roads and serried ranks of good huts. There were canteens for the men and there was also a giant mess for the officers. A busy town had sprung up in the salty wilderness, and there were even Wrens about on roads where before only the male of the species had been seen.

We berthed alongside the depot ship and I was asked to dine with the Commander-in-Chief, Home Fleet, Admiral Fraser, in the Flagship H.M.S. *King George V*. Naturally I was considerably put out at the failure of Rosegarden. It would have been bad enough if the news could have been confined to my own Western Approaches Command. As it was all the northern Commands, the Home Fleet, and even Rosyth, which had operated some of the aircraft, had been concerned. Admiral Fraser could not have been more kind and sympathetic, and his kindness did much to revive my spirits. At least he understood what we had been up against; and I was sure that our own Admiral would do that too, however disappointed he might be in the result.

The next day I went to Hatston for my aircraft. It was a vile day with visibility not much more than two hundred yards, and in the rain and mist the plane, an Airspeed Oxford, looked a most dreary conveyance. Meeting the pilot in the mess, he told me that he did not want to fly. I could not have agreed more profoundly. We had lunch together instead, but during the meal he was called to the telephone. We were told that we must fly down because very important people were coming up from the Admiralty to meet us.

We climbed reluctantly into the plane, and could see only a little more than half-way down the runway. The pilot turned to me and said that he hoped these very important people would stay up for the funeral. They would lend tone to the proceedings. He then let in the clutch, or whatever you do with an aircraft, and we shot off savagely into the mist.

After a minute of seeing nothing I said to the pilot, 'When do we get off the ground?'

'We are off.'

'Oh.' It did not seem reasonable. I could still see nothing.

In quick succession we nearly hit a lighthouse, a ship in the Pentland Firth and then the cliffs of Duncansby Head. This last was too much. I wanted to know why we did not stay at a safe height and go by navigation instead of sight; but apparently there was no navigation equipment other than our eyes. I began to realize why the smaller aircraft were always so unsure of their position, but was not enamoured of the method of learning. We followed the cliff edge all the way down the coast of Invernesshire, and then along by Nairn to Peterhead.

Peterhead proved a headache because the local barrage-balloon people, who had been told that there was no flying, had got all the balloons up; and we nearly stopped there for ever. However after Aberdeen we ran into clear weather, and landed at Donnibristle just before three o'clock. Here, because there was 'no flying', they had dug a trench across the runway, and we had to hop over it.

After that the conference was rather an anti-climax. There were all sorts of high-ranking officers, and I found myself the only representative of Commander-in-Chief, Home Fleet, and Commander-in-Chief, Western Approaches. I was too tired to be polite, and spoke my mind about what I had been trying to do. No one seemed surprised or to disagree; and that was the end of Operation Rosegarden. I never heard it mentioned again.

It was interesting to see how the theoretically perfect plan had fallen down in practice—particularly in waters which must always be vital for the defence of these islands. If war should come again to Britain it seems certain that submarines will once more be used to cut off our sea-borne supplies; and most if not all of them will have to pass through that same Rosegarden. There are only two places where U-Boats can be met with any degree of certainty. One is when they are nibbling at the bait, which is the convoy, and the other is when they are forced to take some particular passage to their base. How to kill in this area was a problem we never solved in the last war. It is to be hoped that improved aircraft co-operation and improved, and much larger, hunting vessels will be available next time.

After the conference I was offered the same aircraft in which to return. I declined hastily, and went back by train and the Scapa Ferry. I am not a birdman.

We rejoined the group in Londonderry, and after our more serious cracks and leaks had been welded up we all sailed to Roseneath at the entrance to the Kyles of Bute, which is the first turning to your left after passing Cumbrae Light on the way up the Clyde.

The British submarine service had been giving a very good account of itself up and down the Mediterranean, particularly in attacks on fast shipping off the Italian coast. The Italians had a number of small high-speed destroyers, and in order to defeat our submarines they had learnt to create a physical barrier around their small convoys.

The torpedo is like the shell in only one way. Both are fired out of a tube. Beyond that the similarity ceases, for the shell travels at hundreds of miles an hour, and does its journey in a time that is measured in seconds. The torpedo on the other hand travels at a speed little more than twice that of a fast merchantman, and its time is reckoned in minutes. The position from which a submarine can launch a successful attack is very restricted. It lies roughly one mile from the target at an angle of forty-five degrees to its course. If destroyers are zig-zagging at very high speed on either bow of the convoy, it is very difficult for the submarine captain to carry out his attack, because he must not only raise his periscope to see the target, but must also do so in order to keep a lookout for the destroyers. The more he raises his periscope the more likely he is to be seen. Our business at Roseneath was to pretend to be Italian destroyers escorting a merchantman, while our young submarine captains learnt their business.

It was a wonderful period from the point of view of ship handling. We would steam up and down Loch Long in close order at thirty knots, by night as well as by day. We learnt to carry out all the usual evolutions, and a lot of new ones especially asked for because the Italians employed them. We achieved a standard of ship handling rare even in peace time, when the need for economy prohibits continuous steaming at high speed.

We learnt to carry out the most intricate of the zig-zag diagrams together and in close order. We could even maintain a continuous weave. It was exhilarating work, and lovely to the eye, for no more beautiful ships than mine were ever built. The design of the *Hood*, of the heavy cruisers *Hawkins* and *Frobisher* and of the 'S Class' destroyers all came at the same time. These ships represent a period when beauty of line coincided with the dictates of efficiency. In my opinion, no modern ships, with the possible exception of certain destroyers of the immediate pre-war period, were so beautiful; and the later craft lacked the flowing lines of their predecessors, and were less feminine in appearance. The 'S Class' were at their best at high speed. The five bow waves level with, or spread out like wings, above the five fo'c's'les. The ships would lean over in unison as their rudders bit into the water. Sterns would swing in a wide arc, smoothing the crisp curls of the sea to a sheet of satin. Slowly the narrow hulls would right themselves as the ships settled to the new course; and the group would still be in perfect station.

I don't know how we avoided a fatal accident to the submarines we were teaching. There were many narrow escapes, and the danger was a real worry to the commanding officers of the ships; for even if you are only carrying out your instructions it is not pleasant to run down one of your own submarines. The strain began to tell on some of us, and I know that for this reason alone I heartily wished myself elsewhere.

The whole place bore an air of tension, for the depot ship near which we moored when in harbour was the school for these submariners. When we met them we were impressed by the strain to which these young men were being subjected. However well they carried it off, one could see it fixed permanently upon their brows. I suppose each branch of the many services thinks that it carries the brunt of the stress of war. The truth is that it falls on all—not continuously, but shifting first to one branch, then to another. What the airman achieves one day is matched the next by the sailor, and on the day after that by the submariner. Lastly all are saved by the foot-soldier who walks into the enemy country and says to the rest of us 'You can go home now chaps. We've won.'

We went back to Londonderry for a boiler-clean and I took the opportunity of going to see Max Horton again. It was the first time that I had seen him since Rosegarden closed down. He promised me something better. There would soon be big changes in the groups, as the new 'Captain Class' frigates were coming across from the American yards and the 'River Class' frigates from our own.

He ended by saying, 'In any case I look upon you as one of the spare Senior Officers. Wherever I may send you temporarily you can be sure of another group of your own one day.'

Before I left the group I was to have the pleasure of welcoming another R.N.V.R. officer, Lieutenant-Commander E. Playne, who had been appointed to *Sardonyx*. I heard also that Lieutenant-Commander Norman Wood (like myself from the Mersey Division), had been given a 'Hunt Class' destroyer. The Volunteer Navy was justifying the faith of those Naval officers who had championed our cause. They had not always been many, for there had always been some who thought that the R.N.V.R. could never be employed afloat, except as junior officers. Fortunately our supporters had been powerful, both in debate and in authority.

I had hardly got back to *Shikari* when I was told to take her round to Grangemouth to dry dock; and when I berthed her there I found a letter appointing me to command of H.M.S. *Warwick* to relieve Commander McCleves R.N.R.

I went down to Liverpool to join the *Warwick* in October 1943.

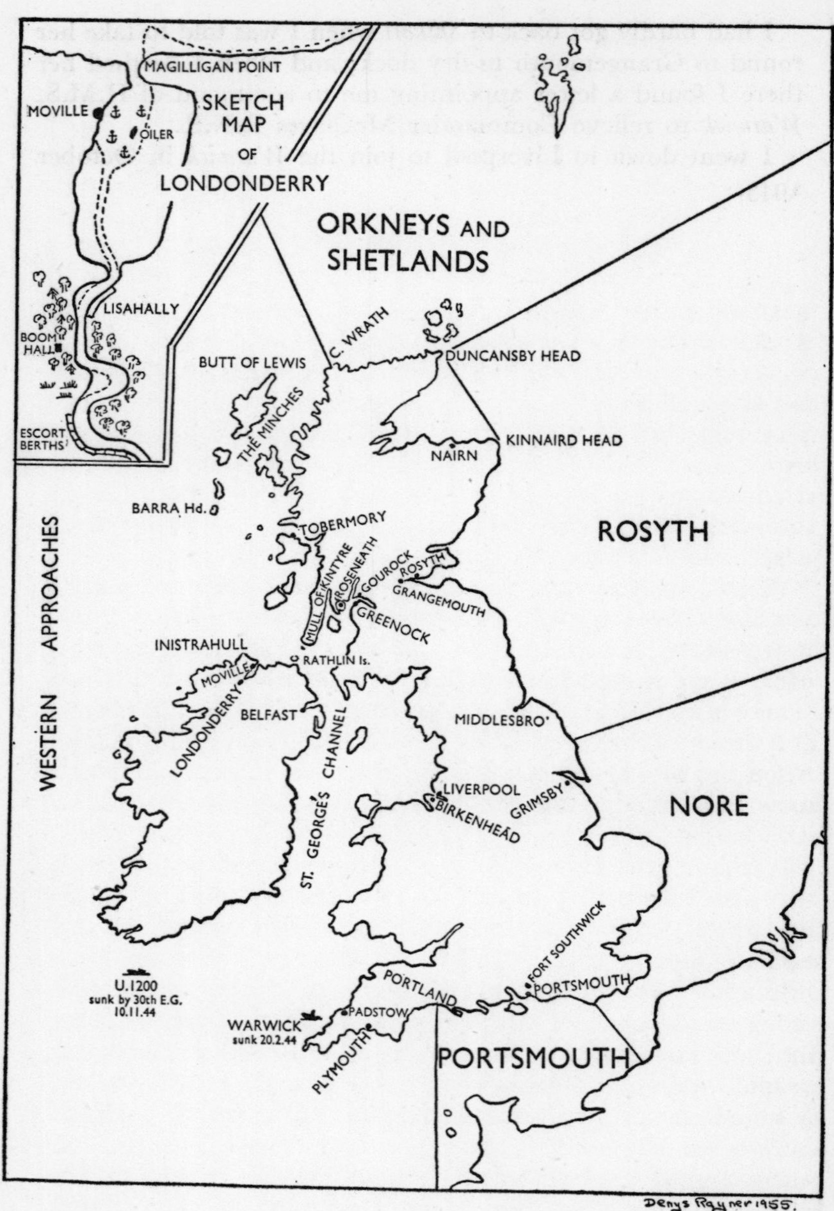
SKETCH MAP OF LONDONDERRY
MAGILLIGAN POINT
MOVILLE
OILER
LISAHALLY
BOOM HALL
ESCORT BERTHS
ORKNEYS AND SHETLANDS
C. WRATH
DUNCANSBY HEAD
BUTT OF LEWIS
THE MINCHES
KINNAIRD HEAD
NAIRN
BARRA Hd.
TOBERMORY
ROSYTH
MULL OF KINTYRE
ROSENEATH
GOUROCK
ROSYTH
GRANGEMOUTH
GREENOCK
WESTERN APPROACHES
INISTRAHULL
RATHLIN Is.
MOVILLE
LONDONDERRY
BELFAST
ST. GEORGE'S CHANNEL
MIDDLESBRO'
LIVERPOOL
BIRKENHEAD
GRIMSBY
NORE
FORT SOUTHWICK
PORTSMOUTH
PORTLAND
PADSTOW
PLYMOUTH
U.1200 sunk by 30th E.G. 10.11.44
WARWICK sunk 20.2.44
PORTSMOUTH
Denys Rayner 1955.

Chapter VII

THE U-BOAT IN THE ATLANTIC

In the middle of September 1943 the war against the U-boat passed through a decisive stage. Four of the escorts of one convoy were then hit by torpedoes. Grand Admiral Doenitz had altered his tactics, and had ordered that our escorts were to be regarded as equally important targets to the merchantmen. That is not to say that torpedoes had never been fired at an escort by a frightened U-Boat in an attempt to frustrate an attack upon itself. What is meant is that in a choice of targets the emphasis had shifted.

When I learnt of the sinkings, I was reminded of a remark made by Commander Howard-Johnston at a conference, when he was asked to what extent a Captain should hazard his own vessel when attacking a U-Boat. Howard-Johnston replied, 'There is no risk yet. The U-Boat is out to sink merchantmen. You are a confounded nuisance to its Captain, not a target. When the first escort vessel is torpedoed deliberately you will know that the Hun is beaten and the war is won. Everything else after that date is just a mopping up operation.'

It is now obvious that H-J's prescience was correct. It may be worth considering briefly what it was that had so transformed the outlook since the days when defeat stared us in the face. I suggest that it is best defined by the word 'co-ordination'. By that means the escorts had been formed into strong teams in which each knew what was expected of him, and how his neighbour would act. By forging the new joint weapon—half naval, half air—Admiral Max Horton had given us something we had never had before. We had the help of shore-based aircraft as far out over the Atlantic as they could reach, and in the 'air gap' we had recently started to use Swordfish aircraft carried in light escort carriers. These were mostly converted liners, and thanks to the intrepid skill of the young men who manned their aircraft they were proving extraordinarily effective. The dynamic personality of our 'Max' had provided the punch to carry through these reforms.

The word co-ordination was certainly the answer to our question, but it was not the whole answer. The rest of it was much more complex. To understand what had happened it is necessary to consider the whole strategy of anti-U-Boat warfare.

In what I have so far written I have purposely not put the reader in the position of a U-Boat captain about to attack a convoy. The reader thus probably finds himself in the same sort of confusion that we were in until the Western Approaches Tactical School dispersed the fog in our minds.

The war was being fought against the U-Boat in a way for which pre-war training had not prepared us. We had been taught to locate and hunt the submerged enemy by means of the asdic, and we had greatly over-estimated the killing power of our depth-charges against a welded pressure hull. For various reasons our naval constructors had not looked with favour on welded construction, and our own pre-war submarines had pressure hulls formed of plates which were joined together by riveted straps. It was assumed that what would damage that type of construction would be even more effective against a welded hull. In practice the weld proved much more difficult to break than our own construction, so that instead of obtaining a kill at sixty feet as we had been taught to expect, it was found that we must get a depth-charge to explode much closer.

It must be remembered that depth-charges always had to be aimed in two dimensions—in depth as well as in plan; and that while our asdic gave us a good chance of putting our depth-charges down correctly for plan, it was a much more difficult problem to gauge the depth at which they should be set to explode. In the shoal waters of the North Sea or in our own coastal waters this last was fairly easy, because the enemy had very little room in which to manœuvre for depth, but in the deep waters of the Atlantic he could be up to six hundred feet below the surface—five times the height of the Nelson column in Trafalgar Square. Naturally our depth-charges took time to sink to such a depth, and in two minutes at four knots the U-Boat would travel over six hundred feet.

If one asks a landsman what method a U-boat uses to attack, he is almost sure to reply that it strikes from beneath the surface. But the U-Boats we had to fight against generally worked by night in the wide and deep waters of the great oceans; and for the first two years of the war they usually worked on the surface running on their diesel engines. This gave them a speed rather better than the best that a corvette could do, and two knots faster than a trawler. The U-Boat was held above water only by the air in his tanks, which supported him like a diver's bell. To dive he had only to open air valves on the top of those tanks, and in a matter of seconds he would sink below the surface. In effect he was using his submarine as a torpedo-boat, and moreover one which was faster than the bulk of the escort force. After he had fired his torpedoes he would either creep into the depths, or stay on the surface and escape.

To put a U-Boat down was to blind it, for its periscope was virtually useless by night, and in any case its horizon was then greatly restricted. Therefore all our early efforts were concentrated on making the U-Boat dive. This was not only done because the enemy was less dangerous when down below, but because we then held it in the element in which we had been taught to kill it. As soon as an attack developed we would do our utmost to turn night into day by firing star shell, and flare rockets, to frighten the U-Boat and put it down.

The arrival of radar gave us the upper hand, because then we had an unseen eye always watching for the enemy. Of course I speak in generalities. The target picked up by the radar could be other things beside a U-Boat. In those first terrible years the seas were full of the wreckage of war, and many a radar echo would, on investigation, turn out to be a ship's lifeboat, with or without survivors. But by and large the introduction of radar was the beginning of the end of the Hun's summer holiday.

Before the war I had done a month's anti-submarine training, but all the escort work that I had been taught had dealt with small organized parties of ships all zig-zagging together. We had learnt the stations for the escorts from naval publications which showed pictures of neat little convoys protected adequately by as many escorts as there were ships in the convoy. In the Western Ocean our work in no way conformed to such a pattern. There we would perhaps have two destroyers and four corvettes to escort eighty merchantmen spread over forty square miles of sea. After two weeks in the Atlantic gales it would be surprising if the complicated electrical devices would be working equally well in all the escort vessels of a group, and in some cases they would not be working at all. This made complete nonsense of the pretty little pictures in the books, and Senior Officers could only do the best they could with the material they had.

It was also very difficult indeed for the Senior Officer to keep track of what was happening—partly for a psychological reason, and partly for a practical one. Let me take the reader for a short time on to the bridge of a corvette escorting a convoy. We will call her the *Pansy*, and put her on the starboard quarter, where she is five or six miles from the Senior Officer. At night wireless silence is of course only broken in an emergency. The officer of the watch is told by the asdic hut that they have an echo outside the screen at a distance of a thousand yards on the starboard beam of the corvette. The officer of the watch calls the captain, who slows the speed of the ship while he investigates the contact. At that same moment the radar office reports a small echo astern of the convoy, and adds that it could be a U-Boat. Troubles never occur singly. The captain decides to carry out a 'pounce' attack on the asdic contact, and then to turn the ship and illuminate the radar contact with star shell.

He runs in to attack, and just as he has given the order 'Fire' he hears whistling noises in the asdic. They denote a shoal of fish. He presses the cease-fire gong—but too late. Depth-charges have already rolled from the after rails. He swings the ship round, orders a range and bearing and fires star shell. The depth-charges explode astern, and his star shell bursts ahead of him to reveal a lifeboat bucketing over the sea. The whole thing has been a false alarm—or rather two false alarms; but with twenty merchantmen at his corner of the convoy, he must act first and ask questions afterwards. He slinks back to his escorting position, and because he does not want to be thought an alarmist sort of chap who goes off on a hair-spring trigger, he says nothing. Perhaps he hopes that in the thick weather no one will have heard his 'feu de joie'.

But the exploding charges were heard on his asdic set by the Senior Officer, although he did not know their bearing; and the star shell were dimly seen by him astern of the convoy. They could have been fired by either of the wing corvettes or by the destroyer astern. The fog of war has descended with a vengeance!

Then ten minutes later a ship is torpedoed in the centre of the convoy, quickly followed by another. How many U-Boats are there? And where should the Senior Officer place his escorts to catch the enemy? And how can he prevent others arriving to join the party? And was that really a false alarm astern of the convoy? Such are the questions he has to answer, and to answer quickly.

In the first two years of the war the Senior Officer had to work out all such problems in his head, with very little guidance from the text books. That he could do so, and did so, is a tribute to the courage and skill of the early Group Commanders.

When the Tactical School started in November 1942, Captain Roberts used models to try out the various tactics employed by the individual Group Commanders. Very soon he was able to issue a comprehensive series of orders and manoeuvres, which provided a common doctrine throughout the Western Approaches. This at once emphasized the need for something more positive than the Senior Officer's brain to provide as broad a view of what was happening as could be seen on the floor of the tactical room. Plotting the positions of the other escorts, the convoy, and the U-Boats all by hand was a very inferior method, and it was therefore decided to fit, firstly in the Senior Officers' ships and later in all escorts, a wonderful device known as a 'Plot'. This was connected to the gyro compass of the ship and to the electric log, so that it made a spot of light travel over the paper to correspond exactly with the passage of the ship herself over the surface of the sea. Working from this spot of light a 'range and bearing arm' could be swung round to plot the position of any object detected by radar or asdic. This helped enormously in identifying and classifying any target. For instance, had the *Pansy* been able to plot her radar contact astern of the convoy she would have found in a very short time that the object was stationary; and was gradually dropping astern of the convoy; it could not have been a U-Boat, and she would not have fired star shell. The same applies to her asdic contact. A tight body of fish such as would give an asdic echo, travels only very slowly, and here again a plot would have told the Captain that he was probably wrong in thinking it an enemy.

We will however assume that *Pansy* has had her little bit of fun and fireworks, and go with the Senior Officer of the escort to the plot, to find the answers to the questions posed above.

On the plot is a large blue arrow marking the direction of the wind. It is pointing towards the port beam of the convoy. He will at once disregard *Pansy's* firework party because no man, and least of all a U-Boat Commander looking for darkened ships on a murky night, likes to make an approach from the down-wind side of the convoy, because his bridge will be smothered in spray. The Senior Officer's radar set already shows him that two of the convoy are out of station. These are the torpedoed merchantmen. He picks up a pair of dividers and finds that they are three miles apart. It is therefore more than probable that two U-Boats have got inside the screen, and by now have almost certainly dived. But before searching for them he must prevent any other U-Boats arriving. So he orders 'Carry out Operation "Buttercup"' to the two escort vessels on the port side, and adds an arc of the compass. They will then illuminate this arc with star shell. Even though one of the escorts does not belong to his own group, he can rely on her carrying out an order that is well-known to all. He now has to deal with the two U-Boats. He has a destroyer astern, so he orders her and the excitable child *Pansy* to search up-wind from one wreck, and the remaining corvette on the starboard bow to search up-wind of the other. He would have liked to send another escort to help the single ship, but he has no one left except himself, and until he receives further news he will probably remain in the van of the convoy. He has sent his escorts to search up-wind of the torpedoed ships for two reasons. Firstly because a U-Boat will submerge more quickly if moving into a sea, and after getting into the middle of the convoy her captain will want to get below as quickly as possible. The second reason is that surface vessels travelling slowly tend to drift down-wind, and by steaming in the opposite direction the U-Boat will open the gap between him and them as rapidly as possible.

The two corvettes carrying out 'Buttercup' suddenly break wireless silence, scrambling over the words with excitement, 'Two U-Boats five miles on the port beam of the convoy'. It is soon followed by another signal 'U-Boats have dived'.

Probably the Admiralty will have warned the Escort Commander earlier in the day that four U-Boats are in the vicinity of the convoy. All four have now been plotted, and all are below the surface. The initiative has passed to Commander Blank, and for an hour he may hunt all four submarines. After that he will have to go back to the convoy; but even if the enemy is not directly attacked, he will probably not surface again until daybreak.

The arrival of radar, the work of the Tactical Schools, the supply of the 'Plot', and the standardized orders for the conduct of Atlantic convoys, such were the nails in the coffin of the U-Boat when it was attacking a convoy.

To carry out a deliberate 'Pack Attack' the U-Boats had to sight the convoy during the day, and then shadow it from below the horizon, while they gradually worked round to get up-wind of the convoy by nightfall. But once air cover had been provided this game became increasingly difficult for them to play. In 1943 they might at any time suddenly find an aircraft over them, homing a Support Group of escorts to their position. Once Max Horton had passed to the offensive he gave his enemy no rest. After scoring big successes in March 1943 Doenitz suffered very heavy losses in the early summer. Even in the 'gap' the U-Boats were now liable to observation and attack from the air. The shore-based long-range aircraft had arrived, and many convoys also carried their air escorts along with them in the small escort-carriers. The forging of the air-sea weapon was complete, and Doenitz was beaten for the time being. He withdrew the U-Boats from the convoy routes until he had a new weapon ready. This was the 'Homing' torpedo. If an escort guided by radar rushed at a U-Boat out of the darkness, the enemy fired one of these new toys, and stood by to watch the bang. It was fitted with an acoustic device in the nose so that it 'homed' its way to the propellers of the attacking ship. It cost us four escort vessels before we found out what it was.

The 'Homing' torpedo was not a decisive weapon, but it did temporarily have the effect of reducing the hunting crafts' effectiveness, because for their own safety they could not use full speed. To reduce speed was to reduce our effectiveness—in other words to reduce Max Horton's strength. But fortunately the number of our escorts was rising rapidly at that time.

Such was the position in the autumn of 1943. Gone were the days when the U-Boats could hold conferences in the middle of the Atlantic. Their targets had become very difficult to find. The German Admiralty had to try to guess the course of our convoys with what help they could get from their own long-range aircraft, and from the reports of U-Boats especially sent out to watch. From those reports the enemy would order other U-Boats to go to various positions in the hope of intercepting the convoy at night. For the Germans it was an unsatisfactory period, with very little to show for the killings that the Support Groups made. The ball was as heavily weighted in our favour at the end of 1943 as it had been weighted in that of the enemy two years earlier.

How then did Commander Howard-Johnston and his B.12 group manage in the summer of 1941 to bring all those convoys through the danger zone without the loss of a single ship?

To praise one man is by no means to belittle others who may have been less fortunate. I know only what B.12 group did, because in the period of which I speak I served only under Howard-Johnston. When I think back fourteen years, I think of him more as a contemporary than as a man who must have been at least six or seven years older than I. Fair haired, of medium stature, he had the figure of a young man. Perhaps the strongest memory I have of him is the terrific enthusiasm with which he approached every problem, however remotely concerned with the efficiency or happiness of his group. The gold braid on the peak of his commander's cap was always new and bright; and if he was very much the Senior Officer of the group, he was also very much the leader of a schoolboy's 'gang'. Indeed it was because of this latter quality that his group would have followed him anywhere. I never remember receiving a signal from him which caused irritation. If I made a mistake he would tell me how he thought I should have handled the matter and never, even after the most tiring convoy, did his messages become snappy. We were as proud of belonging to B.12 group as I know H-J was of his command. Although he flogged us nearly to death in a never ending search for efficiency, the period I spent in the group remains my happiest time in the Service; and I realized afterwards that everything that I had learnt about the handling of a group at sea I owed to H-J, so that in course of time my own groups were really a reflection of B.12.

In those early days we had no radar and no plot, and our most used weapon was that of bluff.

I have told why it was usual for the U-Boats to stalk a convoy towards dusk; why they would stay on the surface and use their speed to get into an attacking position for the night, and that if there was any wind they would be on the up-wind side of the convoy. To counter those tactics towards dusk we would send out a destroyer for some twenty miles to put down the shadowers. When they had been forced under, the course of the convoy would be altered forty-five degrees in the down-wind direction. At midnight the course would be altered back to the original one, but the convoy would then be twelve miles further down-wind than the enemy would expect, and in the dark his chances of making contact would be much slimmer. Later, as the first immature radar sets were developed, the destroyer could remain away longer, and find its way back after dark. This greatly improved the chances of avoiding an attack.

With no more orders from the commodore than a blast on the siren, which was repeated by the leading ships of columns, fifty or sixty lumbering merchantmen would execute a forty-five degree turn with the precision of guardsmen on parade. It was a sight which never ceased to thrill—particularly when the second turn at midnight was made in the darkness of a rainy night. We became intensely proud of our charges, and would be genuinely sorry if one of them did not hear the signal, and had to be driven back to her station.

When the Germans had gathered many U-Boats round a convoy H-J would, in addition to making the side step, arrange a little demonstration to keep the enemy employed during the night. Two corvettes would be sent off some twelve miles from the convoy's original track and twenty-four from its new track, and there they would stage a fire-work display. Rockets would be sent up to simulate signals from a torpedoed ship, star shell also would be fired, and a depth-charge or two dropped by way of sound effect. Sometimes a tar barrel would be lit and set afloat. The U-Boat captains, who were on the surface and looking for a convoy that had mysteriously evaporated, would see our 'Brock's Benefit' and conclude that the convoy was there. But when they arrived it would be twenty-four miles away, with dawn getting nearer every hour.

Now all such stratagems were things of the past. Radar and aircraft were better and more sure, and with their help we had passed from the defensive to the offensive. Escort groups now worked with air support. The seas were scoured by special hunting groups which, having no convoy to look after, could devote all their energies to the destruction of the enemy. The Hun had been harried and chased from the ocean. He went down to the Caribbean, and until those waters too were made unhealthy for him he enjoyed an Indian Summer there. Then the U-Boats turned against the escorts, and we knew that we had won the first round.

What was Doenitz up to? One does not become a Grand Admiral in the German Navy for nothing. He had a trick or two to play yet. In the second round he threw punches that were at least as dangerous to the Allied nations as anything he had done before. In my opinion the second round was a period of stalemate, with both sides sparring for an opening which neither was strong enough to make. On the face of it Doenitz was doing very little damage, but in fact we who hunted his U-Boats knew that we only just contained them.

At the end of 1943 Doenitz produced the Homing Torpedo; in 1944 he produced the Schnorkel; and for 1945 he had the Walter-engined U-Boat. As we have seen, the homing torpedo was not a decisive weapon. The Schnorkel was another matter. It enabled the U-Boat to run on its diesel engines when submerged, by breathing through a large air tube the top of which was fitted with a flap valve. Before its invention it was impossible for the U-Boat to use its diesels except on the surface; and it could only charge the batteries for its electric motors by running the diesels. Before the Schnorkel they had to surface, if only to charge batteries, for four hours out of every twenty-four. With the Schnorkel they need never surface. When the U-Boats surrendered at the end of the war it was found that some had been submerged for six weeks, and were covered with a film of green weed such as forms on a ship's bottom in harbour.

Using the Schnorkel the U-Boats came inshore, and re-visited places from which we had driven them in the first two or three months of the war. With the Schnorkel they could travel underwater almost as fast as an escort vessel. It has been told how our aircraft kept the U-Boats down, and once this had been accomplished they could see very little in the wide spaces of the Atlantic. But if they worked submerged off one of the busy corners where all traffic passes, such as Portland Bill in the Channel, Cape Wrath at the north-west corner of Scotland, or Rathlin Island at the north-east corner of Ireland, they could hardly avoid making many sightings each day.

A U-Boat is a very expensive weapon, and it would be immensely wasteful to allow it to cruise about aimlessly, without paying its way by the destruction of its enemies. In as much as Doenitz achieved only slight successes with his Schnorkel-fitted boats, it can be claimed that he was beaten as surely in the second round as in the first; but that is to go back to a purely defensive attitude against the U-Boat. In terms of the offensive against them, which can only be measured by the number that we destroyed then the 'honours' were fairly even.

The Walter U-Boat which Doenitz planned to use in 1945, had an engine driven by an entirely new fuel—hydrogen peroxide burnt with diesel oil. It could travel submerged at twenty knots for short periods; and it did not have to stay at periscope depth like a Schnorkel boat. If we assume that a Support Group would have arrived one hour after a U-Boat sighting report, the area to be swept would be some fifty square miles of sea. But the much faster Walter boat would increase the zone to be swept to no less than 1,200 square miles. This really would reduce the possibility of finding it to a matter of pure chance. Luckily for us none of these boats were ready for operations when the war ended; but it can hardly be doubted that it was a most threatening development.

On our side, the back-room boys had not of course been idle, and the new anti-submarine vessels such as the 'Castle' Class Corvettes bore much the same relation to the early anti-submarine trawlers as the modern rifle bears to the long bow. Whereas *Loch Tulla* had fired by art, intuition, and a large slice of luck, *Pevensey Castle's* attacks were controlled by instruments throughout.

The asdic was fitted about one third of the ship's length from the bow, where the water noises caused by her own movement were least. Its beam went down into the water at an angle of about sixty degrees from the surface. With a U-Boat at a depth up to seventy-five feet, contact could be held until the target was about one hundred feet away from the bow of the hunting ship. But at the great depth to which the modern boat could dive, contact would frequently be lost when the hunting craft was a hundred yards away. As the depth-charges could only be dropped or fired from the stern of the attacking ship, there was thus a considerable 'blind zone' which the ship had to cover after she had lost contact. In addition to this the depth-charges took time to sink to the estimated depth of the enemy, so that an alert U-Boat captain who took prompt evasive action when he heard propeller noises getting close, had a good chance of making a large enough alteration of course so that he would be at a safe distance when the charges exploded.

To overcome this handicap to the attacker the first thing was to arrange a permanent plot so that the plotting officer could detect at once any change in the direction of the target. The next was to fire while still in contact ahead by throwing explosive charges in front of the attacking ship, instead of dropping them from her stern. The first weapon designed on this entirely new principle was known as the 'Hedgehog'. It threw twenty-four small bombs which would explode on striking the hull of the submarine. The 'Hedgehog' however suffered from being rather complicated, was too exposed to weather, and its bombs were too small to have a good chance of killing the U-Boat; but it was a development on the right lines. Its successor the 'Squid' threw fewer but heavier bombs to a greater distance; and they were arranged to explode at an accurate depth. This latter was a much more effective weapon.

Before the advent of ahead-firing Captain Walker had perfected a technique for defeating the last-minute evasion of the U-Boat, by attacking with three or more ships in line abreast about fifty yards apart. This had proved a most successful method, but it could only be used by 'support groups' who had no convoy to protect. In his mass attacks up to eighty depth-charges were fired with only a few seconds between each explosion. With the new 'Squid' my 30th Escort Group slew U.1200 with the expenditure of only three charges. Such an advance in the technique of killing was amazing. Unfortunately there had been no parallel advance in the technique of finding the U-Boat, for the speed of the hunting craft had advanced very little.

It is true that we could probably have killed the twenty knot Walter boat if we could have found it. But to find it with the number and type of ships we then had would have been a very chancy affair, and I for one was glad that victory saved us from the need to make the attempt.

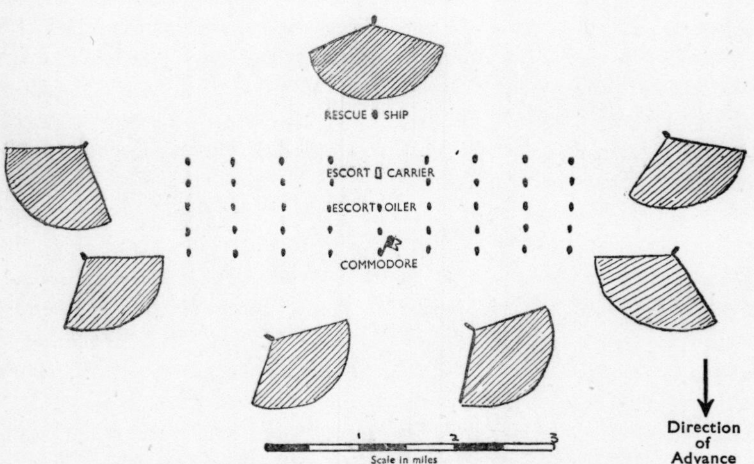

TYPICAL ATLANTIC CONVOY IN NINE COLUMNS
1000 YDS. BETWEEN COLUMNS. 500 YDS. BETWEEN SHIPS.
SEVEN ESCORTS ZIGZAGGING INDEPENDENTLY.

By night there would be two escorts astern and only one ahead of convoy. Shaded areas indicate limits of Asdic Sweep in favourable weather conditions.

Such then in barest outline, were the developments in ships and weapons which both sides made while the tide of battle ebbed and flowed in the Atlantic. Sometimes one side held the advantage, sometimes the other; but looking back on it today it seems clear that our scientists and Service staffs did succeed in countering any new weapon that the enemy had so far brought into the battle. There had been a time when the news that U-Boats were shadowing the convoy had sent a shiver of apprehension through all concerned with the safety of the merchantmen. By the beginning of 1944 such news was greeted with delight, so great was our confidence in the new weapons that had been put into our hands.

Chapter VIII

WARWICK

The destroyer *Warwick* had been Admiral Keyes' flagship on St. George's Day, 1918, at Zeebrugge, and on the wardroom bulkhead was a plaque commemorating her service there. Because of the effect on my life of the reproduction of the attack which I had seen at the Wembley Exhibition, I always felt a special bond of sympathy between the ship and myself. Some people may hold that it is impossible for an inanimate object either to feel sympathy or to possess an atmosphere; but with this I disagree. Admittedly a ship, of herself, can have no human qualities; but the men who have lived in her leave behind them either an aura of happiness or the gloom of unhappiness, either of which becomes as much a part of the ship as her own steel structure. *Warwick* had so happy an atmosphere as to be almost startling. As soon as your foot touched her deck you became aware of it. She radiated a human warmth from the whole of her slim figure.

She was the first ship I had taken over in a state of full efficiency. *Loch Tulla* and *Verbena* had been empty hulls before commissioning, and *Shikari* had been peculiar as far as the crew were concerned. By contrast *Warwick* was a proper ship. Her previous captain, Commander McCleves, was one of the very best of R.N.R.s—and that is high praise indeed. Everything in the ship was as I would have it. She had just returned from ocean escort, and was lying alongside the wall in Gladstone Dock, Liverpool, looking trim and smart. I walked down to the dock, the better to savour the taste of the first encounter with my new command. I know of nothing quite so exciting as the first meeting between a captain and the ship which will be his own as soon as he has climbed the narrow gangway to her deck. So rapidly is the enigma of her character resolved, and by so many little things will he judge her, that by the time he reaches the shore end of the gang-plank he will know a very great deal about her, and will even have hazarded a guess at her sea-kindliness and how she should be handled.

As our weapons became more and more complicated and numerous it became ever more difficult to house all the new ratings in the older ships. *Shikari*, whose original complement had been just over one hundred men, was carrying one hundred and forty. The *Warwick* originally had called for one hundred and twenty men to fight her; but when I joined her she had one hundred and seventy.

To accommodate this increase she had been converted to an escort destroyer. This had involved taking out the forward funnel and boiler-room. In the lower half of the space thus cleared an additional oil fuel tank had been built to increase her range, and above this was a new mess-deck for the stokers. To make more room in the fo'c's'le, the galley had been brought outside and placed where the forward funnel had been.

This conversion only reduced her speed from thirty to twenty-five knots, and she really would have been a very fine escort vessel if the hull had not been so old and leaky. It might be thought that small leaks would not be very serious, because any water that came in could easily be pumped out again. But a large proportion of a destroyer's bottom is lined with the oil fuel tanks, and a very little sea water in them will so contaminate the fuel that it is extremely difficult to burn.

After *Shikari* my new command seemed immense. For once I could stand upright, my comfort was assured. The Captain's harbour quarters stretched right across the ship, and unlike *Shikari's* the sleeping cabin was separate from the day cabin. Although I would never see anything of either when the ship was at sea, this would make a great difference to my time in harbour. At sea too I would be much more comfortable, for my sea cabin was close enough to the upper bridge to enable me to get there instantly if called. As the whole bridge was much higher than *Shikari's* I would no longer suffer from the continual slop of water that had always swirled about the floor of my last sea cabin.

As my favourite recreation in harbour was to hold dinner parties, both to repay the hospitality of the many friends I had made, and to enjoy the pleasure of good wine in good company, it was a great boon to have a home that was adequate for entertaining. I had always taken with me my photographs, and some good pictures, and had collected a number of 'objets d'art' in my wanderings. My greatest prize was my collection of old Arab and Persian horse-bits that I had made on my trip to the North-West Frontier of India. Much to the amusement of my 'bearer' I had combed the bazaars of little towns which had not seen a European for years, in search of these trophies. 'And why does the Commander Sahib pay four rupees for a broken old piece like this when he can go to the blacksmith and buy a new one for three?' the bearer had asked me; nor did my enthusiasm over an exquisitely worked piece, at least two centuries old convince him.

Because I could never see why fighting a war should make one less appreciative of the better things in life, my steward had orders to keep a constant supply of fresh flowers in the big vases. I took great pride in the appearance of my cabin and even after all my things had been lost with the ship, I never regretted that I had taken them with me. There were of course officers who thought that a spartan simplicity was the proper way of life in war-time. I myself could never see why anyone should make themselves less comfortable than they had to be, nor could I believe that stoicism in any way added to efficiency. Rather did I find that if I made a pleasant home of my cabin the ship's company realised that I wished to make a home of the ship herself. A ship is a strange place, and your sailor the strangest of mortals. Although he himself is forbidden to take alcohol aboard, or to have lady visitors except on special occasions, there is nothing he likes better than to see his officers having a party—so long as it is kept within bounds. The sailor at heart is a prude. So far you may go, and he will spare no trouble to see that your guests enjoy themselves; but if a party is allowed to go too far there will be serious trouble at once. If you invite no friends aboard and live like a recluse, he will think that you are unnatural and be unhappy because of it. He wants you to behave as you would in your own house and with your own family.

Commander Y. McCleves, D.S.O., D.S.C., R.D., had been one of the original Unit Commanders. He had graduated, as I had done, through command of his own group to a corvette, and then to the *Warwick*. Out of all the original Unit and Group Commanders there were now only two left in the Western Ocean, Commander Wemyss, R.N., then serving in the *Wild Goose*, and myself.

I found that *Warwick* was due for refit, and was only waiting for a signal to tell her where she could be dry-docked. In a day or two came the order for us to sail for Grimsby, and at the same time a telephone message from the Chief of Staff to Commander-in-Chief, Western Approaches, calling for me to see him. He told me that the Tactical School had just put forward a theory that each group should have two senior officers—one on the bridge of the group leader and the other down in the plot. As soon as I had seen *Warwick* safely into the dockyard hands at Grimsby he wanted me to join Commander R. C. Boyle, R.N., in the destroyer *Havelock*, and to make a trip with him to Newfoundland and back. If I would go he wanted both of us to make a report on how the idea worked in practice. Commander Boyle was the senior officer of my own B.5 group, but because *Warwick* had been taken away to refit before I joined her I had not yet met him. On paper it seemed a reasonable idea, but I thought that both Boyle and I would have to exercise a lot of self-control if we were to avoid a quarrel. As however there seemed no way of avoiding this 'trial by experience' I said that I would go.

When I had taken *Warwick* round to Grimsby I went straight across England to join *Havelock*, and we sailed within an hour of my getting aboard. As I feared the scheme proved quite unworkable. In the last chapter I explained how in a U-Boat attack the 'plot' could tell exactly what was happening, and could judge what should be done. Commander Boyle on his bridge was in the same position as the reader before the purpose of the plot was explained; whereas I, from the plot, was controlling everything, including the movements of Commander Boyle's own ship. Not even a saint could stand having his own ship moved by someone else, far less the Senior Officer of a group of ships. It would have been bad enough if we had possessed similar temperaments, but in fact we were poles apart. Boyle was slow, accurate and very meticulous. Everything he did must be weighed up and considered most carefully; and he was very neat and tidy. I am impetuous, and inclined to be slap-dash; and no one has ever said that I am tidy. We disagreed about every mortal thing, even about the type of sherry we should drink. There was only one point on which we were united—that the scheme of dual control was the craziest idea we had ever been asked to try. That we never quarrelled is a tribute to our background, and to the discipline of the service. In separate ships we would have been complementary to each other, and could have made an excellent team; for he was my senior officer and I would then have carried out the orders I received. If I learnt anything from this strange interlude it was that 'he who controls the plot controls the whole battle'.

After this abortive effort the next idea from the Tactical School was to put the senior officer of the group in the plot, and give him a captain to look after the ship. Although this was better than the scheme which Boyle and I turned down it was still not the ideal solution, because the ships were not big enough to carry a Senior Officer and a Captain. The obvious answer, which was the one finally chosen, was to give the Senior Officer a very experienced First Lieutenant who could handle the ship in action. The former then retired to the plot, and dealt with the problems as a whole.

Although we passed through waters where U-Boats were known to be working in quite large numbers, no attack was made on either convoy. This, though possibly fortunate for our friendship, was unhelpful in the matter of gaining experience. However, there were enough sighting reports from our aircraft, and enough manoeuvrings by the escorts to keep the enemy down, for us to form a reliable opinion that the scheme was unworkable. On my return I went to see the Chief of Staff to ask his advice about my report, because I felt sure that it was going to be very much against the idea we had been trying out. He told me that Boyle had already sent in one sulphurous document, and he saw no reason why I should have to write another. I rather think the result was only what he himself had expected.

We sailed again eastbound from St. John's, Newfoundland, on Boxing Day, 1943. As soon as I was back I spent one night at my home, where I arrived with two frozen salmon, and then rushed over to Grimsby to get *Warwick* ready for a convoy due to sail early in January.

We should have left Grimsby on the 11th, but delays occurred and we did not get away until the 13th, which was the day on which the convoy left Liverpool. However, by dint of pushing her along at her best speed we managed to catch up while the merchantmen were still forming up off the north coast of Ireland.

The convoy was a fast one, and was supposed to make nine knots; but already a westerly gale was rising, and the ships were having great difficulty in getting into their stations. It had been blowing hard from the west for the last fortnight, and a very big westerly swell was running. January 1944 produced the worst weather of the whole war. For escort we had *Havelock* (Senior Officer), three more destroyers, *Warwick*, *Vimy* and *Volunteer*, and two Belgian-manned corvettes, the *Buttercup* and *Godetia*.

That convoy never formed up. We could not get them into their stations that night, and by morning we were all virtually hove to. In the first twenty-four hours we made eighty miles to the westward. The second day we were down to fifty-two miles; and on the third we made only forty—a fraction over one and a half knots. The weather showed no improvement, and the seas got steadily worse. *Havelock* sprung her mainmast, and went off to Iceland for repairs. This left me as Senior Officer of the Escort. Ten of the merchant ships had returned to England with cracks appearing in their superstructures, and fifteen were straggling we knew not where. The convoy was reduced from about fifty to twenty-five ships, spread over miles of sea; and the escorts were more or less out of touch with each other.

As the seas were breaking over the upper deck and green water, two and three feet deep, was sweeping across *Warwick* between the after-house and the 3-inch H.A. gun, I brought the watch-keeping officers forward to sleep in the sick-bay under the bridge, and closed the upper deck to traffic. At the very slow speed which the convoy was making my ship was unmanageable. I had to go faster, and this meant making a broad zig-zag if I was to keep station on the convoy. We were thus constantly altering course, and steaming at an angle to the mountainous seas, instead of heading more comfortably into them. Soon after the upper deck had been closed the motor boat was swept clean out of the davits; half an hour later the whaler on the other side went the same way. We then discovered that all the drinking water was in the fore-part of the ship, and all the bread in the after-part. We solved that one by using a rocket gun to get a line from the bridge to the stern of the ship, and rigging a breeches-buoy. We then exchanged water for bread.

Soon after daylight on the following morning the engineer officer telephoned from the engine room to say that he thought something on deck must have carried away, because a lot of water was coming down through holes in the deck above him. I went to the after end of the bridge and looked over but could see nothing wrong. When I got back to the compass platform, the First Lieutenant was just being relieved for the forenoon watch. Before he went below for his breakfast I said:

'Number One, the Chief thinks something has carried away abaft the funnel, as water is pouring into his engine room. I've had a look but I can't see anything missing. You might have a look yourself and see if anything has gone, because I think that he's imagining things.'

I watched his oilskin-clad figure as he moved cautiously aft, clinging to hand-holds as she rolled, until he disappeared from view behind the asdic hut. Soon he was coming back again, excitedly, and much less carefully. Above the wind he shouted:

'The 3-inch gun's gone—platform and all.'

It had too—whipped clean out of her. The gun and platform had been carried over the side without even bending a guard-rail to show where they had passed.

The following morning, our fifth at sea, both *Vimy* and *Volunteer* reported weather damage and as the convoy was reduced to about twenty ships I ordered the destroyers back to England. The two corvettes were much better suited to this weather than the destroyers, and could still manoeuvre fairly easily. I therefore sent them round to count how many children remained in the bed, and to find out if the escort oiler was still with us. One corvette came back with a count of twenty, and the other with twenty-one—but the escort oiler was not among them. As we did not carry enough fuel to cross the Atlantic without replenishing, this was a serious matter.

The following night was, if anything, even worse than its predecessors; and at dawn we had only eight ships of the convoy in sight. I made a signal to Commander-in-Chief, Western Approaches.

'Convoy scattered by continuous gale. Have only eight merchant ships with me. *Warwick* will have to be dry docked on return as all fuel tanks are leaking. No U-Boat can operate in this weather. Request permission to return.'

That afternoon I received the answer, 'Approved'. Having collected the two corvettes we put our stern to the wind and with revolutions for seven knots on the engines, but actually making ten through the water, we started for home. The Belgians had put up a very good show indeed. Their mess decks might smell peculiar to our Anglo-Saxon noses, but they were both very efficient little ships, and very anxious indeed to please.

Although landsmen may imagine that it can be done, it is of course impossible for an ocean-going ship to travel faster than the waves. A big wave travels at forty-five knots, which is faster than the speed of any such ship. Even if you could steam at, or near the speed of the waves, the down-drag of your propellers would be so great that a following sea would break aboard instead of lifting the stern.

Now at last we could open the upper deck to traffic, and the ship rode much more easily. But as the enormous waves came up astern and passed under us, the hull was bending so much that the steering rods from the wheelhouse to the steering engine were continually jamming; and the big watertight bulkheads between the engine and boiler rooms were popping like biscuit tins. The noise could be heard even on the upper deck. After supper I was standing wedged in the port after corner of the bridge. The seas were quite stupendous. They would roar up astern of us, huge mountains with a curling crest five or six feet deep in foam. Up would go our stern and down went the bow; as the wave passed under us the stern would sink until, looking aft the following wave appeared twice as high as it really was—and its true height was quite enough to be frightening. It was the first time in my life that I had ever felt the wind to be distinctly less when we were in the troughs than on the crests. By any standard it was thrilling to see the way this slim craft

Passing through the convoy.

'Evening.' Two escort vessels can be seen on the horizon.

H.M.S. *Highlander*. One of six destroyers building for the Brazilian navy. Taken over and completed for Britain. At the time this photograph was taken she had been converted for escort work.

'River' Class frigate, H.M.S. *Helmsdale*.

would cock up her tail to mock the elemental fury that the westerly gale flung at her.

As I was watching I became aware of a sudden change. The sky behind me to the north-west had blackened to an intensity that was appalling. Even in the darkness of the gale the seas had been plainly visible. Now, against that new and unearthly blackness they were becoming startlingly light in colour, so that the ship herself showed up ever more clearly against the pale waters. It was while I was considering this phenomenon that I first saw the line squall. It can then only have been about a mile away, and coming down from the north-west at something over eighty miles an hour. From the many old books about sailing ships which I had read I was aware of the terrible power of these squalls. They could catch sailing ships aback and whip the masts clean out of them; for they brought with them a sudden shift of wind of anything from forty-five to ninety degrees. I had seen minor squalls, but never one like this. It was plainly marked by a single foam-topped wave, as high and as fierce as the westerly ones which we were riding. As I waited I realised that one of the old seas would meet this new one just at our stern. Breathlessly I watched. The stern went up and up—and then she broached to, just as a dinghy will do when landing on an open beach. She slewed right round to take the foaming wall of water full on her side.

I had felt her start to swing, and realised instinctively that the helmsman had lost control of her. Before she went over I was already half way down the weather ladder to the wheel-house deck. For a sickening minute while I struggled with the door she lay right over. I did not know it then, but learnt afterwards, that water was pouring into the forward messdecks, and that our elderly bosun—a most God-fearing man—was nearly drowning in the lavatory. 'Up to his neck in water and swearing most horrid, Sir,' as it was reported to me later.

I got the door open, and there in the centre of the wheel-house was the untended wheel. In the far corner was a muddle of legs and arms, which was the helmsman and the bridge messenger. I launched myself towards the engine room tele-graphs, and more by good luck than good management succeeded in getting a toe and hand hold that would support me. I rang down for full astern on the starboard engine and stopped the port engine. As I did so I heard the cry of 'man overboard'; but I could do nothing. My first duty was to the ship. I could feel her vibrating as the starboard engine began to run astern. Glory be—she was coming up! The compass bowl, which had been jammed, was swinging freely in the binnacle again, and slowly the compass card began to creep round as she brought her head to the eastward. She took one more sickening roll and then seemed happier. I took the wheel and rang down for seventy revolutions ahead on both engines.

'Wheelhouse—Forebridge,' I called up the voicepiece.

'Forebridge.'

'I'm down here Mac, at the wheel.'

'Thank God, Sir. We thought it was you that was overboard.'

'I'll stay down here and steer her myself.'

'What about the man overboard Sir? Don't yet know who it is—but someone was certainly seen to go.'

'Sorry—I dare not risk it. I'm afraid the men won't like it, but I can't jeopardise the whole for one; and we'd never find him now. I'll keep the wheel until the sea has settled down.'

I steered her all night, and found that by putting on the wheel I needed before the rods could jam I could keep her pretty well on her course. With the dawn at last came signs of the wind moderating. The wheel was jamming less and less, and the quartermaster of the forenoon watch was a helmsman I could trust. I handed over the wheel to him, and had my breakfast.

As I feared the men were grumbling. I sent for the coxswain. He was a fine man, and did not like having to tell me what he must—if I pressed him. In the end he told me that the men felt that I should have turned back and searched for their shipmate. I wrote a notice and gave it to the coxswain to put on the ship's notice board.

'Decisions are mine—not yours. I shall have to answer for my decision to the Board of Enquiry that will certainly be called. Until the decision of the Board is known you must refrain, for the good of the ship, from criticizing. I will say only what I shall say to the Board, "That to have turned the ship at that time and in that sea, would have been hazardous in the extreme, and I would not place 170 men in such jeopardy to save one who, even if found, would I am sure have been beyond our aid." I would have preferred to have said this to you personally but I cannot leave the bridge.'

Half an hour after this notice had been on the board the coxswain, bosun, and chief stoker came on the bridge to see me. They were a deputation to say 'thank you', and to tell me that the ship's company wanted to apologize for any hard words that I might have overheard.

Later that morning we came across a large tanker, which, damaged by the heavy weather, was going home. She had been torpedoed previously, but the repair was giving trouble. As she had already started to break in two, we signalled for a tug. We stayed with her until off Barra Head, where we were met by the ocean tug to whom we handed over the merchant ship. We had not left her half an hour when she broke clean in half and sank. The tug picked up all her crew.

We were ordered to Londonderry, and then to Ardrossan to dry-dock. We had only left dock on the 12th January, and it was then the 22nd. B.5 Group had been pretty well decimated by that gale. All four destroyers were weather-damaged, the three older ones badly. Only the two corvettes were left. I went down to Liverpool as soon as we had docked to see the Admiral.

'I'm afraid those old destroyers are no longer fit for the western ocean,' he told me and added, 'I've got a number of new escorts coming over from the United States; and I am being asked to provide some destroyers for the Plymouth Command to help with the invasion, and to beat up the German E-Boats which are working out of the Channel Islands against our traffic along the south coast. Our own M.T.B.'s cannot compete with the weather there, and the E-Boats need a lesson. You'll have one or two more "V & W's" [such ships as *Warwick*], and all your old "S Class". It should be quite a party.'

With business in the U-Boat trade so slack just then, and the invasion obviously planned for that summer the idea had attractions.

'Shall we still be in the Western Approaches Command?' I asked.

'Yes, you'll still belong to me. You'll just be loaned to Plymouth.'

'And can I have the hedgehog taken out of her, and the forward 4-inch gun replaced Sir?'

'You can have anything you can squeeze out of anybody.'

I went in search of a 4-inch gun. The most likely place to start seemed to be the Admiralty. So I went off down to London. I was wrong. After wandering round many passages, and seeing a number of very serious-minded officers who obviously considered that I was a dangerous lunatic, I went north. After a day or two searching round Glasgow I at last found a gun that had actually been taken out of a 'V & W' destroyer. To get a gun that does not belong to you was, I discovered, one of the most difficult of undertakings. All sorts of people had an interest in it, and most of them wanted me to 'put it in writing', and they would 'put it up' to someone else.

'My dear man,' I would exclaim, 'the ship sails on Sunday, and it's Tuesday now. Do you really think we've time to exchange "billets-doux" on the subject of a cannon that must be delivered alongside by Friday afternoon?'

The gun arrived in a contractor's lorry at two o'clock on the Friday, and we sailed on Sunday, 13th February. There is an old sailor's saying that you should not sail on a Sunday, and the meaning of the 13th is always clear. We swung our compasses, carried out firing tests on the new 4-inch and on the 3-inch high-angle gun which had been issued to replace the one lost overboard, and sailed for Plymouth on the 17th. We arrived on the afternoon of the 19th, and I went ashore to call on Captain (D). His office overlooked the river, and from there he could see everything that went on.

'I must congratulate you on your ship. I've not seen a destroyer enter harbour like that since the early days. I like to see things done smartly. Of course you've been here before.'

'Only up here once Sir, when I got *Tiger's* whaler foul of the ferry.'

'Oh well, I'll be seeing a lot of you I don't doubt. Just at the moment the Commander-in-Chief wants to see you. There's a car outside.'

As a matter of fact *Warwick* did look very smart. Not since *Verbena* had painted herself from truck to waterline three years before in Gibraltar, had I ever been able to paint my ship all over at the one time. In Ardrossan we had the whole crew aboard, because they had only just finished refit leave; and it had been the obvious job to give them.

I called on the Admiral and was told that I was to take *Scimitar* with me, and intercept a U-Boat which was expected off the west coast of Cornwall. As I told him that my asdic set had not been behaving in a very satisfactory way, the staff anti-submarine officer, Commander J. W. Heath, R.N., was sent for in a hurry and told to go to sea with us to look after it.

We rounded Land's End about ten that night with the 'S Class' destroyer in company, and started to patrol the beat. This was a new sort of war for us. Convoys in long lines of two columns were passing up and down the war channel, and the sea was littered with fishing vessels of all sizes. As our radar screen was confused with the echoes from the small craft a determined U-Boat could have done what he liked.

Next morning we were still sweeping in line abreast. It was a lovely clear morning, with bright sun, but bitterly cold. After 'Sunday Morning Rounds' I spent an hour practising radar control of the guns, and painting the arcs of fire of each gun on the gyro-repeater compass on the upper bridge. If we were to tackle E-Boats we must shift our main interest in life from asdics to guns. At midday I sent for the Engineer Officer and the First Lieutenant to protest about the state of the stokers' messdeck at 'rounds' that morning. I also sent a message to the asdic officer of my own ship and to Commander Heath to say that I was not satisfied with the asdic, and would they please do something about it. As all these officers had gathered in the wardroom before lunch I unwittingly saved their lives when I brought them forward. Then the anti-submarine officer telephoned from the asdic compartment to say that he would like to shut down the set for half an hour, and I agreed. I then turned to the First Lieutenant and the Engineer Officer to discuss the messdeck problem.

The sky suddenly turned to flame and the ship gave a violent shudder. Then the flame had gone, and as far as I could see everything was strangely the same. Looking ahead, I could see something floating and turning over in the water like a giant metallic whale. As I looked it rolled over further still and I could make out our own pennant numbers painted on it. I was dumb-founded. It seemed beyond reason. I ran to the after side of the bridge and looked over. The ship ended just aft of the engine room—everything abaft that had gone. What I had seen ahead of us *had really been the ship's own stern.* There were small fires all over the upper deck. The First Lieutenant was down there organizing the fire parties. He saw me and called, 'Will you abandon ship Sir?'

'Not bloody likely, Number One. Get those fires out, and then all the life-saving equipment over the side and secured by boat-ropes. We'll not get out till we have to.'

I went back to the compass platform.

'Signalman.'

'Sir?'

'Make to "*Scimitar*—I think I've been torpedoed". Then get down to the main deck. Yeoman, you go too—but first take all your books down to the wireless cabinet. Collect all the charts you can lay your hands on, and push them in there as well, and lock the door.'

The officer of the watch was still standing by the compass. I wondered how much longer he was going to stand there.

'Must have been hit in the magazine—the stern's been blown clean off,' I told him.

He leant forward to the wheelhouse voicepipe and called down 'Stop both.'

'Both wizzers have been blown to glory.' I could not help laughing. 'Better get down to the main deck and give Number One a hand.'

When he had gone I was all alone on the bridge. It was strangely quiet. I took off my sea boots and tried to blow up my inflatable life jacket. It would not fill with air. I put my hand behind my back and found that both the rubber tube and my jacket had been cut, I supposed by some flying fragment. I had often complained that life jackets were left lying about the wheelhouse, so perhaps there would be one there now. I went down to see. But no, my recent words had taken effect. I seized a 'sorbo' cushion, and tucked it into the jacket of my battle dress. It gave me a feminine silhouette, but it could be a help if the worst was to happen. I went out on to the wheelhouse deck. The ship was upright and apparently floating well.

The carley-floats were by then all over the side, and secured by boat-ropes. The First Lieutenant had all the small fires out. We might save her yet.

I could hear a high windy sort of noise that I could not place. The deck began to take on an angle—suddenly—so suddenly. She was almost on her side. I was slithering, grasping all sorts of unlikely things. My world had turned through ninety degrees. I just caught sight of Harries, the navigator, going over the high side of the main deck. He had a polished wooden box in either hand, the chronometer and the sextant. I wished that I had someone to laugh with over that one. I jumped for the galley funnel which was now parallel with the water and about two foot clear, and flat-footed it to the end. I could see water pouring into the main funnel. It made a guggling sound, like an enormous bath drain. The sea around me was covered with bobbing heads. I paused at the end of my small funnel to look at the faces. They were laughing as if this were part of some gigantic fun fair. The men called to me.

'Come on Sir. The water's lovely.'

'I'm waiting for the *Skylark*,' I shouted back. But the galley funnel dipped, and I was swimming too—madly. The man beside me turned to look over his shoulder, 'She's going!'

I turned to look. He was right. Her bow was pointed at the sky. 'Swim like hell—suction,' I shouted back. We swam like hell. I turned once more, but now there were very, very few bobbing heads behind me. I swam on. The destroyer of my old group was passing through us. I could see her men at action stations. They were attacking. They were attacking the wreck of the *Warwick*! I screamed at them in my frenzy. Wherever else the U-Boat might have been it could not have been there. The depth-charges sailed up into the air. Funny how they wobbled from side to side, I'd never noticed that before. When, I wondered, would they explode? It was like being punched in the chest, not as bad as I had expected. I swam on. Things were a bit hazy. I was not as interested in going places as I had been. I could only see waves and more waves, and I wished that they would stop coming. I did not really care any more. Then I felt hands grasp my shoulders and a voice say, 'Christ, it's the skipper. Give me a hand to get the bastard in,' and I was dragged into a carley-float which was more than crowded to capacity.

'Is there an officer here?' I gasped.

'Yes Sir. MacIndoe.'

'Then for God's sake get some of the men over the side and lashed in the beckets, or this thing will capsize. Put me back again if you like. Take charge, I'm all in.'

I had always feared that the smaller carley-floats would capsize, for I had experimented with bathing parties and found them remarkably unstable. They are so easy to get away from a ship, and appear to offer such a good chance of rescue, that they nearly always end by being overcrowded. I had evolved a plan, and had always seen that all the carley-floats in the ship were fitted with a number of lengths of rope, about six feet long, which were spliced at intervals to the jack-stay running round the edge of the float. If it should become overcrowded, a number of men could then stay in the water, pass the ropes round their bodies under the arms, and tie them again to the jackstay. In this way the whole balance of the float was greatly improved, and almost double the number of men could be carried.

MacIndoe went over first, and found it much warmer in than out. A number of others followed his lead, and soon we were riding the waves very easily. About two hundred yards away we could see another laden float. They had not followed our example, and it looked hopelessly top-heavy. It must in fact have capsized, and then no one could have found the strength to climb back again. It was empty when we ourselves were picked up by the steam fishing vessel *Lady Luck* and taken to Padstow.

In the tiny bunkroom of the fishing-boat twelve men and a red-hot bogey stove were tightly packed, while the cook handed round cups of scalding tea. It was almost an hour's steaming to the harbour. By the time we were half way there we were getting some heat back into our numbed bodies and I, for one, had taken off my wet clothes. When we got in the captain of the drifter lent me a mackintosh in which to go ashore. Admiral A. G. Crauford, Resident Naval Officer, Padstow, met us as we berthed. As we walked across the quay to R.N.O.'s office, three other trawlers were rounding the headland. We looked for more, but could see none. He lent me a MacDonald tartan rug with which to cover my nakedness, and an ancient cap which he had worn in World War One. It had a very small peak, and set on my head above the rug must have given me a very odd appearance; for my legs and feet, bare and brown as a nigger's from the fuel oil, were sticking out below. I suppose it was this oil film which saved my life, because it was two hours before I could go up to the Air Station myself. The wind was from the east, and it was only just not freezing. After I had telephoned to Captain (D), Plymouth, we went back to the jetty. I wanted to meet the men as they came ashore, and to make a list of names as soon as possible. As the tide was falling, the other three fishing boats had been unable to get alongside, and so we had to have the men brought ashore in a motor boat. I could not believe at first that the three trawlers held all the survivors, but the skippers told me that only four trawlers had gone to the scene of the torpedoing, and that no boats had been seen making for other ports. There was no other conclusion but that the ninety-four names I had was the sum total of survivors.

The explosion of *Warwick's* magazine had been seen by many people, including a number of naval aircrews from St. Merryn Naval Air Station. When we landed we found that transport had been arranged, and everything organized for our comfort. The men were put straight into the buses and taken to the Air Station. When we had seen them all off Admiral Crauford and I went round the four trawlers to thank the skippers; and he then took me up to the wardroom mess in his own car.

They gave us a wonderful reception at St. Merryn. The Commander helped me to try to get the oil fuel off. We tried everything—Vim, soap, even high octane petrol. The last was the most successful, but it stung terribly on the tender parts of my body. After a meal I heard that our Bosun was in hospital nearby, so borrowed a car and drove over to see him. He was a reservist, and an elderly man—too old for the rigours of that day. He was in a very low state, but could recognise me. I was glad that I had come. He slipped his moorings peacefully in the night—just shock. In the evening the Padre held a special service for us. It was entirely voluntary but every man was there. That night I sent a telegram to my wife, 'Rumour is a lying jade.'

Sub-Lieutenant D. H. Harries, R.N.R., the navigator, survived but neither the sextant nor the chronometer did so. He trod water for twenty minutes holding both, and then decided that one would have to go. After considerable thought he let go the chronometer because he reckoned that, although a more expensive instrument, it would also cost more to repair. After another spell of keeping himself and the sextant above the waves, he was forced to the unwelcome conclusion that it too would have to be jettisoned. But the moment his fingers relaxed their hold a hand grasped his shoulder and he was hauled into a raft, madly trying to get at the sextant, which was then sinking into the depths. The seaman who had hold of him thought he had gone 'nuts' and knocked him out.

The next day we were taken by bus to Plymouth. It was extraordinary how the ship's company remained a crew. Discipline was perfect, and they sang all the way. It was not bawdy tunes they sang, but old west country songs, Widdicombe Fair and The Jolly Plough Boy, and a lot I had never heard before. They might have been an excursion party. Or was there something more behind the singing, a something intangible and utterly remote—a spirit of companionship born of a common experience? As we drove through the sunlit Cornish lanes I remember thinking, 'I am sorry for the Hun. I should not like to have to fight against men like these.' With the coxswain getting the men fallen in, we were still 'Warwicks', still a ship's company when we tumbled out of the buses on the parade ground at Devonport Barracks. The men were coming to their own officers for help too. I remember one man, a very small and rather elderly reservist, who took such a very small size in boots, that even the resources of Devonport Barracks were defeated. We telephoned to the local Superintendent of W.R.N.S., and she had a pair of Wren's shoes sent down within half an hour.

A Board of Enquiry was held in the Captain's cabin of H.M.S. *Glasgow*; for service custom dictates that this should be done, not only to ensure that all the safety precautions were carried out but as a check on the discipline of officers and men, and to learn any lessons. There was only one other query. Could it have been a mine from our own minefield? Fortunately Harries remembered the bearings of a fix he had taken a few minutes before, and this removed all doubts on that score. Also the German wireless had claimed us as a sinking. There seems no doubt that the U-Boat we were looking for had fired a homing torpedo at us. It had hit us just forward of the propellers, and exploded the after magazine. *Warwick* would have continued to float had the after engine-room bulkhead not collapsed.

When the President of the Board had told us that he would not require any more evidence, we were free to go on our survivors' leave. That evening for the last time we mustered the Warwicks. The Coxswain came to me, 'I've twenty-three requestmen, Sir.' He was fingering a bundle of request forms.

'Requestmen Coxswain? I can't possibly deal with requestmen now. Anyway I don't believe I've the power to do so—even if there was time. What on earth do they want?'

'They all ask to be drafted to your next ship Sir.'

The men's request was of course fantastic, but their thought kept me warm on the long journey home. I arrived back the next evening, and the following morning went to Liverpool to see the Admiral. He rose from his chair when I was shown in, 'I'm sorry about this, Rayner.'

'So am I Sir. Can you give me another ship?'

'Of course if you want one. But I thought you could do with a shore job for a bit. You've had a long spell.'

'If you'll trust me with another ship Sir?'

'Certainly.' He sat down and waved me to the other chair. 'You'll be a better commanding officer for having lost one ship. You can go over to America and take a Captain Class Frigate. Work her up in Bermuda, and have a good rest while you are over there.'

'A Captain Class Frigate!' There was horror in my voice.

'Why not? They're wonderful ships.'

'But I don't want to go round the Atlantic with "U.S.A." stamped on my backside Sir.'

He looked at me from those queer eyes, which however bright they might seem, always hid what he was really thinking.

'What *do* you want?'

'A destroyer with two funnels.'

'Good God, Rayner, I've only got very few of those left, and the R.N. fellows are after them all the time.'

'Anything that can sink a U-Boat's good enough for me Sir. But destroyers with two funnels are what I really like.'

I left him and went home. I had hardly got inside the door when the telephone bell rang. I answered it. I knew at once it was from Commander-in-Chief's office. I could hear the operator saying, 'The Admiral's secretary wants you Sir,' and then her announcing my name. A voice addressed me,

'Rayner?'

'Yes.'

'Could you be at Troon by tomorrow night?'

I did a bit of quick thinking.

'If it's got two funnels, yes,' I answered.

'It has'—pause—'it means giving up your survivors' leave.' The soft voice tempted. But I was ready for that one.

'I bet it's in dock for repairs or refit, and I'll take my wife with me.'

'I can tell the Admiral you'll take her then?'

'You can tell the Admiral from me that he knows damn well I will.'

'Right. You are appointed *Highlander* in Command. A signal will be made to the ship, and you'll get confirmation in due course. Good luck to you.'

I was on the jetty at Troon the following night. There before me lay the dream that had come true. Not a relic from World War One but a powerful modern destroyer completed in 1940. There were only three of them left now, *Highlander*, *Havelock*, *Hesperus*—for *Harvester* had been sunk by a U-Boat two months before. What ships they were! At the beginning of the war there had been nine similar ships already commissioned for our own Navy and six more, slightly modified, were building for the Brazilian Government. The latter had been taken over and completed as British ships. *Highlander* was one of the six. They had just a little more headroom than their sister ships, because the Brazilians had insisted that they should have big 'punkah' fans in the living spaces. She really was the most beautifully fitted warship I had ever seen. She had been built as the 'leader' of the six ships, and her cabin fittings, if a little old fashioned to our eyes, were quite exceptional. The Captain's day cabin was about eighteen feet by fifteen, and panelled in mahogany; and there was a green-tiled bathroom and lavatory for his own use, and beyond that was a sleeping cabin with a polished brass cot. The Brazilian Navy certainly did itself well. As a 'leader' she carried personal crockery for the Captain's table, white fluted china with a thin rim of gold round the edge of the cups, saucers and plates. She was fitted out almost like a yacht. At sea, too, I would be much more comfortable than in any previous ship. My sea cabin was big enough to stow an easy chair alongside the bunk, and there was a knee-hole desk and drawers. It may seem curious that I should consider my personal comfort so much, but few people are so spartan that they would not have been as pleased as I was with my new ship.

As a matter of fact I had not brought my wife up with me at first, as I had discovered that the ship could not be ready for three weeks. We had decided that I should go on alone and spend three or four days getting the reins into my hands. She would join me as soon as I was settled.

I had wondered why there had been so much insistence on my getting to Troon that night if the ship was not sailing for three weeks. The first thing that the Officer of the Day told me when I went aboard was that the new First Lieutenant had joined half an hour before, and he added that the new Engineer Officer was expected at any moment. So that was the way of it. There was a general reshuffle, and we were to be given the chance to get to know each other. I often wondered how much Max Horton knew about what went on in the individual ships of his command. Once his personal assistant said to me, 'Max knows everything.' Sometimes I believed he did—even down to things you would not think an Admiral would trouble his head about. And yet I wonder whether such matters are so small? A little cog that sticks may stop a vast machine. So too in a Naval Command; and the Admiral is there to see that his machine never stops anywhere.

Chapter IX

HIGHLANDER

As I was shown to my quarters I could see the First Lieutenant unpacking in his cabin next door. He came in at once to introduce himself, and together we went round the ship. It did not take me long to learn that I was very fortunate in my Number One—Lieutenant H. E. G. Atkins R.N. Some men, like some ships, remain a doubt in your mind for days and weeks, even in the close association of shipboard life. Others at once make an indelible impression—favourable or unfavourable. With Atkins there was never any doubt. He was tall, smart and almost too good-looking to be true, but without any trace of effeminacy. He had the same wild charm that I had known so well in *Verbena's* First Lieutenant and, because I remembered Jack Hunter's smile, I felt that I had known Atkins for months.

I think we both fell in love with the ship when we went round her; but I think we both came back to my cabin a little worried at the atmosphere we had encountered, when we had stopped two or three of the men to ask questions. There had been a noticeable lack of interest in us, and after all the pair of us were going to be rather important to them for the next few months. I thought this decidedly odd, and was just wondering whether I should say anything to Atkins, when there was a heavy knock at the door. In answer to my call a tall and elderly Commissioned Engineer pushed the curtain aside. Our new 'Chief' came in very slowly, for he was a big man in every way.

At that first meeting I saw only the outward appearance. Garner was slow of movement, and chary of speech. Had he been a Scot one would have used the word 'dour' in speaking of him. But we very soon discovered that it would have been a most unsuitable word to describe a character which was so open, and which became ever more charming as our friendship grew. I use the word friendship carefully and deliberately, for even if love of *Highlander* was the common bond which was to join the three of us together as partners, there did grow up between us a very real friendship.

The 'Chief' was a good twenty years older than the average age of the wardroom officers. More than thirty years ago he had joined the Navy as a boy, and he had retired on pension before the outbreak of war with the rank of Commissioned Engineer. This he told us was his first sea-going job since recall, and we were to learn that he was at heart a seaman. I was soon to discover that he shared with me a veritable passion for handling the 2,000-ton ship in a way which would have been considered reckless had anyone else been in charge of the engines.

At sea he was always to be seen wearing such spotless white overalls that one wondered how many times a day he must change, and how many of his stokers were kept busy washing the extraordinary number of those garments that he possessed. Even when we borrowed half a dozen to clothe the chorus of the concert party it had no visible effect on the capacity of the 'Chief's' wardrobe.

When entering or leaving harbour I could see the flash of white overalls as he stood in his favourite vantage point abaft the after funnel. From there he could look down through a convenient hatch to the 'starting platform' of his beloved engine room, and he could also watch how I was handling the ship. No wartime Captain ever had a more exacting audience. He had seen much service in destroyers of the Mediterranean Fleet, and nothing short of a faultless performance on my part would satisfy his craving for perfection. As I ran down the bridge ladder after berthing the ship and hurried along the upper deck to my harbour cabin in the stern, I would see him waiting for me.

'Well done Chief,' I'd say, knowing full well that it was really for this that he was still standing there. The little commendation meant everything to such a perfectionist.

'Ah, I don't know Sir. My lads are still just a little too slow in getting those engines astern for my liking.'

'Damn it, Chief, I felt them going astern immediately the telegraphs had rung.'

'Ah, but it's the seconds that count handling a ship at that speed. You know Sir, if only my lads had got her astern just a second or two earlier, and if we'd given her just a few more revolutions, say 180 instead of 150, you wouldn't have needed to give her that extra little kick with the wheel hard over—we'd have been right alongside and secured Sir.'

'Are you suggesting I alter my standing orders to use 180 revolutions instead of 150 for "half ahead" and "half astern"?'

'Well, we could try it Sir.'

'You'll get me court-martialled for hazarding the ship. Bring your copy of "Captain's Orders" to my cabin, and I'll initial the alteration.'

So he made me 'drive' *Highlander* as a destroyer should be handled. But I could not have done it with anyone else.

At first he had said that he was too old to join in the wardroom parties, but I do not think it was really age which made him say that. He was a very moral man, and I fancy that he feared our parties would be a little wild. When he discovered that there was no vice in us, and that our enterprises were only the result of high spirits, he would easily be persuaded to leave his cabin for a corner chair in the wardroom. Like Mr. Badger in the 'Wind in the Willows', he would sit the whole evening through with an avuncular smile on his lips, watching the children at play. He was guide, philosopher, and friend to all of us—a very fine engineer, a first-class officer and a delightful companion.

Happily before I left the ship I was able to recommend him for, and to see him given, the promotion he so much deserved, and which would make so great a difference to his pension in the future. When the last handshake came and he said to me 'I have so much to thank you for,' I was able to answer from the bottom of my heart 'And I to thank you for Chief. I shall never forget our partnership in handling *Highlander*.'

But when we first met in Troon all this still lay in the future. All I knew when I climbed into my cot that night was that I was happy enough with all my officers, and my ship—but the men were a question mark.

It was worse than that. The following day we discovered

A typical winter gale that could go on for days on end.

'Castle' Class corvette.

American-built 'Captain' Class frigate.

there was something wrong. The defaulters' list was as long as your arm, and there were twenty or more requests for 'permission to change to another ship'.

We waited for two days and then the three of us—myself, the First Lieutenant and the Engineer Officer, held a conference in my cabin.

'You know,' I told them, 'I think it's just something that's been allowed to grow up between the officers and the men. They are thoroughly "browned off". After all the poor beast has had a new Captain almost every quarter. You can hardly expect her to be a happy ship. Let's tear up everything and start afresh.'

The Engineer Officer goggled at me 'What, Sir? Tear up the defaulters' list?'

'Yes, Chief, the whole damned lot. And pardon all men under punishment.'

'But we've two or three who are second class for conduct.' (Meaning men who have lost certain very valuable privileges for continual misbehaviour.)

'But you can't do that, Sir,' from the First Lieutenant.

'Of course I can—so long as they remain in my ship. And of course the whole thing is dependent on their allowing me to tear up these ruddy requests for draft.'

Next morning I 'cleared lower deck'. The whole ship's company was mustered closely round the 4-inch H.A. gun, so that I could use that as a platform.

'I want to speak to you. I'm used to having a happy ship. There's something wrong in this one. I don't know what it is. I want to put it right. I want to see you chaps with smiles on your faces. I haven't seen one since I came aboard. Now I'll tell you what I'm going to do. There's a defaulter's list here which is quite fantastic. I think ten per cent of the ship's company are waiting for my first "Captain's Defaulters" and there's another ten per cent under punishment. I've got the list here. At the present time one man in five of the ship's company is either under punishment or waiting to see what I'm going to give them. We can't run a ship that way. Now I'll tell you what I'm going to do. Of course I can't do anything where pay has already been stopped; but this I can do. I can tear up these lists, and we'll start afresh. That goes for the second class for conduct boys too—but there's a tag to it.' I could see that I'd got their interest, and I could see the curiosity in their faces. 'Well you didn't think I was such a fool as to do that for nothing did you? There are two things I want from you. To hear no more about draft chits. In future the only way out of *Highlander* will be by promotion. We'll start classes for leading hand as soon as we leave Troon, and I want to see you make this ship the happiest out of 'Derry. Now can I tear up these papers?' I held out the bundle of request forms, and looked round. I had them guessing. They did not know what to make of it, but the tension was easing. There was something almost tangible growing between officers and men while I stood there. Laughing, I was able to tease them.

'Come on, what shall I do with them?'

They were laughing too.

'All right, I won't make you say it. I can see the answer. Number One, take these and stuff them where they belong. No, on second thoughts don't do that—you'll block it up. Give 'em to the Chief. He'll burn 'em in something or other.'

I got a roar of laughter then, but held up my hand for silence.

'Now, before I get down I just want to say this. There are two things I won't have. One is missing the ship on sailing. I want you back whatever state you're in. The other is inefficiency. And just one thing more, you must remember that a very important part of an officer's job is to look after his men. If you want anything go to your divisional officer, and he'll sort it out for you—and if he can't, I will. I don't care how long "Captain's Requestmen" takes, so long as "Captain's Defaulters" are non-existent.'

We had found the trouble. There had been too many changes. She had been a senior officer's ship, carrying a senior officer's staff, for so long that no one had spared the time for her own men. We turned up the most extraordinary tales; men who had muddles over pay that had not been cleared up for years; medals and clasps not applied for; promotions not made. The twenty odd requests for draft were replaced by a pile of chits for all sorts of things. We set up a special 'bureau' for requests, and we badgered everyone we could think of to get matters put right. One Stoker Petty Officer got £94 back pay, and there were many smaller amounts. One result was that the next quarter's punishment returns were almost nil. As there were practically no defaulters the coxswain (who is also the ship's policeman), now had time to spare. We put him in charge of the ship's concert party.

The town of Perth had 'adopted' the ship, and while we lay in Troon we sent an invitation to the Mayor to bring some of the city notables over to lunch, and to see the ship. When they arrived they produced three bagpipes as a present. Apparently some previous Commanding Officer with a musical ear had asked for them. I accepted the gift as gracefully as my astonishment would allow. I fear though that they must have seen the look of consternation on my face when the gigantic parcel—it was almost a four foot cube—was opened on the upper deck because it was too big to go down the hatchway to the wardroom. Then they asked me what *I* would like for the ship, and I plumped for a silk ensign to use on Sunday mornings. An old Naval custom, now more or less extinct. *Hood* had been the last ship I had seen with one. In due course it arrived, thanks to the kindness of the citizens of Perth. It proved to be just one of the many little things which made *Highlander* into the ship she was to become.

We always seemed to be in trouble with musical instruments and the wardroom hatch. It was never big enough for the curious selection, varying from a piano to a harp, which the officers brought aboard from time to time.

In the middle of March we were sailed to Tobermory for a week's 'refresher' course. With a crew already trained we had no trouble with the 'Terror of Tobermory' and having passed successfully, we went to join B.4 Group in Londonderry.

We had decided that, as we could not learn to blow our bagpipes ourselves, we would put three sailors to stand on the searchlight platform holding them in what we hoped was the correct 'blowing position'. With a powerful loud hailer rigged on the searchlight playing pipe tunes, they gave a most realistic performance. This had been exercised with good effect in Tobermory.

It was a lovely spring afternoon when we steamed up-river to Londonderry. Boom Hall with its green lawns falling down to the river, had been taken over for the Wren ratings, and there were quite a number sitting outside on the grass. We gave them the chance to hear our pipes as we passed. The reception was so enthusiastic that we thought we would provide them with an encore. Shutting off the loud hailer we turned the ship round and went silently down river, made another turn, and then went past once more with the pipes playing and the pipers on the searchlight platform—and a great deal faster than I had ever taken a ship up there before. *Highlander* was excellent for entering harbour with plenty of speed, because until she was travelling about fifteen knots she made almost no wash. The encore performance really did bring the Wrens out by the hundred.

It is difficult to say at what moment something which has been going wrong will suddenly be found to be going right. From some point or other the *Highlander* never looked back. It was as though the lid had been removed, and all the frustrated good ideas bubbled out at the same time. Although these ideas seemed to spring spontaneously from the messdecks, an officer was always somewhere roped in to help. Football and hockey teams came into existence and played regularly. The boats were always in the water in harbour. Ship's company dances were held when we were in Londonderry, and to these a large wardroom party would go, quite sure that we could 'let our hair down' without affecting tomorrow's discipline. At sea we had quiz teams competing over the 'intercom' in the dog watches. A debating society flourished, and there always seemed to be rehearsals going on somewhere for the coxwain's concert party, which included two excellent 'tap dancers', or the ship's 'comb band'.

My own contribution was to organize a gunnery competition with the 4.7-inch armament. No less than twelve teams from various parts of the ship took part. The officers' crew, who had won their first and second rounds, got a bye into the final; and their opponents would be the winner of either 'B gun's' proper crew or a crew from the stokers' mess. The crew of 'B gun' really thought themselves first-class. It was quite a shock to them when the stokers won after a re-fire, and even more of a shock when the officers beat the stokers in the final—which was all as it should be. The method of holding the competition was this. A smoke shell was fired from the forrard gun to burst at about 8,000 yards, and the competitors from the after gun then had to fire six fused rounds against a time limit. On the bridge I fixed up a ring sight which I kept trained on the smoke target, and marked the bursts of the fused shell as one would a rifle target. With the ship travelling fast and beam-on to the sea it was a very good practice, and soon after we had fired the last competition a German aircraft showed up and got the shock of his life.

The Germans had just developed a small V.1. 'buzz bomb' which could be steered by the parent aircraft until it was close to the target, when a radar device in the bomb's nose took over and brought it down to hit. Either the Hun had misjudged his distance, or he had not allowed for an escort having the 4.7-inch guns of *Highlander*. He launched his toy at us out of the sun one evening, but we gave him such a shaking that he lost control of the bomb and it fell into the sea half-way between us and the aircraft. One of his friends was back again the same night, but our radar picked him up and we opened fire. Although we could not see him we must have shot pretty close, because once again we frightened him off. These aircraft were working from Bordeaux, and once they had got their fingers on a convoy they could be quite a nuisance. They not only carried the miniature 'buzz bomb' but also a float which they dropped some miles ahead of the convoy. This float sent out wireless signals, and the U-Boats would 'home' on to it. Bordeaux sent another attacker the next morning, but our escort carrier had its aircraft up in time for that one, and they shot him down. *Highlander* was sent to pick up the pieces, but there was very little to find.

The ship's improvement was not all in the entertainment line. Results came too. We won the group regatta, and headed the group football league. Twelve of the seamen who passed a group board for leading seamen were *Highlanders*, out of a total of fourteen. Six of our leading seamen passed for Petty Officer, and I started fifteen 'C.W. papers' to set those young men off on the road to becoming officers.

I now entered a period of idyllic existence. My ship was thoroughly happy and efficient, and I could do things with her that I had never attempted, even with the very much smaller *Shikari*. No heaving line dared fall short when we were going alongside, or if it should there would be another in the air even before the first fell to the water. We comfortably broke the time record for oiling at sea, thanks to the First Lieutenant's excellent work on the fo'c's'le. The only thing missing were the U-Boats.

In February and March the U-Boats from Brest had taken a severe caning from Captain Walker's 2nd Support Group, and thereafter they were very much on the defensive. In the summer many of them were withdrawn, to take up their anti-invasion stations, or to have the new 'Schnorkel' fitted. There were just enough at sea to make us feel that we were doing a worthwhile job, but with constant air cover from our own escort carriers, and the long-range patrols from shore-based Coastal Command, the U-Boats were a beaten team.

Commander C. W. McMullen R.N. was the Senior Officer of B.4 Escort Group in the 'River' Class Frigate *Helmsdale*. *Highlander* was second in command, and our job a regular trip to Gibraltar and back, with a convoy each way. The route had now been greatly shortened and we went down about the meridian of 15° west, thus taking only ten days on passage. In 1941 the distance and time had been twice as long. This gave us ten days at sea and five in harbour at Gibraltar. The weather was kind, and at both ends we had excellent ports. There were bathing and parties at Gibraltar, and parties and more parties at Londonderry. I had always been fortunate in our North of Ireland base, since on my first visit I had met a very charming family from whom I could always be sure of a welcome. To amuse my officers there were now plenty of Wrens. The Western Approaches Wrens liked to think that they were a hand-picked selection, as I suppose in some respects they were. They certainly provided the officers with a great deal of companionship, and contrary to what some war novels would have us believe, there was almost no 'boy-girl' trouble at all. For one thing there was not time, and for another each girl had so many 'beaux' that when one sailed away for three or four weeks another would be steaming up the river. The girls all knew exactly when the various ships could be expected, and would arrange their schedules accordingly. It really was an astonishing tribute to the men and girls at Londonderry that, in the whole history of the base, there was, as far as I know, only one incident that should never have happened—

and that was not in a ship of the Londonderry Escort Force, but a stranger who did not know the rules.

Commodore Simpson and his staff had hammered out a most sensible routine. If the wardroom wanted to give a party, they would make a signal to the Commodore repeated to the First Officer W.R.N.S. requesting the pleasure of the company of so many W.R.N.S. Officers, and giving the date and time. When an 'approved' signal had been received, you would telephone up the First Officer W.R.N.S. and tell her whom you had arranged to invite. In due course they arrived aboard, and although they had to wear uniform aboard the ships, they were allowed to wear long frocks in the Allied Officers' Club. One imagines that the W.R.N.S. Officer in charge had her side of the situation pretty well organized, and that any Wren showing signs of losing control was hastily removed to some other base. I suppose too, that she had a pretty good idea of the behaviour of the various wardrooms to which her charges were let out. In any case the men and girls would have got together. To acknowledge this fact and provide an organization to control it, was a most successful psychological manoeuvre. Our base was fortunate in that, being so very isolated it could, and did make rules to suit itself. I know that its ships were the envy of less fortunate ones, based on other ports.

Londonderry base had always been first-class ever since the early days, when Captain Ruck-Keene had built it out of nothing. It had the advantages of a foreign station in its freedom to go its own way, and also the advantage of being near enough to the storehouse of the United Kingdom to get adequate supplies for the ships. Under Commodore Simpson a really remarkable series of training devices had been built. There was a dome-shaped construction on whose white walls, and by the use of a cinematograph machine, enemy aircraft could be made to come in at all angles of attack; while the men under training handled a gun fitted with a light. Pressing the trigger produced blobs of light just where the bullets would have gone in practice, and by a cunning mechanism both the time of flight of the bullet and the speed of the target were allowed for. It was a most realistic toy, and great fun to use.

Another booth in 'Simpson's Fun Fair' offered even more exciting attractions. This piece was called 'A Night Attack

Teacher'. It consisted of the bridge of a ship, built in the centre of a hall which could be made completely dark. You went to it with your entire bridge staff, officer of the watch, look-outs, signalmen, yeoman of Signals. Down below was a model wheelhouse where your coxswain was stationed, and in a cabin behind was the automatic plot manned by your own Plotting Officer and his crew. At the word 'go' you would probably be given a radar range and bearing, and when you had turned your ship's head in that direction you would give the order to fire star shell. Immediately a flash of magnesium powder would be touched off just below the bridge, for all the world like the flash of a real gun. Then a little light would appear gently sinking in the darkness, and if you were lucky you'd see a surfaced U-Boat in the camera-obscura that surrounded the hall. Everything that ever happened in the Western Ocean could be put on that machine. If you got your ship too near the convoy the directing officer would give you a radar range and bearing, and on looking that way you would dimly discern a line of merchantmen. It came quite fantastically near to producing the real effect.

In yet another booth, the asdic game was played. Here complete asdic sets, coupled to the inevitable automatic plot produced all the effects of an attack. Days in harbour with the ship to look after, and parties going off to this or that instruction, were never idle ones. About once every two months the group as a whole would go to *Philante*, the training ship for the Western Approaches. Before the war she had been Mr. Tom Sopwith's steam yacht. She was now based on Belfast Lough, and had with her a British submarine to give our asdic and radar ratings practice in detecting submerged or surfaced U-Boats. By that time Admiral Sir Percy Noble's dictum of 'training and more training' was really bearing fruit. Now behind the front line of sea-going ships was a vast array of training officers and their staffs. Most of these training devices were under the management of officers who had served at sea in the earlier years, and really knew what they were talking about.

All the summer of 1944 we ran the convoy to Gibraltar without interference from the U-Boats. *Highlander* did have one little expedition of her own. Two days from Gibraltar at the end of June we received a signal detaching us from B.4 Group to 'proceed with all despatch to a position fifty miles north of Cape Finisterre'. Full of excitement we bustled off without the slightest idea why we had been sent. It appeared unhealthily close to Bordeaux and the German air force. When we arrived in position about ten o'clock at night we found a cloudless sky and a brilliant moon. We had hardly been there for half an hour when the radar office reported an aircraft circling us at five miles. In that moonlight we should have been a sitting target, if it had chosen to attack. The radar operator reported that 'it was not one of ours'. That did not, of course, necessarily mean that it was a German. It could have been a Spaniard, although that seemed unlikely as it did not appear to be burning navigation lights. To prevent the pilot getting a view of *Highlander* I kept her bows always pointing at him, so that even when up-moon of him he would only see a triangular blob in the moon path, and would not be able to recognize our unmistakably British silhouette. Because I had only an anti-surface vessel radar which gave only a very rough idea of the target's height, and only our own makeshift radar control of the guns, I would rather not fight an enemy aircraft in the dark. For some reason the Admiralty wished *Highlander* to be in that position. Presumably not to be sunk there.

It was a silly situation. He wanted to know what I was, and I was most curious to find out what he was; and neither of us could do a thing about it. He was the first to lose patience, and the radar reported him closing rapidly. As he came from the down-moon side he had me full in the moon path. He also had my bows pointing towards him. When he was about a mile away I switched on the mast-head and side lights at full peace time brilliancy. He roared over us and no bombs fell. My experts told me that it was a four-engined Junkers 290, and that his bomb doors were open. I confess I am not too good at telling one aircraft from another. I only know that he was much too low to be pleasant. He seemed satisfied with our lights, and winged away towards France.

Recognition from air to ship is always difficult, and I was reminded of a tale told in the early days of the war when four British destroyers were carrying out a sweep into the Skagerrak between Denmark and Norway. As one of the ships had developed a defect they were rather late coming back. Some British Blenheim bombers saw them by daylight, and went in to bomb. As they did so the party were sighted by some patrolling German Heinkels, who thought the British planes were bombing German destroyers, so came down from the clouds and obligingly chased the Blenheims away.

We settled down to wait for our appointment, but nothing came. Midnight passed and we still had no orders. One o'clock, two o'clock, and then at last a signal to return to Gibraltar 'with all despatch'. We heard afterwards that H.M. the King had been flying home after reviewing the army in North Africa, and that destroyers had been stationed every fifty miles along the route. I was glad we had played no longer with that Junkers.

I called the Engineer Officer in the engine-room.

'Return to Gibraltar with all despatch. Do you hear that, Chief? You've been moaning for long enough that you've never had an opportunity to see how many revolutions you can get out of your engines. Here's your chance to flash up the third boiler and try. I'll put three hundred revolutions on the telegraph but you can do as many as you like.'

Our course was straight up the moon path, in a dead calm sea, with a long lazy swell coming up from the south. From the bridge the water ahead looked like corrugated glass. The ship began to tremble. The electric log ticked faster as the speed increased—a metronome of speed. She leapt from the top of each swell and sheets of golden spray shot out as she flung herself into the trough.

From the engine-room, 'Third boiler connected Sir.'

'Good show Chief. Let's see what you can get out of her.'

I put down the hand-set and turned to the Officer of the Watch. 'You know old "Chiefy" is like a boy. I swear he loses thirty years every time he goes down the engine-room hatch.'

'Yes Sir, and he's beginning to lose 'em down the wardroom hatch too. How the Wrens love the old boy! He's always got one on each arm of his chair when we have a party now.'

I laughed. 'Yes I noticed that. You'd better get the First Lieutenant to order an extra Wren next time, if the Chief is always going to appropriate a couple.'

The engine-room phone buzzed again.

'Yes Chief. . . . Three three o. That's fine. What is her record? Do you know? . . . Oh, she's never been any faster, but you hope you'll be able to squeeze her up another ten. . . . No I'm not going to turn in—far too exciting. When you're happy down there come up here. We have cocoa in half an hour.'

I replaced the hand-set telephone.

A few minutes later he was calling again.

'Just holding three four o, Sir.'

'Well done you! . . . No, I'm sorry I've no speed for three hundred and forty revolutions on the speed board. The last figure is three hundred and thirty, which gives her thirty-six knots. I'd say that another ten revolutions should give her another knot. Come up and feel what it's like.'

Very soon his tall white figure showed round the edge of the asdic hut just as the ship hurled herself over a wave, and two great wings of water were momentarily poised on either side of the bow. The plunge had set him tottering forward to clutch at the binnacle. He stood there with a rapt expression of sheer delight on his face. We gave him cocoa, and then he had to hurry away to see how 'his lads' were treating the two whirring monsters that were almost like children to him. When he had gone, I went down to the fo'c's'le deck, took a line from the bosun's locker and fastened it round my waist. I then went forward as far as the capstan, where I made the other end fast to a link of the anchor chain. Then I crawled forward on hands and knees until I could grasp the bull-ring right in the eyes of the ship, and look down the stem to the water rushing below me.

I do not think I have ever been in a position so thrilling, and so utterly beautiful. Behind me, startingly white in the moonlight, rose the tiered outline of the destroyer. I could look from the fo'c's'le deck to 'B gun' deck with its flaring blast shields, and to the signal deck and the high forebridge, where the armour-plate glass windshields reflected back the moonlight. Ahead of me stretched a golden pathway, and below were gleaming pits into which the ship rushed. The bows were plunging until the surface of the sea was barely twelve inches from my face. The next moment, as she rose out of the swell, I could see almost down to where the stem turned into the keel. At one moment I was only a foot above the sea, which was rushing to meet me at forty-two miles an hour, at the next I was suspended thirty foot above it. Woosh!—and she would plunge her throbbing stem into the wave. A pause, and then she would fling herself forward, dripping golden moonlit water. I could have lain there content for hours, watching her bow tearing the waves apart, while behind me the air was filled with the steady whine of the boiler-room fans.

While I was in the very eyes of the ship we ran through a school of porpoise, and I was amazed to see that even at the speed we were travelling, they could make some attempt to gambol alongside, although they could not hold us for long. It was the best chance I ever had to gauge the speed of these fish with the lovely movements, and I put their maximum at fifty miles an hour with an endurance of barely a minute. At forty-two miles an hour they seemed capable of holding us for about five minutes before they dropped astern, so that their capacity for maintaining maximum speed is about the same as that of a racehorse.

As the examination for leading seamen was due to take place the first day after arrival we were very keen to reach Gibraltar not far behind the rest of the group. Actually we found the convoy just entering the Straits, and we stormed through them at full speed. We entered harbour before they did.

We also had a new toy to play with in the shape of a seine net. Looking through books I had discovered that a destroyer was entitled to one, and had promptly ordered it for use in Gibraltar and also at Moville at the mouth of the Foyle. Of course we had only the very vaguest idea how to use it, and when it arrived there appeared to be much more of it than we had expected. We had no chance until the following Sunday. There was only one possible place on 'The Rock' from which it could be used. This was the bathing beach on the Mediterranean shore, which was reached by a long tunnel. We could not carry the net through the tunnel, and we hoped that our catch would be too big to carry back that way. So we decided to take the ship herself round, with any of the officers of the other ships of the group who wanted to see the fun, and towing the *Helmsdale's* and the *Foley's* motor boats. We thought that we should need at least three motor boats to haul such a big net out to sea and back to the shore. So *Highlander* asked for permission to go to sea for exercises, and towed the motor boats round the point to anchor off the bathing beach.

We put a large picnic party ashore in the afternoon, and the net. The first haul was not a success as the net fouled some obstruction, but the second was a great improvement. We took hundreds of beautiful fish, ten laughing Wrens, and three Paymaster Commanders livid with rage. They were not caught separately, but all bundled up together—fish, Paymasters and Wrens; and the fish scales stuck like glue. The ship's company enjoyed a fish supper; the wardroom officers enjoyed the Wrens; and the three Paymasters reported me to the Commander-in-Chief. Of course no one could do anything about it, because there was no rule against seine netting from the beach; and after all it was an exercise.

But I fear that the Staff decided to black-list the whole of B.4 group, and from that time onwards we were continually in trouble at Gibraltar. We were going through one of those periods when everything that the group did would turn into an escapade of some sort or other, and the more the Staff looked down their noses at us, the worse were the things that happened. We had a wonderful crowd in that group, and *Highlander's* big wardroom was always a seething mass of officers. To avoid the strain which so much entertaining would have thrown on the purses of our own officers they had, at my suggestion, made their friends honorary members of our mess. This made a lot of work for our doctor, who was mess secretary, and had to render and collect the many mess bills, but it made our wardroom into a sort of club for the group. Consequently most of the wild parties started in *Highlander*, and I got the blame.

On the way home the Chief had much trouble with the amount of fresh water that the ship's company was using. With tropical whites to wash after leaving Gibraltar, and no time for washing them in harbour, we were using far more water than the ship's evaporators could produce. Notices on the ship's board had no effect at all. The Chief came to see me on the bridge.

'It really is desperate, Sir. We shall be out of fresh water before we reach Londonderry.'

'How much,' I asked, 'must be saved to satisfy you, Chief?'

'We must cut the consumption down by half, Sir.'

'Signalman.'

'Sir.'

'Give me a signal pad please.'

I wrote out yet another notice and handed it to the Chief who, with a broad smile on his face, took it away to the ship's notice board. But the water situation did not improve. Two days later in the forenoon watch the bosun's mate could have been heard piping round the ship, 'Messdeck sweepers muster abreast the whaler with all buckets from their messes.'

There the Chief, with a party of grinning engine-room artificers, waited for them. Armed with punches and heavy hammers they cut a neat round hole half-way up each bucket, and the water consumption was restored to a level with which our evaporators could cope. I had wondered just how the sailors would take it, but I need have had no fear. They were intensely amused at their mutilated buckets, and were even seen to show them with pride to other ships. For ever afterwards anything which was not a great deal of good would be referred to as being 'as much use as a *Highlander's* bucket'.

On the way home the great invasion of D Day began, and we all wondered whether the U-Boats would show their teeth in retaliation. But they remained as quiet as ever. We were all amazed at the surprise achieved in this great operation, because when we were in Gibraltar and a number of the Captains had been in Commander McMullen's cabin, someone had raised the question where exactly it would be staged. We had sent for the Channel charts, and had decided that there was only one place which we could conceivably recommend. It was there that the landing was actually made. One can only remark once again that the German is essentially a land-based animal, or he would undoubtedly have protected the eastern side of the Cherbourg peninsula much more heavily.

For the next convoy to Gibraltar *Helmsdale* was away for boiler cleaning, and I was Senior Officer of the group. We had a very uneventful passage down, and all tied up together in the harbour—*Highlander*, the 'Captain' Class Frigate *Foley* (Lieutenant-Commander Charles Bird, R.N.V.R.), and four 'Castle' Class Corvettes.

Charles was a particular friend of mine. He was a long-service R.N.V.R. from the Bristol Division, and ran a very efficient ship. Among many idiosyncrasies—for he was by way of being an individualist—was his fixed determination never to alter the time in his ship, but always to keep British double-summer time, however far west he might go. There was some point in this, because the constant changes of one hour daily did mean shuffling the watches round to keep them fair for all. Charles decided against such nonsense, with the result that once, when we had been diverted a long way further west than usual, his ship's company would breakfast at noon and have their evening meal at midnight local time. Of course what he did in his own ship made no difference to the rest of us, but one received some very queer signals from the *Foley*. After tea in the dog watches was a very good time to experiment with new radar plotting techniques, but one had to remember what time it was aboard the *Foley* before asking him to co-operate. Otherwise a signal asking for a 'radar-run' might bring the rather plaintive reply, 'If you say so; but can't you let a fellow have his afternoon sleep in peace?'

I have introduced Charles because he figured largely in the events during the five days in Gibraltar, when the group reached its high-water mark of unpopularity with the Admiral's Staff.

We berthed there on a Wednesday, and as our concert party's first major performance was to take place the next day, we reberthed *Highlander* in the morning between two of the corvettes. We thus created more vantage points overlooking the stage, which had been built on our main deck. By the time the concert was due to begin our own decks and the ships on either side of us were crowded with men, and a large number of copies of *Highlander's* song had been distributed.

From the stage curtain came repeated blows with a hammer on some metallic object, and when the curtain went up a caricature of myself was seen to be busy with a hammer and punch and pile of buckets.

A policeman came on the stage.

'Hoh! and what are you a-doing of?'

'I'm making buckets for the *Highlander*.'

'The *Highlander*—what's the *Highlander*?'

'What—you never heard tell of the *Highlander*?—Oh! we'll sing you a song about her.' He signed to the chorus who came on singing the song which had been chosen in a competition open to all the crew. It was the combined work of the four quartermasters and they had shared quite a substantial prize between them for their effort.

SHIP'S SONG

Now there is a Ship in the British Navy,
She's nifty, she's sturdy, she's always at sea.
For the boys that are on her
Are good to the core,
For they are the lads of the H.44![1]

Chorus: *All together please!*

Highlander, *Highlander*,
I ain't said a word about half what's occurred,
What yer say, what yer say?
The aircraft and U-Boats get out of our way.

Now whenever you see her she's always in trim,
Out of the harbour or whether she's in.
When she's on manoeuvres the boys don't get sore,
For they are the lads of the H.44!

Chorus all together.

Sometimes in harbour the boys have to paint,
Some are all for it and some of 'em ain't;
But when they are finished they all step ashore.
For they are the lads of the H.44!

Chorus all together.

I'll give you an outline of some of the crew
Some of them old hands and some of them new:
I'll start with the Skipper, and his word is law.
But he's one of the lads of the H.44!

Chorus all together.

[1] *Highlander's* pennant numbers.

Now he's a Three-Ringer and he's got a set,[1]
If he got a draft chit the lads they would fret.
He's been with the Ship now just three months or more.
He's one of the lads of the H.44!

Chorus all together.

Then comes our Jimmy,[2] he's a bit of a lad,
And he's a lot better than others we've had.
He joins in our sports when we have tug-of-war,
For he's one of the lads of the H.44!

Chorus all together.

Now next we have Shorty, young L*oo*tenant Grieve,
When he's got the middle he'll always relieve
His oppos[3] on time and never before,
For he's one of the lads of the H.44!

Chorus all together.

Now next comes the Gunner, his name's Mr. Bray,
When he goes on leave, how he'd like to stay.
He'd stay for a week, or a fortnight or more,
For he's one of the lads of the H.44!

Chorus: *All together please!*

Highlander, Highlander,
I ain't said a word about half what's occurred,
What yer say, what yer say?
The aircraft and U-Boats get out of our way.

It was a very good concert. It is surprising how much real talent can be found among any body of men, once their natural shyness has been broken down.

The next day, Thursday, we moved the ship back to our usual shore-side berth, and that night I dined ashore with Charles Bird. When we got back to the ships we found an enormous party in progress in *Highlander's* wardroom. The

[1] A 'set' is Navy slang for a beard.
[2] 'Jimmy' is another term for the First Lieutenant, really 'Jimmy-the-One'.
[3] 'Opposite number', in this case the previous Officer of the Watch.

night was hot, and the atmosphere down below was almost unbearable. A number of Wrens from the Cypher Office were aboard, and someone had suggested taking the motor boat away for a breath of fresh air. The boat was just leaving the ship's side as Charles and I got back, and I was persuaded to jump into her at the last minute, and to take the wheel. Somebody unknown had brought along some thunderflashes (small fireworks), and that person slipped one over the side. It went off underwater with quite a bang, and made the girls scream. Even more interesting, it produced the most wonderful circle of phosphorescence. The girls were quite enchanted by this—so we fired some more. We then went on round the harbour admiring the sudden activity on the part of the soldiers, who seemed to be having some sort of 'field day'. Searchlights suddenly sprang up all over the place, their long pencils of light searching the night. It really was a wonderful sight. We had never realized how many searchlights were hidden about the fortress.

When we got back alongside and the quartermaster had taken our boat-rope, a signal pad was handed down into the boat for me to read. It was from Commander-in-Chief, 'Am informed your motor boat firing charges in harbour. Report name of officer concerned forthwith.'

The girls had already left the boat. I stopped the men and showed them the signal. I looked round. In the boat were most of the Captains of the group, and at least half the First Lieutenants. I made a list of the names. 'What about the girls, Sir?' I waved the list. 'I've got eleven names here and my own, no one will believe that there were at least eleven girls aboard as well. I'm going up to the Staff Office to hand in the list personally.'

I went up to the Office. The Staff Captain on duty administered one of the biggest 'dressing-downs' I have ever received. It made me feel like a whipped schoolboy. Apparently the whole garrison had 'stood to' or as we should say 'gone to action stations'. Even the Governor and Commanding General had been 'alerted'. The soldiers had mistaken our underwater explosions for an attack by the enemy, and the Admiral had ordered the arrest of the officer concerned. However they could not arrest all the Commanding Officers of an Escort Group, and half the First Lieutenants as well. I was told that Commander-in-Chief, Western Approaches would be informed of every detail, and that he would deal with us on our return.

When I got back to the ship it was to find the Commanding Officers in my cabin. 'Anyway I've kept the girls out of it', I told them. 'They wanted to put whoever was responsible under arrest, but they can't lock us all up. Apparently the whole garrison went to "action stations", and even the Governor was "alerted".'

'How do you alert a Governor?'

'Probably by giving him a shot of Benzedrine.'

'Or a shot of his own excellent sherry.' This last was an allusion to a case of Governor's sherry that I had wangled from the cellars of Saccone and Speed.

'Anyhow, go away all of you. You cause me nothing but sorrow.' I turned all but Charles out of my cabin.

'Is this serious?' he asked.

'Very serious for me. I was the Senior Officer in the boat, and for my sins I'm in charge of the lot of you. Pity McMullen is boiler cleaning, or he'd probably have been there too.'

'What about this wedding tomorrow? Shall we go?' One of the staff was marrying one of the cypher Wrens, and there was to be a big reception at the Yacht Club. We had both been invited.

'Of course—unless you feel like throwing thunderflashes at the bride, in which case I won't take you.'

'As we arranged—by boat?'

'Of course. We'll use mine—not that American thing that you use for a boat. I can make our motor boat as smart as a "barge". Do you know they told me that we didn't know how to behave like Naval Officers? At any rate we'll turn out the smartest boat in Gibraltar.'

The next morning, Saturday, I had to carry out one of the periodic inspections of a ship in the group. Because the men were generally on leave when we were in Londonderry, one ship was inspected each time we visited Gibraltar. Before I left I had told Atkins that I wanted the motor boat to be quite perfect by three o'clock.

And she was. The wartime coating of paint had been scraped off the brasswork, and it shone with pre-war brilliance.

Boathook-staves and floorboards had been scrubbed to a wonderful whiteness. The heads of the boathooks shone like gold. In the stern-sheets were white canvas cushions piped with blue, and a little fringe of canvas hung from the after canopy.

It was a wonderful present from the ship's company, who of course knew all about the trouble. I don't know how many men had laboured at her, but she could have lain off the starboard ladder of a fleet flagship, and no one could have found a fault in her. As I followed Charles down into the boat I wondered how many more times I should hear the side 'piped' for me. It was a sobering thought. Standing amidships at the wheel was a burly and familiar figure, his hand raised in salute as I stepped into the boat. 'Coxs'n, what are you dressed up like that for?' *Highlander's* chief petty officer coxswain was dressed as a leading seaman. 'Well Sir, I couldn't trust any of these young fellows to handle the boat properly, Sir. They haven't the experience you see. They may be all right for ordinary work; but we don't want anything to go wrong Sir, not today, Sir.'

'That's terribly nice of you Coxs'n.'

'And I've got Petty Officer ——, Petty Officer —— as bowman and stern-sheetman, and Stoker Petty Officer —— is at the engine.'

'In other words the Petty Officers' Mess is having an afternoon out?'

'Yes Sir.'

'Well, I hope you'll all come to my cabin at six o'clock for a drink, and since you've taken to impersonation, you can bring the motor boat's proper crew along with you. Carry on Coxswain.'

As we crossed the harbour to run into the Yacht Club jetty we could see boats from the many other ships discharging guests. Good, bad and indifferent boats. We lay off waiting our turn. At last it came. The bowman was standing with his head and shoulders through the flap in the forward canopy. The stern-sheetman had clambered aft, and was in the stern. Boathooks had been tossed right up out of hand—and caught again. Sitting under the canopy I could talk through the open flap to the coxswain.

'You take her in fast, Coxs'n.'

'You used to scare me with the ship, Sir.'

'Did I?'

'Yes, Sir—not now Sir.'

There is a special bond between Captain and coxswain. It is he who takes the wheel in action, and when entering or leaving harbour. One of the most comforting sounds I know is the voice of your trusted coxswain coming up the voice-pipe, 'Coxs'n at the wheel, Sir.' It is a guarantee of efficiency. He is the man who turns your orders into fact—the projection of your own personality.

The engine gong in the boat sounded three times. The propeller churned in reverse, causing a flurry of white water to appear under the stern. The tinkling sound of the gong, and the propeller stopped. The boat lay rocking gently as our wash overtook us. The two boathooks dropped as one, to catch the ring bolts in the jetty. I jumped ashore, followed by Charles.

'Thank you Coxs'n—an excellent alongside. Lie off for me please, I'll be about an hour.'

Our arrival was observed all right. Eyes followed the motor boat as she went astern.

Commander G. O. Symonds, who had been Anti-Submarine Officer to Howard-Johnston in the *Malcolm* hurried to meet us.

'Quite worthy of B.12—but for God's sake be careful. The Staff Captains want to shoot you, but they can't think how.'

'They are going to pass the gun to Max Horton, and let him do the shooting,' I told him.

With only the Sunday left before we were to sail, we thought that we must have seen the last of trouble, but it was not to be. We held our Sunday morning Divisions on the jetty alongside the ship, and after I had inspected the men I went back aboard leaving the First Lieutenant to muster the church party and march them round. Before entering the Cathedral they had to march past the Admiral who, with Captain (D) and a number of the staff, took the salute. The Captains of the individual ships were meant to be there as well, and those from our group were all going to cross the harbour in *Highlander's* motor boat to save the walk round. Suddenly I heard Atkins run down the ladder and go into his cabin. I hurried after him.

'What's wrong Number One?'

'Fell over a wire and sat in a pool of oil—I've got to change my shorts, stockings and shoes, Sir.'

'All right—I'll send the men off. You can run after them.'

I had then rushed on to the jetty, seized the party nearest to the road and ordered 'Left turn—quick march!'—and off they had gone.

As I got back to the ship Atkins was rushing down the gangway. He took one horrified glance and wailed, 'Oh Sir, you've sent the wrong party. We're only supposed to send forty men and there's at least a hundred and fifty in what you've sent—Roman Catholics and all sorts.'

'Well it's too late to change now. You'll have to run like a stag to catch 'em up.'

We took the motor boat across the harbour and hurried to our vantage point outside the Cathedral. Already ships' companies were marching along the road. Small parties of thirteen file—perhaps double that size from the cruisers. Then came a number from other destroyers, each of forty men. *Highlander's* came into view. They were the last party. The men were obviously enjoying the joke hugely. It could be seen in the way they swung along, making those that had gone before look like the 'detailed' parties they were. For this parade the *Highlanders* considered themselves volunteers. They went by with a wonderful swing—but there were four times as many as there should have been. Captain (D) turned to me. 'That's a hell of a big church party.'

Fixing my eyes on some point in space and hoping I could keep a straight face I answered:

'Yes Sir. Very religious ship, Sir.'

As one of the corvette Captains said afterwards, 'It sounded as if Captain (D) had suffered an underwater explosion.'

So the *Highlanders* marched into the Cathedral, the believers with the disbelievers. But they jammed. Half in and half out of the west door they stopped, while harassed vergers rushed to fetch more chairs to put in the aisles.

As a matter of fact there was some justification for referring to her as a 'religious' ship. On our first Sunday at sea Number One had come to me and suggested holding a Church service. I had never before had a ship where we had either the room or the proper atmosphere, and in any case I have always believed that such things should be voluntary. I had answered Atkins that we would certainly try it out, but that it must be understood by the men that attendance was not obligatory. An hour later, when church had been 'rigged' in the big messdeck, I went down to conduct the service, and was amazed to find there almost every man who was not on watch. It was such an obvious success that on the following Sunday we drew upon the concert party to form a choir; and from thenceforward was added another sound that might be heard aboard in the dog watches at sea—the ship's choir practising the hymns for the following Sunday.

I heaved a sigh of relief when we sailed on the Monday; but we had not yet finished with Gibraltar, nor they with us. We had hardly been at sea for an hour, and were waiting off Europa Point for our convoy from the Mediterranean, when our gyro-compass developed a serious defect and we rushed back into harbour to get a gyro-engineer to repair it. We had arrived back before our signal explaining the position had been delivered from the signal tower. Without waiting for a berthing signal we went alongside, so fast that a crowd ran out from Captain (D)'s office, which overlooked the jetty, to see the crash. However, by the time his Staff Officer arrived to enquire what was the matter, I was already ashore telephoning to the Engineer's Office. We finally left for good two hours later, and caught up our convoy. Half-way home we received a signal ordering the convoy to enter St. George's Channel from the south-west instead of going the long way round the north of Ireland. Brest had fallen, and there was no longer any need to fear U-Boats in the Bay of Biscay. On arrival at Londonderry I was not surprised to hear that I was to report to Commander-in-Chief, Western Approaches, at once. I left for Liverpool that night.

First I called on the Chief of Staff, who looked up from his papers and said, 'Admiral wants to see you.' I was afraid so. A little further on I came across a secretary who said joyfully, 'Oh come in and wait here, the Admiral wants to see you.' It was getting monotonous. I met the Admiral's Personal Assistant, a very charming W.R.N.S. Officer. She said, 'The Admiral wants——'

'Yes I know that one, "the Admiral wants to see you". I've a very good mind to run home to mother. I don't like your school, and I haven't padded my backside.'

'Why, what have you been up to?'

'Don't you know?'

She laughed and answered 'Max knows everything. Come on—your turn now.'

I went in to the Presence.

'Rayner, the U-Boats are coming inshore. The 'Castle' Class Corvettes have been out with the various groups, and they should be efficient units by now. I'm putting the first six into a Support Group—the 30th. I want you to be the Senior Officer. Well, what is it?'

'This letter, Sir—the one Commander-in-Chief, Gibraltar, has written to you? He has sent me a copy.'

The Admiral looked across his desk at me and said rather testily and without a smile, 'Oh that. I don't take any notice of that. Where was I? And don't interrupt me again.' He continued, 'They are the finest anti-submarine vessels we have. They have everything, the squid, the new radar, the new asdic, a special echo-sounder, and the new wireless navigational machine which will fix your position to fifty yards any time of the day or night.'

Relieved as I was about my own position, I was sure that there was a catch in it somewhere.

'I can keep *Highlander* as Senior Officer's ship?' I asked.

'You can *not*.' His mouth was set to bite, but seeing my consternation he paused, and I blurted out,

'I think I'd rather have *Highlander*.'

'You're crazy—these are the finest anti-U-Boat ships in the world.'

'But I love *Highlander*.'

He looked at me angrily, and then suddenly his face softened, and for a moment I saw a Max Horton that I did not know existed. I have said earlier that quite by chance I should discover the key to the enigma of that great man's character. He lived mainly for those things which he had conjured into being. At any rate he understood my desire to cling to *Highlander*.

'Don't make it harder for me. You've got to go.' It might have been a father talking to his child.

'All right, Sir—and thank you.'

'Good luck to you. Let me know as soon as the group is ready for sea—I need you.'

I was half way to the door. 'Was it a good party, Rayner?'

'A bloody good party, Sir!'

Max's eyes twinkled.

I went back to Londonderry and called on Commodore (D).

'So you're going to leave *Highlander* and have a group of your own?'

'Yes Sir, I hate doing it, but I suppose it's inevitable.'

'If you ask me it's a damn good thing you're not going to Gibraltar again. I've got a letter from Captain (D) about you.'

'From Captain (D) Sir!' I exclaimed. 'I knew you'd had a copy of a letter from the Admiral.'

'Oh yes. I had that one too, but that was to Commander-in-Chief, Western Approaches. This one was just to me—something about your entering harbour at twelve knots.'

'It's not true Sir.'

'What speed were you doing then?'

'One four o revolutions, sir—fifteen knots.'

'Well you see what I mean? You've made Gibraltar too warm for you. Get some leave, and join your group in a week's time, and you might like to know that Commander-in-Chief has recommended you for your qualified status as a Commander. You'll be the first Volunteer Reserve officer to get that.' (I had lost my status on promotion for one could quite logically be only given equality in the rank you held at the time.)

Highlander gave me a wonderful send off. When the taxi arrived to take me away it was fitted with drag ropes. Half the ship's company towed it down the main street of Londonderry, with the rest running behind. It should have been one of the happiest moments of my life, but it was the saddest.

Chapter X

PEVENSEY CASTLE AND SENIOR OFFICER 30TH ESCORT GROUP

After I left *Highlander* I was never happy at sea. I had given her everything that I had, and my first impressions of the 30th Escort Group did nothing to mitigate the deep sadness I had felt when I left my *Highlander*. I there found a different world of officers and men. My three destroyers all had a very big percentage of long-service naval ratings in their crews. *Loch Tulla* had been manned by a crew of reservists, and *Verbena's* men had been half long-service and half reservists.

The 30th Escort Group was manned almost entirely by 'Hostilities Only' officers and ratings. Of the officers I could make neither top nor tail. Although they were the legatees of the robust tradition of the Western Approaches, they were totally different from their forbears in background, outlook and training. This does not mean that they were inefficient, for they certainly were not. They were merely the products of the Radar Age. As I looked round the wardroom table at my new Commanding Officers, I realized just how much we had changed during five years of war. The ages of the Captains in the original escort groups had spanned more than twenty years; I doubted if two years separated the youngest from the oldest of these young men. Responsibility sat rather heavily on shoulders not yet broad enough to bear the weight. They were terribly serious, and inclined to be worried over such matters as the correct way to fill up forms and make returns. In some measure this was justified, for at that stage of the war the long fingers of bureaucracy were reaching out to the front line, and the burden of 'form filling' was increasing every month. One could no longer bring a gale-damaged ship into harbour and write-off everything that could not be accounted for as 'lost in bad weather'; nor could one explain a deficiency in the rum return by merely noting 'supplied to survivors' against the amount short. In the years that now seemed so long ago a corvette had done just that to the tune of ten gallons, only to discover the missing jars some weeks later stowed under the towing hawser in the tiller flat. As they could not re-enter these in the ledger they had no option but to distribute the rum round the various wardrooms in the group.

In 1941 our eyes may have been red with salt water and heavy with lack of sleep; but at least we laughed. It was obvious that one would never receive from these new ships signals such as had set us all rocking with laughter years before. I remembered a day in a full Atlantic gale when a corvette had approached close to *Verbena* to pass a long visual signal. She had been flinging herself half out of the water as she came round the corner of the convoy, and we had made to her 'I can see your dome,' (referring to the asdic dome which was fixed to the ship's keel almost beneath the bridge). The reply came back like a flash, 'How indelicate of you to mention it.'

Perhaps in fairness to my new group I should admit that the fault may well have lain equally with myself, for already I was beginning to look backwards to a time when I imagined that things had been better. We had all been living at such a pace, burning ourselves up, that perhaps we were already developing some of the characteristics of the elderly. There were, however, one or two deep and fundamental differences between us. I doubt if any of the officers in the 30th Escort Group had ever kept a watch without radar. This device had certainly been largely responsible for the destruction of the enemy's U-Boats, and it had greatly relieved the strain on officers; but its arrival marked a rubicon in our lives. Either you had experience of the Western Ocean convoys before radar—or you had not. Those who became officers after this revolutionary change took place could never know the satisfaction which their fore-runners had experienced when sound judgment and good seamanship—helped perhaps by a slice of luck—brought success. Never would they have the thrill of closing the position where they hoped to find the convoy after a night spent on extended patrol, and hearing the look-out cry 'Merchantmen on the starboard bow Sir,' just when they were expected. Even the science of navigation also had suffered the same war-change, for the 'Loran' wireless navigational system had destroyed much of the artistry in a sailor's work. His business of finding his way across the great waters had been reduced to a matter of twiddling dials and looking up the answer in books. True, his life was made easier; but how dearly he paid for his ease! He could never know the joy of making the correct landfall after days without sight of sun or stars. It was more efficient—but I defy anyone to argue that it was more fun.

The men too were very different. They were all much of an age; and the Petty Officers and Leading Seamen were distinguished mainly for their greater intelligence and education than for having stronger or better characters. I do not think there was anyone in the whole group who, like my two ratings in *Verbena*, would have crawled back to the ship on their hands and knees rather than miss her on sailing. They would either never have been in such a state or, if they were, would probably not have bothered to return. In my former ships I had always known every man aboard by name; but in my new job I doubt if I ever knew more than a score of names. One circumstance in particular helped to put me out of touch with the men. I had a Captain in the ship in which I was living as Senior Officer. We were back to the old Unit Commander-Skipper problem and, with both in the same ship it could never really be made to work. It was not fair to either side, if only because the ships themselves were not big enough to house the two in comfort. After years of having my own steward, sea cabin, and chart table, and losing my own rubber or pencil on the bridge, I would now lose the Captain's pencil, or find that he had carried off my rubber in his pocket. To make matters even more difficult there was a ship's navigator as well as my own staff navigator. All four of us who had an interest in the ship's position had to use the one chart table. It is curious how the Navy always seems to lean towards the Senior Officer living in a ship commanded by someone else. I suppose it all springs from what one might term 'The Admiral complex'. But while the group commander of anti-submarine trawlers and the senior officer of a group of escorts did perform some of the functions of an Admiral in a minor key, I feel that authority may have overlooked the fact that the working quarters of a real Admiral and his staff are wholly separated from those of the Flag Captain and the ships officers. If the two of them had to live and work cheek by jowl, as we had to do, friction would surely occur. I was just as sorry for my captain as I was for myself.

None the less, and no matter how deep were my regrets at the changes, it is beyond doubt that without radar and navigational wireless we could not have won the upper hand over the enemy; for we now had to face up to the new U-Boat, which was working inshore with the aid of its Schnorkel. One impudent devil had actually torpedoed a merchantman right on our own doorstep, and within sight of the entrance to the River Foyle. The 30th Escort Group went to sea to try to find it.

Working close to the shore gave us a very busy time. Not only was it necessary that every manoeuvre should be safe for all the ships of the group, but we were also continually investigating asdic echoes. There were hundreds of 'contacts' around the coast—old wrecks, rocks, and tide rips. If we declared them 'non-submarine' then they had to be accurately charted. If we found something new in waters which we had worked over before, we might reasonably suppose it to be a U-Boat. Unfortunately where the tide runs fast a lot of contacts were caused by tidal eddies; and as they all changed with the tide they caused great confusion.

During this first patrol we attacked, with our 'squid', a very likely contact, which proved to be the wreck of a tanker carrying high octane fuel. The petrol was ignited by the bursting of our charges, and the ship was surrounded by flames two or three hundred feet in height. The Captain fortunately rang down for full ahead, and we got out just in time; but the paint was burnt from the ship's side as if it had been taken off with a blow lamp. This episode scared me much more than the loss of *Warwick* had done. I had now been in continuous command for more than five years, and I began to wonder if I was getting tired. But I was looking for a U-Boat to pay me back for *Warwick*. Until I got one I would manage somehow.

We patrolled the north western approaches to the St. George's Channel for a fortnight, and then went back to Londonderry. I went to see Commodore (D) about the difficulties over my command, and found him full of sympathy. I asked him to allow me to be my own Captain, and to give me a secretary to help with the paper work. He agreed to this, and as a new corvette was in need of a captain *Pevensey's* was sent to her. I did not therefore feel that he had lost his command on account of me. The new plan was quite a workable one. I had a staff navigator to help with handling the group, and a writer who could take down what I said in shorthand and quickly produce a reasonably accurate report. Unfortunately for my happiness the ship was a brute to handle. She was underpowered, and so a bad sea-boat; her radar and other new toys made her windage excessive; and she blew down-wind like a rubber ball whenever speed was reduced to investigate a contact. It was then impossible to keep her bows to the sea, and she would lie beam-on rolling like a pig, with her asdic crew as much concerned in remaining on their stools as in classifying the echo with which they were in contact. Had she had the two engines for which I believe this class of corvette was originally designed, she would have been a very fine little hunting vessel. Unfortunately they were all built with only the one engine. Although she was half as big again as *Verbena,* she had only the same 1,200 horsepower. To make machinery taxed the manufacturing power of war-time Britain much more than building ships' hulls. Her anti-submarine equipment, however, was first class.

The U-Boats were then operating south of Ireland, looking for our convoys at their point of greatest density. By saturating that focus of shipping with hunting vessels and aircraft we were preventing them doing much damage; but we were not succeeding in killing many of them. One felt that with just a little more determination they could do a great deal of harm, for no matter how hard we all tried, our efforts reaped very little reward. These U-Boats with their Schnorkels and homing torpedoes were just about as different from the early boats as *Pevensey Castle* was from *Loch Tulla*; so the final result was about the same. Only the great benefit of unlimited airpower kept the balance in our favour.

Our next assignment was a patrol off the south coast of Ireland. The trip started badly in the first week of November 1944. We had hardly gone two miles down river from our berth when the coxswain handed over the wheel without telling me. I was in the habit of taking a pilot for the passage of that difficult river, although I would never allow him to berth or unberth the ship. As we passed down the tree-lined glade below Londonderry I heard the pilot give the order 'starboard ten', and saw the bow start to swing to port. He increased the wheel to starboard twenty, the ship took a sudden sheer across the channel to port—and she struck. I jumped on to the compass platform, and rang down for full astern. With the strong ebb tide under us she heeled over as she swung round, quivered for a moment, and then slid off into deep water. I stopped the engines, and sent the First Lieutenant down to see if she was holed. He reported by telephone from the asdic cabinet in the bottom of the ship that she appeared to have suffered no damage.

A very shaken voice, 'Coxswain at the wheel, Sir.'

'Where the hell have you been?'

'Heads [lavatory], Sir.'

'I'll deal with you afterwards.'

I turned her round, went alongside the oiling jetty at Lisahally, and telephoned to Londonderry for a diver to inspect the stem. By the mercy of providence it appeared that we had hit the only soft spot between Londonderry and the oiling jetty. Even the river pilot had not known that there was a patch of mud there. Investigation proved that the coxswain, a very young petty officer, had handed over the wheel to the quartermaster, and the latter had put it the wrong way.

We arrived in our patrol area off the south coast of Ireland on the 9th November. Our instructions were little more than to 'seek out and destroy the enemy wherever he may be found'. We were told when convoys would be passing through and were expected to sweep the seas ahead of them, and to be on the spot in case of attack. We also had to co-operate with the air patrols, in case they should want anything investigated. Beyond that we were left free to go and look round our beat, and to smell out the U-Boats. If we spent time investigating every possible asdic contact, we found that we moved so slowly over the ground that even the most sleepy of U-Boats would have got out of our way. I had a theory that they would generally be doing something, rather than just drifting aimlessly; and that if they were moving they would give a good asdic contact. We therefore concentrated on keeping the group steaming as fast as we could through the water. If any ship obtained an echo which was doubtful that ship alone would stop to classify the contact. The rest of us closed our ranks and moved on, leaving the investigator to catch up afterwards.

By the night of the 10th November we had swept through our beat once from the westward, and shortly after dark we had turned to a westerly course. At ten o'clock I was lying down in my sea cabin. On the bulkhead above the foot of my bunk was a repeater from the radar scan. I had only to turn over on my back to see the relative positions of all my ships. By night at sea we were, of course, either in complete darkness in the wheelhouse and sea cabin, or had only the smallest of red lights. The group, of four ships, was disposed to port and starboard of *Pevensey Castle*; one ship to the north, two ships to the south of her. On the radar scan the bright little blobs which were the ships glowed brightly, as the pencil of light that represented the ever-searching beam of the radar caught them. They faded slowly when the beam had passed and were rekindled as it came round again, just before they became difficult to see. Round and round swept the beam. Fascinated and half asleep I watched. The night was very calm, and the ship rolled slightly and steadily. I was mesmerized by the revolving beam, and lulled by the gentle motion of the ship. Suddenly I thought that beyond the wing ship I could see a little spot of light. Yes, there it was again—a momentary flash as the beam passed over it. Thoroughly awake now I picked up the telephone to the radar office.

'Is that an echo about 145 degrees, I should say about 10,000 yards beyond *Portchester Castle*?'

I watched the beam sweep round investigating it, probing the night like a finger.

'Yes Sir. It's a very small echo, but quite distinct. Never seen one like it before, Sir. Conditions are very funny tonight. Anomalous propagation, Sir.'

'What's that? For God's sake don't blind me with science. Tell me in simple words.'

'Well, Sir, you might detect an echo tonight much further than you would normally expect to.'

H.M.S. *Pevensey Castle* escaping from the pillar of smoke and flame after she had with her 'squid' attacked and set fire to the wreck of a tanker containing high octane fuel in 180 feet of water 25 miles NNE of Inistrahull. The ship can just be seen to the left of the smoke. Her funnel and bridge were about 50 and the top of the mast about 70 feet above the water. Using the foregoing as data the top of the smoke pillar must have been about 1,200 feet high.

Escort carrier. From these very small carriers the airmen 'took off' and 'flew on' in often appallingly bad weather conditions.

'Will that apply to all ships?'

'Can't say Sir. I believe it varies from set to set.'

'What you really mean is that although we normally reckon that a surfaced U-Boat would be picked up at five miles, for some odd reason your set might pick one up very much further away tonight. Is that it?'

'Yes Sir.'

'Thank you. Watch that echo. It interests me a lot.'

'Watch the echo, Sir.'

I took up another telephone. It was the short wave 'intercom' set for talking to the other ships.

'Calling *Portchester Castle*. Can you get a radar contact bearing around 100 degrees from you about 10,000 yards?'

I waited for the reply.

'Sorry, no.'

'I've got it very clearly on my set. I'm going to watch it. Will you keep a special look-out on that bearing please? I'll let you know if anything further happens.'

I sent for the staff navigator to plot the echo. Very soon he reported back, 'Target is on a slightly converging course to our own. Its speed seems about the same as ours, possibly a little faster.'

I called *Portchester Castle* again, 'Can you pick it up yet?'

Reply: 'Sorry, not yet.'

I called all commanding officers and told them to 'stand by'. 'I have very interesting echo, bearing 147 degrees 19,000 yards.'

I settled down to think. The target was a single unit. It must be a small one, or *Portchester Castle* would certainly have picked it up. We had met no fishing vessels, and if it were a fisherman it would be burning lights; and again *Portchester Castle* would have seen it. There seemed no answer but that it was the U-Boat for which I had searched for five years. What was more it was a most accommodating one, and was actually engaged in stalking us in the belief that we were a convoy.

I picked up the 'intercom' again.

'Ships are to form very slowly on to line of bearing 105 to 285 degrees. Course 240 degrees speed 10 knots. Manoeuvre to be completed within thirty minutes.'

Previously they had been disposed at right angles to our course. When they had taken up the new disposition the axis of the group would lie at an angle of 45 degrees to the direction of our advance.

I lay back and watched the radar. The little echo was by now quite clear, and I could see my ships begin to form on to the new bearing. This was the way to fight a war, lying on my back in a warm cabin. Some minutes later the navigator called me from the plot.

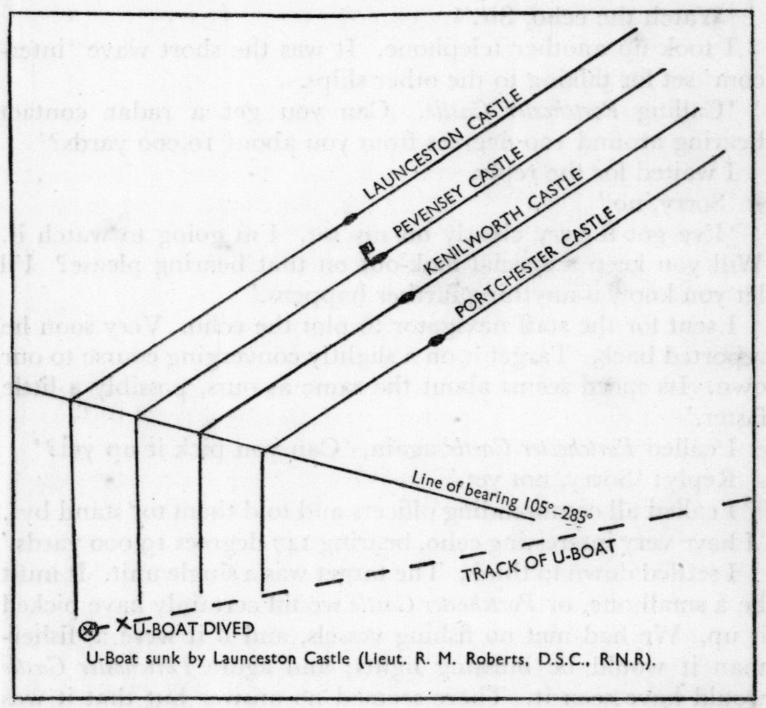

U-Boat sunk by Launceston Castle (Lieut. R. M. Roberts, D.S.C., R.N.R).

'That echo is hunting us.'

'I agree absolutely. His captain probably thinks we are a convoy. You know his radar is very good for "range", but very bad for "direction". All he will be able to see is five little blips on his scan. With this very low cloud layer he is probably banking on there being no aircraft about. If only one of the other ships could get him too. Watch him and let me know the moment he makes an alteration of course.'

Yes, I would be much happier if only one of the other ships would confirm it. I called up the radar office again.

'What's the range now?'

'16,000 Sir.'

I called the navigator in the plot.

'What speed do you reckon he's making?'

'A fraction over fourteen knots.'

Portchester Castle called me, 'Confirm your contact—very small echo but firm. Shall I investigate?'

'No. Stay in bed until I tell you to get up.'

I called all ships.

'My appreciation is that the target bearing 150 degrees 15,000 yards from me is a U-Boat. I intend to hold this course until target bears 180 degrees then turn together by blue turn to 180 degrees. This will put him in the middle of our sweep. Tally-ho, chaps! Tally-ho!'

Signal from *Portchester Castle*: 'He is stalking me.'

I replied: 'I agree. One bait is as good as another.'

From *Launceston Castle*: 'I confirm your contact.'

From *Kenilworth Castle*: 'I've got him too.'

I signalled to the group to reduce speed to six knots. This might catch the enemy unawares, because his plot would not detect the reduction of speed for some time and his bearing from me would draw very quickly forward to 180 degrees, which is where I wanted it to be.

His bearing was indeed altering fast—from 165 to 170 degrees. If I altered the group then he would be inside the net. Oh, I was going to catch this one! I called all ships.

'Stand by for blue turn. If you have not already done so your ships should be at action stations. Target bears 178 degrees 10,000 yards from me.'

I made to *Portchester Castle*: 'How does target bear from you?'

Reply: '230 degrees, 3,000 yards.'

He's in the net! I made to the group, 'Blue 180. Speed 12 knots. Forrard on—Forrard on!' and to my own bridge, 'Port fifteen. Steady on 180 degrees. I've made Blue 180 to the group.'

The staff navigator called me, 'Are you coming to the plot, Sir?'

'I think not. I'm very happy here, and I want to watch this I'll be up as soon as he dives.'

Looking at the radar, I could now see the little dots that were the ships start to change shape as they altered course. The target was still there—or was he? I knelt on the bunk. It was fading—it had gone.

From *Portchester Castle:* 'Lost contact. Reckon he's dived.'

From *Launceston Castle:* 'I've still got a very small target in the same position.—Could be a periscope—180 degrees, 2,500 yards.'

From *Launceston Castle:* 'Very strange roaring noise on asdics.'

I made to her, 'Probably a torpedo. Am keeping fingers crossed.'

From *Launceston Castle:* 'Have asdic contact 182 degrees range 1,500 yards. Shall I attack?'

I replied, 'Yes please. I will send *Portchester* to help you.' And to the group, '*Portchester* assist *Launceston* as hunting ships. *Pevensey* and *Kenilworth* are to form square search round diving position. Legs of box—four miles.'

A dull underwater thud.

I called *Launceston Castle*, 'Was that you?'

Reply: 'Not made by me.'

'Consider it was torpedo exploding on the bottom. Target is a U-Boat all right.'

From *Launceston Castle*: 'Am attacking.' A long reverberation shakes the ocean. I went up to the bridge. I could hear the attacking ships chattering away to each other, 'Are you still in contact?' 'Yes, loud and clear.' 'Do you smell oil?' 'Lots of it, all round me.' 'Are you in contact too?' 'Yes—plain as a daisy.'

When we were out on the sides of the box search I called up the hunting ships, 'So long as you two can hold contact I do not propose to attack again until dawn. We might get survivors.' And to *Launceston Castle* alone, 'What is your assessment of attack?'

'Absolute copy-book. Have wonderful trace, both range and depth. Target is on the bottom now.'

'Buoy the position as closely as you can. We've got to stay here for seventy-two hours.'

The following morning I took *Pevensey Castle* over the U-Boat, and obtained a lovely trace on the echo-sounder. The boat was lying on the bottom with a slight list to starboard. I then carried out a careful attack with our squid, and blew to the surface a tin of oil with a Hamburg address on it. There were a lot of big air bubbles and a smell of diesel oil; but no survivors. We stayed there for three days, and then continued our patrol for another fourteen days.

We went back to Londonderry by the St. George's Channel at the end of the patrol. I had been suffering from a feeling of lassitude ever since the U-Boat episode. When we had rounded Rathlin Island and were approaching the entrance to the River Foyle about an hour after sunset, we found a full gale blowing from the north. The river mouth is on the west side of Lough Foyle, and the mouth of the lough is closed, except for the river, by a long sandy spit called Magilligan Point, which runs like a breakwater right across as far as the narrow river entrance. As we approached the mouth of the river we had the sea on our beam, and the sand spit for a lee shore less than a mile away. Suddenly the ship's head swung violently to port.

'What the hell are you doing with her, quartermaster?'

'Ship won't answer the wheel, Sir.'

I telephoned at once to the engine-room, 'Chief, there's something wrong with the steering engine. Better get there dam' quickly and let me know what's happening. Hurry or you'll be swimming. We've a lee shore under us.'

A few minutes later, but it seemed years, the Chief telephoned from the steering flat, 'Bad break. Will have to put her in hand steering.'

'Can I go astern?'

'No Sir, the rudder is right over to port, and if there's pressure on it we'll never get the hand steering connected.'

'Be as quick as you can—you haven't much time.'

I had hoped to improve matters by going astern, because most single screw ships will then put their sterns up-wind. But with the rudder hard over to port it would have been useless to do so. There was nothing I could do but wait, and pray that the Chief would get the hand steering fixed in time.

I told the First Lieutenant to muster the men in the waist with their life jackets, and blew up my own. Unlike the time when I had tried to blow it up on *Warwick's* bridge, it now held the air. I wedged myself in a corner. The motion was quite indescribable. I began to think,—'An eye for an eye, a tooth for——' Better not start to think like that—better not to think at all.

Signal from *Portchester Castle*: 'Am preparing to take you in tow.'

Reply: 'Thank you, no. We are rolling too heavily to handle towing gear. I am very near to touching. We must not lose two ships. If I go ashore please make signal to coastguard to meet swimming party.'

I looked over the side, and shone an Aldis lamp on to the waves. The water was brown with churned up sand. It could only be a question of minutes. The telephone from the steering flat buzzed.

'Hand steering connected, Sir.'

It could hardly have been a quarter of an hour since the steering engine had broken down.

'Starboard thirty, full ahead.'

Rolling horribly she brought her bow up into the wind. The group were scattered, steaming into the sea, holding their own with the waves, and waiting to see what would happen to us. As we limped slowly through the entrance they formed up astern. The Engineer Officer came on to the bridge, 'Serious defect Sir. Only the dockyard can mend it.' I was shivering so much that I must hold on to the rail to stand upright.

I told the group to anchor, and to follow me up-river the following morning. I went up that night and, as I was in hand steering, I made a signal for a tug to assist me to berth. We were alongside shortly after ten o'clock, and I went down to my cabin.

'Well,' I said to myself, 'this is it—you are round the bend.' It was true. I could no longer trust my own body to obey orders. Catching sight of myself in the glass made me pause. There had been a time when people ashore had said, 'You look very young to be a Commander,' but they hadn't been saying that recently. There wasn't now any reason why they should. The candle was burned out. I went on to the jetty to telephone to the Commodore. I knew he would be in even at that late hour, because it was Max Horton's habit to do his telephoning after his own dinner. I told the Commodore.

'I've expected this for months. When do you want to be relieved?'

'If it must be—the sooner the better Sir.'

'I can do you a relief by noon the day after tomorrow.'

'Thank you Sir.'

'Come and see me tomorrow morning—and congratulations on your U-Boat.'

I went back and lay long in a bath. Two days later I went ashore for the last time from my own ship. It was five years and two months since I had stepped on to *Loch Tulla's* deck.

Chapter XI

SENIOR OFFICER OF ESCORTS (CHAIRBORNE)

In fact it was to take me much longer to leave Londonderry than I had at first thought. There were a great number of things which would be completed more quickly if I continued to handle them myself. Also there were certain formalities by way of visits to the doctors. Even though the executive side might know full well that an officer had become too tired for further service afloat, and should be given a spell ashore, they must obviously seek confirmation from the medical branch. It was greatly to the credit of the Navy that an officer who felt his efficiency to be sinking could always go to his seniors, and talk to them quite frankly without any fear that he would not receive a sympathetic hearing.

It was early December when I eventually arrived home. On the way through Liverpool I had called on Max Horton.

'I'm terribly sorry to let the side down like this, Sir.'

'What does the doctor say, Rayner?'

'Three weeks' sick leave, Sir.'

'Will you be fit for sea again then?'

'I very much doubt it, Sir. There is nothing physically wrong with me—I've just lost my nerve for the sea. Can you find me a job in the Command?'

'As a matter of fact I can. The U-Boats are coming right inshore now, and often my groups are working under the control of other commands, Portsmouth, Plymouth, Rosyth, and even the Nore. The two Channel Commands, Portsmouth and Plymouth, will I think be the scene of a last desperate attempt to cut the life line to the continent. The staff in those two commands don't understand the limitations of the groups, or their capabilities. Already some dam' fool has sent a signal to a group of Castle Class Corvettes ordering an impossible course and speed in bad weather. Result—six asdic domes punctured, and the whole group must be dry-docked. I've just had Admiralty approval to send a Senior Officer of Escorts to each Command to which the groups are attached. I am sending Pryse (Commander H. L. Pryse, R.N.R.) to Plymouth, and you could go to Portsmouth. Let me see—three weeks' leave. That will be just right. You'll report to Commander-in-Chief, Portsmouth on the 1st of January. You'll have to use a lot of tact I expect. Remember you are my ambassador. If you want any help get on to my Chief of Staff right away.'

The reader can imagine how grateful I was to be given such an appointment, for one of the most bitter pills that I had to swallow was that after five years of 'grooming' I had lasted only two months before I cracked. The chance to do something so obviously useful was the best medicine I could have been given.

I enjoyed a splendid three weeks, including Christmas, with my family. I had not been at home for more than ten days consecutively in five years. After Christmas and before the New Year I saw the Chief of Staff, Western Approaches, and then joined Commander-in-Chief, Portsmouth's staff at Fort Southwick on the 1st January 1945.

This was my first appointment to a staff. Until then I had always been on the other side of the great divide between those who sail in ships carrying out the orders of the various staffs, and the shore-based officers who plan the operations. How many times had I railed against the staff officer who, shut in the warm operations room where no winds blew, nor rain nor snow penetrated, had ordered me to take my ship down the River Foyle in a blinding snowstorm? Once I had even gone so far as to telephone to Jove in the fastness of his Olympus.

'Don't you ever open the scuttles in that fug-house of yours and see what's going on outside? Do you really expect me to hazard my ship by taking her down the Foyle in a snowstorm when I can't even see my own bows?'

Jove was at least prepared to talk.

'I'm sorry, but I've got to have a ship at sea off Inistrahull tomorrow morning at six o'clock to take the Clyde portion of the convoy. All the convoy escorts have weather damage, and we've got to have them mended and back at sea in a week.'

'Well, let me wait for a couple of hours until I have the flood tide against me all the way. If I can't see then, I can at least anchor without the ship turning round on her cable. Agree to that and I'll promise to be there on time.'

And so we compromised on that occasion. But I also remembered incidents which, in my conceit, I felt that I would have handled quite differently if I had been in the operations room myself. I was now about to find out if I had been right. I felt very much of a new boy, and had only the vaguest idea of what would be expected of me. To make matters worse I was a representative of another Command, and a great deal would depend on the amount of co-operation I could extract from my new colleagues. At once I was made to realize that my personal position might be extremely difficult. All the Commanders on the staff were Royal Navy men, but only held the rank of 'Acting Commander'. They were fifteen to twenty years older than myself. Most, if not all of them, had left the Navy before the war with the rank of Lieutenant-Commander, and had been given Acting Commander's rank on their recall. They were a very high powered team, and had been at Fort Southwick for the assault on Normandy. There was some reason for them to think that they could well compete with the arrival of a few U-Boats in the Command, without any help from the Western Approaches. To my consternation I found that because of my 'qualified status' I was actually the senior Commander at Fort Southwick. I would have thrust on me such dignities as President of the Mess, and would have to sit at the head of the table; and my arrival meant that one of them would have to leave his cabin. These things may appear trivial and petty when a war is being fought, but when men are herded together they are not to be dismissed lightly. Friction anywhere can spoil the work of the whole machine.

The President of the Wardroom Mess invited me to his cabin after tea. On the way we passed my baggage in the hall. It was still waiting for a decision about my cabin.

'This is very awkward,' he said, waving me to a chair.

'Yes—I can see that. I would very much rather that it had not happened.'

We sat and thought for a bit and then I said, 'Look, you people all think that I'm on Commander-in-Chief, Portsmouth's staff. But in fact I'm not. The Admiralty has only appointed me to Portsmouth because I had to be borne on the books of the *Victory* for pay. I belong to Western Approaches. Obviously I can't belong to both. Let us look at it in this way—I don't belong to your household. I'm a guest, come to do some specialist work; and so long as I have a cabin to myself, *I* don't care whether it is in the Senior Officers' Tunnel or not.' Honour was satisfied, and neither the table nor cabin plan had to be changed.

The actual duties were something quite new to me. Radar had completely changed what little I had been taught about staff work before the war. At that time if ships were ordered to patrol certain waters the manner of doing this was left entirely to the initiative and skill of the Senior Officer. Now with radar covering almost the whole Channel, the staff could plot the minute-by-minute position of the ships, and could see how their orders were being carried out. What is more they could actually guide (or interfere with) the tactical conduct of operations at sea. Taking a leaf from the book of the Royal Air Force, they could control their ships in the same manner as the R.A.F. handled fighters—vectoring the groups on to the enemy. Once again, as when Commander Boyle and I had sailed together in *Havelock*, I discovered that he who controlled the plot controlled the battle.

I always had three or four groups from the Western Approaches, totalling fifteen to twenty frigates or corvettes, as well as the Portsmouth command's own anti-submarine force of twenty-five trawlers, and about a dozen asdic fitted Motor Torpedo-Boats. With these I had to provide close escorts for the outward-and homeward-bound convoys passing through the command, and also patrol the entire area. I must guide the hunt that followed an aircraft sighting report or an enemy attack; and I had to maintain very close relations with Coastal Command, to see that their patrols dovetailed in with those of the surface vessels.

The anti-submarine trawlers were operated by a W.R.N.S. officer, 1st Officer Audrey Parker. I think she was the only Wren officer to be given an operational job. She sat at the next table to mine in the office, and we worked together in perfect harmony. She really knew about ships, and had it not been for this partnership I could never have left the Fort, even for the hour's bicycling exercise which I forced myself to take every day. One never knew when the enemy would appear. The plot was many feet underground, and had no daylight whatsoever. This seemed to make one unconscious of the passing hours and if interesting operations were being carried out it was tempting to stay down in the tunnel for very long periods. Only the insistent clamour of one's stomach would drag one away, probably to find that breakfast, lunch or dinner in the wardroom was long since over; and coffee and buns in the canteen was then the only way to satisfy one's hunger.

As Fort Southwick was some way from the ships, I hardly ever saw my friends when they were in harbour. However, when a very particular friend did bring his 'Captain' Class Frigate in with a defect that would take some considerable time for the dockyard to repair, I strained every nerve to get aboard his ship. For this 'operation' I co-opted Audrey Parker, and we arranged a system of cars and motor boats in case I was needed back in the Plot. When the day came for my expedition I sent a signal to the Captain telling him I was coming aboard, and asked if he could give me lunch. On telephoning to the signal tower to make certain that my signal had been sent, I was surprised to learn that they were having difficulty in passing it. It sounded so unlike that ship's usual efficiency that I began to wonder if her Captain had been changed. However, after some time it was reported that the signal had been passed, and I left the Fort.

When the motor boat arrived alongside there was no sign of life aboard. No quartermaster to take a line—nobody. I scrambled aboard, and in the silence of the deserted ship could hear the clatter of the signal lamp. It stopped, and the Captain's head appeared over the rail of the bridge high above me.

'Sorry not to be down to meet you. I was just taking a signal. Do come up.'

'What,' I shouted back, 'All that way? What's wrong with your cabin?'

'I'll tell you when you get here.' His head was withdrawn.

I clambered up three or four ladders until I reached the open bridge, rather breathless from lack of practice. I had met nobody on the way up.

'And what have you done with the ship's company?' I asked my host when at last I sat down on the compass platform.

'Well as a matter of fact they are all on leave.'

'Good God! Every one of them?' I exclaimed.

'Yes,' he nodded with great seriousness, 'You see I gave one watch leave until the 10th, and naturally gave the other watch leave from the 10th. What I overlooked was that those going on leave today would want to go in the morning, and of course those returning won't get back until the afternoon. So there isn't anybody aboard in the meanwhile.'

'Just like that?' I asked.

'Just like that,' he agreed.

'You're a ruddy marvel. That's what you are. And so we are to have our lunch up here in the March winds so that the Captain can keep signal watch?'

'That's right,' he said, 'You don't mind do you? I've got just one bottle left of that wine you like so much.'

'Of course not—but how I wish you were "operational"! I'd love to order you to sea, and find out what you'd make of that one! Can you imagine the newspaper headings, "Captain goes to sea alone in 1,500 ton Frigate"!'

When the motor boat came back for me in two hours' time, he did come down from the bridge to see me 'over the side'.

'I'm going to send you one heck of a long signal' I shouted as the boat drew away from the ship's side.

'I shan't read it—only the time of origin. The signalmen can ask for a "repeat" when they get back from leave.'

In the Western Ocean I had always been able to get some sleep after lunch. Only once, in the case of the torpedoing of the *Salopian*, had I ever heard of the enemy starting an attack in the afternoon. Also the hours from 4 a.m. to 8 a.m. were nearly always clear for sleep, unless you were helping to clean up a mess made earlier in the night. It almost seemed as though the German captains played to a 'convention' as far as those times were concerned. I was soon to discover that the plot knew no such off-periods. For the first three weeks I slept only in snatches, because sighting reports followed each other almost continuously, and whether they were suspected to be true or false, they must all be investigated with equal care. Fortunately we had an excellent Chief of Staff in Commodore

R. V. Symonds-Tayler, R.N. I had first met him when he was First Lieutenant of the *Hood* in 1932, and I was serving in the same ship. He gave me a remarkably free hand, and under him I really found myself enjoying life in a way which I would not have believed possible away from the sea.

The enemy always kept at least two U-Boats in the area. Sometimes, if my opposite number at Plymouth, Commander Pryse, made things too hot for one of his visitors, the U-Boat would slip over the frontier to see if things were quieter in my part of the Channel. Whereupon I would chase him back again. Similarly I would sometimes drive one over to Pryse's side of the net, but he would very soon return it to me. We kept about forty ships and four aircraft continuously searching for the U-Boats in the waters roughly bounded by a line due south from Dover to one due south from Portland Bill. But we only killed two in four months. One we killed outright after it had attacked and sunk a merchant vessel, and one we attacked after an aircraft sighting report, and drove it into a mine field.

Against these slight successes we only lost two merchantmen —the one already mentioned, and another which might possibly have been sunk by one of our own contact mines which had broken adrift. There was a conflict of opinion over the cause of this loss. I maintained that the weather had been far too bad for a submerged attack, and that although the attack could have been carried out by a surfaced U-Boat I was sure that it would not have dared to surface there, however bad the weather.

As we were the nearest naval plot to London we were always being surprised by special parties of notables who wanted to see what a plot was like, or to study some aspect of D Day. One such party was actually standing round the plot, having it all explained to them, when the merchant ship was torpedoed and we laid on the groups to kill the U-Boat. These particular officers came from the Polish Navy. They were being groomed to go back home to teach their re-formed Navy how to do things. From our point of view the actual sinking of a merchantman caused no more fuss than an aircraft sighting report, and we were all well drilled by this time in the routine to be carried out. Two Escort Groups were covering the convoy.

One was sent to hunt the U-Boat, and the other was spread round the limits of the zone which the enemy could have reached. It was our lucky morning. The U-Boat was caught and despatched. The group that did the killing was left to watch the wreck. Survivors from the merchantman were picked up and brought in, and the second group was sent off on another patrol. To us it was a busy morning which, although it started badly, had a successful conclusion—no more. But our guests were amazed.

Afterwards in the Wardroom one told me, 'You English are a very *calm* race. I do not understand you at all. There is no excitement, no——,' he waved his arms, unable to find a word —'It is not natural. A ship is torpedoed. A Wren is sitting beside the plot. She has such nice legs—she puts a red disc on the plot. She is so calm. No one shouts. You write out the signals. The ships are moved on the plot, and still there is no excitement. The Wren sits swinging her nice legs. When the U-Boat is sunk the Wren still goes on sitting there, and you say to me so quietly, "Come on, let's go and have a drink." I think you English are the most dangerous people to fight in the whole world.'

I was rather taken aback by this fulsomeness. 'You're going to Liverpool next aren't you? You'll see the plot at Derby House. That really is a big one. It covers the whole North Atlantic, but it's not on a table like the one here. It's on a wall and the Wrens have to go up tall ladders to mark the positions.

'The Wrens go up ladders?' he asked eagerly.

I saw the way his mind worked.

'But they wear trousers,' I told him.

When I had first joined a big staff which included both sexes in almost equal numbers, I had wondered just how they would work together. I wondered still more when, after my conversation with the Mess President, I found myself given a cabin on the other side of the Fort, where the ten rooms were occupied by five Wrens and five junior naval officers.

I wonder if there is another country in the world where such an arrangement could have been made without trouble developing. Beyond the fact that the ladies were inclined to occupy the one bathroom for rather longer than one would suppose necessary to clean the human body, they were excellent companions. Their feminine touch made their cabins into something nicer than a mere hole in the ground equipped with the usual naval chest of drawers, wardrobe and bed. Most of the girls had stoves of some sort, and it was more than usual to find a cocoa party in progress. Just occasionally high spirits would break out, and for a short time chaos would reign while sponges, pillows and human bodies flew up and down the long corridor. But such outbreaks were few and far between. Nearly everybody in the tunnel, except Audrey Parker and I, was a watchkeeper; and we were practically in 'watch and watch'. If one of us was not down in the Plot the other was. The chance to sleep was too valuable to be thrown away. I mention this only because so many books written after the war have suggested the exact opposite. The women in our services not only released men to active duties, but contributed a very special sum of their own to final victory. While marriages certainly grew out of many war-time encounters, of what is sometimes mis-called romance there was very little at all.

But to return to the war, the truth of it was that we were using a relatively enormous force, and had achieved the destruction of two submarines; but the continuous threat of attack in our coastal waters had also achieved virtually nothing. I declare that the second round was a draw, with both sides impotent to damage the other. But the Walter-engined high-speed U-Boat was only just round the corner. What would have happened if that weapon had arrived? It was nearly always an aircraft which sighted the U-Boats' Schnorkels, and they would attack by dropping one or perhaps two depth-charges. Nearly all these reports were made at night, and the aircraft attack was little more than a warning to the U-Boat that he had been observed. We would throw round the position such a net of A/S vessels that he would know himself surrounded, and so would become ever more cautious. Given a clean bottom with no wrecks to mislead the hunting vessels, and no tide-rips to upset the asdics, he would have been 'dead mutton' very quickly. But with the wrecks of the first World War, the wrecks of D Day and those of the second World War to confuse us, and the water full of tide-rips, he escaped us time and time again. True we held him on the defensive. But the net we threw round him could not have enclosed the new U-Boat, which could travel faster under water than our hunting craft could travel on the surface.

We had taken our soldiers from Dunkirk, Norway and Crete. We had supplied them at Tobruk and Benghazi, and escorted their supplies over the long route round the Cape. We had landed a vast army in North Africa, and seen it ferried across to Sicily and Salerno. We had guarded the approaches to the D Day invasion, and now the soldiers repaid our efforts. They brought Germany to her knees, and the third round of the U-Boat battle was never fought. When Germany fell, the first Walter boat was nearly ready for sea. She was scuttled in harbour by the Germans, and raised by us so that her secrets were revealed.

The two U-Boats that surrendered in the Portsmouth command were in excellent condition, outside and within. Morale was good, and their crews waited only for the new boats. They may have hoped that if the war had gone another six months they would prove the saviours of their nation. Such hopes of course were nonsensical. Germany was utterly defeated.

EPILOGUE

So there you have it—the war as seen by an amateur sailor, who was fortunate enough to take advantage of the training the Navy offered, so that when war came he was capable of taking command of a ship. If there was one thing that the war taught me, it was to appreciate the innate decency of the many hundreds of men, from all walks of life and from all parts of the Commonwealth, who served in my ships. In the whole time I was at sea I only once had to deal with an offence which would have incurred a prison sentence if it had been committed ashore; and we never sailed short-handed because men did not return from their leave.

If few women figure in these pages it is because they were barely discernible against the background of the ships themselves, each of whom had—or so it appeared to me—a character as complex and as interesting as that of a woman. *Loch Tulla* was the diligent nursemaid, who would take me for a nice walk round the islands and bring me back for tea. *Verbena* the busy housewife. *Shikari* the rather raffish thoroughbred of whom my mother would have said 'A very nice girl, but (and you knew the sting was coming) just a little unreliable I always think.' *Warwick* the widowed lady who had once been a girl herself. *Highlander* the best-loved, in the prime of her life. Lastly *Pevensey Castle*. Poor little *Pevensey*! The girl who had been to the university; the blue stocking; the one who had everything—but had not yet learned how to live.

On the 14th May 1945 Admiral Sir Max Horton made the following signal. It was the last one to be put in my 'In' basket at Fort Southwick, for I was leaving that night for home, and my desk was empty. The groups had gone back to the ports on which they were based. The Command itself was closing down and, although one was glad that the long, weary war was over, one felt a sharp pang of regret that the life we had led was ending. It was more than the finish of a chapter. The book that held such tales of friendship, heroism, and endurance was being closed, and put away for ever. From henceforward it would only live in the memories of many men.

'To: F.O.I.C.'s and N.O.I.C.'s in W.A. From: C.-in-C. W.A. Pass to all ships and establishments.

'In saying goodbye to the Command it gives me great pleasure to communicate the following letter which I have received from the Admiralty.

' "Before the Western Approaches Command comes to an end Their Lordships wish to place on record their recognition of the large part which it has played in the war with Germany now successfully completed. The Command has participated in virtually every form of Naval activity and in most on a large scale.

' "In the campaign against the U-Boats and in trade protection it has been pre-eminent and its record in this vital sphere will form one of the enduring chapters of the Naval history of this Kingdom.

' "Never has the existence of the Nation encountered so grievous a maritime threat as the German attack on its shipping during the years 1939–45, and with the triumph over that threat the name of the Western Approaches Command will always be pre-eminently associated. All who have been members of the Command, whether afloat or ashore, are entitled to take pride in the contribution which it has made to the long and bitter struggle which has so recently been brought to a victorious conclusion."

'I thank you all for your loyal help and support and send you my best wishes for the future.'

INDEX

INDEX

T

U

V

ILLUSTRIOUS

by

Kenneth Poolman

Author of The Kelly *and* Faith, Hope and Charity

On 10th December, 1954, a great ship joined the Reserve Fleet. She is H.M.S. *Illustrious*, the famous aircraft-carrier, veteran of Mediterranean and Far Eastern battles in World War II. This book is her story.

With the help of men who served in her, and in particular of one officer who commanded a squadron of her aircraft, Kenneth Poolman recalls the classic actions and personal heroism that make this ship's record among the finest in the Royal Navy. This officer led his Corsairs in the great attacks on Sabang, and through his eyes we see the assaults on Surabaya, Port Blair and Belawan. Later, with *Illustrious* as the spearhead of the British Pacific Fleet, come attacks on the vital Japanese oil refineries in Sumatra and the invasion of Okinawa. These actions were the climax to a career in which the ship had already won laurels in the Battle of Taranto and the Malta Convoys, which are also vividly described.

The theme and the author are admirably matched and Mr. Poolman does full justice to every dramatic moment—the time off Formosa when a "Kamikaze" suicide plane is seen heading straight for the ship, or the pilot who tries to land on a pitching deck in a badly shot-up aircraft with the fear of crashing in flames or diving into the sea. These and other stories are told with his accustomed skill and feeling for men who had to endure the tense, uncomfortable conditions of war at sea and in the air.

CHALLENGE ME THE RACE

by

Mike Hawthorn

The author of this book is a young man of twenty-six. Since his sixteenth birthday he has risen from being the owner of a 30/- motor cycle to his present position as Britain's top racing motorist and holder of third place in last year's World Championship.

Into these ten years he has packed a lifetime of experience in the field of motor racing. His first racing car was an old Riley given to him by his father who himself had been a racing driver. The first thing Hawthorn did was to beat his father when they both entered the Brighton speed trials. After a successful season in the Riley he was given a bigger car and performed so well in his first race at Goodwood that he beat the world champion Fangio.

The Italians were so astonished that Ferrari invited Hawthorn to drive for them. In 1953 he won the major Grand Prix of the season and became the first Englishman to have won such a race for over thirty years.

Since then his name has become a household word both in this country and on the Continent.

Hawthorn has written his book with such descriptive skill that the reader sits beside the driver from the starting grid to the chequered flag. No other racing driver has ever before, in such colourful and dramatic writing, captured the fascination and pageantry of a Grand Prix.

His chapter on the tragic Le Mans race of 1955 was written during his rest periods while it was actually in progress. At the time he said: "I wanted above all else to blot out the mental shock of the terrible accident, and I found that forcing myself to put down on paper my impressions of the race as seen from hour to hour from behind the wheel was the most effective method."

GUNBOAT 658

by

L. C. Reynolds

Motor Gunboat 658 fought her battles in the Mediterranean. For two years, from the fall of Tunisia until she received the surrender of a flotilla of German E-boats in the last week of the war, she sought the enemy in his own waters, far behind the line of battle ashore.

North Africa, Malta, Sicily, Sardinia and Corsica, Elba and the Italian coast from La Spezia to Naples—all were familiar to her. Her second year of operations was spent in the Adriatic, mainly among the picturesque islands of Dalmatia. There she worked with the Yugoslav Partisans as the Germans were gradually forced to withdraw northwards.

Gunboat 658 was typical of many of the Navy's MTBs and MGBs. Her life was a kaleidoscope of intense action, of exasperation and excitement, of disappointment and success. She was manned almost entirely by amateur sailors—both officers and men. When she set out for the Mediterranean from South Wales, undertaking a voyage of 1,600 miles to start her commission, only four of the thirty ratings had ever been to sea before.

The author served in her through all her adventures. As a newly commissioned R.N.V.R. Midshipman, he watched her being built in a West Country yard. Six months later he became her First Lieutenant, and soon after his twenty-first birthday he was commanding her on operations.

The spirit of the men of Gunboat 658 was reflected in her own personality. She had one, without a doubt. She was a proud and happy ship, and her crew were proud to serve in her.

Demy *Illustrated* 16*s. net*

K-MEN

The Adventures of the German Frogmen and Midget Submariners

by

C. D. Bekker

Author of Swastika at Sea

This book tells the whole exciting story of how the Germans, influenced by the British X-craft attack on the *Tirpitz* and the Italian frogmen in the Mediterranean, formed what they called naval "Kommandos" and used them in daring exploits against the Western Allies and the Russians in the later stages of the last war. The Kommandos not only operated as frogmen but also they manned midget submarines and human torpedoes and piloted explosive boats by remote control.

The author, himself a former German naval officer, spent nearly two years interviewing surviving K-men, and in these pages he recounts their dangerous and often fatal task with a skill which brings to life the tension and the risks they had to run. The K-men's objectives ranged from ships of the Allied invasion fleet and the bridges and harbours vital to the invading forces to pirate warfare in the Adriatic Sea and operations against the Russians in the river Oder.

This thrilling account of the K-men's adventures will be read with the greatest interest by those who enjoyed such books as *U-boat 977* and *Swastika at Sea.*

Demy *Profusely Illustrated* 16*s. net*

THE LAUGHING COW

A U-Boat Captain's Story

by

Jost Metzler

A thrilling story of the exploits of the German U-boat U 69 during the Second World War. Lieutenant-Commander Metzler ranked with Prien and Kretschmer as one of the best U-boat aces. *The Laughing Cow,* as his submarine was called from its emblem, was finally sunk in 1943 under a new commander.

It is interesting to read such a human document as this from the enemy's side. The crew carried out some extremely daring exploits and their duties took them all over the world—to the American coast, the Indian Ocean and almost to the ice barrier. The terror of attacks with depth charges, of being chased by destroyers, and the hardships in the cramped space of a submarine are magnificently portrayed. It is an historical, graphic and true document of sea warfare.

Demy *Illustrated* 15*s. net*

NINTH TIME LUCKY

by

Elios Toschi

An officer in the Italian navy, Elios Toschi was also an inventor of the Italian human torpedoes which disabled the battleships *Valiant* and *Queen Elizabeth* in Alexandria harbour in 1941. It was during an attempt of his own to penetrate the harbour that the submarine carrying his torpedoes was located by a British destroyer, depth-charged and forced to surface. Toschi was rescued by the destroyer and taken prisoner.

Sent to a transit camp in Egypt, he immediately started making plans to escape, but the tunnel he was building under the barbed wire could not be completed before he was transferred to India. From camps in India he made repeated efforts to get away. On one occasion he escaped from a camp at the foot of the Himalayas, living among the local shepherds while trying to reach Kashmir or Afghanistan. Each time he was recaptured. At last he was successful: disguised as a Pathan, he travelled across the breadth of India by train and reached the Portuguese island of Diu.

Toschi's account of his adventures holds the imagination from first to last, and the stories of his escapes are enriched by fascinating descriptions of his surroundings and the natives among whom he lived.

Demy *Illustrated* 16*s. net*

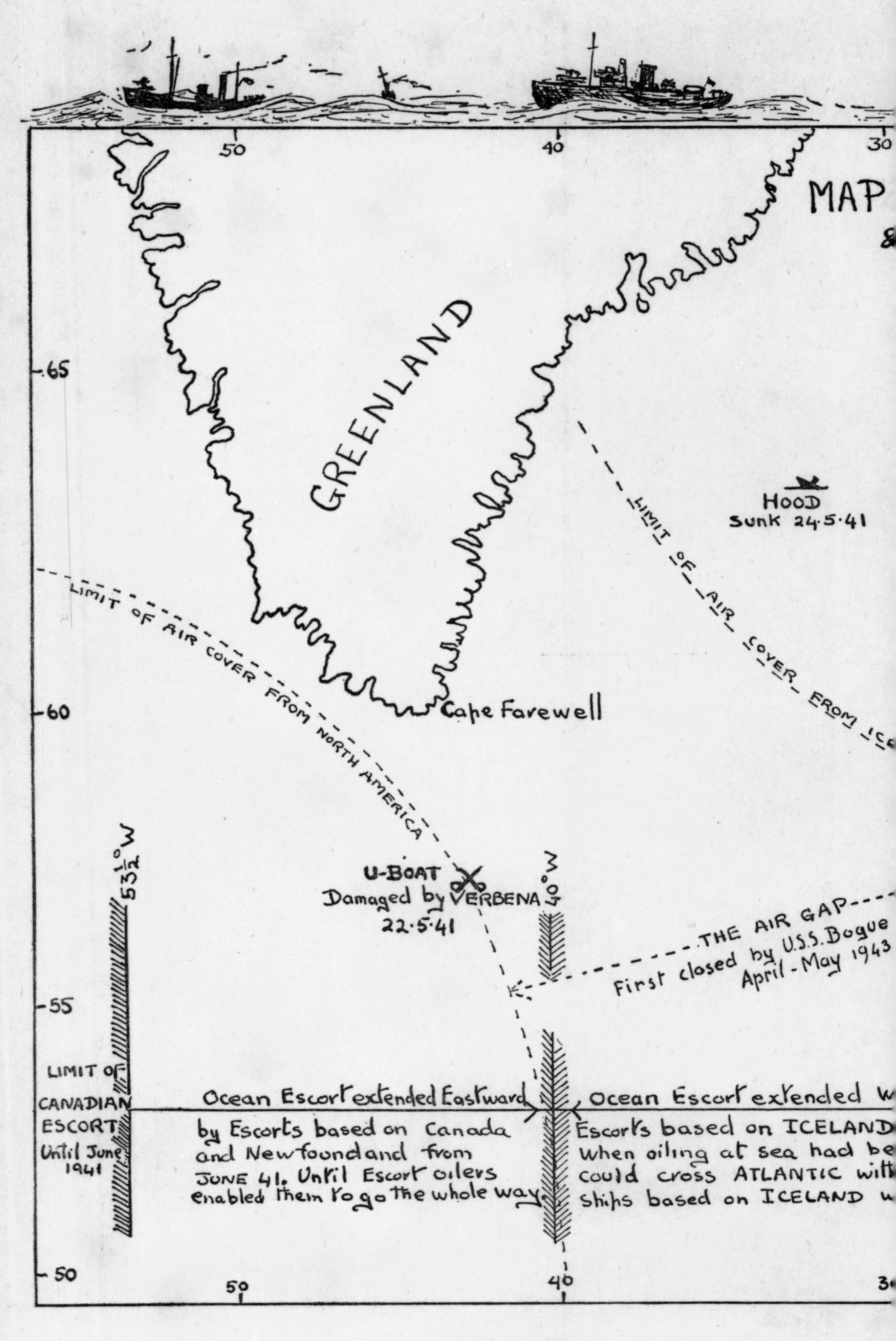
MAP
50
40
30
GREENLAND
65
60
55
50
HOOD
Sunk 24.5.41
LIMIT OF AIR COVER FROM ICE
LIMIT OF AIR COVER FROM NORTH AMERICA
Cape Farewell
U-BOAT
Damaged by VERBENA
22.5.41
53½° W
40° W
THE AIR GAP
First closed by U.S.S. Bogue
April - May 1943
LIMIT OF CANADIAN ESCORT Until June 1941
Ocean Escort extended Eastward
by Escorts based on Canada and Newfoundland from JUNE 41. Until Escort oilers enabled them to go the whole way.
Ocean Escort extended W
Escorts based on ICELAND
when oiling at sea had be
could cross ATLANTIC with
ships based on ICELAND w
50
40